This Guide
offers a DRIP
as special op
you will find
lio of high-q
own schedule and financial ability.

Indeed, you will learn exactly how to get a DRIP account
open, in whose name the account should be registered, and, once
enrolled, how much (or little) you may invest, where and when to
send your investment, whether there will be service fees—and
other information to help you select companies in which to invest
over the long term.

# CONTENTS

# What Are DRIPs?

Direct investment plans, also known as dividend reinvestment plans (DRPs or DRIPs), are plans offered by about 1,300 companies to enable shareholders to invest cash and/or dividends directly to buy additional shares of the company's stock. Each company makes its own decisions as to how its plan will operate.

Plans accept investments according to a preset schedule. Some plans invest quarterly, on the dividend payment date; others invest once or twice each month, and some invest as often as every week or even every day. Some plans require that dividends be reinvested. Some permit partial reinvestment; others will send you a check if you choose not to have any dividends reinvested, but will still permit you to make cash purchases. In general, an investment can be as little as $10 or $25 or as much as $5,000, and even more. Investments are sent to the company's transfer agent (which, in some cases, is the company itself) by check, money order, or even by wire. And a growing number of companies accept instructions to debit funds automatically from the investor's bank account according to the investor's instructions.

## Why Are They Valuable?

Direct investment plans make it possible to invest without a broker. Therefore, you can accumulate shares slowly instead of paying a commission and buying into the company all at once. They make it possible to employ two important investment strategies (which otherwise could be accomplished only through a mutual fund)--dollar-cost averaging and diversification. Why are these strategies important? Many people get burned as investors. They buy at the top and sell at the bottom. That's because emotions play such a large part in investment decisions.

Diversification will help you overcome the effect of your emotions. When some of your stocks are lagging, others may be gaining. That way, you won't feel so much pressure to sell the laggards (assuming that all things are equal, you would want to be buying those shares when they are lagging, not selling them). And dollar-cost averaging will impose discipline on your investing. You decide in advance how many dollars you intend to invest and how often. Then you continue on this schedule regardless of the market prices of the stocks you own.

These techniques have particular application at this time. Newer investors may be unable to resist reacting to their first taste of a bear market, especially since many of them have become spoiled by the unusual success of the past five years. This is especially true for investors who did not experience the flat year for stocks in 1994, the recessions of 1990 and 1991, or the "crash" of 1987...let alone the extended bear market of 1973-74. What escapes them is the simple fact that bear markets are normal and the extended bull market we had been enjoying was an unusual phenomenon. Although the stock markets have historically returned 10-11% annually, that average return includes many great years, and a fair amount of negative ones, as well. What it boils down to is that patience is an important attribute for investors--and dollar-cost averaging and broad diversification make it easier to withstand the temptation to act impetuously.

At times, certain industries will be in favor while others are out of favor. Will the growth of the Internet mean that people will buy fewer Sara Lee cheesecakes? Will you? That's why we recommend that you establish a strategy and stay with it. Indeed, if you adhere strictly to a dollar-cost averaging strategy with a well-diversified portfolio of stocks, you will buy more shares when stocks are at bargain prices.

## Diversification Is Usually Costly

Wide diversification of assets may seem to be possible only for people who have a lot of money to invest or for those who invest in mutual funds. Investors who use a broker tend to buy round lots (100 shares). Therefore, without substantial funds, it is difficult to diversify. And mutual funds have drawbacks, such as hefty fees, lack of control, and "forced" capital gains distributions. Worst of all, most fund investors usually have no idea what companies the fund owns at any given time.

## Dollar-Cost Averaging

By employing a strict dollar-cost averaging strategy, you invest a fixed number of dollars on a regular basis regardless of how many shares those dollars buy. This strategy, in effect, forces you to buy more shares when prices are low and fewer shares when they are high. Buy Low, Sell High! You also spread your investment risk because you don't have to buy 100 shares at a time--and risk buying at the worst possible time.

## Summary

If you accept that by dollar-cost averaging you will improve the results you achieve as an investor, and that by diversifying your investments among many different companies you will reduce your exposure to losses, your only problem may be how to do this on a limited budget. If you were to make small, regular investments in several different companies through a broker, commissions might account for more of the investment than the stock itself! That's why we recommend that you make your investments through company-sponsored DRIPs. Within these plans, dividends and optional cash are invested (based on the market price of the stock on the investment date), usually without commissions or service fees.

## DRPs, DRIPs, or DSPPs?

The explosion in the number of people using direct investment plans has led to an unfortunate blurring of terminology, and it would be easy to be tripped up by mislabeling. This is especially true in the highly promoted area of direct-enrollment plans, which allow nonshareholders to make their first investment directly through the transfer agent in order to open a DRIP account.

Some people have attached the term "no-load" to any plan that allows direct enrollment by nonshareholders. Unfortunately, the direct-enrollment feature is offered by the less desirable plans--in that most of these plans charge fees for each cash and/or dividend investment. In addition, the vast majority of these direct-enrollment plans charge an enrollment fee of $10 or $15.

In itself, the enrollment fee is not an important factor. Indeed, we recommend an enrollment service offered by Temper of the Times Communications, Inc., that charges a fee for its service. That service contacts the transfer agent on your behalf and handles the transactions for you: It purchases the minimum number of shares to allow you to qualify as a shareholder of record. It gets the share or shares registered in your name. It contacts the transfer agent to get your account opened. And when it has been accomplished, it confirms that fact to you. Otherwise, you can go directly to the transfer agent. However, the companies that don't require shareholder status for entry generally request an initial investment of $250-$1,000 and charge an ongoing fee for each subsequent investment.

In short, the "no-load" or direct-enrollment plans are actually the ones that are less investor-friendly. For each and every subsequent cash investment, they typically charge $5, plus commissions--and often even levy fees to reinvest your dividends! We believe the term "no-load" is being abused when it is associated with these high-fee plans.

## Direct Purchase, Direct Investment, or Direct Stock Purchase Plan

A similar misuse of terminology involves the broader phrases "direct purchase," "direct investment," and "direct stock purchase plan." These terms all describe investment plans offered by companies that enable investors to purchase shares directly through the company without going through a stockbroker.

The three terms may be said to represent the three different methods of obtaining the initial share(s) in the company before entering the plan. One way is through a traditional broker. The customer must request that the shares be registered in his or her name and not in "street name." The customer must then contact the transfer agent for the company and request enrollment in the plan. A second way, which is available for about 584 companies, is through the transfer agent for the company. By investing a certain dollar amount (generally from $250 to $1,000), the customer can request enrollment directly from the transfer agent (but remember, this can be done, in general, only for companies that charge fees for subsequent investments). The third way, which is available for virtually every company, is through an enrollment service offered by Temper of the Times Communications, Inc. For a modest fee, the Temper Enrollment Service will open DRIP accounts by transferring the share or shares required to qualify the investor to join the plan as a shareholder.

### Shareholder Enrollment vs. Direct Enrollment

As mentioned above, once enrolled--whether by becoming a shareholder first, going through the transfer agent where available, or utilizing the enrollment service offered by Temper of the Times Communications, Inc.--the customer will be able to make further optional cash investments through the plan. This is a substantial advantage if the plan does not charge fees.

The Temper Enrollment Service is a fully licensed broker/dealership that specializes in DRIP enrollments. When Temper opens the account, the customer will become enrolled as a shareholder (usually with a single share). Although there is no ongoing charge by Temper, if the company plan charges fees, the investor will pay these fees regardless of whether he or she joined the plan through the transfer agent or used the Temper service to become a shareholder. Investors should calculate the effect of the fees on the amount they invest.

In summary, the only ways in which direct-enrollment plans differ from traditional DRIPs is that they tend to charge ongoing fees for each investment and you can buy your first shares through the transfer agent for the company. Thus, traditional DRIPs require shareholder status and don't charge fees (Intel, Coca-Cola, Paychex, Harley-Davidson, 3M, and General Motors, for instance) whereas direct-enrollment plans don't require shareholder status and do charge fees (e.g., IBM, Mattel, McDonald's, Disney, and Ford).

### Entering a DRIP as a Shareholder

Perhaps you are already a shareholder of a company that has a plan. If the shares are registered in "street name" (held in a brokerage account), the company will not recognize you as a shareholder. In that case, ask your broker to get the shares reissued in your name--this usually means asking for a certificate. Then contact the transfer agent or the company's shareholder relations department and request a DRIP enrollment form. Generally, you can make your first optional cash investment when you return the form.

If you are not already a shareholder, you can buy the number of shares necessary to enter the DRIP as a shareholder by going to a traditional broker or by using the enrollment service offered by Temper of the Times Communications, Inc. The number of shares required by each company in order to qualify for its plan is shown in the prospectus details starting on page 30. This information is also available at www.moneypaper.com and www.directinvesting.com.

### The Temper Enrollment Service

Unlike traditional broker/dealers, the Temper Enrollment Service provides a very efficient way to get a DRIP account opened. Traditional brokers generally make purchases in street name, which does not qualify the customer to join the plan as a shareholder. Temper buys the initial qualifying share(s) (or up to 100 shares) in the customer's name and deals with the transfer agent to get the account open. It charges a one-time fee for the service and receives no further fees for subsequent investments. Although The Moneypaper Inc. is not involved with the operations at Temper. Temper is an affiliated company which was organized to help Moneypaper subscribers qualify for DRIPs. Temper opens an account for an individual, purchases the share or shares required to qualify for a direct investment plan, has the DRIP account opened in the customer's name, and sends the customer notices in accordance with NASD reporting rules. An order form for the Temper Enrollment Service is available online at www.moneypaper.com and www.directinvesting.com. Orders can be placed online, or by mail by printing out the form. You can also call for an enrollment order form at 1-800-295-2550.

# Unusual Plans

Some companies that offer DRIPs require the investor to acquire more than one share to have dividends reinvested but only one share to make optional cash investments. This allows the investor to join the plan with one share and then make optional cash investments to accumulate the additional shares needed to qualify for the reinvestment of dividends. These companies include:

| Company Name | Shares Needed for Optional Cash | Shares Needed to Reinvest Dividends |
|---|---|---|
| * American States Water | 1 | 15 |
| * AmerUs Group Co. | 1 | 100 |
| * Anadarko Petroleum Corp. | 1 | 25 |
| * Annaly Mortgage Mgmt., Inc. | 1 | 25 |
| * BellSouth Corp. | 1 | 5 |
| * Blue Chip Value Fund, Inc. | 1 | 50 |
| * Boeing Co. (The) | 1 | 50 |
| * Clayton Homes, Inc. | 1 | 10 |
| * Coastal Financial Corp. | 1 | 250 |
| * Computer Associates Int'l | 1 | 50 |
| * Curtiss-Wright Corp. | 1 | 20 |
| Dime Bancorp, Inc. | 1 | 100 |
| * Equity Office Properties Trust | 1 | 10 |
| * Estee Lauder Companies Inc. | 1 | 10 |
| * Granite Construction Inc. | 1 | 25 |
| * Greenpoint Financial | 1 | 100 |
| * Heinz (H.J.) | 1 | 10 |
| * Hershey Foods | 1 | 10 |
| * International Paper | 1 | 25 |
| * Mack-Cali Realty Corp. | 1 | 50 |
| * Manufactured Home Communities | 1 | 10 |
| * McGraw-Hill Cos. | 1 | 5 |
| * Mellon Financial Corp. | 1 | 5 |
| * Middlesex Water Co. | 1 | 10 |
| * Pier 1 Imports Inc. | 1 | 10 |
| * PPG Industries | 1 | 10 |
| * Reader's Digest Assn., Inc. | 1 | 10 |
| * Reader's Digest Assn., Inc. | 1 | 10 |
| * Sanderson Farms, Inc. | 1 | 10 |
| United Investors Realty Trust | 1 | 50 |
| * Valspar Corp | 1 | 25 |
| * York International Corp. | 1 | 100 |

**\* Available through the Temper Enrollment Service**

# Foreign Investors

There are currently 778 U.S. companies that allow foreign investors to participate in their DRIPs (see Company Listings starting on page 30). All funds must be in U.S. currency. The enrollment procedure is the same as for U.S. citizens, except that a W-8 tax form must be filed so that taxes are not withheld from dividend distributions. (You may contact *The Moneypaper* for W-8 forms, call 1-800-388-9993.) Foreign investors should keep in mind, though, that they may face tax obligations on the dividends and company-paid fees in their own country, just as U.S. investors do here. Also, if their local bank charges for currency conversions, they should factor in this cost in making their investment decisions. A section on foreign investing is available online at www.moneypaper.com.

## Fees for Investing Cash and/or Dividends

Of the 778 U.S. companies that offer DRIPs to foreigners, 545 do not charge fees for cash investments and/or dividend reinvestments, and of the remaining 233, 98 charge low fees. That leaves only 135 companies that levy high fees. Those are the companies that people who want to make frequent and/or small investments should avoid.

In this Guide, companies that don't charge investment and/or reinvestment fees are shown with the symbol of a heart (♥). You'll see that the vast majority of companies don't charge fees. (Companies that offer no-fee DRIPs are shown in boldface online at www.moneypaper.com and www.directinvesting.com.)

## ADRs with High Fees

A number of transfer agents have aggressively sought to bring foreign companies to the U.S. market as American Depository Receipts (ADRs). Their underlying reason is to create fee income. As a result, we now see a lot of DRIPs for ADR companies. These plans are sponsored not by the companies themselves, but by the agents. Morgan Guaranty, with its "Shareholder Services Plan"; the Bank of New York, with its "Global BuyDirect" program; and Citibank, with its "Direct Investment," have taken a "cookie-cutter" approach by setting up programs that charge the same fees for all of their client companies. You will find a listing of ADR companies offered through agent-sponsored plans on page 174 of this Guide. Some of these companies are offered by the Temper Enrollment Service and are indicated by asterisks in the general listing.

## Closed-End Funds

Direct investment plans are offered for a number of closed-end funds, some of which specialize in foreign or domestic stocks, while others invest in bonds. Closed-end funds differ from "normal" mutual funds in that a limited, fixed number of shares are authorized and they trade on a stock exchange, just like a stock. Unlike a stock, however, they feature a net asset value (NAV) and the exchange price can represent a discount or premium to that NAV. They also charge annual fees, and many pay distributions only once or twice a year, at which time you can invest additional funds along with your reinvestment. Since a fund manager is in charge of buying and selling securities, fund investors lack control over their investments, which may also be subject to currency fluctuations (for international funds) or interest rate volatility (for bond funds). A listing of closed-end funds that offer DRIPs can be found on page 173, and if a fund is offered by the Temper Enrollment Service, it will be indicated by an asterisk and included in the general listing.

## Automatic Investing

One of the easiest ways to engage in dollar-cost averaging is to set up automatic investing transfers from your bank account to a DRIP. Companies that provide this option are shown in the general listing, as well as in the Companies Listed by Industry.

But be aware that some plans charge fees for this option, and in some cases the minimum monthly debits may be a greater commitment than you want to make.

Over the past several years, the number of companies offering automatic investing has grown to about 700. Of these, 300 do not charge for the service. However, some agents, notably First Chicago Trust Company, routinely charge a $2 fee to process automatic debits.

Some direct-enrollment plans may be causing confusion on this issue, since they may charge less for automatic investments than they do for accepting checks...a reversal of sorts compared with the traditional DRIP. Generally, the direct-enrollment plans, which charge a $5 fee for every investment by check, allow automatic investing for a lower fee, often $1 or $2. Unfortunately, at least one agent seems to be using this feature as an automatic way to get an interest-free loan from the investor. Money is deducted from the investor's bank account weeks in advance of the investment date. If you notice this happening, you might want to discontinue the authorization and/or complain to the company about its agent's practices.

# Paying Taxes

Reinvesting dividends doesn't exempt you from paying taxes on them in the year they are "paid." This should come as no surprise, since dividends are a form of income, and the IRS expects you to report all income. Remember to include the amount you earned as part of your cost basis, since it was used to buy more shares. or fractions of shares. Also, be sure to add the amount of the dividend (on which you are taxed) to your cost basis, so you won't overstate your capital gains when you eventually sell the shares. Each year, corporations must send you a Form 1099 if you earn more than $10 in dividends, and the same information is sent to the government. (Note that if you earn less than $10 from a particular company, you still owe taxes on the income...but a Form 1099 is not required.)

### When the Company Pays Fees on Your Behalf

Each Form 1099 may also show an amount classified as "additional income," which is included in the total reported. This amount represents amounts paid on your behalf by the company, such as fees and commissions charged by the transfer agent. (Companies that pay fees and/or commissions for you are indicated in the company listings with an exclamation point [!] under "div" or "cash," e.g., "comm!") Although it may appear to be "phantom" income, the amounts are costs that the company paid on your behalf, and, therefore, are considered income to you. Like reinvested dividends, you should include these amounts in your cost basis, which will keep you from overstating your capital gains when you sell.

In some cases, we may describe a plan as "no-fee" when, in fact, there is a fee, but the company is paying it for you. One way to understand this is to imagine that the transfer agent demands to be paid, say, $1 on each investment you make, but the company steps in and gives you the dollar, which you in turn pay to the agent. By giving you the dollar, the company is, in effect, paying you an additional dividend. But because there is no net cost to you, we have decided to call the plan a no-fee or no-cost plan.

### Dividends and Fees Paid Add to Your Cost Basis

The importance of including these dividends becomes clear when you eventually sell shares and need to calculate capital gains. Although it may seem unfair to report (and be taxed on) additional, seemingly "phantom," income, each dollar of income also represents an additional dollar of cost basis, and the difference between your cost basis and net proceeds is the amount of capital gains when you sell.

Some companies' statements show company-paid fees throughout the year, while others do not. This is why it's advisable to reconcile your records each year upon receipt of the Form 1099, which companies are required to mail by January 31 of the following year. While you may not wish to wait until February or later to file your tax return, it may be a good idea to wait until you can confirm these amounts. And as you begin to receive larger dividend payments on your portfolio, you may find that the tax liability is more likely to require that you send money to the IRS, rather than being due a refund, so filing closer to the April 15 deadline may be more advantageous. Setting aside a small reserve to pay additional taxes may also be a good move.

# Creating a DRIP Portfolio

Where to start? Oil stocks deserve representation in the average portfolio. Most other industries throughout the global economy depend on oil. Select from among the big household brand names--ExxonMobil, for example. Investors may view utilities as incapable of producing significant gains. However, with deregulation in this industry, the options for these companies are expanding, as is their opportunity to expand their businesses. Pick utilities that are fee-free. Many of the companies in the telecommunications industry have DRIPs and would be appropriate candidates for a small portfolio. And everyone must eat. Every day! This is another of those basic, unavoidable facts of life. There are a large number of great food companies with DRIPs. To round out a five-stock portfolio, pick from another basic group, such as a drug company, a paper company, a bank stock, a retailer, or a diversified manufacturer. Always strive for quality, industry leaders whose products have broad brand-name recognition.

The listing of stocks based on industry, which begins on page 16, will be helpful in establishing a diversified portfolio (you can become enrolled in the company plan through the Temper Enrollment Service if an asterisk appears before the company name). One test you can use if you are unsure about a company is to ask yourself some questions: Do I own any of the company's products? Would I like to own any of its products? If I do own the products, would I buy them again?

Once you are enrolled in a company's DRIP, you can make additional investments without brokerage commissions by sending funds to the transfer agent with the tear-off portion of each statement.

## Tiny Investments Are Possible

Virtually everyone can afford to put money into stocks to fund his or her retirement. There are 137 companies that will accept investments of $10 or less. Among them are such companies as Abbott Labs, Avon Products, Clorox, Coca-Cola Co., General Mills, General Electric, Philip Morris, Sara Lee, and TRW. With as little as $100 a month (or $100 a quarter), one could accumulate shares in all these companies over a period of years without paying any service fees. Hundreds of other plans accept as little as $25 a month. So a 10-stock portfolio could be funded every month (or every quarter) with just $250.

## Huge Investments Are Possible

In general, we don't recommend DRIPs for large investments, but it nevertheless is true that investors could use these plans to invest millions without paying a cent in commissions or fees!

Although some companies restrict investments to a maximum of $1,000 a month, about 687 companies permit you to invest $5,000 or more a month (that is, at least $60,000 per year per company). These include such companies as Anheuser-Busch, Coca-Cola, Colgate-Palmolive, and Eastman Kodak. And about 343 of these companies allow monthly investments of $10,000 or more .

# Selling Shares Through the DRIP

We believe that the primary advantage of DRIPs is that they enable the investor to accumulate shares slowly by making frequent purchases. Although we don't think that selling through the DRIP is necessarily an advantage, there have been some recent changes to the plans that make selling through them more feasible. In the past, shareholders could mail a sell order to the transfer agent, who would sell the shares on a monthly or quarterly basis. However, some transfer agents are now accepting sell orders over the phone, and even more companies are selling shares on a weekly or daily basis. Most companies charge a fee for this service, but you may benefit from a lower institutional commission rate (commission rates are typically 10-12 cents a share).

The company listings also indicate the selling practices of each company. We have included details of how a company accepts sell orders, when the orders are executed, and at what price shares are sold. These are listed at the end of each company's fee structure (the company listings start on page 30). If a company does not offer to sell shares through the DRIP, N/O appears in the listing. If we were unable to obtain the information, N/A appears there. For the companies that don't offer exact selling times, we have listed "irregularly." These companies may hold shares until there is a round lot to sell, or they may wait until other investors are buying and then sell the shares to them.

Keep in mind that by selling through the plan, you may miss selling at the best price.

## Investor-Friendly Selling Practices

Below we have listed some of the companies that offer excellent selling features—they accept sell orders by phone and execute the orders daily. Please confirm these practices before you sell as the provisions of the plans can change without much notice. One caution: Don't let the ease of selling shares encourage you to engage in trading, which will cost you money and trigger tax obligations. Your reason for using DRIPs should always be to build wealth over the long term.

### Companies that sell by phone on a daily basis

* AAR Corp.
* Acadia Realty Trust
* ADC Telecommunications, Inc.
* Aetna Inc.
* Alcoa
* Allstate Corp.
* American Electric Power
* American Home Products
* American States Water
* AmerUs Group Co.
* Ametek, Inc.
* Anheuser-Busch Cos.
* Arch Coal, Inc.
* ArvinMeritor Inc.

* Associated Banc-Corp
* Avista Corp.
* AXA SA
* Ball Corp.
* Bandag Inc.
* Bandag Inc.
* Bank One Corp.
* Beckman Coulter Inc.
* Becton Dickinson & Co.
* Bemis Co., Inc.
* Black & Decker
* BorgWarner Inc.
* BP plc
* Brandywine Realty Trust

Brookline Bancorp, Inc.
* Brown-Forman Corp.
* Brown-Forman Corp.
* Burlington Northern Santa Fe Corp.
* Calgon Carbon Corp.
* Campbell Soup Co.
Canada Southern Petroleum
* Capital One Financial Corp.
* Carver Bancorp, Inc.
* Caterpillar, Inc.
* CH Energy Group, Inc.
* Charter One Financial Inc.
* Chubb Corp.
* CIGNA Corp.
* Citizens Banking Corp.
* Citizens & Northern Corporation
* Cleveland-Cliffs Inc.
* Clorox
* CNF Transportation Inc.
Coastal Caribbean Oils & Minerals, Ltd.
* Coca-Cola Co. (The)
* Coca-Cola Enterprises Inc.
* Conoco Inc.
* Conoco Inc.
* Corn Products International, Inc.
* Crane Co.
* Crown Cork & Seal Co., Inc.
* Delta Air Lines, Inc.
* Donegal Group Inc.
* Donnelley (RR) & Sons Co.
* DPL Inc.
* DuPont (E.I.)
Eastern Co. (The)
* Eastman Chemical Co.
* Eastman Kodak
* Eaton Corp.
Electronic Data Systems
Empire District Electric Co.
* Energen Corp.
* Enron Corp.
* Estee Lauder Companies Inc.
* Exelon Corporation
* Fannie Mae
* Federal Signal Corp.
* FedEx Corp.
* First American Corp. (The)
* First Niagara Financial Group, Inc.
* FirstMerit Corp.
* Ford Motor Co.
* Freddie Mac
* Gabelli Convertible Securities Fund, Inc.
* Gabelli Equity Trust, Inc.
* Gabelli Global Multimedia Trust
* Gardner Denver Inc.
* Georgia-Pacific Group
* Gillette
* Goodyear Tire & Rubber
* Gray Communications Systems, Inc.
Great Atlantic & Pacific Tea Co., Inc. (The)
* Green Mountain Power
* Guidant Corp.
* Harland (John H.) Co.
* Herman Miller, Inc.
* Hibernia Corp.
* HRPT Properties Trust
* International Business Machines
* Intimate Brands, Inc.
* Investors Financial Services Corp.
* iStar Financial Inc.
* Johnson Controls
* Johnson & Johnson
JPS Industries, Inc.
* Keyspan Energy Corp.
* La-Z-Boy, Inc.
* Liberty ALL-STAR Equity Fund
* Liberty ALL-STAR Growth Fund, Inc.
* Lilly (Eli) & Co.
* LION Inc.
Lockheed Martin
* Louisiana-Pacific Corp.
* LSB Bancshares, Inc.

Lubrizol Corp.
Lucent Technologies Inc.
* MacDermid, Inc.
* Macerich Co.
* Magellan Petroleum Corp.
* Marriott International, Inc.
* McDermott International Inc.
* McDonald's Corp.
* MDU Resources Group
* Meadowbrook Insurance Group
* Merck & Co., Inc.
* Mid-State Bancshares
* Mills Corp. (The)
* MONY Group Inc. (The)
* National Service Industries, Inc.
* Nationwide Financial Services
NCR Corp.
* New Jersey Resources Corp.
* Newell Rubbermaid Inc.
* Newport Corp.
* Nike, Inc.
* Nokia Corp.
* North Fork Bancorp
* Ohio Casualty Corp.
* Old Republic International Corp.
* Omnicare, Inc.
* ONEOK, Inc.
* Pan Pacific Retail Properties, Inc.
* Paychex, Inc.
* Penney (J.C.)
* People's Bank
* PepsiAmericas, Inc.
* Pharmacia Corp.
* Philadelphia Suburban Corp.
* Philip Morris
* Pitney Bowes
* PolyOne Corp.
* PPG Industries
* Prentiss Properties Trust
* Progress Energy
* Providian Financial
* Regions Financial Corp.
* SBC Communications
* Schawk, Inc.
* Sears, Roebuck & Co.
* Sempra Energy
* Sky Financial Group
* Snap-on Inc.
* Solutia Inc.
* Southwestern Energy Co.
* St. Paul Cos. (The)
* State Street Corp.
* Sunoco Inc.
* Target Corp.
* Temple-Inland
* Tennant Co.
* Textron, Inc.
* Thomas & Betts Corp.
Timber Co. (The)
* Tyson Foods
* Unitrin, Inc.
* Unocal Corp.
* UNUMProvident Corp.
* USEC Inc.
* UtiliCorp United Inc.
* Venator Group
* Visteon Corp.
* Volvo AB
* Vulcan Materials Co.
* W Holding Co.
* W.P. Carey & Co.
* Wal-Mart Stores
* Washington REIT
* Wells Fargo & Co.
Western Digital Corp.
* Whirlpool Corp.
* Winn-Dixie Stores, Inc.
* Wisconsin Energy Corp.
* Yahoo! Inc.
* Zweig Fund (The)

**\* Available through the Temper Enrollment Service**

### You May Prefer to Sell Through a Broker

Once you have accumulated a round lot (100 shares) within a direct investment plan, it makes sense to ask the transfer agent to have those shares certificated and sent to you. Some transfer agents take longer than others, and at best it will take a week or two. (If you have a single share in storage at home, ask that 99 shares be certificated so that you can get rid of that one share when you sell a round lot.)

With your certificate immediately available to you, you can call your broker and place a sell order whenever you wish, as long as the broker doesn't require you to deposit the certificate first. With a broker, you can set your own selling price or sell at the (current) market price. Be careful about depositing the certificate into a brokerage account because the shares could immediately revert to "street name," in which case dividends would no longer be reinvested by the plan, but instead would be paid to the broker (and credited to your brokerage account).

# IRAs and DRIPs

Some DRIP companies will act as custodian of an IRA. Otherwise, to invest IRA funds in a DRIP, you must find an institution that will act as custodian for your IRA. Unfortunately, most IRA custodians simply won't invest in DRIPs, as a practical matter.

However, if you have a good relationship with your bank, it may agree to invest your IRA funds into DRIPs. In that case, you would deposit your IRA funds in the bank in an account registered in the name of your IRA. The account would be called something like "XYZ Bank, custodian for John Doe under IRA plan dated XXX."

Then you would establish an account in the DRIP in the name of the IRA, and have the bank withdraw funds from your IRA account and send them to a broker to buy the qualifying share or shares in the company whose plan you want to join. The Temper Enrollment Service is set up to handle such requests and will provide you with a form to give to the bank. Once the DRIP has been established in the name of your IRA, you can have the bank transfer as much money into the company plan as you wish, up to the maximum allowed by the plan. Advise your banker when to make your voluntary transfer from the bank money-market IRA account to the company DRIP account.

### The Roth IRA

As limited as the options are for combining "regular" IRAs and DRIPs, they are even more limited for the new

Roth IRA. Only a few of the companies that will act as a custodian have instituted a Roth IRA option.

If you can arrange it, though, the new Roth IRA can be superior to a traditional IRA because the assets in the account not only will grow on a tax-deferred basis, but will be completely free of taxation when you eventually withdraw them. However, the yearly contribution is not deductible.

## Companies That Act as Custodians for IRAs

The following companies will open IRAs through their DRIPs. (A small service fee may apply.)

| | | |
|---|---|---|
| Allstate C orp. | ⊘ | *auto* |
| American Electric Power | ♥ | *auto* |
| Atmos Energy Corp. | ♥ | *auto* |
| Blue Chip Value Fund, Inc. | | *auto* |
| Campbell Soup Co. | ⊘ | *auto* |
| Connecticut Water Service Inc. | ♥ | *auto* |
| Exxon Mobil Corp. | ♥ | *auto* |
| Fannie Mae | ⊘ | *auto* |
| Ford Motor Co. | ⊘ | *auto* |
| Hershey Foods | ⊘ | *auto* |
| Interchange Financial Services | | *auto* |
| Intimate Brands, Inc. | ⊘ | *auto* |
| Lucent Technologies Inc. | ⊘ | *auto* |
| McDonald's Corp. | ⊘ | *auto* |
| MidSouth Bancorp, Inc. | ♥ | *auto* |
| ONEOK, Inc. | ♥ | *auto* |
| Philadelphia Suburban Corp. | ♥ | *auto* |
| ProLogis Trust | ♥ | *auto* |
| SBC Communications | | *auto* |
| Sears, Roebuck & Co. | ⊘ | *auto* |
| South Financial Group, Inc. (The) | ♥ | *auto* |
| Thornburg Mortgage, Inc. | ♥ | |
| UtiliCorp United Inc. | ♥ | *auto* |
| Verizon Communications, Inc. | | *auto* |
| Wal-Mart Stores | ⊘ | *auto* |
| Westbank Corp. | ♥ | |

⊘ indicates high fees for investing and/or reinvesting. ♥ indicates that there is no charge for investing cash or reinvesting dividends. An "*auto*" is displayed when a plan will automatically withdraw funds from your bank account to buy shares of the company's stock.

# Listing of companies
# By Industry

You can become enrolled in the companies shown below with an ★ through the Temper Enrollment service.

Companies shown below with a ♥ DO NOT charge fees to invest and reinvest dividends.

Companies that provide automatic withdraws from your bank account to fund your DRIP account are shown below with *auto.*

## Advertising
* Cadmus Communications Corp. ♥
  Havas Advertising *auto*
* Interpublic Group of Cos.
* Schawk, Inc. ♥ *auto*
  Scoot.com plc *auto*

## Agriculture
* ConAgra Foods, Inc. ♥ *auto*
  Cresud S.A.C.I.F. y A. *auto*
* DuPont (E.I.)
  Norsk Hydro A.S. *auto*
* Pharmacia Corp. *auto*
  Savia SA de C.V. *auto*

## Apparel
* Angelica Corp. ♥
  Benetton Grp. SpA *auto*
* Brown Shoe Co., Inc. ♥
  Fila Holding S.p.A. *auto*
* Hartmarx Corp. ♥
* Kellwood Co. ♥
* Liz Claiborne, Inc. ♥ *auto*
* Russell Corp. ♥
* Sara Lee Corp. ♥
* Stride Rite Corp. (The)
* VF Corp.
  Wacoal Corp. *auto*

## Auction
* Sotheby's Holdings, Inc. ♥

## Automotive
* Applied Industrial Technologies, Inc. ♥
* ArvinMeritor Inc. ♥ *auto*
* Barnes Group Inc. ♥
* BorgWarner Inc. ♥ *auto*
* Carlisle Companies Inc. ♥
  DaimlerChrysler AG *auto*
* Dana Corp. ♥
* Delphi Automotive Systems Corp. *auto*
  Ducati Motor Holding *auto*
* Federal Signal Corp. ♥ *auto*
* Federal-Mogul
  Fiat SpA *auto*
* Ford Motor Co. *auto*
* GenCorp Inc. ♥ *auto*

* General Motors ♥ *auto*
* Genuine Parts Co. ♥
* Harley-Davidson ♥
* Honeywell International Inc. ♥
* Johnson Controls ♥ *auto*
* Lear Corp.
* Modine Manufacturing Co. ♥ *auto*
* Pennzoil-Quaker State Co. ♥ *auto*
* Pep Boys ♥
* Reynolds & Reynolds Co. A ♥ *auto*
* Superior Industries Int'l, Inc. ♥
* Teleflex Inc. ♥
  Tenneco Automotive *auto*
* Textron, Inc. ♥ *auto*
  Toyota Motor Corp. *auto*
* TRW Inc. ♥
* United Technologies ♥
* Visteon Corp. *auto*
* Volvo AB B *auto*

## Banking
* Abington Bancorp, Inc. *auto*
  ABN AMRO Holdings N.V. *auto*
* Allegiant Bancorp, Inc.
  Allied Irish Banks, plc *auto*
* Amcore Financial, Inc. ♥ *auto*
* American Financial Holdings, Inc. ♥ *auto*
* American National Bankshares Inc. ♥
* AmeriServ Financial, Inc. ♥
* AmSouth Bancorp. ♥
  Andover Bancorp, Inc. ♥
* Arrow Financial Corp. ♥ *auto*
* Associated Banc-Corp *auto*
  Banco BHIF, SA *auto*
  Banco Bilbao Vizcaya *auto*
  Banco Comercial Portugues SA ADS *auto*
  Banco Ganadero (common) *auto*
  Banco Ind. Colombiano, SA *auto*
  Banco Rio de la Plata, SA *auto*
  Banco Santiago *auto*
* BancorpConnecticut Inc. ♥
* BancorpSouth, Inc. ♥ *auto*
  BancWest Corp. ♥ *auto*
* Bank Mutual Corp. ♥
* Bank of America Corp. ♥ *auto*
* Bank of Granite Corp. ♥ *auto*

# Companies Listed by Industry (continued)

Bank of Ireland *auto*
* Bank of Montreal ♥
* Bank of New York ♥ *auto*
Bank of Tokyo-Mitsubishi *auto*
* Bank One Corp. ♥ *auto*
Bank West Financial Corp. ♥
* Banknorth Group, Inc. ♥
Barclays Bank plc *auto*
* BB&T Corp. ♥ *auto*
* BostonFed Bancorp, Inc. ♥
* Bridge View Bancorp ♥
Brookline Bancorp, Inc. *auto*
* BSB Bancorp, Inc. ♥ *auto*
* C & F Financial Corp. ♥ *auto*
* Camco Financial Corp. ♥
Canadian Imperial Bank of Commerce ♥
* Capital City Bank Group ♥
* Capital Directions, Inc. ♥
* Capital One Financial Corp. ♥ *auto*
* Capitol Bancorp Ltd. ♥
* Carver Bancorp, Inc. *auto*
* Cathay Bancorp, Inc. ♥
* CCFNB Bancorp, Inc. ♥
* Cecil Bancorp, Inc. ♥ *auto*
* Center Bancorp, Inc. ♥
* Charter One Financial Inc.
* Chemical Financial Corp. ♥
* Chemung Financial Corp. ♥
* Chester Valley Bancorp ♥
* Chittenden Corp. ♥
* ChoiceOne Financial Services, Inc. ♥
* Citizens Banking Corp. ♥
* Citizens & Northern Corporation *auto*
* City Holding Co. ♥
CNB Financial Corp. ♥
* Coastal Financial Corp. ♥ *auto*
* Codorus Valley Bancorp, Inc. ♥ *auto*
* Colonial BancGroup, Inc. (The) ♥
* Colony Bankcorp, Inc. ♥
* Columbia Bancorp ♥
* Comerica Inc. ♥
* Commerce Bancorp, Inc. ♥
* Commonwealth Bank
* Commonwealth Bankshares, Inc. ♥
Community Bank System, Inc. ♥ *auto*
* Community Banks, Inc. ♥ *auto*
* Community First Bankshares ♥
* Community Savings Bankshares, Inc. ♥
* Compass Bancshares, Inc.
* Cornerstone Bancorp, Inc. ♥
* Cortland Bancorp ♥ *auto*
* CoVest Bancshares, Inc. ♥
* Crescent Banking Company ♥
* DCB Financial Corp. ♥
Dime Bancorp, Inc.
* Eagle Bancshares, Inc. ♥
* ESB Financial Corp. ♥
Espirito Santo Financial Grp., SA *auto*
* Exchange Bancshares, Inc. ♥
* F & M Bancorp ♥
F.N.B. Corp. ♥ *auto*
* Farmers National Banc Corp. ♥

* FFLC Bancorp, Inc. ♥ *auto*
* Fidelity Bancorp ♥
* Fidelity Bankshares, Inc. ♥
* Fidelity National Corp.
* Fifth Third Bancorp *auto*
* First Bancorp ♥ *auto*
* First Bell Bancorp, Inc. ♥
* First Charter Corp. ♥ *auto*
* First Chester County Corp. ♥
* First Colonial Group, Inc. ♥
* First Commonwealth Financial ♥ *auto*
* First Federal Capital Corp. ♥
* First Financial Bancorp ♥
* First Financial Holdings Inc. ♥ *auto*
* First Indiana Corp. ♥
* First Keystone Financial
* First Leesport Bancorp, Inc. ♥ *auto*
* First M & F Corp. ♥ *auto*
First Merchants Corp. ♥
* First Midwest Bancorp, Inc. ♥
* First Nat'l Community Bancorp, Inc. ♥
* First Niagara Financial Group, Inc. ♥ *auto*
First State Bancorp. ♥
* First Tennessee National Corp. ♥
* First Union Corp. ♥ *auto*
* First United Corp. ♥
* First Virginia Banks, Inc. ♥ *auto*
* FIRSTFED Bancorp, Inc. ♥ *auto*
* FirstMerit Corp. ♥
* Flag Financial Corp. ♥ *auto*
* FleetBoston Financial Corp. ♥
* FNB Financial Services Corp. ♥
* Foothill Independent Bancorp ♥
* Four Oaks Fincorp, Inc. ♥
* Franklin Bank ♥
* Fulton Bank ♥
* GA Financial, Inc. ♥
* GB&T Bancshares, Inc. ♥
* German American Bancorp ♥ *auto*
* Glacier Bancorp, Inc. ♥
* Great Southern Bancorp, Inc.
* Greater Bay Bancorp ♥
* Greater Community Bancorp ♥
* Greenpoint Financial *auto*
* Guaranty Federal Bancshares Inc. ♥
* Habersham Bancorp ♥
* Hancock Holding Co. ♥ *auto*
* Harleysville Savings Financial Corp. ♥
* Hawaiian Electric Ind. *auto*
* Hibernia Corp. ♥
* HMN Financial, Inc. ♥ *auto*
* Horizon Financial Corp. ♥
* HSBC Holding plc *auto*
* Hudson United Bancorp ♥ *auto*
* Huntington Bancshares Inc. ♥ *auto*
* Independent Bank Corp. ♥ *auto*
Independent Bank Corp. (MA) ♥
* Independent Community Bank ♥
* Indiana United Bancorp ♥
* Integra Bank Corp. ♥ *auto*
* Interchange Financial Services *auto*
* Juniata Valley Financial Corp. ♥

## Companies Listed by Industry (continued)

* KeyCorp ♥
* Lakeland Financial Corp. ♥
* LCNB Corp. *auto*
* Long Island Financial Corp. *auto*
* LNB Bancorp, Inc. ♥ *auto*
* LSB Bancshares, Inc. *auto*
* M & T Bank Corp. *auto*
* Mahaska Investment Co. ♥
* Marshall & Ilsley Corp. ♥ *auto*
* MASSBANK Corp. ♥
* Mayflower Cooperative Bank ♥
* Medford Bancorp, Inc. ♥
* Mellon Financial Corp. ♥ *auto*
* Mercantile Bankshares Corp. ♥
* Merchants Bancshares, Inc. ♥
* MetroCorp Bancshares, Inc. ♥
* Mid-State Bancshares *auto*
* MidSouth Bancorp, Inc. ♥ *auto*
* Mystic Financial, Inc. ♥
  National Australia Bank Ltd. *auto*
* National City Corp. ♥ *auto*
* National Commerce Financial ♥
* Newmil Bancorp, Inc. ♥
* North Fork Bancorp ♥
* Northeast PA Financial Corp. ♥
* Northwest Bancorp, Inc. ♥
* OceanFirst Financial Corp. ♥
* Old National Bancorp *auto*
* PAB Bankshares, Inc. ♥
* Pacific Century Financial Corp. ♥ *auto*
* Patriot Bank Corp. ♥ *auto*
* Penns Woods Bancorp, Inc. ♥
* Pennsylvania Commerce Bancorp, Inc. ♥
* People's Bank ♥
* Peoples Bancorp of NC *auto*
* Peoples BancTrust Co., Inc. ♥
* Peoples First, Inc. ♥
* PNC Financial Services Group ♥ *auto*
* Pocahontas Bancorp, Inc. ♥
* Popular, Inc. ♥
* Promistar Financial Corporation ♥
* Provident Bankshares Corp. ♥
* Redwood Empire Bancorp ♥ *auto*
* Regions Financial Corp. ♥ *auto*
* Republic Bancorp Inc. ♥
* Roslyn Bancorp, Inc.
* Rurban Financial Corp. ♥ *auto*
* S.Y. Bancorp, Inc. ♥
* S&T Bancorp, Inc. ♥
* Sandy Spring Bancorp ♥
  Santander Central Hispano Bank & Trust Ltd. *auto*
  Scotiabank ♥
* Seacoast Financial Services Corp. ♥ *auto*
* Second Bancorp, Inc. ♥
* Slade's Ferry Bancorp ♥ *auto*
* SNB Bancshares, Inc. ♥
  Sonoma Valley Bank *auto*
* South Financial Group, Inc. (The) ♥ *auto*
* Southern Financial Bancorp, Inc. ♥
* Southern Michigan Bancorp ♥
* Southtrust Corp. ♥ *auto*
* Southwest Georgia Financial Corp. ♥ *auto*

* Sovereign Bancorp Inc. ♥
* State Bancorp, Inc. ♥
* Sterling Bancorp ♥
* Sterling Financial Corp. ♥
* Stifel Financial Corp. ♥
* Suffolk Bancorp ♥
* Sun Bancorp, Inc. ♥ *auto*
* SunTrust Banks Inc. ♥ *auto*
* Susquehanna Bancshares *auto*
* Sussex Bancorp ♥
* Synovus Financial Corp. *auto*
* TCF Financial Corp.
* Teche Holding Company ♥
* Thistle Group Holding Co. ♥
* Tompkins Trustco, Inc. ♥
* TriCo Bancshares ♥
* Troy Financial Corp.
* TrustCo Bank Corp NY ♥ *auto*
* U.S. Bancorp ♥ *auto*
* UMB Financial Corp. ♥
* UNB Corp. ♥
* Union National Financial Corp. ♥
* Union Planters National Bank ♥
* UnionBanCal Corp. ♥
* United Bancorp, Inc. ♥
* United Bankshares, Inc. ♥
* United Community Financial Corp. ♥
* United National Bancorp ♥ *auto*
* Unity Bancorp, Inc. ♥
* Univest Corp. of Pennsylvania ♥ *auto*
* Valley National Bancorp ♥ *auto*
  Vista Bancorp, Inc. ♥
* W Holding Co. *auto*
* Warwick Community Bancorp, Inc. ♥
* Washington Mutual, Inc. ♥ *auto*
* Washington Trust Bancorp, Inc. ♥ *auto*
* Waypoint Financial Corp.
* WebsterFinancial Corp. ♥
* Wells Fargo & Co. *auto*
* WesBanco, Inc. ♥ *auto*
* Westamerica Bancorporation ♥
* Westbank Corp. ♥
  Westpac Banking Corp. *auto*
* Whitney Holding Co. ♥
* Wilmington Trust Co. ♥ *auto*

## Building

* Ashland Inc. ♥
* Carlisle Companies Inc. ♥
  Chicago Bridge & Iron Co. N.V. *auto*
* Clayton Homes, Inc. ♥
* Crane Co. ♥
  Empresas ICA, SA de C.V. *auto*
* Foster Wheeler Ltd. ♥
* Granite Construction Inc.
  Grupo Tribasa *auto*
* Hanson plc
* Home Depot *auto*
* Johnson Controls ♥ *auto*
* Lowe's Cos., Inc. *auto*
  Maderas y Sinteticos Sociedad Anonima *auto*
* Masco Corp. ♥
* Massey Energy Company

## Companies Listed by Industry (continued)

* McDermott International Inc. *auto*
  Sawako Corp. *auto*
* Sherwin Williams Co. ♥
* Thomas Industries ♥
* Vulcan Materials Co. *auto*

### Chemical

* Avery Dennison Corp. *auto*
  BOC Group plc (The) *auto*
* BP plc ♥ *auto*
* Cabot Corp. ♥
* Calgon Carbon Corp. *auto*
* Crompton Corp. ♥
* Dow Chemical ♥
* DuPont (E.I.)
* Eastman Chemical Co. *auto*
* Ecolab Inc. ♥
* Engelhard Corp. ♥
* Ethyl Corp. ♥
* Exxon Mobil Corp. ♥ *auto*
* Ferro Corp. ♥
* Fuller (H.B.) ♥ *auto*
* GenCorp Inc. ♥ *auto*
* Goodrich Corporation ♥
* Grace (W.R.) ♥
* Hercules, Inc.
* Honeywell International Inc. ♥
  Imperial Chemical Ind. plc *auto*
* International Flavors & Fragrances ♥
* Kerr-McGee ♥
  Lubrizol Corp. *auto*
* Lyondell Chemical Co. ♥
* MacDermid, Inc.
* Millipore Corp. ♥
* Minnesota Mining & Manufacturing ♥ *auto*
* National Service Industries, Inc. *auto*
* Occidental Petroleum Corp. ♥
* Olin Corp.
* OM Group ♥
* Omnova Solutions Inc. ♥ *auto*
* Phillips Petroleum Co. ♥ *auto*
* PolyOne Corp. *auto*
* PPG Industries *auto*
* Praxair, Inc. ♥
* Quaker Chemical Corp. ♥ *auto*
  Royal Dutch Petroleum Co. *auto*
* RPM, Inc. ♥ *auto*
  Sinopec Beijing Yanhua Petrochemical Co. Ltd. *auto*
  Sociedad Quimica y Minera *auto*
* Solutia Inc. *auto*
* Sunoco Inc. *auto*
* Unocal Corp.
* USEC Inc. *auto*
* Valspar Corp *auto*
* Vulcan Materials Co. *auto*
* Westvaco Corp. ♥ *auto*

### Computer

* American Software, Inc. A ♥
  ARM Holdings plc *auto*
* Avnet, Inc. ♥
  Baltimore Technologies plc *auto*
* Compaq Computer *auto*

* Computer Associates Int'l
  Corning Inc. ♥ *auto*
  Dassault Systemes SA *auto*
* Data Research Associates, Inc. ♥
  ECsoft Group plc *auto*
  Eidos plc *auto*
  Electronic Data Systems *auto*
  Formula Systems Ltd. *auto*
* Hewlett-Packard *auto*
  Ilog SA *auto*
  Insignia Solutions plc *auto*
* Intel Corp. ♥ *auto*
* International Business Machines *auto*
  Logitech International SA *auto*
  Macronix Int'l. Co. Ltd. *auto*
  Merant plc *auto*
* Motorola, Inc. *auto*
* National Data Corp. ♥
  NCR Corp. *auto*
  NEC Corp. *auto*
  Nice Systems Ltd. *auto*
* Paychex, Inc. ♥ *auto*
  SmartForce plc *auto*
  Western Digital Corp. *auto*
* Yahoo! Inc. *auto*

### Consumer

* American Greetings Corp. A ♥ *auto*
* American Home Products *auto*
  Aracruz Celulose SA *auto*
* Avon Products, Inc. ♥
* Black & Decker ♥ *auto*
* Blyth, Inc. ♥
* Bristol-Myers Squibb
* Brown-Forman Corp. A ♥
* Brown-Forman Corp. B ♥
  Canon Inc. *auto*
* Church & Dwight ♥
* Clorox ♥ *auto*
* Colgate-Palmolive ♥ *auto*
  De Rigo S.p.A. *auto*
  Eastern Co. (The) *auto*
  Electrolux, AB B *auto*
* Enesco Group, Inc. ♥
* Estee Lauder Companies Inc. *auto*
* Fortune Brands ♥
* General Electric *auto*
* Gillette *auto*
  Grupo Casa Saba SA de C.V. *auto*
* Harland (John H.) Co. *auto*
* Hasbro Inc. ♥ *auto*
* Huffy Corp. *auto*
  Industrie Natuzzi SPA ADS *auto*
* Johnson & Johnson ♥ *auto*
* Kimberly-Clark Corp. ♥
  Koninklijke Philips Electronics NV *auto*
* La-Z-Boy, Inc. *auto*
* Lancaster Colony Corp. ♥
* Libbey Inc. *auto*
  Luxottica Grp. ADS *auto*
  LVMH Moet Hennessy L.V. *auto*
  Matsushita Electric Ind. Co.,Ltd. *auto*
* Mattel Inc. *auto*

**19**

## Companies Listed by Industry (continued)

* Maytag Corp. ♥ *auto*
* McKesson Corporation ♥ *auto*
* Minnesota Mining & Manufacturing ♥ *auto*
* Moore Corp. Ltd. ♥
* Myers Industries, Inc. ♥
* Nature's Sunshine Products, Inc. ♥
* New England Business Service, Inc. *auto*
* Newell Rubbermaid Inc. *auto*
* Nike, Inc. B *auto*
  Orbital Engine Corp. Ltd. *auto*
* Pfizer Inc. ♥ *auto*
  Pioneer Electronic Corp. *auto*
* Pioneer Standard Electronics ♥
* Procter & Gamble *auto*
* Rowe Cos. (The) ♥
* Sara Lee Corp. ♥
* Schering-Plough Corp. ♥
  Sony Corp. *auto*
* Stanley Works *auto*
  TDK Corp. *auto*
  Thomson Multimedia *auto*
  Tomkins plc *auto*
* Toro Co. (The) ♥
  Unilever N.V. *auto*
  Unilever plc *auto*
  Waterford Wedgewood plc *auto*
* Whirlpool Corp. *auto*

### Defense

* AAR Corp. *auto*
* Ball Corp. ♥
* Barnes Group Inc. ♥
* Crane Co. ♥
* Curtiss-Wright Corp. *auto*
  DaimlerChrysler AG *auto*
* GenCorp Inc. ♥ *auto*
* Goodrich Corporation ♥
* Honeywell International Inc. ♥
* ITT Industries ♥ *auto*
* Kaman Corp. A *auto*
* Lockheed Martin ♥ *auto*
  Newport News Shipbuilding *auto*
* Northrop Grumman Corp. ♥
* Parker-Hannifin Corp. ♥
* Raytheon Co. A ♥
* Rockwell Automation *auto*
* Teleflex Inc. ♥
* Textron, Inc. ♥ *auto*
* TRW Inc. ♥
* United Industrial Corp. ♥
* United Technologies ♥

### Drugs

* Abbott Labs. ♥
  Akzo Nobel NV *auto*
* Allergan, Inc. ♥ *auto*
* AMCOL International ♥
* American Home Products *auto*
  AstraZeneca Group plc *auto*
* Aventis
  Biora AB *auto*
* Bristol-Myers Squibb
  Cantab Pharmaceuticals plc *auto*

* DuPont (E.I.)
  ELAN Corp., plc *auto*
  Fresenius Medical Care AG *auto*
  GlaxoSmithKline plc *auto*
  Grupo Casa Saba SA de C.V. *auto*
* Johnson & Johnson ♥ *auto*
* Lilly (Eli) & Co. *auto*
* McKesson Corporation ♥ *auto*
* Merck & Co., Inc. *auto*
* Mylan Laboratories ♥
  Novo Nordisk A/S B *auto*
  Novogen Ltd. *auto*
* Pfizer Inc. ♥*auto*
* Pharmacia Corp. *auto*
* Schering-Plough Corp. ♥
  Shire Pharmaceuticals plc *auto*

### Electric

* Avnet, Inc. ♥
* AVX Corp. ♥
* Baldor Electric Co. ♥
  British Energy plc *auto*
* Cooper Industries ♥
* Emerson Electric Co. ♥
* Federal Signal Corp. ♥ *auto*
* GenCorp Inc. ♥ *auto*
* General Electric *auto*
* Harris Corp. ♥ *auto*
* Hubbell, Inc. B ♥
* Hubbell, Inc. A ♥
* ITT Industries ♥ *auto*
* Johnson Controls ♥ *auto*
* Keithley Instruments ♥
  Makita *auto*
  Matsushita Electric Ind. Co.,Ltd. *auto*
* Motorola, Inc. *auto*
* National Service Industries, Inc. *auto*
  NEC Corp. *auto*
* Pioneer Standard Electronics ♥
* Raytheon Co. A ♥
* Rockwell Automation *auto*
* Scientific-Atlanta ♥
  Sony Corp. *auto*
  TDK Corp. *auto*
* Technitrol Inc. ♥
* Tektronix *auto*
* TRW Inc. ♥
* Tyco International Ltd. ♥ *auto*

### Financial

* Advanta Corp. B ♥
* Aetna Inc.
  AFP Provida *auto*
* American Express Co. *auto*
  AMVESCAP plc *auto*
* Astoria Financial Corp. ♥
  Banco Bilbao Vizcaya *auto*
  Bank of Ireland *auto*
* Bank of Montreal ♥
  Bank of Tokyo-Mitsubishi *auto*
* Bank One Corp. ♥ *auto*
* BB&T Corp. ♥ *auto*
* Block (H&R)

## Companies Listed by Industry (continued)

Canadian Imperial Bank of Commerce ♥
* Capital One Financial Corp. ♥ *auto*
* Capital Southwest Corp. ♥ *auto*
* Charter Municipal Mortgage Acceptance Co. ♥
* Countrywide Credit Industries, Inc. ♥
* Equifax *auto*
* Fannie Mae *auto*
* FINOVA Group Inc. (The) ♥ *auto*
* First American Corp. (The) ♥ *auto*
* First Union Corp. ♥ *auto*
* FirstMerit Corp. ♥
* FleetBoston Financial Corp. ♥
* Franklin Resources, Inc. ♥
* Freddie Mac *auto*
* GATX Corp. ♥
* General Electric *auto*
* Hartford Financial Services Group Inc ♥
* Household International, Inc. ♥
* IndyMac Bancorp ♥
* Investors Financial Services Corp. *auto*
* Jefferson-Pilot Corp. ♥
* KeyCorp ♥
* Lehman Brothers Holdings Inc. ♥ *auto*
* Lincoln National Corp. *auto*
* Marsh & McLennan Co., Inc.
* Medallion Financial Group ♥
* Mellon Financial Corp. ♥ *auto*
  Merrill Lynch
* Morgan Stanley Dean Witter & Co. ♥ *auto*
* Municipal Mortgage & Equity, L.L.C. ♥
* Nationwide Financial ServicesA *auto*
  New York Broker Deutschland *auto*
* Paychex, Inc. ♥ *auto*
* Pennrock Financial Services Corp. ♥
* PMC Capital, Inc.
* Providian Financial *auto*
  Sanpaolo di Torino-IMI *auto*
  Santander Central Hispano Bank & Trust Ltd. *auto*
* Schwab (Charles) Corp. ♥ *auto*
* Sky Financial Group *auto*
* St. Paul Cos. (The) ♥
* State Street Corp. *auto*
* Stilwell Financial, Inc.
* Synovus Financial Corp. *auto*
* TCF Financial Corp.
* Temple-Inland ♥
* Textron, Inc. ♥ *auto*
* Tompkins Trustco, Inc. ♥
* Torchmark Corp.
* Total System Services, Inc. *auto*
* Union Planters National Bank ♥
* Unitrin, Inc. *auto*
* Wells Fargo & Co. *auto*
* Wilmington Trust Co. ♥ *auto*
* Zions Bancorp ♥

### Food & Beverage
* Anheuser-Busch Cos. ♥
* Bob Evans Farms ♥ *auto*
* Boston Beer Co. (The) *auto*
* Brown-Forman Corp. A ♥
* Brown-Forman Corp. B ♥
  Cadbury Schweppes plc *auto*

* Campbell Soup Co. *auto*
* Coca-Cola Bottling Co. Consolidated *auto*
* Coca-Cola Co. (The) ♥ *auto*
* Coca-Cola Enterprises Inc. ♥ *auto*
  Coca-Cola FEMSA *auto*
  Compania Cervecerias Unida SA *auto*
* ConAgra Foods, Inc. ♥ *auto*
* Corn Products International, Inc. *auto*
  Dean Foods Co. ♥
  Diageo plc ADS *auto*
  Formula Co. ♥ *auto*
* General Mills ♥ *auto*
  Great Atlantic & Pacific Tea Co., Inc. (The) *auto*
  Groupe Danone *auto*
* Heinz (H.J.) ♥ *auto*
* Hershey Foods *auto*
* Hormel Foods Corp. ♥ *auto*
  Industrias Bachoco *auto*
* International Multifoods Corp. ♥
* Interstate Bakeries Corp. ♥
* Kellogg ♥ *auto*
* Lance, Inc.
  LVMH Moet Hennessy L.V. *auto*
* McCormick & Co.
  Molson Companies Ltd. A ♥
  Molson Companies Ltd. B ♥
* Nestle SA
  Pepsi-Gemex, SA de C.V. *auto*
* PepsiAmericas, Inc. *auto*
* PepsiCo Inc. ♥
* Philip Morris ♥ *auto*
  Reliv International, Inc. *auto*
* Sanderson Farms, Inc. *auto*
* Sara Lee Corp. ♥
* Sensient Technologies Corp. ♥
* Smucker (J.M.) ♥
* Tyson Foods A ♥ *auto*
  Unilever N.V. *auto*
  Unilever plc *auto*
  Vina Concha y Toro, SA *auto*
* Wrigley (Wm. Jr.) Co. ♥

### Food Service
* 7-Eleven, Inc. *auto*
* Fleming Companies, Inc. ♥
* Marriott International, Inc. A *auto*
* Nash Finch Co. ♥
* Pizza Inn, Inc. ♥
* Supervalu, Inc. ♥
* Sysco Corp. *auto*

### Hotels & Gaming
* Canadian Pacific Ltd. ♥
* Marcus Corp. (The) ♥
* Marriott International, Inc. A *auto*

### Insurance
  AEGON N.V. *auto*
* Aetna Inc. x
* AFLAC Inc. ♥ *auto*
* Alfa Corp. ♥
* Allstate Corp. *auto*
  American General Corp. ♥ *auto*

# Companies Listed by Industry (continued)

* AmerUs Group Co. *auto*
* Aon Corp. ♥
* AXA SA *auto*
* BB&T Corp. ♥ *auto*
  Canadian Imperial Bank of Commerce ♥
* Chubb Corp. *auto*
* CIGNA Corp. ♥
* Cincinnati Financial Corp.
* Donegal Group Inc. A ♥ *auto*
* EMC Insurance Group ♥
* FBL Financial Group, Inc. A ♥ *auto*
  Frontier Insurance Group, Inc. *auto*
* Harleysville Group, Inc. ♥
* Hartford Financial Services Group Inc ♥
  ING Groep N.V. *auto*
* Jefferson-Pilot Corp. ♥
* LabOne, Inc. ♥
* Lincoln National Corp. *auto*
* Marsh & McLennan Co., Inc.
* Meadowbrook Insurance Group ♥ *auto*
* MONY Group Inc. (The) *auto*
* Nationwide Financial Services A *auto*
* Ohio Casualty Corp. *auto*
* Old Republic International Corp. ♥
* Omnicare, Inc. ♥
* Protective Life Corp. ♥
  Prudential plc *auto*
* RLI Corp. ♥
  SCOR *auto*
* Selective Insurance Group ♥
* St. Paul Cos. (The) ♥
* State Auto Financial Corp. ♥
* Torchmark Corp.
* Union Planters National Bank ♥
* Unitrin, Inc. *auto*
* UNUMProvident Corp. *auto*
* Zions Bancorp ♥

## Machinery

* Applied Industrial Technologies, Inc. ♥
* Briggs & Stratton Corp. ♥
* Caterpillar, Inc. *auto*
* Chart Industries ♥
  CNH Global N.V. *auto*
* Crane Co. ♥
* Cummins Inc. ♥ *auto*
* Curtiss-Wright Corp. *auto*
* Deere & Company *auto*
* Donaldson Co., Inc. ♥
* Flowserve Corp. ♥
* Foster Wheeler Ltd. ♥
* Gardner Denver Inc. *auto*
* GATX Corp. ♥
* Gorman-Rupp Co. ♥
* Graco, Inc. ♥
* Honeywell International Inc. ♥
* Ingersoll-Rand ♥
* ITT Industries ♥ *auto*
* Kaman Corp. A *auto*
* Manitowoc Co. ♥
* Met-Pro Corp. ♥ *auto*
  Metso Corp. *auto*
* Milacron, Inc. ♥

* Millipore Corp. ♥
* Myers Industries, Inc. ♥
* Nordson Corp. ♥
* Pall Corp. ♥
* Parker-Hannifin Corp. ♥
* Pentair, Inc. ♥ *auto*
  Pfeiffer Vacuum Technology AG *auto*
* Robbins & Myers, Inc. ♥
* SIFCO Industries, Inc. ♥
* Smith (A.O.) Corp. B ♥
* Snap-on Inc. ♥ *auto*
* Stanley Works *auto*
* Technitrol Inc. ♥
* Tennant Co. ♥
* Textron, Inc. ♥ *auto*
* Toro Co. (The) ♥
* Twin Disc, Inc. ♥
* Tyco International Ltd. ♥ *auto*
* United Technologies ♥
* Woodward Governor Co. ♥
* York International Corp. *auto*

## Manufacturing

* AAR Corp. *auto*
* Albany International A ♥
* Allegheny Technologies Inc. *auto*
  Ametek, Inc. *auto*
  ARCADIS NV *auto*
  ASM Lithography Holding NV *auto*
* Aviall, Inc. ♥
* Bandag Inc. A ♥
* Bandag Inc. ♥
  BE Semiconductor Industries *auto*
* Boeing Co. (The) *auto*
* Briggs & Stratton Corp. ♥
  Chase Corp. *auto*
* CLARCOR Inc. ♥
  Columbus McKinnon Corp. *auto*
  Compania Cervecerias Unida SA *auto*
  CRH plc *auto*
  CSR Ltd. *auto*
  Delta Galil Industries *auto*
* Donaldson Co., Inc. ♥
  Eastern Co. (The) *auto*
* Eaton Corp. ♥ *auto*
  Epcos AG *auto*
* General Electric *auto*
* Harsco Corp. ♥
* Hillenbrand Industries *auto*
* Illinois Tool Works, Inc. ♥
* Insteel Industries, Inc. ♥
  JPS Industries, Inc. *auto*
* Kennametal, Inc. ♥
* Knape & Vogt Manufacturing Co. ♥
  Koor Industries Ltd. *auto*
  Kyocera Corp. *auto*
* La-Z-Boy, Inc. *auto*
  Laboratorio Chile S.A. *auto*
* LESCO, Inc. ♥
* Lockheed Martin ♥ *auto*
  Maderas y Sinteticos Sociedad Anonima *auto*
* Middleton Doll Company ♥
* Modine Manufacturing Co. ♥ *auto*

## Companies Listed by Industry (continued)

* Molex, Inc. A *auto*
* Newport Corp. *auto*
* Northrop Grumman Corp. ♥
  Pacific Dunlop Ltd. *auto*
* PerkinElmer Inc. ♥
* Raven Industries, Inc. ♥ *auto*
* Snap-on Inc. ♥ *auto*
  STMicroelectronics NV *auto*
  SunSource, Inc. ♥
* Thomas & Betts Corp. ♥
  Tomkins plc *auto*
* Tredegar Corp. ♥
* United Industrial Corp. ♥

### Media

  Anntenna TV *auto*
* Banta Corp. ♥ *auto*
* Bowne & Co., Inc. ♥ *auto*
  Carlton Communications plc *auto*
  Digitale Telekabel AG *auto*
* Donnelley (RR) & Sons Co. ♥
* Dow Jones & Co. ♥ *auto*
* E.W. Scripps Co. A ♥ *auto*
  Elsevier N.V. *auto*
* Gannett Co., Inc. ♥ *auto*
* General Electric *auto*
* Gray Communications Systems, Inc.B *auto*
  Gray Communications Systems, Inc.A *auto*
* Jefferson-Pilot Corp. ♥
* Knight Ridder Inc. ♥
  Matav-Cable Systems Media *auto*
* McGraw-Hill Cos. ♥ *auto*
* Media General, Inc. A ♥
  Modern Times Group *auto*
* New York Times Co. A ♥
* NTELOS Inc.
  Rank Group plc (The) *auto*
* Reader's Digest Assn., Inc. A *auto*
* Reader's Digest Assn., Inc. B *auto*
  Reed International plc *auto*
  Reuters Group plc *auto*
  Trader.com NV *auto*
* Tribune Co. *auto*
  TV Azteca *auto*
  Vivendi Universal *auto*
  Walt Disney Co. *auto*

### Medical

* Abbott Labs. ♥
* Allergan, Inc. ♥ *auto*
* Bausch & Lomb ♥
* Baxter International Inc. ♥
* Beckman Coulter Inc. ♥ *auto*
* Becton Dickinson & Co. *auto*
* Bristol-Myers Squibb
* Chemed Corp. ♥ *auto*
  ELAN Corp., plc  A
  Flamel Technologies *auto*
* Guidant Corp. *auto*
* Hillenbrand Industries *auto*
* Invacare ♥
* Johnson & Johnson ♥ *auto*
* McKesson Corporation ♥ *auto*

  MDS Inc. ♥
* Medtronic, Inc. ♥ *auto*
* Meridian Bioscience, Inc.
* Millipore Corp. ♥
* Omnicare, Inc. ♥
* Owens & Minor, Inc. ♥
* Pfizer Inc. ♥ *auto*
* Pharmacia Corp. *auto*
  Senetek plc ADS *auto*
  Sulzer Medica *auto*
* Teleflex Inc. ♥
* Tenet Healthcare Corp. ♥
* Tyco International Ltd. ♥ *auto*
* West Pharmaceutical Services Inc. ♥
  Xenova Grp. plc *auto*

### Metal Fabricating

* AK Steel Holding Corp. ♥
* Alcan Inc. ♥
* Alcoa ♥ *auto*
* Amcast Industrial Corp. ♥
* Barnes Group Inc. ♥
* Bethlehem Steel Corporation ♥
* Birmingham Steel Corp. ♥
  Carpenter Technology Corp. *auto*
* Castle (A.M.) & Co. ♥
  Eastern Co. (The) *auto*
  Grupo Imsa, SA de C.V. *auto*
* Inco Limited ♥
* IPSCO Inc. ♥
  Ispat International N.V. *auto*
* Kennametal, Inc. ♥
* Nucor Corp. ♥
* Phelps Dodge *auto*
  Pohang Iron & Steel Co. Ltd. *auto*
* Quanex Corp. ♥ *auto*
* Schnitzer Steel Industries, Inc. ♥ *auto*
* SIFCO Industries, Inc. ♥
* Timken Co. *auto*
  Tubos de Acero de Mexico SA *auto*
  USX-U.S. Steel Group ♥ *auto*
* Worthington Industries ♥ *auto*

### Metals & Mining

  Agnico-Eagle Mines Ltd. ♥
* Alcan Inc. ♥
* Alcoa ♥ *auto*
* ALLETE ♥ *auto*
  Anglogold Ltd. *auto*
* Arch Coal, Inc. ♥ *auto*
  Ashanti Goldfields Co. *auto*
* Brush Engineered Materials Inc. ♥
* Cleveland-Cliffs Inc. ♥ *auto*
  Compania de Minas Buenaventura *auto*
  Durban Roodeport Deep Ltd. *auto*
* Engelhard Corp. ♥
* Hanson plc
  Harmony Gold Mining Co. Ltd. *auto*
  Homestake Mining Co.
* Inco Limited ♥
  Lihir Gold Ltd. ADS *auto*
* MDU Resources Group ♥ *auto*
* Montana Power Co. (The) *auto*

23

## Companies Listed by Industry (continued)

Norsk Hydro A.S. *auto*
* Phelps Dodge *auto*
  Rangold & Exploration Co. *auto*
  Rio Tinto plc *auto*
* Ryerson Tull Inc. ♥
* Southern Peru Copper Corp. ♥
* TECO Energy ♥
* Unocal Corp.
  Yanzhou Coal Mining Co. Ltd. *auto*

### Natural Gas

* AGL Resources Inc. ♥ *auto*
* Cabot Corp. ♥
* Chesapeake Utilities Corp. ♥
* Duke Energy ♥ *auto*
* El Paso Corporation ♥ *auto*
* Enbridge, Inc. ♥
* Enron Corp. ♥ *auto*
* Equitable Resources Inc. ♥
* Kinder Morgan, Inc. ♥ *auto*
* National Fuel Gas ♥ *auto*
* Occidental Petroleum Corp. ♥
* ONEOK, Inc. ♥ *auto*
* Questar Corp. *auto*
* Southern Union Co. *auto*
* Southwestern Energy Co. *auto*
* TransCanada Pipelines Ltd. ♥
* UGI Corp. ♥
* UtiliCorp United Inc. ♥ *auto*
* Westcoast Energy Inc. ♥

### Office Equipment

* Avery Dennison Corp. *auto*
  Canon Inc. *auto*
* Diebold, Inc. *auto*
* Fortune Brands ♥
* Harris Corp. ♥ *auto*
* Herman Miller, Inc. *auto*
* Hewlett-Packard *auto*
* IKON Office Solutions, Inc.
* Nashua Corp. ♥
  Oce-van der Grinten N.V. *auto*
* Office Depot, Inc. *auto*
* Pitney Bowes ♥
* Reynolds & Reynolds Co. A ♥ *auto*
* Standard Register ♥ *auto*
* Tektronix *auto*
  Xeikon, N.V. *auto*
* Xerox Corp. ♥

### Oil & Gas

  Alberta Energy Co. Ltd. ♥
* Amerada Hess ♥
* Anadarko Petroleum Corp. ♥ *auto*
* Apache Corp. ♥
* Ashland Inc. ♥
* Baker Hughes Inc. ♥
* BP plc ♥ *auto*
  Canada Southern Petroleum *auto*
* Canadian Pacific Ltd. ♥
* Chevron Corp. *auto*
  Coastal Caribbean Oils & Minerals, Ltd. *auto*
* Conoco Inc. B ♥ *auto*

* Conoco Inc. A ♥ *auto*
* Dynegy Inc. A ♥ *auto*
* Enbridge, Inc. ♥
* Energen Corp. ♥ *auto*
  ENI SpA *auto*
  EON AG *auto*
* Equitable Resources Inc. ♥
* Exxon Mobil Corp. ♥ *auto*
* Imperial Oil Ltd.
* Kerr-McGee ♥
* Lyondell Chemical Co. ♥
* Magellan Petroleum Corp. *auto*
* National Fuel Gas ♥ *auto*
  Norsk Hydro A.S. *auto*
  OAO Tatneft *auto*
* Occidental Petroleum Corp. ♥
* ONEOK, Inc. ♥ *auto*
  PetroChina Co. *auto*
* Phillips Petroleum Co. ♥ *auto*
* Pride International, Inc. ♥
  Repsol S.A. ADS *auto*
  Royal Dutch Petroleum Co. *auto*
  Santos Ltd. *auto*
* Shell Trans. & Trading Co. plc ADR
  Sinopec Shanghai Petrochemical *auto*
* Southwestern Energy Co. *auto*
* Suncor Energy Inc. ♥
* Sunoco Inc. *auto*
  Texaco Inc. *auto*
* Tidewater Inc.
  Total Fina Elf SA *auto*
* Transocean Sedco Forex *auto*
  Ultramar Diamond Shamrock ♥
* Unocal Corp.
  USX-Marathon Group ♥ *auto*
* XTO Energy Inc. ♥ *auto*

### Packaging

* Ball Corp. ♥
* Bemis Co., Inc. ♥
* Caraustar Industries, Inc. *auto*
* Chesapeake Corp. ♥
* CLARCOR Inc. ♥
* Crown Cork & Seal Co., Inc. ♥ *auto*
  Grupo Industrial Durango, SA *auto*
* International Paper ♥ *auto*
  Jefferson Smurfit plc *auto*
* Mead Corp. *auto*
  Savia SA de C.V. *auto*
* Sonoco Products Co. *auto*
* West Pharmaceutical Services Inc. ♥
* Westvaco Corp. ♥ *auto*

### Paper & Lumber

* ALLETE ♥ *auto*
  AMCOR Ltd. *auto*
* Boise Cascade Corp.
* Bowater Inc. ♥
* Chesapeake Corp. ♥
* Crown Pacific Partners LP ♥
* Georgia-Pacific Group *auto*
  Grupo Industrial Durango, SA *auto*
* International Paper ♥ *auto*

## Companies Listed by Industry (continued)

* Kimberly-Clark Corp. ♥
* Louisiana-Pacific Corp. ♥
* Mead Corp. *auto*
* Potlatch Corp. ♥
* Rayonier Inc.
  Sappi Ltd. *auto*
* Temple-Inland ♥
* Universal Corp. ♥ *auto*
* Wausau-Mosinee Paper Corp. ♥
* Westvaco Corp. ♥ *auto*
* Weyerhaeuser Co.

### Personnel Services

  Adecco SA *auto*
* Chemed Corp. ♥ *auto*
* Kelly Services, Inc. A *auto*
* Manpower ♥
* Paychex, Inc. ♥ *auto*
* ServiceMaster Co. ♥ *auto*

### Photography

* Eastman Kodak *auto*
* Polaroid Corp.

### Real Estate Investment Trusts

  Acadia Realty Trust *auto*
* AMB Property Corp. ♥
* AMLI Residential Properties ♥
* Annaly Mortgage Mgmt., Inc. ♥ *auto*
* Anthracite Capital ♥ *auto*
* Anworth Mortgage Asset Corp. ♥
* Archstone Communities Trust ♥ *auto*
* Associated Estates Realty Corp. ♥ *auto*
* AvalonBay Communities, Inc. ♥
* Bedford Property Investors ♥ *auto*
* BNP Residential Properties, Inc. ♥
* Boston Properties, Inc. ♥ *auto*
* Boykin Lodging Co. ♥
* Brandywine Realty Trust ♥ *auto*
* BRE Properties, Inc. ♥ *auto*
* Cabot Industrial Trust *auto*
* Camden Property Trust ♥
* Capital Automotive REIT ♥ *auto*
* CarrAmerica
* CBL & Associates Properties, Inc. ♥
* CenterPoint Properties Trust ♥
  Charles E. Smith Res. Rlty. Inc. ♥
* Colonial Properties Trust *auto*
* Cornerstone Realty Income Trust, Inc. ♥ *auto*
* Crown American Realty Trust ♥ *auto*
* Developers Diversified Realty ♥
* Duke Realty Corporation ♥ *auto*
* Entertainment Properties Trust ♥ *auto*
* Equity Office Properties Trust ♥ *auto*
* Equity Residential Prop. Trust ♥
* Essex Property Trust, Inc. *auto*
* Federal Realty Investment Trust ♥ *auto*
* General Growth Properties ♥
* Glenborough Realty Trust *auto*

* Glimcher Realty Trust ♥
* Health Care Property Investors, Inc. ♥ *auto*
* Health Care REIT ♥
* Healthcare Realty Trust ♥
* Highwoods Properties, Inc. ♥
* Home Properties of NY ♥ *auto*
* Hospitality Properties Trust ♥
* HRPT Properties Trust ♥
* Innkeepers USA Trust ♥
* iStar Financial Inc. ♥ *auto*
* Jameson Inns, Inc. ♥
* JDN Realty Corp. ♥
* Karmont Realty Trust ♥
* Kilroy Realty Corp. ♥
* Kimco Realty Corp. *auto*
* La Quinta Companies ♥
* LaSalle Hotel Properties ♥
* Liberty Property Trust ♥ *auto*
* LTC Properties, Inc.
* Macerich Co. ♥ *auto*
* Mack-Cali Realty Corp. ♥ *auto*
* Manufactured Home Communities ♥
* Maxus Realty Trust Inc.
* Mid-America Apt. Communities, Inc. ♥
* Mills Corp. (The) *auto*
* Monmouth Capital Corp. ♥
* Monmouth REIT ♥
* National Health Investors ♥
* New Plan Excel Realty Trust ♥
* Omega Healthcare Investor ♥ *auto*
* Pan Pacific Retail Properties, Inc. ♥ *auto*
* Parkway Properties Inc. ♥ *auto*
* Pennsylvania REIT ♥
* Prentiss Properties Trust *auto*
* Presidential Realty B ♥
* ProLogis Trust ♥ *auto*
* Redwood Trust, Inc. ♥
* Rouse Co. ♥
* Senior Housing Properties Trust ♥
* Sizeler Property Investors Inc. *auto*
* Sovran Self Storage, Inc. ♥
* Storage USA, Inc. ♥
* Summit Properties ♥
* Tanger Factory Outlet Centers, Inc. ♥
* Taubman Centers, Inc. *auto*
* Thornburg Mortgage, Inc. ♥
* United Dominion Realty Trust ♥
  United Investors Realty Trust ♥ *auto*
* Universal Health Realty Income Trust ♥
* Washington REIT *auto*
* Weingarten Realty Investors A ♥ *auto*
* Winston Hotels, Inc. ♥ *auto*

### Recreation

* Anheuser-Busch Cos. ♥
* Brunswick Corp. ♥
* Callaway Golf Co. ♥

# Companies Listed by Industry (continued)

* Cedar Fair L.P. ♥
Ducati Motor Holding *auto*
* Fortune Brands ♥
* Harley-Davidson ♥
* Hasbro Inc. ♥ *auto*
* Huffy Corp. *auto*
* Kaman Corp. A *auto*
* Marcus Corp. (The) ♥
* Mattel Inc. *auto*
P&O Princess Cruises plc *auto*
Rank Group plc (The) *auto*
* Sea Containers Ltd. A ♥
Walt Disney Co. *auto*
Zindart Ltd. *auto*

## Restaurant

* Bob Evans Farms ♥ *auto*
* CBRL Group, Inc. ♥
* Darden Restaurants
Diageo plc ADS *auto*
* Luby's Inc. ♥
* Marcus Corp. (The) ♥
* McDonald's Corp. *auto*
* Piccadilly Cafeterias Inc. ♥
* Sea Containers Ltd. A ♥
* Tricon Global Restaurants, Inc. *auto*
* Wendy's International, Inc. ♥ *auto*

## Retail

* Albertson's, Inc.
Blue Square-Israel Ltd. *auto*
* Brown Shoe Co., Inc. ♥
* Casey's General Store ♥ *auto*
* CBRL Group, Inc. ♥
Companhia Brasileira de Distribuicao *auto*
* Compaq Computer *auto*
* CPI Corp. ♥
* CVS Corp. A
* Dollar General Corp. *auto*
* Fleming Companies, Inc. ♥
* Genuine Parts Co. ♥
Grupo Elektra, SA de C.V. *auto*
* Home Depot *auto*
* Intimate Brands, Inc. A *auto*
* Jacobson Stores Inc. ♥
* Kmart Corp. *auto*
* Limited (The) ♥
* Longs Drug Stores *auto*
* Lowe's Cos., Inc. *auto*
* Marsh Supermarkets A ♥
* Marsh Supermarkets B ♥
* May Dept. Stores Co.
* Michaels Stores ♥
* Nash Finch Co. ♥
* Neiman Marcus Group A ♥
* Neiman Marcus Group B ♥
* Penney (J.C.) *auto*
* Pep Boys ♥
* Pier 1 Imports Inc. ♥ *auto*
* RadioShack Corp. *auto*
Rite Aid Corp. ♥
Royal Ahold *auto*
* Ruddick Corp ♥

* Sears, Roebuck & Co. *auto*
Signet Group plc *auto*
* Stride Rite Corp. (The)
Super-Sol Ltd. *auto*
Supermercados Unimarc SA *auto*
* Supervalu, Inc. ♥
* Target Corp. *auto*
* Venator Group ♥
* Wal-Mart Stores *auto*
* Walgreen Co. *auto*
* Weis Markets, Inc. ♥
* Winn-Dixie Stores, Inc. ♥ *auto*

## Services-Misc.

* Bowne & Co., Inc. ♥ *auto*
* Paychex, Inc. ♥ *auto*
* Reynolds & Reynolds Co. A ♥ *auto*
* Schawk, Inc. ♥ *auto*
* ServiceMaster Co. ♥ *auto*
* Strayer Education Inc. ♥
Telewest Communications plc *auto*

## Services-Real Estate

IRSA Inversiones y Representaciones SA *auto*
* W.P. Carey & Co. ♥ *auto*

## Telecommunications

* ADC Telecommunications, Inc. *auto*
Alcatel Alsthom SA *auto*
Aliant Inc. ♥
* ALLTEL Corp. ♥ *auto*
APT Satellite *auto*
Asia Satellite Tele. Holdings Ltd. *auto*
* AT&T Corp. *auto*
* Avaya Inc. *auto*
* BCE Inc. ♥
* BellSouth Corp. ♥ *auto*
British Telecommunications plc *auto*
* BroadWing Inc. ♥
* CenturyTel, Inc. ♥ *auto*
China Telecom Ltd. *auto*
* Citizens Communications B *auto*
* Conestoga Enterprises, Inc. ♥
Corning Inc. ♥ *auto*
* D&E Communications, Inc. ♥
Deutsche Telekom AG *auto*
Embratel Participacoes SA *auto*
Emcee Broadcast Products, Inc. *auto*
Empresas Telex-Chile *auto*
Equant NV *auto*
France Telecom *auto*
General Cable *auto*
* Global Crossing Ltd. ♥
Groupe AB ADS *auto*
* Harris Corp. ♥ *auto*
Jazztel plc *auto*
* LION Inc. *auto*
LM Ericsson Telephone Co. *auto*
Lucent Technologies Inc. *auto*
Magyar Tavkozlesi Rt. (MATAV) *auto*
Marconi plc *auto*
* Montana Power Co. (The) *auto*
* Motorola, Inc. *auto*

## Companies Listed by Industry (continued)

Movil@ccess SA de CV *auto*
Nera A.S. ADS *auto*
Nippon Telephone & Telegraph Corp. *auto*
\* Nokia Corp. *auto*
Nuevo Grupo Iusacell *auto*
OAO Rostelecom *auto*
P.T. IndoSat *auto*
P.T. Pasifik Satelit Nusantara *auto*
P.T. Telkom *auto*
Portugal Telecom *auto*
\* SBC Communications *auto*
\* Scientific-Atlanta ♥
\* Sprint Corp. (FON Group) ♥
STET Hellas Telecomm. SA *auto*
Tele Celular Sul Participacoes SA *auto*
Tele Centro Oeste Celular Participacoes SA *auto*
Tele Leste Celular Participacoes SA *auto*
Tele Nordesto Celular Participacoes SA *auto*
Tele Norte Celular Participacoes SA *auto*
Tele Norte Leste Participacoes SA *auto*
Tele Sudeste Celular Participacoes SA *auto*
Tele2 AB *auto*
Telecom Argentina Stet-France Telecom SA *auto*
Telecom Corp. of New Zealand Ltd. *auto*
Telecom Italia SpA *auto*
Telecomunicacoes Brasileiras SA *auto*
Telefonica del Peru SA *auto*
Telefonos de Mexico, SA de C.V. *auto*
Telemig Celular Participacoes SA *auto*
\* Telephone & Data Systems ♥
Telesp Celular Participacoes SA *auto*
Telesp Participacoes SA *auto*
Telstra Corp. Ltd. *auto*
\* TELUS Corporation ♥
Tricom, SA *auto*
\* Verizon Communications, Inc. *auto*
VersaTel Telecom Int'l N.V. *auto*
VimpelCom *auto*
Vodafone Group plc *auto*
Wavecom SA *auto*

### Textile
\* Russell Corp. ♥
\* Tredegar Corp. ♥

### Tires & Rubber
\* Carlisle Companies Inc. ♥
\* Goodyear Tire & Rubber *auto*

### Tobacco
British American Tobacco plc
Gallaher Group plc *auto*
Imperial Tobacco Group plc *auto*
\* Philip Morris ♥ *auto*
\* R.J. Reynolds Tobacco Holdings, Inc. *auto*
Savia SA de C.V. *auto*
\* Standard Commercial Corp. ♥
Swedish Match AB *auto*
\* Universal Corp. ♥ *auto*
\* UST Inc. ♥

### Transportation
Anangel-American Shipholdings Ltd. *auto*

\* Arnold Industries, Inc. ♥
British Airways plc *auto*
\* Burlington Northern Santa Fe Corp.
\* Canadian Pacific Ltd. ♥
China Eastern Airlines Corp. *auto*
China Southern Airlines Co. Ltd. *auto*
\* CNF Transportation Inc.
\* Consolidated Freightways Corp. *auto*
\* CSX Corp. ♥
\* Delta Air Lines, Inc. *auto*
\* FedEx Corp. *auto*
\* GATX Corp. ♥
\* Greif Brothers Corp. A ♥
Guangshen Railway Co. Ltd. *auto*
\* Manitowoc Co. ♥
Newport News Shipbuilding *auto*
\* Nicor Inc. ♥
\* Norfolk Southern Corp.
\* Roadway Corporation *auto*
Ryanair *auto*
\* Ryder System, Inc. ♥
\* Sea Containers Ltd. A ♥
\* Tidewater Inc.
\* UAL Corp. *auto*
\* Union Pacific Corp. ♥

### Utility-Electric
\* Allegheny Energy
\* ALLETE ♥ *auto*
\* Alliant Energy Corp. ♥ *auto*
\* Ameren Corp. *auto*
\* American Electric Power ♥ *auto*
\* Avista Corp.
\* Black Hills Corp. ♥
\* Central Vermont Public Service *auto*
\* CH Energy Group, Inc. ♥ *auto*
\* Cinergy Corp. ♥ *auto*
\* CLECO Corp. ♥
\* CMS Energy ♥ *auto*
Companhia Paranaense de Energia *auto*
\* Consolidated Edison
\* Constellation Energy Group, Inc.
\* Dominion Resources ♥ *auto*
\* DPL Inc. ♥
\* DQE *auto*
\* DTE Energy Co.
\* Duke Energy ♥ *auto*
\* Edison International ♥ *auto*
\* Empire District Electric Co. *auto*
Endesa SA *auto*
Energis plc *auto*
\* Energy East Corp. ♥
\* Enron Corp. ♥ *auto*
\* Entergy Corp.
\* Exelon Corporation *auto*
\* FirstEnergy *auto*
\* Florida Public Utilities Co. ♥
\* FPL Group, Inc. ♥
\* Green Mountain Power ♥
\* Hawaiian Electric Ind. *auto*
Huaneng Power Int'l, Inc. *auto*
\* IDACORP, Inc.
International Power plc *auto*

## Companies Listed by Industry (continued)

* Kansas City Power & Light *auto*
  Korea Electric Power Corp. *auto*
* Madison Gas & Electric Co. *auto*
* MDU Resources Group ♥ *auto*
* Montana Power Co. (The) *auto*
* NiSource Inc. ♥
* NorthWestern Corp. ♥ *auto*
* NSTAR ♥ *auto*
* OGE Energy Corp. ♥ *auto*
* Otter Tail Corporation ♥
* Pinnacle West Capital Corp. *auto*
* Potomac Electric Power ♥
  PowerGen plc *auto*
* PPL Corp. ♥
* Progress Energy *auto*
* Public Service Co. of NM *auto*
* Public Service Enterprise Group ♥ *auto*
* Puget Energy, Inc.
* Reliant Energy *auto*
* SCANA Corp. *auto*
  Scottish Power UK plc *auto*
* Sempra Energy ♥ *auto*
* Sierra Pacific Resources
* Southern Co. ♥ *auto*
* TECO Energy ♥
  Transalta Corp. ♥
* TXU Corp. ♥ *auto*
* UGI Corp. ♥
* UIL Holdings Corp. *auto*
* UniSource Energy Corp. ♥ *auto*
* Unitil Corp. ♥
* UtiliCorp United Inc. ♥ *auto*
* Vectren Corp. ♥ *auto*
  Western Resources, Inc. ♥ *auto*
* Wisconsin Energy Corp. ♥ *auto*
* WPS Resources Corp. ♥ *auto*
* Xcel Energy Inc. ♥ *auto*

### Utility-Natural Gas

* AGL Resources Inc. ♥ *auto*
* Allegheny Energy
* Alliant Energy Corp. ♥ *auto*
* Ameren Corp. *auto*
* Atmos Energy Corp. ♥ *auto*
* Avista Corp.
  BC Gas, Inc. ♥
* Cascade Natural Gas ♥
* CH Energy Group, Inc. ♥ *auto*
* Chesapeake Utilities Corp. ♥
* Cinergy Corp. ♥ *auto*
* CLECO Corp. ♥
* Consolidated Edison
* Constellation Energy Group, Inc.
* Delta Natural Gas Co., Inc. ♥
* Duke Energy ♥ *auto*
* Energen Corp. ♥ *auto*
* Energy East Corp. ♥
* EnergySouth, Inc. ♥
* Florida Public Utilities Co. ♥
* Keyspan Energy Corp. ♥ *auto*
* Laclede Gas Co. ♥
* Madison Gas & Electric Co. *auto*
* MDU Resources Group ♥ *auto*

* Montana Power Co. (The) *auto*
* National Fuel Gas ♥ *auto*
* New Jersey Resources Corp. ♥ *auto*
* Nicor Inc. ♥
* NiSource Inc. ♥
* Northwest Natural Gas Co. ♥ *auto*
* NorthWestern Corp. ♥ *auto*
* NUI Corp. ♥ *auto*
* OGE Energy Corp. ♥ *auto*
* ONEOK, Inc. ♥ *auto*
* Peoples Energy Corp. ♥ *auto*
* Piedmont Natural Gas ♥ *auto*
* Public Service Co. of NM *auto*
* Public Service Enterprise Group ♥ *auto*
* Puget Energy, Inc.
* Questar Corp. *auto*
* Reliant Energy *auto*
* RGC Resources Inc. ♥ *auto*
* SCANA Corp. *auto*
* SEMCO Energy Inc. ♥ *auto*
* Sempra Energy ♥ *auto*
* Sierra Pacific Resources
* South Jersey Industries, Inc. ♥
* Southwest Gas Corp. ♥ *auto*
* UGI Corp. ♥
* Unitil Corp. ♥
* UtiliCorp United Inc. ♥ *auto*
* Vectren Corp. ♥ *auto*
  Western Resources, Inc. ♥ *auto*
* WGL Holdings, Inc.
* Wisconsin Energy Corp. ♥ *auto*
* WPS Resources Corp. ♥ *auto*
* Xcel Energy Inc. ♥ *auto*

### Utility-Water

* ALLETE ♥ *auto*
* American States Water ♥ *auto*
* American Water Works ♥
* Artesian Resources Corp. A ♥
* California Water Service Group ♥ *auto*
* Connecticut Water Service Inc. ♥ *auto*
* Middlesex Water Co. ♥
* NiSource Inc. ♥
* Pennichuck Corp. ♥
* Philadelphia Suburban Corp. ♥ *auto*
* Sierra Pacific Resources
* Southwest Water Co. ♥

### Waste Removal
* Waste Management, Inc. *auto*

# How to Read the Company Listings in the Following Section

## Left-Hand Column

\* An asterisk before the COMPANY NAME indicates that enrollment is available through the **Temper Enrollment Service**. Stock symbol and exchange.

    **N/A:** Information not available to us  **N/O:** Not offered by company

    **H:** 52-week high price  **L:** 52-week low price

    **Rec:** Recent price

    **Div:** The annual dividend (divide by 4 for quarterly dividend). A dividend may be paid in the form of corporate stock.

        *STK:* Dividend is paid in the form of stock.

    **Paid on:** Indicates the months and approximate days when the dividends are paid.

    **Since:** The year when the company started paying dividends.

## Center Column

Company name, company industry, company address, agent's name and phone number, minimum and maximum cash investments allowed, investment frequency, and the first opportunity to invest each year.

A heart symbol ♥ means the company does not charge fees for investing or reinvesting. A prohibit symbol ⊘ means the company charges high fees.

**Note:** BankBoston, Boston Eq., First Chicago Trust, State Street Bank, and Wachovia are all divisions of EquiServe.

    *Amounts shown in center column:* Dollar amounts shown indicate the minimum and maximum investments accepted—per year, per quarter, per month, or per week.

    **Fees:** Any service fees levied by a company are included in that company's listing.

        *Div:* Fee charged when dividends are reinvested.

        *Cash:* Fee charged for cash investments.

        *Auto Inv:* Fee charged when automatic investments are made.

        *Cert:* Fee charged for issuing a certificate.

        *Term:* Fee charged to terminate an account.

        *Selling:* Indicates when shares are sold, how sell orders can be placed, at what price shares are sold, and the fee the company charges to sell shares through the plan.

        *Comm:* Broker's commission

! An exclamation point on the FEES line indicates that the fee is <u>paid by the company</u>.

## Right-Hand Column

**Shares to qualify:** Indicates the minimum number of shares required to open a DRIP in that company to make optional cash investments.

    **de** A "de" after SHARES TO QUALIFY indicates direct enrollment through the transfer agent (and often results in fees for investing cash). The number in parentheses is the minimum investment required.

    **de/restricted** A "de/restricted" means direct enrollment is available only under certain conditions.

    **Safekeeping:** Indicates that plan accepts certificated shares.

    **Accepts foreign:** Foreign investors (Yes or No).

    **Auto inv.:** Automatically withdraws of money from your bank to make optional cash investments.

    **Disc.:** Offers a discount from market price.

    *Div:* Indicates that a discount is given when dividends are reinvested.

    *Cash:* Indicates that a discount is given when optional cash investments are made.

*Do not become enrolled in a DRIP unless you plan to make subsequent investments to acquire additional shares. Dividends earned on only the minimum shares to qualify will not result in meaningful accumulation.*

# Listing of companies with

# Direct Investment Plans

✷ An asterisk indicates that plan enrollment can be handled through the Temper Enrollment Service (see page 180). Once enrolled, subsequent investments can be made without a broker. Call 1-800-295-2550 or visit www.directinvesting.com.

---

| ✶ | **7-Eleven, Inc.** ⊗ | |
|---|---|---|
| **SE/NYSE** | **Convenience food stores** | **Shares to qualify:** 1 /de ($250) |
| H: 14.62 | 2711 N. Haskell Ave. | **Safekeeping:** Yes |
| L: 8.00 | Dallas. TX 75204 | **Accepts foreign:** Yes |
| **Rec:** 12.81 | Computershare Investor Svcs.      877-360-5464 | **Auto. inv.:** Yes |
| **Div.:** 0.00 | $100 - $120,000/year | **Disc.:** No |
| **Paid on:** | Every 5 days beginning varies | |
| N/0 | FEES: Div: n/o;  Cash: $5 + 10¢/sh.;  Auto. Inv.: $1.50 + 10¢/sh.; Cert: $5;  Term: $10 + | |
| **Since:**-- | 10¢/sh.; Sells within 5 bus. days, by mail or fax, at market, for $10 + 10¢/sh. | |

---

| ✶ | **AAR Corp.** ⊗ | |
|---|---|---|
| **AIR/NYSE** | **Aviation parts & services** | **Shares to qualify:** 1 |
| H: 17.45 | 1 AAR Pl.,1100 North Wood Dale Rd. | **Safekeeping:** Yes |
| L: 9.75 | Wood Dale. IL 60191 | **Accepts foreign:** Yes |
| **Rec:** 16.55 | First Chicago Trust     800-446-2617 | **Auto. inv.:** Yes |
| **Div.:** 0.34 | $50 - $250,000/year | **Disc.:** No |
| **Paid on:** | Every 30 days beginning 1/2 | |
| 3.6.9.12-5 | FEES: Div: $0!;  Cash: $5 + 3¢/sh.;  Auto. Inv.: $2 + 3¢/sh.; Cert: $0!;  Term: $0; Sells daily, | |
| **Since:**1973 | by mail, fax , or phone, at market, for $15 + 12¢/sh. | |

---

| ✶ | **Abbott Labs.** ♥ | |
|---|---|---|
| **ABT/NYSE** | **Drugs, health care** | **Shares to qualify:** 1 |
| H: 56.25 | 100 Abbott Park Rd., Dept. 312, AP6D2 | **Safekeeping:** Yes |
| L: 39.31 | Abbott Park. IL 60064-3500 | **Accepts foreign:** Yes |
| **Rec:** 52.25 | Boston Eq.     888-332-2268 | **Auto. inv.:** No |
| **Div.:** 0.84 | $10 - $5,000/quarter | **Disc.:** No |
| **Paid on:** | Every 45 days beginning 2/15 | |
| 2.5.8.11-15 | FEES: Div: $0!; Cash: $0!; Cert: $0!; Term: $0; Sells within 10 bus. days, by mail or phone, | |
| **Since:**1926 | at market, for 15¢/sh. | |

---

| ✶ | **Aberdeen Asia-Pacific Income Fund, Inc.** | |
|---|---|---|
| **FAX/ASE** | **Closed-end fund** | **Shares to qualify:** 1 |
| H: 4.62 | c/o Aberdeen Asset, 45 Broadway, 31st Fl. | **Safekeeping:** Yes |
| L: 3.66 | New York. NY 10006 | **Accepts foreign:** Yes |
| **Rec:** 4.11 | State St. Bank     800-451-6788 | **Auto. inv.:** No |
| **Div.:** 0.54 | $100 - $unlimited | **Disc.:** Div 5% Cash: 0% |
| **Paid on:** | Every 30 days beginning 1/15 | |
| MONTHLY-15 | FEES: Div: $0; Cash: 75¢ + 2¢/sh.; Cert: $0; Term: $2.50 + 15¢/sh.; Sells irregularly, by | |
| **Since:**N/A | mail or phone, at market, for $2.50 + 15¢/sh. | |

---

## ✱ Aberdeen Australia Equity Fund, Inc.

| | | |
|---|---|---|
| **IAF/ASE** | **Closed-end fund** | **Shares to qualify:** 1 |
| H: 6.62 | c/o Aberdeen Asset, 45 Broadway, 31st Fl. | **Safekeeping:** Yes |
| L: 5.20 | New York. NY 10006 | **Accepts foreign:** Yes |
| **Rec:** 5.89 | State St. Bank     800-451-6788 | **Auto. inv.:** No |
| **Div.:** 0.65 | $100 - $unlimited | **Disc.:** Div 5% Cash: 0% |
| **Paid on:** | Every 30 days beginning 1/15 | |
| MONTHLY-13 | FEES: Div: $0!; Cash: 75¢ + 2¢/sh.; Cert: $0; Term: $2.50 + 15¢/sh.; Sells irregularly, by | |
| **Since:** N/A | mail or phone, at market, for $2.50 + 15¢/sh. | |

## ✱ Aberdeen Commonwealth Income Fund, Inc.

| | | |
|---|---|---|
| **FCO/NYSE** | **Closed-end fund** | **Shares to qualify:** 1 |
| H: 9.56 | c/o Aberdeen Asset, 45 Broadway, 31st Fl. | **Safekeeping:** Yes |
| L: 8.18 | New York. NY 10006 | **Accepts foreign:** Yes |
| **Rec:** 8.92 | State St. Bank     800-426-5523 | **Auto. inv.:** No |
| **Div.:** 0.84 | $100 - $unlimited | **Disc.:** Div 5% Cash: 0% |
| **Paid on:** | Every 30 days beginning 1/15 | |
| MONTHLY-13 | FEES: Div: $0!; Cash: 75¢ + 2¢/sh.; Cert: $0; Term: $2.50 + 15¢/sh.; Sells irregularly, by | |
| **Since:** N/A | mail or phone, at market, for $2.50 + 15¢/sh. | |

## ✱ Abington Bancorp, Inc.

| | | |
|---|---|---|
| **ABBK/NASD** | **Bank holding company** | **Shares to qualify:** 1 |
| H: 17.00 | 536 Washington St., Box 2006 | **Safekeeping:** Yes |
| L: 8.75 | Abington. MA 02351 | **Accepts foreign:** No |
| **Rec:** 16.30 | Registrar & Transfer     800-368-5948 | **Auto. inv.:** Yes |
| **Div.:** 0.40 | $250 - $unlimited | **Disc.:** No |
| **Paid on:** | Every 90 days beginning 1/23 | |
| 1.4.7.10-23 | FEES: Div: $0!; Cash: $1; Auto. Inv.: $1; Cert: $0!; Term: $0; Sells weekly, by mail, at | |
| **Since:** 1988 | market, for $5 + comm. | |

## Acadia Realty Trust

| | | |
|---|---|---|
| **AKR/NYSE** | **REIT** | **Shares to qualify:** 1 /de ($250) |
| H: 7.22 | 20 Soundview Marketplace | **Safekeeping:** Yes |
| L: 5.50 | Port Washington. NY 11050 | **Accepts foreign:** Yes |
| **Rec:** 6.97 | American Stock Transfer     800-278-4353 | **Auto. inv.:** Yes |
| **Div.:** 0.48 | $25 - $10,000/investment | **Disc.:** No |
| **Paid on:** | Every day days beginning daily | |
| 1.4.7.10-17 | FEES: Div: 2% to $1.50 + 10¢/sh.; Cash: $2.50 + 10¢/sh.; Auto. Inv.: $2.50 + 10¢/sh.; | |
| **Since:** 1999 | Cert: $0; Term: $7.50 + 10¢/sh.; Sells daily, by phone, mail, fax, or Internet, at market, for | |
| | $7.50 + 10¢/sh. | |

## ✱ Adams Express Co.

| | | |
|---|---|---|
| **ADX/NYSE** | **Closed-end fund** | **Shares to qualify:** 1 /de ($500) |
| H: 27.04 | 7 St. Paul St., Ste. 1140 | **Safekeeping:** Yes |
| L: 16.01 | Baltimore. MD 21202 | **Accepts foreign:** Yes |
| **Rec:** 16.90 | Bank of New York     800-432-8224 | **Auto. inv.:** Yes |
| **Div.:** 0.16 | $50 - $25,000/investment | **Disc.:** No |
| **Paid on:** | Every day days beginning daily | |
| 3.6.9-1 & 12-27 | FEES: Div: 10% to $2.50 + 5¢/sh.; Cash: $2.50 + 5¢/sh.; Auto. Inv.: $2.50 + 5¢/sh.; | |
| **Since:** N/A | Cert: $0; Term: $10 + 5¢/sh.; Sells weekly, by mail, fax or phone, at avg. price, for $10 + | |
| | 5¢/sh. | |

## ✱ ADC Telecommunications, Inc. ⊗

| | | |
|---|---|---|
| **ADCT/NASD** | **Communications equipment** | **Shares to qualify:** 1 /de ($500) |
| H: 47.25 | 12501 Whitewater Dr. | **Safekeeping:** Yes |
| L: 4.41 | Minnetonka. MN 55343 | **Accepts foreign:** Yes |
| **Rec:** 4.74 | Computershare Investor Svcs.     800-929-6782 | **Auto. inv.:** Yes |
| **Div.:** 0.00 | $50 - $250,000/year | **Disc.:** No |
| **Paid on:** | Every 5 days beginning varies | |
| DIV. SUSP. | FEES: Div: n/o; Cash: $5 + 5¢/sh.; Auto. Inv.: $2 + 5¢/sh.; Cert: $10; Term: $0; Sells | |
| **Since:** -- | daily, by phone, mail, fax, or Internet, at avg. price, for $10 + 15¢/sh. | |

## ✱ Advanta Corp.-B ♥

| | | |
|---|---|---|
| **ADVNB/NAS** | **Mkts. consumer fin'l prods.** | **Shares to qualify:** 25 /de ($1500) |
| H: 17.10 | Welsh and McKean Rds., Box 844 | **Safekeeping:** Yes |
| L: 4.12 | Spring House. PA 19477 | **Accepts foreign:** Yes |
| **Rec:** 11.52 | Mellon Inv. Svcs.     800-851-9673 | **Auto. inv.:** No |
| **Div.:** 0.30 | $50 - $3,000/month | **Disc.:** No |
| **Paid on:** | Every 30 days beginning 1/18 | |
| 3.6.9.12-18 | FEES: Div: $0!; Cash: $0!; Cert: $0!; Term: $0; Sells weekly, by mail, at market, for $15 + | |
| **Since:** 1992 | 12¢/sh. | |

---

✱ DRIP enrollment through Temper Enrollment Service (see page 180).     **31**

## Aetna Inc. ⊗

**AET/NYSE** — Insurance, retirement svcs.

H: 70.00
L: 23.01
Rec: 26.52
Div.: 0.80
Paid on: DECEMBER-14
Since: 1934

151 Farmington Ave.
Hartford. CT 06156

First Chicago Trust    800-446-2617

$50 - $250,000/year
Every 7 days beginning varies

**Shares to qualify:** 1 /de
**Safekeeping:** Yes
**Accepts foreign:** Yes
**Auto. inv.:** Yes
**Disc.:** No

FEES: Div: 5% to $3 + 10¢/sh.; Cash: $5 + 10¢/sh.; Auto. Inv.: $1 + 10¢/sh.; Cert: $0; Term: $0; Sells daily, by phone or mail, at market, for $15 + 12¢/sh.

---

## AFLAC Inc. ♥

**AFL/NYSE** — Insurance

H: 37.46
L: 23.38
Rec: 27.40
Div.: 0.20
Paid on: 3.6.9.12-1
Since: 1973

1932 Wynnton Rd.
Columbus. GA 31999

AFLAC Inc.    800-235-2667

$50 - $120,000/year
Every 15 days beginning 1/12

**Shares to qualify:** 1 /de ($1000)
**Safekeeping:** Yes
**Accepts foreign:** Yes
**Auto. inv.:** Yes
**Disc.:** No

FEES: Div: $0; Cash: $0; Auto. Inv.: $0; Cert: $0; Term: $0; Sells within 5 bus. days, by mail or fax, at market, for 5¢/sh.

---

## AGL Resources Inc. ♥

**ATG/NYSE** — Natural gas holding co.

H: 24.42
L: 17.93
Rec: 24.42
Div.: 1.08
Paid on: 3.6.9.12-1
Since: 1939

Box 4569
Atlanta. GA 30302-4569

State St. Bank    800-633-4236

$25 - $5,000/month
Every 15 days beginning 1/2

**Shares to qualify:** 1 /de ($250)
**Safekeeping:** Yes
**Accepts foreign:** Yes
**Auto. inv.:** Yes
**Disc.:** No

FEES: Div: $0!; Cash: $0!; Auto. Inv.: $0; Cert: $0!; Term: $0; Sells within 10 bus. days, by mail, at market, for comm.

---

## Air Products & Chemicals, Inc. ⊗

**APD/NYSE** — Industrial gases

H: 49.00
L: 30.50
Rec: 42.09
Div.: 0.80
Paid on: 2.5.8.11-10
Since: 1954

7201 Hamilton Blvd.
Allentown. PA 18195-1501

First Chicago Trust    800-519-3111

$100 - $200,000/year
Every 5 days beginning varies

**Shares to qualify:** 1 /de ($500)
**Safekeeping:** Yes
**Accepts foreign:** Yes
**Auto. inv.:** Yes
**Disc.:** No

FEES: Div: 5% to $3 + 3¢/sh.; Cash: $5 + 10¢/sh.; Auto. Inv.: $2 + 10¢/sh.; Cert: $0; Term: $0; Sells within 5 bus. days, by mail or phone, at avg. price, for $10 + 12¢/sh.

---

## AK Steel Holding Corp. ♥

**AKS/NYSE** — Integrated steel producer

H: 15.00
L: 7.50
Rec: 13.35
Div.: 0.25
Paid on: 2.5.8.11-15
Since: 1995

703 Curtis St.
Middeltown. OH 45053-0001

Fifth Third Bancorp    800-837-2755

$25 - $4,000/month
Every 30 days beginning 1/15

**Shares to qualify:** 1
**Safekeeping:** Yes
**Accepts foreign:** Yes
**Auto. inv.:** No
**Disc.:** No

FEES: Div: $0!; Cash: $0!; Cert: $0!; Term: $5 + comm.; Sells weekly, by mail or fax, at market, for $5 + comm.

---

## Albany International-A ♥

**AIN/NYSE** — Mfr. of paper, machinery, clothing

H: 23.00
L: 9.62
Rec: 20.30
Div.: 0.00
Paid on: DIV.SUSP.
Since: --

Box 1907
Albany. NY 12201-1907

Computershare Investor Svcs.    312-360-5395

$10 - $5,000/month
Every 30 days beginning 1/2

**Shares to qualify:** 1
**Safekeeping:** Yes
**Accepts foreign:** No
**Auto. inv.:** No
**Disc.:** No

FEES: Div: n/o; Cash: $0!; Cert: $0!; Term: $0; Sells weekly, by mail or fax, at market, for $10 + 8¢/sh.

---

## Albemarle Corp. ♥

**ALB/NYSE** — Mfr. special and fine chemicals

H: 26.12
L: 18.50
Rec: 20.89
Div.: 0.52
Paid on: 1.4.7.10-1
Since: 1994

451 Florida St.
Baton Rouge. LA 70801

Computershare Investor Svcs.    312-360-5146

$25 - $1,000/month
Every 30 days beginning 1/2

**Shares to qualify:** 1
**Safekeeping:** No
**Accepts foreign:** Yes
**Auto. inv.:** No
**Disc.:** No

FEES: Div: $0; Cash: $0; Cert: $0; Term: $0; Sells irregularly, by mail, at market, for 7¢/sh.

---

✱ DRIP enrollment through Temper Enrollment Service (see page 180).          **32**

## Albertson's, Inc. ⊗ *

**ABS/NYSE** — Retail food & drug chain

H: 34.05
L: 20.06
**Rec:** 32.98
**Div.:** 0.76
**Paid on:**
2.5.8.11-10
**Since:** 1960

250 Parkcenter Blvd., Box 20
Boise. ID 83726

Mellon Inv. Svcs.    888-788-5081
$30 - $30,000/quarter
Every 90 days beginning 2/25

FEES: Div: $0; Cash: $5 + 12¢/sh.; Cert: $15; Term: $15; Sells weekly, by mail , at avg. price, for $15 + comm.

**Shares to qualify:** 15
**Safekeeping:** Yes
**Accepts foreign:** Yes
**Auto. inv.:** No
**Disc.:** No

---

## Alcan Inc. ♥ *

**AL/NYSE** — Mining

H: 48.75
L: 28.18
**Rec:** 35.49
**Div.:** 0.60
**Paid on:**
3.6.9.12-20
**Since:** 1939

Box 6090
Montreal. Que.  H3C 3A7 Canada

Mellon Inv. Svcs.    800-387-0825
$100 - $9,000/quarter
Every 30 days beginning 1/15

FEES: Div: $0; Cash: $0; Cert: $0; Term: $0,Does not sell through the plan

**Shares to qualify:** 1
**Safekeeping:** No
**Accepts foreign:** Yes
**Auto. inv.:** No
**Disc.:** No

---

## Alcoa ♥ *

**AA/NYSE** — Metals

H: 45.71
L: 23.12
**Rec:** 37.01
**Div.:** 0.60
**Paid on:**
2.5.8.11-25
**Since:** 1939

6603 West Broad St.
Richmond. VA 23230

First Chicago Trust    800-317-4445
$25 - $5,000/month
Every 30 days beginning 1/25

FEES: Div: $0!; Cash: $0!; Auto. Inv.: $1; Cert: $0!; Term: $10 + 12¢/sh.; Sells daily, by mail or phone, at avg. price, for $10 + 12¢/sh.

**Shares to qualify:** 1
**Safekeeping:** Yes
**Accepts foreign:** Yes
**Auto. inv.:** Yes
**Disc.:** No

---

## Alfa Corp. ♥ *

**ALFA/NASD** — Insurance holding co.

H: 32.69
L: 16.37
**Rec:** 23.31
**Div.:** 0.58
**Paid on:**
3.6.9.12-1
**Since:** 1974

2108 East South Blvd., Box 11000
Montaomerv. AL 36191

Bank of New York    800-524-4458
$25 - $5,000/quarter
Every 90 days beginning 3/1

FEES: Div: $0; Cash: $0; Cert: $0; Term: $0; Sells irregularly, by mail, at market, for comm.

**Shares to qualify:** 1
**Safekeeping:** Yes
**Accepts foreign:** Yes
**Auto. inv.:** No
**Disc.:** No

---

## Aliant Inc. ♥

**AITO/TSE** — Communications

H: 39.70
L: 29.51
**Rec:** 32.76
**Div.:** 0.90
**Paid on:**
3.6.9.12-30
**Since:** 1912

Box 1113, Station Central RPO
Halifax. NS B3J 2X1 Canada

Mellon Inv. Svcs.    800-387-0825
$0 - $10,000/quarter Cdn.
Every 90 days beginning 3/30

FEES: Div: $0!; Cash: $0!; Cert: $0!; Term: $0,Does not sell through the plan

**Shares to qualify:** 1
**Safekeeping:** No
**Accepts foreign:** Yes
**Auto. inv.:** No
**Disc.:** No

---

## Allegheny Energy ⊗ *

**AYE/NYSE** — Utility-electric & gas

H: 55.09
L: 33.12
**Rec:** 44.07
**Div.:** 1.72
**Paid on:**
3.6.9.12-31
**Since:** 1935

10435 Downsville Pike
Hagerstown. MD 21740-1766

Mellon Inv. Svcs.    800-648-8389
$50 - $10,000/quarter
Every 90 days beginning 3/31

FEES: Div: 3% to $3; Cash: $3; Cert: $0!; Term: $0; Sells weekly, by mail , at market, for $15 + comm.

**Shares to qualify:** 1
**Safekeeping:** Yes
**Accepts foreign:** Yes
**Auto. inv.:** No
**Disc.:** No

---

## Allegheny Technologies Inc. *

**ATI/NYSE** — Mfr. of specialty materials, industrial

H: 22.62
L: 12.50
**Rec:** 19.13
**Div.:** 0.80
**Paid on:**
3.6.9.12-28
**Since:** 1996

1000 Six PPG Pl.
Pittsburah. PA  15222-5479

Mellon Inv. Svcs.    800-406-4850
$100 - $10,000/month
Every 7 days beginning varies

FEES: Div: $0; Cash: 12¢/sh.; Auto. Inv.: $0; Cert: $0; Term: $15 + 12¢/sh.; Sells weekly, by mail or phone, at market, for $15 + 12¢/sh.

**Shares to qualify:** 15 /de ($1000)
**Safekeeping:** Yes
**Accepts foreign:** Yes
**Auto. inv.:** Yes
**Disc.:** No

---

* DRIP enrollment through Temper Enrollment Service (see page 180).      **33**

## ✳ **Allegiant Bancorp, Inc.**

| | | |
|---|---|---|
| **ALLE/NASD** | **Bank holding company** | **Shares to qualify:** 1 |
| H: 14.49 | 2122 Kratky Rd. | **Safekeeping:** No |
| L: 8.00 | St. Louis. MO 63114 | **Accepts foreign:** Yes |
| **Rec:** 14.45 | UMB Bank, N.A.    816-860-7888 | **Auto. inv.:**No |
| **Div.:** 0.24 | $100 - $15,000/quarter | **Disc.:** No |
| **Paid on:** | Every 90 days beginning 1/30 | |
| 1.4.7.10-1 | FEES: Div: $0; Cash: $1 + comm.; Cert: $0; Term: $2 + comm.; Sells daily, by mail, at | |
| **Since:**N/A | market, for $2 + comm. | |

---

## ✳ **Allergan, Inc. ♥**

| | | |
|---|---|---|
| **AGN/NYSE** | **Drugs, eye & skin care prods.** | **Shares to qualify:** 1 |
| H: 101.12 | Box 19534 | **Safekeeping:** Yes |
| L: 59.00 | Irvine. CA 92623-9534 | **Accepts foreign:** Yes |
| **Rec:** 72.50 | First Chicago Trust    201-324-1644 | **Auto. inv.:**Yes |
| **Div.:** 0.36 | $10 - $50,000/year | **Disc.:** No |
| **Paid on:** | Every 30 days beginning 1/10 | |
| 3.6.9.12-10 | FEES: Div: $0!; Cash: $0!; Auto. Inv.: $1; Cert: $0!; Term: $0; Sells daily, by mail, at | |
| **Since:**1989 | market, for $10 + 12¢/sh. | |

---

## ✳ **ALLETE ♥**

| | | |
|---|---|---|
| **ALE/NYSE** | **Utility-electric** | **Shares to qualify:** 1 /de ($250) |
| H: 26.13 | 30 West Superior St. | **Safekeeping:** Yes |
| L: 20.12 | Duluth. MN  55802-2093 | **Accepts foreign:** No |
| **Rec:** 24.63 | ALLETE    800-535-3056 | **Auto. inv.:**Yes |
| **Div.:** 1.07 | $10 - $100,000/year | **Disc.:** No |
| **Paid on:** | Every 30 days beginning 1/1 | |
| 3.6.9.12-1 | FEES: Div: $0!; Cash: $0!; Auto. Inv.: $0; Cert: $0!; Term: $0; Sells within 5 bus. days, by | |
| **Since:**1948 | mail or fax, at market, for $5 | |

---

## ✳ **Alliant Energy Corp. ♥**

| | | |
|---|---|---|
| **LNT/NYSE** | **Utility-electric, gas** | **Shares to qualify:** 1 /de ($250) |
| H: 33.20 | 222 W. Washington Ave. | **Safekeeping:** Yes |
| L: 27.62 | Madison. WI  53703 | **Accepts foreign:** No |
| **Rec:** 29.55 | Alliant Energy    800-356-5343 | **Auto. inv.:**Yes |
| **Div.:** 2.00 | $25 - $120,000/year | **Disc.:** No |
| **Paid on:** | Every 30 days beginning 1/15 | |
| 2.5.8.11-15 | FEES: Div: $0!; Cash: $0!; Auto. Inv.: $0; Cert: $0!; Term: $0; Sells weekly, by mail, at | |
| **Since:**1946 | market, for 2.5¢/sh. | |

---

## ✳ **Allmerica Securities Trust**

| | | |
|---|---|---|
| **ALM/NYSE** | **Corporate bond fund** | **Shares to qualify:** 1 |
| H: 11.00 | 440 Lincoln St. | **Safekeeping:** Yes |
| L: 9.25 | Worcester. MA 01653 | **Accepts foreign:** Yes |
| **Rec:** 10.40 | Bank of New York    800-432-8224 | **Auto. inv.:**No |
| **Div.:** 0.73 | $25 - $1,000/month | **Disc.:** No |
| **Paid on:** | Every 30 days beginning 1/2 | |
| 3.6.9.12-31 | FEES: Div: $0!; Cash: $1 + 5¢/sh. ; Cert: $0; Term: $0!,Does not sell through the plan | |
| **Since:**N/A | | |

---

## ✳ **Allstate Corp. ⊗**

| | | |
|---|---|---|
| **ALL/NYSE** | **Insurance** | **Shares to qualify:** 1 /de ($500) |
| H: 45.90 | 3075 Sanders Rd., Ste. G2C | **Safekeeping:** Yes |
| L: 28.31 | Northbrook. IL 60062-7127 | **Accepts foreign:** Yes |
| **Rec:** 33.40 | First Chicago Trust    800-355-5191 | **Auto. inv.:**Yes |
| **Div.:** 0.76 | $100 - $150,000/year | **Disc.:** No |
| **Paid on:** | Every 7 days beginning 1/7 | |
| VARIES | FEES: Div: 5% to $3 + 3¢/sh.; Cash: 5% to $5 + 3¢/sh.; Auto. Inv.: 3¢/sh.; Cert: $0; | |
| **Since:**1993 | Term: $0; Sells daily, by mail or phone, at avg. price, for $15 + 12¢/sh. | |

---

## ✳ **ALLTEL Corp. ♥**

| | | |
|---|---|---|
| **AT/NYSE** | **Telecommunications** | **Shares to qualify:** 1 |
| H: 68.68 | One Allied Dr. | **Safekeeping:** Yes |
| L: 47.75 | Little Rock. AR 72202 | **Accepts foreign:** No |
| **Rec:** 61.41 | First Union Nat'l Bank    888-243-5445 | **Auto. inv.:**Yes |
| **Div.:** 1.32 | $50 - $25,000/quarter | **Disc.:** No |
| **Paid on:** | Every 30 days beginning 1/2 | |
| 1.4.7.10-3 | FEES: Div: $0!; Cash: $0!; Auto. Inv.: $0; Cert: $0!; Term: $5; Sells weekly, by mail, at | |
| **Since:**1961 | market, for comm. | |

---

✳ DRIP enrollment through Temper Enrollment Service (see page 180).     **34**

## ✳ AMB Property Corp. ♥

| | |
|---|---|
| **AMB/NYSE** | **REIT** |
| H: 26.10 | 505 Montgomery St., 5th Fl. |
| L: 22.50 | San Francisco. CA 94111 |
| **Rec:** 26.05 | BankBoston    800-331-9474 |
| **Div.:** 1.58 | $500 - $5,000/month |
| **Paid on:** | Every 30 days beginning 1/20 |
| 1.4.7.10-15 | FEES: Div $0!; Cash: $0!; Cert: $0!; Term: $0; Sells weekly, by mail or phone, at avg. price, |
| **Since:** 1997 | for comm. |

**Shares to qualify:** 1 /de ($500)
**Safekeeping:** Yes
**Accepts foreign:** Yes
**Auto. inv.:** No
**Disc.:** Cash: 0-5%

---

## ✳ Amcast Industrial Corp. ♥

| | |
|---|---|
| **AIZ/NYSE** | **Manufacturing** |
| H: 14.18 | 7887 Washington Village Dr. |
| L: 7.81 | Davton. OH 45459 |
| **Rec:** 8.55 | National City Bank    800-622-6757 |
| **Div.:** 0.00 | $25 - $1,000/month |
| **Paid on:** | Every 90 days beginning 3/1 |
| DIV. SUSP. | FEES: Div: n/o; Cash: $0; Cert: $0; Term: $10 + 12¢/sh.; Sells daily, by mail, at market, for |
| **Since:** -- | $10 + 12¢/sh. |

**Shares to qualify:** 1
**Safekeeping:** Yes
**Accepts foreign:** No
**Auto. inv.:** No
**Disc.:** No

---

## ✳ AMCOL International ♥

| | |
|---|---|
| **ACO/NYSE** | **Produces minerals, specialty** |
| H: 7.81 | 1500 West Shure Dr. |
| L: 2.87 | Arlington Heights. IL 60004-7803 |
| **Rec:** 6.35 | American Stock Transfer    800-937-5449 |
| **Div.:** 0.06 | $25 - $2,000/month |
| **Paid on:** | Every 30 days beginning 1/4 |
| 3.6.9.12-10 | FEES: Div $0!; Cash: $0!; Cert: $0!; Term: $0; Sells weekly, by mail, at market, for 2¢/sh. |
| **Since:** 1937 | |

**Shares to qualify:** 1
**Safekeeping:** Yes
**Accepts foreign:** Yes
**Auto. inv.:** No
**Disc.:** No

---

## ✳ Amcore Financial, Inc. ♥

| | |
|---|---|
| **AMFI/NASD** | **Banking, mortgage, finance** |
| H: 24.05 | 501 Seventh St., Box 1537 |
| L: 15.87 | Rockford. IL 61104 |
| **Rec:** 22.25 | Wells Fargo Bank    800-468-9716 |
| **Div.:** 0.64 | $10 - $7,500/quarter |
| **Paid on:** | Every 30 days beginning 1/2 |
| 3.6.9.12-10 | FEES: Div: $0!; Cash: $0!; Auto. Inv.: $0; Does not sell through the plan |
| **Since:** 1983 | |

**Shares to qualify:** 1
**Safekeeping:** No
**Accepts foreign:** Yes
**Auto. inv.:** Yes
**Disc.:** No

---

## ✳ Amerada Hess ♥

| | |
|---|---|
| **AHC/NYSE** | **Oil & gas** |
| H: 90.40 | 1185 Ave. of the Americas |
| L: 58.12 | New York. NY 10036 |
| **Rec:** 76.73 | Bank of New York    800-524-4458 |
| **Div.:** 1.20 | $50 - $5,000/quarter |
| **Paid on:** | Every 30 days beginning 1/30 |
| 1.3.6.9-30 | FEES: Div: $0!; Cash: $0!; Cert: $5; Term: $0; Sells daily, by mail, at market, for $1 |
| **Since:** 1922 | |

**Shares to qualify:** 1
**Safekeeping:** Yes
**Accepts foreign:** No
**Auto. inv.:** No
**Disc.:** No

---

## ✳ Ameren Corp.

| | |
|---|---|
| **AEE/NYSE** | **Utility-electric, gas** |
| H: 46.93 | Box 66887 |
| L: 37.31 | St. Louis. MO 63166-6887 |
| **Rec:** 39.96 | Ameren Services Co.    800-255-2237 |
| **Div.:** 2.54 | $25 - $120,000/year |
| **Paid on:** | Every 15 days beginning varies |
| 3.6.9.12-31 | FEES: Div: 4¢/sh.; Cash: 4¢/sh.; Auto. Inv.: $0; Cert: $0; Term: $0; Sells weekly, by mail, |
| **Since:** 1906 | phone or fax, at market, for 4¢/sh. |

**Shares to qualify:** 1 /de ($250)
**Safekeeping:** Yes
**Accepts foreign:** Yes
**Auto. inv.:** Yes
**Disc.:** No

---

## ✳ American Electric Power ♥

| | |
|---|---|
| **AEP/NYSE** | **Utility-electric** |
| H: 51.20 | 1 Riverside Plaza, Box 6631 |
| L: 34.31 | Columbus. OH 43215 |
| **Rec:** 45.24 | First Chicago Trust    800-328-6955 |
| **Div.:** 2.40 | $25 - $150,000/year |
| **Paid on:** | Every 7 days beginning varies |
| 3.6.9.12-10 | FEES: Div: $0; Cash: $0; Auto. Inv.: $0; Cert: $0; Term: $0; Sells daily, by phone or mail, |
| **Since:** 1909 | at market, for $5 + 12¢/sh. |

**Shares to qualify:** 1 /de ($250)
**Safekeeping:** Yes
**Accepts foreign:** Yes
**Auto. inv.:** Yes
**Disc.:** No

---

✳ DRIP enrollment through Temper Enrollment Service (see page 180).    **35**

## American Express Co. ⊗

**AXP/NYSE**

**Financial services**

World Financial Ctr.
New York. NY 10285

Mellon Inv. Svcs.   800-463-5911

$50 - $10,000/month

Every 30 days beginning 1/10

H: 63.00
L: 34.00
**Rec:** 39.85

**Div.:** 0.32
**Paid on:**
2.5.8.11-10
**Since:** 1870

**Shares to qualify:** 10 /de ($1000)
**Safekeeping:** Yes
**Accepts foreign:** Yes
**Auto. inv.:** Yes
**Disc.:** No

FEES: Div: 10% to 75¢ + 6¢/sh.; Cash: $5 + 6¢/sh.; Auto. Inv.: $3 + 6¢/sh.; Cert: $0;
Term: $0; Sells weekly, by mail or phone, at market, for $10 + 12¢/sh.

---

## American Financial Holdings, Inc. ♥

**AMFH/NAS**

**Bank holding co.**

Box 174
New Britian. CT 06050

American Stock Transfer   800-937-5449

$50 - $20,000/month

Every 30 days beginning 1/15

H: 25.00
L: 16.87
**Rec:** 24.86

**Div.:** 0.66
**Paid on:**
2.5.8.11-18
**Since:** N/A

**Shares to qualify:** 1
**Safekeeping:** Yes
**Accepts foreign:** Yes
**Auto. inv.:** Yes
**Disc.:** No

FEES: Div: $0!; Cash: $0!; Auto. Inv.: $0; Cert: $0!; Term: $0; Sells weekly, by mail, at
market, for $10 + 4¢/sh.

---

## American Greetings Corp.-A ♥

**AM/NYSE**

**Consumer products, cards & gift**

One American Rd.
Cleveland. OH 44144-2398

National City Bank   800-622-6757

$100 - $10,000/quarter

Every 30 days beginning 3/10

H: 20.12
L: 8.18
**Rec:** 11.43

**Div.:** 0.40
**Paid on:**
3.6.9.12-10
**Since:** 1950

**Shares to qualify:** 10
**Safekeeping:** Yes
**Accepts foreign:** No
**Auto. inv.:** No
**Disc.:** No

FEES: Div: $0!; Cash: $0!; Cert: $5; Term: $5; Sells weekly, by mail, at market, for $5 +
comm.

---

## American Home Products ⊗

**AHP/NYSE**

**Pharmaceuticals & consumer products**

5 Giralda Farms
Madison. NJ 07940

Mellon Inv. Svcs.   800-565-2067

$50 - $120,000/year

Every 7 days beginning varies

H: 65.25
L: 30.37
**Rec:** 50.99

**Div.:** 0.92
**Paid on:**
3.6.9.12-1
**Since:** 1919

**Shares to qualify:** 1 /de ($500)
**Safekeeping:** Yes
**Accepts foreign:** Yes
**Auto. inv.:** Yes
**Disc.:** No

FEES: Div: 5% to $3 ; Cash: $5 + 5¢/sh.; Auto. Inv.: $2 + 5¢/sh.; Cert: $0; Term: $0;
Sells daily, by phone, mail, fax, or Internet, at market, for $15 + 12¢/sh.

---

## American National Bankshares Inc. ♥

**AMNB/NAS**

**Bank holding company**

628 Main St., Box 191
Danville. VA 24543-0191

American National Bankshares   804-773-2220

$200 - $3,500/quarter

Every 90 days beginning 3/1

H: 25.00
L: 9.00
**Rec:** 19.00

**Div.:** 0.68
**Paid on:**
3.6.9.12-24
**Since:** N/A

**Shares to qualify:** 1
**Safekeeping:** No
**Accepts foreign:** No
**Auto. inv.:** No
**Disc.:** No

FEES: Div: $0!; Cash: $0!; Cert: $0; Term: $0,Does not sell through the plan

---

## American Software, Inc.-A ♥

**AMSWA/NA**

**Software**

470 East Paces Ferry Rd.
Atlanta. GA 30305

First Union Nat'l Bank   800-829-8432

$25 - $2,500/quarter

Every 90 days beginning 3/20

H: 6.68
L: 1.06
**Rec:** 1.68

**Div.:** 0.00
**Paid on:**
DIV. SUSP.
**Since:** --

**Shares to qualify:** 1
**Safekeeping:** Yes
**Accepts foreign:** No
**Auto. inv.:** No
**Disc.:** No

FEES: Div: $0; Cash: $0; Cert: $0; Term: $0; Sells irregularly, by mail, at market, for comm.

---

## American States Water ♥

**AWR/NYSE**

**Utility-water**

630 East Foothill Blvd.
San Dimas. CA 91773-1212

Mellon Inv. Svcs.   888-816-6998

$100 - $20,000/month

Every 7 days beginning Monday

H: 37.93
L: 25.00
**Rec:** 35.70

**Div.:** 1.30
**Paid on:**
3.6.9.12-1
**Since:** 1931

**Shares to qualify:** 1 /de ($500)
**Safekeeping:** Yes
**Accepts foreign:** No
**Auto. inv.:** Yes
**Disc.:** No

FEES: Div: $0; Cash: $0; Auto. Inv.: $0; Cert: $0; Term: $0; Sells daily, by mail or phone,
at avg. price, for $15 + 12¢/sh.

---

## ✳ American Water Works ♥

**AWK/NYSE**
**H:** 34.75
**L:** 23.31
**Rec:** 33.52
**Div.:** 0.94
**Paid on:**
2.5.8.11-15
**Since:** 1948

**Utility-water**
Box 1770
Voorhees. NJ 08043

BankBoston    877-987-9757
$100 - $5,000/month
Every 30 days beginning 1/15
FEES: Div: $0!; Cash: $0!; Cert: $0; Term: $1 to $10 + comm.; Sells daily, by mail, at market, for $1 to $10 + comm.

**Shares to qualify:** 1 /de ($100)
**Safekeeping:** Yes
**Accepts foreign:** Yes
**Auto. inv.:** No
**Disc.:** Div 2% Cash: 2%

---

## ✳ AmeriServ Financial, Inc. ♥

**ASRV/NASD**
**H:** 5.99
**L:** 3.62
**Rec:** 5.48
**Div.:** 0.36
**Paid on:**
1.4.7.10-3
**Since:** N/A

**Banking**
Main & Franklin, Box 430
Johnstown. PA 15907-0430

Boston Eq.    800-730-4001
$10 - $2,000/month
Every 30 days beginning 1/2
FEES: Div: $0!; Cash: $0!; Cert: $0; Term: $0; Sells daily, by mail or Internet, at market, for $10 + comm.

**Shares to qualify:** 1
**Safekeeping:** Yes
**Accepts foreign:** Yes
**Auto. inv.:** No
**Disc.:** No

---

## ✳ AmerUs Group Co. ⊗

**AMH/NYSE**
**H:** 37.00
**L:** 23.25
**Rec:** 31.35
**Div.:** 0.40
**Paid on:**
11-30
**Since:** 1997

**Insurance holding co.**
699 Walnut St.
Des Moines. IA 50309

Mellon Inv. Svcs.    800-304-9709
$50 - $15,000/month
Every 7 days beginning varies
FEES: Div: 5% to $2.50; Cash: $5 + 12¢/sh.; Auto. Inv.: $3 + 12¢/sh.; Cert: $0; Term: $15 + 12¢/sh.; Sells daily, by phone, mail, fax, or Internet, at market, for $15 + 12¢/sh.

**Shares to qualify:** 1 /de ($1000)
**Safekeeping:** Yes
**Accepts foreign:** Yes
**Auto. inv.:** Yes
**Disc.:** No

---

## Ametek, Inc.

**AME/NYSE**
**H:** 33.47
**L:** 19.87
**Rec:** 33.47
**Div.:** 0.24
**Paid on:**
3.6.9.12-30
**Since:** 1942

**Mfr. of electric motors & instruments**
37 N. Valley Rd., Bldg. 4
Paoli. PA 19301

American Stock Transfer    877-854-0864
$25 - $10,000/investment
Every 1 days beginning daily
FEES: Div: 2% to $1.50 + 10¢/sh.; Cash: $2.50 + 10¢/sh.; Auto. Inv.: $2.50 + 10¢/sh.; Cert: $0; Term: $7.50 + 10¢/sh.; Sells daily, by phone, mail, fax, or Internet, at market, for $7.50 + 10¢/sh.

**Shares to qualify:** 1 /de ($500)
**Safekeeping:** Yes
**Accepts foreign:** Yes
**Auto. inv.:** Yes
**Disc.:** No

---

## ✳ AMLI Residential Properties ♥

**AML/NYSE**
**H:** 25.31
**L:** 20.12
**Rec:** 23.59
**Div.:** 1.88
**Paid on:**
2.5.8.11-25
**Since:** 1994

**REIT**
125 S. Wacker Dr., Ste. 3100
Chicago. IL 60606

BankBoston    800-730-6001
$10 - $25,000/quarter
Every 90 days beginning 2/25
FEES: Div: $0!; Cash: $0!; Cert: $0!; Term: $0; Sells within 10 bus. days, by mail, at market, for 0

**Shares to qualify:** 1
**Safekeeping:** Yes
**Accepts foreign:** Yes
**Auto. inv.:** No
**Disc.:** No

---

## ✳ AmSouth Bancorp. ♥

**ASO/NYSE**
**H:** 20.20
**L:** 11.68
**Rec:** 20.15
**Div.:** 0.84
**Paid on:**
1.4.7.10-1
**Since:** 1943

**Banking**
Box 11007
Birmingham. AL 35288

Bank of New York    800-524-4458
$10 - $5,000/quarter
Every 90 days beginning 1/2
FEES: Div: $0!; Cash: $0!; Cert: $0!; Term: $0; Sells irregularly, by mail, at market, for $0

**Shares to qualify:** 1
**Safekeeping:** Yes
**Accepts foreign:** Yes
**Auto. inv.:** No
**Disc.:** No

---

## ✳ Anadarko Petroleum Corp. ♥

**APC/NYSE**
**H:** 75.95
**L:** 46.52
**Rec:** 55.20
**Div.:** 0.20
**Paid on:**
3.6.9.12-25
**Since:** 1986

**Oil & gas**
17001 Northchase Dr., Box 1330
Houston. TX 77251-1330

Mellon Inv. Svcs.    800-851-9677
$50 - $10,000
Every 30 days beginning varies
FEES: Div: $0; Cash: $0; Cert: $0; Term: $0,Does not sell through the plan

**Shares to qualify:** 1 /de ($1000)
**Safekeeping:** Yes
**Accepts foreign:** Yes
**Auto. inv.:** Yes
**Disc.:** Div 5% Cash: 0%

---

## Andover Bancorp, Inc. ♥

**ANDB/NASD**
H: 53.35
L: 27.75
**Rec:** 53.05
**Div.:** 1.08
**Paid on:**
2.5.8.11-15
**Since:** N/A

Savings banks
61 Main St., Box 2005
Andover. MA 01810

Boston Eq.     800-730-4001
$25 - $1,800/month
Every 30 days beginning 1/2

**Shares to qualify:** 1
**Safekeeping:** Yes
**Accepts foreign:** Yes
**Auto. inv.:** No
**Disc.:** No

FEES: Div: $0!; Cash: $0!; Cert: $0!; Term: $0; Sells within 10 bus. days, by mail, at avg. price, for 5% to $5 + comm.

---

## * Angelica Corp. ♥

**AGL/NYSE**
H: 14.00
L: 7.68
**Rec:** 12.70
**Div.:** 0.32
**Paid on:**
1.4.7.10-1
**Since:** 1954

Uniforms
424 South Woods Mill Rd.
Chesterfield. MO 63017

UMB Bank, N.A.    800-884-4225
$10 - $3,000/quarter
Every 90 days beginning 2/1

**Shares to qualify:** 1
**Safekeeping:** Yes
**Accepts foreign:** Yes
**Auto. inv.:** No
**Disc.:** No

FEES: Div: $0!; Cash: $0!; Cert: $0; Term: $0; Sells weekly, by mail, at market, for $2 + comm.

---

## * Anheuser-Busch Cos. ♥

**BUD/NYSE**
H: 49.87
L: 36.75
**Rec:** 42.05
**Div.:** 0.72
**Paid on:**
3.6.9.12-9
**Since:** 1932

Food & beverages, brewers
One Busch Pl.
St. Louis. MO 63118

Mellon Inv. Svcs.    888-213-0964
$25 - $5,000/month
Every 30 days beginning 1/9

**Shares to qualify:** 1
**Safekeeping:** Yes
**Accepts foreign:** Yes
**Auto. inv.:** No
**Disc.:** No

FEES: Div: $0!; Cash: $0!; Cert: $0!; Term: $0; Sells daily, by mail or phone, at avg. price, for 5¢/sh.

---

## * Annaly Mortgage Mgmt., Inc. ♥

**NLY/NYSE**
H: 14.50
L: 7.87
**Rec:** 14.41
**Div.:** 1.60
**Paid on:**
1.4.7.10-27
**Since:** 1998

REIT
12 East 41st St., Ste. 700
New York. NY 10017

Mellon Inv. Svcs.    800-301-5234
$250 - $10,000/month
Every 30 days beginning 1/25

**Shares to qualify:** 1 /de ($1000)
**Safekeeping:** Yes
**Accepts foreign:** Yes
**Auto. inv.:** Yes
**Disc.:** Div: 0-3% Cash:
0-3%

FEES: Div: $0!; Cash: $0!; Auto. Inv.: $0; Cert: $0!; Term: $15 + 12¢/sh.; Sells monthly, by mail, at market, for $15 + 12¢/sh.

---

## * Anthracite Capital ♥

**AHR/NYSE**
H: 11.65
L: 7.12
**Rec:** 11.14
**Div.:** 1.28
**Paid on:**
1.4.7.10-15
**Since:** 1998

REIT
345 Park Ave.
New York. NY 10154

Bank of New York    800-524-4458
$100 - $5,000/month
Every 30 days beginning varies

**Shares to qualify:** 1 /de ($250)
**Safekeeping:** Yes
**Accepts foreign:** Yes
**Auto. inv.:** Yes
**Disc.:** Div: 0%-5%
Cash: 0-5%

FEES: Div: $0!; Cash: $0!; Auto. Inv.: $0; Cert: $0!; Term: $10 + 10¢/sh.; Sells weekly, by mail, at avg. price, for $10 +10¢/sh.

---

## * Anworth Mortgage Asset Corp. ♥

**ANH/ASE**
H: 8.08
L: 3.87
**Rec:** 7.10
**Div.:** 0.44
**Paid on:**
1.4.7.10-11
**Since:** N/A

REIT
1299 Ocean Ave., Ste. 200
Santa Monica. CA 90401

Continental Stock Transfer    212-509-4000
$100 - $5,000/month
Every 30 days beginning 3rd from last day each

**Shares to qualify:** 1 /de ($500)
**Safekeeping:** Yes
**Accepts foreign:** Yes
**Auto. inv.:** No
**Disc.:** Div: 5% Cash:
0-5%

FEES: Div: $0!; Cash: $0!; Cert: $0!; Term: $2.50 + comm.; Sells weekly, by mail, at market, for $2.50 + comm.

---

## * Aon Corp. ♥

**AOC/NYSE**
H: 42.31
L: 28.12
**Rec:** 38.80
**Div.:** 0.90
**Paid on:**
2.5.8.11-15
**Since:** 1950

Insurance
123 North Wacker Dr.
Chicago. IL 60606

First Chicago Trust    800-446-2617
$20 - $1,000/month
Every 30 days beginning 1/15

**Shares to qualify:** 1
**Safekeeping:** Yes
**Accepts foreign:** Yes
**Auto. inv.:** No
**Disc.:** No

FEES: Div: $0!; Cash: $0!; Cert: $0!; Term: $10 + 12¢/sh.; Sells daily, by mail, at market, for $10 + 12¢/sh.

---

## * Apache Corp. ♥

**APA/NYSE**
H: 74.18
L: 44.30
**Rec:** 49.66
**Div.:** 0.56
**Paid on:**
12-15
**Since:** 1965

Oil exploration

2000 Post Oak Blvd., Ste. 100
Houston. TX 77056-4400

Wells Fargo Bank    800-468-9716
$50 - $5,000/quarter
Every 30 days beginning 1/31
FEES: Div: $0!; Cash: $0!; Cert: $0!; Term: $0; Sells within 5 bus. days, by mail or fax, at market, for $10 + 10¢/sh.

**Shares to qualify:** 1
**Safekeeping:** Yes
**Accepts foreign:** Yes
**Auto. inv.:** No
**Disc.:** No

---

## * Applied Industrial Technologies, Inc.  ♥

**AIT/NYSE**
H: 21.00
L: 15.65
**Rec:** 17.93
**Div.:** 0.48
**Paid on:**
3.6.9.12-1
**Since:** 1963

Dist. bearings & power transmissions

1 Applied Plaza
Cleveland. OH 44115

Computershare Investor Svcs.    800-988-5291
$10 - $1,000/month
Every 30 days beginning 1/2
FEES: Div: $0!; Cash: $0!; Cert: $5; Term: $10; Sells within 5 bus. days, by mail, at market, for $10

**Shares to qualify:** 1
**Safekeeping:** Yes
**Accepts foreign:** Yes
**Auto. inv.:** No
**Disc.:** No

---

## * Arch Chemicals, Inc. ⊗

**ARJ/NYSE**
H: 23.99
L: 15.62
**Rec:** 20.13
**Div.:** 0.80
**Paid on:**
3.6.9.12-10
**Since:** 1999

Specialty chemical services

501 Merritt 7, Box 5204
Norwalk. CT 06856-5204

First Chicago Trust    800-446-2617
$50 - $250,000/year
Every 5 days beginning varies
FEES: Div: $0; Cash: $5 + 3¢/sh.; Auto. Inv.: $2 + 3¢/sh.; Cert: $0; Term: $15 + 12¢/sh.; Sells within 5 bus. days, by phone, mail, fax, or Internet, at market, for $15 + 12¢/sh.

**Shares to qualify:** 1 /de ($500)
**Safekeeping:** Yes
**Accepts foreign:** Yes
**Auto. inv.:** Yes
**Disc.:** No

---

## * Arch Coal, Inc. ♥

**ACI/NYSE**
H: 38.40
L: 7.00
**Rec:** 17.45
**Div.:** 0.23
**Paid on:**
3.6.9.12-15
**Since:** 1988

Metal, coal mining

CityPlace One, Ste. 300
St. Louis. MO 63141

First Chicago Trust    800-317-4445
$25 - $100,000/year
Every 30 days beginning 1/15
FEES: Div: $0!; Cash: $0!; Auto. Inv.: $1; Cert: $0!; Term: $15 + 12¢/sh.; Sells daily, by mail or phone, at market, for $15 + 12¢/sh.

**Shares to qualify:** 1
**Safekeeping:** Yes
**Accepts foreign:** Yes
**Auto. inv.:** Yes
**Disc.:** No

---

## * Archstone Communities Trust ♥

**ASN/NYSE**
H: 26.56
L: 21.87
**Rec:** 26.48
**Div.:** 1.64
**Paid on:**
2.5.8.11-27
**Since:** N/A

Real estate operations

7670 S. Chester St., Ste.100
Englewood. CO 80112

Mellon Inv. Svcs.    800-842-7629
$200 - $5,000/month
Every 30 days beginning varies
FEES: Div: $0!; Cash: $0!; Auto. Inv.: $0; Cert: $0!; Term: $15 + 12¢/sh.; Sells weekly, by mail, at market, for $15 + 12¢/sh.

**Shares to qualify:** 1 /de ($200)
**Safekeeping:** Yes
**Accepts foreign:** Yes
**Auto. inv.:** Yes
**Disc.:** Div 0% Cash: 2%

---

## * Argentina Fund Inc. (The)

**AF/NYSE**
H: 12.85
L: 9.08
**Rec:** 9.97
**Div.:** 0.23
**Paid on:**
1-14
**Since:** N/A

Closed-end fund

345 Park Ave.
New York. NY 10154

Kemper Service Co.    800-621-1048
$100 - $3,000/investment
Every 180 days beginning 2/15
FEES: Div: $0; Cash: 75¢ + comm.; Cert: $0; Term: $0; Sells irregularly, by mail or phone, at market, for $2.50 + comm.

**Shares to qualify:** 1
**Safekeeping:** No
**Accepts foreign:** Yes
**Auto. inv.:** No
**Disc.:** Div 0-5% Cash: 0%

---

## * Arnold Industries, Inc. ♥

**AIND/NASD**
H: 21.25
L: 14.10
**Rec:** 19.25
**Div.:** 0.44
**Paid on:**
3.6.9.12-1
**Since:** 1972

Trucking

Box 210
Lebanon. PA 17042

Registrar & Transfer    800-368-5948
$25 - $3,000/quarter
Every 90 days beginning 3/2
FEES: Div: $0!; Cash: $0!; Cert: $0!; Term: $2.50,Does not sell through the plan

**Shares to qualify:** 1
**Safekeeping:** Yes
**Accepts foreign:** No
**Auto. inv.:** No
**Disc.:** No

---

* DRIP enrollment through Temper Enrollment Service (see page 180).    **39**

## Arrow Financial Corp. ♥

**AROW/NAS** | **Banking**

H: 28.63
L: 14.75
**Rec:** 28.53

**Div.:** 0.92
**Paid on:**
3.6.9.12-15
**Since:** N/A

250 Glen St.
Glens Falls. NY 12801

American Stock Transfer    800-937-5449
$100 - $10,000/quarter
Every 30 days beginning 1/15

FEES: Div: $0!; Cash: $0!; Auto. Inv.: $0; Cert: $0!; Term: $0!; Sells daily, by mail, fax or Internet, at market, for $0!

**Shares to qualify:** 1 /de ($300)
**Safekeeping:** Yes
**Accepts foreign:** Yes
**Auto. inv.:** Yes
**Disc.:** No

---

## Artesian Resources Corp.-A ♥

**ARTNA/NAS** | **Utility-water**

H: 27.25
L: 21.50
**Rec:** 24.55

**Div.:** 1.12
**Paid on:**
2.5.8.11-24
**Since:** N/A

664 Churchmans Rd.
Newark. DE 19702-1934

Registrar & Transfer    800-368-5948
$100 - $10,000/quarter
Every 30 days beginning 1/20

FEES: Div: $0!; Cash: $0!; Cert: $0!; Term: $0!; Sells daily, by mail, at market, for $0!

**Shares to qualify:** 1
**Safekeeping:** Yes
**Accepts foreign:** Yes
**Auto. inv.:** No
**Disc.:** No

---

## ArvinMeritor Inc. ♥

**ARM/NYSE** | **Automotive**

H: 21.87
L: 8.87
**Rec:** 20.15

**Div.:** 0.40
**Paid on:**
3.6.9.12-30
**Since:** 1925

2135 West Maple Rd.
Troy. MI 48084-7186

First Chicago Trust    800-519-3111
$50 - $100,000/year
Every 7 days beginning varies

FEES: Div: $0!; Cash: $0!; Auto. Inv.: $0; Cert: $0!; Term: $15 + 12¢/sh.; Sells daily, by mail or phone, at market, for $15 + 12¢/sh.

**Shares to qualify:** 1 /de ($500)
**Safekeeping:** Yes
**Accepts foreign:** Yes
**Auto. inv.:** Yes
**Disc.:** No

---

## ASA Ltd.

**ASA/NYSE** | **Closed-end fund**

H: 22.90
L: 14.06
**Rec:** 18.20

**Div.:** 0.60
**Paid on:**
2.5.8.11-24
**Since:** N/A

c/o LGN Assoc., Box 269
Florham Park. NJ 07932

First Chicago Trust    201-324-0498
$50 - $3,000/quarter
Every 90 days beginning 2/24

FEES: Div: 5% to $2.50; Cash: 5% to $2.50 ; Cert: $0; Term: $10 + 12¢/sh.; Sells daily, by mail, at market, for $10 + 12¢/sh.

**Shares to qualify:** 1
**Safekeeping:** Yes
**Accepts foreign:** Yes
**Auto. inv.:** No
**Disc.:** No

---

## Ashland Inc. ♥

**ASH/NYSE** | **Oil refining, marketing**

H: 44.25
L: 30.62
**Rec:** 40.65

**Div.:** 1.10
**Paid on:**
3.6.9.12-15
**Since:** 1936

Box 391
Ashland. KY 41105-0391

National City Bank    800-622-6757
$25 - $5,000/month
Every 7 days beginning varies

FEES: Div: $0!; Cash: $0!; Cert: $0!; Term: $0; Sells weekly, by mail or fax, at market, for $10 + comm.

**Shares to qualify:** 1 /de ($250)
**Safekeeping:** Yes
**Accepts foreign:** Yes
**Auto. inv.:** No
**Disc.:** No

---

## Associated Banc-Corp ⊗

**ASBC/NASD** | **Bank holding company**

H: 36.25
L: 21.50
**Rec:** 36.08

**Div.:** 1.24
**Paid on:**
2.5.8.11-15
**Since:** 1970

1200 Hansen Rd., Box 13307
Green Bav. WI 54307-3307

First Chicago Trust    800-446-2617
$50 - $50,000/year
Every 30 days beginning 1/15

FEES: Div: 5% to $3; Cash: $5 + 3¢/sh.; Auto. Inv.: $2 + 3¢/sh.; Cert: $0!; Term: $15 + 12¢/sh.; Sells daily, by phone, mail, fax, or Internet, at market, for $15 + 12¢/sh.

**Shares to qualify:** 1
**Safekeeping:** Yes
**Accepts foreign:** Yes
**Auto. inv.:** Yes
**Disc.:** No

---

## Associated Estates Realty Corp. ♥

**AEC/NYSE** | **REIT**

H: 10.72
L: 7.50
**Rec:** 10.09

**Div.:** 1.00
**Paid on:**
2.5.8.11-1
**Since:** 1994

5025 Swetland Ct.
Cleveland. OH 44143

National City Bank    800-622-6757
$100 - $5,000/month
Every 30 days beginning 1/2

FEES: Div: $0; Cash: $0; Auto. Inv.: $2; Cert: $0; Term: $0; Sells monthly, by mail, at market, for 8¢ to 20¢/sh.

**Shares to qualify:** 1
**Safekeeping:** Yes
**Accepts foreign:** Yes
**Auto. inv.:** Yes
**Disc.:** No

---

## Astoria Financial Corp. ♥

ASFC/NASD

**Savings and loan**

H: 61.75
L: 31.25
**Rec:** 61.09

One Astoria Federal Plaza
Lake Success. NY 11042-1085

Mellon Inv. Svcs.     800-526-0801

**Div.:** 1.24
**Paid on:**
3.6.9.12-1
**Since:** N/A

$50 - $5,000/quarter
Every 90 days beginning 3/12

**Shares to qualify:** 1
**Safekeeping:** Yes
**Accepts foreign:** Yes
**Auto. inv.:** No
**Disc.:** No

FEES: Div: $0!; Cash: $0!; Cert: $5; Term: $15; Sells weekly, by mail or phone, at market, for $15

---

## AT&T Corp. ⊗

T/NYSE

**Telecommunications**

H: 32.93
L: 16.50
**Rec:** 19.58

295 N. Maple Ave., Rm. 3351
Basking Ridge. NJ 07920

Boston Eq.     800-348-8288

**Div.:** 0.15
**Paid on:**
2.5.8.11-1
**Since:** 1881

$100 - $250,000/year
Every 7 days beginning varies

**Shares to qualify:** 1
**Safekeeping:** Yes
**Accepts foreign:** Yes
**Auto. inv.:** Yes
**Disc.:** No

FEES: Div: 10% to $1; Cash: $5; Auto. Inv.: $5; Cert: $0; Term: $0; Sells weekly, by mail, fax , or phone, at avg. price, for $20 + comm.

---

## Atmos Energy Corp. ♥

ATO/NYSE

**Utility-gas and propane**

H: 26.25
L: 19.18
**Rec:** 21.26

Box 650205
Dallas. TX 75265-0205

BankBoston     800-543-3038

**Div.:** 1.16
**Paid on:**
3.6.9.12-10
**Since:** 1984

$25 - $100,000/year
Every 7 days beginning varies

**Shares to qualify:** 1 /de ($200)
**Safekeeping:** Yes
**Accepts foreign:** Yes
**Auto. inv.:** Yes
**Disc.:** Div 3% Cash: 0%

FEES: Div: $0!; Cash: $0!; Auto. Inv.: $0; Cert: $0!; Term: $0; Sells within 10 bus. days, by mail, at market, for $15 + 5¢/sh.

---

## Austria Fund (The)

OST/NYSE

**Closed-end fund**

H: 11.43
L: 5.96
**Rec:** 6.81

c/o All. Capital,1345 Ave. of the Americas
New York. NY 10105-0302

State St. Bank     800-219-4218

**Div.:** 0.65
**Paid on:**
1-10
**Since:** N/A

$100 - $unlimited
Every 180 days beginning 1/15

**Shares to qualify:** 1
**Safekeeping:** No
**Accepts foreign:** Yes
**Auto. inv.:** No
**Disc.:** Div 5% Cash: 0%

FEES: Div: $0; Cash: 75¢; Cert: $0; Term: $0; Sells irregularly, by mail, at market, for $2.50 + 15¢/sh.

---

## AvalonBay Communities, Inc. ♥

AVB/NYSE

**Real estate operations**

H: 50.62
L: 42.45
**Rec:** 49.90

2900 Eisenhower Ave., Ste. 300
Alexandria. VA 22314

First Union Nat'l Bank     800-829-8432

**Div.:** 2.56
**Paid on:**
1.4.7.10-15
**Since:** N/A

$100 - $100,000/quarter
Every 90 days beginning 1/18

**Shares to qualify:** 1
**Safekeeping:** Yes
**Accepts foreign:** No
**Auto. inv.:** No
**Disc.:** Div 3% Cash: 0%

FEES: Div: $0; Cash: $0; Cert: $0; Term: $0; Sells within 10 bus. days, by mail, at market, for 5¢/sh.

---

## Avaya Inc. ⊗

AV/NYSE

**Telecommunications**

H: 26.00
L: 9.87
**Rec:** 11.52

211 Mount Airy Rd.
Basking Ridge. NJ 07920

Bank of New York     866-222-8292

**Div.:** 0.00
**Paid on:**
N/0
**Since:** N/A

$125 - $50,000/investment
Every 7 days beginning varies

**Shares to qualify:** 1 /de ($1500)
**Safekeeping:** Yes
**Accepts foreign:** Yes
**Auto. inv.:** Yes
**Disc.:** No

FEES: Div: n/o; Cash: $5 + 12¢/sh.; Auto. Inv.: $2.50 + 12¢/sh.; Cert: $0; Term: $15 + 12¢/sh.; Sells daily, by mail or phone, at market, for $15 + 12¢/sh.

---

## Aventis

AVE/NYSE

**Chemicals, drugs**

H: 87.50
L: 66.62
**Rec:** 75.98

c/o Citibank Shrhldr. Svcs., Box 2502
Jersey City. NJ 07303-2502

Citibank     800-808-8010

**Div.:** 0.44
**Paid on:**
6-15
**Since:** 1993

$50 - $100,000/year
Every 30 days beginning varies

**Shares to qualify:** 1
**Safekeeping:** Yes
**Accepts foreign:** No
**Auto. inv.:** No
**Disc.:** No

FEES: Div: comm.; Cash: $2.50 + comm.; Cert: $0; Term: $0; Sells irregularly, by mail, at market, for $3 + comm.

---

✱ DRIP enrollment through Temper Enrollment Service (see page 180).     **41**

## ✱ Avery Dennison Corp. ⊗

**Adhesives, specialty chemicals**

| | | |
|---|---|---|
| **AVY/NYSE** | Box 7090 | **Shares to qualify:** 1 /de ($500) |
| H: 60.50 | Pasadena. CA 91109-7090 | **Safekeeping:** Yes |
| L: 41.12 | | **Accepts foreign:** Yes |
| **Rec:** 49.77 | First Chicago Trust    800-756-8200 | **Auto. inv.:** Yes |
| **Div.:** 1.20 | $100 - $12,500/month | **Disc.:** No |
| **Paid on:** | Every 7 days beginning varies | |
| 3.6.9.12-15 | | |
| **Since:** 1964 | FEES: Div $0!; Cash: $5 + 3¢/sh.; Auto. Inv.: $2 + 3¢/sh.; Cert: $0!; Term: $0; Sells daily, by mail, at market, for $15 + 12¢/sh. | |

## ✱ Aviall, Inc. ♥

**Aviation services**

| | | |
|---|---|---|
| **AVL/NYSE** | 2075 Diplomat Dr. | **Shares to qualify:** 10 |
| H: 11.25 | Dallas. TX 75234-8999 | **Safekeeping:** Yes |
| L: 4.50 | | **Accepts foreign:** Yes |
| **Rec:** 10.81 | Boston Eq.    800-730-4001 | **Auto. inv.:** No |
| **Div.:** 0.00 | $25 - $15,000/quarter | **Disc.:** No |
| **Paid on:** | Every 30 days beginning 1/2 | |
| DIV. SUSP. | | |
| **Since:** -- | FEES: Div $0!; Cash: $0!; Cert: $0!; Term: $0; Sells 3 bus. days after receipt, by mail, at market, for $1 to $10 | |

## ✱ Avista Corp.

**Hydroelectric, gas utility**

| | | |
|---|---|---|
| **AVA/NYSE** | Box 3727 | **Shares to qualify:** 1 |
| H: 30.43 | Spokane. WA 99220-3727 | **Safekeeping:** Yes |
| L: 15.00 | | **Accepts foreign:** Yes |
| **Rec:** 17.48 | Bank of New York    800-642-7365 | **Auto. inv.:** No |
| **Div.:** 0.48 | $0 - $100,000/year | **Disc.:** No |
| **Paid on:** | Every 30 days beginning 1/15 | |
| 3.6.9.12-15 | | |
| **Since:** 1898 | FEES: Div 4¢/sh.; Cash: 4¢/sh.; Cert: $0; Term: $0; Sells daily, by mail or phone, at market, for 4¢/sh. | |

## ✱ Avnet, Inc. ♥

**Electronics**

| | | |
|---|---|---|
| **AVT/NYSE** | 2211 South 47th St. | **Shares to qualify:** 1 |
| H: 32.56 | Phoenix. AZ 85034 | **Safekeeping:** Yes |
| L: 17.18 | | **Accepts foreign:** Yes |
| **Rec:** 25.06 | Wells Fargo Bank    800-468-9716 | **Auto. inv.:** No |
| **Div.:** 0.30 | $10 - $unlimited | **Disc.:** No |
| **Paid on:** | Every 45 days beginning 1/2 | |
| 1.4.7.10 | | |
| **Since:** 1961 | FEES: Div $0; Cash: $0; Cert: $0; Term: $0; Sells weekly, by mail, fax, or telephone, at market, for comm. | |

## ✱ Avon Products, Inc. ♥

**Cosmetics, fragrance, jewelry, gift prod.**

| | | |
|---|---|---|
| **AVP/NYSE** | 1345 Ave. of the Americas | **Shares to qualify:** 1 |
| H: 49.75 | New York. NY 10105-0196 | **Safekeeping:** Yes |
| L: 35.00 | | **Accepts foreign:** Yes |
| **Rec:** 44.97 | First Chicago Trust    201-324-0498 | **Auto. inv.:** No |
| **Div.:** 0.76 | $10 - $5,000/month | **Disc.:** No |
| **Paid on:** | Every 30 days beginning 1/2 | |
| 3.6.9.12-1 | | |
| **Since:** 1919 | FEES: Div $0!; Cash: $0!; Cert: $0!; Term: $0; Sells daily, by mail, at market, for $5 + 12¢/sh. | |

## ✱ AVX Corp. ♥

**Electronic instr. & controls**

| | | |
|---|---|---|
| **AVX/NYSE** | Box 867 | **Shares to qualify:** 1 |
| H: 31.75 | Mvrtle Beach. SC 29578 | **Safekeeping:** Yes |
| L: 15.12 | | **Accepts foreign:** Yes |
| **Rec:** 21.64 | American Stock Transfer    800-937-5449 | **Auto. inv.:** No |
| **Div.:** 0.15 | $20 - $2,000/month | **Disc.:** No |
| **Paid on:** | Every 30 days beginning 1/2 | |
| 2.5.8.11-10 | | |
| **Since:** 1995 | FEES: Div $0; Cash: $0; Cert: $0; Term: comm.; Sells irregularly, by mail, at market, for comm. | |

## ✱ AXA SA

**Insurance**

| | | |
|---|---|---|
| **AXA/NYSE** | c/o FCT, EquiServe, Box 2590 | **Shares to qualify:** 1 |
| H: 39.87 | Jersev Citv. NJ 07303-2590 | **Safekeeping:** Yes |
| L: 24.57 | | **Accepts foreign:** Yes |
| **Rec:** 29.53 | First Chicago Trust    800-437-8736 | **Auto. inv.:** Yes |
| **Div.:** 0.49 | $25 - $100,000/year | **Disc.:** No |
| **Paid on:** | Every 7 days beginning varies | |
| 5-16 | | |
| **Since:** NA | FEES: Div 50¢; Cash: $0!; Auto. Inv.: $0; Cert: $0!; Term: $10 + 12¢/sh.; Sells daily, by phone, mail, fax, or Internet, at market, for $10 + 12¢/sh. | |

✱ DRIP enrollment through Temper Enrollment Service (see page 180).

## Baker Hughes Inc. ♥

**\***

**BHI/NYSE**

H: 45.29
L: 29.80
**Rec:** 33.39

**Div.:** 0.46
**Paid on:**
2.5.8.11-26
**Since:** 1987

**Oil, gas, & mining, equip. svcs.**

Box 4740
Houston. TX 77210-4740

Mellon Inv. Svcs.     888-216-8057
$10 - $350/month
Every 30 days beginning 1/20

FEES: Div: $0!; Cash: $0!; Cert: $0; Term: $0; Sells weekly, by mail or phone, at market, for $15 + 10¢/sh.

**Shares to qualify:** 1
**Safekeeping:** Yes
**Accepts foreign:** Yes
**Auto. inv.:** No
**Disc.:** No

---

## Baldor Electric Co. ♥

**\***

**BEZ/NYSE**

H: 25.15
L: 18.37
**Rec:** 21.79

**Div.:** 0.52
**Paid on:**
3.6.9.12-VARIES
**Since:** 1938

**Designs, mfrs. & mkts. electric motors**

Box 2400
Fort Smith. AR 72902-2400

Continental Stock Transfer     800-509-5586
$50 - $10,000/month
Every 30 days beginning 1/2

FEES: Div: $0!; Cash: $0!; Cert: $0!; Term: $0; Sells daily, by mail, at market, for comm.

**Shares to qualify:** 1
**Safekeeping:** Yes
**Accepts foreign:** Yes
**Auto. inv.:** No
**Disc.:** No

---

## Ball Corp. ♥

**\***

**BLL/NYSE**

H: 51.15
L: 28.56
**Rec:** 48.38

**Div.:** 0.60
**Paid on:**
3.6.9.12-15
**Since:** 1958

**Aerospace, metal and packaging**

10 Longs Peak Dr.
Broomfield. CO 80021

First Chicago Trust     800-446-2617
$25 - $3,000/quarter
Every 30 days beginning 1/15

FEES: Div: $0!; Cash: $0!; Cert: $0!; Term: $0; Sells daily, by mail, fax , or phone, at avg. price, for $10 + 12¢/sh.

**Shares to qualify:** 1
**Safekeeping:** No
**Accepts foreign:** Yes
**Auto. inv.:** No
**Disc.:** Div: 5% Cash: 0%

---

## BancorpConnecticut Inc. ♥

**\***

**BKCT/NASD**

H: 20.05
L: 12.62
**Rec:** 20.00

**Div.:** 0.76
**Paid on:**
2.5.8.11-15
**Since:** N/A

**Bank holding company**

121 Main St.
Southington. CT  06489

American Stock Transfer     800-278-4353
$100 - $10,000/quarter
Every 90 days beginning 2/15

FEES: Div: $0!; Cash: $0!; Cert: $0!; Term: 4¢/sh.; Sells weekly, by mail, at market, for 4¢/sh.

**Shares to qualify:** 1
**Safekeeping:** Yes
**Accepts foreign:** Yes
**Auto. inv.:** No
**Disc.:** No

---

## BancorpSouth, Inc. ♥

**\***

**BXS/NYSE**

H: 17.00
L: 11.87
**Rec:** 16.50

**Div.:** 0.56
**Paid on:**
1.4.7.10-3
**Since:** 1945

**Banking**

Box 789
Tupelo. MS 38802

SunTrust Bank, Atlanta     800-568-3476
$25 - $5,000/quarter
Every 90 days beginning 4/1

FEES: Div: $0!; Cash: $0!; Auto. Inv.: $0; Cert: $0; Term: $0; Sells weekly, by mail, at market, for $0!

**Shares to qualify:** 1
**Safekeeping:** No
**Accepts foreign:** Yes
**Auto. inv.:** Yes
**Disc.:** No

---

## Bancroft Convertible Fund, Inc. ⊗

**\***

**BCV/ASE**

H: 24.62
L: 18.31
**Rec:** 21.09

**Div.:** 0.84
**Paid on:**
3.6.9.12-30
**Since:** N/A

**Closed-end fund**

c/o Davis-Dinsmore, 65 Madison Ave., Ste. 550
Morristown. NJ  07960-7308

American Stock Transfer     800-937-5449
$25 - $5,000/month
Every 30 days beginning 1/30

FEES: Div: $0; Cash: 5% to $3 + comm.; Cert: $0; Term: fee + comm.; Sells monthly, by mail, at market, for fee + comm.

**Shares to qualify:** 1
**Safekeeping:** No
**Accepts foreign:** Yes
**Auto. inv.:** No
**Disc.:** No

---

## BancWest Corp. ♥

**BWE/NASD**

H: 34.99
L: 16.75
**Rec:** 34.96

**Div.:** 0.76
**Paid on:**
3.6.9.12-15
**Since:** 1929

**Banking**

999 Bishop St., 29th fl.
Honolulu. HI 96813

American Stock Transfer     800-278-4353
$50 - $10,0000/quarter
Every 30 days beginning 1/5

FEES: Div: $0!; Cash: $0!; Auto. Inv.: $0; Cert: $0!; Term: $15; Sells within 10 bus. days, by mail, fax or phone, at market, for comm.

**Shares to qualify:** 25
**Safekeeping:** Yes
**Accepts foreign:** Yes
**Auto. inv.:** Yes
**Disc.:** No

---

## ✶ Bandag Inc.-A ♥

**BDGA/NYSE** — Manufacturing

H: 38.68
L: 20.90
**Rec:** 24.30

**Div.:** 1.22
**Paid on:**
1.4.7.10-21
**Since:**1976

2905 N. Hwy. 61
Muscatine. IA 52761-5886

BankBoston      800-730-4001
$50 - $10,000/quarter
Every 30 days beginning 1/20

FEES: Div: $0!; Cash: $0!; Cert: $0!; Term: $0; Sells daily, by mail, phone or fax, at avg. price, for $1 to $10 + comm.

**Shares to qualify:** 1
**Safekeeping:** Yes
**Accepts foreign:** Yes
**Auto. inv.:** No
**Disc.:** No

---

## ✶ Bandag Inc. ♥

**BDG/NYSE** — Manufacturing

H: 46.75
L: 25.70
**Rec:** 29.10

**Div.:** 1.22
**Paid on:**
1.4.7.10-21
**Since:**1976

2905 N. Hwy. 61
Muscatine. IA 52761-5886

BankBoston      800-730-4001
$50 - $10,000/quarter
Every 30 days beginning 1/20

FEES: Div: $0!; Cash: $0!; Cert: $0!; Term: $0!; Sells daily, by mail, phone or fax, at avg. price, for $1 to $10 + comm.

**Shares to qualify:** 1
**Safekeeping:** Yes
**Accepts foreign:** Yes
**Auto. inv.:** No
**Disc.:** No

---

## ✶ Bank Mutual Corp. ♥

**BKMU/NAS** — Bank holding co.

H: 15.75
L: 7.75
**Rec:** 15.75

**Div.:** 0.28
**Paid on:**
3.6.9.12-5
**Since:**2001

4949 W. Brown Deer Rd., Box 245034
Milwaukee. WI 53224-9534

Registrar & Transfer      800-368-5948
$100 - $2,500/quarter
Every 90 days beginning 3/5

FEES: Div: $0!; Cash: $0!; Cert: $0!; Term: $10 + comm.; Sells within 10 bus. days, by mail, at avg. price, for $10 + comm.

**Shares to qualify:** 50
**Safekeeping:** Yes
**Accepts foreign:** Yes
**Auto. inv.:** No
**Disc.:** No

---

## ✶ Bank of America Corp. ♥

**BAC/NYSE** — Banking

H: 64.70
L: 36.31
**Rec:** 62.90

**Div.:** 2.24
**Paid on:**
3.6.9.12-4TH FRI.
**Since:**1903

100 North Tryon St., 18th Fl.
Charlotte. NC 28255

Mellon Inv. Svcs.      800-642-9855
$50 - $120,000/year
Every 7 days beginning varies

FEES: Div: $0; Cash: $0; Auto. Inv.: $0; Cert: $0; Term: $0; Sells weekly, by mail or phone, at avg. price, for $15 + 8¢/sh.

**Shares to qualify:** 1 /de ($1000)
**Safekeeping:** Yes
**Accepts foreign:** Yes
**Auto. inv.:** Yes
**Disc.:** No

---

## ✶ Bank of Granite Corp. ♥

**GRAN/NASD** — Bank holding company

H: 23.93
L: 18.86
**Rec:** 21.60

**Div.:** 0.48
**Paid on:**
1.4.7.10-30
**Since:**N/A

Box 128
Granite Falls. NC 28630

Registrar & Transfer      800-368-5948
$100 - $2,000/quarter
Every 90 days beginning 1/30

FEES: Div: $0!; Cash: $0!; Auto. Inv.: $0; Does not sell through the plan

**Shares to qualify:** 100
**Safekeeping:** Yes
**Accepts foreign:** Yes
**Auto. inv.:** Yes
**Disc.:** No

---

## ✶ Bank of Montreal ♥

**BMO/NYSE** — Banking

H: 29.15
L: 20.18
**Rec:** 26.82

**Div.:** 0.73
**Paid on:**
2.5.8.11-30
**Since:**1829

100 King St. W., 21st Fl.
Toronto. Ont. M5X 1A1 Canada

Bank of Montreal (The Trust Co.      800-332-0095
$0 - $40,000/year
Every 30 days beginning 1/31

FEES: Div: $0!; Cash: $0!; Cert: $0!; Term: $0!; Sells irregularly, by mail or fax, at market, for comm.

**Shares to qualify:** 1
**Safekeeping:** No
**Accepts foreign:** Yes
**Auto. inv.:** No
**Disc.:** No

---

## ✶ Bank of New York ♥

**BK/NYSE** — Banking

H: 59.37
L: 40.15
**Rec:** 45.45

**Div.:** 0.72
**Paid on:**
2.5.8.11-4
**Since:**1785

One Wall St., 31st Fl.
New York. NY 10286

Bank of New York      800-432-0140
$50 - $150,000/year
Every 7 days beginning varies

FEES: Div: $0!; Cash: $0!; Auto. Inv.: $0; Cert: $0!; Term: $10 + 5¢/sh.; Sells weekly, by mail or phone, at market, for $10 + 5¢/sh.

**Shares to qualify:** 1 /de ($1000)
**Safekeeping:** Yes
**Accepts foreign:** Yes
**Auto. inv.:** Yes
**Disc.:** No

---

✶ DRIP enrollment through Temper Enrollment Service (see page 180).      **44**

## ✳ Bank One Corp. ♥

**ONE/NYSE**
H: 41.56
L: 30.75
**Rec:** 38.42
**Div.:** 0.84
**Paid on:**
1.4.7.10-1
**Since:** 1935

**Banking**
1 Bank One Plaza, MC- IL1-0738
Chicago. IL 60670-0738
First Chicago Trust      888-764-5592
$25 - $5,000/month
Every 30 days beginning varies
FEES: Div: $0!; Cash: $0!; Auto. Inv.: $0; Cert: $0; Term: $0; Sells daily, by mail or phone, at market, for $10 + 12¢/sh.

**Shares to qualify:** 1
**Safekeeping:** Yes
**Accepts foreign:** Yes
**Auto. inv.:** Yes
**Disc.:** No

---

## Bank West Financial Corp. ♥

**BWFC/NAS**
H: 11.40
L: 5.75
**Rec:** 11.36
**Div.:** 0.24
**Paid on:**
2.6.8.11-22
**Since:** N/A

**Bank holding co.**
2185 Three Mile Road N.W.
Grand Rapids. MI 49544
Registrar & Transfer      800-368-5948
$100 - $5,000/quarter
Every 90 days beginning 2/22
FEES: Div: $0!; Cash: $0!; Cert: $0!; Term: $10,Does not sell through the plan

**Shares to qualify:** 100
**Safekeeping:** No
**Accepts foreign:** Yes
**Auto. inv.:** No
**Disc.:** No

---

## ✳ Banknorth Group, Inc. ♥

**BKNG/NASD**
H: 23.68
L: 15.56
**Rec:** 23.60
**Div.:** 0.52
**Paid on:**
2.5.8.11-14
**Since:** 1994

**Bank holding co.**
Box 9540
Portland. ME 04112
American Stock Transfer      800-278-4353
$100 - $5,000/quarter
Every 90 days beginning 2/5
FEES: Div: $0!; Cash: $0!; Cert: $0!; Term: 4¢/sh.; Sells weekly, by mail, at market, for 4¢/sh.

**Shares to qualify:** 1
**Safekeeping:** Yes
**Accepts foreign:** Yes
**Auto. inv.:** No
**Disc.:** No

---

## ✳ Banta Corp. ♥

**BN/NYSE**
H: 29.99
L: 19.68
**Rec:** 29.66
**Div.:** 0.64
**Paid on:**
2.5.8.11-1
**Since:** 1927

**Printing**
Box 8003
Menasha. WI 54952-8003
Firstar Bank      800-637-7549
$25 - $7,500/quarter
Every 30 days beginning 1/2
FEES: Div: $0; Cash: $0; Auto. Inv.: $0; Cert: $0;  Term: $0; Sells irregularly, by mail, at market, for comm.

**Shares to qualify:** 1
**Safekeeping:** Yes
**Accepts foreign:** Yes
**Auto. inv.:** Yes
**Disc.:** No

---

## ✳ Barnes Group Inc. ♥

**B/NYSE**
H: 24.85
L: 17.62
**Rec:** 22.10
**Div.:** 0.80
**Paid on:**
3.6.9.12-10
**Since:** 1934

**Precision metal parts mfg. and dist.**
123 Main St., Box 489
Bristol. CT 06011-0489
Mellon Inv. Svcs.      800-801-9519
$10 - $10,000/quarter
Every 90 days beginning 3/10
FEES: Div: $0!; Cash: $0!; Cert: $0!; Term: $0; Sells weekly, by mail , at avg. price, for comm.

**Shares to qualify:** 1
**Safekeeping:** No
**Accepts foreign:** No
**Auto. inv.:** No
**Disc.:** No

---

## ✳ Bausch & Lomb ♥

**BOL/NYSE**
H: 60.00
L: 32.95
**Rec:** 35.21
**Div.:** 1.04
**Paid on:**
1.4.7.10-1
**Since:** 1952

**Health care and pharmaceuticals**
One Bausch & Lomb Pl.
Rochester. NY 14604-2701
Mellon Inv. Svcs.      888-581-9377
$25 - $60,000/year
Every 30 days beginning 1/2
FEES: Div: $0!; Cash: $0!; Cert: $0!; Term: $0; Sells weekly, by mail or fax, at market, for $15 + 8¢/sh.

**Shares to qualify:** 1
**Safekeeping:** Yes
**Accepts foreign:** No
**Auto. inv.:** No
**Disc.:** No

---

## ✳ Baxter International Inc. ♥

**BAX/NYSE**
H: 54.50
L: 36.81
**Rec:** 49.56
**Div.:** 0.58
**Paid on:**
DEC-31
**Since:** 1934

**Health care**
One Baxter Pkwy.
Deerfield. IL 60015-4633
First Chicago Trust      800-446-2617
$25 - $25,000/year
Every 30 days beginning 1/4
FEES: Div: $0!; Cash: $0!; Cert: $0; Term: 12¢/sh.; Sells daily, by mail or fax, at market, for 12¢/sh.

**Shares to qualify:** 1
**Safekeeping:** Yes
**Accepts foreign:** Yes
**Auto. inv.:** No
**Disc.:** No

---

✳ DRIP enrollment through Temper Enrollment Service (see page 180).      **45**

## BB&T Corp. ♥

| | |
|---|---|
| BBT/NYSE | **Banking** |
| H: 38.43 | Box 1489 |
| L: 25.93 | Lumberton. NC 28359-1489 |
| Rec: 38.00 | Branch Banking & Trust    800-682-6902 |
| Div.: 1.04 | $25 - $10,000/month |
| Paid on: | Every 15 days beginning varies |
| 2.5.8.11-1 | |
| Since:1934 | |

**Shares to qualify:** 1
**Safekeeping:** Yes
**Accepts foreign:** No
**Auto. inv.:** Yes
**Disc.:** No

FEES: Div: $0;  Cash: $0;  Auto. Inv.: $0;  Cert: $0;  Term: $0; Sells bimonthly, by mail or fax, at avg. price, for 7¢/sh.

---

## BCE Inc. ♥

| | |
|---|---|
| BCE/NYSE | **Telecommunications** |
| H: 29.56 | 1000 Rue de La Gauchetiere W., # 3700 |
| L: 21.00 | Montreal. Que. H3B 4Y7 Canada |
| Rec: 26.91 | Computershare Trust Co. of    800-558-0046 |
| Div.: 0.78 | $0 - $20,000/year (Cdn.) |
| Paid on: | Every 30 days beginning 1/15 |
| 1.4.7.10-15 | |
| Since:1881 | |

**Shares to qualify:** 1
**Safekeeping:** No
**Accepts foreign:** Yes
**Auto. inv.:** No
**Disc.:** No

FEES: Div: $0!;  Cash: $0!;  Cert: $0!;  Term: $0; Sells daily, by mail or fax, at avg. price, for 3¢/sh.

---

## Beckman Coulter Inc. ♥

| | |
|---|---|
| BEC/NYSE | **Mfr. lab instr.** |
| H: 46.71 | 4300 N. Harbor Blvd., M/S A-38-C, Box 3100 |
| L: 32.62 | Fullerton. CA 92834-3100 |
| Rec: 44.57 | First Chicago Trust    201-324-1644 |
| Div.: 0.34 | $10 - $60,000/year |
| Paid on: | Every 30 days beginning 1/8 |
| 3.6.9.12-1 | |
| Since:1989 | |

**Shares to qualify:** 1
**Safekeeping:** Yes
**Accepts foreign:** Yes
**Auto. inv.:** Yes
**Disc.:** No

FEES: Div: $0!;  Cash: $0!;  Auto. Inv.: $0;  Cert: $0!;  Term: $0; Sells daily, by mail, fax , or phone, at market, for $0

---

## Becton Dickinson & Co.

| | |
|---|---|
| BDX/NYSE | **Health care** |
| H: 39.25 | 1 Becton Dr. |
| L: 21.75 | Franklin Lakes. NJ 07417-1880 |
| Rec: 34.78 | First Chicago Trust    800-955-4743 |
| Div.: 0.38 | $50 - $unlimited |
| Paid on: | Every 7 days beginning varies |
| 3.6.9-30 & 1-1 | |
| Since:1909 | |

**Shares to qualify:** 1 /de ($250)
**Safekeeping:** Yes
**Accepts foreign:** Yes
**Auto. inv.:** Yes
**Disc.:** No

FEES: Div: 3¢/sh.;  Cash: 3¢/sh.;  Auto. Inv.: 3¢/sh.; Cert: $0;  Term: $0; Sells daily, by mail or phone, at market, for $15 + 15¢/sh.

---

## Bedford Property Investors ♥

| | |
|---|---|
| BED/NYSE | **Real estate, commercial** |
| H: 21.76 | 270 Lafayette Circle |
| L: 18.00 | Lafayette. CA 94549 |
| Rec: 21.76 | First Chicago Trust    800-756-8200 |
| Div.: 1.80 | $100 - $5,000/month |
| Paid on: | Every 30 days beginning 1/15 |
| 1.4.7.10-15 | |
| Since:1993 | |

**Shares to qualify:** 1 /de ($1000)
**Safekeeping:** Yes
**Accepts foreign:** Yes
**Auto. inv.:** Yes
**Disc.:** No

FEES: Div: $0;  Cash: $0;  Auto. Inv.: $0;  Cert: $0;  Term: $0; Sells weekly, by mail or phone, at market, for $15 + 12¢/sh.

---

## BellSouth Corp. ♥

| | |
|---|---|
| BLS/NYSE | **Telecommunications** |
| H: 50.62 | 1155 Peachtree St. N.E., Rm.14B06 |
| L: 35.50 | Atlanta. GA 30309-3610 |
| Rec: 40.11 | Mellon Inv. Svcs.    800-631-6001 |
| Div.: 0.76 | $50 - $100,000/year |
| Paid on: | Every 7 days beginning varies |
| 2.5.8.11-1 | |
| Since:1984 | |

**Shares to qualify:** 1 /de ($500)
**Safekeeping:** Yes
**Accepts foreign:** Yes
**Auto. inv.:** Yes
**Disc.:** No

FEES: Div: $0!;  Cash: $0!;  Auto. Inv.: $0;  Cert: $0!;  Term: $0; Sells weekly, by phone, mail, fax, or Internet, at avg. price, for $10 + 8¢/sh.

---

## Bemis Co., Inc. ♥

| | |
|---|---|
| BMS/NYSE | **Packaging** |
| H: 44.64 | 222 South Ninth St., Ste. 2300 |
| L: 22.93 | Minneapolis. MN 55402-4099 |
| Rec: 42.35 | Wells Fargo Bank    800-468-9716 |
| Div.: 1.00 | $25 - $10,000/quarter |
| Paid on: | Every 30 days beginning 1/2 |
| 3.6.9.12-1 | |
| Since:1922 | |

**Shares to qualify:** 1
**Safekeeping:** Yes
**Accepts foreign:** No
**Auto. inv.:** No
**Disc.:** No

FEES: Div: $0;  Cash: $0;  Cert: $0;  Term: $0; Sells daily, by mail, fax , or phone, at avg. price, for $10 + 10¢/sh.

---

## * Bethlehem Steel Corporation ♥

**BS/NYSE**

**Steel**

H: 4.31
L: 1.62
**Rec:** 2.06

**Div.:** 0.00
**Paid on:**
DIV. SUSP.
**Since:** --

1170 Eighth Ave.
Bethlehem. PA 18016-7699

First Chicago Trust    201-324-1225

$10 - $3,000/month

Every 30 days beginning 1/2

FEES: Div: n/o; Cash: $0!; Cert: $0!; Term: $10 + 12¢/sh.; Sells daily, by mail, at market, for $10 + 12¢/sh.

**Shares to qualify:** 1
**Safekeeping:** Yes
**Accepts foreign:** No
**Auto. inv.:** No
**Disc.:** No

---

## * Birmingham Steel Corp. ♥

**BIR/NYSE**

**Produces steel & steel products**

H: 3.37
L: 0.60
**Rec:** 1.05

**Div.:** 0.00
**Paid on:**
DIV. SUSP.
**Since:** --

1000 Urban Center Dr., Ste. 300
Birmingham. AL 35242-2516

First Union Nat'l Bank    800-829-8432

$20 - $2,000/month

Every 30 days beginning 1/5

FEES: Div: n/o ; Cash: $0!; Cert: $0!; Term: $0; Sells bimonthly, by mail, at market, for fee + 5¢/sh.

**Shares to qualify:** 1
**Safekeeping:** Yes
**Accepts foreign:** Yes
**Auto. inv.:** No
**Disc.:** No

---

## * Black & Decker ♥

**BDK/NYSE**

**Home appl. & power tools**

H: 46.95
L: 27.56
**Rec:** 41.88

**Div.:** 0.48
**Paid on:**
3.6.9.12-30
**Since:** 1937

701 East Joppa Rd., TW 266
Towson. MD 21286

First Chicago Trust    800-519-3111

$50 - $60,000/year

Every 30 days beginning 1/28

FEES: Div: $0; Cash: $0; Auto. Inv.: $1; Cert: $0; Term: $0; Sells daily, by phone or mail, at market, for $10 + comm.

**Shares to qualify:** 1
**Safekeeping:** Yes
**Accepts foreign:** Yes
**Auto. inv.:** Yes
**Disc.:** No

---

## * Black Hills Corp. ♥

**BKH/NYSE**

**Utility-electric**

H: 58.50
L: 24.12
**Rec:** 37.15

**Div.:** 1.12
**Paid on:**
3.6.9.12-1
**Since:** 1942

Box 1400
Rapid Citv. SD 57709

Wells Fargo Bank    800-468-9716

$200 - $50,000/quarter

Every 30 days beginning 1/2

FEES: Div: $0; Cash: $0; Cert: $0; Term: $0; Sells weekly, by mail , at avg. price, for $10 + 10¢/sh.

**Shares to qualify:** 1
**Safekeeping:** Yes
**Accepts foreign:** Yes
**Auto. inv.:** No
**Disc.:** No

---

## * Block (H&R)

**HRB/NYSE**

**Tax & financial services**

H: 36.40
L: 15.65
**Rec:** 34.86

**Div.:** 0.64
**Paid on:**
1.4.7.10-1
**Since:** 1962

4400 Main St.
Kansas Citv. MO 64111

Mellon Inv. Svcs.    888-213-0968

$25 - $2,000/month

Every 30 days beginning last bus. day

FEES: Div: 7¢/sh.; Cash: 3¢/sh.; Cert: $0; Term: $0; Sells 10 to12 bus.days, by mail or phone, at market, for 7¢/sh.

**Shares to qualify:** 1
**Safekeeping:** Yes
**Accepts foreign:** Yes
**Auto. inv.:** No
**Disc.:** No

---

## * Blue Chip Value Fund, Inc.

**BLU/NYSE**

**Closed-end fund**

H: 8.68
L: 6.60
**Rec:** 7.84

**Div.:** 0.80
**Paid on:**
1.4.7.10-30
**Since:** N/A

1225 17th St., 26th Fl.
Denver. CO 80202

Mellon Inv. Svcs.    800-288-9541

$50 - $10,000/month

Every 30 days beginning last bus. day

FEES: Div: $0!; Cash: 2¢ to 4¢/sh.; Auto. Inv.: 2¢ to 4¢/sh.; Cert: $0!; Term: $0!; Sells within 5 bus. days, by mail, at market, for 2¢ to 4¢/sh.

**Shares to qualify:** 1
**Safekeeping:** Yes
**Accepts foreign:** Yes
**Auto. inv.:** Yes
**Disc.:** No

---

## * Blyth, Inc. ⊗

**BTH/NYSE**

**Mfrs. and dist. candles & home**

H: 30.37
L: 21.06
**Rec:** 23.15

**Div.:** 0.20
**Paid on:**
5-15. 11-15
**Since:** 2000

100 Field Point Rd.
Greenwich. CT 06830

First Chicago Trust    800-446-2617

$50 - $10,000/month

Every 30 days beginning varies

FEES: Div: 10¢/sh.; Cash: $5 + 10¢/sh.; Auto. Inv.: $1.50 + 10¢/sh.; Cert: $5; Term: $10 + 10¢/sh.; Sells within 5 bus. days, by mail, at avg. price, for $10 + 10¢/sh.

**Shares to qualify:** 1 /de ($250)
**Safekeeping:** Yes
**Accepts foreign:** Yes
**Auto. inv.:** Yes
**Disc.:** No

---

* DRIP enrollment through Temper Enrollment Service (see page 180).    **47**

## ❋ BNP Residential Properties, Inc. ♥

**BNP/ASE**
H: 10.65
L: 7.25
**Rec:** 10.44
**Div.:** 1.24
**Paid on:**
2.5.8.11-15
**Since:** 1987

REIT
3850 One First Union Ctr.
Charlotte. NC 28202-6032
First Union Nat'l Bank     800-829-8432
$25 - $10,000/quarter
Every 90 days beginning 2/15
FEES: Div: $0; Cash: $0; Cert: $0; Term: $0; Sells within 10 bus. days, by mail or fax, at market, for comm.

Shares to qualify: 1
Safekeeping: Yes
Accepts foreign: Yes
Auto. inv.: No
Disc.: No

---

## ❋ Bob Evans Farms ♥

**BOBE/NASD**
H: 21.68
L: 15.43
**Rec:** 19.25
**Div.:** 0.36
**Paid on:**
3.6.9.12-1
**Since:** 1964

Restaurant & sausage mfg.
3776 S. High St.
Columbus. OH 43207-0863
Bob Evans Farms Inc.     614-492-4952
$50 - $20,000/month
Every 15 days beginning 1/2
FEES: Div: $0!; Cash: $0!; Auto. Inv.: $0; Cert: $0!; Term: $0; Sells within 10 bus. days, by mail or fax, at market, for 10¢/sh.

Shares to qualify: 1 /de ($100)
Safekeeping: Yes
Accepts foreign: Yes
Auto. inv.: Yes
Disc.: No

---

## ❋ Boeing Co. (The)

**BA/NYSE**
H: 70.93
L: 45.31
**Rec:** 56.85
**Div.:** 0.68
**Paid on:**
3.6.9.12-6
**Since:** 1942

Aerospace
Box 3707, MC 13-08
Seattle. WA 98124-2207
BankBoston     888-777-0923
$50 - $100,000/year
Every 7 days beginning Friday
FEES: Div: $1 + comm.; Cash: $1 + comm.; Auto. Inv.: $0; Cert: $0; Term: $0; Sells daily, by mail, at avg. price, for $10 + 5¢/sh.

Shares to qualify: 1
Safekeeping: Yes
Accepts foreign: Yes
Auto. inv.: Yes
Disc.: No

---

## ❋ Boise Cascade Corp.

**BCC/NYSE**
H: 38.00
L: 21.75
**Rec:** 35.49
**Div.:** 0.60
**Paid on:**
1.4.7.10-15
**Since:** 1935

Paper & lumber products
1111 West Jefferson St., Box 50
Boise. ID 83728-0001
Boise Cascade Corp.     800-544-6473
$10 - $unlimited
Every 30 days beginning 1/15
FEES: Div: comm.; Cash: comm.; Cert: $0!; Term: $0; Sells monthly, by mail or fax, at market, for comm.

Shares to qualify: 1
Safekeeping: Yes
Accepts foreign: Yes
Auto. inv.: No
Disc.: No

---

## ❋ BorgWarner Inc. ♥

**BWA/NYSE**
H: 55.19
L: 31.00
**Rec:** 53.95
**Div.:** 0.60
**Paid on:**
2.5.8.11-17
**Since:** 1994

Auto powertrain components
200 South Michigan Ave.
Chicago. IL 60604
Mellon Inv. Svcs.     800-851-4229
$50 - $120,000/year
Every 7 days beginning varies
FEES: Div: $0; Cash: $0; Auto. Inv.: $0; Cert: $0; Term: $15 + 12¢/sh.; Sells daily, by mail or phone, at market, for $15 + 12¢/sh.

Shares to qualify: 1 /de ($500)
Safekeeping: Yes
Accepts foreign: Yes
Auto. inv.: Yes
Disc.: No

---

## ❋ Boston Beer Co. (The) ⊗

**SAM/NYSE**
H: 10.70
L: 7.50
**Rec:** 10.63
**Div.:** 0.00
**Paid on:**
DIV. SUSP.
**Since:** --

Beer
75 Arlington St.
Boston. MA 02116
Mellon Inv. Svcs.     888-877-2890
$50 - $10,000/month
Every 7 days beginning varies
FEES: Div: n/o; Cash: $3 + 12¢/sh.; Auto. Inv.: $3 + 12¢/sh.; Cert: $0; Term: $25 + 12¢/sh.; Sells weekly, by mail or phone, at market, for $25 + 12¢/sh.

Shares to qualify: 1 /de ($500)
Safekeeping: Yes
Accepts foreign: Yes
Auto. inv.: Yes
Disc.: No

---

## ❋ Boston Properties, Inc. ♥

**BXP/NYSE**
H: 44.87
L: 36.00
**Rec:** 39.90
**Div.:** 2.32
**Paid on:**
1.4.7.10-28
**Since:** 1997

REIT
800 Boylston St.
Boston. MA 02199
BankBoston     888-485-2389
$100 - $25,000/quarter
Every 90 days beginning 1/28
FEES: Div: $0; Cash: $0; Auto. Inv.: $0; Cert: $0; Term: $15 + comm.; Sells within 10 bus. days, at avg. price, for $15 + comm.

Shares to qualify: 1 /de ($100)
Safekeeping: Yes
Accepts foreign: Yes
Auto. inv.: Yes
Disc.: Div 3% Cash: 0%

---

## ✳ BostonFed Bancorp, Inc. ♥

**BFD/ASE** — **Bank holding company**

H: 25.00
L: 14.75
**Rec:** 23.20

**Div.:** 0.60
**Paid on:**
2.5.8.11-18
**Since:** 1996

17 New England Executive Park
Burlington. MA 01803

BankBoston     800-688-2372
$75 - $7,500/quarter
Every 30 days beginning 1st bus. day

**Shares to qualify:** 1
**Safekeeping:** Yes
**Accepts foreign:** Yes
**Auto. inv.:** No
**Disc.:** No

FEES: Div: $0!; Cash: $0!; Cert: $0!; Term: $10 + 15¢/sh.; Sells within 5 bus. days, by mail, at market, for $10 + 15¢/sh.

---

## ✳ Bowater Inc. ♥

**BOW/NYSE** — **Paper**

H: 58.75
L: 42.65
**Rec:** 45.85

**Div.:** 0.80
**Paid on:**
1.4.7.10-3
**Since:** 1984

55 E. Camperdown Way, Box 1028
Greenville. SC 29602

Bank of New York     888-269-8845
$100 - $5,000/month
Every 30 days beginning 1/2

**Shares to qualify:** 1
**Safekeeping:** No
**Accepts foreign:** Yes
**Auto. inv.:** No
**Disc.:** No

FEES: Div: $0; Cash: $0; Cert: $0; Term: $0; Sells weekly, by mail, at market, for $0

---

## ✳ Bowne & Co., Inc. ♥

**BNE/NYSE** — **Printing services**

H: 12.50
L: 7.87
**Rec:** 11.68

**Div.:** 0.22
**Paid on:**
2.5.8.10-25
**Since:** N/A

345 Hudson St.
New York. NY 10014

Bank of New York     800-524-4458
$50 - $100,000/year
Every 7 days beginning varies

**Shares to qualify:** 1 /de ($500)
**Safekeeping:** Yes
**Accepts foreign:** Yes
**Auto. inv.:** Yes
**Disc.:** No

FEES: Div: $0!; Cash: $0!; Auto. Inv.: $0; Cert: $0!; Term: $0; Sells weekly, by mail, at market, for $15 + 12¢/sh.

---

## ✳ Boykin Lodging Co. ♥

**BOY/NYSE** — **REIT**

H: 12.98
L: 8.50
**Rec:** 11.20

**Div.:** 1.46
**Paid on:**
2.5.8.11-4
**Since:** 1997

45 W. Prospect Ave., Ste. 1500
Cleveland. OH 44115

National City Bank     800-622-6757
$50 - $5,000/month
Every 30 days beginning 1/10

**Shares to qualify:** 1 /de ($2000)
**Safekeeping:** Yes
**Accepts foreign:** Yes
**Auto. inv.:** No
**Disc.:** Div 2% Cash: 2%

FEES: Div: $0!; Cash: $0!; Cert: $0!; Term: $0; Sells weekly, by mail, at market, for $5 + comm.

---

## ✳ BP plc ♥

**BP/NYSE** — **Oil & gas, petrochemicals**

H: 57.81
L: 45.12
**Rec:** 50.92

**Div.:** 1.47
**Paid on:**
4.6.9.12-10
**Since:** 1917

c/o Morgan Guaranty Trust, Box 842006
Boston. MA 02284-2006

Morgan Guaranty Trust Co.     877-638-5672
$50 - $150,000/year
Every 3 days beginning varies

**Shares to qualify:** 3 /de ($250)
**Safekeeping:** Yes
**Accepts foreign:** No
**Auto. inv.:** Yes
**Disc.:** No

FEES: Div: $0; Cash: $0; Auto. Inv.: $0; Cert: $0; Term: $10 + 12¢/sh.; Sells daily, by mail or phone, at market, for $10 + 12¢/sh.

---

## ✳ Brandywine Realty Trust ♥

**BDN/NYSE** — **REIT**

H: 22.80
L: 18.00
**Rec:** 22.60

**Div.:** 1.64
**Paid on:**
1.4.7.10-15
**Since:** N/A

14 Campus Blvd.
Newtown Square. PA 19073

First Chicago Trust     800-317-4445
$100 - $10,000/month
Every 30 days beginning 1/30

**Shares to qualify:** 1
**Safekeeping:** Yes
**Accepts foreign:** Yes
**Auto. inv.:** Yes
**Disc.:** Div 0% Cash: 0%-5%

FEES: Div: $0!; Cash: $0!; Auto. Inv.: $0; Cert: $0!; Term: $0; Sells daily, by phone, mail, fax, or Internet, at market, for $15 + 12¢/sh.

---

## ✳ Brazil Fund, Inc. (The)

**BZF/NYSE** — **Closed-end fund**

H: 19.25
L: 13.30
**Rec:** 14.50

**Div.:** 0.42
**Paid on:**
3-31
**Since:** N/A

c/o Zurich Scudder Inv., 345 Park Ave.
New York. NY 10154

Kemper Service Co.     800-621-1048
$100 - $3,000/semiannually
Every 180 days beginning 2/15

**Shares to qualify:** 1
**Safekeeping:** No
**Accepts foreign:** No
**Auto. inv.:** No
**Disc.:** Div 5% Cash: 0%

FEES: Div: $0!; Cash: $1 + comm.; Cert: $0; Term: $0; Sells within 10 bus. days, by mail, at market, for 5% to $3.50 + comm.

---

## Brazilian Equity Fund (The), Inc. ⊗

**BZL/NYSE** | Closed-end fund

H: 6.43
L: 4.25
Rec: 4.41

Div.: 0.12
Paid on:
JANUARY-15
Since: N/A

c/o Credit Suisse, 466 Lexington Ave.
New York. NY 10017

Boston Eq.      800-730-6001
$100 - $100,000/year
Every 7 days beginning Wednesday

Shares to qualify: 1 /de ($250)
Safekeeping: Yes
Accepts foreign: Yes
Auto. inv.: Yes
Disc.: No

FEES: Div: $0; Cash: $5 + 8¢/sh.; Auto. Inv.: $5 + 8¢/sh.; Cert: $0; Term: $0; Sells weekly, by mail, at avg. price, for $10 + 15¢/sh.

---

## BRE Properties, Inc. ♥

**BRE/NYSE** | REIT

H: 33.62
L: 26.20
Rec: 31.45

Div.: 1.86
Paid on:
3.6.9.12-27
Since: 1970

44 Montgomery St., 44th Fl.
San Francisco. CA 94104-4809

Mellon Inv. Svcs.      800-368-8392
$100 - $10,000/month
Every 7 days beginning varies

Shares to qualify: 1 /de ($500)
Safekeeping: Yes
Accepts foreign: Yes
Auto. inv.: No
Disc.: No

FEES: Div: $0!; Cash: $0!; Auto. Inv.: $0; Cert: $0!; Term: $15 + 12¢/sh.; Sells weekly, by mail or phone, at avg. price, for $15 + 12¢/sh.

---

## Bridge View Bancorp ♥

**BVB/ASE** | Bank holding co.

H: 17.95
L: 11.81
Rec: 15.70

Div.: 0.40
Paid on:
2.5.8.11-1
Since: N/A

457 Sylvan Ave.
Englewood Cliffs. NJ 07632

American Stock Transfer      800-937-5449
$100 - $5,000/quarter
Every 90 days beginning 2/1

Shares to qualify: 1
Safekeeping: Yes
Accepts foreign: Yes
Auto. inv.: No
Disc.: No

FEES: Div: $0!; Cash: $0!; Cert: $0!; Term: $10 + 4¢/sh.; Sells upon termination, by mail, at market, for $10 + 4¢/sh.

---

## Briggs & Stratton Corp. ♥

**BGG/NYSE** | Mfr. small gas engines

H: 48.37
L: 30.37
Rec: 40.65

Div.: 1.24
Paid on:
1.4.6.10-VARIES
Since: 1929

Box 702
Milwaukee. WI 53201-0702

Firstar Bank      800-637-7549
$25 - $5,000/quarter
Every 30 days beginning 1/2

Shares to qualify: 1
Safekeeping: Yes
Accepts foreign: Yes
Auto. inv.: No
Disc.: No

FEES: Div: $0; Cash: $0; Cert: $0; Term: $0; Sells biweekly, by mail or fax, at market, for comm.

---

## Bristol-Myers Squibb ⊗

**BMY/NYSE** | Pharmaceutical & consumer products

H: 74.87
L: 49.93
Rec: 56.70

Div.: 1.10
Paid on:
2.5.8.11-1
Since: 1933

345 Park Ave.
New York. NY 10154-0037

Mellon Inv. Svcs.      888-552-8493
$105 - $10,025/month
Every 7 days beginning Wed.

Shares to qualify: 50
Safekeeping: Yes
Accepts foreign: Yes
Auto. inv.: No
Disc.: No

FEES: Div: 4% to $5; Cash: $4.20 to $25; Cert: $5; Term: $15 + 5¢/sh.; Sells daily, by mail, at market, for $15 + 5¢/sh.

---

## BroadWing Inc. ♥

**BRW/NYSE** | Telecommunications

H: 30.00
L: 15.40
Rec: 20.73

Div.: 0.40
Paid on:
2.5.8.11-1
Since: N/A

201 E. Fourth St., Ste. 102-850
Cincinnati. OH 45202

Fifth Third Bancorp      800-837-2755
$25 - $5,000/month
Every 30 days beginning 1/2

Shares to qualify: 1
Safekeeping: No
Accepts foreign: Yes
Auto. inv.: No
Disc.: No

FEES: Div: $0!; Cash: $0!; Cert: $0!; Term: $0; Sells weekly, by mail, at market, for comm.

---

## Brookline Bancorp, Inc.

**BRKL/NASD** | Bank holding co.

H: 16.90
L: 10.25
Rec: 15.55

Div.: 0.64
Paid on:
2.5.8.11-15
Since: 1998

160 Washington St.
Brookline. MA 02147

American Stock Transfer      800-937-5449
$25 - $10,000/investment
Every day days beginning daily

Shares to qualify: 1 /de ($1000)
Safekeeping: Yes
Accepts foreign: Yes
Auto. inv.: Yes
Disc.: No

FEES: Div: 2% to $1.50 + 10¢/sh.; Cash: $2.50 + 10¢/sh.; Auto. Inv.: $2.50 + 10¢/sh.; Cert: $0; Term: $7.50 + 10¢/sh.; Sells daily, by phone, mail, fax, or Internet, at market, for $7.50 + 10¢/sh.

---

✳ DRIP enrollment through Temper Enrollment Service (see page 180).      **50**

## Brown Shoe Co., Inc. ♥

**BWS/NYSE**
H: 20.50
L: 8.43
**Rec:** 15.10
**Div.:** 0.40
**Paid on:**
1.4.7.10-1
**Since:** 1923

Shoes
Box 29
St. Louis. MO 63166-0029
First Chicago Trust    800-446-2617
$25 - $1,000/month
Every 30 days beginning 1/2

**Shares to qualify:** 1
**Safekeeping:** Yes
**Accepts foreign:** Yes
**Auto. inv.:** No
**Disc.:** No

FEES: Div: $0; Cash: $0; Cert: $0; Term: $0; Sells weekly, by mail or fax, at market, for $10 + 12¢/sh.

---

## Brown-Forman Corp. -B ♥

**BFB/NYSE**
H: 72.00
L: 50.43
**Rec:** 66.30
**Div.:** 1.32
**Paid on:**
1.4.7.10-1
**Since:** 1960

Beverages, liquors, consumer durables
850 Dixie Hwy.
Louisville. KY 40210
First Chicago Trust    201-324-0498
$50 - $3,000/quarter
Every 30 days beginning 1/2

**Shares to qualify:** 1
**Safekeeping:** No
**Accepts foreign:** Yes
**Auto. inv.:** No
**Disc.:** No

FEES: Div: $0!; Cash: $0!; Cert: $0; Term: $0; Sells daily, by phone, at market, for $15 + 12¢/sh.

---

## Brown-Forman Corp. -A ♥

**BFA/NYSE**
H: 71.00
L: 49.75
**Rec:** 67.37
**Div.:** 1.32
**Paid on:**
1.4.7.10-1
**Since:** 1945

Beverages, liquors, consumer durables
850 Dixie Hwy.
Louisville. KY 40210
First Chicago Trust    201-324-0498
$50 - $3,000/quarter
Every 30 days beginning 1/2

**Shares to qualify:** 1
**Safekeeping:** No
**Accepts foreign:** Yes
**Auto. inv.:** No
**Disc.:** No

FEES: Div: $0!; Cash: $0!; Cert: $0; Term: $0; Sells daily, by phone, at market, for $15 + 12¢/sh.

---

## Brunswick Corp. ♥

**BC/NYSE**
H: 25.01
L: 14.81
**Rec:** 21.90
**Div.:** 0.50
**Paid on:**
3.6.9.12-15
**Since:** 1969

Recreation prod.
1 North Field Ct.
Lake Forest. IL 60045-4811
Brunswick Corp.    800-546-9420
$10 - $2,000/month
Every 30 days beginning 1/14

**Shares to qualify:** 1
**Safekeeping:** Yes
**Accepts foreign:** Yes
**Auto. inv.:** No
**Disc.:** No

FEES: Div: $0!; Cash: $0!; Cert: $0!; Term: $0; Sells bimonthly, by mail, fax or Internet, at market, for 3¢/sh.

---

## Brush Engineered Materials Inc. ♥

**BW/NYSE**
H: 24.31
L: 15.27
**Rec:** 15.50
**Div.:** 0.48
**Paid on:**
3.6.9.12-30
**Since:** 1972

Engineered materials
17876 St. Clair Ave.
Cleveland. OH 44110
National City Bank    800-622-6757
$25 - $5,000/quarter
Every 30 days beginning 1/26

**Shares to qualify:** 1
**Safekeeping:** Yes
**Accepts foreign:** Yes
**Auto. inv.:** No
**Disc.:** No

FEES: Div: $0!; Cash: $0!; Cert: $0!; Term: $5 + comm.,Does not sell through the plan

---

## BSB Bancorp, Inc. ♥

**BSBN/NASD**
H: 25.04
L: 10.98
**Rec:** 24.25
**Div.:** 1.00
**Paid on:**
3.6.9.12-10
**Since:** N/A

Banking
Box 1056
Binghamton. NY 13902
American Stock Transfer    800-937-5449
$50 - $5,000/month
Every 30 days beginning 1/10

**Shares to qualify:** 1
**Safekeeping:** Yes
**Accepts foreign:** Yes
**Auto. inv.:** Yes
**Disc.:** No

FEES: Div: $0; Cash: $0; Auto. Inv.: $0; Cert: $0; Term: $0; Sells weekly, by mail, at market, for 4¢/sh.

---

## Burlington Northern Santa Fe Corp.

**BNI/NYSE**
H: 34.00
L: 20.37
**Rec:** 26.63
**Div.:** 0.48
**Paid on:**
1.4.7.10-1
**Since:** 1940

Railroad
2650 Lou Menk Dr., 2nd Fl.
Fort Worth. TX 76131-2830
First Chicago Trust    800-526-5678
$50 - $60,000/year
Every 30 days beginning varies

**Shares to qualify:** 1
**Safekeeping:** Yes
**Accepts foreign:** Yes
**Auto. inv.:** No
**Disc.:** No

FEES: Div: 5% to $2.50; Cash: 5% to $2.50; Cert: $0; Term: $0; Sells daily, by phone or mail, at market, for $10 + 12¢/sh.

---

✽ DRIP enrollment through Temper Enrollment Service (see page 180).    **51**

## ✳ C & F Financial Corp. ♥

**CFFI/NASD** | **Bank holding company** | **Shares to qualify:** 1
H: 18.00 | Eighth & Main St. | **Safekeeping:** No
L: 14.00 | West Point. VA 23181 | **Accepts foreign:** Yes
**Rec:** 18.00 | American Stock Transfer 800-278-4353 | **Auto. inv.:** Yes
**Div.:** 0.56 | $100 - $1,000/month | **Disc.:** No
**Paid on:** | Every 30 days beginning 1/4
1.4.7.10-1 | FEES: Div: $0!; Cash: $0!; Auto. Inv.: $0; Cert: $0!; Term: $10 + 4¢/sh.; Sells weekly, by
**Since:** N/A | mail, at market, for $10 + 4¢/sh.

## ✳ Cabot Corp. ♥

**CBT/NYSE** | **Chemicals** | **Shares to qualify:** 1
H: 39.50 | 2 Seaport Lane., Ste. 1300 | **Safekeeping:** Yes
L: 18.18 | Boston. MA 02210-2019 | **Accepts foreign:** Yes
**Rec:** 38.92 | Boston Eq. 800-730-4001 | **Auto. inv.:** No
**Div.:** 0.52 | $10 - $10,000/quarter | **Disc.:** No
**Paid on:** | Every 45 days beginning 3/1
3.6.9.12-9 | FEES: Div: $0; Cash: $0; Cert: $0; Term: $0; Sells within 10 bus. days, by mail or phone, at
**Since:** 1931 | market, for $0

## ✳ Cabot Industrial Trust

**CTR/NYSE** | **REIT** | **Shares to qualify:** 1 /de ($200)
H: 21.42 | 2 Center Plaza, Ste. 200 | **Safekeeping:** Yes
L: 18.00 | Boston. MA 02108-1906 | **Accepts foreign:** Yes
**Rec:** 20.99 | BankBoston 877-228-7006 | **Auto. inv.:** Yes
**Div.:** 1.48 | $50 - $5,000/month | **Disc.:** Div 0% Cash:
**Paid on:** | Every 30 days beginning varies | 0-5%
1.4.7.10-VARIES | FEES: Div: $0; Cash: 5¢/sh.; Auto. Inv.: 5¢/sh.; Cert: $0; Term: $0; Sells within 3 bus.
**Since:** 1998 | days, by mail, at market, for $15 + 12¢/sh.

## ✳ Cadmus Communications Corp. ♥

**CDMS/NAS** | **Printing, mktg., publ. & graphic arts** | **Shares to qualify:** 1
H: 12.30 | 1801 Bayberry Ct., Ste. 200 | **Safekeeping:** Yes
L: 5.50 | Richmond. VA 23226 | **Accepts foreign:** No
**Rec:** 10.49 | First Union Nat'l Bank 800-829-8432 | **Auto. inv.:** No
**Div.:** 0.20 | $25 - $3,000/quarter | **Disc.:** No
**Paid on:** | Every 90 days beginning 3/1
3.6.9.12-6 | FEES: Div: $0; Cash: $0; Cert: $0; Term: $25; Sells 1st & 15th, by mail or fax, at market, for
**Since:** 1941 | $5

## ✳ Calgon Carbon Corp. ⊗

**CCC/NYSE** | **Chemical manufacturing** | **Shares to qualify:** 1 /de ($250)
H: 9.43 | Box 717 | **Safekeeping:** Yes
L: 4.75 | Pittsburgh. PA 15230-0717 | **Accepts foreign:** Yes
**Rec:** 8.03 | First Chicago Trust 800-317-4445 | **Auto. inv.:** Yes
**Div.:** 0.20 | $50 - $350,000/year | **Disc.:** No
**Paid on:** | Every 5 days beginning varies
1.4.7.10-18 | FEES: Div: $0!; Cash: $5 + 3¢/sh.; Auto. Inv.: $2 + 3¢/sh.; Cert: $0!; Term: $15 +
**Since:** 1987 | 12¢/sh.; Sells daily, by mail or phone, at market, for $15 + 12¢/sh.

## ✳ California Water Service Group ♥

**CWT/NYSE** | **Utility-water** | **Shares to qualify:** 1 /de ($500)
H: 28.60 | 1720 North First St. | **Safekeeping:** Yes
L: 22.87 | San Jose. CA 95112-4598 | **Accepts foreign:** Yes
**Rec:** 24.00 | BankBoston 800-736-3001 | **Auto. inv.:** Yes
**Div.:** 3.34 | $100 - $20,000/month | **Disc.:** No
**Paid on:** | Every 7 days beginning Wed.
2.5.8.11-15 | FEES: Div: $0; Cash: $0; Auto. Inv.: $0; Cert: $0; Term: $0; Sells varies, by mail, at market,
**Since:** 1926 | for $10 to $15 + comm.

## ✳ Callaway Golf Co. ♥

**ELY/NYSE** | **Mfr. golf clubs** | **Shares to qualify:** 1
H: 27.18 | 2180 Rutherford Rd. | **Safekeeping:** Yes
L: 12.62 | Carlsbad. CA 92008-7328 | **Accepts foreign:** Yes
**Rec:** 15.70 | Mellon Inv. Svcs. 800-368-7068 | **Auto. inv.:** No
**Div.:** 0.28 | $50 - $5,000/quarter | **Disc.:** No
**Paid on:** | Every 30 days beginning 1/15
2.5.8.11-VARIES | FEES: Div: $0; Cash: $0; Cert: $15; Term: $15 + comm.; Sells weekly, by mail or phone, at
**Since:** 1993 | market, for $15 + comm.

---

## Camco Financial Corp. ♥

| | | |
|---|---|---|
| * | | |
| **CAFI/NASD** | **Bank holding co.** | **Shares to qualify:** 1 |
| H: 14.59 | 6901 Glenn Hwy. | **Safekeeping:** Yes |
| L: 8.37 | Cambridge, OH 43725 | **Accepts foreign:** Yes |
| **Rec:** 13.45 | Registrar & Transfer   800-368-5948 | **Auto. inv.:** No |
| **Div.:** 0.48 | $100 - $3,000/quarter | **Disc.:** No |
| **Paid on:** | Every 30 days beginning 1/20 | |
| 1.4.7.10-19 | FEES: Div: $0; Cash: $0; Cert: $0; Term: $15; Sells weekly, by mail, at market, for $15 + | |
| **Since:** N/A | comm. | |

## Camden Property Trust ♥

| | | |
|---|---|---|
| * | | |
| **CPT/NYSE** | **REIT** | **Shares to qualify:** 1 |
| H: 38.04 | 3 Greenway Plz., Ste.1300 | **Safekeeping:** No |
| L: 28.06 | Houston, TX 77046 | **Accepts foreign:** Yes |
| **Rec:** 38.04 | American Stock Transfer   800-278-4353 | **Auto. inv.:** No |
| **Div.:** 2.44 | $100 - $10,000/quarter | **Disc.:** No |
| **Paid on:** | Every 90 days beginning 1/19 | |
| 1.4.7.10-18 | FEES: Div: $0; Cash: $0; Cert: $0; Term: $0; Sells irregularly, by mail, at market, for comm. | |
| **Since:** 1993 | | |

## Campbell Soup Co. ⊗

| | | |
|---|---|---|
| * | | |
| **CPB/NYSE** | **Food proc.** | **Shares to qualify:** 1 /de ($500) |
| H: 35.43 | Campbell Pl. | **Safekeeping:** Yes |
| L: 23.75 | Camden, NJ 08103-1799 | **Accepts foreign:** Yes |
| **Rec:** 25.99 | First Chicago Trust   800-446-2617 | **Auto. inv.:** Yes |
| **Div.:** 0.90 | $50 - $350,000/year | **Disc.:** No |
| **Paid on:** | Every 5 days beginning 1/5 | |
| 1.4.7.10-31 | FEES: Div: 5% to $3 + 10¢/sh.; Cash: $5 + 3¢/sh.; Auto. Inv.: $2 + 3¢/sh.; Cert: $0!; | |
| **Since:** 1954 | Term: $15 + 12¢/sh.; Sells daily, by mail or phone, at market, for $15 + 12¢/sh. | |

## Canada Southern Petroleum

| | | |
|---|---|---|
| **CSPLF/NAS** | **Oil & gas exploration** | **Shares to qualify:** 1 /de ($250) |
| H: 9.87 | 1 Palliser Sq., Ste. 1410, 125 9th Ave., S.E. | **Safekeeping:** Yes |
| L: 3.06 | Calgary, Alta. T2G 0P6 Canada | **Accepts foreign:** Yes |
| **Rec:** 8.51 | American Stock Transfer   800-278-4353 | **Auto. inv.:** Yes |
| **Div.:** 0.00 | $25 - $10,000/daily | **Disc.:** No |
| **Paid on:** | Every day days beginning daily | |
| N/0 | FEES: Div: n/o; Cash: $2.50 + 10¢/sh.; Auto. Inv.: $2.50 + 10¢/sh.; Cert: $0;  Term: | |
| **Since:** N/A | $7.50 + 10¢/sh.; Sells daily, by phone, mail, fax, or Internet, at market, for $7.50 + | |
| | 10¢/sh. | |

## Canadian Pacific Ltd. ♥

| | | |
|---|---|---|
| * | | |
| **CP/NYSE** | **Transportation, energy, & hotels** | **Shares to qualify:** 1 |
| H: 43.63 | 1800 Bankers Hall East, 855-2nd St. S.W. | **Safekeeping:** No |
| L: 25.50 | Calgary, Alta.T2P 4Z5 Canada | **Accepts foreign:** Yes |
| **Rec:** 39.21 | Bank of Montreal   800-332-0095 | **Auto. inv.:** No |
| **Div.:** 0.37 | $0 - $30,000/year Cdn. | **Disc.:** No |
| **Paid on:** | Every 30 days beginning 1/28 | |
| 1.4.7.10-28 | FEES: Div: $0!; Cash: $0!; Cert: $0!; Term: $0,Does not sell through the plan | |
| **Since:** 1944 | | |

## Capital Automotive REIT ♥

| | | |
|---|---|---|
| * | | |
| **CARS/NASD** | **REIT** | **Shares to qualify:** 1 /de ($500) |
| H: 19.97 | c/o Fincl. Relations Bd., 675 Third Ave. | **Safekeeping:** Yes |
| L: 12.00 | New York. NY 10017 | **Accepts foreign:** Yes |
| **Rec:** 17.20 | American Stock Transfer   800-278-4353 | **Auto. inv.:** Yes |
| **Div.:** 1.55 | $500 - $10,000/month | **Disc.:** Div 3% Cash: 3% |
| **Paid on:** | Every 30 days beginning 1/1 | |
| 1.4.7.10-31 | FEES: Div: $0!; Cash: $0!; Auto. Inv.: $0; Cert: $0!; Term: 4¢/sh.; Sells within 10 bus. | |
| **Since:** N/A | days, by mail, at market, for 4¢/sh. | |

## Capital City Bank Group ♥

| | | |
|---|---|---|
| * | | |
| **CCBG/NASD** | **Bank holding company** | **Shares to qualify:** 1 |
| H: 26.75 | 217 North Monroe St. | **Safekeeping:** Yes |
| L: 18.75 | Tallahassee. FL 32301 | **Accepts foreign:** Yes |
| **Rec:** 23.83 | American Stock Transfer   800-278-4353 | **Auto. inv.:** No |
| **Div.:** 0.59 | $100 - $2,500/quarter | **Disc.:** No |
| **Paid on:** | Every 30 days beginning 3/26 | |
| 3.6.9.12-26 | FEES: Div: $0!; Cash: $0!; Cert: $0!; Term: $0; Sells within 3 bus. days, by mail, at market, | |
| **Since:** N/A | for 4¢/sh. | |

---

## ✶ Capital Directions, Inc. ♥

**CTDN/OTC** — Bank holding company

H: 40.50
L: 36.25
**Rec:** 39.25
**Div.:** 1.40
**Paid on:**
1.4.7.10-30
**Since:** N/A

322 South Jefferson St.
Mason. MI 48856

American Stock Transfer     800-937-5449
$10 - $12,000/year
Every 90 days beginning 1/30

FEES: Div: $0!; Cash: $0!; Cert: $0!; Term: $0,Does not sell through the plan

**Shares to qualify:** 1
**Safekeeping:** Yes
**Accepts foreign:** Yes
**Auto. inv.:** No
**Disc.:** No

---

## ✶ Capital One Financial Corp. ♥

**COF/NYSE** — Bank card issuer svcs.

H: 73.25
L: 45.87
**Rec:** 62.02
**Div.:** 0.11
**Paid on:**
2.5.8.11-20
**Since:** 1995

2980 Fairview Park Dr., Ste.1300
Falls Church. VA 22042-4525

First Chicago Trust     800-446-2617
$50 - $5,000/month
Every 30 days beginning 1/20

FEES: Div: $0!; Cash: $0!; Auto. Inv.: $1; Cert: $0; Term: $15 + 12¢/sh.; Sells daily, by mail or phone, at market, for $15 + 12¢/sh.

**Shares to qualify:** 1
**Safekeeping:** Yes
**Accepts foreign:** Yes
**Auto. inv.:** Yes
**Disc.:** No

---

## ✶ Capital Southwest Corp. ♥

**CSWC/NAS** — Venture capital investment

H: 69.00
L: 50.62
**Rec:** 67.40
**Div.:** 0.40
**Paid on:**
2.5.8.11-31
**Since:** N/A

12900 Preston Rd., Ste. 700
Dallas. TX 75230

American Stock Transfer     800-937-5449
$100 - $10,000/month
Every 30 days beginning 1/31

FEES: Div: $0!; Cash: $0!; Auto. Inv.: $0; Does not sell through the plan

**Shares to qualify:** 25
**Safekeeping:** Yes
**Accepts foreign:** Yes
**Auto. inv.:** Yes
**Disc.:** No

---

## ✶ Capitol Bancorp Ltd. ♥

**CBCL/NASD** — Banking

H: 16.75
L: 8.75
**Rec:** 15.75
**Div.:** 0.40
**Paid on:**
3.6.9.12-1
**Since:** 1941

200 Washington Sq. North
Lansing. MI 48933

UMB Bank, N.A.     800-884-4225
$50 - $5,000/quarter
Every 30 days beginning 1/19

FEES: Div: $0!; Cash: $0!; Cert: $0!; Term: $5; Sells monthly, by mail, at market, for $5 + comm.

**Shares to qualify:** 1
**Safekeeping:** Yes
**Accepts foreign:** Yes
**Auto. inv.:** No
**Disc.:** No

---

## ✶ Caraustar Industries, Inc.

**CSAR/NASD** — Recycled packaging

H: 16.00
L: 6.35
**Rec:** 9.94
**Div.:** 0.12
**Paid on:**
1.4.7.10-7
**Since:** N/A

Box 115
Austell. GA 30106

Bank of New York     800-524-4458
$50 - $300,000/year
Every 30 days beginning 1/31

FEES: Div: $0; Cash: 10¢/sh.; Auto. Inv.: 10¢/sh.; Cert: $0; Term: $5 + 10¢/sh.; Sells weekly, by mail, at market, for $5 + 10¢/sh.

**Shares to qualify:** 1 /de ($250)
**Safekeeping:** Yes
**Accepts foreign:** Yes
**Auto. inv.:** Yes
**Disc.:** No

---

## ✶ Carlisle Companies Inc. ♥

**CSL/NYSE** — Diversified manufacturing

H: 46.93
L: 30.28
**Rec:** 36.77
**Div.:** 0.84
**Paid on:**
3.6.9.12-1
**Since:** 1950

250 South Clinton St., Ste. 201
Syracuse. NY 13202-1258

Computershare Investor Svcs.     800-897-9071
$10 - $3,000/quarter
Every 30 days beginning 1/2

FEES: Div: $0!; Cash: $0!; Cert: $0!; Term: $1 + 10¢/sh.; Sells daily, by mail, at avg. price, for $1 + 10¢/sh.

**Shares to qualify:** 1
**Safekeeping:** Yes
**Accepts foreign:** Yes
**Auto. inv.:** No
**Disc.:** No

---

## Carpenter Technology Corp.

**CRS/NYSE** — Metals

H: 38.25
L: 25.35
**Rec:** 28.20
**Div.:** 1.32
**Paid on:**
3.6.9.12-1
**Since:** 1907

1047 North Park Rd.
Wyomissing. PA 19610

American Stock Transfer     800-937-5449
$25 - $20,000/investment
Every day days beginning daily

FEES: Div: $0!; Cash: $2.50 + 10¢/sh.; Auto. Inv.: $2.50 + 10¢/sh.; Cert: $0!; Term: $7.50 + 10¢/sh.; Sells weekly, by phone, mail, fax, or Internet, at avg. price, for $7.50 + 10¢/sh.

**Shares to qualify:** 1 /de ($250)
**Safekeeping:** Yes
**Accepts foreign:** Yes
**Auto. inv.:** Yes
**Disc.:** No

---

✶ DRIP enrollment through Temper Enrollment Service (see page 180).

## * CarrAmerica ♥

| | |
|---|---|
| CRE/NYSE | **Real estate operations** |
| H: 32.48 | 1850 K St., N.W. |
| L: 27.00 | Washington, DC 20006 |
| **Rec:** 32.48 | |
| **Div.:** 1.85 | Boston Eq. 781-575-3100 |
| **Paid on:** | $25 - $25,000/year |
| 3.6.9.12-4 | Every 30 days beginning 1/30 |
| **Since:** N/A | |

**Shares to qualify:** 1
**Safekeeping:** Yes
**Accepts foreign:** No
**Auto. inv.:** No
**Disc.:** No

FEES: Div: $0!; Cash: $0!; Cert: $0!; Term: $0; Sells weekly, by mail or phone, at market, for $1 to $10 +comm.

## * Carver Bancorp, Inc.

| | |
|---|---|
| CNY/ASE | **Bank holding company** |
| H: 10.37 | 75 West 125th St. |
| L: 7.25 | New York, NY 10027 |
| **Rec:** 9.59 | |
| **Div.:** 0.10 | American Stock Transfer 800-278-4353 |
| **Paid on:** | $100 - $10,000/week |
| 3.6.9.12-15 | Every 7 days beginning varies |
| **Since:** N/A | |

**Shares to qualify:** 1 /de ($200)
**Safekeeping:** Yes
**Accepts foreign:** Yes
**Auto. inv.:** Yes
**Disc.:** No

FEES: Div: $0; Cash: $2.50 + 10¢/sh.; Auto. Inv.: $1 + 10¢/sh.; Cert: $0; Term: $7.50 + 10¢/sh.; Sells daily, by mail or phone, at market, for $7.50 + 10¢/sh.

## * Cascade Natural Gas ♥

| | |
|---|---|
| CGC/NYSE | **Utility-gas** |
| H: 21.70 | 222 Fairview Ave. North |
| L: 15.50 | Seattle, WA 98109 |
| **Rec:** 20.36 | |
| **Div.:** 0.96 | Bank of New York 888-269-8845 |
| **Paid on:** | $50 - $20,000/year |
| 2.5.8.11-15 | Every 30 days beginning 1/15 |
| **Since:** 1964 | |

**Shares to qualify:** 1 /de ($250)
**Safekeeping:** Yes
**Accepts foreign:** Yes
**Auto. inv.:** No
**Disc.:** No

FEES: Div: $0!; Cash: $0!; Cert: $0; Term: $0; Sells daily, by mail, at avg. price, for $5 + 10¢/sh.

## * Casey's General Store ♥

| | |
|---|---|
| CASY/NASD | **Convenience stores** |
| H: 15.00 | One Convenience Blvd. |
| L: 10.12 | Ankeny, IA 50021 |
| **Rec:** 14.03 | |
| **Div.:** 0.08 | UMB Bank, N.A. 816-860-7891 |
| **Paid on:** | $50 - $10,000/quarter |
| 2.5.8.11-15 | Every 30 days beginning 1/15 |
| **Since:** 1990 | |

**Shares to qualify:** 1
**Safekeeping:** Yes
**Accepts foreign:** Yes
**Auto. inv.:** Yes
**Disc.:** No

FEES: Div: $0!; Cash: $0!; Auto. Inv.: $0; Cert: $0!; Term: $0!; Sells daily, by mail, at avg. price, for $5 + comm.

## * Castle (A.M.) & Co. ♥

| | |
|---|---|
| CAS/ASE | **Metals service distribution centers** |
| H: 14.50 | 3400 North Wolf Rd. |
| L: 8.00 | Franklin Park, IL 60131 |
| **Rec:** 11.00 | |
| **Div.:** 0.48 | American Stock Transfer 800-937-5449 |
| **Paid on:** | $100 - $10,000/quarter |
| 2.5.8.11-14 | Every 90 days beginning varies |
| **Since:** 1934 | |

**Shares to qualify:** 1
**Safekeeping:** No
**Accepts foreign:** Yes
**Auto. inv.:** No
**Disc.:** No

FEES: Div: $0!; Cash: $0!; Cert: $0!; Term: $0,Does not sell through the plan

## * Caterpillar, Inc. ⊗

| | |
|---|---|
| CAT/NYSE | **Heavy machinery** |
| H: 56.83 | 100 N.E. Adams St. |
| L: 29.00 | Peoria, IL 61629 |
| **Rec:** 53.65 | |
| **Div.:** 1.40 | First Chicago Trust 800-446-2617 |
| **Paid on:** | $50 - $350,000/year |
| 2.5.8.11-20 | Every 5 days beginning varies |
| **Since:** 1914 | |

**Shares to qualify:** 1 /de ($500)
**Safekeeping:** Yes
**Accepts foreign:** Yes
**Auto. inv.:** Yes
**Disc.:** No

FEES: Div: 5% to $3 + 3¢/sh.; Cash: $5 + 3¢/sh.; Auto. Inv.: $2 + 3¢/sh.; Cert: $0; Term: $0; Sells daily, by phone or mail, at market, for $15 + 12¢/sh.

## * Cathay Bancorp, Inc. ♥

| | |
|---|---|
| CATY/NASD | **Bank holding company** |
| H: 64.50 | 777 North Broadway |
| L: 43.62 | Los Angeles, CA 90012 |
| **Rec:** 56.00 | |
| **Div.:** 1.00 | American Stock Transfer 800-937-5449 |
| **Paid on:** | $600 - $15,000/quarter |
| 1.4.7.10-20 | Every 30 days beginning varies |
| **Since:** 1991 | |

**Shares to qualify:** 1
**Safekeeping:** Yes
**Accepts foreign:** Yes
**Auto. inv.:** No
**Disc.:** Div 5% Cash: 0%

FEES: Div: $0!; Cash: $0!; Cert: $0; Term: $0,Does not sell through the plan

## ✳ CBL & Associates Properties, Inc. ♥

| | |
|---|---|
| **CBL/NYSE** | REIT |
| H: 31.28 | One Park Pl., 6148 Lee Hwy., Ste. 300 |
| L: 22.43 | Chattanooga. TN 37421-6511 |
| **Rec:** 31.15 | SunTrust Bank, Atlanta    800-568-3476 |
| **Div.:** 2.13 | $100 - $5,000/quarter |
| **Paid on:** | Every 30 days beginning 1/15 |
| 1.4.7.10-24 | |
| **Since:** 1993 | |

**Shares to qualify:** 1
**Safekeeping:** Yes
**Accepts foreign:** Yes
**Auto. inv.:** No
**Disc.:** Div: 5% Cash: 0%

FEES: Div: $0; Cash: $0; Cert: $0; Term: $0; Sells within 10 bus. days, by mail, at market, for 5% to $10 + comm.

---

## ✳ CBRL Group, Inc. ♥

| | |
|---|---|
| **CBRL/NASD** | Restaurant, gift shop |
| H: 24.25 | Box 787 |
| L: 11.87 | Lebanon. TN 37088-0787 |
| **Rec:** 18.97 | SunTrust Bank, Atlanta    800-568-3476 |
| **Div.:** 0.02 | $100 - $5,000/quarter |
| **Paid on:** | Every 30 days beginning 1/30 |
| 1-3 | |
| **Since:** 1972 | |

**Shares to qualify:** 1
**Safekeeping:** Yes
**Accepts foreign:** Yes
**Auto. inv.:** No
**Disc.:** No

FEES: Div: $0; Cash: $0; Cert: $0; Term: $0; Sells within 10 bus.days , by mail, at avg. price, for $0

---

## ✳ CCFNB Bancorp, Inc. ♥

| | |
|---|---|
| **CCFN/OTC** | Banking |
| H: 24.00 | 232 East St. |
| L: 16.37 | Bloomsburg. PA 17815 |
| **Rec:** 23.75 | American Stock Transfer    800-937-5449 |
| **Div.:** 0.60 | $25 - $1,500/quarter |
| **Paid on:** | Every 90 days beginning 1/15 |
| 3.6.9.12-VARIES | |
| **Since:** N/A | |

**Shares to qualify:** 1
**Safekeeping:** No
**Accepts foreign:** Yes
**Auto. inv.:** No
**Disc.:** No

FEES: Div: $0; Cash: $0; Cert: $0; Term: $0; Sells irregularly, by mail, at market, for comm.

---

## ✳ Cecil Bancorp, Inc. ♥

| | |
|---|---|
| **CECB/OTC** | Banking |
| H: 20.00 | 127 North St., Box 568 |
| L: 16.62 | Elkton. MD 21922 |
| **Rec:** 19.00 | Registrar & Transfer    800-368-5948 |
| **Div.:** 0.40 | $300 - $2,500/quarter |
| **Paid on:** | Every 30 days beginning last bus. day of each month |
| 3.6.9.12-31 | |
| **Since:** N/A | |

**Shares to qualify:** 50
**Safekeeping:** Yes
**Accepts foreign:** Yes
**Auto. inv.:** Yes
**Disc.:** No

FEES: Div: $0!; Cash: $0!; Auto. Inv.: $0; Cert: $5; Term: $10 + comm.; Sells weekly, by mail, at market, for $10 + comm.

---

## ✳ Cedar Fair L.P. ♥

| | |
|---|---|
| **FUN/NYSE** | Retail, amusement parks |
| H: 23.50 | One Cedar Point Dr. |
| L: 17.62 | Sandusky. OH 44870-5259 |
| **Rec:** 19.30 | American Stock Transfer    800-278-4352 |
| **Div.:** 1.56 | $50 - $5,000/quarter |
| **Paid on:** | Every 30 days beginning 1/15 |
| 2.5.8.11-15 | |
| **Since:** 1987 | |

**Shares to qualify:** 50
**Safekeeping:** Yes
**Accepts foreign:** Yes
**Auto. inv.:** No
**Disc.:** No

FEES: Div: $0!; Cash: $0!; Cert: $0; Term: $5 + 4¢/sh.; Sells daily, by mail, at market, for $5 + 4¢/sh.

---

## ✳ Center Bancorp, Inc. ♥

| | |
|---|---|
| **CNBC/NASD** | Regional banks |
| H: 22.75 | 2455 Morris Ave. |
| L: 11.42 | Union. NJ 07083 |
| **Rec:** 17.85 | American Stock Transfer    800-937-5449 |
| **Div.:** 0.60 | $100 - $30,000/year |
| **Paid on:** | Every 30 days beginning 1/2 |
| 2.5.8.11-1 | |
| **Since:** N/A | |

**Shares to qualify:** 1
**Safekeeping:** Yes
**Accepts foreign:** Yes
**Auto. inv.:** No
**Disc.:** No

FEES: Div: $0!; Cash: $0!; Cert: $0!; Term: $0; Sells daily, by mail, at market, for comm.

---

## ✳ CenterPoint Properties Trust ♥

| | |
|---|---|
| **CNT/NYSE** | REIT |
| H: 50.90 | 1808 Swift Dr. |
| L: 42.37 | Oak Brook. IL 60523-1501 |
| **Rec:** 48.30 | First Chicago Trust    800-446-2617 |
| **Div.:** 2.10 | $25 - $100,000/year |
| **Paid on:** | Every 90 days beginning 3/30 |
| 1.4.7.10-31 | |
| **Since:** 1994 | |

**Shares to qualify:** 1
**Safekeeping:** Yes
**Accepts foreign:** Yes
**Auto. inv.:** No
**Disc.:** No

FEES: Div: $0!; Cash: $0!; Cert: $0!; Term: 12¢/sh.; Sells daily, by mail, at market, for $10 + 12¢/sh.

---

## Central European Equity Fund

**CEE/NYSE**

| | |
|---|---|
| H: 14.55 | |
| L: 9.85 | |
| **Rec:** 10.31 | |
| **Div.:** 0.14 | |
| **Paid on:** | |
| 1-13 | |
| **Since:** NA | |

**Closed-end fund**

c/o Deutsche Bk.Securities, 280 Park Ave., 7-East
New York. NY 10017

Investors Bank & Trust Co.      800-356-2754
$100 - $36,000/year
Every 30 days beginning 1/15

FEES: Div: $0!; Cash: comm.; Cert: $0!; Term: $0,Does not sell through the plan

Shares to qualify: 1
Safekeeping: Yes
Accepts foreign: Yes
Auto. inv.: No
Disc.: No

---

## Central Vermont Public Service

**CV/NYSE**

| | |
|---|---|
| H: 19.64 | |
| L: 9.75 | |
| **Rec:** 18.45 | |
| **Div.:** 0.88 | |
| **Paid on:** | |
| 2.5.8.11-15 | |
| **Since:** 1944 | |

**Utility-electric**

77 Grove St.
Rutland. VT 05701

BankBoston      800-736-3001
$100 - $6,000/quarter
Every 30 days beginning 1/15

FEES: Div: 5¢/sh.; Cash: 5¢/sh.; Auto. Inv.: $0; Cert: $0; Term: $0; Sells within 10 bus. days, by mail, at avg. price, for 10¢/sh.

Shares to qualify: 1 /de ($250)
Safekeeping: Yes
Accepts foreign: Yes
Auto. inv.: Yes
Disc.: No

---

## CenturyTel, Inc. ♥

**CTL/NYSE**

| | |
|---|---|
| H: 39.87 | |
| L: 25.25 | |
| **Rec:** 30.47 | |
| **Div.:** 0.20 | |
| **Paid on:** | |
| 3.6.9.12-17 | |
| **Since:** 1974 | |

**Telecommunications**

Box 4065
Monroe. LA 71211-4065

Computershare Investor Svcs.      800-969-6718
$25 - $150,000/year
Every 7 days beginning varies

FEES: Div: $0!; Cash: $0!; Auto. Inv.: $0; Cert: $0!; Term: $0; Sells within 10 bus. days, by mail or fax, at avg. price, for comm.

Shares to qualify: 1
Safekeeping: Yes
Accepts foreign: Yes
Auto. inv.: Yes
Disc.: No

---

## CH Energy Group, Inc. ♥

**CHG/NYSE**

| | |
|---|---|
| H: 46.31 | |
| L: 35.00 | |
| **Rec:** 42.98 | |
| **Div.:** 2.16 | |
| **Paid on:** | |
| 2.5.8.11-1 | |
| **Since:** 1903 | |

**Utility-electric, gas**

284 South Ave.
Poughkeepsie. NY 12601-4879

First Chicago Trust      800-428-9578
$50 - $150,000/year
Every 30 days beginning 1/2

FEES: Div: $0!; Cash: $0!; Auto. Inv.: $0; Cert: $0!; Term: $0; Sells daily, by mail or phone, at market, for $10 + 12¢/sh.

Shares to qualify: 1 /de ($100)
Safekeeping: Yes
Accepts foreign: Yes
Auto. inv.: Yes
Disc.: No

---

## Charles E. Smith Res. Rlty. Inc. ♥

**SRW/NYSE**

| | |
|---|---|
| H: 52.00 | |
| L: 40.00 | |
| **Rec:** 51.75 | |
| **Div.:** 2.34 | |
| **Paid on:** | |
| 2.5.8.11-16 | |
| **Since:** 1994 | |

**REIT**

2345 Crystal Dr.
Arlington. VA 22202

First Union Nat'l Bank      800-829-8432
$200 - $25,000/year
Every 30 days beginning 1/15

FEES: Div: $0; Cash: $0; Cert: $0; Term: $0; Sells daily, by mail, at market, for 5¢/sh.

Shares to qualify: 1
Safekeeping: Yes
Accepts foreign: Yes
Auto. inv.: No
Disc.: No

---

## Chart Industries ♥

**CTI/NYSE**

| | |
|---|---|
| H: 6.00 | |
| L: 3.15 | |
| **Rec:** 3.45 | |
| **Div.:** 0.00 | |
| **Paid on:** | |
| DIV. SUSP. | |
| **Since:** -- | |

**Mfr. custom-built industrial eq.**

5885 Landerbrook Dr., Ste.150
Cleveland. OH 44124

National City Bank      800-622-6757
$10 - $5,000/month
Every 30 days beginning 1/15

FEES: Div: n/o; Cash: $0; Cert: $0; Term: $0; Sells weekly, by mail, at market, for 20¢/sh.

Shares to qualify: 1
Safekeeping: Yes
Accepts foreign: Yes
Auto. inv.: No
Disc.: No

---

## Charter Municipal Mortgage Acceptance Co. ♥

**CHC/ASE**

| | |
|---|---|
| H: 16.10 | |
| L: 12.40 | |
| **Rec:** 15.54 | |
| **Div.:** 1.10 | |
| **Paid on:** | |
| 2.5.8.11-15 | |
| **Since:** 1998 | |

**Consumer financial svcs.**

625 Madison Ave.
New York. NY 10022

EquiServe      800-730-6001
$500 - $12,500/quarter
Every 90 days beginning 2/15

FEES: Div: $0!; Cash: $0!; Cert: $0!; Term: $0; Sells daily, by mail, at market, for $15 + 12¢/sh.

Shares to qualify: 1
Safekeeping: Yes
Accepts foreign: Yes
Auto. inv.: No
Disc.: No

---

## Charter One Financial Inc. ⊗

**CF/NYSE**
H: 32.98
L: 19.87
**Rec:** 31.50

**Div.:** 0.80
**Paid on:**
2.5.8.11-20
**Since:** 1988

**Banking**

1215 Superior Ave.
Cleveland. OH 44114

BankBoston    800-733-5001
$50 - $5,000/month
Every 30 days beginning 1/20

FEES: Div: $0; Cash: $5; Cert: $0; Term: $0; Sells daily, by mail or phone, at market, for $15 + comm.

**Shares to qualify:** 10
**Safekeeping:** Yes
**Accepts foreign:** No
**Auto. inv.:** No
**Disc.:** No

---

## Chase Corp.

**CCF/ASE**
H: 14.25
L: 9.00
**Rec:** 12.81

**Div.:** 0.36
**Paid on:**
NOV.-VARIES
**Since:** 1993

**Industrial mfr.**

26 Summer St.
Bridgewater. MA 02324

American Stock Transfer    877-253-6849
$25 - $10,000/week
Every 7 days beginning varies

FEES: Div: 2% to $1.50 + 10¢/sh.; Cash: $2.50 +10¢/sh.; Auto. Inv.: $2.50 + 10¢/sh.; Cert: $0; Term: $7.50 + 10¢/sh.; Sells weekly, by mail or phone, at market, for $7.50 + 10¢/sh.

**Shares to qualify:** 1 /de ($250)
**Safekeeping:** Yes
**Accepts foreign:** Yes
**Auto. inv.:** Yes
**Disc.:** No

---

## Chemed Corp. ♥

**CHE/NYSE**
H: 39.25
L: 26.50
**Rec:** 31.15

**Div.:** 0.44
**Paid on:**
3.9.12-10 &
**Since:** 1971

**Diversified services**

2600 Chemed Ctr., 255 East Fifth St.
Cincinnati. OH 45202-4726

Wells Fargo Bank    800-468-9716
$50 - $5,000/month
Every 30 days beginning 1/10

FEES: Div: $0!; Cash: $0!; Auto. Inv.: $0; Cert: $5; Term: $5; Sells irregularly, by mail or phone, at market, for $5 + comm.

**Shares to qualify:** 25
**Safekeeping:** Yes
**Accepts foreign:** Yes
**Auto. inv.:** Yes
**Disc.:** No

---

## Chemical Financial Corp. ♥

**CHFC/NASD**
H: 30.40
L: 19.31
**Rec:** 27.74

**Div.:** 0.96
**Paid on:**
3.6.9.12-17
**Since:** 1997

**Banking**

Box 569
Midland. MI 48640-0569

Computershare Investor Svcs.    800-942-5909
$10 - $3,000/quarter
Every 15 days beginning 1/18

FEES: Div: $0; Cash: $0; Cert: $0; Term: $5; Sells weekly, by mail or fax, at market, for $0

**Shares to qualify:** 1
**Safekeeping:** Yes
**Accepts foreign:** Yes
**Auto. inv.:** No
**Disc.:** No

---

## Chemung Financial Corp. ♥

**CHMG/OTC**
H: 25.00
L: 19.05
**Rec:** 25.00

**Div.:** 0.88
**Paid on:**
1.4.7.10-1
**Since:** N/A

**Bank holding company**

One Chemung Canal Plaza
Elmira. NY 14902

American Stock Transfer    800-937-5449
$25 - $2,000/quarter
Every 90 days beginning varies

FEES: Div: $0; Cash: $0; Cert: $0; Term: $0,Does not sell through the plan

**Shares to qualify:** 1
**Safekeeping:** Yes
**Accepts foreign:** Yes
**Auto. inv.:** No
**Disc.:** No

---

## Chesapeake Corp. ♥

**CSK/NYSE**
H: 28.36
L: 16.75
**Rec:** 28.36

**Div.:** 0.88
**Paid on:**
2.5.8.11-15
**Since:** 1933

**Packaging**

1021 East Cary St., Box 2350
Richmond. VA 23218-2350

Computershare Investor Svcs.    312-360-5163
$10 - $5,000/quarter
Every 30 days beginning 1/15

FEES: Div: $0; Cash: $0; Cert: $0; Term: $0; Sells irregularly, by mail, at market, for 7¢ to 10¢/sh.

**Shares to qualify:** 1
**Safekeeping:** No
**Accepts foreign:** Yes
**Auto. inv.:** No
**Disc.:** No

---

## Chesapeake Utilities Corp. ♥

**CPK/NYSE**
H: 19.55
L: 16.62
**Rec:** 18.45

**Div.:** 1.10
**Paid on:**
1.4.7.10-5
**Since:** 1961

**Natural gas**

909 Silver Lake Blvd.
Dover. DE 19904

Boston Eq.    800-736-3001
$50 - $15,000/quarter
Every 30 days beginning 1/5

FEES: Div: $0; Cash: $0; Cert: $0; Term: $0; Sells within 3 bus. days, by mail, at market, for comm.

**Shares to qualify:** 1
**Safekeeping:** Yes
**Accepts foreign:** Yes
**Auto. inv.:** No
**Disc.:** No

---

## ∗ Chester Valley Bancorp ♥

**CVAL/NASD**
H: 28.25
L: 12.66
**Rec:** 13.75

**Div.:** 0.36
**Paid on:**
3.6.9.12-21
**Since:** 1991

Savings and loan
100 East Lancaster Ave.
Downinaton. PA 19335

American Stock Transfer    800-937-5449
$50 - $10,000/year
Every 90 days beginning 3/17

FEES: Div: $0;  Cash: $0;  Cert: $0;  Term: $0,Does not sell through the plan

**Shares to qualify:** 1
**Safekeeping:** Yes
**Accepts foreign:** No
**Auto. inv.:** No
**Disc.:** Div 5% Cash: 5%

---

## ∗ Chevron Corp. ⊗

**CHV/NYSE**
H: 98.49
L: 78.18
**Rec:** 91.75

**Div.:** 2.60
**Paid on:**
3.6.9.12-10
**Since:** 1912

Oil refining, marketing
575 Market St., Rm. 3440
San Francisco. CA 94105-2856

Mellon Inv. Svcs.    800-368-8357
$50 - $100,000/year
Every 5 days beginning 1/2

FEES: Div: 5% to $2.50 + 8¢/sh.;  Cash: $3 + 8¢/sh.;  Auto. Inv.: $1.50 + 8¢/sh.; Cert: $0;
Term: $10 + 8¢/sh.; Sells weekly, by mail or phone, at market, for $10 + 8¢/sh.

**Shares to qualify:** 1 /de ($250)
**Safekeeping:** Yes
**Accepts foreign:** Yes
**Auto. inv.:** Yes
**Disc.:** No

---

## ∗ Chile Fund (The), Inc. ⊗

**CH/NYSE**
H: 10.00
L: 8.18
**Rec:** 8.80

**Div.:** 0.55
**Paid on:**
1.4.7.10-27
**Since:** 1997

Closed-end fund
c/o Credit Suisse, 466 Lexington Ave.
New York. NY 10017

BankBoston    800-730-6001
$100 - $100,000/year
Every 5 days beginning Wed.

FEES: Div: $0!;  Cash: $5 + 8¢/sh.;  Auto. Inv.: $5 + 8¢/sh.; Cert: $0!; Term: $0; Sells
weekly, by mail, at market, for $10 +15¢/sh.

**Shares to qualify:** 1 /de ($250)
**Safekeeping:** Yes
**Accepts foreign:** Yes
**Auto. inv.:** Yes
**Disc.:** No

---

## ∗ Chittenden Corp. ♥

**CHZ/NYSE**
H: 34.31
L: 22.75
**Rec:** 34.11

**Div.:** 0.96
**Paid on:**
2.5.8.11-15
**Since:** N/A

Banking
Box 820
Burlinaton. VT 05401

BankBoston    800-969-3386
$25 - $10,000/quarter
Every 90 days beginning 2/21

FEES: Div: $0!;  Cash: $0!;  Cert: $0!; Term: $0; Sells within 10 bus. days, by mail, at market,
for $1 to $10

**Shares to qualify:** 1
**Safekeeping:** Yes
**Accepts foreign:** Yes
**Auto. inv.:** No
**Disc.:** No

---

## ∗ ChoiceOne Financial Services, Inc. ♥

**COFS/OTC**
H: 14.80
L: 11.43
**Rec:** 14.25

**Div.:** 0.68
**Paid on:**
3.6.9.12-30
**Since:** N/A

Bank holding co.
109 E. Division St., Box 186
Sparta. MI 49345

Registrar & Transfer    800-866-1340
$25 - $1,000/quarter
Every 30 days beginning 1/15

FEES: Div: $0!;  Cash: $0!;  Cert: $0!; Term: $10,Does not sell through the plan

**Shares to qualify:** 1
**Safekeeping:** Yes
**Accepts foreign:** No
**Auto. inv.:** No
**Disc.:** No

---

## ∗ Chubb Corp. ⊗

**CB/NYSE**
H: 90.25
L: 53.30
**Rec:** 59.43

**Div.:** 1.36
**Paid on:**
1.4.7.10-4
**Since:** 1902

Insurance
15 Mountain View Rd., Box 1615
Warren. NJ 07061-1615

First Chicago Trust    800-317-4445
$10 - $60,000/year
Every 30 days beginning 1/10

FEES: Div: 5% to $3;  Cash: 5% to $3;  Auto. Inv.: $1; Cert: $0;  Term: $0; Sells daily, by
mail or phone, at market, for $10 + 12¢/sh.

**Shares to qualify:** 1
**Safekeeping:** Yes
**Accepts foreign:** Yes
**Auto. inv.:** Yes
**Disc.:** No

---

## ∗ Church & Dwight ♥

**CHD/NYSE**
H: 27.00
L: 15.62
**Rec:** 26.24

**Div.:** 0.30
**Paid on:**
3.6.9.12-1
**Since:** 1901

Consumer products
469 N. Harrison St.
Princeton. NJ 08543-5297

Mellon Inv. Svcs.    800-851-9677
$250 - $5,000/quarter
Every 90 days beginning varies

FEES: Div: $0!;  Cash: $0!;  Cert: $5; Term: $15 + comm.; Sells daily, by mail, at market, for
$15 + comm.

**Shares to qualify:** 1
**Safekeeping:** Yes
**Accepts foreign:** Yes
**Auto. inv.:** No
**Disc.:** No

---

## ✱ CIGNA Corp. ♥

**CI/NYSE**
H: 136.75
L: 86.48
**Rec:** 89.85
**Div.:** 1.28
**Paid on:**
1.4.7.10-10
**Since:** 1867

**Insurance**
1601 Chestnut St., TL37A
Philadelphia. PA 19192

First Chicago Trust    800-317-4445
$10 - $5,000/month
Every 30 days beginning 1/10
FEES: Div: $0!; Cash: $0!; Cert: $0!; Term: $15 +12¢/sh.; Sells daily, by phone or mail, at market, for $15 + 12¢/sh.

**Shares to qualify:** 1
**Safekeeping:** Yes
**Accepts foreign:** Yes
**Auto. inv.:** No
**Disc.:** No

---

## ✱ Cincinnati Financial Corp. ⊗

**CINF/NASD**
H: 42.92
L: 32.56
**Rec:** 39.89
**Div.:** 0.84
**Paid on:**
1.4.7.10-15
**Since:** 1954

**Insurance**
Box 145496
Fairfield. OH 45250-5496

Fifth Third Bancorp    800-837-2755
$25 - $5,000/month
Every 30 days beginning 1/8
FEES: Div: 5% to $3; Cash: $3; Cert: $0; Term: $0; Sells weekly, by mail, at market, for $0!

**Shares to qualify:** 1
**Safekeeping:** Yes
**Accepts foreign:** No
**Auto. inv.:** No
**Disc.:** No

---

## ✱ Cinergy Corp. ♥

**CIN/NYSE**
H: 35.60
L: 27.68
**Rec:** 31.75
**Div.:** 1.80
**Paid on:**
2.5.8.11-15
**Since:** 1994

**Utility-electric, gas**
Box 900
Cincinnati. OH 45201-0900

Cinergy Corp.    800-325-2945
$25 - $100,000/year
Every 30 days beginning 1/15
FEES: Div: $0!; Cash: $0!; Auto. Inv.: $0; Cert: $0!; Term: $0; Sells weekly, by mail or fax, at avg. price, for 4¢/sh.

**Shares to qualify:** 1 /de ($250)
**Safekeeping:** Yes
**Accepts foreign:** Yes
**Auto. inv.:** Yes
**Disc.:** No

---

## ✱ Citizens Banking Corp. ♥

**CBCF/NASD**
H: 30.90
L: 20.06
**Rec:** 30.45
**Div.:** 1.10
**Paid on:**
2.5.8.11-7
**Since:** 1935

**Banking**
328 S. Saginaw St., Inv, Relations 002066
Flint. MI 48502-2401

Computershare Investor Svcs.    877-795-0772
$25 - $2,000/month
Every 30 days beginning 1/15
FEES: Div: $0!; Cash: $0!; Cert: $0!; Term: $10; Sells daily, by mail or phone, at market, for 10¢/sh.

**Shares to qualify:** 1
**Safekeeping:** Yes
**Accepts foreign:** No
**Auto. inv.:** No
**Disc.:** No

---

## ✱ Citizens Communications-B ⊗

**CZN/NYSE**
H: 16.93
L: 10.90
**Rec:** 11.34
**Div.:** 0.00
**Paid on:**
DIV. SUSP.
**Since:** --

**Telecommunications**
3 High Ridge Park
Stamford. CT 06905-1390

Illinois Stock Transfer    800-757-5755
$100 - $25,000/quarter
Every 30 days beginning 1/18
FEES: Div: n/o; Cash: $6 + 2¢/sh.; Auto. Inv.: $0; Cert: $0; Term: $0; Sells weekly, by mail or fax, at avg. price, for $15 + 2¢/sh.

**Shares to qualify:** 1
**Safekeeping:** Yes
**Accepts foreign:** No
**Auto. inv.:** Yes
**Disc.:** No

---

## ✱ Citizens & Northern Corporation

**CZNC/OTC**
H: 23.51
L: 19.50
**Rec:** 21.90
**Div.:** 1.04
**Paid on:**
1.4.7.10-20
**Since:** N/A

**Bank holding co.**
90-92 Main St., Box 58
Wellsboro. PA 16901

American Stock Transfer    800-937-5449
$25 - $10,000/investment
Every day days beginning daily
FEES: Div: 2% to $2.50 + 10¢/sh.; Cash: $2.50 + 10¢/sh.; Auto. Inv.: $2.50 + 10¢/sh.; Cert: $0; Term: $15 + 10¢/sh.; Sells daily, by phone, mail, fax, or Internet, at market, for $15 + 10¢/sh.

**Shares to qualify:** 1 /de ($250)
**Safekeeping:** Yes
**Accepts foreign:** No
**Auto. inv.:** Yes
**Disc.:** No

---

## ✱ City Holding Co. ♥

**CHCO/NASD**
H: 14.64
L: 4.87
**Rec:** 11.25
**Div.:** 0.32
**Paid on:**
3.6.9.12-15
**Since:** N/A

**Banking**
25 Gatewater Rd.
Cross Lanes. WV 25313

SunTrust Bank, Atlanta    800-568-3476
$50 - $5,000/quarter
Every 90 days beginning 3/15
FEES: Div: $0!; Cash: $0!; Cert: $0; Term: $5,Does not sell through the plan

**Shares to qualify:** 1
**Safekeeping:** Yes
**Accepts foreign:** Yes
**Auto. inv.:** No
**Disc.:** No

---

## ✱ CLARCOR Inc. ♥

**CLC/NYSE**
Manufacturing, filters, packaging

H: 27.00
L: 16.87
**Rec:** 26.90

2323 6th St., Box 7007
Rockford. IL 61125

First Chicago Trust    800-446-2617
$25 - $3,000/month

**Div.:** 0.47
**Paid on:**
1.4.7.10-28
**Since:** 1921

Every 30 days beginning 1/31

FEES: Div $0!; Cash: $0!; Cert: $0!; Term: $0; Sells within 10 bus. days, by mail, at market, for $0

**Shares to qualify:** 1
**Safekeeping:** No
**Accepts foreign:** No
**Auto. inv.:** No
**Disc.:** No

---

## ✱ Clayton Homes, Inc. ♥

**CMH/NYSE**
Mobile home manufacturer

H: 16.55
L: 8.31
**Rec:** 16.00

Box 15169
Knoxville. TN 37901

American Stock Transfer    800-278-4353
$100 - $5,000/quarter

**Div.:** 0.06
**Paid on:**
1.4.7.10-19
**Since:** 1995

Every 15 days beginning 5th & 20th /month

FEES: Div: $0; Cash: $0; Cert: $0; Term: $0; Sells weekly, by mail, at market, for 4¢/sh.

**Shares to qualify:** 1
**Safekeeping:** Yes
**Accepts foreign:** Yes
**Auto. inv.:** No
**Disc.:** No

---

## ✱ CLECO Corp. ♥

**CNL/NYSE**
Utility-electric, gas

H: 28.25
L: 19.62
**Rec:** 21.99

Box 5000
Pineville. LA 71361-5000

First Chicago Trust    201-324-0137
$25 - $5,000/month

**Div.:** 0.88
**Paid on:**
2.5.8.11-15
**Since:** 1935

Every 30 days beginning 1/2

FEES: Div: $0!; Cash: $0!; Cert: $0!; Term: $0; Sells daily, by mail or fax, at market, for $10 + comm.

**Shares to qualify:** 1
**Safekeeping:** Yes
**Accepts foreign:** No
**Auto. inv.:** No
**Disc.:** No

---

## ✱ Cleveland-Cliffs Inc. ♥

**CLF/NYSE**
Metals

H: 27.25
L: 13.68
**Rec:** 16.57

1100 Superior Ave., 18th Fl.
Cleveland. OH 44114-2589

First Chicago Trust    800-446-2617
$20 - $30,000/year

**Div.:** 0.40
**Paid on:**
3.6.9.12-1
**Since:** 1989

Every 30 days beginning 1/2

FEES: Div: $0!; Cash: $0!; Auto. Inv.: $1; Cert: $0!; Term: $0; Sells daily, by mail, fax , or phone, at market, for $5 + 12¢/sh.

**Shares to qualify:** 1
**Safekeeping:** Yes
**Accepts foreign:** No
**Auto. inv.:** Yes
**Disc.:** No

---

## ✱ Clorox ♥

**CLX/NYSE**
Consumer products

H: 48.62
L: 28.37
**Rec:** 36.02

1221 Broadway
Oakland. CA 94612

First Chicago Trust    201-324-1644
$10 - $60,000/year

**Div.:** 0.84
**Paid on:**
2.5.8.11-15
**Since:** 1968

Every 30 days beginning 1/15

FEES: Div: $0; Cash: $0; Auto. Inv.: $1; Cert: $0; Term: $10 + 12¢/sh.; Sells daily, by phone or mail, at market, for $10 + 12¢/sh.

**Shares to qualify:** 1
**Safekeeping:** Yes
**Accepts foreign:** Yes
**Auto. inv.:** Yes
**Disc.:** No

---

## ✱ CMS Energy ♥

**CMS/NYSE**
Utility-electric

H: 32.25
L: 24.15
**Rec:** 24.59

212 W. Michigan Ave.
Jackson. MI 49201-2277

CMS Investor Services Dept.    517-788-1868
$25 - $250,000/year

**Div.:** 1.46
**Paid on:**
2.5.8.11-22
**Since:** 1989

Every 7 days beginning varies

FEES: Div: $0!; Cash: $0!; Auto. Inv.: $0; Cert: $0!; Term: $0; Sells weekly, by phone, mail, fax, or Internet, at market, for 5¢/sh.

**Shares to qualify:** 1 /de ($500)
**Safekeeping:** Yes
**Accepts foreign:** Yes
**Auto. inv.:** Yes
**Disc.:** No

---

## CNB Financial Corp. ♥

**CNBF/NASD**
Community banks

H: 19.75
L: 7.25
**Rec:** 18.71

24 Church St.
Canaioharie. NY 13317

CNB Financial Corp    518-673-3243
$10 - $3,000/quarter

**Div.:** 0.36
**Paid on:**
3.6.9.12-10
**Since:** 1993

Every 90 days beginning 3/10

FEES: Div: $0!; Cash: $0!; Cert: $0; Term: $0,Does not sell through the plan

**Shares to qualify:** 1
**Safekeeping:** No
**Accepts foreign:** Yes
**Auto. inv.:** No
**Disc.:** No

---

## ❋ CNF Transportation Inc. ⊗

**CNF/NYSE** | Transportation

H: 39.87
L: 20.18
**Rec:** 31.50

3240 Hillview Ave.
Palo Alto. CA 94304

**Div.:** 0.40
**Paid on:**
3.6.9.12-15
**Since:**1995

First Chicago Trust    800-756-8200
$25 - $60,000/year
Every 30 days beginning 1/15

**Shares to qualify:** 1
**Safekeeping:** Yes
**Accepts foreign:** Yes
**Auto. inv.:** No
**Disc.:** No

FEES: Div: 5% to $3; Cash: 5% to $3 + 3¢/sh.; Cert: $0!; Term: $15 + 12¢/sh.; Sells daily, by mail or phone, at market, for $15 + 12¢/sh.

---

## Coastal Caribbean Oils & Minerals, Ltd.

**COCBF/OTC** | Oil & gas operations

H: 2.50
L: 0.62
**Rec:** 1.01

Clarendon House, Church St.
Hamilton. HM 11. Bermuda

**Div.:** 0.00
**Paid on:**
DIV. SUSP.
**Since:**--

American Stock Transfer    877-854-0852
$25 - $10,000/investment
Every day days beginning daily

**Shares to qualify:** 1 /de ($250)
**Safekeeping:** Yes
**Accepts foreign:** Yes
**Auto. inv.:** Yes
**Disc.:** No

FEES: Div: n/o; Cash: $2.50 + 10¢/sh.; Auto. Inv.: $2.50 + 10¢/sh.; Cert: $0; Term: $7.50 + 10¢/sh.; Sells daily, by phone, mail, fax, or Internet, at market, for $7.50 + 10¢/sh.

---

## ❋ Coastal Financial Corp. ♥

**CFCP/NASD** | Savings & loan holding company

H: 15.75
L: 5.00
**Rec:** 15.00

2619 Oak St.
Myrtle Beach. SC 29577

**Div.:** 0.15
**Paid on:**
1.4.7.10-14
**Since:**N/A

Registrar & Transfer    800-866-1340x
$25 - $1,000/quarter
Every 90 days beginning 1/15

**Shares to qualify:** 1
**Safekeeping:** Yes
**Accepts foreign:** Yes
**Auto. inv.:** Yes
**Disc.:** Div: 3% Cash: 3%

FEES: Div: $0!; Cash: $0!; Auto. Inv.: $0; Cert: $5; Term: $10; Sells weekly, by mail, at market, for 0

---

## ❋ Coca-Cola Bottling Co. Consolidated

**COKE/NASD** | Soft drink distr.

H: 45.12
L: 32.04
**Rec:** 37.90

Box 31487
Charlotte. NC 28231

**Div.:** 1.00
**Paid on:**
3.6.9.12-9
**Since:**1967

First Union Nat'l Bank    800-829-8432
$10 - $1,000/month
Every 30 days beginning 1/5

**Shares to qualify:** 1
**Safekeeping:** Yes
**Accepts foreign:** No
**Auto. inv.:** Yes
**Disc.:** No

FEES: Div: 4% to $2.50 ; Cash: 4% to $2.50 ; Auto. Inv.: $0; Cert: $0; Term: $0; Sells bimonthly, by mail, at avg. price, for 4% to $2.50

---

## ❋ Coca-Cola Co. (The) ♥

**KO/NYSE** | Beverages

H: 63.37
L: 42.37
**Rec:** 45.67

One Coca-Cola Plz.
Atlanta. GA 30313

**Div.:** 0.72
**Paid on:**
4.7.10-1 &
**Since:**1920

First Chicago Trust    888-265-3747
$10 - $125,000/year
Every 30 days beginning 1st bus. day

**Shares to qualify:** 1
**Safekeeping:** Yes
**Accepts foreign:** Yes
**Auto. inv.:** Yes
**Disc.:** No

FEES: Div: $0!; Cash: $0!; Auto. Inv.: $1; Cert: $0!; Term: $0; Sells daily, by phone, mail, fax, or Internet, at market, for $10 + 12¢/sh.

---

## ❋ Coca-Cola Enterprises Inc. ♥

**CCE/NYSE** | Nonalcoholic bev. bottling co.

H: 23.90
L: 14.01
**Rec:** 15.00

Box 723040
Atlanta. GA 31139-0040

**Div.:** 0.16
**Paid on:**
4.7.10.12-VARIE
**Since:**1986

First Chicago Trust    800-418-4223
$10 - $100,000/year
Every 15 days beginning 1st & 15th

**Shares to qualify:** 1
**Safekeeping:** Yes
**Accepts foreign:** Yes
**Auto. inv.:** Yes
**Disc.:** No

FEES: Div: $0!; Cash: $0!; Auto. Inv.: $1; Cert: $0!; Term: $0; Sells daily, by mail or phone, at market, for $10 + 12¢/sh.

---

## ❋ Codorus Valley Bancorp, Inc. ♥

**CVLY/NASD** | Bank holding company

H: 18.09
L: 10.35
**Rec:** 14.90

105 Leader Heights Rd., Box 2887
York. PA 17405-2887

**Div.:** 0.48
**Paid on:**
2.5.8.11-11
**Since:**N/A

Wells Fargo Bank    800-468-9716
$100 - $3,000/quarter
Every 90 days beginning 2/26

**Shares to qualify:** 1
**Safekeeping:** Yes
**Accepts foreign:** Yes
**Auto. inv.:** Yes
**Disc.:** No

FEES: Div: $0!; Cash: $0!; Auto. Inv.: $0; Cert: $0!; Term: $5 + 8¢/sh.; Sells monthly, by mail, at market, for $5 + 8¢/sh.

---

## Colgate-Palmolive ♥

**CL/NYSE** | **Household products**

H: 65.69
L: 42.50
**Rec:** 53.50

300 Park Ave.
New York. NY 10022-7499

**Div.:** 0.72
**Paid on:**
2.5.8.11-15
**Since:** 1895

First Chicago Trust    800-756-8700
$20 - $60,000/year
Every 30 days beginning 1/15

**Shares to qualify:** 1
**Safekeeping:** Yes
**Accepts foreign:** Yes
**Auto. inv.:** Yes
**Disc.:** No

FEES: Div: $0!; Cash: $0!; Auto. Inv.: $1; Cert: $0!; Term: $0; Sells irregularly, by mail, at market, for $15 + 12¢/sh.

---

## Colonial BancGroup, Inc. (The) ♥

**CNB/NYSE** | **Banking**

H: 14.94
L: 8.18
**Rec:** 14.53

Box 1108
Montgomery. AL 36101

**Div.:** 0.48
**Paid on:**
2.5.8.11-11
**Since:** 1981

SunTrust Bank, Atlanta    800-568-3476
$10 - $120,000/year
Every 30 days beginning varies

**Shares to qualify:** 1
**Safekeeping:** Yes
**Accepts foreign:** Yes
**Auto. inv.:** No
**Disc.:** No

FEES: Div: $0!; Cash: $0!; Cert: $0!; Term: $0; Sells weekly, by mail or fax, at market, for comm.

---

## Colonial Properties Trust ♥

**CLP/NYSE** | **REIT**

H: 30.99
L: 24.00
**Rec:** 30.19

2101 6th Ave. North, Ste. 750
Birmingham. AL 35203

**Div.:** 2.52
**Paid on:**
2.5.8.11-3
**Since:** 1994

BankBoston    800-730-6001
$200 - $25,000/year
Every 30 days beginning 1/7

**Shares to qualify:** 1
**Safekeeping:** Yes
**Accepts foreign:** Yes
**Auto. inv.:** Yes
**Disc.:** Div 5% Cash: 5%

FEES: Div: $0; Cash: $0; Auto. Inv.: $0; Cert: $0; Term: $10 + 5¢/sh.; Sells within 5 bus. days, by mail, at market, for $10 + 5¢/sh.

---

## Colony Bankcorp, Inc. ♥

**CBAN/NASD** | **Bank holding company**

H: 13.00
L: 9.37
**Rec:** 11.65

115 S. Grant St., Box 989
Fitzgerald. GA 31750

**Div.:** 0.24
**Paid on:**
1.4.7.10-16
**Since:** N/A

SunTrust Bank, Atlanta    800-568-3476
$25 - $5,000/quarter
Every 90 days beginning varies

**Shares to qualify:** 1
**Safekeeping:** No
**Accepts foreign:** No
**Auto. inv.:** No
**Disc.:** No

FEES: Div: $0; Cash: $0; Cert: $0; Term: $0; Sells Tuesdays & Fridays, by mail, at market, for 8¢/sh.

---

## Columbia Bancorp ♥

**CBMD/NAS** | **Banking**

H: 16.31
L: 9.50
**Rec:** 15.90

9151 Baltimore Nat'l Pike
Ellicott City. MD 21042

**Div.:** 0.40
**Paid on:**
1.4.7.10-5
**Since:** 1994

Registrar & Transfer    800-368-5948
$250 - $2,500/quarter
Every 90 days beginning 1/5

**Shares to qualify:** 1
**Safekeeping:** No
**Accepts foreign:** Yes
**Auto. inv.:** No
**Disc.:** Div 3% Cash: 0%

FEES: Div: $0!; Cash: $0!; Cert: $10; Term: $10; Sells monthly, by mail, at market, for $10 + comm.

---

## Columbus McKinnon Corp.

**CMCO/NAS** | **Mfr. of capital goods**

H: 15.50
L: 6.75
**Rec:** 9.90

140 John James Audubon Pkwy.
Amherst. NY 14228

**Div.:** 0.28
**Paid on:**
1.4.7.10-6
**Since:** N/A

American Stock Transfer    800-278-4353
$25 - $10,000/week
Every 7 days beginning varies

**Shares to qualify:** 1 /de ($250)
**Safekeeping:** Yes
**Accepts foreign:** Yes
**Auto. inv.:** Yes
**Disc.:** No

FEES: Div: 2% to $1.50 + 10¢/sh.; Cash: $2.50 +10¢/sh.; Auto. Inv.: $1 + 10¢/sh.; Cert: $0; Term: $7.50 + 10¢/sh.; Sells weekly, by mail or phone, at market, for $7.50 + 10¢/sh.

---

## Comerica Inc. ♥

**CMA/NYSE** | **Banking**

H: 65.15
L: 47.18
**Rec:** 62.46

500 Woodward Ave., MC 3391
Detroit. MI 48226

**Div.:** 1.76
**Paid on:**
1.4.7.10-1
**Since:** 1936

Wells Fargo Bank    800-468-9716
$10 - $3,000/quarter
Every 90 days beginning 1/2

**Shares to qualify:** 1
**Safekeeping:** Yes
**Accepts foreign:** No
**Auto. inv.:** No
**Disc.:** No

FEES: Div: $0!; Cash: $0!; Cert: $0!; Term: $10 + 10¢/sh.; Sells daily, by mail, at market, for $10 + 10¢/sh.

---

## ✳ Commerce Bancorp, Inc. ♥

**CBH/NYSE** | Bank holding company

H: 77.90
L: 49.56
**Rec:** 74.11

**Div.:** 1.10
**Paid on:**
1.4.7.10-20
**Since:** 1984

1701 Route 70 East
Cherry Hill. NJ 08034-5400

Mellon Inv. Svcs.       888-470-5884
$100 - $3,000/month
Every 30 days beginning 1/15
FEES: Div: $0!; Cash: $0!; Cert: $0!; Term: $0; Sells weekly, by mail, at market, for $15 + 12¢/sh.

Shares to qualify: 1
Safekeeping: Yes
Accepts foreign: Yes
Auto. inv.: No
Disc.: Div 3% Cash: 3%

---

## ✳ Commonwealth Bank ⊗

**CMSB/NAS** | Banking

H: 22.10
L: 13.25
**Rec:** 21.00

**Div.:** 0.56
**Paid on:**
1.4.7.10-15
**Since:** N/A

2 West Lafayette St.
Morristown. PA 19401

Registrar & Transfer       800-368-5948
$100 - $2,500/quarter
Every 30 days beginning 1/15
FEES: Div: $0; Cash: $5; Cert: $5; Term: $5 to $15; Sells irregularly, by mail, at market, for $15

Shares to qualify: 1
Safekeeping: Yes
Accepts foreign: Yes
Auto. inv.: No
Disc.: No

---

## ✳ Commonwealth Bankshares, Inc. ♥

**CWBS/OTC** | Banking

H: 7.50
L: 4.90
**Rec:** 6.35

**Div.:** 0.14
**Paid on:**
3.6.9.12-14
**Since:** N/A

403 Boush St.
Norfolk. VA 23510

Commonwealth Bank       757-446-6914
$25 - $20,000/quarter
Every 90 days beginning 3/31
FEES: Div: $0!; Cash: $0!; Cert: $0!; Term: $0; Sells within 10 bus. days, by mail, at market, for 0

Shares to qualify: 1
Safekeeping: Yes
Accepts foreign: Yes
Auto. inv.: No
Disc.: Div 5% Cash: 0%

---

## Community Bank System, Inc. ♥

**CBU/NYSE** | Banking

H: 29.65
L: 22.00
**Rec:** 27.05

**Div.:** 1.08
**Paid on:**
1.4.7.10-10
**Since:** 1983

5790 Widewaters Pkwy.
DeWitt. NY 13214

American Stock Transfer       800-278-4353
$25 - $10,000/investment
Every 7 days beginning varies
FEES: Div: $0; Cash: $0; Auto. Inv.: $0; Cert: $0; Term: $7.50 + 10¢/sh.; Sells weekly, by phone, mail, fax, or Internet, at market, for $7.50 + 10¢/sh.

Shares to qualify: 1 /de ($250)
Safekeeping: Yes
Accepts foreign: Yes
Auto. inv.: Yes
Disc.: No

---

## ✳ Community Banks, Inc. ♥

**CTY/ASE** | Bank holding company

H: 29.85
L: 18.21
**Rec:** 26.15

**Div.:** 0.68
**Paid on:**
1.4.7.10-1
**Since:** 1988

150 Market Sq.
Millersburg. PA 17061

Wells Fargo Bank       800-468-9716
$100 - $5,000/quarter
Every 90 days beginning 1/2
FEES: Div: $0!; Cash: $0!; Auto. Inv.: $0; Cert: $0!; Term: $10 + 12¢/sh.; Sells within 15 bus. days, by mail or fax, at market, for $5 + 12¢/sh.

Shares to qualify: 1
Safekeeping: No
Accepts foreign: Yes
Auto. inv.: Yes
Disc.: Div 5% Cash: 5%

---

## ✳ Community First Bankshares ♥

**CFBX/NASD** | Banking

H: 25.50
L: 14.75
**Rec:** 25.00

**Div.:** 0.72
**Paid on:**
3.6.9.12-15
**Since:** N/A

520 Main Ave.
Fargo. ND 58124-0001

Wells Fargo Bank       800-468-9716
$25 - $3,000/quarter
Every 30 days beginning 1/15
FEES: Div: $0!; Cash: $0!; Cert: $0; Term: $0; Sells daily, by mail or fax, at market, for $10 + 10¢/sh.

Shares to qualify: 1
Safekeeping: Yes
Accepts foreign: Yes
Auto. inv.: No
Disc.: No

---

## ✳ Community Savings Bankshares, Inc. ♥

**CMSV/NASD** | Financial

H: 16.35
L: 11.93
**Rec:** 16.20

**Div.:** 0.44
**Paid on:**
N/A
**Since:** 1994

660 U.S. Hwy. One, Box 14547
North Palm Beach. FL 33408-0547

Mellon Inv. Svcs.       800-526-0801
$25 - $5,000/month
Every 30 days beginning 1/2
FEES: Div: $0!; Cash: $0!; Cert: $0; Term: $15 + 6¢/sh.; Sells within 2 bus. days, by mail or fax, at market, for $15 + 6¢/sh.

Shares to qualify: 1
Safekeeping: Yes
Accepts foreign: Yes
Auto. inv.: No
Disc.: No

---

## Compaq Computer ⊗

**CPO/NYSE** | **Manufacturer of personal computers**

H: 35.00
L: 13.20
**Rec:** 15.00
**Div.:** 0.10
**Paid on:**
1.4.7.10-20
**Since:** 1998

Box 692000, MS110312
Houston. TX 77269-2000

State St. Bank    888-218-4373
$50 - $10,000/month
Every 7 days beginning Tuesday

**Shares to qualify:** 1 /de ($250)
**Safekeeping:** Yes
**Accepts foreign:** Yes
**Auto. inv.:** Yes
**Disc.:** No

FEES: Div: $0; Cash: $5 + 4¢/ sh.; Auto. Inv.: $2.50 + 4¢/ sh.; Cert: $0; Term: $0; Sells daily, by mail, at avg. price, for $10 + 7¢/sh.

---

## Compass Bancshares, Inc.

**CBSS/NASD** | **Banking**

H: 28.40
L: 16.43
**Rec:** 28.01
**Div.:** 0.92
**Paid on:**
1.4.7.10-1
**Since:** 1981

15 South 20th St.
Birmingham. AL 35233

Continental Stock Transfer    212-509-4000
$25 - $500/month
Every 30 days beginning 1/2

**Shares to qualify:** 1
**Safekeeping:** Yes
**Accepts foreign:** No
**Auto. inv.:** No
**Disc.:** No

FEES: Div: 5% to 2.50; Cash: 5% to 2.50; Cert: $0; Term: $0; Sells within 10 bus. days , by mail, at market, for 5% to 2.50

---

## Computer Associates Int'l

**CA/NYSE** | **Computer software**

H: 39.03
L: 18.12
**Rec:** 33.83
**Div.:** 0.08
**Paid on:**
1.7-1
**Since:** 1990

One Computer Associates Plaza
Islandia. NY 11749

Mellon Inv. Svcs.    800-244-7155
$25 - $3,000/month
Every 30 days beginning 1/5

**Shares to qualify:** 1
**Safekeeping:** Yes
**Accepts foreign:** Yes
**Auto. inv.:** No
**Disc.:** No

FEES: Div: $1.50 + 6¢ to 10¢/sh.; Cash: $1.50 + 6¢ to10¢/sh.; Cert: $0; Term: $5 + 6¢ to 10¢/sh.; Sells weekly, by mail or phone, at market, for $5 + 3¢ to 18¢/sh.

---

## ConAgra Foods, Inc. ♥

**CAG/NYSE** | **Food**

H: 26.18
L: 17.50
**Rec:** 21.39
**Div.:** 0.90
**Paid on:**
3.6.9.12-1
**Since:** 1976

One ConAgra Dr.
Omaha. NE 68102

Wells Fargo Bank    800-214-0349
$50 - $50,000/year
Every 15 days beginning 1/2

**Shares to qualify:** 1
**Safekeeping:** Yes
**Accepts foreign:** Yes
**Auto. inv.:** Yes
**Disc.:** No

FEES: Div: $0!; Cash: $0!; Auto. Inv.: $0; Cert: $0!; Term: $10 + 15¢/sh.; Sells daily, by mail or fax, at market, for $10 + 15¢/sh.

---

## Conestoga Enterprises, Inc. ♥

**CENI/NASD** | **Communications services**

H: 38.75
L: 13.37
**Rec:** 35.14
**Div.:** 0.84
**Paid on:**
3.6.9.12-15
**Since:** N/A

202 East First St.
Birdsboro. PA 19508

Conestoga Enterprises    610-582-8711
$100 - $2,500/quarter
Every 90 days beginning 3/15

**Shares to qualify:** 1
**Safekeeping:** No
**Accepts foreign:** No
**Auto. inv.:** No
**Disc.:** No

FEES: Div: $0; Cash: $0; Cert: $0; Term: $0,Does not sell through the plan

---

## Connecticut Water Service Inc. ♥

**CTWS/NASD** | **Utility-water**

H: 40.74
L: 28.00
**Rec:** 36.40
**Div.:** 1.20
**Paid on:**
3.6.9.12-15
**Since:** 1956

93 West Main St.
Clinton. CT 06413

State St. Bank    800-426-5523
$25 - $1,000/month
Every 30 days beginning 1/2

**Shares to qualify:** 1 /de
**Safekeeping:** Yes
**Accepts foreign:** Yes
**Auto. inv.:** Yes
**Disc.:** No

FEES: Div: $0; Cash: $0; Auto. Inv.: $0; Cert: $0; Term: $5 ; Sells within 4 bus. days, by phone or mail, at market, for $5 + comm.

---

## Conoco Inc.-B ♥

**COCB/NYSE** | **Oil & gas exploration & development**

H: 33.35
L: 23.18
**Rec:** 29.83
**Div.:** 0.76
**Paid on:**
3.6.9.12-11
**Since:** N/A

Box 2197
Houston. TX 77252-2197

First Chicago Trust    800-317-4445
$50 - $250,000/year
Every 5 days beginning varies

**Shares to qualify:** 1 /de ($250)
**Safekeeping:** Yes
**Accepts foreign:** Yes
**Auto. inv.:** Yes
**Disc.:** No

FEES: Div: $0!; Cash: $0!; Auto. Inv.: $0; Cert: $0; Term: $0; Sells daily, by phone, mail, fax, or Internet, at market, for $10 + 12¢/sh.

---

✱ DRIP enrollment through Temper Enrollment Service (see page 180). **65**

## ✱ Conoco Inc.-A ♥

**COCA/NYSE**
Oil & gas exploration, development, &

| | |
|---|---|
| H: 32.99 | 600 N. Dairy Ashford |
| L: 21.93 | Houston. TX 77079 |
| Rec: 29.70 | First Chicago Trust    800-317-4445 |
| Div.: 0.76 | $50 - $250,000/year |
| Paid on: | Every 5 days beginning varies |
| 3.6.9.12-11 | |
| Since: N/A | FEES: Div $0!; Cash: $0!; Auto. Inv.: $0; Cert: $0; Term: $10 + 12¢/sh.; Sells daily, by phone, mail, fax, or Internet, at market, for $10 + 12¢/sh. |

Shares to qualify: 1
Safekeeping: Yes
Accepts foreign: Yes
Auto. inv.: Yes
Disc.: No

---

## ✱ Consolidated Edison

**ED/NYSE**
Utility-electric, gas

| | |
|---|---|
| H: 41.79 | 4 Irving Pl., Rm. 206-S |
| L: 30.12 | New York. NY 10003 |
| Rec: 41.79 | Bank of New York    800-522-5522 |
| Div.: 2.20 | $100 - $24,000/year |
| Paid on: | Every 7 days beginning varies |
| 3.6.9.12-15 | |
| Since: 1885 | FEES: Div: $0; Cash: $2; Cert: $0; Term: $2 + 10¢/sh.; Sells weekly, by mail, at market, for $2 + 10¢/sh. |

Shares to qualify: 50
Safekeeping: Yes
Accepts foreign: Yes
Auto. inv.: No
Disc.: No

---

## ✱ Consolidated Freightways Corp.

**CFWY/NASD**
Trucking & air freight

| | |
|---|---|
| H: 9.10 | 175 Linfield Dr. |
| L: 3.25 | Menlo Park. CA 94025 |
| Rec: 6.05 | Bank of New York    800-524-4458 |
| Div.: 0.00 | $25 - $50,000/year |
| Paid on: | Every 7 days beginning varies |
| DIV. SUSP. | |
| Since: -- | FEES: Div: $0; Cash: $2 + 5¢/sh.; Auto. Inv.: $2 + 5¢/sh.; Cert: $0; Term: $0; Sells weekly, by mail, at avg. price, for $10 + 5¢/sh. |

Shares to qualify: 1 /de ($100)
Safekeeping: Yes
Accepts foreign: Yes
Auto. inv.: Yes
Disc.: No

---

## ✱ Constellation Energy Group, Inc.

**CEG/NYSE**
Utility-electric

| | |
|---|---|
| H: 52.06 | 39 W. Lexington St. |
| L: 29.00 | Baltimore. MD 21201 |
| Rec: 30.01 | Constellation Energy Group    800-258-0499 |
| Div.: 0.48 | $25 - $100,000/year |
| Paid on: | Every 30 days beginning 1/2 |
| 1.4.7.10-1 | |
| Since: 1910 | FEES: Div: 2.5¢ to 4¢/sh.; Cash: 2.5¢ to 4¢/sh.; Cert: $0; Term: $0; Sells biweekly, by mail, at avg. price, for $5 + 2.5¢ to 4¢/sh. |

Shares to qualify: 1
Safekeeping: Yes
Accepts foreign: Yes
Auto. inv.: No
Disc.: No

---

## ✱ Cooper Industries ♥

**CBE/NYSE**
Mfr. of electrical prods. & tools

| | |
|---|---|
| H: 60.45 | Box 4446 |
| L: 31.61 | Houston. TX 77210-4446 |
| Rec: 57.78 | First Chicago Trust    800-446-2617 |
| Div.: 1.40 | $25 - $24,000/year |
| Paid on: | Every 30 days beginning 1/2 |
| 1.4.7.10-1 | |
| Since: 1947 | FEES: Div: $0; Cash: $0; Cert: $0; Term: $0; Sells daily, by mail, at avg. price, for $10 + 12¢/sh. |

Shares to qualify: 1
Safekeeping: No
Accepts foreign: Yes
Auto. inv.: No
Disc.: No

---

## ✱ Corn Products International, Inc. ⊗

**CPO/NYSE**
Corn refining, products

| | |
|---|---|
| H: 32.00 | 6500 South Archer Ave. |
| L: 19.00 | Bedford Park. IL 60501 |
| Rec: 30.06 | First Chicago Trust    800-446-2617 |
| Div.: 0.40 | $100 - $350,000/year |
| Paid on: | Every 30 days beginning 1/25 |
| 1.4.7.10-25 | |
| Since: 1998 | FEES: Div: 5% to $3 + 3¢/sh.; Cash: $5 + 3¢/sh.; Auto. Inv.: $2 + 3¢/sh.; Cert: $0!; Term: $15 + 10¢/sh.; Sells daily, by mail or phone, at market, for $15 + 10¢/sh. |

Shares to qualify: 1
Safekeeping: Yes
Accepts foreign: Yes
Auto. inv.: Yes
Disc.: No

---

## ✱ Cornerstone Bancorp, Inc. ♥

**CBN/ASE**
Bank holding company

| | |
|---|---|
| H: 17.75 | 550 Summer St. |
| L: 11.87 | Stamford. CT 06901 |
| Rec: 17.25 | American Stock Transfer    800-278-4353 |
| Div.: 0.45 | $50 - $5,000/quarter |
| Paid on: | Every 90 days beginning 1/15 |
| 1.4.7.10-15 | |
| Since: 1995 | FEES: Div: $0; Cash: $0; Cert: $0; Term: 4¢/sh.; Sells weekly, by mail, at market, for 4¢/sh. |

Shares to qualify: 50
Safekeeping: Yes
Accepts foreign: Yes
Auto. inv.: No
Disc.: No

---

✱ DRIP enrollment through Temper Enrollment Service (see page 180).

## Cornerstone Realty Income Trust, Inc. ♥

**TCR/NYSE**
H: 11.60
L: 10.20
**Rec:** 11.03
**Div.:** 1.12
**Paid on:**
1.4.7.10-1
**Since:** 1997

REIT

306 E. Main St.
Richmond. VA 23219

First Union Nat'l Bank    800-829-8432
$50 - $15,000/quarter
Every 90 days beginning 1/2

FEES: Div: $0!; Cash: $0!; Auto. Inv.: $0; Cert: $0!; Term: comm.; Sells weekly, by mail, at avg. price, for comm.

Shares to qualify: 1
Safekeeping: Yes
Accepts foreign: Yes
Auto. inv.: Yes
Disc.: No

---

## Cortland Bancorp ♥

**CLDB/OTC**
H: 22.00
L: 15.62
**Rec:** 19.00
**Div.:** 0.88
**Paid on:**
1-1.7-1
**Since:** N/A

Banking

194 West Main St.
Cortland. OH 44410

Cortland Savings Bank    330-637-8040
$100 - $1,000/year
Every 180 days beginning 6/1

FEES: Div: $0; Cash: $0; Auto. Inv.: $0; Does not sell through the plan

Shares to qualify: 1
Safekeeping: Yes
Accepts foreign: No
Auto. inv.: Yes
Disc.: No

---

## Countrywide Credit Industries, Inc. ♥

**CCR/NYSE**
H: 52.00
L: 31.50
**Rec:** 43.30
**Div.:** 0.40
**Paid on:**
1.4.8.11-1
**Since:** 1979

Mortgage banking & financial svcs.

4500 Park Granada Blvd., MS CH-19
Calabasas. CA 91302

Bank of New York    800-524-4458
$100 - $3,000/month
Every 30 days beginning varies

FEES: Div: $0; Cash: $0; Cert: $0; Term: comm.; Sells daily, by mail, at market, for comm.

Shares to qualify: 1
Safekeeping: Yes
Accepts foreign: Yes
Auto. inv.: No
Disc.: Div 0-5% Cash:
0-5%

---

## CoVest Bancshares, Inc. ♥

**COVB/NASD**
H: 17.90
L: 10.87
**Rec:** 17.32
**Div.:** 0.32
**Paid on:**
3.6.9.12-30
**Since:** 1995

Banking

749 Lee St.
Des Plaines. IL 60016

Computershare Investor Svcs.    312-360-5106
$25 - $5,000/quarter
Every 90 days beginning 3/30

FEES: Div: $0!; Cash: $0!; Cert: $0!; Term: $0; Sells weekly, by mail or fax, at market, for 5% to $3 + 7¢/sh.

Shares to qualify: 1
Safekeeping: Yes
Accepts foreign: Yes
Auto. inv.: No
Disc.: No

---

## CPI Corp. ♥

**CPY/NYSE**
H: 25.00
L: 18.30
**Rec:** 20.50
**Div.:** 0.56
**Paid on:**
2.5.8.11-25
**Since:** 1985

Portrait studio and wall decor

1706 Washington Ave.
St. Louis. MO 63103-1717

Computershare Investor Svcs.    800-441-9673
$10 - $10,000/quarter
Every 90 days beginning 2/25

FEES: Div: $0!; Cash: $0!; Cert: $0!; Term: $5 + 5¢ to 7¢/sh.; Sells weekly, by mail, at market, for $5 + 5¢ to 7¢/sh.

Shares to qualify: 1
Safekeeping: Yes
Accepts foreign: Yes
Auto. inv.: No
Disc.: No

---

## Crane Co. ♥

**CR/NYSE**
H: 32.25
L: 20.87
**Rec:** 30.10
**Div.:** 0.40
**Paid on:**
3.6.9.12-14
**Since:** 1939

Manufacturing

100 First Stamford Pl.
Stamford. CT 06902

First Chicago Trust    800-446-2617
$10 - $5,000/month
Every 30 days beginning 1/14

FEES: Div: $0!; Cash: $0!; Cert: $0!; Term: 12¢/sh.; Sells daily, by mail, fax , or phone, at market, for $10 + 12¢/sh.

Shares to qualify: 1
Safekeeping: Yes
Accepts foreign: No
Auto. inv.: No
Disc.: No

---

## Crescent Banking Company ♥

**CSNT/NASD**
H: 13.45
L: 8.87
**Rec:** 13.00
**Div.:** 0.31
**Paid on:**
2.5.8.11-20
**Since:** N/A

Banking

Box 668
Jasper. GA 30143

Crescent Bank & Trust    706-692-2424
$50 - $2,500/month
Every 30 days beginning 1/2

FEES: Div: $0; Cash: $0; Cert: $0; Term: $10,Does not sell through the plan

Shares to qualify: 1 /de ($500)
Safekeeping: Yes
Accepts foreign: Yes
Auto. inv.: No
Disc.: No

---

## ✳ Crompton Corp. ♥

**CK/NYSE**
**H:** 12.18
**L:** 6.93
**Rec:** 9.26
**Div.:** 0.20
**Paid on:** N/A
**Since:** 1933

**Specialty chemicals**

One American Ln.
Greenwich. CT 06831

Mellon Inv. Svcs.    877-698-6867
$30 - $3,000/quarter
Every 30 days beginning last bus. day

FEES: Div: $0!; Cash: $0!; Cert: $0!; Term: $0; Sells weekly, by mail or phone, at market, for $5 + comm.

**Shares to qualify:** 50
**Safekeeping:** Yes
**Accepts foreign:** No
**Auto. inv.:** No
**Disc.:** No

---

## ✳ Crown American Realty Trust ♥

**CWN/NYSE**
**H:** 8.72
**L:** 5.12
**Rec:** 8.30
**Div.:** 0.84
**Paid on:** 3.6.9.12-17
**Since:** 1993

**REIT**

Pasquerilla Plaza
Johnstown. PA 15901

American Stock Transfer    800-278-4353
$100 - $5,000/quarter
Every 30 days beginning last Tues. of each month

FEES: Div: $0!; Cash: $0!; Auto. Inv.: $0; Cert: $0!; Term: $0; Sells weekly, by mail, at market, for comm.

**Shares to qualify:** 1 /de ($100)
**Safekeeping:** Yes
**Accepts foreign:** Yes
**Auto. inv.:** Yes
**Disc.:** No

---

## ✳ Crown Cork & Seal Co., Inc. ♥

**CCK/NYSE**
**H:** 14.62
**L:** 2.51
**Rec:** 3.80
**Div.:** 0.00
**Paid on:** DIV. SUSP.
**Since:** --

**Packaging**

One Crown Way
Philadelphia. PA 19154-4599

First Chicago Trust    800-317-4445
$25 - $25,000/year
Every 30 days beginning 1/20

FEES: Div: n/o; Cash: $0; Auto. Inv.: $1; Cert: $0; Term: $10 + 12¢/sh.; Sells daily, by phone or mail, at avg. price, for $10 + 12¢/sh.

**Shares to qualify:** 1
**Safekeeping:** Yes
**Accepts foreign:** Yes
**Auto. inv.:** Yes
**Disc.:** No

---

## ✳ Crown Pacific Partners LP ♥

**CRO/NASDA**
**H:** 20.50
**L:** 6.55
**Rec:** 8.10
**Div.:** 2.26
**Paid on:** 1.4.7.10-14
**Since:** N/A

**Manufacturer of wood products**

121 S.W. Morrison St., Ste. 1500
Portland. OR 97204

American Stock Transfer    212-936-5100
$50 - $500/month
Every 30 days beginning varies

FEES: Div: $0!; Cash: $0!; Cert: $0!; Term: $15 + 4¢/sh.; Sells weekly, by mail, at market, for $15 + 4¢/sh.

**Shares to qualify:** 1
**Safekeeping:** Yes
**Accepts foreign:** Yes
**Auto. inv.:** No
**Disc.:** No

---

## ✳ CSX Corp. ♥

**CSX/NYSE**
**H:** 41.30
**L:** 20.06
**Rec:** 39.40
**Div.:** 0.40
**Paid on:** 3.6.9.12-15
**Since:** 1922

**Transportation, railroad**

Box 85629
Richmond. VA 23285-5629

Computershare Investor Svcs.    800-521-5571
$50 - $10,000/month
Every 7 days beginning varies

FEES: Div: $0!; Cash: $0!; Auto. Inv.: $0; Cert: $0!; Term: $0; Sells weekly, by mail or fax, at avg. price, for $10 + 15¢/sh.

**Shares to qualify:** 1 /de ($500)
**Safekeeping:** Yes
**Accepts foreign:** Yes
**Auto. inv.:** Yes
**Disc.:** No

---

## ✳ Cummins Inc. ♥

**CUM/NYSE**
**H:** 45.50
**L:** 28.50
**Rec:** 41.03
**Div.:** 1.20
**Paid on:** 3.6.9.12-15
**Since:** 1948

**Machinery**

Box 3005, MC 60118
Columbus. IN 47202-3005

Wells Fargo Bank    800-468-9716
$10 - $24,000/year
Every 30 days beginning 1/15

FEES: Div: $0!; Cash: $0!; Auto. Inv.: $0; Cert: $0!; Term: $10 + 12¢/sh.; Sells daily, by mail or fax, at market, for $10 + 12¢/sh.

**Shares to qualify:** 1
**Safekeeping:** Yes
**Accepts foreign:** Yes
**Auto. inv.:** No
**Disc.:** No

---

## ✳ Curtiss-Wright Corp. ⊗

**CW/NYSE**
**H:** 53.70
**L:** 42.31
**Rec:** 49.95
**Div.:** 0.52
**Paid on:** 1.4.7.10-31
**Since:** 1974

**Equipment for aerospace and defense**

1200 Wall St. West
Lyndhurst. NJ 07071

Mellon Inv. Svcs.    800-416-3743
$100 - $10,000/month
Every 7 days beginning varies

FEES: Div: 5% to $2.50 + 12¢/sh.; Cash: $5 + 12¢/sh.; Auto. Inv.: $0; Cert: $0; Term: $0; Sells weekly, by mail or phone, at market, for $15 + 12¢/sh.

**Shares to qualify:** 1 /de ($2000)
**Safekeeping:** Yes
**Accepts foreign:** No
**Auto. inv.:** Yes
**Disc.:** No

---

✳ DRIP enrollment through Temper Enrollment Service (see page 180).    **68**

## CVS Corp.

**\***
**CVS/NYSE**
H: 63.75
L: 33.25
**Rec:** 36.05
**Div.:** 0.23
**Paid on:**
2.5.8.11-3
**Since:** N/A

**Retail drugstore chain**
670 White Plains Rd., Ste. 210
Scarsdale. NY 10583

Bank of New York      877-287-7526
$100 - $50,000/inv.
Every 7 days beginning varies

**Shares to qualify:** 1 /de ($100)
**Safekeeping:** Yes
**Accepts foreign:** Yes
**Auto. inv.:** Yes
**Disc.:** No

FEES: Div: $0; Cash: $2.50 + 10¢/sh.; Auto. Inv.: $1 + 10¢/sh.; Cert: $7.50; Term: $10 + 10¢/sh.; Sells weekly, by mail or phone, at market, for $10 + 10¢/sh.

---

## D&E Communications, Inc. ♥

**\***
**DECC/NASD**
H: 28.00
L: 16.50
**Rec:** 24.75
**Div.:** 0.50
**Paid on:**
3.6.9.12-15
**Since:** N/A

**Communications**
124 East Main St.
Ephrata. PA 17522

D&E Communications Inc.      717-738-8304
$100 - $5,000/quarter
Every 90 days beginning 1/15

**Shares to qualify:** 1
**Safekeeping:** No
**Accepts foreign:** Yes
**Auto. inv.:** No
**Disc.:** No

FEES: Div: $0!; Cash: $0!; Cert: $0!; Term: $0,Does not sell through the plan

---

## Dana Corp. ♥

**\***
**DCN/NYSE**
H: 27.68
L: 12.81
**Rec:** 24.60
**Div.:** 1.24
**Paid on:**
3.6.9.12-15
**Since:** 1936

**Mfr. auto parts**
Box 1000
Toledo. OH 43637

Mellon Inv. Svcs.      800-298-6810
$25 - $2,000/month
Every 30 days beginning 1/15

**Shares to qualify:** 1
**Safekeeping:** Yes
**Accepts foreign:** Yes
**Auto. inv.:** No
**Disc.:** No

FEES: Div: $0; Cash: $0; Cert: $0; Term: $0; Sells semiweekly, by mail or phone, at market, for $15

---

## Darden Restaurants ⊗

**\***
**DRI/NYSE**
H: 32.50
L: 16.50
**Rec:** 27.80
**Div.:** 0.08
**Paid on:**
5.11-1
**Since:** 1997

**Restaurants**
Box 593330
Orlando. FL 32859-3330

First Union Nat'l Bank      800-829-8432
$50 - $25,000/quarter
Every 7 days beginning varies

**Shares to qualify:** 50 /de ($1000)
**Safekeeping:** Yes
**Accepts foreign:** No
**Auto. inv.:** No
**Disc.:** No

FEES: Div: 5% to $5 + 10¢/sh.; Cash: $5 + 10¢/sh.; Cert: $0; Term: $0; Sells weekly, by mail, at market, for $15 + 10¢/sh.

---

## Data Research Associates, Inc. ♥

**\***
**DRAI/NASD**
H: 10.97
L: 4.62
**Rec:** 10.89
**Div.:** 0.12
**Paid on:**
1-28
**Since:** N/A

**Software & hardware svcs.**
1276 North Warson Rd., Box 8495
St. Louis. MO 63132-1806

Computershare Investor Svcs.      312-360-5291
$25 - $25,000/year
Every 30 days beginning 1/15

**Shares to qualify:** 1
**Safekeeping:** Yes
**Accepts foreign:** Yes
**Auto. inv.:** No
**Disc.:** Div: 5% Cash: 0%

FEES: Div: $0!; Cash: $0!; Cert: $0!; Term: $10 + comm.; Sells weekly, by mail, at market, for $10 + comm.

---

## DCB Financial Corp. ♥

**\***
**DCBF/OTC**
H: 14.10
L: 9.75
**Rec:** 14.00
**Div.:** 0.32
**Paid on:**
2.5.8.11-15
**Since:** N/A

**Bank holding company**
41 N. Sandusky St.
Delaware. OH 43015

Delaware County Bank      740-363-1133
$100 - $2,000/quarter
Every 90 days beginning 2/15

**Shares to qualify:** 1
**Safekeeping:** Yes
**Accepts foreign:** Yes
**Auto. inv.:** No
**Disc.:** No

FEES: Div: $0; Cash: $0; Cert: $0; Term: comm.; Sells within 10 bus. days, by mail, at market, for comm.

---

## DCB Financial Corp ♥

**\***
**DCBF/OTC**
H: 14.10
L: 9.75
**Rec:** 14.10
**Div.:** 0.32
**Paid on:**
2.5.8.11-16
**Since:** N/A

**Bank holding co.**
41 N. Sandusky St.
Delaware. OH 43015

Delaware County Bank & Trust      740-363-1133
$100 - $2,000/quarter
Every 90 days beginning 2/16

**Shares to qualify:** 1
**Safekeeping:** Yes
**Accepts foreign:** Yes
**Auto. inv.:** No
**Disc.:** No

FEES: Div: $0!; Cash: $0!; Cert: $0!; Term: $0; Sells within 10 bus. days, by mail, at market, for comm.

---

## Dean Foods Co. ♥

| | |
|---|---|
| **DF/NYSE** | **Food** |
| H: 42.90 | 3600 N. River Rd. |
| L: 26.00 | Franklin Park. IL 60131 |
| **Rec:** 41.40 | Mellon Inv. Svcs.    877-785-9660 |
| **Div.:** 0.90 | $25 - $3,000/quarter |
| **Paid on:** | Every 90 days beginning 3/15 |
| 3.6.9.12-15 | FEES: Div: $0!; Cash: $0!; Cert: $0!; Term: 7¢/sh.,Does not sell through the plan |
| **Since:** 1941 | |

**Shares to qualify:** 25
**Safekeeping:** Yes
**Accepts foreign:** No
**Auto. inv.:** No
**Disc.:** No

---

## ✳ Deere & Company ⊗

| | |
|---|---|
| **DE/NYSE** | **Machinery** |
| H: 47.12 | One John Deere Pl. |
| L: 30.68 | Moline. IL 61265-8098 |
| **Rec:** 42.51 | Bank of New York   800-268-7369 |
| **Div.:** 0.88 | $100 - $10,000/month |
| **Paid on:** | Every 7 days beginning varies |
| 2.5.8.11-1 | FEES: Div: 5% to $3 + 5¢/sh.; Cash: $3 + 5¢/sh.; Auto. Inv.: $1; Cert: $0!; Term: $0; |
| **Since:** 1940 | Sells daily, by mail, at market, for $10 + 5¢/sh |

**Shares to qualify:** 1 /de ($500)
**Safekeeping:** Yes
**Accepts foreign:** Yes
**Auto. inv.:** Yes
**Disc.:** No

---

## ✳ Delphi Automotive Systems Corp. ⊗

| | |
|---|---|
| **DPH/NYSE** | **Manufacturer of automotive parts** |
| H: 17.50 | 5725 Delphi Dr., M/C 483-400-521 |
| L: 10.50 | Troy. MI 48098-2815 |
| **Rec:** 15.99 | Bank of New York   800-818-6599 |
| **Div.:** 0.28 | $50 - $350,000/year |
| **Paid on:** | Every 7 days beginning Wed. |
| 1.4.7.10-20 | FEES: Div: 5% to $3 + 4¢/sh.; Cash: $5 + 4¢/sh.; Auto. Inv.: 4¢/sh.; Cert: $0; Term: $15 |
| **Since:** 1999 | + 7¢/sh.; Sells within 2 bus. days, by mail or phone, at avg. price, for $15 + 7¢/sh. |

**Shares to qualify:** 1 /de ($500)
**Safekeeping:** Yes
**Accepts foreign:** Yes
**Auto. inv.:** Yes
**Disc.:** No

---

## ✳ Delta Air Lines, Inc. ⊗

| | |
|---|---|
| **DAL/NYSE** | **Airline services** |
| H: 53.25 | Box 20706, Dept. 829 |
| L: 37.51 | Atlanta. GA 30320-6001 |
| **Rec:** 43.00 | First Chicago Trust   201-324-1225 |
| **Div.:** 0.10 | $50 - $100,000/year |
| **Paid on:** | Every 5 days beginning varies |
| 3.6.9.12-1 | FEES: Div: $0!; Cash: $5 + 3¢/sh.; Auto. Inv.: $2 + 3¢/sh.; Cert: $0; Term: $0; Sells daily, |
| **Since:** 1938 | by phone, mail, fax, or Internet, at market, for $15 + 12¢/sh. |

**Shares to qualify:** 1 /de ($250)
**Safekeeping:** Yes
**Accepts foreign:** Yes
**Auto. inv.:** Yes
**Disc.:** No

---

## ✳ Delta Natural Gas Co., Inc. ♥

| | |
|---|---|
| **DGAS/NASD** | **Utility-gas** |
| H: 20.75 | 3617 Lexington Rd. |
| L: 15.87 | Winchester. KY 40391 |
| **Rec:** 19.36 | Fifth Third Bancorp   800-837-2755 |
| **Div.:** 1.14 | $25 - $50,000/year |
| **Paid on:** | Every 30 days beginning 1/15 |
| 3.6.9.12-15 | FEES: Div: $0; Cash: $0; Cert: $0; Term: $0,Does not sell through the plan |
| **Since:** 1964 | |

**Shares to qualify:** 1
**Safekeeping:** Yes
**Accepts foreign:** Yes
**Auto. inv.:** No
**Disc.:** No

---

## ✳ Developers Diversified Realty ♥

| | |
|---|---|
| **DDR/NYSE** | **REIT** |
| H: 18.60 | 3300 Enterprise Pkwy. |
| L: 11.62 | Beachwood. OH 44122 |
| **Rec:** 18.50 | National City Bank   800-622-6757 |
| **Div.:** 1.48 | $100 - $5,000/quarter |
| **Paid on:** | Every 90 days beginning 3/31 |
| 3.6.9.12-31 | FEES: Div: $0!; Cash: $0!; Cert: $0!; Term: $0!; Sells weekly, by mail, at market, for comm. |
| **Since:** 1993 | |

**Shares to qualify:** 1
**Safekeeping:** Yes
**Accepts foreign:** No
**Auto. inv.:** No
**Disc.:** No

---

## ✳ Diebold, Inc.

| | |
|---|---|
| **DBD/NYSE** | **Self-service prods., security equip.** |
| H: 36.37 | 5995 Mayfair Rd., Box 3077 |
| L: 22.93 | North Canton. OH 44720-8077 |
| **Rec:** 34.80 | Bank of New York   800-432-0140 |
| **Div.:** 0.64 | $50 - $10,000/month |
| **Paid on:** | Every 7 days beginning varies |
| 3.6.9.12-11 | FEES: Div: $0!; Cash: $1 + 10¢/sh.; Auto. Inv.: $1 + 10¢/sh.; Cert: $0!; Term: $10 + |
| **Since:** 1954 | 10¢/sh.; Sells weekly, by mail or phone, at market, for $10 + 10¢/sh. |

**Shares to qualify:** 1 /de ($500)
**Safekeeping:** Yes
**Accepts foreign:** Yes
**Auto. inv.:** Yes
**Disc.:** No

---

## Dime Bancorp, Inc.

**Bank holding co.**

DME/NYSE
H: 42.58
L: 17.06
**Rec:** 41.70
**Div.:** 0.48
**Paid on:**
3.6.9.12-6
**Since:**1997

589 Fifth Ave.
New York. NY 10017-1977

BankBoston     800-730-4001
$50 - $15,000/quarter
Every 30 days beginning 1/20

**Shares to qualify:** 1
**Safekeeping:** No
**Accepts foreign:** Yes
**Auto. inv.:** No
**Disc.:** No

FEES: Div: $0; Cash: 5% to $2.50 + 5¢/sh.; Cert: $0; Term: $10 + 15¢/sh.; Sells daily, by mail, at market, for $10 + 15¢/sh.

---

* ## Dollar General Corp.

**Discount retailer**

DG/NYSE
H: 24.05
L: 13.43
**Rec:** 17.37
**Div.:** 0.13
**Paid on:**
2.5.8.11-24
**Since:**1975

104 Woodmont Blvd., Ste. 500
Nashville. TN 37205

Registrar & Transfer     800-368-5948
$0 - $7,500/month
Every 30 days beginning 1/24

**Shares to qualify:** 1 /de ($50)
**Safekeeping:** Yes
**Accepts foreign:** Yes
**Auto. inv.:** Yes
**Disc.:** No

FEES: Div: $0; Cash: $1 + 4¢/sh.; Auto. Inv.: 75¢ + 4¢/sh.; Cert: $0; Term: $5 ; Sells weekly, by mail or fax, at avg. price, for $10 + 4¢/sh.

---

* ## Dominion Resources ♥

**Utility-electric**

D/NYSE
H: 69.99
L: 49.06
**Rec:** 61.50
**Div.:** 2.58
**Paid on:**
3.6.9.12-20
**Since:**1925

Box 26532
Richmond. VA 23261-6532

Dominion Resources     800-552-4034
$40 - $100,000/quarter
Every 15 days beginning 1/5

**Shares to qualify:** 5 /de ($250)
**Safekeeping:** Yes
**Accepts foreign:** Yes
**Auto. inv.:** Yes
**Disc.:** No

FEES: Div: $0; Cash: $0; Auto. Inv.: $0; Cert: $0; Term: 13¢/sh.; Sells weekly, by mail or fax, at market, for 13¢/sh.

---

* ## Donaldson Co., Inc. ♥

**Diesel engine & filtration products**

DCI/NYSE
H: 33.05
L: 19.75
**Rec:** 30.00
**Div.:** 0.30
**Paid on:**
3.6.9.12-13
**Since:**1956

Box 1299, MS101
Minneapolis. MN 55440

Wells Fargo Bank     800-468-9716
$10 - $1,000/month
Every 30 days beginning 1/14

**Shares to qualify:** 1
**Safekeeping:** Yes
**Accepts foreign:** Yes
**Auto. inv.:** No
**Disc.:** No

FEES: Div: $0; Cash: $0; Cert: $0; Term: $10 + 10¢/sh.; Sells daily, by mail, at market, for $10 + 10¢/sh.

---

* ## Donegal Group Inc.-A ♥

**Insurance holding co.**

DGICA/NAS
H: 14.50
L: 10.15
**Rec:** 13.45
**Div.:** 0.40
**Paid on:**
2.5.8.11-30
**Since:**N/A

1195 River Rd., Box 302
Marietta. PA 17547-0302

First Chicago Trust     800-317-4445
$25 - $12,000/year
Every 30 days beginning 1/15

**Shares to qualify:** 1
**Safekeeping:** Yes
**Accepts foreign:** Yes
**Auto. inv.:** Yes
**Disc.:** No

FEES: Div: $0!; Cash: $0!; Auto. Inv.: $2; Cert: $0!; Term: $15 + 12¢/sh.; Sells daily, by phone, mail, fax, or Internet, at market, for $15 + 12¢/sh.

---

* ## Donnelley (RR) & Sons Co. ♥

**Printing**

DNY/NYSE
H: 31.90
L: 21.06
**Rec:** 29.58
**Div.:** 0.96
**Paid on:**
3.6.9.12-1
**Since:**1911

77 West Wacker Dr.
Chicago. IL 60601-1696

First Chicago Trust     800-446-2617
$10 - $60,000/year
Every 30 days beginning 1/2

**Shares to qualify:** 1
**Safekeeping:** Yes
**Accepts foreign:** Yes
**Auto. inv.:** No
**Disc.:** No

FEES: Div: $0!; Cash: $0!; Cert: $0!; Term: 12¢/sh.; Sells daily, by phone or mail, at market, for $10 + 12¢/sh.

---

* ## Dow Chemical ♥

**Chemicals**

DOW/NYSE
H: 39.67
L: 23.00
**Rec:** 35.35
**Div.:** 1.16
**Paid on:**
1.4.7.10-30
**Since:**1912

2030 Dow Ctr.
Midland. MI 48674

Boston Eq.     800-369-5606
$25 - $25,000/quarter
Every 15 days beginning 1/15

**Shares to qualify:** 1
**Safekeeping:** Yes
**Accepts foreign:** Yes
**Auto. inv.:** No
**Disc.:** No

FEES: Div: $0!; Cash: $0!; Cert: $0; Term: $10 + comm.; Sells within 5 bus. days, by mail or phone, at market, for $10 + comm.

---

## Dow Jones & Co. ♥

**DJ/NYSE**
H: 69.62
L: 48.10
**Rec:** 57.48
**Div.:** 1.00
**Paid on:**
3.6.9.12-1
**Since:** 1906

**Publishing**
200 Liberty St.
New York. NY 10281
Mellon Inv. Svcs.     800-851-4228
$100 - $10,000/month
Every 30 days beginning 1/2
FEES: Div $0!; Cash: $0!; Auto. Inv.: $0!; Cert: $0!; Term: $0; Sells weekly, by mail or phone, at market, for $15 + 12¢/sh.

**Shares to qualify:** 10 /de ($1000)
**Safekeeping:** Yes
**Accepts foreign:** Yes
**Auto. inv.:** Yes
**Disc.:** No

---

## DPL Inc. ♥

**DPL/NYSE**
H: 33.81
L: 22.85
**Rec:** 25.64
**Div.:** 0.94
**Paid on:**
3.6.9.12-1
**Since:** 1919

**Utility-electric**
Box 8825
Dayton. OH 45401
Boston Eq.     800-736-3001
$25 - $1,000/quarter
Every 90 days beginning 3/1
FEES: Div: $0; Cash: $0; Cert: $0; Term: $0; Sells daily, by phone, mail, fax, or Internet, at avg. price, for 15¢/sh.

**Shares to qualify:** 1
**Safekeeping:** No
**Accepts foreign:** Yes
**Auto. inv.:** No
**Disc.:** No

---

## DQE

**DQE/NYSE**
H: 43.01
L: 19.28
**Rec:** 22.57
**Div.:** 1.68
**Paid on:**
1.4.7.10-1
**Since:** 1952

**Utility-electric**
400 Fairway Dr., Ste. 100
Moon Township. PA 15108
DQE Shareholder Services     800-247-0400
$10 - $5,000/month
Every 30 days beginning 1/2
FEES: Div: 5¢/sh.; Cash: 5¢/sh.; Auto. Inv.: $0; Cert: $0; Term: $0; Sells weekly, by mail or fax, at market, for 7¢/sh.

**Shares to qualify:** 1 /de ($100)
**Safekeeping:** Yes
**Accepts foreign:** Yes
**Auto. inv.:** Yes
**Disc.:** No

---

## Dresdner RCM Global Strategic Income Fund

**DSF/NYSE**
H: 7.47
L: 6.37
**Rec:** 6.83
**Div.:** 0.72
**Paid on:**
MONTHLY
**Since:** N/A

**Closed-end fund**
Four Embarcadero Ctr., Ste. 3000
San Francisco. CA 94111-4189
Boston Eq.     800-730-6001
$100 - $3,000/quarter
Every 90 days beginning 2/15
FEES: Div: comm.; Cash: comm.; Cert: $0; Term: $0; Sells daily, by mail, at avg. price, for comm.

**Shares to qualify:** 1
**Safekeeping:** No
**Accepts foreign:** Yes
**Disc.:** Div 5% Cash: 0%

---

## DTE Energy Co.

**DTE/NYSE**
H: 47.13
L: 32.62
**Rec:** 42.43
**Div.:** 2.06
**Paid on:**
1.4.7.10-15
**Since:** 1909

**Utility-electric**
2000 2nd Ave.
Detroit. MI 48226-1279
DTE Energy Company     800-551-5009
$25 - $100,000/year
Every 30 days beginning 1/10
FEES: Div: $1 + 4¢/sh.; Cash: $1 + 4¢/sh.; Cert: $0; Term: $0; Sells weekly, by mail, at market, for 12.5¢/sh.

**Shares to qualify:** 1 /de ($100)
**Safekeeping:** Yes
**Accepts foreign:** No
**Auto. inv.:** No
**Disc.:** No

---

## Duff & Phelps Utilities Income Inc.

**DNP/NYSE**
H: 11.20
L: 9.50
**Rec:** 10.98
**Div.:** 0.78
**Paid on:**
MONTHLY-10
**Since:** 1987

**Closed-end fund**
55 East Monroe St.
Chicago. IL 60603-5802
Bank of New York     877-381-2537
$100 - $5,000/month
Every 30 days beginning 1/10
FEES: Div: $0; Cash: $2.50 + 7¢/sh.; Cert: $0; Term: $5; Sells weekly, by mail, at market, for $2.50 + 7¢/sh.

**Shares to qualify:** 1
**Safekeeping:** Yes
**Accepts foreign:** No
**Auto. inv.:** No
**Disc.:** Div 0-5% Cash: 0%

---

## Duke Energy ♥

**DUK/NYSE**
H: 47.74
L: 32.40
**Rec:** 37.97
**Div.:** 1.10
**Paid on:**
3.6.9.12-16
**Since:** 1926

**Energy services**
Box 1005
Charlotte. NC 28201-1005
Duke Energy Corp.     800-488-3853
$50 - $100,000/month
Every 15 days beginning varies
FEES: Div: $0!; Cash: $0!; Auto. Inv.: $0; Cert: $0!; Term: $0; Sells weekly, by mail or fax, at market, for 5¢/sh.

**Shares to qualify:** 1 /de ($250)
**Safekeeping:** Yes
**Accepts foreign:** Yes
**Auto. inv.:** Yes
**Disc.:** No

---

✱ DRIP enrollment through Temper Enrollment Service (see page 180).     72

## Duke Realty Corporation ♥

| | |
|---|---|
| DRE/NYSE | REIT |
| H: 25.86 | 600 E. 96th St., Ste. 100 |
| L: 21.85 | Indianapolis. IN 46240 |
| Rec: 25.45 | American Stock Transfer  800-278-4353 |
| Div.: 1.80 | $50 - $20,000/month |
| Paid on: | Every 15 days beginning 1/15 |
| 2.5.8.11-30 | FEES: Div: $0!; Cash: $0!; Auto. Inv.: $0; Cert: $0!; Term: $0; Sells within 5 bus. days, by |
| Since:1986 | mail, at avg. price, for 5¢ to 10¢/sh. |

**Shares to qualify:** 1 /de ($250)
**Safekeeping:** Yes
**Accepts foreign:** Yes
**Auto. inv.:** Yes
**Disc.:** No

---

## DuPont (E.I.) ⊗

| | |
|---|---|
| DD/NYSE | Chemicals, oil, gas |
| H: 50.68 | 1007 Market St., D-11018 |
| L: 38.18 | Wilminaton. DE 19898 |
| Rec: 42.07 | First Chicago Trust  888-983-8766 |
| Div.: 1.40 | $20 - $5,000/month |
| Paid on: | Every 30 days beginning varies |
| 3.6.9.12.12-14 | FEES: Div: 5% to $3 + 10¢/sh.; Cash: 5% to $3 + 3¢/sh.; Cert: $0; Term: $0; Sells daily, |
| Since:1904 | by mail or phone, at market, for $10 + 12¢/sh. |

**Shares to qualify:** 1
**Safekeeping:** Yes
**Accepts foreign:** Yes
**Auto. inv.:** No
**Disc.:** No

---

## Dynegy Inc.-A ♥

| | |
|---|---|
| DYN/NYSE | Energy products |
| H: 59.87 | 1000 Louisiana St., Ste. 5800 |
| L: 36.59 | Houston. TX 77002-5050 |
| Rec: 44.59 | Mellon Inv. Svcs.  888-921-5563 |
| Div.: 0.30 | $100 - $10,000/month |
| Paid on: | Every 15 days beginning varies |
| 3.6.9.12-15 | FEES: Div: $0!; Cash: $0!; Auto. Inv.: $0; Cert: $0!; Term: $0; Sells within 5 bus. days, by |
| Since:1994 | mail or phone, at market, for 8¢/sh. |

**Shares to qualify:** 1 /de ($250)
**Safekeeping:** Yes
**Accepts foreign:** Yes
**Auto. inv.:** Yes
**Disc.:** No

---

## E.W. Scripps Co.-A ♥

| | |
|---|---|
| SSP/NYSE | Printing & publishing |
| H: 71.70 | Box 5380 |
| L: 47.43 | Cincinnati. OH 45201 |
| Rec: 71.27 | Fifth Third Bancorp  800-837-2755 |
| Div.: 0.60 | $100 - $2,500/quarter |
| Paid on: | Every 90 days beginning varies |
| 3.6.9.12-VARIES | FEES: Div: $0!; Cash: $0!; Auto. Inv.: $0; Cert: $0!; Term: $15 + comm.; Sells weekly, by |
| Since:1922 | mail, at avg. price, for $15 + comm. |

**Shares to qualify:** 1
**Safekeeping:** Yes
**Accepts foreign:** Yes
**Auto. inv.:** Yes
**Disc.:** No

---

## Eagle Bancshares, Inc. ♥

| | |
|---|---|
| EBSI/NASD | Savings and loan |
| H: 16.01 | 4305 Lynburn Dr. |
| L: 9.18 | Tucker. GA 30884-4441 |
| Rec: 14.20 | SunTrust Bank, Atlanta  800-568-3476 |
| Div.: 0.00 | $25 - $5,000/quarter |
| Paid on: | Every 90 days beginning 1/21 |
| DIV. SUSP. | FEES: Div: n/o; Cash: $0!; Cert: $0!; Term: $10; Sells weekly, by mail, at market, for comm. |
| Since:-- | |

**Shares to qualify:** 1
**Safekeeping:** Yes
**Accepts foreign:** Yes
**Auto. inv.:** No
**Disc.:** No

---

## Eastern Co. (The)

| | |
|---|---|
| EML/ASE | Mfr. locks & security hardware |
| H: 17.05 | 112 Bridge St., Box 460 |
| L: 11.25 | Nauaatuck. CT 06770-0460 |
| Rec: 14.50 | American Stock Transfer  800-937-5449 |
| Div.: 0.44 | $25 - $10,000/investment |
| Paid on: | Every day days beginning daily |
| 3.6.9.12-15 | FEES: Div: $0!; Cash: 10¢/sh.; Auto. Inv.: $0; Cert: $0!; Term: $15 + 10¢/sh.; Sells daily, |
| Since:1940 | by mail or phone, at market, for $15 + 10¢/sh. |

**Shares to qualify:** 1 /de ($250)
**Safekeeping:** Yes
**Accepts foreign:** Yes
**Auto. inv.:** Yes
**Disc.:** No

---

## Eastman Chemical Co.

| | |
|---|---|
| EMN/NYSE | Chemical manufacturer |
| H: 55.65 | 100 North Eastman Rd.. Box 511 |
| L: 35.06 | Kinasport. TN 37662-5075 |
| Rec: 42.62 | American Stock Transfer  800-937-5449 |
| Div.: 1.76 | $0 - $60,000/year |
| Paid on: | Every 7 days beginning Wed. |
| 1.4.7.10-3 | FEES: Div: 2% to $2.50 + 10¢/sh.; Cash: $2.50 + 10¢/sh.; Auto. Inv.: $2.50 + 10¢/sh.; |
| Since:1994 | Cert: $0; Term: $15 + 12¢/sh.; Sells daily, by phone, mail, fax, or Internet, at market, for $15 + 12¢/sh. |

**Shares to qualify:** 1
**Safekeeping:** Yes
**Accepts foreign:** No
**Auto. inv.:** Yes
**Disc.:** No

---

## ✳ Eastman Kodak ⊗

**EK/NYSE**
H: 65.68
L: 35.31
**Rec:** 43.65

**Div.:** 1.76
**Paid on:**
1.4.7.10-1
**Since:** 1902

**Photography, imaging**
343 State St.
Rochester. NY 14650

BankBoston    800-253-6057
$50 - $120,000/year
Every Tues. & Fri. days beginning Tuesday

FEES: Div: 5% to $3 ; Cash: $5 + 5¢/sh.; Auto. Inv.: $2 + 5¢/sh.; Cert: $0; Term: $15 + 12¢/sh.; Sells daily, by mail or phone, at avg. price, for $15 + 12¢/sh.

**Shares to qualify:** 1 /de ($150)
**Safekeeping:** Yes
**Accepts foreign:** Yes
**Auto. inv.:** Yes
**Disc.:** No

---

## ✳ Eaton Corp. ♥

**ETN/NYSE**
H: 81.43
L: 57.50
**Rec:** 76.47

**Div.:** 1.76
**Paid on:**
2.5.8.11-25
**Since:** 1923

**Diversified manufacturing**
Eaton Ctr.
Cleveland. OH 44114-2584

First Chicago Trust    800-317-4445
$10 - $60,000/year
Every 30 days beginning 1/25

FEES: Div: $0!; Cash: $0!; Auto. Inv.: $1; Cert: $0!; Term: $5; Sells daily, by mail or phone, at market, for $10 + comm.

**Shares to qualify:** 1
**Safekeeping:** Yes
**Accepts foreign:** Yes
**Auto. inv.:** Yes
**Disc.:** No

---

## ✳ Ecolab Inc. ♥

**ECL/NYSE**
H: 45.68
L: 33.25
**Rec:** 39.71

**Div.:** 0.52
**Paid on:**
1.4.7.10-15
**Since:** 1936

**Cleaning & sanitizing products**
370 Wabasha St. N.
St. Paul. MN 55102-1390

First Chicago Trust    201-324-0313
$10 - $60,000/year
Every 30 days beginning 1/15

FEES: Div: $0; Cash: $0; Cert: $0; Term: comm.; Sells irregularly, by mail, at market, for $10 + comm.

**Shares to qualify:** 1
**Safekeeping:** Yes
**Accepts foreign:** Yes
**Auto. inv.:** No
**Disc.:** No

---

## ✳ Edison International ♥

**EIX/NYSE**
H: 26.62
L: 6.25
**Rec:** 14.01

**Div.:** 0.00
**Paid on:**
DIV. SUSP.
**Since:** --

**Utility-electric**
Box 400
Rosemead. CA 91770

Wells Fargo Bank    800-347-8625
$25 - $10,000/month
Every 30 days beginning varies

FEES: Div: n/o; Cash: $0!; Auto. Inv.: $0; Cert: $0!; Term: $0; Sells weekly, by mail or fax, at market, for 3.5¢/sh.

**Shares to qualify:** 1
**Safekeeping:** Yes
**Accepts foreign:** Yes
**Auto. inv.:** Yes
**Disc.:** No

---

## ✳ El Paso Corporation ♥

**EPG/NYSE**
H: 75.30
L: 44.50
**Rec:** 46.37

**Div.:** 0.85
**Paid on:**
1.4.7.10-1
**Since:** 1992

**Natural gas**
1001 Louisiana St., Box 2511
Houston. TX 77252-2511

BankBoston    800-736-3001
$50 - $10,000/month
Every 15 days beginning 1st & 15th

FEES: Div: $0!; Cash: $0!; Auto. Inv.: $0; Cert: $0!; Term: $0; Sells within 10 days, by mail, phone or Internet, at market, for $1 to $10 + comm.

**Shares to qualify:** 1
**Safekeeping:** Yes
**Accepts foreign:** Yes
**Auto. inv.:** Yes
**Disc.:** No

---

## Electronic Data Systems

**EDS/NYSE**
H: 67.40
L: 39.43
**Rec:** 61.80

**Div.:** 0.60
**Paid on:**
3.6.9.12-10
**Since:** 1984

**Computer system services**
5400 Legacy Dr., H1-2D-05
Plano. TX 75024-3199

American Stock Transfer    800-250-5016
$25 - $10,000/month
Every day days beginning daily

FEES: Div: 2% to $1.50 + 10¢/sh.; Cash: $2.50 + 10¢/sh.; Auto. Inv.: $2.50 + 10¢/sh.; Cert: $0; Term: $7.50 + 10¢/sh.; Sells daily, by phone, mail or internet, at avg. price, for $7.50 + 10¢/sh.

**Shares to qualify:** 1 /de ($250)
**Safekeeping:** Yes
**Accepts foreign:** Yes
**Auto. inv.:** Yes
**Disc.:** No

---

## Ellsworth Convertible Growth & Income Fund ♥

**ECF/ASE**
H: 10.43
L: 7.50
**Rec:** 8.94

**Div.:** 0.40
**Paid on:**
2.5.8.11-VARIES
**Since:** 1986

**Convertible bond fund**
65 Madison Ave., 5th Fl.
Morristown, NJ 07960

Bank of New York    800-432-8224
$100 - $1,000/month
Every 30 days beginning 1/15

FEES: Div: $0!; Cash: $0!; Cert: $0; Term: $0!; Sells irregularly, by mail, at market, for comm.

**Shares to qualify:** 1
**Safekeeping:** No
**Accepts foreign:** Yes
**Auto. inv.:** No
**Disc.:** No

---

## * EMC Insurance Group ♥

**EMCI/NASD**

H: 15.85
L: 8.50
**Rec:** 13.35

**Div.:** 0.60
**Paid on:**
3.6.9.12-26
**Since:** 1982

**Insurance holding co.**

717 Mulberry St.
Des Moines. IA 50309

UMB Bank, N.A.     800-884-4225
$50 - $5,000/month
Every 90 days beginning 3/23

FEES: Div $0!; Cash: $0!; Cert: $0!; Term: $0; Sells daily, by mail, at market, for $5 + comm.

**Shares to qualify:** 1
**Safekeeping:** Yes
**Accepts foreign:** Yes
**Auto. inv.:** No
**Disc.:** No

---

## Emcee Broadcast Products, Inc.

**ECIN/NASD**

H: 4.37
L: 0.44
**Rec:** 1.05

**Div.:** 0.00
**Paid on:**
DIV. SUSP.
**Since:** --

**Communications equipment**

Box 68
White Haven. PA 18661-0068

American Stock Transfer     800-937-5449
$50 - $10,000/investment
Every 7 days beginning 1/2

FEES: Div: n/o; Cash: $2.50 + 10¢/sh.; Auto. Inv.: $2.50 + 10¢/sh.; Cert: $0; Term: $0;
Sells weekly, by mail or fax, at market, for $7.50 + 10¢/sh.

**Shares to qualify:** 1 /de ($100)
**Safekeeping:** Yes
**Accepts foreign:** Yes
**Auto. inv.:** Yes
**Disc.:** No

---

## * Emerging Markets Floating Rate Fund Inc. (The)

**EFL/NYSE**

H: 13.50
L: 11.12
**Rec:** 12.45

**Div.:** 1.47
**Paid on:**
MONTHLY-24
**Since:** N/A

**Closed-end fund**

7 World Trade Ctr., 38th Fl.
New York. NY 10048

American Stock Transfer     800-937-5449
$250 - $unlimited
Every 30 days beginning 1st bus. day

FEES: Div: $0; Cash: comm.; Cert: $0; Term: $0,Does not sell through the plan

**Shares to qualify:** 1
**Safekeeping:** No
**Accepts foreign:** Yes
**Auto. inv.:** No
**Disc.:** No

---

## * Emerging Markets Income Fund Inc. (The)

**EMD/NYSE**

H: 14.85
L: 11.00
**Rec:** 13.00

**Div.:** 1.65
**Paid on:**
3.6.9.12-24
**Since:** N/A

**Closed-end fund**

7 World Trade Ctr., 38th Fl.
New York. NY 10048

American Stock Transfer     800-937-5449
$250 - $unlimited
Every 30 days beginning 1st bus. day

FEES: Div: $0; Cash: comm.; Cert: $0; Term: $2.50 + comm.,Does not sell through the plan

**Shares to qualify:** 1
**Safekeeping:** No
**Accepts foreign:** Yes
**Auto. inv.:** No
**Disc.:** No

---

## * Emerging Markets Income II Fund Inc. (The)

**EDF/NYSE**

H: 13.13
L: 10.25
**Rec:** 12.36

**Div.:** 1.65
**Paid on:**
3.6.9.12-24
**Since:** N/A

**Closed-end fund**

7 World Trade Ctr., 38th Fl.
New York. NY 10048

American Stock Transfer     800-937-5449
$250 - $unlimited
Every 30 days beginning 1st bus. day

FEES: Div: $0; Cash: comm.; Cert: $0; Term: $0,Does not sell through the plan

**Shares to qualify:** 1
**Safekeeping:** No
**Accepts foreign:** Yes
**Auto. inv.:** No
**Disc.:** No

---

## * Emerging Markets Telecomm. Fund, Inc. (The) ⊗

**ETF/NYSE**

H: 14.68
L: 7.08
**Rec:** 7.50

**Div.:** 3.09
**Paid on:**
1.4.7.10-27
**Since:** N/A

**Closed-end fund**

c/o Credit Suisse, 153 E. 53 St., 58th Fl.
New York. NY 10022

BankBoston     800-730-6001
$100 - $100,000/year
Every 7 days beginning Wed.

FEES: Div: $0; Cash: $5 + 8¢/sh.; Auto. Inv.: $5 + 8¢/sh.; Cert: $0; Term: $10 + 15¢/sh.;
Sells within 4 bus. days, by mail, at avg. price, for $10 + 15¢/sh.

**Shares to qualify:** 1 /de ($250)
**Safekeeping:** Yes
**Accepts foreign:** Yes
**Auto. inv.:** Yes
**Disc.:** No

---

## * Emerson Electric Co. ♥

**EMR/NYSE**

H: 79.75
L: 51.00
**Rec:** 56.80

**Div.:** 1.53
**Paid on:**
3.6.9.12-10
**Since:** 1947

**Electric equipment**

8000 W. Florissant, Box 4100
St. Louis. MO 63136

Mellon Inv. Svcs.     888-213-0970
$50 - $120,000/year
Every 15 days beginning 1/10

FEES: Div $0!; Cash: $0!; Cert: $0; Term: $0; Sells weekly, by mail or phone, at market, for
$5 + comm.

**Shares to qualify:** 1
**Safekeeping:** Yes
**Accepts foreign:** Yes
**Auto. inv.:** No
**Disc.:** No

---

* DRIP enrollment through Temper Enrollment Service (see page 180).     **75**

## Empire District Electric Co. ⊗

**EDE/NYSE** | Utility-electric | **Shares to qualify:** 1
H: 30.75 | 602 Joplin St. | **Safekeeping:** Yes
L: 17.50 | Joplin. MO 64801 | **Accepts foreign:** Yes
**Rec:** 19.92 | | **Auto. inv.:** Yes
**Div.:** 1.28 | Mellon Inv. Svcs.    888-261-6784 | **Disc.:** Div 3%
**Paid on:** | $50 - $125,000/year |
3.6.9.12-15 | Every 5 days beginning varies |
**Since:** N/A | FEES: Div: $0; Cash: $5 + 12¢/sh.; Auto. Inv.: $2 + 12¢/sh.; Cert: $0; Term: $15 + 12¢/sh.; Sells daily, by mail or phone, at market, for $15 + 12¢/sh.

## Enbridge, Inc. ♥

**ENBR/NASD** | Pipeline operator | **Shares to qualify:** 1
H: 28.87 | 2900 Canada Trust Twr., 421-7 Ave. S.W. | **Safekeeping:** No
L: 21.50 | Calgary. Alta. T2P 4K9 Canada | **Accepts foreign:** Yes
**Rec:** 27.02 | | **Auto. inv.:** No
**Div.:** 0.91 | Mellon Inv. Svcs.    800-387-0825 | **Disc.:** Div 5% Cash: 0%
**Paid on:** | $0 - $5,000/quarter Cdn. |
3.6.9.12-1 | Every 90 days beginning 3/1 |
**Since:** 1952 | FEES: Div: $0; Cash: $0; Cert: $0; Term: $0; Sells within 3 weeks, by mail, at avg. price, for comm.

## Energen Corp. ♥

**EGN/NYSE** | Utility-gas, oil & gas exploration & prod. | **Shares to qualify:** 1 /de ($250)
H: 40.25 | 605 Richard Arrington, Jr. Blvd. N | **Safekeeping:** Yes
L: 22.18 | Birmingham. AL 35203-2707 | **Accepts foreign:** Yes
**Rec:** 26.83 | | **Auto. inv.:** Yes
**Div.:** 0.70 | First Chicago Trust    888-764-5603 | **Disc.:** No
**Paid on:** | $25 - $250,000/year |
3.6.9.12-1 | Every 7 days beginning varies |
**Since:** 1953 | FEES: Div: $0; Cash: $0!; Auto. Inv.: $0; Cert: $0; Term: $15 + 12¢/sh.; Sells daily, by mail, fax , or phone, at avg. price, for $15 + 12¢/sh.

## Energy East Corp. ♥

**EAS/NYSE** | Utility-electric, gas | **Shares to qualify:** 1
H: 23.50 | Box 3200 | **Safekeeping:** Yes
L: 16.96 | Ithaca. NY 14852-3200 | **Accepts foreign:** Yes
**Rec:** 19.80 | | **Auto. inv.:** No
**Div.:** 0.92 | Energy East Corp.    800-225-5643 | **Disc.:** No
**Paid on:** | $25 - $100,000/year |
2.5.8.11-15 | Every 30 days beginning 1st bus. day |
**Since:** 1949 | FEES: Div: $0!; Cash: $0!; Cert: $0!; Term: $0; Sells weekly, by mail, at avg. price, for 7¢ to 8¢/sh.

## EnergySouth, Inc. ♥

**ENSI/NASD** | Utility-gas | **Shares to qualify:** 1
H: 23.37 | Box 2607 | **Safekeeping:** Yes
L: 18.00 | Mobile. AL 36652 | **Accepts foreign:** Yes
**Rec:** 20.73 | | **Auto. inv.:** No
**Div.:** 1.04 | Boston Eq.    800-736-3001 | **Disc.:** No
**Paid on:** | $25 - $5,000/quarter |
1.4.7.10-1 | Every 30 days beginning 1/2 |
**Since:** 1945 | FEES: Div: $0; Cash: $0; Cert: $0; Term: $0; Sells irregularly, by mail, at market, for comm.

## Enesco Group, Inc. ♥

**ENC/NYSE** | Giftware, collectibles, consumer | **Shares to qualify:** 1
H: 7.31 | 225 Windsor Dr. | **Safekeeping:** Yes
L: 4.25 | Itasca. IL 60143 | **Accepts foreign:** Yes
**Rec:** 6.44 | | **Auto. inv.:** No
**Div.:** 0.00 | Mellon Inv. Svcs.    800-288-9541 | **Disc.:** No
**Paid on:** | $10 - $5,000/quarter |
DIV. SUSP. | Every 90 days beginning 1/2 |
**Since:** -- | FEES: Div: n/o; Cash: $0!; Cert: $0!; Term: $15 + comm.; Sells within 5 bus. days, by mail or phone, at market, for $15 + comm.

## Engelhard Corp. ♥

**EC/NYSE** | Specialty chemicals | **Shares to qualify:** 1
H: 29.20 | 101 Wood Ave., Box 770 | **Safekeeping:** Yes
L: 15.06 | Iselin. NJ 08830 | **Accepts foreign:** No
**Rec:** 26.45 | | **Auto. inv.:** No
**Div.:** 0.40 | Mellon Inv. Svcs.    800-851-9677 | **Disc.:** No
**Paid on:** | $10 - $3,000/month |
3.6.9.12-31 | Every 30 days beginning 1/30 |
**Since:** 1981 | FEES: Div: $0; Cash: $0; Cert: $0; Term: $0; Sells weekly, by mail or phone, at market, for $5 + comm.

---

✳ DRIP enrollment through Temper Enrollment Service (see page 180).     76

## ✲ Enron Corp. ♥

| | |
|---|---|
| **ENE/NYSE** | **Gas distr. & electricity** |
| H: 90.75 | Box 1188, Ste. 4926B |
| L: 42.00 | Houston. TX 77251-1188 |
| **Rec:** 42.81 | First Chicago Trust     800-519-3111 |
| **Div.:** 0.50 | $25 - $120,000/year |
| **Paid on:** | Every 7 days beginning Wed. |
| 3.6.9.12-20 | |
| **Since:**1935 | |

**Shares to qualify:** 1 /de ($250)
**Safekeeping:** Yes
**Accepts foreign:** Yes
**Auto. inv.:** Yes
**Disc.:** No

FEES: Div: $0!; Cash: $0!; Auto. Inv.: $1; Cert: $0!; Term: $0; Sells daily, by phone or mail, at avg. price, for $15 + 12¢/sh.

---

## ✲ Entergy Corp. ⊗

| | |
|---|---|
| **ETR/NYSE** | **Utility-electric** |
| H: 44.67 | Box 61000 |
| L: 30.31 | New Orleans. LA 70161 |
| **Rec:** 37.75 | Mellon Inv. Svcs.     800-333-4368 |
| **Div.:** 1.26 | $100 - $3,000/month |
| **Paid on:** | Every 30 days beginning 1/4 |
| 3.6.9.12-1 | |
| **Since:**1988 | |

**Shares to qualify:** 1 /de ($1000)
**Safekeeping:** Yes
**Accepts foreign:** No
**Auto. inv.:** No
**Disc.:** No

FEES: Div: $0; Cash: $5 + comm.; Cert: $0; Term: $0; Sells biweekly, by mail or phone, at market, for $15 + 12¢/sh.

---

## ✲ Entertainment Properties Trust ♥

| | |
|---|---|
| **EPR/NYSE** | **REIT** |
| H: 18.65 | 30 Pershing Rd., Ste. 201 |
| L: 10.00 | Kansas Citv. MO 64108 |
| **Rec:** 17.65 | UMB Bank, N.A.     800-884-4225 |
| **Div.:** 1.80 | $50 - $100,000/year |
| **Paid on:** | Every 30 days beginning 1/15 |
| 1.4.7.10-15 | |
| **Since:**1998 | |

**Shares to qualify:** 1 /de ($200)
**Safekeeping:** Yes
**Accepts foreign:** No
**Auto. inv.:** Yes
**Disc.:** No

FEES: Div: $0!; Cash: $0!; Auto. Inv.: $0!; Cert: $0!; Term: $10; Sells monthly, by mail, at market, for $10

---

## ✲ Equifax ⊗

| | |
|---|---|
| **EFX/NYSE** | **Business information services** |
| H: 38.76 | Box 4081 |
| L: 20.60 | Atlanta. GA 30302 |
| **Rec:** 24.99 | SunTrust Bank, Atlanta     800-568-3476 |
| **Div.:** 0.08 | $50 - $10,000/month |
| **Paid on:** | Every 7 days beginning Wed. |
| 3.6.9.12-15 | |
| **Since:**1913 | |

**Shares to qualify:** 1 /de ($500)
**Safekeeping:** Yes
**Accepts foreign:** Yes
**Auto. inv.:** Yes
**Disc.:** No

FEES: Div: $0; Cash: $5 + 7¢/sh.; Auto. Inv.: $0; Cert: $0; Term: $15 + 7¢/sh.; Sells Thursday, by mail or fax, at market, for $15 + 7¢/sh.

---

## ✲ Equitable Resources Inc. ♥

| | |
|---|---|
| **EOT/NYSE** | **Energy company** |
| H: 40.49 | One Oxford Center, Ste. 3300, 301 Grant St. |
| L: 27.25 | Pittsburgh. PA 15219 |
| **Rec:** 32.92 | Mellon Inv. Svcs.     800-589-9026 |
| **Div.:** 0.64 | $25 - $5,000/month |
| **Paid on:** | Every 30 days beginning 1/2 |
| 3.6.9.12-1 | |
| **Since:**1950 | |

**Shares to qualify:** 1
**Safekeeping:** Yes
**Accepts foreign:** Yes
**Auto. inv.:** No
**Disc.:** No

FEES: Div: $0!; Cash: $0!; Cert: $2.50; Term: $7.50; Sells weekly, by mail , at market, for $5 + 10¢/sh.

---

## ✲ Equity Office Properties Trust ♥

| | |
|---|---|
| **EOP/NYSE** | **REIT** |
| H: 33.50 | Two N. Riverside Plaza, Ste. 2200 |
| L: 26.20 | Chicago. Il 60606 |
| **Rec:** 30.95 | BankBoston     888-752-4831 |
| **Div.:** 2.00 | $250 - $5,000/month |
| **Paid on:** | Every 30 days beginning 1/14 |
| 4.7.10.12-10 | |
| **Since:**1997 | |

**Shares to qualify:** 1 /de ($1000)
**Safekeeping:** Yes
**Accepts foreign:** Yes
**Auto. inv.:** Yes
**Disc.:** No

FEES: Div: $0!; Cash: $0!; Auto. Inv.: $0; Cert: $0!; Term: $15 + 12¢/sh. ; Sells within 3 bus. days, by mail, at market, for $15 + 12¢/sh.

---

## ✲ Equity Residential Prop. Trust ♥

| | |
|---|---|
| **EOR/NYSE** | **REIT** |
| H: 57.85 | Two North Riverside Plaza, Ste. 600 |
| L: 44.50 | Chicago. IL 60606 |
| **Rec:** 57.50 | BankBoston     800-733-5001 |
| **Div.:** 1.73 | $250 - $5,000/month |
| **Paid on:** | Every 30 days beginning 1/7 |
| 4.7.10.12-14 | |
| **Since:**N/A | |

**Shares to qualify:** 1 /de ($250)
**Safekeeping:** Yes
**Accepts foreign:** Yes
**Auto. inv.:** No
**Disc.:** Div: 0-5% Cash:
0%

FEES: Div: $0; Cash: $0; Cert: $0; Term: $0; Sells within 10 days, by mail, at market, for $10 + 15¢/sh.

---

✲ DRIP enrollment through Temper Enrollment Service (see page 180).     77

## ESB Financial Corp. ♥

| | |
|---|---|
| ESBF/NASD | **Banking** |
| H: 13.55 | 600 Lawrence Ave. |
| L: 7.60 | Ellwood City. PA 16117-1930 |
| **Rec:** 12.95 | Registrar & Transfer   800-368-5948 |
| **Div.:** 0.40 | $25 - $15,000/quarter |
| **Paid on:** | Every 30 days beginning 1/25 |
| 1.4.7.10-25 | |
| **Since:** N/A | |

**Shares to qualify:** 1
**Safekeeping:** No
**Accepts foreign:** Yes
**Auto. inv.:** No
**Disc.:** No

FEES: Div: $0!; Cash: $0!; Cert: $5; Term: $10 + comm., Does not sell through the plan

---

## Essex Property Trust, Inc. ⊗

| | |
|---|---|
| ESS/NYSE | **REIT** |
| H: 57.75 | 925 E. Meadow Dr. |
| L: 42.28 | Palo Alto. CA 94303 |
| **Rec:** 52.85 | BankBoston   800-730-6001 |
| **Div.:** 2.80 | $100 - $20,000/month |
| **Paid on:** | Every 7 days beginning Friday |
| 1.4.7.10-15 | |
| **Since:** 1994 | |

**Shares to qualify:** 1 /de ($100)
**Safekeeping:** Yes
**Accepts foreign:** Yes
**Auto. inv.:** Yes
**Disc.:** No

FEES: Div: $0; Cash: $5; Auto. Inv.: $5; Cert: $0; Term: $10 + 15¢/sh.; Sells within 10 bus. days, by mail, at avg. price, for $10 + 15¢/sh.

---

## Estee Lauder Companies Inc. ⊗

| | |
|---|---|
| EL/NYSE | **Personel health products, cosmetics** |
| H: 47.25 | 767 5th Ave. |
| L: 33.18 | New York. NY 10153 |
| **Rec:** 38.47 | Mellon Inv. Svcs.   888-860-6295 |
| **Div.:** 0.20 | $100 - $10,000/month |
| **Paid on:** | Every 7 days beginning varies |
| 1.4.7.10-6 | |
| **Since:** 2000 | |

**Shares to qualify:** 1 /de ($250)
**Safekeeping:** Yes
**Accepts foreign:** Yes
**Auto. inv.:** Yes
**Disc.:** No

FEES: Div: $0!; Cash: $5 + 12¢/sh.; Auto. Inv.: $3 + 12¢/sh.; Cert: $0!; Term: $15 + 12¢/sh.; Sells daily, by mail or phone, at market, for $15 + 12¢/sh.

---

## Ethyl Corp. ♥

| | |
|---|---|
| EY/NYSE | **Chemicals** |
| H: 2.43 | Box 2189 |
| L: 0.99 | Richmond. VA 23218-2189 |
| **Rec:** 1.23 | Computershare Investor Svcs.   800-625-5191 |
| **Div.:** 0.00 | $25 - $1,000/month |
| **Paid on:** | Every 30 days beginning 1/2 |
| DIV. SUSP. | |
| **Since:** -- | |

**Shares to qualify:** 1
**Safekeeping:** No
**Accepts foreign:** No
**Auto. inv.:** No
**Disc.:** No

FEES: Div: n/o; Cash: $0; Cert: $0; Term: $0; Sells weekly, by mail or fax, at market, for comm.

---

## Exchange Bancshares, Inc. ♥

| | |
|---|---|
| EBLO/OTC | **Banking** |
| H: 25.00 | 237 Main St., Box 177 |
| L: 17.00 | Luckev. OH 43443 |
| **Rec:** 18.25 | Illinois Stock Transfer   800-757-5755 |
| **Div.:** 0.40 | $25 - $500/semiannually |
| **Paid on:** | Every 180 days beginning 6/15 |
| 6-15 &12-15 | |
| **Since:** N/A | |

**Shares to qualify:** 25
**Safekeeping:** No
**Accepts foreign:** No
**Auto. inv.:** No
**Disc.:** No

FEES: Div: $0!; Cash: $0!; Cert: $0!; Term: $5, Does not sell through the plan

---

## Exelon Corporation

| | |
|---|---|
| EXC/NYSE | **Utility-electric** |
| H: 71.00 | Box 805398 |
| L: 45.37 | Chicago. IL 60680-5398 |
| **Rec:** 55.33 | First Chicago Trust   800-626-8729 |
| **Div.:** 1.69 | $25 - $60,000/year |
| **Paid on:** | Every 30 days beginning 1/10 |
| 3.6.9.12-10 | |
| **Since:** 1902 | |

**Shares to qualify:** 1
**Safekeeping:** Yes
**Accepts foreign:** Yes
**Auto. inv.:** Yes
**Disc.:** No

FEES: Div: $0!; Cash: 10¢/sh.; Auto. Inv.: $0; Cert: $0!; Term: $0; Sells daily, by mail, fax, or phone, at market, for 10¢/sh.

---

## Exxon Mobil Corp. ♥

| | |
|---|---|
| XOM/NYSE | **Oil refining** |
| H: 47.71 | Box 140369 |
| L: 37.60 | Irving. TX 75014-0369 |
| **Rec:** 41.35 | BankBoston   800-252-1800 |
| **Div.:** 0.92 | $50 - $200,000/year |
| **Paid on:** | Every 7 days beginning Thursday |
| 3.6.9.12-10 | |
| **Since:** 1882 | |

**Shares to qualify:** 1 /de ($250)
**Safekeeping:** Yes
**Accepts foreign:** Yes
**Auto. inv.:** Yes
**Disc.:** No

FEES: Div: $0; Cash: $0; Auto. Inv.: $0; Cert: $0; Term: $0; Sells weekly, by mail or fax, at avg. price, for $5 + 5¢/sh.

---

✱ DRIP enrollment through Temper Enrollment Service (see page 180).   **78**

## ✱ F & M Bancorp ♥

**FMBN/NAS**
H: 29.99
L: 17.50
**Rec:** 26.66

**Div.:** 1.08
**Paid on:**
2.5.8.11-1
**Since:** 1984

**Bank holding company**
110 Thomas Johnson Dr., Box 518
Frederick. MD 21705

Wells Fargo Bank      800-468-9716
$25 - $3,000/quarter
Every 90 days beginning 1/2
FEES: Div: $0!; Cash: $0!; Cert: $0!; Term: $10 + 10¢/sh.; Sells daily, by mail or fax, at market, for $10 + 10¢/sh.

**Shares to qualify:** 1
**Safekeeping:** No
**Accepts foreign:** Yes
**Auto. inv.:** No
**Disc.:** Div 5% Cash: 0%

---

## ✱ Fannie Mae ⊗

**FNM/NYSE**
H: 89.37
L: 52.06
**Rec:** 84.40

**Div.:** 1.20
**Paid on:**
2.5.8.11-25
**Since:** 1956

**Mortgage and financing**
3900 Wisconsin Ave. NW
Washington. DC 20016

First Chicago Trust      800-910-8277
$25 - $250,000/year
Every 7 days beginning varies
FEES: Div: $0; Cash: $5; Auto. Inv.: $2; Cert: $0; Term: $0; Sells daily, by mail or phone, at market, for $15 + 12¢/sh.

**Shares to qualify:** 1 /de ($250)
**Safekeeping:** Yes
**Accepts foreign:** Yes
**Auto. inv.:** Yes
**Disc.:** No

---

## Farmers National Banc Corp. ♥

**FMNB/OTC**
H: 10.60
L: 7.00
**Rec:** 9.93

**Div.:** 0.52
**Paid on:**
3.6.9.12-30
**Since:** N/A

**Bank holding company**
20 South Broad St., Box 555
Canfield. OH 44406

Farmers National Bank of      330-533-3341
$0 - $1,000/quarter
Every 90 days beginning 3/12
FEES: Div: $0; Cash: $0; Cert: $0; Term: $0,Does not sell through the plan

**Shares to qualify:** 1
**Safekeeping:** Yes
**Accepts foreign:** Yes
**Auto. inv.:** No
**Disc.:** No

---

## ✱ FBL Financial Group, Inc.-A

**FFG/NYSE**
H: 18.99
L: 12.12
**Rec:** 18.25

**Div.:** 0.40
**Paid on:**
3.6.9.12-31
**Since:** 1996

**Markets and distributes insurance**
5400 University Ave.
West Des Moines. IA 50266

Mellon Inv. Svcs.      888-213-0965
$50 - $150,000/year
Every 5 days beginning varies
FEES: Div: $0; Cash: $5 + 3¢/sh.; Auto. Inv.: $2 + 3¢/sh.; Cert: $0; Term: $15 + 12¢/sh.; Sells daily, by mail or phone, at avg. price, for $15 + 12¢/sh.

**Shares to qualify:** 1 /de ($250)
**Safekeeping:** Yes
**Accepts foreign:** No
**Auto. inv.:** Yes
**Disc.:** No

---

## ✱ Federal Realty Investment Trust ♥

**FRT/NYSE**
H: 22.78
L: 18.75
**Rec:** 22.78

**Div.:** 1.88
**Paid on:**
1.4.7.10-15
**Since:** 1962

**REIT**
1626 East Jefferson St.
Rockville. MD 20852-4041

American Stock Transfer      800-937-5449
$50 - $15,000/quarter
Every 30 days beginning 1/15
FEES: Div: $0; Cash: $0; Auto. Inv.: $0; Cert: $0; Term: $0; Sells weekly, by mail, at market, for comm.

**Shares to qualify:** 1
**Safekeeping:** Yes
**Accepts foreign:** Yes
**Auto. inv.:** Yes
**Disc.:** No

---

## ✱ Federal Signal Corp. ♥

**FSS/NYSE**
H: 24.63
L: 17.06
**Rec:** 21.11

**Div.:** 0.78
**Paid on:**
1.4.7.10-3
**Since:** 1948

**Elec. equip., vehicles, tools & signs**
1415 West 22nd St.
Oak Brook. IL 60523-2004

First Chicago Trust      800-446-2617
$100 - $5,000/month
Every 30 days beginning 1/2
FEES: Div: $0!; Cash: $0!; Auto. Inv.: $2; Cert: $0!; Term: $15 + 12¢/sh.; Sells daily, by mail or phone, at market, for $15 + 12¢/sh.

**Shares to qualify:** 50
**Safekeeping:** Yes
**Accepts foreign:** Yes
**Auto. inv.:** Yes
**Disc.:** No

---

## ✱ Federal-Mogul ⊗

**FMO/NYSE**
H: 12.06
L: 1.01
**Rec:** 1.07

**Div.:** 0.01
**Paid on:**
3.6.9.12-12
**Since:** 1936

**Auto parts**
26555 Northwestern Hwy.
Southfield. MI 48034

Bank of New York      800-524-4458
$10 - $25,000/year
Every 30 days beginning 1/11
FEES: Div: 5% to $3; Cash: 5% to $3; Cert: $5; Term: $5; Sells weekly, by mail, at avg. price, for $5 + comm.

**Shares to qualify:** 1
**Safekeeping:** Yes
**Accepts foreign:** Yes
**Auto. inv.:** No
**Disc.:** No

---

## FedEx Corp. ⊗

**FDX/NYSE**
H: 49.85
L: 35.50
**Rec:** 39.97
**Div.:** 0.00
**Paid on:**
N/0
**Since:** N/0

**Package delivery service**
942 South Shady Grove Rd.
Memphis. TN 38120
First Chicago Trust    800-446-2617
$100 - $250,000/year
Every 5 days beginning varies
FEES: Div: 5% to $3 + 3¢/sh.; Cash: $5 + 3¢/sh.; Auto. Inv.: $2 + 3¢/sh.; Cert: $0; Term: $15 + 9¢/sh.; Sells daily, by phone, mail, fax, or Internet, at market, for $15 + 9¢/sh.

**Shares to qualify:** 1 /de ($1000)
**Safekeeping:** Yes
**Accepts foreign:** Yes
**Auto. inv.:** Yes
**Disc.:** No

---

## Ferro Corp. ♥

**FOE/NYSE**
H: 24.70
L: 17.62
**Rec:** 22.59
**Div.:** 0.58
**Paid on:**
3.6.9.12-10
**Since:** 1939

**Specialty chemicals**
1000 Lakeside Ave., Box 147000
Cleveland. OH 44114-7000
National City Bank    800-622-6757
$10 - $3,000/month
Every 30 days beginning 1/2
FEES: Div: $0; Cash: $0; Cert: $0; Term: comm.; Sells irregularly, by mail, at market, for comm.

**Shares to qualify:** 1
**Safekeeping:** Yes
**Accepts foreign:** Yes
**Auto. inv.:** No
**Disc.:** No

---

## FFLC Bancorp, Inc. ♥

**FFLC/NASD**
H: 21.30
L: 13.12
**Rec:** 20.38
**Div.:** 0.52
**Paid on:**
2.5.8.11-1
**Since:** N/A

**Bank holding company**
800 N. Blvd. West, Box 490420
Leesburg. FL 34749-0420
Registrar & Transfer    800-368-5948
$100 - $100,000/year
Every 30 days beginning 1st bus. day of each month
FEES: Div: $0!; Cash: $0!; Auto. Inv.: $0; Cert: $5; Term: $10 + comm.; Sells weekly, by mail, at market, for $10 + comm.

**Shares to qualify:** 50
**Safekeeping:** Yes
**Accepts foreign:** Yes
**Auto. inv.:** Yes
**Disc.:** No

---

## Fidelity Bancorp ♥

**FSBI/NASD**
H: 17.00
L: 10.50
**Rec:** 16.65
**Div.:** 0.40
**Paid on:**
2.5.8.11-31
**Since:** 1988

**Bank holding company**
1009 Perry Hwy.
Pittsburgh. PA 15237-2105
Registrar & Transfer    800-866-1340
$10 - $3,500/quarter
Every 90 days beginning 2/10
FEES: Div: $0; Cash: $0; Cert: $0; Term: $0; Sells daily, by mail, at market, for comm.

**Shares to qualify:** 1
**Safekeeping:** Yes
**Accepts foreign:** Yes
**Auto. inv.:** No
**Disc.:** No

---

## Fidelity Bankshares, Inc. ♥

**FFFL/NASD**
H: 14.40
L: 7.13
**Rec:** 14.00
**Div.:** 0.40
**Paid on:**
1.4.7.10-15
**Since:** 1995

**Bank holding company**
218 Datura St.
West Palm Beach. FL 33401
American Stock Transfer    800-937-5449
$100 - $15,000/quarter
Every 90 days beginning 1/15
FEES: Div: $0!; Cash: $0!; Cert: $0!; Term: $0,Does not sell through the plan

**Shares to qualify:** 50
**Safekeeping:** Yes
**Accepts foreign:** Yes
**Auto. inv.:** No
**Disc.:** No

---

## Fidelity National Corp.

**LION/NASD**
H: 8.00
L: 4.75
**Rec:** 7.05
**Div.:** 0.20
**Paid on:**
3.6.9.12-28
**Since:** N/A

**Bank holding company**
3490 Piedmont Rd., Ste. 1550
Atlanta. GA 30305
Bank of New York    800-524-4458
$100 - $50,000/quarter
Every 30 days beginning 1/15
FEES: Div: $0!; Cash: $2 + 6¢/sh.; Cert: $5; Term: $5 + 6¢/sh.; Sells daily, by mail, at avg. price, for $5 + 6¢/sh.

**Shares to qualify:** 100
**Safekeeping:** Yes
**Accepts foreign:** Yes
**Auto. inv.:** No
**Disc.:** No

---

## Fifth Third Bancorp ⊗

**FITB/NASD**
H: 64.11
L: 42.93
**Rec:** 62.90
**Div.:** 0.80
**Paid on:**
1.4.7.10-15
**Since:** 1952

**Banking**
38 Fountain Sq. Plz., MS 10AT
Cincinnati. OH 45263
Fifth Third Bancorp    800-837-2755
$50 - $10,000/month
Every 15 days beginning varies
FEES: Div: 5% to $3 + 4¢/sh.; Cash: $3 + 4¢/sh.; Auto. Inv.: $2 + 4¢/sh.; Cert: $10; Term: $10; Sells weekly, by mail, at market, for $10 + 4¢/sh.

**Shares to qualify:** 1 /de ($500)
**Safekeeping:** Yes
**Accepts foreign:** Yes
**Auto. inv.:** Yes
**Disc.:** No

---

✱ DRIP enrollment through Temper Enrollment Service (see page 180).    **80**

## * FINOVA Group Inc. (The) ♥

**FNV/NYSE** | **Commercial finance**

H: 10.93
L: 0.47
**Rec:** 3.46

4800 N. Scottsdale Rd.
Scottsdale. AZ 85251-7623

Computershare Investor Svcs.   888-445-6428

**Div.:** 0.00
**Paid on:**
DIV. SUSP.
**Since:**--

$50 - $25,000/quarter
Every 7 days beginning varies

**Shares to qualify:** 1 /de ($500)
**Safekeeping:** Yes
**Accepts foreign:** Yes
**Auto. inv.:** Yes
**Disc.:** No

FEES: Div: n/o; Cash: $0!; Auto. Inv.: $0; Cert: $0!; Term: $0; Sells every 5 bus. days, by mail, at avg. price, for $10 + 8¢/sh.

---

## * First American Corp. (The) ♥

**FAF/NYSE** | **Financial services**

H: 35.49
L: 15.12
**Rec:** 17.60

1 First American Way
Santa Ana. CA 92707

Wells Fargo Bank   800-468-9716

**Div.:** 0.28
**Paid on:**
1.4.7.10-15
**Since:** N/A

$50 - $5,000/quarter
Every 5 days beginning varies

**Shares to qualify:** 1 /de ($250)
**Safekeeping:** Yes
**Accepts foreign:** Yes
**Auto. inv.:** Yes
**Disc.:** No

FEES: Div: $0!; Cash: $0!; Auto. Inv.: $0; Cert: $10; Term: $10 + 15¢/sh.; Sells daily, by mail or phone, at market, for $10 + 15¢/sh.

---

## * First Bancorp ♥

**FBNC/NASD** | **Bank holding company**

H: 28.08
L: 12.62
**Rec:** 23.79

341 North Main St., Box 508
Troy. NC 27371-0508

Registrar & Transfer   800-368-5948

**Div.:** 0.88
**Paid on:**
1.4.7.10-25
**Since:** N/A

$25 - $2,500/quarter
Every 30 days beginning 1/25

**Shares to qualify:** 1
**Safekeeping:** Yes
**Accepts foreign:** Yes
**Auto. inv.:** Yes
**Disc.:** No

FEES: Div: $0; Cash: $0; Auto. Inv.: $0; Cert: $0; Term: $0; Sells monthly, by mail, at market, for 6¢ to 8¢/sh.

---

## * First Bell Bancorp, Inc. ♥

**FBBC/NASD** | **Bank holding company**

H: 16.37
L: 11.93
**Rec:** 14.68

532 Lincoln Ave.
Pittsburgh. PA 15202

Registrar & Transfer   800-368-5948

**Div.:** 0.48
**Paid on:**
1.4.7.10-21
**Since:** N/A

$50 - $3,000/quarter
Every 90 days beginning 1/21

**Shares to qualify:** 1
**Safekeeping:** No
**Accepts foreign:** Yes
**Auto. inv.:** No
**Disc.:** No

FEES: Div: $0!; Cash: $0!; Cert: $0!; Term: $20,Does not sell through the plan

---

## * First Charter Corp. ♥

**FCTR/NASD** | **Banking**

H: 18.75
L: 12.75
**Rec:** 18.05

Box 37937
Charlotte. NC 28237

Registrar & Transfer   800-368-5948

**Div.:** 0.72
**Paid on:**
1.4.7.10-18
**Since:** N/A

$25 - $3,000/quarter
Every 30 days beginning 1/15

**Shares to qualify:** 1
**Safekeeping:** Yes
**Accepts foreign:** Yes
**Auto. inv.:** Yes
**Disc.:** No

FEES: Div: $0; Cash: $0; Auto. Inv.: $0; Cert: $0; Term: $15; Sells irregularly, by mail, at market, for $0

---

## * First Chester County Corp. ♥

**FCEC/OTC** | **Bank holding company**

H: 18.75
L: 13.62
**Rec:** 17.25

9 North High St., Box 523
West Chester. PA 19381

Registrar & Transfer   800-368-5948

**Div.:** 0.52
**Paid on:**
1.4.7.10-1
**Since:** N/A

$25 - $2,000/month
Every 30 days beginning 1/2

**Shares to qualify:** 1
**Safekeeping:** Yes
**Accepts foreign:** Yes
**Auto. inv.:** No
**Disc.:** No

FEES: Div: $0!; Cash: $0!; Cert: $0!; Term: $0; Sells within 15 bus. days, by mail, at market, for comm.

---

## * First Colonial Group, Inc. ♥

**FTCG/NASD** | **Banking**

H: 17.00
L: 11.42
**Rec:** 16.90

76 South Main St.
Nazareth. PA 18064-2053

Nazareth National Bank   610-746-7317

**Div.:** 0.76
**Paid on:**
2.5.8.11-22
**Since:** 1897

$100 - $1,000/quarter
Every 90 days beginning 2/22

**Shares to qualify:** 1
**Safekeeping:** Yes
**Accepts foreign:** N/A
**Auto. inv.:** No
**Disc.:** Div 5% Cash: 5%

FEES: Div: $0; Cash: $0; Cert: $0; Term: $0,Does not sell through the plan

---

## ✳ First Commonwealth Financial ♥

**FCF/NYSE**
H: 15.10
L: 8.81
**Rec:** 11.20

**Div.:** 0.58
**Paid on:**
1.4.7.10-15
**Since:** 1987

**Banking**
Box 400
Indiana. PA 15701-0400
Bank of New York      800-524-4458
$50 - $120,000/year
Every 7 days beginning varies

**Shares to qualify:** 1 /de ($500)
**Safekeeping:** Yes
**Accepts foreign:** Yes
**Auto. inv.:** Yes
**Disc.:** Div: 10% Cash:
0%

FEES: Div: $0!; Cash: $0!; Auto. Inv.: $1; Cert: $0!; Term: $0; Sells weekly, by mail, at avg. price, for $10 + 10¢/sh.

## ✳ First Federal Capital Corp. ♥

**FTFC/NASD**
H: 16.81
L: 10.87
**Rec:** 15.85

**Div.:** 0.48
**Paid on:**
3.6.9.12
**Since:** 1991

**Banking**
605 State St., Box 1868
La Crosse. WI 54602
Wells Fargo Bank      800-468-9716
$50 - $5,000/quarter
Every 90 days beginning 3/1

**Shares to qualify:** 1
**Safekeeping:** Yes
**Accepts foreign:** Yes
**Auto. inv.:** No
**Disc.:** No

FEES: Div: $0!; Cash: $0!; Cert: $0!; Term: $0; Sells daily, by mail or fax, at market, for $10 + 10¢/sh.

## ✳ First Financial Bancorp ♥

**FFBC/NASD**
H: 17.44
L: 13.33
**Rec:** 16.74

**Div.:** 0.60
**Paid on:**
1.4.7.10-1
**Since:** N/A

**Bank holding company**
300 High St.
Hamilton. OH 45011
Registrar & Transfer      800-368-5948
$100 - $5,000/quarter
Every 90 days beginning 1/4

**Shares to qualify:** 25
**Safekeeping:** Yes
**Accepts foreign:** Yes
**Auto. inv.:** No
**Disc.:** No

FEES: Div: $0!; Cash: $3/quarter; Cert: $5; Term: $0; Sells within 5 bus. days, by mail, at market, for comm.

## ✳ First Financial Holdings Inc. ♥

**FFCH/NASD**
H: 24.98
L: 13.75
**Rec:** 24.23

**Div.:** 0.62
**Paid on:**
2.5.8.11
**Since:** 1986

**Savings and loan holding co.**
Box 118068
Charleston. SC 29423-8068
Registrar & Transfer      800-368-5948
$100 - $5,000/month
Every 7 days beginning varies

**Shares to qualify:** 1 /de ($250)
**Safekeeping:** Yes
**Accepts foreign:** Yes
**Auto. inv.:** Yes
**Disc.:** No

FEES: Div: $0!; Cash: $0!; Auto. Inv.: $0; Cert: $0!; Term: $3.50 + comm.; Sells irregularly, by mail, at market, for $3.50 + comm.

## ✳ First Indiana Corp. ♥

**FISB/NASD**
H: 27.00
L: 19.68
**Rec:** 25.35

**Div.:** 0.64
**Paid on:**
3.6.9.12-15
**Since:** N/A

**Savings banks**
135 North Pennsylvania St.
Indianapolis. IN 46204
Computershare Investor Svcs.      312-461-5545
$100 - $5,000/quarter
Every 90 days beginning 3/15

**Shares to qualify:** 1
**Safekeeping:** No
**Accepts foreign:** Yes
**Auto. inv.:** No
**Disc.:** No

FEES: Div: $0!; Cash: $0!; Cert: $0!; Term: $5 + comm.,Does not sell through the plan

## ✳ First Keystone Financial ⊗

**FKFS/NASD**
H: 14.50
L: 9.93
**Rec:** 13.65

**Div.:** 0.32
**Paid on:**
1.4.7.10-2
**Since:** N/A

**Bank holding co.**
22 West State St.
Media. PA 19063
Registrar & Transfer      800-368-5948
$100 - $2,500/quarter
Every 90 days beginning 1/2

**Shares to qualify:** 1
**Safekeeping:** Yes
**Accepts foreign:** Yes
**Auto. inv.:** No
**Disc.:** No

FEES: Div: $0!; Cash: $5; Cert: $0; Term: $15 + comm.; Sells 10 bus. days, by mail, at avg. price, for $15 + comm.

## ✳ First Leesport Bancorp, Inc. ♥

**FLPB/NASD**
H: 16.75
L: 12.62
**Rec:** 16.10

**Div.:** 0.60
**Paid on:**
1.4.7.10-15
**Since:** N/A

**Bank holding company**
Box 741
Leesport. PA 19533
American Stock Transfer      800-278-4353
$50 - $5,000/month
Every 30 days beginning 1/15

**Shares to qualify:** 1
**Safekeeping:** Yes
**Accepts foreign:** Yes
**Auto. inv.:** Yes
**Disc.:** No

FEES: Div: $0!; Cash: $0!; Auto. Inv.: $0; Cert: $0!; Term: $0; Sells weekly, by mail, at market, for 4¢/sh.

---

✳ DRIP enrollment through Temper Enrollment Service (see page 180).

## ✳ First M & F Corp. ♥

**FMFC/NASD** — Bank holding company

| | |
|---|---|
| H: 28.00 | 221 E. Washington St., Box 520 |
| L: 16.00 | Kosciusko. MS 39090 |
| **Rec:** 22.50 | Registrar & Transfer    800-368-5948 |
| **Div.:** 1.00 | $50 - $5,000/quarter |
| **Paid on:** | Every 30 days beginning 1/30 |
| 3.6.9.12-31 | |
| **Since:** N/A | FEES: Div $0!; Cash: $0!; Auto. Inv.: $0!; Cert: $0!; Term: $10 + comm.; Sells within 10 bus. days, by mail, at avg. price, for $10 + comm. |

**Shares to qualify:** 100
**Safekeeping:** Yes
**Accepts foreign:** Yes
**Auto. inv.:** Yes
**Disc.:** No

---

## ✳ First Midwest Bancorp, Inc. ♥

**FMBI/NASD** — Banking

| | |
|---|---|
| H: 33.94 | 300 Park Blvd., Ste. 405 |
| L: 22.00 | Itasca. IL 60143-9768 |
| **Rec:** 33.94 | Mellon Inv. Svcs.    888-581-9376 |
| **Div.:** 0.80 | $100 - $5,000/quarter |
| **Paid on:** | Every 30 days beginning 1/30 |
| 1.4.7.10-25 | |
| **Since:** 1983 | FEES: Div $0; Cash: $0; Cert: $0; Term: $0; Sells weekly, by mail, fax , or phone, at market, for $10 +12¢/sh. |

**Shares to qualify:** 1
**Safekeeping:** Yes
**Accepts foreign:** No
**Auto. inv.:** No
**Disc.:** No

---

## ✳ First Nat'l Community Bancorp, Inc. ♥

**FNCB/NASD** — Bank holding company

| | |
|---|---|
| H: 35.00 | 102 East Drinker St. |
| L: 27.37 | Dunmore. PA 18512-2491 |
| **Rec:** 33.75 | Registrar & Transfer    800-368-5948 |
| **Div.:** 0.84 | $100 - $2,500/quarter |
| **Paid on:** | Every 90 days beginning 3/15 |
| 3.6.9.12-15 | |
| **Since:** N/A | FEES: Div $0!; Cash: $0!; Cert: $0!; Term: $10; Sells within 10 bus. days, by mail, at market, for $10 |

**Shares to qualify:** 1
**Safekeeping:** Yes
**Accepts foreign:** Yes
**Auto. inv.:** No
**Disc.:** Div 5% Cash: 5%

---

## ✳ First Niagara Financial Group, Inc. ♥

**FNFG/NASD** — Bank holding co.

| | |
|---|---|
| H: 16.75 | 6950 S. Transit Rd., Box 514 |
| L: 8.75 | Lockport. NY 14095-0514 |
| **Rec:** 16.23 | Mellon Inv. Svcs.    877-785-9670 |
| **Div.:** 0.36 | $50 - $60,000/year |
| **Paid on:** | Every 5 days beginning varies |
| 2.5.8.11-22 | |
| **Since:** N/A | FEES: Div $0!; Cash: $0!; Auto. Inv.: $0; Cert: $0!; Term: $15 + 12¢/sh.; Sells daily, by mail or phone, at market, for $15 + 12¢/sh. |

**Shares to qualify:** 1 /de ($150)
**Safekeeping:** Yes
**Accepts foreign:** Yes
**Auto. inv.:** Yes
**Disc.:** No

---

## ✳ First Tennessee National Corp. ♥

**FTN/NYSE** — Banking

| | |
|---|---|
| H: 36.80 | Box 84 |
| L: 18.75 | Memphis. TN 38101-0084 |
| **Rec:** 34.20 | Wells Fargo Bank    800-468-9716 |
| **Div.:** 0.88 | $25 - $10,000/quarter |
| **Paid on:** | Every 30 days beginning 1/2 |
| 1.4.7.10-1 | |
| **Since:** 1896 | FEES: Div $0; Cash: $0; Cert: $0; Term: $10 + 10¢/sh.; Sells weekly, by mail, at market, for $10 + 10¢/sh. |

**Shares to qualify:** 1
**Safekeeping:** Yes
**Accepts foreign:** Yes
**Auto. inv.:** No
**Disc.:** No

---

## ✳ First Union Corp. ♥

**FTU/NYSE** — Banking

| | |
|---|---|
| H: 36.00 | 301 S. College St. |
| L: 23.50 | Charlotte. NC 28254-0040 |
| **Rec:** 35.96 | First Union Nat'l Bank    800-347-1246 |
| **Div.:** 0.96 | $25 - $2,000/month |
| **Paid on:** | Every 30 days beginning 1/15 |
| 3.6.9.12-15 | |
| **Since:** 1977 | FEES: Div $0!; Cash: $0!; Auto. Inv.: $0; Cert: $0!; Term: $0!; Sells monthly, by mail, at market, for $0! |

**Shares to qualify:** 10
**Safekeeping:** Yes
**Accepts foreign:** Yes
**Auto. inv.:** Yes
**Disc.:** Div 1% Cash: 0%

---

## ✳ First United Corp. ♥

**FUNC/NASD** — Regional banks

| | |
|---|---|
| H: 16.48 | 19 South Second St. |
| L: 9.00 | Oakland. MD 21550 |
| **Rec:** 16.30 | Mellon Inv. Svcs.    800-953-2593 |
| **Div.:** 0.66 | $50 - $10,000/quarter |
| **Paid on:** | Every 90 days beginning 2/1 |
| 2.5.8.11-1 | |
| **Since:** N/A | FEES: Div $0!; Cash: $0!; Cert: $0!; Term: $3.50 + comm.; Sells weekly, by mail or phone, at market, for $3.50 + comm. |

**Shares to qualify:** 1
**Safekeeping:** Yes
**Accepts foreign:** No
**Auto. inv.:** No
**Disc.:** No

---

## ✱ First Virginia Banks, Inc. ♥

**FVB/NYSE** | **Banking** | **Shares to qualify:** 1
H: 49.25 | 6400 Arlington Blvd. | **Safekeeping:** Yes
L: 37.00 | Falls Church. VA 22042-2336 | **Accepts foreign:** Yes
**Rec:** 47.50 | | **Auto. inv.:** Yes
| Registrar & Transfer      800-368-5948 | **Disc.:** No
**Div.:** 1.56 | $25 - $5,000/quarter |
**Paid on:** | Every 30 days beginning 1/2 |
1.4.7.10-VARIES | FEES: Div $0!; Cash: $0!; Auto. Inv.: $0; Does not sell through the plan |
**Since:** 1959 | |

## ✱ FirstEnergy

**FE/NYSE** | **Utility-electric** | **Shares to qualify:** 1 /de ($250)
H: 32.85 | 76 South Main St. | **Safekeeping:** Yes
L: 22.93 | Akron. OH 44308-1890 | **Accepts foreign:** Yes
**Rec:** 30.42 | | **Auto. inv.:** Yes
| FirstEnergy Corp. Investor      800-736-3402 | **Disc.:** No
**Div.:** 1.50 | $25 - $100,000/year |
**Paid on:** | Every 15 days beginning 1/2 |
3.6.9.12-1 | FEES: Div 9¢/sh.; Cash: 9¢/sh.; Auto. Inv.: $0; Cert: $0; Term: $0; Sells biweekly, by mail, |
**Since:** N/A | fax , or phone, at avg. price, for 9¢/sh. |

## ✱ FIRSTFED Bancorp, Inc. ♥

**FFDB/NASD** | **Banking** | **Shares to qualify:** 1
H: 10.00 | 1630 Fourth Ave. North | **Safekeeping:** Yes
L: 7.00 | Bessemer. AL 35020 | **Accepts foreign:** Yes
**Rec:** 9.25 | | **Auto. inv.:** Yes
| Registrar & Transfer      800-368-5948 | **Disc.:** Div 5% Cash: 0%
**Div.:** 0.28 | $50 - $2,000/month |
**Paid on:** | Every 30 days beginning 1/10 |
1.4.7.10-10 | FEES: Div: $0; Cash: $0; Auto. Inv.: $0; Cert: $0; Term: $0; Sells monthly, by mail, at |
**Since:** N/A | market, for comm. |

## ✱ FirstMerit Corp. ♥

**FMER/NASD** | **Banking** | **Shares to qualify:** 1
H: 27.75 | III Cascade Plaza | **Safekeeping:** Yes
L: 19.18 | Akron. OH 44308-1103 | **Accepts foreign:** Yes
**Rec:** 25.25 | | **Auto. inv.:** No
| FirstMerit Bank, N.A.      888-384-6388 | **Disc.:** No
**Div.:** 0.92 | $25 - $5,000/quarter |
**Paid on:** | Every 90 days beginning 3/12 |
3.6.9.12-15 | FEES: Div: $0; Cash: $0; Cert: $0; Term: $0; Sells daily, by phone, at market, for $2.50 + |
**Since:** 1982 | comm. |

## ✱ Flag Financial Corp. ♥

**FLAG/NASD** | **Bank holding co.** | **Shares to qualify:** 1
H: 7.93 | Box 3007 | **Safekeeping:** Yes
L: 4.12 | LaGrange. GA 30241 | **Accepts foreign:** Yes
**Rec:** 7.29 | | **Auto. inv.:** Yes
| Registrar & Transfer      800-368-5948 | **Disc.:** No
**Div.:** 0.24 | $25 - $2,000/month |
**Paid on:** | Every 30 days beginning 1/2 |
1.4.7.10-1 | FEES: Div: $0!; Cash: $0!; Auto. Inv.: $0; Cert: $0; Term: $0; Sells daily, by mail, at market, |
**Since:** N/A | for $0 |

## ✱ FleetBoston Financial Corp. ♥

**FBF/NYSE** | **Banking** | **Shares to qualify:** 1
H: 43.99 | One Federal St. | **Safekeeping:** No
L: 31.75 | Boston. MA 02110-2010 | **Accepts foreign:** No
**Rec:** 38.42 | | **Auto. inv.:** No
| First Chicago Trust      800-317-4445 | **Disc.:** No
**Div.:** 1.32 | $10 - $10,000/quarter |
**Paid on:** | Every 30 days beginning 1st bus. day |
1.4.7.10-1 | FEES: Div: $0!; Cash: $0!; Cert: $0!; Term: $0,Does not sell through the plan |
**Since:** 1791 | |

## ✱ Fleming Companies, Inc. ♥

**FLM/NYSE** | **Food marketing, distribution** | **Shares to qualify:** 1
H: 37.89 | Box 26647 | **Safekeeping:** Yes
L: 10.31 | Oklahoma City. OK 73126-0647 | **Accepts foreign:** Yes
**Rec:** 32.00 | | **Auto. inv.:** No
| First Chicago Trust      800-317-4445 | **Disc.:** Div 5% Cash: 0%
**Div.:** 0.08 | $25 - $5,000/quarter |
**Paid on:** | Every 30 days beginning 1/10 |
3.6.9.12-10 | FEES: Div: $0!; Cash: $0!; Cert: $0!; Term: $0; Sells within 10 bus. days, by mail or fax, at |
**Since:** 1917 | market, for 10¢/sh. |

## * Florida Public Utilities Co. ♥

**FPU/ASE**
H: 17.62
L: 13.75
**Rec:** 16.15
**Div.:** 0.74
**Paid on:**
1.4.7.10-1
**Since:** N/A

**Utility-electric, gas**

Box 3395
West Palm Beach. FL 33402-3395

American Stock Transfer      800-937-5449
$25 - $2,000/quarter
Every 90 days beginning 1/2

FEES: Div: $0!; Cash: $0!; Cert: $0!; Term: $2.50 ; Sells irregularly, by mail, at market, for $2.50

**Shares to qualify:** 1
**Safekeeping:** No
**Accepts foreign:** Yes
**Auto. inv.:** No
**Disc.:** No

---

## * Flowserve Corp. ♥

**FLS/NYSE**
H: 33.30
L: 15.68
**Rec:** 25.29
**Div.:** 0.56
**Paid on:**
3.6.9.12-10
**Since:** 1935

**Corrosion resist. equipment**

222 W. Las Colinas Blvd., Ste.1500
Irving. TX 75039

National City Bank      800-622-6757
$25 - $1,000/quarter
Every 90 days beginning 3/1

FEES: Div: $0; Cash: $0; Cert: $0; Term: $0; Sells weekly, by mail or fax, at market, for $3

**Shares to qualify:** 1
**Safekeeping:** Yes
**Accepts foreign:** Yes
**Auto. inv.:** No
**Disc.:** No

---

## * FNB Financial Services Corp. ♥

**FNBF/NASD**
H: 15.52
L: 9.56
**Rec:** 14.50
**Div.:** 0.52
**Paid on:**
3.6.9.12-31
**Since:** N/A

**Banking**

Box 2037
Reidsville. NC 27320

Registrar & Transfer      800-368-5948
$25 - $10,000/month
Every 30 days beginning 1/2

FEES: Div: $0; Cash: $0; Cert: $0; Term: $0; Sells within 10 bus. days, by mail, at market, for 6¢ to 12¢/sh.

**Shares to qualify:** 1
**Safekeeping:** Yes
**Accepts foreign:** Yes
**Auto. inv.:** No
**Disc.:** No

---

## * Foothill Independent Bancorp ♥

**FOOT/NASD**
H: 13.25
L: 8.87
**Rec:** 13.00
**Div.:** 0.40
**Paid on:**
1.4.7.10-27
**Since:** N/A

**Banking**

510 South Grand Ave.
Glendora. CA 91741

Mellon Inv. Svcs.      800-356-2017
$100 - $10,000/quarter
Every 30 days beginning 1/27

FEES: Div: $0; Cash: $0; Cert: $0; Term: $0; Sells weekly, by mail, at market, for $15

**Shares to qualify:** 1
**Safekeeping:** Yes
**Accepts foreign:** No
**Auto. inv.:** No
**Disc.:** No

---

## * Ford Motor Co. ⊗

**F/NYSE**
H: 31.42
L: 21.68
**Rec:** 24.77
**Div.:** 1.20
**Paid on:**
3.6.9.12-1
**Since:** 1983

**Automotive**

The American Rd., Box 1899
Dearborn. MI 48121-1899

First Chicago Trust      800-279-1237
$50 - $250,000/year
Every 7 days beginning varies

FEES: Div: 5% to $5 + 3¢/sh.; Cash: $5 + 3¢/sh.; Auto. Inv.: $1 + 3¢/sh.; Cert: $0; Term: $0; Sells daily, by phone, mail, fax, or Internet, at avg. price, for $15 + 12¢/sh.

**Shares to qualify:** 1 /de ($1000)
**Safekeeping:** Yes
**Accepts foreign:** Yes
**Auto. inv.:** Yes
**Disc.:** No

---

## * Fortune Brands ♥

**FO/NYSE**
H: 38.49
L: 23.50
**Rec:** 37.30
**Div.:** 0.96
**Paid on:**
3.6.9.12-1
**Since:** 1905

**Consumer products**

300 Tower Pkwy.
Lincolnshire. IL 60069-3665

Bank of New York      800-225-2719
$50 - $15,000/quarter
Every 30 days beginning 1/2

FEES: Div: $0!; Cash: $0!; Cert: $0!; Term: $0; Sells Friday, by mail, at market, for 10¢/sh.

**Shares to qualify:** 1
**Safekeeping:** Yes
**Accepts foreign:** Yes
**Auto. inv.:** No
**Disc.:** No

---

## * Foster Wheeler Ltd. ♥

**FWC/NYSE**
H: 18.75
L: 3.93
**Rec:** 7.36
**Div.:** 0.24
**Paid on:**
3.6.9.12-15
**Since:** 1960

**Engineering, construction**

Perryville Corp. Park
Clinton. NJ 08809-4000

Mellon Inv. Svcs.      800-851-9677
$10 - $unlimited
Every 30 days beginning 1/4

FEES: Div: $0!; Cash: $0!; Cert: $0!; Term: $3.50 + comm.; Sells within 5 bus. days, by mail or phone, at market, for $3.50 + comm.

**Shares to qualify:** 1
**Safekeeping:** No
**Accepts foreign:** Yes
**Auto. inv.:** No
**Disc.:** No

---

* DRIP enrollment through Temper Enrollment Service (see page 180).      **85**

## ✱ Four Oaks Fincorp, Inc. ♥

**FOFN/OTC**
H: 26.87
L: 20.00
**Rec:** 24.00
**Div.:** 0.36
**Paid on:**
3.6.9.12-8
**Since:** N/A

Bank holding company
6144 U.S. 301 South, Box 309
Four Oaks. NC 27524
Branch Banking & Trust    800-213-4314
$20 - $500/quarter
Every 90 days beginning 3/8
FEES: Div: $0!; Cash: $0!; Cert: $0!; Term: $0!; Sells quarterly, by mail, at market, for $0!

**Shares to qualify:** 1
**Safekeeping:** Yes
**Accepts foreign:** Yes
**Auto. inv.:** No
**Disc.:** No

---

## ✱ FPL Group, Inc. ♥

**FPL/NYSE**
H: 73.00
L: 52.12
**Rec:** 53.40
**Div.:** 2.24
**Paid on:**
2.5.8.11-15
**Since:** 1944

Utility-electric
700 Universe Blvd., Box 14000
Juno Beach. FL 33408-0420
Boston Eq.    888-218-4392
$100 - $100,000/year
Every 90 days beginning 2/15
FEES: Div: $0!; Cash: $0!; Cert: $0!; Term: $0; Sells weekly, by mail or phone, at market, for 4¢/sh.

**Shares to qualify:** 1
**Safekeeping:** Yes
**Accepts foreign:** Yes
**Auto. inv.:** No
**Disc.:** No

---

## ✱ Franklin Bank ♥

**FSVB/NASD**
H: 17.00
L: 7.93
**Rec:** 16.75
**Div.:** 0.28
**Paid on:**
2.5.8.11-20
**Since:** N/A

Banking
24725 W. Twelve Mile Rd., Box 5006
Southfield. MI 48086-5006
BankBoston    800-257-1770
$100 - $5,000/quarter
Every 90 days beginning 2/20
FEES: Div: $0!; Cash: $0!; Cert: $0!; Term: $10 + comm.; Sells within 3 bus. days, by mail, at market, for $10 + comm.

**Shares to qualify:** 1
**Safekeeping:** Yes
**Accepts foreign:** Yes
**Auto. inv.:** No
**Disc.:** No

---

## ✱ Franklin Resources, Inc. ♥

**BEN/NYSE**
H: 48.30
L: 33.93
**Rec:** 42.76
**Div.:** 0.26
**Paid on:**
1.4.7.10-15
**Since:** 1981

Financial
777 Mariners Island Blvd.
San Mateo. CA 94404
Bank of New York    800-524-4458
$100 - $50,000/month
Every 30 days beginning 1/15
FEES: Div: $0!; Cash: $0!; Cert: $0!; Term: $3; Sells weekly, by mail or fax, at market, for $3 + comm.

**Shares to qualify:** 1
**Safekeeping:** Yes
**Accepts foreign:** Yes
**Auto. inv.:** No
**Disc.:** No

---

## ✱ Freddie Mac ⊗

**FRE/NYSE**
H: 70.35
L: 40.62
**Rec:** 68.75
**Div.:** 0.80
**Paid on:**
3.6.9.12-31
**Since:** N/A

Mortgage lending
8200 Jones Branch Dr.
McLean. VA 22102
First Chicago Trust    800-519-3111
$25 - $250,000/year
Every 5 days beginning varies
FEES: Div: $0!; Cash: $5 + 3¢/sh.; Auto. Inv.: $2 + 3¢/sh.; Cert: $0!; Term: $15 + 12¢/sh.; Sells daily, by phone, mail, fax, or Internet, at market, for $15 + 12¢/sh.

**Shares to qualify:** 1 /de ($250)
**Safekeeping:** Yes
**Accepts foreign:** Yes
**Auto. inv.:** Yes
**Disc.:** No

---

## Frontier Insurance Group, Inc.

**FTER/OTC**
H: .87
L: 0.01
**Rec:** 0.02
**Div.:** 0.00
**Paid on:**
DIV. SUSP.
**Since:** --

Property and casualty insurance
195 Lake Louise Marie Rd.
Rock Hill. NY 12775
American Stock Transfer    800-278-4353
$25 - $10,000/investment
Every 7 days beginning varies
FEES: Div: $0; Cash: $2.50 + 10¢/sh.; Auto. Inv.: $2.50 + 10¢/sh.; Cert: $0; Term: $0; Sells weekly, by mail, at market, for $7.50 + 10¢/sh.

**Shares to qualify:** 1 /de ($250)
**Safekeeping:** Yes
**Accepts foreign:** Yes
**Auto. inv.:** Yes
**Disc.:** No

---

## ✱ Fuller (H.B.) ♥

**FULL/NASD**
H: 54.68
L: 28.12
**Rec:** 52.45
**Div.:** 0.86
**Paid on:**
2.5.8.11-10
**Since:** 1953

Chemicals
Box 64683
St. Paul. MN 55164-0683
Wells Fargo Bank    800-468-9716
$25 - $6,000/month
Every 30 days beginning 1/10
FEES: Div: $0!; Cash: $0; Auto. Inv.: $0; Cert: $0; Term: $0; Sells daily, by mail, at market, for $10 + 10¢/sh.

**Shares to qualify:** 1
**Safekeeping:** Yes
**Accepts foreign:** Yes
**Auto. inv.:** Yes
**Disc.:** Div: 3% Cash: 0%

---

## ✱ **Fulton Bank ♥**

**FULT/NASD** | **Banking**
H: 23.00
L: 18.27
**Rec:** 22.35

Box 4887
Lancaster. PA 17604-4887

**Div.:** 0.68
**Paid on:**
1.4.7.10-15
**Since:**1920

Fulton Bank    800-626-0255
$25 - $5,000/month
Every 30 days beginning 1/15
FEES: Div $0!; Cash: $0!; Cert: $0!; Term: $0!; Sells within 15 days, by mail, at market, for $35 + 10¢/sh.

**Shares to qualify:** 1
**Safekeeping:** Yes
**Accepts foreign:** Yes
**Auto. inv.:** No
**Disc.:** No

---

## ✱ **GA Financial, Inc. ♥**

**GAF/ASE** | **Banking**
H: 17.00
L: 12.12
**Rec:** 16.35

4750 Clairton Blvd.
Pittsburgh. PA 15236

**Div.:** 0.72
**Paid on:**
2.5.8.11-21
**Since:**1996

Registrar & Transfer    800-368-5948
$100 - $2,500/quarter
Every 90 days beginning 2/20
FEES: Div: $0!; Cash: $0!; Cert: $0!; Term: $20; Sells daily, by mail, at market, for $20

**Shares to qualify:** 50
**Safekeeping:** Yes
**Accepts foreign:** Yes
**Auto. inv.:** No
**Disc.:** No

---

## ✱ **Gabelli Convertible Securities Fund, Inc.**

**GCV/NYSE** | **Closed-end fund**
H: 11.60
L: 8.62
**Rec:** 11.10

One Corporate Ctr.
Rve. NY 10580-1434

**Div.:** 0.80
**Paid on:**
3.6.9.12-28
**Since:**1989

State St. Bank    800-336-6983
$250 - $10,000/month
Every 15 days beginning 1/2
FEES: Div: $0; Cash: 75¢ + comm.; Cert: $0; Term: $0; Sells daily, by mail or phone, at avg. price, for $2.50 + 10¢/sh.

**Shares to qualify:** 1
**Safekeeping:** Yes
**Accepts foreign:** Yes
**Auto. inv.:** No
**Disc.:** No

---

## ✱ **Gabelli Equity Trust Inc.**

**GAB/NYSE** | **Closed-end fund**
H: 12.68
L: 10.00
**Rec:** 11.11

One Corporate Ctr.
Rve. NY 10580-1434

**Div.:** 1.08
**Paid on:**
3.6.9.12-27
**Since:**1986

State St. Bank    800-336-6983
$250 - $10,000/month
Every 30 days beginning 1/15
FEES: Div: $0; Cash: 75¢ + comm.; Cert: $0; Term: $0; Sells daily, by phone or mail, at market, for $2.50 + 10¢/sh.

**Shares to qualify:** 1
**Safekeeping:** Yes
**Accepts foreign:** Yes
**Auto. inv.:** No
**Disc.:** No

---

## ✱ **Gabelli Global Multimedia Trust**

**GGT/NYSE** | **Closed-end fund**
H: 14.75
L: 9.32
**Rec:** 10.00

One Corporate Ctr.
Rve. NY 10580-1434

**Div.:** 0.01
**Paid on:**
12/28
**Since:**1986

State St. Bank    800-336-6983
$250 - $10,000/month
Every 15 days beginning 1/1
FEES: Div: $0; Cash: 75¢ + comm.; Cert: $0; Term: $0; Sells daily, by mail or phone, at avg. price, for $2.50 + 10¢/sh.

**Shares to qualify:** 1
**Safekeeping:** Yes
**Accepts foreign:** Yes
**Auto. inv.:** No
**Disc.:** No

---

## ✱ **Gannett Co., Inc. ♥**

**GCI/NYSE** | **Publishing, broadcasting**
H: 70.02
L: 48.37
**Rec:** 67.21

1100 Wilson Blvd.
Arlington. VA 22234

**Div.:** 0.88
**Paid on:**
1.4.7.10-1
**Since:**1929

Wells Fargo Bank    800-778-3299
$10 - $5,000/month
Every 30 days beginning 1/2
FEES: Div: $0!; Cash: $0!; Auto. Inv.: $0; Cert: $0!; Term: $0; Sells daily, by mail or fax, at market, for $10 + 10¢/sh.

**Shares to qualify:** 1
**Safekeeping:** Yes
**Accepts foreign:** Yes
**Auto. inv.:** Yes
**Disc.:** No

---

## ✱ **Gardner Denver Inc. ⊗**

**GDI/NYSE** | **Capital goods**
H: 23.70
L: 14.43
**Rec:** 22.80

1800 Gardner Exp.
Quincv. IL 62301

**Div.:** 0.00
**Paid on:**
DIV. SUSP.
**Since:**--

First Chicago Trust    800-317-4445
$25 - $150,000/year
Every 7 days beginning varies
FEES: Div: n/o; Cash: $5 + 12¢/sh.; Auto. Inv.: $5 to $20 +12¢/sh.; Cert: $0; Term: $0; Sells daily, by mail or phone, at avg. price, for $10 + 12¢/sh.

**Shares to qualify:** 1
**Safekeeping:** Yes
**Accepts foreign:** Yes
**Auto. inv.:** Yes
**Disc.:** No

---

✱ DRIP enrollment through Temper Enrollment Service (see page 180).    **87**

## ✱ GATX Corp. ♥

**GMT/NYSE** — Railcar leasing equip. financing

H: 50.50
L: 36.31
**Rec:** 40.05

**Div.:** 1.24
**Paid on:**
3.6.9.12-31
**Since:**1911

500 West Monroe St.
Chicago. IL 60661-3676

Mellon Inv. Svcs.     800-851-9677
$25 - $36,000/year
Every 30 days beginning 1/30

FEES: Div: $0!; Cash: $0!; Cert: $0!; Term: $0; Sells weekly, by mail or phone, at avg. price, for $0!

Shares to qualify: 1
Safekeeping: Yes
Accepts foreign: Yes
Auto. inv.:No
Disc.: No

---

## ✱ GB&T Bancshares, Inc. ♥

**GBTB/NASD** — Banking

H: 20.00
L: 13.65
**Rec:** 17.50

**Div.:** 0.32
**Paid on:**
1.4.7.10-30
**Since:**N/A

500 Jesse Jewell Pkwy., Box 2760
Gainesville. GA  30503

Registrar & Transfer     800-368-5948
$25 - $2,500/quarter
Every 90 days beginning 1/30

FEES: Div: $0; Cash: $0; Cert: $0; Term: $0,Does not sell through the plan

Shares to qualify: 1
Safekeeping: No
Accepts foreign: No
Auto. inv.:No
Disc.: No

---

## ✱ GenCorp Inc. ♥

**GY/NYSE** — Aerospace, auto, & polymer products

H: 14.25
L: 6.87
**Rec:** 13.30

**Div.:** 0.12
**Paid on:**
2.5.8.11-31
**Since:**1937

Box 537012
Sacramento. CA  95853-7012

Bank of New York     800-524-4458
$50 - $10,000/month
Every 7 days beginning varies

FEES: Div: $0!; Cash: $0!; Auto. Inv.: $0; Cert: $5; Term: $0; Sells weekly, by mail, at market, for $5 + 10¢/sh.

Shares to qualify: 1 /de ($500)
Safekeeping: Yes
Accepts foreign: Yes
Auto. inv.:Yes
Disc.: No

---

## ✱ General Electric ⊗

**GE/NYSE** — Elec. equip., broadcasting & fin'l serv.

H: 60.50
L: 36.42
**Rec:** 42.57

**Div.:** 0.64
**Paid on:**
1.4.7.10-25
**Since:**1899

1 River Rd., Bldg. 5, Rm. 5W
Schenectadv. NY  12345

Bank of New York     800-786-2543
$10 - $10,000/week
Every 7 days beginning Wednesday

FEES: Div: $0!; Cash: $3; Auto. Inv.: $1; Cert: $0!; Term: $0; Sells biweekly, by mail or phone, at market price, for $10 + 15¢/sh.

Shares to qualify: 1 /de ($250)
Safekeeping: Yes
Accepts foreign: Yes
Auto. inv.:Yes
Disc.: No

---

## ✱ General Growth Properties ♥

**GGP/NYSE** — REIT

H: 39.36
L: 28.68
**Rec:** 37.35

**Div.:** 2.12
**Paid on:**
1.4.7.10-31
**Since:**1993

110 N. Wacker Dr.
Chicago. IL 60606

Mellon Inv. Svcs.     888-395-8037
$50 - $50,000/month
Every 30 days beginning 1/20

FEES: Div: $0!; Cash: $0!; Cert: $0!; Term: $15 + 12¢/sh.; Sells daily, by mail , at avg. price, for $15 + 12¢/sh.

Shares to qualify: 1 /de ($200)
Safekeeping: Yes
Accepts foreign: Yes
Auto. inv.:No
Disc.: No

---

## ✱ General Mills ♥

**GIS/NYSE** — Foods

H: 46.35
L: 31.37
**Rec:** 44.50

**Div.:** 1.10
**Paid on:**
2.5.8.11-1
**Since:**1928

Box 1113
Minneapolis. MN  55440-1113

Wells Fargo Bank     800-670-4763
$10 - $3,000/quarter
Every 30 days beginning 1/2

FEES: Div: $0!; Cash: $0!; Auto. Inv.: $0; Cert: $0!; Term: $10 + 5¢/sh. ; Sells daily, by mail or fax, at market, for $10 + 5¢/sh.

Shares to qualify: 1
Safekeeping: Yes
Accepts foreign: Yes
Auto. inv.:Yes
Disc.: No

---

## ✱ General Motors ♥

**GM/NYSE** — Automotive

H: 76.62
L: 48.43
**Rec:** 63.46

**Div.:** 2.00
**Paid on:**
3.6.9.12-10
**Since:**1917

300 Renaissance Ctr., Box 300, 482-C38-B71
Detroit. MI 48265-3000

Boston Eq.     800-331-9922
$25 - $150,000/year
Every 7 days beginning Tuesday

FEES: Div: $0!; Cash: $0!; Auto. Inv.: $2; Cert: $0!; Term: $15 + 7¢/sh.; Sells within 5 bus. days, by mail or phone, at avg. price, for $15 + 7¢/sh.

Shares to qualify: 1
Safekeeping: Yes
Accepts foreign: Yes
Auto. inv.:Yes
Disc.: No

---

✱ DRIP enrollment through Temper Enrollment Service (see page 180).     **88**

## ✻ Genuine Parts Co. ♥

**GPC/NYSE**

H: 34.56
L: 18.25
**Rec:** 33.25

**Div.:** 1.14
**Paid on:**
1.4.7.10-1
**Since:** 1948

**Distr. & retails auto parts, electronics**

2999 Circle 75 Pkwy.
Atlanta. GA 30339

SunTrust Bank, Atlanta    800-568-3476
$10 - $3,000/quarter
Every 30 days beginning 1/2

FEES: Div: $0; Cash: $0; Cert: $0; Term: $0; Sells biweekly, by mail, at avg. price, for 9¢/sh.

**Shares to qualify:** 1
**Safekeeping:** Yes
**Accepts foreign:** No
**Auto. inv.:** No
**Disc.:** No

---

## ✻ Georgia-Pacific Group ⊗

**GP/NYSE**

H: 36.99
L: 19.31
**Rec:** 35.88

**Div.:** 0.50
**Paid on:**
3.6.9.12-10
**Since:** 1955

**Pulp, paper, and building products**

133 Peachtree St. N.E., Box 105605
Atlanta. GA 30348

First Chicago Trust    800-519-3111
$25 - $5,000/month
Every 30 days beginning 1/10

FEES: Div: 5% to $3; Cash: 5% to $3; Auto. Inv.: 5% to $3 + $2 comm.; Cert: $0; Term: $10 + 12¢/sh.; Sells daily, by mail, fax , or phone, at avg. price, for $10 + 12¢/sh.

**Shares to qualify:** 1
**Safekeeping:** Yes
**Accepts foreign:** Yes
**Auto. inv.:** Yes
**Disc.:** No

---

## ✻ German American Bancorp ♥

**GABC/NASD**

H: 18.25
L: 11.60
**Rec:** 17.42

**Div.:** 0.56
**Paid on:**
2.5.8.11-20
**Since:** N/A

**Banking**

Box 810
Jasper. IN 47547-0810

UMB Bank, N.A.    800-884-4225
$100 - $100,000/year
Every 30 days beginning 1/15

FEES: Div: $0!; Cash: $0!; Auto. Inv.: $0; Cert: $0!; Term: $5; Sells monthly, by mail, at market, for $5

**Shares to qualify:** 1 /de ($100)
**Safekeeping:** Yes
**Accepts foreign:** Yes
**Auto. inv.:** Yes
**Disc.:** No

---

## ✻ Germany Fund (The)

**GER/NYSE**

H: 14.50
L: 7.75
**Rec:** 8.03

**Div.:** 0.02
**Paid on:**
9. 11-13
**Since:** N/A

**Closed-end fund**

c/o Deutsche Bk.Securities, 280 Park Ave., 7-East
New York. NY 10017

Investors Bank & Trust Co.    800-356-2754
$100 - $36,000/year
Every 30 days beginning 1/15

FEES: Div: $0!; Cash: comm.; Cert: $0!; Term: $0,Does not sell through the plan

**Shares to qualify:** 1
**Safekeeping:** Yes
**Accepts foreign:** Yes
**Auto. inv.:** No
**Disc.:** No

---

## ✻ Gillette ⊗

**G/NYSE**

H: 37.18
L: 24.50
**Rec:** 27.55

**Div.:** 0.65
**Paid on:**
3.6.9.12-5
**Since:** 1917

**Consumer products**

Prudential Twr. Bldg.
Boston. MA 02199

BankBoston    888-218-2841
$100 - $120,000/year
Every 7 days beginning varies

FEES: Div: $0 to $1.25 + 8¢/sh.; Cash: $5 + 8¢/sh.; Auto. Inv.: $2.50 + 8¢/sh.; Cert: $0; Term: $0; Sells daily, by mail, fax , or phone, at avg. price, for $10 + 15¢/sh.

**Shares to qualify:** 10 /de ($1000)
**Safekeeping:** Yes
**Accepts foreign:** Yes
**Auto. inv.:** Yes
**Disc.:** No

---

## ✻ Glacier Bancorp, Inc. ♥

**GBCI/NASD**

H: 19.75
L: 11.00
**Rec:** 18.31

**Div.:** 0.60
**Paid on:**
1.4.7.10-23
**Since:** 1984

**Bank holding company**

49 Commons Loop
Kalispell. MT 59901

Davidson Trust Co.    800-634-5526
$100 - $2,000/quarter
Every 90 days beginning 1/22

FEES: Div: $0!; Cash: $0!; Cert: $0!; Term: $3.50; Sells irregularly, by mail, at market, for $5 + comm.

**Shares to qualify:** 1
**Safekeeping:** No
**Accepts foreign:** Yes
**Auto. inv.:** No
**Disc.:** No

---

## ✻ Glenborough Realty Trust ⊗

**GLB/NYSE**

H: 20.150
L: 14.75
**Rec:** 20.06

**Div.:** 1.68
**Paid on:**
1.4.7.10-10
**Since:** 1996

**Real estate operations**

400 South El Camino Real
San Mateo. CA 94402

Registrar & Transfer    800-338-9151
$100 - $10,000/transaction
Every 7 days beginning varies

FEES: Div: comm.; Cash: $5 + comm.; Auto. Inv.: $0; Cert: $0; Term: $0; Sells daily, by mail, fax, or e-mail, at avg. price, for $7.50 + comm.

**Shares to qualify:** 1 /de ($250)
**Safekeeping:** Yes
**Accepts foreign:** Yes
**Auto. inv.:** Yes
**Disc.:** No

---

## Glimcher Realty Trust ♥

**✳**

**GRT/NYSE**
H: 19.00
L: 11.87
**Rec:** 18.89
**Div.:** 1.92
**Paid on:**
1.4.7.10-15
**Since:** N/A

REIT
20 South Third St.
Columbus. OH 43215-3602
Computershare Investor Svcs.    800-738-4931
$100 - $3,000/quarter
Every 30 days beginning 1/15
FEES: Div: $0; Cash: $0; Cert: $0; Term: $10 + 10¢/sh.; Sells weekly, by mail, at market, for $10 + 10¢/sh.

**Shares to qualify:** 1 /de ($100)
**Safekeeping:** Yes
**Accepts foreign:** Yes
**Auto. inv.:** No
**Disc.:** Cash: 0%-3%

---

## Global Crossing Ltd. ♥

**✳**

**GX/NYSE**
H: 37.75
L: 5.00
**Rec:** 5.88
**Div.:** 0.00
**Paid on:**
N/0
**Since:** N/0

Telecommunications
360 N. Crescent Dr.
Beverly Hills. CA 90210
Boston Eq.    877-425-4259
$25 - $50,000/month
Every 30 days beginning 1/5
FEES: Div: n/o; Cash: $0!; Cert: $0!; Term: $10 + 15¢/sh.; Sells weekly, by mail, fax or phone, at market, for $10 + 15¢/sh.

**Shares to qualify:** 1
**Safekeeping:** Yes
**Accepts foreign:** Yes
**Auto. inv.:** No
**Disc.:** No

---

## Goodrich Corporation ♥

**✳**

**GR/NYSE**
H: 44.50
L: 32.37
**Rec:** 36.27
**Div.:** 1.10
**Paid on:**
1.4.7.10-1
**Since:** 1912

Chemicals & aerospace
4 Coliseum Ctr., 2730 W. Tyvola Rd.
Charlotte. NC 28217-4578
Bank of New York    800-524-4458
$25 - $1,000/month
Every 30 days beginning 1/30
FEES: Div: $0!; Cash: $0!; Cert: $0!; Term: $2 ; Sells weekly, by mail, at market, for $2 + 3¢ to 5¢/sh.

**Shares to qualify:** 1
**Safekeeping:** Yes
**Accepts foreign:** Yes
**Auto. inv.:** No
**Disc.:** No

---

## Goodyear Tire & Rubber

**✳**

**GT/NYSE**
H: 32.10
L: 15.60
**Rec:** 27.48
**Div.:** 1.20
**Paid on:**
3.6.9.12-15
**Since:** 1929

Tire and rubber mfr.
1144 East Market St.
Akron. OH 44316-0001
First Chicago Trust    800-317-4445
$25 - $150,000/year
Every 7 days beginning Friday
FEES: Div: $1 + 3¢/sh.; Cash: 3¢/sh.; Auto. Inv.: $0; Cert: $0!; Term: $15 + 15¢/sh.; Sells daily, by mail or phone, at avg. price, for $15 + 15¢/sh.

**Shares to qualify:** 1 /de ($250)
**Safekeeping:** Yes
**Accepts foreign:** Yes
**Auto. inv.:** Yes
**Disc.:** No

---

## Gorman-Rupp Co. ♥

**✳**

**GRC/ASE**
H: 28.75
L: 15.00
**Rec:** 24.95
**Div.:** 0.64
**Paid on:**
3.6.9.12-10
**Since:** 1968

Mfr. const. & ind'l pumps & parts
Box 1217
Mansfield. OH 44901-1217
National City Bank    800-622-6757
$20 - $1,000/month
Every 30 days beginning 1/10
FEES: Div: $0; Cash: $0; Cert: $0; Term: $0; Sells weekly, by mail or fax, at market, for comm.

**Shares to qualify:** 1
**Safekeeping:** Yes
**Accepts foreign:** Yes
**Auto. inv.:** No
**Disc.:** No

---

## Grace (W.R.) ♥

**✳**

**GRA/NYSE**
H: 10.12
L: 1.25
**Rec:** 1.65
**Div.:** 0.00
**Paid on:**
DIV. SUSP.
**Since:** --

Chemicals
1750 Clint Moore Rd.
Boca Raton. FL 33487-2707
Mellon Inv. Svcs.    800-648-8392
$100 - $100,000/year
Every 30 days beginning 1/10
FEES: Div: $0; Cash: $0; Cert: $5; Term: $5 + $15 + comm.; Sells weekly, by mail, at market, for $15 + 12¢/sh.

**Shares to qualify:** 50
**Safekeeping:** Yes
**Accepts foreign:** Yes
**Auto. inv.:** No
**Disc.:** No

---

## Graco, Inc. ♥

**✳**

**GGG/NYSE**
H: 34.89
L: 20.12
**Rec:** 34.15
**Div.:** 0.40
**Paid on:**
2.5.8.11-1
**Since:** 1970

Mfr. spray equipment
Box 1441
Minneapolis. MN 55440-1441
Wells Fargo Bank    800-468-9716
$25 - $1,000/quarter
Every 30 days beginning 1/15
FEES: Div: $0!; Cash: $0!; Cert: $0!; Term: $0; Sells daily, by mail, at market, for $10 + 10¢/sh.

**Shares to qualify:** 1
**Safekeeping:** Yes
**Accepts foreign:** Yes
**Auto. inv.:** No
**Disc.:** No

---

## Granite Construction Inc. ⊗

**GVA/NYSE**
H: 31.10
L: 14.00
Rec: 23.24
Div.: 0.32
Paid on:
1.4.7.10-20
Since: 1990

**Construction contractrators**
P.O. Box 50085
Watsonville, CA 95077-5085
Mellon Inv. Svcs.    888-884-5090
$100 - $10,000/month
Every 30 days beginning 1/15

Shares to qualify: 1 /de ($3000)
Safekeeping: Yes
Accepts foreign: Yes
Auto. inv.: No
Disc.: No

FEES: Div: $0; Cash: $5 + 12¢/sh.; Cert: $0; Term: $15 + 12¢/sh.; Sells weekly, by mail, at market, for $15 + 12¢/sh.

---

## Gray Communications Systems, Inc.-B

**GCSB/NYSE**
H: 17.65
L: 9.62
Rec: 14.64
Div.: 0.08
Paid on:
3.6.9.12-28
Since: 1992

**TV broadcasting, newspaper publishing**
Box 48
Albany, GA 31702-0048
Mellon Inv. Svcs.    888-835-2869
$100 - $10,000/month
Every 7 days beginning varies

Shares to qualify: 1 /de ($250)
Safekeeping: Yes
Accepts foreign: Yes
Auto. inv.: Yes
Disc.: No

FEES: Div: $0; Cash: 12¢/sh.; Auto. Inv.: 12¢/sh.; Cert: $0; Term: $15 + 12¢/sh.; Sells daily, by mail or phone, at market, for $15 + 12¢/sh.

---

## Great Atlantic & Pacific Tea Co., Inc. (The)

**GAP/NYSE**
H: 18.56
L: 6.00
Rec: 17.92
Div.: 0.40
Paid on:
2.5.8.11-3
Since: 1986

**Retail food**
2 Paragon Dr.
Montvale, NJ 07645
American Stock Transfer    800-937-5449
$25 - $10,000/investment
Every day days beginning daily

Shares to qualify: 1 /de ($100)
Safekeeping: Yes
Accepts foreign: Yes
Auto. inv.: Yes
Disc.: No

FEES: Div: 2% to $1.50 + 10¢/sh.; Cash: $2.50 + 10¢/sh.; Auto. Inv.: $2.50 + 10¢/sh.; Cert: $0; Term: $7.50 + 10¢/sh.; Sells daily, by phone, mail, fax, or Internet, at market, for $7.50 + 10¢/sh.

---

## Great Southern Bancorp, Inc.

**GSBC/NASD**
H: 30.74
L: 14.62
Rec: 30.49
Div.: 0.50
Paid on:
1.4.7.10-24
Since: N/A

**Savings and trust service**
Box 9009
Springfield, MO 65808
Registrar & Transfer    800-368-5948
$25 - $2,500/quarter
Every 90 days beginning 1/2

Shares to qualify: 1
Safekeeping: Yes
Accepts foreign: Yes
Auto. inv.: No
Disc.: No

FEES: Div: 5% to $2.50; Cash: 5% to $2.50; Cert: $0; Term: $0,Does not sell through the plan

---

## Greater Bay Bancorp ♥

**GBBK/NASD**
H: 43.56
L: 20.00
Rec: 26.40
Div.: 0.40
Paid on:
1.4.7.10-15
Since: N/A

**Bank holding company**
400 Emerson St., 3rd Fl.
Palo Alto, CA 94301
Wells Fargo Bank    800-468-9716
$50 - $1,000/month
Every 30 days beginning 1/15

Shares to qualify: 25
Safekeeping: Yes
Accepts foreign: Yes
Auto. inv.: No
Disc.: No

FEES: Div: $0; Cash: $0; Cert: $0; Term: $10 + 15¢/sh.; Sells weekly, by mail, at avg. price, for $10 + 15¢/sh.

---

## Greater Community Bancorp ♥

**GFLS/NASD**
H: 12.38
L: 7.14
Rec: 11.18
Div.: 0.32
Paid on:
1.4.7.10-31
Since: 2000

**Bank holding co.**
55 Union Blvd.
Totowa, NJ 07512
First City Transfer Co.    732-906-9227
$25 - $3,000/quarter
Every 90 days beginning 1/31

Shares to qualify: 1
Safekeeping: Yes
Accepts foreign: Yes
Auto. inv.: No
Disc.: No

FEES: Div: $0; Cash: comm.; Cert: $0; Term: $0; Sells within 3 weeks, by mail, at avg. price, for $0

---

## Green Mountain Power ♥

**GMP/NYSE**
H: 19.50
L: 6.75
Rec: 17.00
Div.: 0.55
Paid on:
3.6.9.12-30
Since: 1951

**Utility-electric**
163 Acorn Lane
Colchester, VT 05446
Mellon Inv. Svcs.    800-851-9677
$50 - $40,000/year
Every 30 days beginning 1/30

Shares to qualify: 1 /de
Safekeeping: Yes
Accepts foreign: Yes
Auto. inv.: No
Disc.: Div 5% Cash: 0%

FEES: Div: $0!; Cash: $0!; Cert: $0!; Term: $0; Sells daily, by mail or phone, at market, for comm.

---

✳ DRIP enrollment through Temper Enrollment Service (see page 180).

## Greenpoint Financial ⊗

**GPT/NYSE**
**H:** 44.19
**L:** 24.18
**Rec:** 43.22
**Div.:** 1.00
**Paid on:**
3.6.9.12-5
**Since:** 1994

Savings bank
90 Park Ave.
New York. NY 10016
Mellon Inv. Svcs.       888-224-2741
$100 - $10,000/month
Every 7 days beginning varies
FEES: Div $0!; Cash: $5 + 12¢/sh.; Auto. Inv.: $5 + 12¢/sh.; Cert: $0; Term: $0; Sells weekly, by mail or phone, at market, for $15 + 12¢/sh.

**Shares to qualify:** 1 /de ($2000)
**Safekeeping:** Yes
**Accepts foreign:** Yes
**Auto. inv.:** Yes
**Disc.:** No

---

## Greif Brothers Corp.-A ♥

**GBCOA/NAS**
**H:** 34.49
**L:** 23.00
**Rec:** 31.77
**Div.:** 0.56
**Paid on:**
1.4.7.10-1
**Since:** 1926

Shipping containers
425 Winter Rd.
Delaware. OH 43015
National City Bank       800-622-6757
$100 - $1,000/month
Every 30 days beginning 1/15
FEES: Div: $0!; Cash: $0!; Cert: $0; Term: $0; Sells weekly, by mail, at market, for comm.

**Shares to qualify:** 1
**Safekeeping:** Yes
**Accepts foreign:** No
**Auto. inv.:** No
**Disc.:** No

---

## Guaranty Federal Bancshares Inc. ♥

**GFED/NASD**
**H:** 13.00
**L:** 10.60
**Rec:** 12.60
**Div.:** 0.48
**Paid on:**
1.4.7.10-15
**Since:** N/A

Bank holding co.
1341 West Battlefield
Springfield. MO 65807
Registrar & Transfer       800-368-5948
$100 - $5,000/semiannually
Every 180 days beginning 1/16
FEES: Div: $0!; Cash: $0!; Cert: $0!; Term: $10; Sells weekly, by mail, at market, for $10 + comm.

**Shares to qualify:** 50
**Safekeeping:** Yes
**Accepts foreign:** Yes
**Auto. inv.:** No
**Disc.:** No

---

## Guidant Corp. ⊗

**GDT/NYSE**
**H:** 71.81
**L:** 26.90
**Rec:** 32.11
**Div.:** 0.00
**Paid on:**
DIV. SUSP.
**Since:** --

Design & mfr. medical devices
111 Monument Cir., 29th Fl., Box 44906
Indianapolis. IN 46204-5129
First Chicago Trust       888-756-3638
$50 - $unlimited
Every 7 days beginning varies
FEES: Div: $0; Cash: 5% to $7.50 + 3¢/sh.; Auto. Inv.: $1 + 3¢/sh.; Cert: $0; Term: $15 + 12¢/sh.; Sells daily, by phone, mail, fax, or Internet, at avg. price, for $15 + 12¢/sh.

**Shares to qualify:** 1 /de ($250)
**Safekeeping:** Yes
**Accepts foreign:** Yes
**Auto. inv.:** Yes
**Disc.:** No

---

## Habersham Bancorp ♥

**HABC/NASD**
**H:** 14.50
**L:** 9.62
**Rec:** 13.01
**Div.:** 0.24
**Paid on:**
3.6.9.12-15
**Since:** N/A

Bank holding company
Box 1980
Cornelia. GA 30531
SunTrust Bank, Atlanta       800-568-3476
$10 - $3,000/quarter
Every 90 days beginning 3/15
FEES: Div: $0!; Cash: $0!; Cert: $0!; Term: comm.; Sells weekly, by mail, at market, for comm.

**Shares to qualify:** 1
**Safekeeping:** Yes
**Accepts foreign:** Yes
**Auto. inv.:** No
**Disc.:** No

---

## Hancock Holding Co. ♥

**HBHC/NASD**
**H:** 44.50
**L:** 28.75
**Rec:** 43.24
**Div.:** 1.12
**Paid on:**
3.6.9.12-15
**Since:** 1967

Banking
Box 4019
Gulfport. MS 39502-4019
Hancock Bank Trust Dept.       228-868-4414
$50 - $5,000/quarter
Every 90 days beginning 3/15
FEES: Div: $0; Cash: $0; Auto. Inv.: $0; Cert: $0; Term: $0; Sells weekly, by mail, at market, for comm.

**Shares to qualify:** 1
**Safekeeping:** No
**Accepts foreign:** No
**Auto. inv.:** Yes
**Disc.:** No

---

## Hanson plc

**HAN/NYSE**
**H:** 38.20
**L:** 22.31
**Rec:** 37.15
**Div.:** 0.71
**Paid on:**
VARIES
**Since:** 1997

Conglomerates
1350 Campus Pkwy.
Neptune. NJ 07753
Citibank       877-248-4237
$50 - $60,000/year
Every 30 days beginning 1/2
FEES: Div: 6¢/sh.; Cash: $2.50 + 6¢/sh.; Cert: $0; Term: $3 + 6¢/sh.; Sells monthly, by mail, at market, for $2.50 + 6¢/sh.

**Shares to qualify:** 1
**Safekeeping:** Yes
**Accepts foreign:** Yes
**Auto. inv.:** No
**Disc.:** No

---

## Harland (John H.) Co. ⊗

**JH/NYSE**
**Printer, financial services provider**

H: 24.00
L: 12.25
**Rec:** 22.00

**Div.:** 0.30
**Paid on:**
3.6.9.12-2
**Since:** 1953

Box 105250
Atlanta, GA 30348

First Chicago Trust     800-519-3111
$50 - $250,000/year
Every 7 days beginning varies

**Shares to qualify:** 1 /de ($500)
**Safekeeping:** Yes
**Accepts foreign:** Yes
**Auto. inv.:** Yes
**Disc.:** No

FEES: Div: $0!; Cash: $5 + 3¢/sh.; Auto. Inv.: $2 + comm.; Cert: $0; Term: $0; Sells daily, by mail, fax , or phone, at avg. price, for $15 + 12¢/sh.

---

## Harley-Davidson ♥

**HDI/NYSE**
**Mfr. motorcycles**

H: 54.35
L: 34.25
**Rec:** 49.49

**Div.:** 0.12
**Paid on:**
3.6.9.12-26
**Since:** 1993

3700 W. Juneau Ave., Box 653
Milwaukee, WI 53201

Computershare Investor Svcs.     866-360-5339
$30 - $5,000/quarter
Every 30 days beginning 1/2

**Shares to qualify:** 1
**Safekeeping:** No
**Accepts foreign:** Yes
**Auto. inv.:** No
**Disc.:** No

FEES: Div: $0!; Cash: $0!; Cert: $0!; Term: $0; Sells daily, by mail or fax, at market, for 2¢ to 5¢/sh.

---

## Harleysville Group, Inc. ♥

**HGIC/NASD**
**Insurance, prop. & casualty**

H: 30.62
L: 18.25
**Rec:** 23.40

**Div.:** 0.56
**Paid on:**
3.6.9.12-30
**Since:** N/A

355 Maple Ave.
Harleysville, PA 19438-2297

Mellon Inv. Svcs.     800-851-9677
$100 - $25,000/year
Every 90 days beginning 3/30

**Shares to qualify:** 1
**Safekeeping:** No
**Accepts foreign:** No
**Auto. inv.:** No
**Disc.:** No

FEES: Div: $0!; Cash: $0!; Cert: $0; Term: comm.; Sells weekly, by mail or phone, at market, for comm.

---

## Harleysville Savings Financial Corp. ♥

**HARL/NASD**
**Savings bank**

H: 17.00
L: 14.12
**Rec:** 17.00

**Div.:** 0.48
**Paid on:**
2.5.8.11-24
**Since:** N/A

271 Main St.
Harleysville, PA 19438

Registrar & Transfer     800-368-5948
$250 - $2,500/quarter
Every 90 days beginning 2/24

**Shares to qualify:** 1
**Safekeeping:** Yes
**Accepts foreign:** Yes
**Auto. inv.:** No
**Disc.:** No

FEES: Div: $0!; Cash: $0!; Cert: $0!; Term: $5,Does not sell through the plan

---

## Harris Corp. ♥

**HRS/NYSE**
**Electronic sys., comm. & office equip.**

H: 33.25
L: 20.75
**Rec:** 29.88

**Div.:** 0.20
**Paid on:**
3.6.9.12
**Since:** 1945

1025 W. NASA Blvd.
Melbourne, FL 32919

Mellon Inv. Svcs.     800-313-9450
$10 - $5,000/quarter
Every 30 days beginning 1/15

**Shares to qualify:** 1
**Safekeeping:** Yes
**Accepts foreign:** Yes
**Auto. inv.:** Yes
**Disc.:** No

FEES: Div: $0!; Cash: $0!; Auto. Inv.: $0; Cert: $0!; Term: $0; Sells within 2 bus. days, by mail or phone, at market, for $0!

---

## Harsco Corp. ♥

**HSC/NYSE**
**Manufacturing & service**

H: 32.40
L: 17.68
**Rec:** 32.40

**Div.:** 0.96
**Paid on:**
2.5.8.11-15
**Since:** 1939

350 Poplar Church Rd., Box 8888
Camp Hill, PA 17001-8888

Mellon Inv. Svcs.     800-526-0801
$10 - $unlimited
Every 30 days beginning 1/15

**Shares to qualify:** 1
**Safekeeping:** Yes
**Accepts foreign:** Yes
**Auto. inv.:** No
**Disc.:** No

FEES: Div: $0!; Cash: $0!; Cert: $0!; Term: $5 + comm.; Sells only for termination, by mail or phone, at market, for $5 + comm.

---

## Hartford Financial Services Group Inc ♥

**HIG/NYSE**
**Multiline insurance**

H: 80.00
L: 53.50
**Rec:** 64.44

**Div.:** 1.00
**Paid on:**
1.4.7.10-1
**Since:** 1995

Hartford Plaza, HO-1-01
Hartford, CT 06115

Bank of New York     800-254-2823
$50 - $5,000/inv.
Every 7 days beginning Monday

**Shares to qualify:** 1
**Safekeeping:** Yes
**Accepts foreign:** Yes
**Auto. inv.:** No
**Disc.:** No

FEES: Div: $0!; Cash: $0!; Cert: $0!; Term: $0; Sells weekly, by mail, at market, for $3 + 7¢/sh.

---

✱ DRIP enrollment through Temper Enrollment Service (see page 180).     **93**

## Hartmarx Corp. ♥

**HMX/NYSE**
H: 3.85
L: 1.90
**Rec:** 1.90
**Div.:** 0.00
**Paid on:**
DIV. SUSP.
**Since:** --

**Apparel, retail clothing**

101 North Wacker Dr.
Chicago. IL 60606

First Chicago Trust     201-324-0498
$25 - $1,000/month
Every 30 days beginning 1/15

FEES: Div $0; Cash: $0; Cert: $0; Term: $0, Does not sell through the plan

**Shares to qualify:** 1
**Safekeeping:** No
**Accepts foreign:** Yes
**Auto. inv.:** No
**Disc.:** No

---

## ✱ Hasbro Inc. ♥

**HAS/NYSE**
H: 16.79
L: 8.37
**Rec:** 15.98
**Div.:** 0.12
**Paid on:**
2.5.8.11-15
**Since:** 1981

**Manufactures toys and games**

1027 Newport Ave., Box 1059
Pawtucket. RI 02862-1059

Boston Eq.     800-733-5001
$25 - $2,000/month
Every 30 days beginning 1/15

FEES: Div: $0!; Cash: $0!; Auto. Inv.: $0; Cert: $0!; Term: $0; Sells daily, by mail, at market, for $10 + 15¢/sh.

**Shares to qualify:** 1
**Safekeeping:** Yes
**Accepts foreign:** No
**Auto. inv.:** Yes
**Disc.:** No

---

## ✱ Hawaiian Electric Ind.

**HE/NYSE**
H: 40.09
L: 31.50
**Rec:** 39.92
**Div.:** 2.48
**Paid on:**
3.6.9.12-10
**Since:** 1901

**Utility-electric, holding co.**

Box 730
Honolulu. HI 96808-0730

Hawaiian Electric Industries Inc.     808-532-5841
$25 - $120,000/year
Every 15 days beginning 1/15 & 1/30

FEES: Div: 3¢/sh. + 50¢/qtr.; Cash: 3¢/sh.; Auto. Inv.: $0; Cert: $0; Term: $0; Sells weekly, by mail or fax, at market, for $15 + 3.2¢/sh.

**Shares to qualify:** 1 /de ($250)
**Safekeeping:** Yes
**Accepts foreign:** Yes
**Auto. inv.:** Yes
**Disc.:** No

---

## ✱ Health Care Property Investors, Inc. ♥

**HCP/NYSE**
H: 36.80
L: 26.12
**Rec:** 34.98
**Div.:** 3.08
**Paid on:**
2.5.8.11-20
**Since:** N/A

**REIT**

4675 MacArthur Ct., 9th Fl.
Newport Beach. CA 92660

Bank of New York     800-524-4458
$100 - $10,000/month
Every 30 days beginning 1/20

FEES: Div: $0!; Cash: $0!; Auto. Inv.: $0; Cert: $0!; Term: $0; Sells within 2 bus. days, by mail or phone, at avg. price, for $15 + 10¢/sh.

**Shares to qualify:** 1 /de ($750)
**Safekeeping:** Yes
**Accepts foreign:** Yes
**Auto. inv.:** Yes
**Disc.:** Div 0%-5%
Cash: 0%-5%

---

## ✱ Health Care REIT ♥

**HCN/NYSE**
H: 25.55
L: 15.93
**Rec:** 25.55
**Div.:** 2.34
**Paid on:**
2.5.8.11-20
**Since:** N/A

**REIT**

1 SeaGate, Ste.1500, Box 1475
Toledo. OH 43603-1475

Mellon Inv. Svcs.     888-216-7206
$50 - $5,000/quarter
Every 90 days beginning 2/20

FEES: Div: $0!; Cash: $0!; Cert: $0!; Term: $15 + comm.; Sells weekly, by mail, at market, for $15 + comm.

**Shares to qualify:** 1
**Safekeeping:** Yes
**Accepts foreign:** Yes
**Auto. inv.:** No
**Disc.:** Div 4% Cash: 4%

---

## ✱ Healthcare Realty Trust ♥

**HR/NYSE**
H: 27.56
L: 17.25
**Rec:** 27.23
**Div.:** 2.32
**Paid on:**
3.6.9.12-7
**Since:** 1993

**REIT**

3310 West End Ave., Ste.700
Nashville. TN 37203

BankBoston     781-575-3400
$25 - $5,000/quarter
Every 90 days beginning 3/7

FEES: Div: $0!; Cash: $0!; Cert: $0!; Term: $0, Does not sell through the plan

**Shares to qualify:** 1
**Safekeeping:** Yes
**Accepts foreign:** Yes
**Auto. inv.:** No
**Disc.:** Div 5% Cash: 0%

---

## ✱ Heinz (H.J.) ♥

**HNZ/NYSE**
H: 48.00
L: 34.00
**Rec:** 43.91
**Div.:** 1.57
**Paid on:**
1.4.7.10-10
**Since:** 1946

**Food processor**

Box 57
Pittsburgh. PA 15230-0057

Mellon Inv. Svcs.     800-253-3399
$50 - $10,000/month
Every 7 days beginning varies

FEES: Div: $0!; Cash: $0!; Auto. Inv.: $0; Cert: $0!; Term: $15 + 12¢/sh.; Sells weekly, by mail or phone, at market, for $15 + 12¢/sh.

**Shares to qualify:** 1 /de ($250)
**Safekeeping:** Yes
**Accepts foreign:** Yes
**Auto. inv.:** Yes
**Disc.:** No

---

## Hercules, Inc. ⊗

**HPC/NYSE**
H: 20.18
L: 10.27
**Rec:** 10.55
**Div.:** 0.00
**Paid on:**
DIV. SUSP.
**Since:** --

**Chemicals & plastics**
Hercules Plaza, 1313 N. Market St.
Wilmington, DE 19894-0001

Mellon Inv. Svcs.    800-237-9980
$50 - $2,000/month
Every 30 days beginning 1/30
FEES: Div: $0!; Cash: $5 + comm.; Cert: $0!; Term: $15 + comm.; Sells monthly, by mail or phone, at market, for $15 + comm.

**Shares to qualify:** 1
**Safekeeping:** No
**Accepts foreign:** No
**Auto. inv.:** No
**Disc.:** No

---

## Herman Miller, Inc. ⊗

**MLHR/NAS**
H: 33.93
L: 18.37
**Rec:** 24.91
**Div.:** 0.14
**Paid on:**
1.4.7.10-15
**Since:** 1945

**Office equipment and systems**
855 East Main Ave., Box 302
Zeeland, MI 49464-0302

First Chicago Trust    800-446-2617
$25 - $60,000/year
Every 30 days beginning 1/15
FEES: Div: $0!; Cash: 5% to $3 + 5¢/sh.; Auto. Inv.: $1 + fee; Cert: $0; Term: $15 + 12¢/sh.; Sells daily, by mail or phone, at market, for $15 + 12¢/sh.

**Shares to qualify:** 1
**Safekeeping:** Yes
**Accepts foreign:** No
**Auto. inv.:** Yes
**Disc.:** No

---

## Hershey Foods ⊗

**HSY/NYSE**
H: 70.15
L: 41.56
**Rec:** 59.47
**Div.:** 1.21
**Paid on:**
3.6.9.12-15
**Since:** 1932

**Mfg. of chocolate & grocery prod.**
100 Crystal Dr., Box 810
Hershey, PA 17033-0810

Mellon Inv. Svcs.    800-851-4216
$100 - $10,000/month
Every 7 days beginning Monday
FEES: Div: $0; Cash: $5 + 12¢/sh.; Auto. Inv.: $3 + 12¢/sh.; Cert: $0; Term: $0; Sells weekly, by mail or phone, at market, for $15 + 12¢/sh.

**Shares to qualify:** 1 /de ($500)
**Safekeeping:** Yes
**Accepts foreign:** Yes
**Auto. inv.:** Yes
**Disc.:** No

---

## Hewlett-Packard

**HWP/NYSE**
H: 63.21
L: 23.45
**Rec:** 25.10
**Div.:** 0.32
**Paid on:**
1.4.7.10-14
**Since:** 1965

**Manufacturer of computer products**
3000 Hanover St.
Palo Alto, CA 94304

Computershare Investor Svcs.    800-286-5977
$50 - $10,000/month
Every 30 days beginning 1/15
FEES: Div: 5% to $2.50 + 8¢/sh.; Cash: $2.50 + 8¢/sh.; Auto. Inv.: $1.25; Cert: $0; Term: $0; Sells weekly, by mail or fax, at avg. price, for $10 + 8¢/sh.

**Shares to qualify:** 10
**Safekeeping:** Yes
**Accepts foreign:** Yes
**Auto. inv.:** Yes
**Disc.:** No

---

## Hibernia Corp. ♥

**HIB/NYSE**
H: 19.11
L: 10.75
**Rec:** 18.81
**Div.:** 0.52
**Paid on:**
2.5.8.11-20
**Since:** 1993

**Banking**
Box 61540
New Orleans, LA 70161

Mellon Inv. Svcs.    800-814-0305
$100 - $3,000/month
Every 30 days beginning 1/20
FEES: Div: $0; Cash: $0; Cert: $0; Term: $0; Sells daily, by mail or phone, at avg. price, for comm.

**Shares to qualify:** 1
**Safekeeping:** Yes
**Accepts foreign:** Yes
**Auto. inv.:** No
**Disc.:** Div 5% Cash: 0%

---

## Highwoods Properties, Inc. ♥

**HIW/NYSE**
H: 26.78
L: 21.00
**Rec:** 25.45
**Div.:** 2.34
**Paid on:**
2.5.8.11-16
**Since:** 1994

**REIT**
3100 Smoketree Ct., Ste. 600
Raleigh, NC 27604-1051

First Union Nat'l Bank    800-829-8432
$25 - $10,000/month
Every 30 days beginning 1/24
FEES: Div: $0!; Cash: $0!; Cert: $0!; Term: $0; Sells within 10 bus. days, by mail, at market, for comm.

**Shares to qualify:** 1
**Safekeeping:** Yes
**Accepts foreign:** Yes
**Auto. inv.:** No
**Disc.:** Div 5% Cash: 0%

---

## Hillenbrand Industries ⊗

**HB/NYSE**
H: 58.51
L: 31.81
**Rec:** 55.65
**Div.:** 0.84
**Paid on:**
2.5.8.11-30
**Since:** 1971

**Hospital equip., caskets, life insurance**
700 State Route 46 East
Batesville, IN 47006-8835

Computershare Investor Svcs.    800-716-3607
$100 - $50,000/month
Every 7 days beginning varies
FEES: Div: $0; Cash: $5 + 10¢/sh.; Auto. Inv.: $2.50 +10¢/sh.; Cert: $0; Term: $0; Sells weekly, by mail, at avg. price, for $10 + 10¢/sh.

**Shares to qualify:** 1 /de ($250)
**Safekeeping:** Yes
**Accepts foreign:** Yes
**Auto. inv.:** Yes
**Disc.:** No

---

✽ DRIP enrollment through Temper Enrollment Service (see page 180).    **95**

## HMN Financial, Inc. ♥

*

| | |
|---|---|
| **HMNF/NAS** | **Bank holding co.** |
| H: 17.15 | 101 North Broadway, Box 231 |
| L: 11.75 | Spring Valley, MN 55975-0231 |
| **Rec:** 16.40 | Wells Fargo Bank 800-468-9716 |
| **Div.:** 0.56 | $50 - $5,000/month |
| **Paid on:** | Every 30 days beginning 1/10 |
| 3.6.9.12-11 | FEES: Div: $0!; Cash: $0!; Auto. Inv.: $0; Cert: $0!; Term: $5 + 15¢/sh.; Sells daily, by |
| **Since:** N/A | mail or fax, at market, for $5 + 15¢/sh. |

Shares to qualify: 1
Safekeeping: Yes
Accepts foreign: Yes
Auto. inv.: Yes
Disc.: No

---

## Home Depot

*

| | |
|---|---|
| **HD/NYSE** | **Retail building materials** |
| H: 60.00 | 2455 Paces Ferry Rd. NW, C17 |
| L: 34.68 | Atlanta, GA 30339-4024 |
| **Rec:** 48.46 | Boston Eq. 800-577-0177 |
| **Div.:** 0.16 | $25 - $100,000/year |
| **Paid on:** | Every Tues./Thurs. days beginning varies |
| 3.6.9.12-24 | FEES: Div: 5% to $2.50 + comm.; Cash: 5% to $2.50 + comm.; Auto. Inv.: 5% to $2.50 + |
| **Since:** 1987 | comm.; Cert: $0; Term: $0; Sells twice per week, by mail, fax or phone, at market, for $10 |
| | + comm. |

Shares to qualify: 1 /de ($250)
Safekeeping: Yes
Accepts foreign: Yes
Auto. inv.: Yes
Disc.: No

---

## Home Properties of NY ♥

| | |
|---|---|
| **HME/NYSE** | **REIT** |
| H: 31.15 | 850 Clinton Sq. |
| L: 25.50 | Rochester, NY 14604 |
| **Rec:** 31.15 | Mellon Inv. Svcs. 888-245-0458 |
| **Div.:** 2.28 | $50 - $1,000/month |
| **Paid on:** | Every 30 days beginning 1/10 |
| 2.5.8.11-24 | FEES: Div: $0!; Cash: $0!; Auto. Inv.: $0; Cert: $0!; Term: $0; Sells weekly, by mail or |
| **Since:** 1994 | phone, at market, for $15 + 12¢/sh. |

Shares to qualify: 1 /de ($2000)
Safekeeping: Yes
Accepts foreign: Yes
Auto. inv.: Yes
Disc.: Div 2% Cash: 2%

---

## Homestake Mining Co. ⊗

| | |
|---|---|
| **HM/NYSE** | **Gold mining** |
| H: 8.40 | 650 California St. |
| L: 3.50 | San Francisco, CA 94108-8150 |
| **Rec:** 8.17 | BankBoston 800-730-4001 |
| **Div.:** 0.05 | $25 - $5,000/quarter |
| **Paid on:** | Every 30 days beginning 1/15 |
| 5-22 & 11-20 | FEES: Div: $0; Cash: $3; Cert: $0; Term: $0; Sells weekly, by mail, at market, for $10 + |
| **Since:** 1946 | 15¢/sh. |

Shares to qualify: 1
Safekeeping: Yes
Accepts foreign: No
Auto. inv.: No
Disc.: No

---

## Honeywell International Inc. ♥

*

| | |
|---|---|
| **HON/NYSE** | **Automotive, chemicals, aerospace** |
| H: 55.68 | 101 Columbia Rd., Box 2245 |
| L: 33.00 | Morristown, NJ 07962-2245 |
| **Rec:** 36.50 | Bank of New York 800-432-0140 |
| **Div.:** 0.75 | $25 - $120,000/year |
| **Paid on:** | Every 30 days beginning 1st bus. day |
| 3.6.9.12-10 | FEES: Div: $0!; Cash: $0!; Cert: $0!; Term: $5; Sells biweekly, by mail, at market, for 5¢/sh. |
| **Since:** 1887 | |

Shares to qualify: 1
Safekeeping: Yes
Accepts foreign: No
Auto. inv.: No
Disc.: No

---

## Horizon Financial Corp. ♥

*

| | |
|---|---|
| **HRZB/NASD** | **Bank holding company** |
| H: 12.20 | 1500 Cornwall Ave., Box 580 |
| L: 7.55 | Bellingham, WA 98227 |
| **Rec:** 12.00 | American Stock Transfer 800-278-4353 |
| **Div.:** 0.48 | $125 - $3,000/quarter |
| **Paid on:** | Every 90 days beginning 2/10 |
| 2.5.8.11-5 | FEES: Div: $0!; Cash: $0!; Cert: $0!; Term: 4¢/sh.; Sells weekly, by mail, at market, for 4¢/sh. |
| **Since:** N/A | |

Shares to qualify: 1
Safekeeping: Yes
Accepts foreign: Yes
Auto. inv.: No
Disc.: No

---

## Hormel Foods Corp. ♥

*

| | |
|---|---|
| **HRL/NYSE** | **Food processor, marketer** |
| H: 25.63 | 1 Hormel Pl. |
| L: 15.06 | Austin, MN 55912-3680 |
| **Rec:** 25.62 | Wells Fargo Bank 877-536-3559 |
| **Div.:** 0.37 | $25 - $20,000/month |
| **Paid on:** | Every 30 days beginning 1/15 |
| 2.5.8.11-15 | FEES: Div: $0!; Cash: $0!; Auto. Inv.: $0; Cert: $0; Term: $10 + 10¢/sh. ; Sells daily, by |
| **Since:** 1928 | mail or fax, at market, for $10 + 10¢/sh. |

Shares to qualify: 1
Safekeeping: Yes
Accepts foreign: Yes
Auto. inv.: Yes
Disc.: No

---

## Hospitality Properties Trust ♥

**HPT/NYSE** | REIT
H: 30.35
L: 20.25
**Rec:** 28.26

400 Centre St.
Newton. MA 02458-2076

State St. Bank  800-426-5523
$0 - $10,000/quarter
Every 90 days beginning 2/19

**Shares to qualify:** 1
**Safekeeping:** No
**Accepts foreign:** Yes
**Auto. inv.:** No
**Disc.:** No

**Div.:** 2.84
**Paid on:**
2.5.8.11-19
**Since:** 1995

FEES: Div $0!; Cash: $0!; Cert: $0!; Term: $2.50 + 15¢/sh.; Sells within 10 bus. days, by mail, at market, for $2.50 + 15¢/sh.

---

## Household International, Inc. ♥

**HI/NYSE** | Financial services
H: 69.98
L: 43.87
**Rec:** 67.13

2700 Sanders Rd.
Prospect Heights. IL  60070-2799

Computershare Investor Svcs.  800-926-2335
$50 - $5,000/quarter
Every 30 days beginning 1/15

**Shares to qualify:** 1
**Safekeeping:** Yes
**Accepts foreign:** Yes
**Auto. inv.:** No
**Disc.:** Div 2.5% Cash: 0%

**Div.:** 0.88
**Paid on:**
1.4.7.10-15
**Since:** 1926

FEES: Div: $0; Cash: $0; Cert: $0; Term: $1 + 7¢/sh.; Sells daily, by mail, at market, for 5¢/sh.

---

## HRPT Properties Trust ♥

**HRP/NYSE** | REIT
H: 10.09
L: 6.12
**Rec:** 8.76

400 Centre St.
Newton. MA 02458

State St. Bank  800-426-5523
$0 - $10,000/quarter
Every 90 days beginning 2/20

**Shares to qualify:** 1
**Safekeeping:** No
**Accepts foreign:** Yes
**Auto. inv.:** No
**Disc.:** No

**Div.:** 0.80
**Paid on:**
2.5.8.11-20
**Since:** 1986

FEES: Div: $0!; Cash: $0!; Cert: $0!; Term: $0; Sells daily, by mail or phone, at market, for $2.50 + 15¢/sh.

---

## HSBC Holding plc ⊗

**HBC/NYSE** | Banking
H: 80.00
L: 55.40
**Rec:** 60.20

c/o BNY,101 Barclay St.,22 West
New York. NY  10286

Bank of New York  888-269-2377
$20 - $60,000/year
Every 30 days beginning 1/7

**Shares to qualify:** 1 /de ($250)
**Safekeeping:** Yes
**Accepts foreign:** Yes
**Auto. inv.:** Yes
**Disc.:** No

**Div.:** 2.11
**Paid on:**
10-7
**Since:** 1999

FEES: Div: 5% to $2.50; Cash: $5 + 12¢/sh.; Auto. Inv.: $0; Cert: $0; Term: $0; Sells daily, by mail, at market, for $5 + 12¢/sh.

---

## Hubbell, Inc. -B ♥

**HUBB/NYSE** | Mfr. elec. equipment
H: 30.98
L: 21.62
**Rec:** 29.35

584 Derby Milford Rd., Box 549
Orange. CT  06477-4024

Mellon Inv. Svcs.  800-851-9677
$100 - $5,000/quarter
Every 30 days beginning 1/15

**Shares to qualify:** 1
**Safekeeping:** Yes
**Accepts foreign:** Yes
**Auto. inv.:** No
**Disc.:** No

**Div.:** 1.32
**Paid on:**
1.4.7.10-11
**Since:** 1934

FEES: Div: $0!; Cash: $0!; Cert: $5; Term: $0; Sells biweekly, by mail , at market, for $15 + comm.

---

## Hubbell, Inc. -A ♥

**HUBA/NYSE** | Mfr. elec. equipment
H: 29.50
L: 21.37
**Rec:** 28.73

584 Derby Milford Rd., Box 549
Orange. CT  06477-4024

Mellon Inv. Svcs.  800-851-9677
$100 - $5,000/quarter
Every 30 days beginning 1/15

**Shares to qualify:** 1
**Safekeeping:** Yes
**Accepts foreign:** Yes
**Auto. inv.:** No
**Disc.:** No

**Div.:** 1.32
**Paid on:**
1.4.7.10-11
**Since:** 1934

FEES: Div: $0!; Cash: $0!; Cert: $5; Term: $0; Sells biweekly, by mail, at market, for $15 + comm.

---

## Hudson United Bancorp ♥

**HU/NYSE** | Banking
H: 28.15
L: 16.93
**Rec:** 27.87

1000 MacArthur Blvd.
Mahwah. NJ 07430

American Stock Transfer  800-278-4353
$10 - $20,000/quarter
Every 30 days beginning 1/31

**Shares to qualify:** 1
**Safekeeping:** Yes
**Accepts foreign:** No
**Auto. inv.:** Yes
**Disc.:** No

**Div.:** 1.00
**Paid on:**
3.6.9.12-1
**Since:** 1952

FEES: Div: $0; Cash: $0; Auto. Inv.: $0; Cert: $0; Term: $0; Sells weekly, by mail, at avg. price, for $0

---

## Huffy Corp. ⊗

**HUF/NYSE**
**H:** 13.68
**L:** 6.01
**Rec:** 8.95
**Div.:** 0.00
**Paid on:**
DIV. SUSP.
**Since:** --

**Recreation & leisure products**
225 Byers Rd.
Miamisburg, OH 45342
LaSalle Bank, NA     800-246-5761
$50 - $100,000/year
Every 5 days beginning varies
FEES: Div: n/o;  Cash: $5 + 10¢/sh.;  Auto. Inv.: $1.50 + 10¢/sh.;  Cert: $0!;  Term: $10 + 10¢/sh.;  Sells weekly, by mail, at market, for $10 + 10¢/sh.

**Shares to qualify:** 1 /de ($500)
**Safekeeping:** Yes
**Accepts foreign:** Yes
**Auto. inv.:** Yes
**Disc.:** No

---

## Huntington Bancshares Inc. ♥

**HBAN/NASD**
**H:** 19.15
**L:** 12.51
**Rec:** 18.90
**Div.:** 0.64
**Paid on:**
1.4.7.10-2
**Since:** 1912

**Banking**
Huntington Ctr., HC0623
Columbus, OH 43287
Computershare Investor Svcs.     800-725-0674
$200 - $10,000/quarter
Every 90 days beginning 1/2
FEES: Div: $0;  Cash: $0;  Auto. Inv.: $0;  Cert: $0;  Term: $0;  Sells weekly, by mail, at market, for $10 + comm.

**Shares to qualify:** 1
**Safekeeping:** Yes
**Accepts foreign:** Yes
**Auto. inv.:** Yes
**Disc.:** No

---

## IDACORP, Inc.

**IDA/NYSE**
**H:** 51.81
**L:** 33.55
**Rec:** 37.23
**Div.:** 1.86
**Paid on:**
2.5.8.11-30
**Since:** 1917

**Utility-electric**
Box 70
Boise, ID 83707
Idaho Power     800-635-5406
$10 - $15,000/quarter
Every 90 days beginning 1/21
FEES: Div: 4¢/sh.;  Cash: 4¢/sh.;  Cert: $0;  Term: 4¢/sh.;  Sells weekly, by mail or fax, at avg. price, for 4¢/sh.

**Shares to qualify:** 1 /de
**Safekeeping:** Yes
**Accepts foreign:** Yes
**Auto. inv.:** No
**Disc.:** No

---

## IKON Office Solutions, Inc.

**IKN/NYSE**
**H:** 9.80
**L:** 2.00
**Rec:** 7.25
**Div.:** 0.16
**Paid on:**
3.6.9.12-10
**Since:** 1965

**Paper, office products**
70 Valley Stream Pkwy.
Malvern, PA 19355
National City Bank     800-622-6757
$25 - $5,000/month
Every 30 days beginning 1/10
FEES: Div: comm.;  Cash: comm.;  Cert: $0;  Term: $0;  Sells weekly, by mail, at market, for $2.50 + comm.

**Shares to qualify:** 1
**Safekeeping:** Yes
**Accepts foreign:** Yes
**Auto. inv.:** No
**Disc.:** No

---

## Illinois Tool Works, Inc. ♥

**ITW/NYSE**
**H:** 71.99
**L:** 49.50
**Rec:** 62.90
**Div.:** 0.88
**Paid on:**
1.4.7.10-25
**Since:** 1962

**Industrial systems**
3600 West Lake Ave.
Glenview, IL 60025
Computershare Investor Svcs.     888-829-7424
$100 - $10,000/month
Every 30 days beginning 1/22
FEES: Div: $0!;  Cash: $0!;  Cert: $0!;  Term: 10¢/sh. + comm.;  Sells weekly, by mail or fax, at market, for 10¢/sh. + comm.

**Shares to qualify:** 1
**Safekeeping:** Yes
**Accepts foreign:** Yes
**Auto. inv.:** No
**Disc.:** No

---

## Imperial Oil Ltd.

**IMO/ASE**
**H:** 28.40
**L:** 22.59
**Rec:** 27.70
**Div.:** 0.54
**Paid on:**
1.4.7.10-1
**Since:** N/A

**Energy**
111 St. Clair Ave. West, Rm.1724
Toronto, Ont. M5W 1K3 Canada
Montreal Trust     212-701-7673
$50 - $5,000/quarter (Cdn.)
Every 90 days beginning 1/4
FEES: Div: comm.;  Cash: comm.;  Cert: $0;  Term: $0,Does not sell through the plan

**Shares to qualify:** 1
**Safekeeping:** No
**Accepts foreign:** Yes
**Auto. inv.:** No
**Disc.:** No

---

## Inco Limited ♥

**N/NYSE**
**H:** 20.60
**L:** 13.93
**Rec:** 15.89
**Div.:** 0.00
**Paid on:**
DIV. SUSP.
**Since:** --

**Metals & mining**
145 King St. West, Ste.1500
Toronto, Ont. M5H 4B7 Canada
Mellon Inv. Svcs.     800-387-0825
$50 - $10,000/quarter
Every 90 days beginning 3/9
FEES: Div: n/o;  Cash: $0!;  Cert: $0!;  Term: $0;  Sells within 10 days, by mail or fax, at market, for comm.

**Shares to qualify:** 1
**Safekeeping:** No
**Accepts foreign:** Yes
**Auto. inv.:** No
**Disc.:** No

---

✳ DRIP enrollment through Temper Enrollment Service (see page 180).

## Independent Bank Corp. ♥

**IBCP/NASD**
H: 27.71
L: 13.80
**Rec:** 27.71

**Div.:** 0.64
**Paid on:**
1.4.7.10-30
**Since:** 1974

**Banking**
230 West Main St., Box 491
Ionia, MI 48846
State St. Bank     800-257-1770
$50 - $5,000/quarter
Every 90 days beginning 1/30
FEES: Div: $0; Cash: $0; Auto. Inv.: $0; Cert: $0; Term: $5 + comm.; Sells irregularly, by mail or phone, at market, for $5 + comm.

**Shares to qualify:** 1
**Safekeeping:** Yes
**Accepts foreign:** No
**Auto. inv.:** Yes
**Disc.:** No

---

## Independent Community Bank ♥

**ICBX/NASD**
H: 34.00
L: 20.00
**Rec:** 32.50

**Div.:** 1.00
**Paid on:**
1.4.7.10-20
**Since:** N/A

**Bank holding co.**
Box 5
Middleburg, VA  20118-0005
Registrar & Transfer     800-368-5948
$100 - $5,000/quarter
Every 3rd Fri. days beginning 1/19
FEES: Div: $0!; Cash: $0!; Cert: $0!; Term: $0; Sells weekly, by mail, at market, for comm.

**Shares to qualify:** 1
**Safekeeping:** Yes
**Accepts foreign:** Yes
**Auto. inv.:** No
**Disc.:**

---

## Indiana United Bancorp ♥

**IUBC/NASD**
H: 18.75
L: 13.33
**Rec:** 18.25

**Div.:** 0.66
**Paid on:**
1.4.7.10-15
**Since:** N/A

**Bank holding co.**
201 N. Broadway, Box 87
Greensburg, IN  47240
Registrar & Transfer     800-368-5948
$25 - $2,500/month
Every 30 days beginning 1/15
FEES: Div: $0!; Cash: $0!; Cert: $5; Term: $0,Does not sell through the plan

**Shares to qualify:** 1
**Safekeeping:** Yes
**Accepts foreign:** Yes
**Auto. inv.:** No
**Disc.:** No

---

## Indonesia Fund, Inc. (The) ⊗

**IF/NYSE**
H: 3.50
L: 1.27
**Rec:** 1.85

**Div.:** 0.04
**Paid on:**
N/A
**Since:** N/A

**Closed-end fund**
c/o Credit Suisse, 153 E. 53 St., 58th Fl.
New York, NY  10022
BankBoston     800-730-6001
$100 - $100,000/year
Every 7 days beginning Wed.
FEES: Div: $0; Cash: $5 + 8¢/sh.; Auto. Inv.: $5 + 8¢/sh.; Cert: $0; Term: $10 + 15¢/sh.; Sells within 4 bus. days, by mail, at avg. price, for $10 + 15¢/sh.

**Shares to qualify:** 1 /de ($250)
**Safekeeping:** Yes
**Accepts foreign:** Yes
**Auto. inv.:** Yes
**Disc.:** No

---

## IndyMac Bancorp ♥

**NDE/NYSE**
H: 30.43
L: 16.31
**Rec:** 27.08

**Div.:** 0.00
**Paid on:**
DIV. SUSP.
**Since:** --

**Financial services**
155 North Lake Ave.
Pasadena, CA  91101-7211
Bank of New York     800-524-4458
$50 - $10,000/month
Every 30 days beginning 1/22
FEES: Div: n/o; Cash: $0; Cert: $0; Term: $0,Does not sell through the plan

**Shares to qualify:** 1
**Safekeeping:** No
**Accepts foreign:** No
**Auto. inv.:** No
**Disc.:** No

---

## Ingersoll-Rand ♥

**IR/NYSE**
H: 50.28
L: 29.50
**Rec:** 42.30

**Div.:** 0.68
**Paid on:**
3.6.9.12-1
**Since:** 1910

**Machinery**
200 Chestnut Ridge Rd.
Woodcliff Lake, NJ  07675
Bank of New York     800-524-4458
$10 - $3,000/quarter
Every 30 days beginning 1/2
FEES: Div: $0!; Cash: $0!; Cert: $0; Term: $0; Sells daily, by mail, at market, for comm.

**Shares to qualify:** 1
**Safekeeping:** Yes
**Accepts foreign:** Yes
**Auto. inv.:** No
**Disc.:** No

---

## Innkeepers USA Trust ♥

**KPA/NYSE**
H: 12.43
L: 9.56
**Rec:** 11.39

**Div.:** 1.20
**Paid on:**
1.4.7.10-VARIES
**Since:** N/A

**Ownership of hotels**
306 Royal Poinciana Way
Palm Beach, FL  33480
Computershare Investor Svcs.     800-942-5909
$250 - $3,000/investment
Every 30 days beginning 4/15
FEES: Div: $0!; Cash: $0!; Cert: $0!; Term: $5 + comm.; Sells monthly, by mail or e-mail, at avg. price, for $5 + comm.

**Shares to qualify:** 1 /de ($250)
**Safekeeping:** Yes
**Accepts foreign:** No
**Auto. inv.:** No
**Disc.:** Div: 4% Cash:
                0-3%

---

## ✲ Insteel Industries, Inc. ♥

**III/NYSE** — **Mfr. wire & wire products**

H: 5.50
L: 0.93
**Rec:** 1.16
**Div.:** 0.00
**Paid on:**
DIV. SUSP.
**Since:**--

1373 Boggs Dr.
Mount Airv. NC 27030

First Union Nat'l Bank   800-829-8432
$10 - $unlimited
Every 30 days beginning 1/5

FEES: Div $0!; Cash: $0!; Cert: $0!; Term: $0; Sells bimonthly, by mail, at market, for 5¢/sh.

**Shares to qualify:** 1
**Safekeeping:** Yes
**Accepts foreign:** Yes
**Auto. inv.:** No
**Disc.:** No

---

## ✲ Integra Bank Corp. ♥

**IBNK/NASD** — **Bank holding company**

H: 27.37
L: 17.75
**Rec:** 25.00
**Div.:** 0.94
**Paid on:**
1.4.7.10-7
**Since:** N/A

21 S.E. Third St., Box 868
Evansville. IN 47705-0868

Integra Bank   812-464-9693
$100 - $10,000/month
Every 30 days beginning 1/7

FEES: Div $0!; Cash: $0!; Auto. Inv.: $0; Cert: $0!; Term: $0; Sells weekly, by mail, at market, for $0!

**Shares to qualify:** 1
**Safekeeping:** Yes
**Accepts foreign:** No
**Auto. inv.:** Yes
**Disc.:** No

---

## ✲ Intel Corp. ♥

**INTC/NASD** — **Computer chips**

H: 75.81
L: 22.25
**Rec:** 29.95
**Div.:** 0.08
**Paid on:**
3.6.9.12-1
**Since:** 1992

2200 Mission College Blvd., RN5-24
Santa Clara. CA 95052

Computershare Investor Svcs.   800-298-0146
$25 - $15,000/month
Every 30 days beginning 1/2

FEES: Div: $0!; Cash: $0!; Auto. Inv.: $0; Cert: $0!; Term: $0; Sells within 10 bus. days, by mail or fax, at avg. price, for $0

**Shares to qualify:** 1
**Safekeeping:** Yes
**Accepts foreign:** Yes
**Auto. inv.:** Yes
**Disc.:** No

---

## ✲ Interchange Financial Services

**IFCJ/NASD** — **Commercial banking**

H: 18.87
L: 12.00
**Rec:** 18.05
**Div.:** 0.54
**Paid on:**
1.4.7.10-20
**Since:** 1981

Park 80 West/Plaza Two
Saddle Brook. NJ 07663

Continental Stock Transfer   212-509-4000
$25 - $unlimited
Every 30 days beginning 1/5

FEES: Div: comm.; Cash: comm.; Auto. Inv.: $0; Cert: $0!; Term: $0!; Sells weekly, by mail or fax, at market, for $1 + comm.

**Shares to qualify:** 1
**Safekeeping:** No
**Accepts foreign:** Yes
**Auto. inv.:** Yes
**Disc.:** No

---

## ✲ International Business Machines ⊗

**IBM/NYSE** — **Mfr. of bus. machines and info. tech.**

H: 134.93
L: 80.06
**Rec:** 104.95
**Div.:** 0.56
**Paid on:**
3.6.9.12-10
**Since:** 1913

New Orchard Rd.
Armonk. NY 10504

First Chicago Trust   888-IBM-6700
$50 - $250,000/year
Every 7 days beginning varies

FEES: Div: 2% to $3; Cash: $5; Auto. Inv.: $1; Cert: $0; Term: $15 + 10¢/sh.; Sells daily, by mail or phone, at market, for $15 + 10¢/sh.

**Shares to qualify:** 1 /de ($500)
**Safekeeping:** Yes
**Accepts foreign:** Yes
**Auto. inv.:** Yes
**Disc.:** No

---

## ✲ International Flavors & Fragrances ♥

**IFF/NYSE** — **Specialty chemicals**

H: 30.10
L: 14.68
**Rec:** 28.88
**Div.:** 0.60
**Paid on:**
1.4.7.10-11
**Since:** 1961

521 West 57th St.
New York. NY 10019-2960

Bank of New York   800-524-4458
$25 - $5,000/month
Every 30 days beginning 1/2

FEES: Div: $0!; Cash: $0!; Cert: $0!; Term: $0; Sells weekly, by phone or mail, at market, for $0

**Shares to qualify:** 1
**Safekeeping:** Yes
**Accepts foreign:** Yes
**Auto. inv.:** No
**Disc.:** No

---

## ✲ International Multifoods Corp. ♥

**IMC/NYSE** — **Food processing**

H: 23.31
L: 15.75
**Rec:** 20.64
**Div.:** 0.80
**Paid on:**
1.4.7.10-15
**Since:** 1923

110 Cheshire Lane, Ste. 300
Minnetonka. MN 55305-1060

Wells Fargo Bank   800-468-9716
$10 - $60,000/year
Every 30 days beginning 1/15

FEES: Div: $0!; Cash: $0!; Cert: $0!; Term: $10 + 10¢/sh. ; Sells daily, by mail, at market, for $10 + 10¢/sh.

**Shares to qualify:** 1
**Safekeeping:** Yes
**Accepts foreign:** No
**Auto. inv.:** No
**Disc.:** No

---

## International Paper ♥

**\***

**IP/NYSE**
H: 43.31
L: 26.31
**Rec:** 39.82
**Div.:** 1.00
**Paid on:**
3.6.9.12-15
**Since:** 1946

Forest products
400 Atlantic St.
Stamford. CT 06921

Mellon Inv. Svcs.　800-678-8715
$50 - $20,000/year
Every 7 days beginning varies

FEES: Div: $0!; Cash: $0!; Auto. Inv.: $0; Cert: $0!; Term: $15 + 12¢/sh.; Sells within 4 bus. days, by mail or phone, at avg. price, for $15 + 12¢/sh.

**Shares to qualify:** 1 /de ($500)
**Safekeeping:** Yes
**Accepts foreign:** Yes
**Auto. inv.:** Yes
**Disc.:** No

---

## Interpublic Group of Cos.

**\***

**IPG/NYSE**
H: 47.43
L: 25.90
**Rec:** 27.88
**Div.:** 0.38
**Paid on:**
3.6.9.12-15
**Since:** 1977

Advertising
1271 Ave. of the Americas
New York. NY 10020

First Chicago Trust　201-324-0498
$10 - $3,000/quarter
Every 90 days beginning 3/15

FEES: Div: 5% to 2.50; Cash: 5% to $2.50; Cert: $0; Term: $10 + 12¢/sh.; Sells daily, by mail or fax, at market, for $10 + 12¢/sh.

**Shares to qualify:** 1
**Safekeeping:** Yes
**Accepts foreign:** No
**Auto. inv.:** No
**Disc.:** No

---

## Interstate Bakeries Corp. ♥

**\***

**IBC/NYSE**
H: 23.83
L: 10.50
**Rec:** 23.83
**Div.:** 0.28
**Paid on:**
2.5.8.11-1
**Since:** 1991

Food & beverage
12 East Armour Blvd., Box 419627
Kansas Citv. MO 64111

UMB Bank, N.A.　816-860-7761
$50 - $3,000/quarter
Every 30 days beginning 1/30

FEES: Div: $0!; Cash: $0!; Cert: $0; Term: $0; Sells daily, by mail, at market, for $10 + 12¢/sh.

**Shares to qualify:** 1
**Safekeeping:** Yes
**Accepts foreign:** Yes
**Auto. inv.:** No
**Disc.:** No

---

## Intimate Brands, Inc.-A ⊗

**\***

**IBI/NYSE**
H: 24.31
L: 12.31
**Rec:** 15.94
**Div.:** 0.28
**Paid on:**
3.6.9.12-15
**Since:** 1995

Women's apparel & lingerie
3 Limited Pkwy., Box 16000
Columbus. OH 43216

First Chicago Trust　800-317-4445
$100 - $250,000/year
Every 7 days beginning varies

FEES: Div: 5% to $3; Cash: $5 + 3¢/sh.; Auto. Inv.: $2 + 3¢/sh.; Cert: $0; Term: $15 + 12¢/sh.; Sells daily, by phone, mail, fax, or Internet, at market, for $15 + 12¢/sh.

**Shares to qualify:** 1 /de ($500)
**Safekeeping:** Yes
**Accepts foreign:** Yes
**Auto. inv.:** Yes
**Disc.:** No

---

## Invacare ♥

**\***

**IVC/NYSE**
H: 40.80
L: 22.56
**Rec:** 37.65
**Div.:** 0.05
**Paid on:**
1.4.7.10-15
**Since:** 1994

Home health care medical equip.
Box 4028
Elvria. OH 44036-2125

National City Bank　800-622-6757
$10 - $5,000/month
Every 30 days beginning 1/15

FEES: Div: $0!; Cash: $0!; Cert: $0!; Term: $2.50; Sells weekly, by mail or fax, at market, for $2.50 + comm.

**Shares to qualify:** 1
**Safekeeping:** Yes
**Accepts foreign:** Yes
**Auto. inv.:** No
**Disc.:** No

---

## Investors Financial Services Corp. ⊗

**\***

**IFIN/NASDA**
H: 96.00
L: 39.43
**Rec:** 71.50
**Div.:** 0.08
**Paid on:**
2.5.8.11-13
**Since:** N/A

Financial
Box 9130
Boston. MA 02117

First Chicago Trust　201-324-0313
$100 - $unlimited
Every 7 days beginning Tuesday

FEES: Div: $0; Cash: $5 + 10¢/sh.; Auto. Inv.: $2 + 10¢/sh.; Cert: $0; Term: 12¢/sh.; Sells daily, by mail or phone, at market, for $15 + 12¢/sh.

**Shares to qualify:** 1 /de ($250)
**Safekeeping:** Yes
**Accepts foreign:** Yes
**Auto. inv.:** No
**Disc.:** No

---

## IPSCO Inc. ♥

**\***

**IPS/NYSE**
H: 16.35
L: 7.31
**Rec:** 12.49
**Div.:** 0.32
**Paid on:**
3.6.9.12-30
**Since:** 1988

Manufacturer of steel products
650 Warrenville Rd., Ste. 500
Lisle. IL 60532

Montreal Trust　888-334-3305
$0 - $5,000/quarter Cdn.
Every 90 days beginning 3/30

FEES: Div: $0!; Cash: $0!; Cert: $0!; Term: $0,Does not sell through the plan

**Shares to qualify:** 1
**Safekeeping:** Yes
**Accepts foreign:** Yes
**Auto. inv.:** No
**Disc.:** No

---

## iStar Financial Inc. ♥

**SFI/NYSE**
H: 28.60
L: 18.43
**Rec:** 27.90

**Div.:** 2.45
**Paid on:**
1.4.7.10-28
**Since:** 1998

**REIT**
1114 Ave. of the Americas, 27th Fl.
New York. NY 10036
First Chicago Trust     800-317-4445
$100 - $10,000/month
Every 30 days beginning 1/18

**Shares to qualify:** 1 /de ($100)
**Safekeeping:** Yes
**Accepts foreign:** Yes
**Auto. inv.:** Yes
**Disc.:** Div: 0-3% Cash:
0%

FEES: Div: $0!; Cash: $0!; Auto. Inv.: $0; Cert: $0!; Term: $15 + 12¢/sh.; Sells daily, by mail or phone, at market, for $15 + 12¢/sh.

---

## Italy Fund Inc. (The) ♥

**ITA/NYSE**
H: 18.75
L: 7.64
**Rec:** 8.00

**Div.:** 0.23
**Paid on:**
12-31
**Since:** N/A

**Closed-end fund**
c/o SSB Fund Mgt., 388 Greenwich St.
New York. NY 10013
First Data Investor Services     800-331-1710
$100 - $3,000/semiannually
Every 180 days beginning 2/15

**Shares to qualify:** 1
**Safekeeping:** No
**Accepts foreign:** Yes
**Auto. inv.:** No
**Disc.:** Div: 5% Cash: 0%

FEES: Div: $0; Cash: $0; Cert: $0; Term: $5; Sells daily, by mail, at market, for $5

---

## ITT Industries ♥

**ITT/NYSE**
H: 49.00
L: 29.75
**Rec:** 43.47

**Div.:** 0.60
**Paid on:**
1.4.7.10-1
**Since:** 1995

**Diversified**
4 West Red Oak Lane
White Plains. NY 10604
Bank of New York     800-254-2823
$50 - $10,000/investment
Every 7 days beginning varies

**Shares to qualify:** 1 /de ($500)
**Safekeeping:** Yes
**Accepts foreign:** Yes
**Auto. inv.:** Yes
**Disc.:** No

FEES: Div: $0!; Cash: $0!; Auto. Inv.: $0; Cert: $5;  Term: $5 + 10¢/sh.; Sells weekly, by mail, at market, for $5 + 10¢/sh.

---

## Jacobson Stores Inc. ♥

**JCBS/NASD**
H: 5.50
L: 2.18
**Rec:** 3.00

**Div.:** 0.00
**Paid on:**
DIV. SUSP.
**Since:** --

**Retail stores**
3333 Sargent Rd.
Jackson. MI 49201-8847
Wells Fargo Bank     800-468-9716
$10 - $1,000/month
Every 30 days beginning 1/10

**Shares to qualify:** 1
**Safekeeping:** Yes
**Accepts foreign:** No
**Auto. inv.:** No
**Disc.:** No

FEES: Div: $0; Cash: $0!; Cert: $0!; Term: $10 + 10¢/sh.,Does not sell through the plan

---

## Jameson Inns, Inc. ♥

**JAMS/NASD**
H: 7.75
L: 5.50
**Rec:** 6.86

**Div.:** 0.98
**Paid on:**
2.5.8.11-20
**Since:** N/A

**REIT**
8 Perimeter Center East, Ste. 8050
Atlanta. GA 30346
First Union Nat'l Bank     800-829-8432
$100 - $5,000/quarter
Every 30 days beginning 1/15

**Shares to qualify:** 1
**Safekeeping:** Yes
**Accepts foreign:** Yes
**Auto. inv.:** No
**Disc.:** Div: 5% Cash: 0%

FEES: Div: $0!; Cash: $0!; Cert: $0!; Term: $0; Sells bimonthly, by mail or fax, at market, for 5¢ to $5

---

## JDN Realty Corp. ♥

**JDN/NYSE**
H: 13.64
L: 9.00
**Rec:** 12.09

**Div.:** 1.20
**Paid on:**
3.6.9.12-24
**Since:** 1994

**REIT**
359 E. Paces Ferry Rd., Ste. 400
Atlanta. GA 30305
First Union Nat'l Bank     800-829-8432
$100 - $10,000/quarter
Every 90 days beginning 1/15

**Shares to qualify:** 1
**Safekeeping:** Yes
**Accepts foreign:** Yes
**Auto. inv.:** No
**Disc.:** Div: 2% Cash: 0%

FEES: Div: $0!; Cash: $0!; Cert: $0!; Term: $0,Does not sell through the plan

---

## Jefferson-Pilot Corp. ♥

**JP/NYSE**
H: 50.58
L: 39.33
**Rec:** 46.92

**Div.:** 1.10
**Paid on:**
3.6.9.12-5
**Since:** 1913

**Insurance holding co.**
100 North Greene St., Box 21008
Greensboro. NC 27420
First Union Nat'l Bank     800-829-8432
$20 - $2,000/month
Every 30 days beginning 1/6

**Shares to qualify:** 1
**Safekeeping:** Yes
**Accepts foreign:** Yes
**Auto. inv.:** No
**Disc.:** No

FEES: Div: $0!; Cash: $0!; Cert: $0!; Term: comm.; Sells bimonthly, by mail, at market, for comm.

---

## Johnson Controls ♥

**JCI/NYSE**

H: 81.70
L: 45.81
**Rec:** 79.49

**Div.:** 1.24
**Paid on:**
3,6,9-30 & 1-2
**Since:** 1887

**Elec. equip., batteries & auto interiors**

5757 N. Green Bay Ave., Box 591
Milwaukee. WI 53201

Wells Fargo Bank     877-602-7397
$50 - $15,000/quarter
Every 7 days beginning Wednesday

FEES: Div: $0; Cash: $0; Auto. Inv.: $0; Cert: $0; Term: $0; Sells daily, by mail, fax or
phone, at market, for $10 + 10¢/sh.

**Shares to qualify:** 1 /de ($250)
**Safekeeping:** Yes
**Accepts foreign:** Yes
**Auto. inv.:** Yes
**Disc.:** No

---

## Johnson & Johnson ♥

**JNJ/NYSE**

H: 55.02
L: 40.25
**Rec:** 55.02

**Div.:** 0.72
**Paid on:**
3,6,9,12-9
**Since:** 1944

**Health care & consumer products**

One Johnson & Johnson Plaza
New Brunswick. NJ 08933

First Chicago Trust     800-328-9033
$25 - $50,000/year
Every 30 days beginning 1/7

FEES: Div: $0!; Cash: $0!; Auto. Inv.: $1; Cert: $0!; Term: $15 + 12¢/sh.; Sells daily, by
mail, fax , or phone, at market, for $15 + 12¢/sh.

**Shares to qualify:** 1
**Safekeeping:** Yes
**Accepts foreign:** Yes
**Auto. inv.:** Yes
**Disc.:** No

---

## JPS Industries, Inc.

**JPST/NASD**

H: 7.49
L: 3.25
**Rec:** 6.40

**Div.:** 0.00
**Paid on:**
N/0
**Since:** --

**Mfr. plastics**

555 N. Pleasantburg Dr., Ste. 202
Greenville. SC 29607

American Stock Transfer     800-937-5449
$25 - $10,000/investment
Every day days beginning daily

FEES: Div: n/o; Cash: $2.50 + 10¢/sh.; Auto. Inv.: $2.50 + 10¢/sh.; Cert: $0; Term:
$7.50 + 10¢/sh.; Sells daily, by phone, mail, fax, or Internet, at market, for $7.50 +
10¢/sh.

**Shares to qualify:** 1 /de ($250)
**Safekeeping:** Yes
**Accepts foreign:** Yes
**Auto. inv.:** Yes
**Disc.:** No

---

## Juniata Valley Financial Corp. ♥

**JUVF/OTC**

H: 27.50
L: 22.50
**Rec:** 27.25

**Div.:** 0.78
**Paid on:**
6,12-1
**Since:** N/A

**Banking**

Box 66
Mifflintown. PA 17059

Juniata Valley Financial Corp.     717-436-8211
$200 - $1,500/semiannually
Every 180 days beginning 6/1

FEES: Div: $0!; Cash: $0!; Cert: fee; Term: fee,Does not sell through the plan

**Shares to qualify:** 1
**Safekeeping:** No
**Accepts foreign:** Yes
**Auto. inv.:** No
**Disc.:** No

---

## Kaman Corp. -A ⊗

**KAMNA/NA**

H: 19.50
L: 11.00
**Rec:** 15.72

**Div.:** 0.44
**Paid on:**
1,4,7.10-17
**Since:** 1971

**Diversified mfr.**

1332 Blue Hills Ave., Box 1
Bloomfield. CT 06002

Mellon Inv. Svcs.     800-227-0291
$50 - $60,000/year
Every 30 days beginning 1/15

FEES: Div: $0!; Cash: $5 + 12¢/sh.; Auto. Inv.: $3 + 12¢/sh.; Cert: $0!; Term: $15 +
12¢/sh.; Sells weekly, by mail or phone, at market, for $15 + 12¢/sh.

**Shares to qualify:** 10 /de ($250)
**Safekeeping:** Yes
**Accepts foreign:** Yes
**Auto. inv.:** Yes
**Disc.:** No

---

## Kansas City Power & Light

**KLT/NYSE**

H: 28.75
L: 23.60
**Rec:** 25.00

**Div.:** 1.66
**Paid on:**
3,6,9,12-20
**Since:** 1921

**Utility-electric**

1201 Walnut St.
Kansas City. MO 64106

UMB Bank, N.A.     816-860-7786
$100 - $5,000/month
Every 30 days beginning 1/20

FEES: Div: 5¢/sh.; Cash: 5¢/sh.; Auto. Inv.: $0; Cert: $0; Term: $0; Sells monthly, by mail,
at market, for $10 + 10¢/sh.

**Shares to qualify:** 1 /de ($500)
**Safekeeping:** Yes
**Accepts foreign:** Yes
**Auto. inv.:** Yes
**Disc.:** No

---

## Keithley Instruments ♥

**KEI/NYSE**

H: 83.93
L: 12.18
**Rec:** 20.75

**Div.:** 0.15
**Paid on:**
3,6,9,12-30
**Since:** 1955

**Maker of electronic test instruments**

28775 Aurora Rd.
Cleveland. OH 44139

National City Bank     800-622-6757
$50 - $10,000/month
Every 7 days beginning varies

FEES: Div: $0; Cash: $0; Cert: $0; Term: $10 + comm.; Sells daily, by mail or fax, at market,
for $10 + comm.

**Shares to qualify:** 1 /de ($250)
**Safekeeping:** Yes
**Accepts foreign:** Yes
**Auto. inv.:** No
**Disc.:** No

---

## Kellogg ♥

**K/NYSE**
H: 31.00
L: 21.56
**Rec:** 30.02
**Div.:** 1.01
**Paid on:**
3.6.9.12-15
**Since:** 1925

**Food**
One Kellogg Sq.
Battle Creek. MI 49016-3599
Wells Fargo Bank  877-910-5385
$25 - $25,000/year
Every 30 days beginning 1/18
FEES: Div: $0; Cash: $0; Auto. Inv.: $0; Cert: $0; Term: $0; Sells irregularly, by mail, at market, for 7¢/sh.

**Shares to qualify:** 1
**Safekeeping:** Yes
**Accepts foreign:** Yes
**Auto. inv.:** Yes
**Disc.:** No

---

## Kellwood Co. ♥

**KWD/NYSE**
H: 25.50
L: 15.12
**Rec:** 20.50
**Div.:** 0.64
**Paid on:**
3.6.9.12-17
**Since:** 1961

**Apparel**
Box 14374
St. Louis. MO 63178
American Stock Transfer  800-937-5449
$25 - $3,000/month
Every 30 days beginning 1/20
FEES: Div: $0; Cash: $0; Cert: $0; Term: $5 + 10¢/sh.; Sells weekly, by mail, at market, for 10¢/sh.

**Shares to qualify:** 1 /de ($100)
**Safekeeping:** Yes
**Accepts foreign:** No
**Auto. inv.:** No
**Disc.:** No

---

## Kelly Services, Inc.-A ⊗

**KELYA/NAS**
H: 29.25
L: 18.50
**Rec:** 25.75
**Div.:** 1.00
**Paid on:**
3.6.9.12-15
**Since:** N/A

**Staffing services**
999 West Big Beaver Rd.
Troy. MI 48084
State St. Bank  800-829-8259
$50 - $100,000/year
Every 7 days beginning Friday
FEES: Div: $0; Cash: $5 + 5¢/sh.; Auto. Inv.: $2 + 5¢/sh.; Cert: $0; Term: $15 +12¢/sh.; Sells daily, by mail, at avg. price, for $15 + 12¢/sh.

**Shares to qualify:** 1 /de ($250)
**Safekeeping:** Yes
**Accepts foreign:** Yes
**Auto. inv.:** Yes
**Disc.:** No

---

## Kennametal, Inc. ♥

**KMT/NYSE**
H: 39.47
L: 22.93
**Rec:** 39.47
**Div.:** 0.68
**Paid on:**
2.5.8.11-25
**Since:** N/A

**Metals fabricating**
Box 231, 1600 Technology Way
Latrobe. PA 15650-0231
Mellon Inv. Svcs.  800-756-3353
$25 - $4,000/quarter
Every 90 days beginning 2/25
FEES: Div: $0!; Cash: $0!; Cert: $0!; Term: $0; Sells within 2 bus. days, by mail , at market, for comm.

**Shares to qualify:** 1
**Safekeeping:** No
**Accepts foreign:** Yes
**Auto. inv.:** No
**Disc.:** Div 5% Cash:
 0%

---

## Kerr-McGee ♥

**KMG/NYSE**
H: 74.10
L: 55.50
**Rec:** 60.83
**Div.:** 1.80
**Paid on:**
1.4.7.10-1
**Since:** 1941

**Oil & gas exploring & production**
Box 25861
Oklahoma Citv. OK 73125
UMB Bank, N.A.  800-884-4225
$10 - $3,000/quarter
Every 30 days beginning 1/2
FEES: Div: $0!; Cash: $0!; Cert: $0!; Term: $0; Sells weekly, by mail, at market, for $0

**Shares to qualify:** 1 /de ($750)
**Safekeeping:** Yes
**Accepts foreign:** Yes
**Auto. inv.:** No
**Disc.:** No

---

## KeyCorp ♥

**KEY/NYSE**
H: 29.25
L: 19.06
**Rec:** 27.26
**Div.:** 1.18
**Paid on:**
3.6.9.12-15
**Since:** 1965

**Banking, financial services**
127 Public Sq., OH-01-27-1113
Cleveland. OH  44114-1306
Computershare Investor Svcs.  800-539-7216
$10 - $10,000/month
Every 30 days beginning 1/15
FEES: Div: $0; Cash: $0; Cert: $0; Term: $10 + comm.; Sells irregularly, by mail, at market, for $10 + comm.

**Shares to qualify:** 1
**Safekeeping:** Yes
**Accepts foreign:** Yes
**Auto. inv.:** No
**Disc.:** No

---

## Keyspan Energy Corp. ♥

**KSE/NYSE**
H: 43.62
L: 29.10
**Rec:** 30.86
**Div.:** 1.78
**Paid on:**
2.5.8.11-1
**Since:** 1949

**Utility-gas**
One MetroTech Ctr.
Brooklvn. NY 11201
First Chicago Trust  800-482-3638
$25 - $150,000/year
Every 7 days beginning Thurs.
FEES: Div: $0!; Cash: $0!; Auto. Inv.: $0; Cert: $0!; Term: $0; Sells daily, by phone, mail, fax, or Internet, at market, for $5 + 5¢/sh.

**Shares to qualify:** 1 /de ($250)
**Safekeeping:** Yes
**Accepts foreign:** Yes
**Auto. inv.:** Yes
**Disc.:** No

---

## ✱ Kilroy Realty Corp. ♥

**KRC/NYSE**
H: 29.25
L: 24.20
**Rec:** 28.34
**Div.:** 1.92
**Paid on:**
1.4.7.10-10
**Since:** 1997

REIT
2250 East Imperial Hwy., Ste. 1200
El Segundo, CA 90245

Mellon Inv. Svcs.     888-816-7506
$100 - $5,000/month
Every 90 days beginning 1/20
FEES: Div: $0!; Cash: $0!; Cert: $0!; Term: $15 + 12¢/sh.; Sells weekly, by mail or phone, at avg. price, for $15 + 12¢/sh.

**Shares to qualify:** 1 /de ($750)
**Safekeeping:** Yes
**Accepts foreign:** Yes
**Auto. inv.:** No
**Disc.:** No

---

## ✱ Kimberly-Clark Corp. ♥

**KMB/NYSE**
H: 73.25
L: 49.93
**Rec:** 60.51
**Div.:** 1.12
**Paid on:**
1.4.7.10-2
**Since:** 1935

Paper, newsprint, & consumer products
Box 619100
Dallas, TX 75261-9100

BankBoston     800-730-4001
$25 - $3,000/quarter
Every 45 days beginning 1/2
FEES: Div: $0!; Cash: $0!; Cert: $0!; Term: $0; Sells within 10 bus. days, by mail, at market, for $1 to $10 + comm.

**Shares to qualify:** 1
**Safekeeping:** Yes
**Accepts foreign:** Yes
**Auto. inv.:** No
**Disc.:** No

---

## ✱ Kimco Realty Corp. ⊗

**KIM/NYSE**
H: 48.93
L: 39.00
**Rec:** 48.93
**Div.:** 2.88
**Paid on:**
1.4.7.10-15
**Since:** 1992

REIT
3333 New Hyde Park Rd., Ste. 100
New Hvde Park. NY 11042

Boston Eq.     877-453-1506
$50 - $250,000/year
Every 7 days beginning Wednesday
FEES: Div: $0!; Cash: $5 + 5¢/sh.; Auto. Inv.: $2 + 5¢/sh.; Cert: $0!;  Term: $15 + 12¢/sh.; Sells within 5 bus. days, by mail or phone, at market, for $15 + 12¢/sh.

**Shares to qualify:** 1 /de ($100)
**Safekeeping:** Yes
**Accepts foreign:** Yes
**Auto. inv.:** Yes
**Disc.:** No

---

## ✱ Kinder Morgan, Inc. ♥

**KMI/NYSE**
H: 60.00
L: 33.37
**Rec:** 52.56
**Div.:** 0.20
**Paid on:**
3.6.9.12-31
**Since:** 1937

Oil & gas, & gas distrib.
500 Dallas, Ste.1000
Houston. TX 77002

First Chicago Trust     800-847-4351
$25 - $8,000/quarter
Every 7 days beginning varies
FEES: Div: $0!; Cash: $0!; Auto. Inv.: $0; Cert: $0!;  Term: $5; Sells weekly, by mail, at market, for $0

**Shares to qualify:** 1
**Safekeeping:** Yes
**Accepts foreign:** Yes
**Auto. inv.:** Yes
**Disc.:** No

---

## ✱ Kmart Corp. ⊗

**KM/NYSE**
H: 13.55
L: 4.75
**Rec:** 12.50
**Div.:** 0.00
**Paid on:**
DIV. SUSP.
**Since:** --

Retail stores
3100 West Big Beaver Rd.
Trov. MI 48084

Boston Eq.     800-336-6981
$50 - $100,000/year
Every Tues. & Thurs. days beginning Tuesday
FEES: Div: n/o; Cash: $5 + 5¢/sh.; Auto. Inv.: $2 + 5¢/sh.; Cert: $0!;  Term: $10 + 12¢/sh.; Sells within 3 bus. days, by phone, mail, fax, or Internet, at market, for $10 + 12¢/sh.

**Shares to qualify:** 1 /de ($250)
**Safekeeping:** Yes
**Accepts foreign:** Yes
**Auto. inv.:** Yes
**Disc.:** No

---

## ✱ Knape & Vogt Manufacturing Co. ♥

**KNAP/NASD**
H: 15.43
L: 11.60
**Rec:** 12.42
**Div.:** 0.66
**Paid on:**
3.6.9.12-3
**Since:** 1934

Manufacturing
2700 Oak Industrial Dr., NE
Grand Rapids. MI 49505

Computershare Investor Svcs.     312-360-5341
$25 - $1,000/month
Every 30 days beginning 1/2
FEES: Div: $0!; Cash: $0!; Cert: $0!; Term: $0; Sells within 10 bus. days, by mail, at market, for fee + comm.

**Shares to qualify:** 1
**Safekeeping:** Yes
**Accepts foreign:** Yes
**Auto. inv.:** No
**Disc.:** No

---

## ✱ Knight Ridder Inc. ♥

**KRI/NYSE**
H: 63.80
L: 44.12
**Rec:** 61.89
**Div.:** 1.00
**Paid on:**
2.5.8.11-12
**Since:** 1941

Newspaper publisher
50 W. San Fernando, Ste. 1500
San Jose. CA 95113

Mellon Inv. Svcs.     800-982-7648
$25 - $10,000/month
Every 7 days beginning Monday
FEES: Div: $0; Cash: $0; Cert: $0; Term: $0; Sells biweekly, by mail or phone, at market, for $15 + 10¢/sh.

**Shares to qualify:** 50
**Safekeeping:** Yes
**Accepts foreign:** Yes
**Auto. inv.:** No
**Disc.:** No

---

## ＊ Korea Fund, Inc. (The)

**KF/NYSE** | Closed-end fund

H: 13.50
L: 8.31
**Rec:** 10.39
**Div.:** 0.00
**Paid on:**
DIV. SUSP.
**Since:**--

345 Park Ave.
New York, NY 10154

Kemper Service Co.     800-621-1048
$100 - $3,000/semiannually
Every 180 days beginning 2/15

**Shares to qualify:** 1
**Safekeeping:** No
**Accepts foreign:** Yes
**Auto. inv.:** No
**Disc.:** Div: 0-5% Cash: 0%

FEES: Div: $0!; Cash: 75¢ + comm.; Cert: $0; Term: $0; Sells within 7 to 10 bus. days , by mail or phone, at avg. price, for $2.50 + comm.

---

## ＊ Kramont Realty Trust ♥

**KRT/NYSE** | REIT

H: 13.80
L: 8.75
**Rec:** 12.87
**Div.:** N/A
**Paid on:**
1.4.7.10-20
**Since:** 2000

580 W. Germantown Pike
Plymouth Meeting, PA 19462

American Stock Transfer     877-322-4940
$100 - $3,000/quarter
Every 30 days beginning 1/15

**Shares to qualify:** 1
**Safekeeping:** Yes
**Accepts foreign:** Yes
**Auto. inv.:** No
**Disc.:** No

FEES: Div: $0!; Cash: $0!; Cert: $0!; Term: $0; Sells weekly, by mail, at market, for $15 + 10¢/sh.

---

## ＊ La Quinta Companies ♥

**LQI/NYSE** | REIT

H: 6.15
L: 2.00
**Rec:** 5.74
**Div.:** 0.00
**Paid on:**
DIV. SUSP.
**Since:**--

909 Hidden Ridge, Ste. 600
Irving, TX 75038

BankBoston     800-730-4001
$100 - $10,000/quarter
Every 90 days beginning 2/15

**Shares to qualify:** 1
**Safekeeping:** No
**Accepts foreign:** No
**Auto. inv.:** No
**Disc.:** No

FEES: Div: n/o; Cash: $0!; Cert: $0!; Term: $0,Does not sell through the plan

---

## ＊ La-Z-Boy, Inc.

**LZB/NYSE** | Furniture manufacturer

H: 20.48
L: 13.00
**Rec:** 20.40
**Div.:** 0.36
**Paid on:**
3.6.9.12-10
**Since:** 1971

1284 North Telegraph Rd.
Monroe. MI 48162-3390

American Stock Transfer     800-937-9449
$25 - $1,000/month
Every day days beginning daily

**Shares to qualify:** 1
**Safekeeping:** Yes
**Accepts foreign:** No
**Auto. inv.:** Yes
**Disc.:** No

FEES: Div: 2 % to $2.50 + 10¢/sh.; Cash: $2.50 + 10¢/sh.; Auto. Inv.: $2.50 + 10¢/sh.; Cert: $0!; Term: $15 + 10¢/sh. Sells daily, by phone, mail, fax, or Internet, at market, for $15 + 10¢/sh.

---

## ＊ LabOne, Inc. ♥

**LABS/NASD** | Insurance, health care services

H: 10.31
L: 4.37
**Rec:** 8.22
**Div.:** 0.00
**Paid on:**
DIV. SUSP.
**Since:**--

10101 Renner Blvd.
Lenexa. KS 66219

American Stock Transfer     800-937-5449
$25 - $5,000/quarter
Every 90 days beginning 3/1

**Shares to qualify:** 1
**Safekeeping:** No
**Accepts foreign:** No
**Auto. inv.:** No
**Disc.:** No

FEES: Div: n/o; Cash: $0!; Cert: $0!; Term: $0; Sells weekly, by mail, at market, for 4¢/sh.

---

## ＊ Laclede Gas Co. ♥

**LG/NYSE** | Utility-gas

H: 25.48
L: 19.62
**Rec:** 22.60
**Div.:** 1.34
**Paid on:**
1.4.7.10-1
**Since:** 1946

720 Olive St.
St. Louis. MO 63101

UMB Bank, N.A.     800-884-4225
$100 - $30,000/year
Every 90 days beginning 1/2

**Shares to qualify:** 1
**Safekeeping:** Yes
**Accepts foreign:** Yes
**Auto. inv.:** No
**Disc.:** No

FEES: Div: $0; Cash: $0; Cert: $0; Term: $10 + comm.; Sells monthly, by mail or phone, at market, for $10 + comm.

---

## ＊ Lakeland Financial Corp. ♥

**LKFN/NASD** | Bank holding co.

H: 17.00
L: 10.31
**Rec:** 16.80
**Div.:** 0.60
**Paid on:**
1.4.7.10-25
**Since:** N/A

202 E. Center St., Box 1387
Warsaw, IN 46581

Lake City Bank     219-267-6144
$100 - $5,000/quarter
Every 90 days beginning varies

**Shares to qualify:** 1
**Safekeeping:** Yes
**Accepts foreign:** Yes
**Auto. inv.:** No
**Disc.:** No

FEES: Div: $0!; Cash: $0!; Cert: $0!; Term: $0; Sells within 5 bus. days, by mail, at market, for comm.

---

＊ DRIP enrollment through Temper Enrollment Service (see page 180).     **106**

## Lancaster Colony Corp. ♥

**LANC/NASD**
H: 34.50
L: 22.37
**Rec:** 34.25

**Div.:** 0.68
**Paid on:**
3.6.9.12-31
**Since:** N/A

Household products
37 West Broad St.
Columbus. OH 43215-4177

American Stock Transfer     800-937-5449
$50 - $20,000/year
Every 30 days beginning 1/10

**Shares to qualify:** 1
**Safekeeping:** Yes
**Accepts foreign:** Yes
**Auto. inv.:** No
**Disc.:** No

FEES: Div: $0!; Cash: $0!; Cert: $0!; Term: $0; Sells daily, by mail, at market, for 4¢/sh.

---

## Lance, Inc.

**LNCE/NASD**
H: 14.40
L: 8.56
**Rec:** 13.05

**Div.:** 0.64
**Paid on:**
2.5.8.11-15
**Since:** 1945

Snack foods, vending machines
Box 32368
Charlotte. NC 28232

First Union Nat'l Bank     800-829-8432
$10 - $1,000/month
Every 30 days beginning 1/15

**Shares to qualify:** 1
**Safekeeping:** Yes
**Accepts foreign:** No
**Auto. inv.:** No
**Disc.:** No

FEES: Div: $0!; Cash: 4% to $2.50; Cert: $0!; Term: $0; Sells daily, by mail, at market, for $0

---

## LaSalle Hotel Properties ♥

**LHO/NYSE**
H: 18.00
L: 13.37
**Rec:** 17.15

**Div.:** 1.56
**Paid on:**
1.5.8.11-15
**Since:** 1998

REIT
4800 Montgomery Ln., Ste. M25
Bethesda. MD 20814

Computershare Investor Svcs.     312-360-5100
$100 - $5,000/month
Every 30 days beginning 1/15

**Shares to qualify:** 1
**Safekeeping:** Yes
**Accepts foreign:** Yes
**Auto. inv.:** No
**Disc.:** No

FEES: Div: $0!; Cash: $0!; Cert: $0!; Term: $10 + comm.; Sells within 5 bus. days, by mail, at market, for $10 + comm.

---

## LCNB Corp. ⊗

**LCNB/OTC**
H: 42.00
L: 32.50
**Rec:** 39.50

**Div.:** 1.80
**Paid on:**
3.6.9.12-15
**Since:** N/A

Bank holding co.
2 North Broadway, Box 59
Lebanon. OH 45036

Computershare Investor Svcs.     312-588-4127
$25 - $25,000/quarter
Every 5 days beginning varies

**Shares to qualify:** 1 /de ($500)
**Safekeeping:** Yes
**Accepts foreign:** Yes
**Auto. inv.:** Yes
**Disc.:** No

FEES: Div: $0!; Cash: $5 + 10¢/sh.; Auto. Inv.: $1.50 + 10¢/sh.; Cert: $0!; Term: $0; Sells within 5 bus. days, by mail, at market, for $10 + 10¢/sh.

---

## Lear Corp.

**LEA/NYSE**
H: 41.46
L: 19.50
**Rec:** 40.81

**Div.:** 0.00
**Paid on:**
N/0
**Since:** N/0

Automotive supplier
21557 Telegraph Rd., Box 5008
Southfield. MI 48086-5008

Bank of New York     800-524-4458
$50 - $150,000/year
Every 30 days beginning 1/25

**Shares to qualify:** 1 /de ($250)
**Safekeeping:** Yes
**Accepts foreign:** Yes
**Auto. inv.:** No
**Disc.:** No

FEES: Div: n/o; Cash: $2; Cert: $5; Term: $5; Sells weekly, by mail, at market, for $5 + 7¢/sh.

---

## Lehman Brothers Holdings Inc. ♥

**LEH/NYSE**
H: 86.20
L: 47.00
**Rec:** 69.20

**Div.:** 0.28
**Paid on:**
2.5.8.11-30
**Since:** 1994

Investment banking
1 World Financial Ctr., 27th Fl.
New York. NY 10281

Bank of New York     800-824-5707
$50 - $175,000/year
Every 7 days beginning varies

**Shares to qualify:** 1 /de ($500)
**Safekeeping:** Yes
**Accepts foreign:** No
**Auto. inv.:** Yes
**Disc.:** No

FEES: Div: $0!; Cash: $0!; Auto. Inv.: $0; Cert: $0!; Term: $10 + 10¢/sh.; Sells daily, by mail, at market, for $10 + 10¢/sh.

---

## LESCO, Inc. ♥

**LSCO/NASD**
H: 18.37
L: 10.56
**Rec:** 11.00

**Div.:** 0.07
**Paid on:**
6-11
**Since:** 1984

Mfr. & dist. of turf grass & lawn equip.
15885 Sprogue Rd.
Strongsville. OH 44136

National City Bank     800-622-6757
$25 - $5,000/month
Every 30 days beginning 1/10

**Shares to qualify:** 1
**Safekeeping:** Yes
**Accepts foreign:** Yes
**Auto. inv.:** No
**Disc.:** No

FEES: Div: $0!; Cash: $0; Cert: $0; Term: $0; Sells weekly, by mail or fax, at avg. price, for 5% to $5

---

## ✳ Libbey Inc.

**Produces glass & ceramic tableware**

**LBY/NYSE**
H: 42.20
L: 26.31
**Rec:** 33.05
**Div.:** 0.30
**Paid on:**
3.6.9.12-6
**Since:** 1993

300 Madison Ave., Box 10060
Toledo. OH 43699-0060

Bank of New York      800-524-4458
$20 - $5,000/investment
Every 7 days beginning Thursday

**Shares to qualify:** 1 /de ($100)
**Safekeeping:** Yes
**Accepts foreign:** Yes
**Auto. inv.:** Yes
**Disc.:** No

FEES: Div 7¢/sh.; Cash: 7¢/sh.; Auto. Inv.: $0; Cert: $5; Term: $0; Sells weekly, by mail, at avg. price, for $5 + 7¢/sh.

---

## ✳ Liberty ALL-STAR Equity Fund

**Closed-end fund**

**USA/NYSE**
H: 13.57
L: 11.31
**Rec:** 12.91
**Div.:** 1.24
**Paid on:**
1.3.7.10-VARIES
**Since:** 1986

c/o Liberty Asset Mgt., 600 Atlantic Ave.
Boston. MA 02210-2214

State St. Bank      800-542-3863
$0 - $unlimited
Every 30 days beginning 1/15

**Shares to qualify:** 1
**Safekeeping:** Yes
**Accepts foreign:** Yes
**Auto. inv.:** No
**Disc.:** No

FEES: Div: comm.; Cash: $1.25 + comm.; Cert: $0; Term: $0; Sells daily, by phone or mail, at market, for $2.50 + comm.

---

## ✳ Liberty ALL-STAR Growth Fund, Inc.

**Closed-end fund**

**ASG/NYSE**
H: 12.56
L: 7.95
**Rec:** 8.93
**Div.:** 0.92
**Paid on:**
1.5.7.10-VARIES
**Since:** 1996

c/o Liberty Asset Mgt., 600 Atlantic Ave.
Boston. MA 02210-2214

State St. Bank      800-542-3863
$100 - $3,000/month
Every 30 days beginning 1/15

**Shares to qualify:** 1
**Safekeeping:** Yes
**Accepts foreign:** Yes
**Auto. inv.:** No
**Disc.:** No

FEES: Div: comm.; Cash: $1.25 + comm.; Cert: $0; Term: $0; Sells daily, by mail or phone, at market, for $2.50 + comm.

---

## ✳ Liberty Property Trust ♥

**REIT**

**LRY/NYSE**
H: 30.38
L: 25.00
**Rec:** 30.38
**Div.:** 2.28
**Paid on:**
1.4.7.10-15
**Since:** 1994

65 Valley Stream Pkwy.
Malvern. PA 19355

Boston Eq.      800-944-2214
$250 - $7,500/month
Every 30 days beginning 1/15

**Shares to qualify:** 10 /de ($1000)
**Safekeeping:** Yes
**Accepts foreign:** No
**Auto. inv.:** Yes
**Disc.:** Div 3% Cash: 0%

FEES: Div: $0; Cash: $0; Auto. Inv.: $0; Cert: $0; Term: $0; Sells daily, by mail, at market, for $10 + comm.

---

## ✳ Lilly (Eli) & Co. ⊗

**Drugs**

**LLY/NYSE**
H: 108.93
L: 66.62
**Rec:** 78.10
**Div.:** 1.12
**Paid on:**
3.6.9.12-10
**Since:** 1885

Lilly Corporate Ctr.-Drop Code 1859
Indianapolis. IN 46285

Wells Fargo Bank      800-833-8699
$50 - $150,000/year
Every 7 days beginning varies

**Shares to qualify:** 1 /de ($1000)
**Safekeeping:** Yes
**Accepts foreign:** Yes
**Auto. inv.:** Yes
**Disc.:** No

FEES: Div: 3% to $3 + 3¢/sh.; Cash: $5 + 3¢/sh.; Auto. Inv.: $2 + 3¢/sh.; Cert: $0; Term: $10 + 12¢/sh.; Sells daily, by mail or phone, at market, for $10 + 12¢/sh.

---

## ✳ Limited (The) ♥

**Retail stores**

**LTD/NYSE**
H: 27.87
L: 14.43
**Rec:** 16.72
**Div.:** 0.30
**Paid on:**
3.6.9.12-14
**Since:** 1970

3 Limited Pkwy.
Columbus. OH 43216

First Chicago Trust      800-317-4445
$30 - $6,000/quarter
Every 45 days beginning 2/5

**Shares to qualify:** 1
**Safekeeping:** No
**Accepts foreign:** No
**Auto. inv.:** No
**Disc.:** No

FEES: Div: $0!; Cash: $0!; Cert: $0!; Term: 12¢/sh.; Sells daily, by mail, at market, for $10 + 12¢/sh.

---

## ✳ Lincoln Nat'l Convert. Securities Fund ♥

**Closed-end fund**

**LNV/NYSE**
H: 19.18
L: 13.53
**Rec:** 15.45
**Div.:** 0.80
**Paid on:**
1-16.4.7.10-31
**Since:** N/A

200 East Berry St.
Fort Wayne. IN 46802

First Chicago Trust      800-317-4445
$100 - $3,000/quarter
Every 90 days beginning 3/7

**Shares to qualify:** 1
**Safekeeping:** Yes
**Accepts foreign:** Yes
**Auto. inv.:** No
**Disc.:** No

FEES: Div: $0!; Cash: $0!; Cert: $0!; Term: 12¢/sh.; Sells daily, by mail, at market, for $10 + 12¢/sh.

---

✳ DRIP enrollment through Temper Enrollment Service (see page 180).      **108**

## Lincoln Nat'l Income Fund ♥

**LND/NYSE** | Closed-end fund

H: 13.20
L: 10.55
**Rec:** 12.83

**Div.:** 1.31
**Paid on:**
1-16.4.7.10-31
**Since:** N/A

c/o Delaware Service Co., 1818 Market St.
Philadelphia. PA 19103

First Chicago Trust     800-317-4445
$100 - $3,000/quarter
Every 90 days beginning 3/7

**Shares to qualify:** 1
**Safekeeping:** Yes
**Accepts foreign:** Yes
**Auto. inv.:** No
**Disc.:** No

FEES: Div: $0!; Cash: $0!; Cert: $0!; Term: 12¢/sh.; Sells daily, by mail, at market, for $10 + 12¢/sh.

---

## Lincoln National Corp. ⊗

**LNC/NYSE** | Insurance

H: 56.37
L: 38.00
**Rec:** 49.82

**Div.:** 1.22
**Paid on:**
2.5.8.11-1
**Since:** 1905

1500 Market St., 39th Fl.
Philadelphia. PA 19102-2112

First Chicago Trust     800-317-4445
$100 - $250,000/year
Every 7 days beginning varies

**Shares to qualify:** 1 /de ($2000)
**Safekeeping:** Yes
**Accepts foreign:** Yes
**Auto. inv.:** Yes
**Disc.:** No

FEES: Div: 5% to $3 + 3¢/sh.; Cash: $5 + 3¢/sh.; Auto. Inv.: $2 + 3¢/sh.; Cert: $0!; Term: $10 + 12¢/sh.; Sells daily, by mail, at market, for $10 + 12¢/sh.

---

## LION Inc. ⊗

**LINN/OTC** | Internet

H: 0.40
L: 0.05
**Rec:** 0.09

**Div.:** N/A
**Paid on:**
N/0
**Since:** --

P.O. Box 18599
Spokane. WA 99228

First Chicago Trust     800-756-8200
$25 - $250,000/year
Every 5 days beginning varies

**Shares to qualify:** 1 /de ($150)
**Safekeeping:** Yes
**Accepts foreign:** Yes
**Auto. inv.:** Yes
**Disc.:** No

FEES: Div: n/o; Cash: $5 + 3¢/sh.; Auto. Inv.: $0; Cert: $0; Term: $15 + 12¢/sh.; Sells daily, by phone, mail, fax, or Internet, at market, for $15 + 12¢/sh.

---

## Liz Claiborne, Inc. ♥

**LIZ/NYSE** | Apparel

H: 54.95
L: 34.37
**Rec:** 52.44

**Div.:** 0.45
**Paid on:**
3.6.9.12-2
**Since:** 1984

One Claiborne Ave.
North Bergen. NJ 07047

First Chicago Trust     201-324-0313
$25 - $60,000/year
Every 30 days beginning 1/30

**Shares to qualify:** 1
**Safekeeping:** Yes
**Accepts foreign:** No
**Auto. inv.:** Yes
**Disc.:** No

FEES: Div: $0!; Cash: $0!; Auto. Inv.: $1; Cert: $0!; Term: $10 + 12¢/sh.; Sells daily, by mail, at market, for $10 + 12¢/sh.

---

## LNB Bancorp, Inc. ♥

**LNBB/NASD** | Bank holding company

H: 23.03
L: 17.64
**Rec:** 20.10

**Div.:** 0.98
**Paid on:**
1.4.7.10-1
**Since:** N/A

457 Broadway
Lorain. OH 44052-1739

Registrar & Transfer     800-368-5948
$50 - $2,500/month
Every 30 days beginning 1/1

**Shares to qualify:** 1 /de ($250)
**Safekeeping:** Yes
**Accepts foreign:** Yes
**Auto. inv.:** Yes
**Disc.:** No

FEES: Div: $0; Cash: $0; Auto. Inv.: $0; Cert: $0; Term: $0; Sells weekly, by mail, at market, for $15 + comm.

---

## Lockheed Martin ♥

**LMT/NYSE** | Aeronautics, electronics, missiles

H: 40.01
L: 27.00
**Rec:** 38.99

**Div.:** 0.44
**Paid on:**
3.6.9.12-30
**Since:** 1995

6801 Rockledge Dr.
Bethesda. MD 20817-1836

First Chicago Trust     800-446-2617
$50 - $unlimited
Every 30 days beginning 1/31

**Shares to qualify:** 1 /de ($250)
**Safekeeping:** Yes
**Accepts foreign:** Yes
**Auto. inv.:** Yes
**Disc.:** No

FEES: Div: $0!; Cash: $0!; Auto. Inv.: $0; Cert: $0!; Term: $10 + 12¢/sh.; Sells daily, by phone, mail, fax, or Internet, at market, for $10 + 12¢/sh.

---

## Long Island Financial Corp. ♥

**LICB/NASD** | Bank holding co.

H: 20.00
L: 11.12
**Rec:** 18.25

**Div.:** 0.32
**Paid on:**
1-1 & 7-1
**Since:** N/A

One Suffolk Sq.
Islandia. NY 11749

Mellon Inv. Svcs.     800-851-9677
$1000 - $10,000/quarter
Every 90 days beginning 1/1

**Shares to qualify:** 1
**Safekeeping:** Yes
**Accepts foreign:** Yes
**Auto. inv.:** No
**Disc.:** No

FEES: Div: $0!; Cash: $0!; Cert: $5; Term: $15; Sells weekly, by mail, at avg. price, for $15

---

## Longs Drug Stores ⊗

**\***

**LDG/NYSE**
H: 32.00
L: 17.56
**Rec:** 21.79
**Div.:** 0.56
**Paid on:**
1,4,7,10-10
**Since:** 1961

**Self-service drug store chain**
141 North Civic Dr.
Walnut Creek, CA 94596
Mellon Inv. Svcs.    888-213-0886
$25 - $5,000/quarter
Every 7 days beginning varies
FEES: Div: 5% to $10; Cash: $5 + 12¢/sh.; Auto. Inv.: $0; Cert: $0; Term: $0; Sells weekly, by mail, at market, for $15 + 12¢/sh.

**Shares to qualify:** 1 /de ($500)
**Safekeeping:** Yes
**Accepts foreign:** Yes
**Auto. inv.:** Yes
**Disc.:** No

---

## Louisiana-Pacific Corp. ♥

**LPX/NYSE**
H: 13.95
L: 7.06
**Rec:** 10.86
**Div.:** 0.20
**Paid on:**
3,6,9,12-1
**Since:** 1973

**Building products**
111 S.W. 5th Ave.
Portland, OR 97204-3601
First Chicago Trust    201-324-1644
$25 - $12,000/year
Every 30 days beginning 1/31
FEES: Div: $0!; Cash: $0!; Cert: $0!; Term: $0; Sells daily, by mail, phone or Internet, at market, for $10 + 12¢/sh.

**Shares to qualify:** 1
**Safekeeping:** Yes
**Accepts foreign:** Yes
**Auto. inv.:** No
**Disc.:** No

---

## Lowe's Cos., Inc.

**\***

**LOW/NYSE**
H: 39.86
L: 17.12
**Rec:** 36.11
**Div.:** 0.08
**Paid on:**
1,4,7,10-31
**Since:** 1961

**Retail**
Box 1111
North Wilkesboro, NC 28656
Wachovia    877-282-1174
$25 - $250,000/year
Every 7 days beginning Thursday
FEES: Div: $0!; Cash: 5% to $2.50 + 5¢/sh.; Auto. Inv.: 5% to $2.50 + 5¢/sh.; Cert: $0!; Term: $0; Sells daily, by mail, at avg. price, for $10 + 12¢/sh.

**Shares to qualify:** 1 /de ($250)
**Safekeeping:** Yes
**Accepts foreign:** Yes
**Auto. inv.:** Yes
**Disc.:** No

---

## LSB Bancshares, Inc. ⊗

**\***

**LXBK/NASD**
H: 15.50
L: 10.37
**Rec:** 13.90
**Div.:** 0.56
**Paid on:**
1,4,7,10-15
**Since:** N/A

**Bank holding company**
Box 867
Lexington, NC 27293-0867
Wachovia    866-367-6351
$50 - $350,000/year
Every 7 days beginning Friday
FEES: Div: $0; Cash: $5 + 5¢/sh.; Auto. Inv.: $2 + 5¢/sh.; Cert: $0; Term: $15 + 12¢/sh.; Sells daily, by phone, mail, fax, or Internet, at market, for $15 + 12¢/sh.

**Shares to qualify:** 1 /de ($250)
**Safekeeping:** Yes
**Accepts foreign:** Yes
**Auto. inv.:** Yes
**Disc.:** No

---

## LTC Properties, Inc.

**LTC/NYSE**
H: 6.37
L: 2.93
**Rec:** 4.80
**Div.:** 1.16
**Paid on:**
3,6,9,12-31
**Since:** 1992

**Health care REIT**
300 Esplanade Dr., Ste.1860
Oxnard, CA 93030
Computershare Investor Svcs.    312-360-5294
$25 - $1,000/month
Every 30 days beginning 1/15
FEES: Div: $0; Cash: comm.; Cert: $0; Term: $0; Sells weekly, by mail, at market, for 8¢/sh.

**Shares to qualify:** 1
**Safekeeping:** Yes
**Accepts foreign:** Yes
**Auto. inv.:** No
**Disc.:** No

---

## Lubrizol Corp.

**LZ/NYSE**
H: 36.25
L: 18.25
**Rec:** 35.90
**Div.:** 1.04
**Paid on:**
3,6,9,12-10
**Since:** N/A

**Chemicals**
29400 Lakeland Blvd.
Wickliffe, OH 44092-2298
American Stock Transfer    877-573-3998
$25 - $10,000/investment
Every 7 days beginning varies
FEES: Div: 2% to $2.50; Cash: $2.50; Auto. Inv.: $2.50; Cert: $0; Term: $15 ; Sells daily, by mail or phone, at market, for $15

**Shares to qualify:** 1 /de ($250)
**Safekeeping:** Yes
**Accepts foreign:** No
**Auto. inv.:** Yes
**Disc.:** No

---

## Luby's Inc. ♥

**\***

**LUB/NYSE**
H: 10.05
L: 3.50
**Rec:** 9.00
**Div.:** 0.00
**Paid on:**
DIV. SUSP.
**Since:** --

**Cafeteria-style restaurants**
2211 Northeast Loop 410, Box 33069
San Antonio, TX 78265-3069
American Stock Transfer    800-937-5449
$20 - $5,000/quarter
Every 30 days beginning 1/2
FEES: Div: n/o; Cash: $0; Cert: $0; Term: comm.; Sells weekly, by mail, at market, for comm.

**Shares to qualify:** 1
**Safekeeping:** Yes
**Accepts foreign:** Yes
**Auto. inv.:** No
**Disc.:** No

---

## Lucent Technologies Inc. ⊗

| | |
|---|---|
| LU/NYSE | **Mfr. telecommunications systems** |
| H: 45.18 | 600 Mountain Ave., Rm. 3D 548 |
| L: 5.04 | Murray Hill. NJ 07974-0636 |
| **Rec:** 6.51 | Bank of New York    888-582-3686 |
| **Div.:** 0.00 | $100 - $50,000/investment |
| **Paid on:** | Every daily days beginning 1/2 |
| DIV. SUSP. | |
| **Since:** -- | |

**Shares to qualify:** 1 /de ($1000)
**Safekeeping:** Yes
**Accepts foreign:** Yes
**Auto. inv.:** Yes
**Disc.:** No

FEES: Div: n/o; Cash: 10% to $2 + 10¢/sh.; Auto. Inv.: $0; Cert: $0; Term: $0; Sells daily, by mail or phone, at market, for $10 + 10¢/sh.

---

## ✶ Lyondell Chemical Co. ♥

| | |
|---|---|
| LYO/NYSE | **Chemicals & refining** |
| H: 17.95 | Box 3646 |
| L: 11.00 | Houston. TX 77253-3646 |
| **Rec:** 14.15 | Bank of New York    800-524-4458 |
| **Div.:** 0.90 | $25 - $10,000/quarter |
| **Paid on:** | Every 90 days beginning 3/15 |
| 3.6.9.12-15 | |
| **Since:** N/A | |

**Shares to qualify:** 1
**Safekeeping:** Yes
**Accepts foreign:** No
**Auto. inv.:** No
**Disc.:** No

FEES: Div: $0; Cash: $0; Cert: $0; Term: $0; Sells irregularly, by mail, at market, for $5 + comm.

---

## ✶ M & T Bank Corp.

| | |
|---|---|
| MTB/NYSE | **Banking** |
| H: 82.11 | One M & T Plaza, 12th Fl., Box 223 |
| L: 46.67 | Buffalo. NY 14203-2399 |
| **Rec:** 79.90 | Boston Eq.    800-730-4001 |
| **Div.:** 1.00 | $10 - $1,000/month |
| **Paid on:** | Every 30 days beginning 1/2 |
| 3.6.9.12-28 | |
| **Since:** N/A | |

**Shares to qualify:** 1
**Safekeeping:** Yes
**Accepts foreign:** No
**Auto. inv.:** Yes
**Disc.:** No

FEES: Div: 5% to $2.50 + comm.; Cash: 5% to $2.50 + comm.; Auto. Inv.: 5% to $2.50 +comm.; Cert: $0; Term: $0; Sells within10 bus. days, by mail, at market, for 5% to $10 + comm.

---

## ✶ MacDermid, Inc.

| | |
|---|---|
| MRD/NYSE | **Industrial metal finishing chemicals** |
| H: 27.00 | 245 Freight St. |
| L: 15.50 | Waterbury. CT 06702 |
| **Rec:** 16.30 | Bank of New York    877-268-5209 |
| **Div.:** 0.08 | $50 - $unlimited |
| **Paid on:** | Every 30 days beginning 1/2 |
| 1.4.7.10-1 | |
| **Since:** N/A | |

**Shares to qualify:** 1
**Safekeeping:** Yes
**Accepts foreign:** Yes
**Auto. inv.:** Yes
**Disc.:** No

FEES: Div: 10% to $1.50 + 10¢/sh.; Cash: $2.50 + 10¢/sh.; Auto. Inv.: $2.50 + 10¢/sh.; Cert: $0; Term: $10 + 10¢/sh.; Sells daily, by mail or phone, at avg. price, for $10 + 10¢/sh.

---

## ✶ Macerich Co. ♥

| | |
|---|---|
| MAC/NYSE | **Real estate operations** |
| H: 25.08 | Box 2172 |
| L: 18.31 | Santa Monica. CA 90407-2172 |
| **Rec:** 24.55 | First Chicago Trust    800-567-0169 |
| **Div.:** 2.12 | $50 - $250,000/year |
| **Paid on:** | Every 7 days beginning varies |
| 3.6.9.12-VARIES | |
| **Since:** 1994 | |

**Shares to qualify:** 1 /de ($250)
**Safekeeping:** Yes
**Accepts foreign:** Yes
**Auto. inv.:** Yes
**Disc.:** No

FEES: Div: $0!; Cash: $0!; Auto. Inv.: $0; Cert: $0!; Term: $0; Sells daily, by mail or phone, at market, for $10 + 12¢/sh.

---

## ✶ Mack-Cali Realty Corp. ♥

| | |
|---|---|
| CLI/NYSE | **REIT** |
| H: 28.87 | 11 Commerce Dr. |
| L: 25.49 | Cranford. NJ 07016 |
| **Rec:** 28.81 | First Chicago Trust    800-317-4445 |
| **Div.:** 2.44 | $100 - $5,000/month |
| **Paid on:** | Every 30 days beginning 3/31 |
| 1.4.7.10-VARIES | |
| **Since:** 1994 | |

**Shares to qualify:** 1 /de ($2000)
**Safekeeping:** Yes
**Accepts foreign:** Yes
**Auto. inv.:** Yes
**Disc.:** No

FEES: Div: $0; Cash: $0; Auto. Inv.: $0; Cert: $0; Term: $15 + 12¢/sh.; Sells weekly, by mail, at market, for $15 + 12¢/sh.

---

## ✶ Madison Gas & Electric Co.

| | |
|---|---|
| MDSN/NAS | **Utility-electric, gas** |
| H: 27.80 | Box 1231 |
| L: 19.25 | Madison. WI 53701-1231 |
| **Rec:** 24.12 | Madison G&E Co.    800-356-6423 |
| **Div.:** 1.32 | $25 - $25,000/quarter |
| **Paid on:** | Every 30 days beginning 1/15 |
| 3.6.9.12-15 | |
| **Since:** 1909 | |

**Shares to qualify:** 1 /de ($50)
**Safekeeping:** Yes
**Accepts foreign:** Yes
**Auto. inv.:** Yes
**Disc.:** No

FEES: Div: comm.; Cash: comm.; Auto. Inv.: $0; Cert: $0; Term: $0; Sells weekly, by phone or mail, at market, for comm.

---

## ✳ Magellan Petroleum Corp.

**MPET/NASD** | **Oil & gas exploration**

H: 1.65
L: 0.71
Rec: 1.08
Div.: 0.00
Paid on:
N/0
Since: N/0

149 Durham Rd., Oak Park-Unit 31
Madison. CT 06443

American Stock Transfer    800-937-5449
$25 - $10,000/investment
Every day days beginning daily

FEES: Div: n/o; Cash: $2.50 + 10¢/sh.; Auto. Inv.: $2.50 + 10¢/sh.; Cert: $0; Term: $7.50 + 10¢/sh. Sells daily, by phone, mail, fax, or Internet, at market, for $7.50 + 10¢/sh.

**Shares to qualify:** 1 /de ($250)
**Safekeeping:** Yes
**Accepts foreign:** Yes
**Auto. inv.:** Yes
**Disc.:** No

---

## ✳ Mahaska Investment Co. ♥

**OSKY/NASD** | **Regional banks**

H: 12.50
L: 7.50
Rec: 11.50
Div.: 0.60
Paid on:
3.6.9.12-15
Since: N/A

222 First Ave. East, Box 1104
Oskaloosa. IA 52577-1104

Illinois Stock Transfer    800-757-5755
$25 - $5,000/month
Every 30 days beginning 1/2

FEES: Div: $0!; Cash: $0!; Cert: $0!; Term: $5 + comm.; Sells within 10 bus. days, by mail, at market, for $3

**Shares to qualify:** 1
**Safekeeping:** Yes
**Accepts foreign:** No
**Auto. inv.:** No
**Disc.:** No

---

## ✳ Manitowoc Co. ♥

**MTW/NYSE** | **Machinery**

H: 31.06
L: 17.62
Rec: 28.25
Div.: 0.30
Paid on:
3.6.9.12-10
Since: 1945

500 South 16th St., Box 66
Manitowoc. WI 54221-0066

First Chicago Trust    800-519-3111
$10 - $60,000/year
Every 30 days beginning 1/10

FEES: Div: $0!; Cash: $0!; Cert: $0!; Term: $0; Sells daily, by mail, at market, for $10 + 12¢/sh.

**Shares to qualify:** 1
**Safekeeping:** Yes
**Accepts foreign:** Yes
**Auto. inv.:** No
**Disc.:** No

---

## ✳ Manpower ♥

**MAN/NYSE** | **Nongovernmental temp. employment**

H: 39.43
L: 27.36
Rec: 32.15
Div.: 0.20
Paid on:
6-14 & 12-14
Since: 1994

5301 N. Ironwood Rd., Box 2053
Milwaukee. WI 53201

Mellon Inv. Svcs.    800-851-9677
$25 - $10,000/year
Every 30 days beginning 1/15

FEES: Div: $0!; Cash: $0!; Cert: $0!; Term: $5 + comm.; Sells biweekly, by mail , at market, for $5 + comm.

**Shares to qualify:** 1
**Safekeeping:** Yes
**Accepts foreign:** Yes
**Auto. inv.:** No
**Disc.:** No

---

## ✳ Manufactured Home Communities ♥

**MHC/NYSE** | **REIT**

H: 29.50
L: 23.50
Rec: 28.67
Div.: 1.78
Paid on:
1.4.7.10-8
Since: 1993

2 North Riverside Plaza, Ste. 800
Chicago. IL 60606

Mellon Inv. Svcs.    888-847-1159
$250 - $5,000/month
Every 30 days beginning 1/14

FEES: Div: $0!; Cash: $0!; Cert: $0!; Term: $15 + 12¢/sh.; Sells within 3 bus. days, by mail, at market, for $15 + 12¢/sh.

**Shares to qualify:** 1 /de ($100)
**Safekeeping:** Yes
**Accepts foreign:** Yes
**Auto. inv.:** No
**Disc.:** Div: 0% Cash:
0-5%

---

## ✳ Marcus Corp. (The) ♥

**MCS/NYSE** | **Hotels, restaurants & movie theaters**

H: 15.72
L: 10.12
Rec: 13.90
Div.: 0.22
Paid on:
2.5.8.11-15
Since: 1983

250 East Wisconsin Ave., Ste.1700
Milwaukee. WI 53202-4220

Firstar Bank    800-637-7549
$100 - $1,500/month
Every 30 days beginning 1/15

FEES: Div: $0; Cash: $0; Cert: $0; Term: $0; Sells biweekly, by mail or fax, at market, for $5 + comm.

**Shares to qualify:** 1
**Safekeeping:** Yes
**Accepts foreign:** Yes
**Auto. inv.:** No
**Disc.:** No

---

## ✳ Marriott International, Inc.-A ⊗

**MAR/NYSE** | **Hotels, food service mgt., time share**

H: 50.50
L: 34.12
Rec: 47.77
Div.: 0.26
Paid on:
1.4.7.10-16
Since: 1993

Marriott Dr.
Washington. DC 20058

First Chicago Trust    800-311-4816
$25 - $350,000/year
Every 5 days beginning varies

FEES: Div: 5% to $3 + 3¢/sh.; Cash: $5 + 3¢/sh.; Auto. Inv.: $2 + 3¢/sh.; Cert: $0; Term: $15 + 12¢/sh.; Sells daily, by mail or phone, at market, for $15 + 12¢/sh.

**Shares to qualify:** 1 /de ($350)
**Safekeeping:** Yes
**Accepts foreign:** Yes
**Auto. inv.:** Yes
**Disc.:** No

---

## Marsh & McLennan Co., Inc.

**Insurance**

MMC/NYSE
H: 135.68
L: 80.30
**Rec:** 101.48

**Div.:** 2.12
**Paid on:**
2.5.8.11-15
**Since:** 1923

1166 Ave. of the Americas
New York. NY 10036

Bank of New York    800-457-8968
$10 - $3,000/quarter
Every 90 days beginning 2/15

**Shares to qualify:** 1
**Safekeeping:** Yes
**Accepts foreign:** No
**Auto. inv.:** No
**Disc.:** No

FEES: Div 5% to $2.50; Cash: 5% to $2.50; Cert: $0; Term: $0; Sells daily, by mail, at market, for $0

---

## Marsh Supermarkets -A ♥

**Supermarkets**

MARSA/NA
H: 16.75
L: 12.96
**Rec:** 15.00

**Div.:** 0.44
**Paid on:**
2.5.8.11-VARIES
**Since:** 1953

9800 Crosspoint Blvd.
Indianapolis. IN 46256-3350

National City Bank    800-622-6757
$100 - $5,000/month
Every 30 days beginning 1/2

**Shares to qualify:** 1
**Safekeeping:** Yes
**Accepts foreign:** Yes
**Auto. inv.:** No
**Disc.:** No

FEES: Div: $0; Cash: $0; Cert: $0; Term: 8¢ to 20¢/sh.; Sells weekly, by mail, at market, for $2.50 + 8¢ to 20¢/sh.

---

## Marsh Supermarkets -B ♥

**Supermarkets**

MARSB/NA
H: 14.00
L: 10.25
**Rec:** 13.60

**Div.:** 0.44
**Paid on:**
2.5.8.11-VARIES
**Since:** 1953

9800 Crosspoint Blvd.
Indianapolis. IN 46256-3350

National City Bank    800-622-6757
$100 - $5,000/month
Every 30 days beginning 1/2

**Shares to qualify:** 1
**Safekeeping:** Yes
**Accepts foreign:** Yes
**Auto. inv.:** No
**Disc.:** No

FEES: Div: $0; Cash: $0; Cert: $0; Term: 8¢ to 20¢/sh.; Sells weekly, by mail, at market, for $2.50 + 8¢ to 20¢/sh.

---

## Marshall & Ilsley Corp. ♥

**Banking**

MI/NYSE
H: 59.93
L: 38.25
**Rec:** 59.15

**Div.:** 1.16
**Paid on:**
3.6.9.12-14
**Since:** 1938

770 N. Water St.
Milwaukee. WI 53202

Continental Stock Transfer    800-529-3163
$25 - $20,000/year
Every 30 days beginning 1/14

**Shares to qualify:** 1
**Safekeeping:** Yes
**Accepts foreign:** No
**Auto. inv.:** Yes
**Disc.:** No

FEES: Div: $0!; Cash: $0!; Auto. Inv.: $0!; Cert: $0!; Term: $0; Sells within 10 bus. days, by mail, at market, for $10

---

## Masco Corp. ♥

**Bldg. & home improvement products**

MAS/NYSE
H: 27.00
L: 14.50
**Rec:** 25.65

**Div.:** 0.52
**Paid on:**
2.5.8.11-4
**Since:** 1944

21001 Van Born Rd.
Taylor. MI 48180

Bank of New York    800-524-4458
$50 - $5,000/month
Every 30 days beginning 1/10

**Shares to qualify:** 1
**Safekeeping:** Yes
**Accepts foreign:** No
**Auto. inv.:** No
**Disc.:** No

FEES: Div: $0!; Cash: $0!; Cert: $0!; Term: comm.; Sells weekly, by mail or fax, at market, for $5 + 5¢/sh.

---

## MASSBANK Corp. ♥

**Banking**

MASB/NAS
H: 40.00
L: 27.87
**Rec:** 39.55

**Div.:** 1.26
**Paid on:**
2.5.8.11
**Since:** 1986

159 Haven St.
Reading. MA 01867

Boston Eq.    800-730-4001
$50 - $5,000/quarter
Every 90 days beginning 2/15

**Shares to qualify:** 1
**Safekeeping:** Yes
**Accepts foreign:** Yes
**Auto. inv.:** No
**Disc.:** No

FEES: Div: $0; Cash: $0; Cert: $0; Term: $0; Sells within 10 bus. days, by mail, at market, for comm.

---

## Massey Energy Company

**Energy & construction**

MEE/NYSE
H: 28.95
L: 8.75
**Rec:** 16.41

**Div.:** 0.16
**Paid on:**
1.4.7.10-15
**Since:** 1974

Box 26765
Richmond. VA 23261

Mellon Inv. Svcs.    800-813-2847
$100 - $10,000/quarter
Every 30 days beginning 1/15

**Shares to qualify:** 50
**Safekeeping:** Yes
**Accepts foreign:** Yes
**Auto. inv.:** No
**Disc.:** No

FEES: Div: $0!; Cash: $1.50 + 7¢/sh.; Cert: $5; Term: $5; Sells weekly, by mail or phone, at market, for $15 + 7¢/sh.

---

✳ DRIP enrollment through Temper Enrollment Service (see page 180). **113**

## ✳ Mattel Inc. ⊗

**MAT/NYSE** — Mfg., marketing toys

H: 19.60
L: 9.75
Rec: 17.41
Div.: 0.36
Paid on:
1.4.7.10-5
Since:1990

333 Continental Blvd.
El Segundo. CA 90245

BankBoston      800-730-4001
$100 - $100,000/year
Every 7 days beginning Wed.

FEES: Div: $0; Cash: $5 + 8¢/sh.; Auto. Inv.: $0; Cert: $0; Term: $0; Sells within 10 bus. days, by mail, at market, for $10 + 15¢/sh.

**Shares to qualify:** 1 /de ($500)
**Safekeeping:** Yes
**Accepts foreign:** Yes
**Auto. inv.:** Yes
**Disc.:** No

---

## ✳ Maxus Realty Trust Inc.

**MRTI/NASD** — REIT

H: 11.05
L: 5.00
Rec: 9.15
Div.: 0.80
Paid on:
3.6.9.12-21
Since:N/A

Box 26730
Kansas Citv. MO 64196

Mellon Inv. Svcs.      888-213-0965
$50 - $unlimited
Every 90 days beginning 3/30

FEES: Div: $0; Cash: 5% to $2.50 + comm.; Cert: $1; Term: $1; Sells weekly, by mail or phone, at market, for comm.

**Shares to qualify:** 1
**Safekeeping:** No
**Accepts foreign:** No
**Auto. inv.:** No
**Disc.:** No

---

## ✳ May Dept. Stores Co.

**MAY/NYSE** — Retail stores

H: 41.25
L: 19.18
Rec: 32.84
Div.: 0.94
Paid on:
3.6.9.12-15
Since:1911

611 Olive St.
St. Louis. MO 63101-1799

Bank of New York      800-524-4458
$25 - $unlimited
Every day days beginning daily

FEES: Div: 5% to $2; Cash: $2; Cert: $2.50; Term: $2.50; Sells irregularly, by mail, at avg. price, for $2.50

**Shares to qualify:** 1
**Safekeeping:** Yes
**Accepts foreign:** Yes
**Auto. inv.:** No
**Disc.:** No

---

## ✳ Mayflower Cooperative Bank ♥

**MFLR/NASD** — Banking

H: 13.34
L: 9.75
Rec: 12.45
Div.: 0.60
Paid on:
3.6.9.12-20
Since:N/A

30 South Main St., Box 311
Middleboro. MA 02346

American Stock Transfer      800-278-4353
$50 - $2,500/quarter
Every 90 days beginning 3/20

FEES: Div: $0!; Cash: $0!; Cert: $0!; Term: $0; Sells weekly , by mail, at market, for comm.

**Shares to qualify:** 1
**Safekeeping:** Yes
**Accepts foreign:** Yes
**Auto. inv.:** No
**Disc.:** No

---

## ✳ Maytag Corp. ♥

**MYG/NYSE** — Home appliances

H: 42.43
L: 25.00
Rec: 32.15
Div.: 0.72
Paid on:
3.6.9.12-15
Since:1946

403 West 4th St. North, Box 39
Newton. IA 50208-0039

Computershare Investor Svcs.      888-237-0935
$25 - $5,000/month
Every 30 days beginning 1/15

FEES: Div: $0!; Cash: $0!; Auto. Inv.: $0; Cert: $0!; Term: 15¢/sh.; Sells weekly, by mail or fax, at market, for 15¢/sh.

**Shares to qualify:** 1
**Safekeeping:** Yes
**Accepts foreign:** Yes
**Auto. inv.:** Yes
**Disc.:** No

---

## ✳ McCormick & Co.

**MKC/NYSE** — Food mfr., spices, teas, & flavorings

H: 45.22
L: 27.62
Rec: 42.49
Div.: 0.80
Paid on:
1-22.4-12.7-12.
Since:1929

18 Loveton Circle
Sparks. MD 21152-6000

Wells Fargo Bank      800-468-9716
$50 - $50,000/year
Every 30 days beginning 1/10

FEES: Div: 5¢/sh.; Cash: 5¢/sh.; Cert: $0; Term: $0; Sells daily, by mail or fax, at market , for $10 + 10¢/sh.

**Shares to qualify:** 1 /de ($250)
**Safekeeping:** Yes
**Accepts foreign:** Yes
**Auto. inv.:** No
**Disc.:** No

---

## ✳ McDermott International Inc. ⊗

**MDR/NYSE** — Engineering & marine construction

H: 16.85
L: 7.37
Rec: 10.70
Div.: 0.00
Paid on:
DIV. SUSP.
Since:--

1450 Poydras St.
New Orleans. LA 70112

First Chicago Trust      800-446-2617
$50 - $250,000/year
Every 7 days beginning varies

FEES: Div: n/o; Cash: $5 + 3¢/sh.; Auto. Inv.: $2 + 3¢/sh.; Cert: $0; Term: $0; Sells daily, by mail or phone, at market, for $15 + 12¢/sh.

**Shares to qualify:** 1 /de ($500)
**Safekeeping:** Yes
**Accepts foreign:** Yes
**Auto. inv.:** Yes
**Disc.:** No

---

## McDonald's Corp. ⊗

**MCD/NYSE**
Restaurants

H: 35.06
L: 24.75
**Rec:** 28.09

**Div.:** 0.21
**Paid on:**
12-2
**Since:** 1976

Inv. Relations, Dept. 300, Kroc Dr.
Oak Brook. IL 60523

First Chicago Trust    800-621-7825
$50 - $250,000/year
Every daily days beginning varies

FEES: Div: 75¢; Cash: $6 + 10¢/sh.; Auto. Inv.: $1.50 + 10¢/sh.; Cert: $0; Term: $0;
Sells daily, by mail, fax , or phone, at market, for $15 + 15¢/sh.

**Shares to qualify:** 10 /de ($500)
**Safekeeping:** Yes
**Accepts foreign:** Yes
**Auto. inv.:** Yes
**Disc.:** No

---

## McGraw-Hill Cos. ♥

**MHP/NYSE**
Publishing & information services

H: 70.87
L: 52.00
**Rec:** 62.20

**Div.:** 0.98
**Paid on:**
3.6.9.12-10
**Since:** 1937

1221 Ave. of the Americas
New York. NY 10020-1095

Mellon Inv. Svcs.    888-201-5538
$100 - $10,000/month
Every 7 days beginning varies

FEES: Div: $0!; Cash: $0!; Auto. Inv.: $0; Cert: $0!; Term: $0; Sells at least weekly, by
phone, mail, fax, or Internet, at market, for $15 + 12¢/sh.

**Shares to qualify:** 1 /de ($500)
**Safekeeping:** Yes
**Accepts foreign:** Yes
**Auto. inv.:** Yes
**Disc.:** No

---

## McKesson Corporation ♥

**MCK/NYSE**
Drugs, consumer products

H: 41.50
L: 23.40
**Rec:** 38.49

**Div.:** 0.24
**Paid on:**
1.4.7.10-1
**Since:** 1995

One Post St.
San Francisco. CA 94104-5296

First Chicago Trust    800-414-6280
$10 - $60,000/year
Every 30 days beginning 1st monthly

FEES: Div: $0!; Cash: $0!; Auto. Inv.: $1; Cert: $0; Term: $0; Sells irregularly, by mail, at
market, for $10 + 12¢/sh.

**Shares to qualify:** 1
**Safekeeping:** Yes
**Accepts foreign:** No
**Auto. inv.:** Yes
**Disc.:** No

---

## MDU Resources Group ♥

**MDU/NYSE**
Mining, oil & gas exploration,

H: 40.37
L: 23.00
**Rec:** 29.79

**Div.:** 0.88
**Paid on:**
1.4.7.10-1
**Since:** 1937

Box 5650
Bismarck. ND 58506-5650

Wells Fargo Bank    877-536-3553
$50 - $5,000/month
Every 30 days beginning 1/1

FEES: Div: $0!; Cash: $0!; Auto. Inv.: $0; Cert: $0!; Term: $0!; Sells daily, by mail, fax , or
phone, at market, for $3 + 15¢/sh.

**Shares to qualify:** 1 /de ($50)
**Safekeeping:** Yes
**Accepts foreign:** No
**Auto. inv.:** Yes
**Disc.:** No

---

## Mead Corp. ⊗

**MEA/NYSE**
Paper, forest prod.

H: 33.00
L: 21.18
**Rec:** 29.52

**Div.:** 0.68
**Paid on:**
3.6.9.12-1
**Since:** 1940

Courthouse Plaza NE
Davton. OH 45463

Boston Eq.    800-730-4001
$25 - $6,000/month
Every 30 days beginning 1/2

FEES: Div: $0!; Cash: $5; Auto. Inv.: $2; Cert: $0!; Term: $0; Sells within 10 bus. days, by
phone, at avg. price, for $15 + 5¢/sh.

**Shares to qualify:** 1
**Safekeeping:** Yes
**Accepts foreign:** Yes
**Auto. inv.:** Yes
**Disc.:** No

---

## Meadowbrook Insurance Group ♥

**MIG/NYSE**
Property and casualty insurance

H: 8.37
L: 2.45
**Rec:** 3.10

**Div.:** 0.12
**Paid on:**
1.4.7.10-9
**Since:** 1996

26600 Telegraph Rd.
Southfield. MI 48075

First Chicago Trust    800-519-3111
$25 - $50,000/year
Every 7 days beginning Wed.

FEES: Div: $0!; Cash: $0!; Auto. Inv.: $0; Cert: $0!; Term: $0; Sells daily, by mail or phone,
at market, for comm.

**Shares to qualify:** 1 /de ($250)
**Safekeeping:** Yes
**Accepts foreign:** Yes
**Auto. inv.:** Yes
**Disc.:** No

---

## Medallion Financial Group ♥

**TAXI/NASD**
Finance company

H: 18.00
L: 8.68
**Rec:** 10.70

**Div.:** 0.60
**Paid on:**
1.4.7.10-11
**Since:** N/A

437 Madison Ave., 38th Fl.
New York. NY 10022

American Stock Transfer    800-278-4353
$25 - $5,000/quarter
Every 90 days beginning 1/11

FEES: Div: $0; Cash: $0; Cert: $0; Term: $10 + 4¢/sh.,Does not sell through the plan

**Shares to qualify:** 1
**Safekeeping:** Yes
**Accepts foreign:** Yes
**Auto. inv.:** No
**Disc.:** No

---

## ✻ Medford Bancorp, Inc. ♥

**MDBK/NAS**
H: 23.10
L: 13.37
**Rec:** 21.98
**Div.:** 0.52
**Paid on:**
1.4.7.10-15
**Since:** 1987

**Banking**
29 High St.
Medford. MA 02155

State St. Bank    800-426-5523
$100 - $1,000/quarter
Every 90 days beginning 1/15

FEES: Div: $0; Cash: $0; Cert: $0; Term: $0; Sells daily, by mail, at market, for comm.

**Shares to qualify:** 1
**Safekeeping:** Yes
**Accepts foreign:** Yes
**Auto. inv.:** No
**Disc.:** No

---

## ✻ Media General, Inc. -A ♥

**MEGA/ASE**
H: 53.50
L: 33.65
**Rec:** 48.05
**Div.:** 0.68
**Paid on:**
3.6.9.12-15
**Since:** 1969

**Newspaper, TV**
Box 85333
Richmond. VA 23293-0001

American Stock Transfer    800-937-5449
$25 - $5,000/month
Every 30 days beginning 1/10

FEES: Div: $0!; Cash: $0!; Cert: $0!; Term: $0; Sells monthly, by mail or fax, at avg. price, for comm.

**Shares to qualify:** 1
**Safekeeping:** Yes
**Accepts foreign:** Yes
**Auto. inv.:** No
**Disc.:** Div 5% Cash: 0%

---

## ✻ Medtronic, Inc. ♥

**MDT/NYSE**
H: 62.00
L: 39.95
**Rec:** 45.13
**Div.:** 0.23
**Paid on:**
1.4.7.10-30
**Since:** 1977

**Medical**
7000 Central Ave. NE
Minneapolis. MN 55432

Wells Fargo Bank    800-468-9716
$25 - $4,000/month
Every 30 days beginning 1/31

FEES: Div: $0; Cash: $0; Auto. Inv.: $0; Cert: $0; Term: $10 + 10¢/sh. ; Sells daily, by mail or fax, at market, for $10 + 10¢/sh.

**Shares to qualify:** 1
**Safekeeping:** Yes
**Accepts foreign:** Yes
**Auto. inv.:** Yes
**Disc.:** No

---

## ✻ Mellon Financial Corp. ♥

**MEL/NYSE**
H: 51.93
L: 34.97
**Rec:** 39.05
**Div.:** 0.96
**Paid on:**
2.5.8.11-15
**Since:** 1895

**Banking**
One Mellon Bank Ctr., Rm. 750
Pittsburgh. PA 15258-0001

Mellon Inv. Svcs.    800-205-7699
$100 - $100,000/year
Every 7 days beginning varies

FEES: Div: $0!; Cash: $0!; Auto. Inv.: $0; Cert: $0!; Term: $0; Sells weekly, by mail or phone, at avg. price, for $15 + 12¢/sh.

**Shares to qualify:** 1 /de ($500)
**Safekeeping:** Yes
**Accepts foreign:** Yes
**Auto. inv.:** Yes
**Disc.:** No

---

## ✻ Mercantile Bankshares Corp. ♥

**MRBK/NAS**
H: 45.12
L: 31.56
**Rec:** 43.49
**Div.:** 1.12
**Paid on:**
3.6.9.12-31
**Since:** 1970

**Banking**
Box 1477
Baltimore. MD 21203

Bank of New York    800-524-4458
$25 - $5,000/quarter
Every 90 days beginning 3/31

FEES: Div: $0!; Cash: $0!; Cert: $0!; Term: $0,Does not sell through the plan

**Shares to qualify:** 1
**Safekeeping:** Yes
**Accepts foreign:** Yes
**Auto. inv.:** No
**Disc.:** Div 5%  Cash: 0%

---

## ✻ Merchants Bancshares, Inc. ♥

**MBVT/NASD**
H: 33.70
L: 19.62
**Rec:** 32.50
**Div.:** 1.32
**Paid on:**
2.5.8.11-18
**Since:** N/A

**Bank holding company**
Box 1009
Burlington. VT 05402

BankBoston    800-426-5523
$25 - $2,500/quarter
Every 90 days beginning 2/18

FEES: Div: $0; Cash: $0; Cert: $0; Term: $2.50 + 15¢/sh.; Sells within 3 bus. days, by mail, at avg. price, for $2.50 + 15¢/sh.

**Shares to qualify:** 1
**Safekeeping:** Yes
**Accepts foreign:** Yes
**Auto. inv.:** No
**Disc.:** No

---

## ✻ Merck & Co., Inc. ⊗

**MRK/NYSE**
H: 96.68
L: 60.35
**Rec:** 69.30
**Div.:** 1.40
**Paid on:**
1.4.7.10-1
**Since:** 1935

**Drugs**
Box 100, (WS 3AB-40)
Whitehouse Station. NJ 08889-0100

Wells Fargo Bank    888-291-3713
$50 - $50,000/year
Every 7 days beginning Tuesday

FEES: Div: 4% to $2 + 1¢/sh.; Cash: $5 + 1¢/sh.; Auto. Inv.: $2 + 1¢/sh.; Cert: $0; Term: $0; Sells daily, by mail, fax , or phone, at avg. price, for $5 + 1¢/sh.

**Shares to qualify:** 1 /de ($350)
**Safekeeping:** Yes
**Accepts foreign:** Yes
**Auto. inv.:** Yes
**Disc.:** No

---

## Meridian Bioscience, Inc. ⊗

**VIVO/NASD** | Mfr. medical diagnostic kits

H: 8.37
L: 2.12
**Rec:** 5.15
**Div.:** 0.26
**Paid on:**
3.6.9.12-8
**Since:** 1990

3471 River Hills Dr.
Cincinnati. OH 45244

Fifth Third Bancorp 800-837-2755
$25 - $1,000/month
Every 30 days beginning 1/30

FEES: Div: 5% to $3; Cash: $3; Cert: $0; Term: comm.; Sells weekly, by mail, at market, for comm.

**Shares to qualify:** 1
**Safekeeping:** Yes
**Accepts foreign:** Yes
**Auto. inv.:** No
**Disc.:** No

---

## Met-Pro Corp. ♥

**MPR/NYSE** | Pollution control, fluid handling, air

H: 15.25
L: 9.56
**Rec:** 13.58
**Div.:** 0.34
**Paid on:**
1.4.7.10-29
**Since:** 1992

Box 144,160 Cassell Rd.
Harleysville. PA 19438

American Stock Transfer 800-278-4353
$100 - $5,000/month
Every 30 days beginning 1/10

FEES: Div: $0!; Cash: $0!; Auto. Inv.: $0; Cert: $0!; Term: $15 + comm.; Sells weekly, by mail or fax, at avg. price, for $15 + comm.

**Shares to qualify:** 10 /de ($1000)
**Safekeeping:** Yes
**Accepts foreign:** Yes
**Auto. inv.:** Yes
**Disc.:** Div: 3% Cash: 0%

---

## MetroCorp Bancshares, Inc. ♥

**MCBI/NASD** | Bank holding company

H: 12.37
L: 6.50
**Rec:** 11.00
**Div.:** 0.24
**Paid on:**
1.4.7.10-15
**Since:** N/A

9600 Bellaire Blvd., Ste. 252
Houston. TX 77036

American Stock Transfer 800-278-4353
$100 - $5,000/quarter
Every 90 days beginning 1/15

FEES: Div: $0!; Cash: $0!; Cert: $0; Term: $15,Does not sell through the plan

**Shares to qualify:** 1
**Safekeeping:** Yes
**Accepts foreign:** Yes
**Auto. inv.:** No
**Disc.:** No

---

## Michaels Stores ♥

**MIKE/NASD** | Retail,specialty arts & crafts and home

H: 49.62
L: 18.00
**Rec:** 38.94
**Div.:** 0.00
**Paid on:**
N/0
**Since:** N/0

Box 619566
Dallas. TX 75261-9566

Computershare Investor Svcs. 800-577-4676
$100 - $2,500/month
Every 30 days beginning 1/19

FEES: Div: $0; Cash: $0; Cert: $0; Term: $0; Sells weekly, by mail, at market, for $10 + 12¢/sh.

**Shares to qualify:** 1 /de ($500)
**Safekeeping:** Yes
**Accepts foreign:** No
**Auto. inv.:** No
**Disc.:** No

---

## Mid-America Apt. Communities, Inc. ♥

**MAA/NYSE** | REIT

H: 26.42
L: 21.25
**Rec:** 25.70
**Div.:** 2.34
**Paid on:**
1.4.7.10.-30
**Since:** 1994

6584 Poplar Ave., Ste. 300
Memphis. TN 38138

First Union Nat'l Bank 800-829-8432
$250 - $5,000/month
Every 30 days beginning 1/31

FEES: Div: $0; Cash: $0; Cert: $0; Term: $0; Sells weekly, by mail or fax, at avg. price, for $0

**Shares to qualify:** 1
**Safekeeping:** Yes
**Accepts foreign:** No
**Auto. inv.:** No
**Disc.:** No

---

## Mid-State Bancshares ⊗

**MDST/NASD** | Banking

H: 18.62
L: 13.28
**Rec:** 16.20
**Div.:** 0.36
**Paid on:**
1.4.7.10-17
**Since:** N/A

1026 Grand Ave., Box 580
Arrovo Grande. CA 93421-0580

Mellon Inv. Svcs. 888-540-9878
$50 - $5,000/month
Every 7 days beginning varies

FEES: Div: $0!; Cash: $5 + 12¢/sh.; Auto. Inv.: $5 + 12¢/sh.; Cert: $0; Term: $15 + 12¢/sh.; Sells daily, by mail or phone, at market, for $15 + 12¢/sh.

**Shares to qualify:** 1 /de ($1000)
**Safekeeping:** Yes
**Accepts foreign:** Yes
**Auto. inv.:** Yes
**Disc.:** No

---

## Middlesex Water Co. ♥

**MSEX/NASD** | Utility-water

H: 37.45
L: 27.00
**Rec:** 32.57
**Div.:** 1.24
**Paid on:**
3.6.9.12-1
**Since:** 1912

Box 1500
Iselin. NJ 08830-0452

Registrar & Transfer 800-368-5948
$25 - $25,000/quarter
Every 30 days beginning 1/2

FEES: Div: $0!; Cash: $0!; Cert: $0!; Term: $0; Sells monthly, by mail, at market, for comm.

**Shares to qualify:** 1
**Safekeeping:** Yes
**Accepts foreign:** Yes
**Auto. inv.:** No
**Disc.:** No

---

## ✳ **Middleton Doll Company ♥**

| | | |
|---|---|---|
| **DOLL/NASD** | **Doll mfr.** | **Shares to qualify:** 1 |
| H: 9.75 | Box 190 | **Safekeeping:** Yes |
| L: 5.87 | Pewaukee. WI 53072-0190 | **Accepts foreign:** Yes |
| **Rec:** 7.00 | Firstar Bank    800-637-7549 | **Auto. inv.:** No |
| **Div.:** 0.65 | $25 - $3,000/quarter | **Disc.:** No |
| **Paid on:** | Every 90 days beginning 2/1 | |
| 2.5.8.11-15 | FEES: Div: $0!; Cash: $0!; Cert: $0!; Term: comm.; Sells biweekly, by mail or fax, at market, | |
| **Since:** 1987 | for comm. | |

## ✳ **MidSouth Bancorp, Inc. ♥**

| | | |
|---|---|---|
| **MSL/ASE** | **Regional banks** | **Shares to qualify:** 25 /de ($1000) |
| H: 11.90 | 102 Versailles Blvd., Versailles Ctr. | **Safekeeping:** Yes |
| L: 7.75 | Lafayette. LA 70501 | **Accepts foreign:** Yes |
| **Rec:** 10.15 | Mellon Inv. Svcs.    888-216-8113 | **Auto. inv.:** Yes |
| **Div.:** 0.20 | $100 - $10,000/quarter | **Disc.:** No |
| **Paid on:** | Every 7 days beginning varies | |
| 1.4.7.10-2 | FEES: Div: $0; Cash: $0; Auto. Inv.: $0; Cert: $0; Term: $0; Sells weekly, by mail or phone, | |
| **Since:** 1995 | at market, for $15 + 12¢/sh. | |

## ✳ **Milacron, Inc. ♥**

| | | |
|---|---|---|
| **MZ/NYSE** | **Machinery, factory supplies** | **Shares to qualify:** 1 |
| H: 22.94 | 2090 Florence Ave. | **Safekeeping:** No |
| L: 13.31 | Cincinnati. OH 45206-2425 | **Accepts foreign:** Yes |
| **Rec:** 18.18 | Mellon Inv. Svcs.    800-426-5754 | **Auto. inv.:** No |
| **Div.:** 0.48 | $25 - $1,000/month | **Disc.:** No |
| **Paid on:** | Every 30 days beginning 1/12 | |
| 3.6.9.12-12 | FEES: Div: $0!; Cash: $0!; Cert: $0!; Term: $0; Sells weekly, by mail or phone, at market, for | |
| **Since:** 1894 | 12¢/sh. | |

## ✳ **Millipore Corp. ♥**

| | | |
|---|---|---|
| **MIL/NYSE** | **Mfr. fluid analyzing equipment** | **Shares to qualify:** 1 |
| H: 66.85 | 80 Ashby Rd. | **Safekeeping:** Yes |
| L: 42.56 | Bedford. MA 01730-2271 | **Accepts foreign:** No |
| **Rec:** 61.92 | Boston Eq.    800-730-4001 | **Auto. inv.:** No |
| **Div.:** 0.44 | $25 - $3,000/quarter | **Disc.:** No |
| **Paid on:** | Every 90 days beginning 1/28 | |
| 1.4.7.10-21 | FEES: Div: $0; Cash: $0; Cert: $0; Term: 5% to $3; Sells within 10 bus. days, by mail, at | |
| **Since:** N/A | market, for comm. | |

## ✳ **Mills Corp. (The) ⊗**

| | | |
|---|---|---|
| **MLS/NYSE** | **REIT** | **Shares to qualify:** 1 /de ($250) |
| H: 25.65 | 1300 Wilson Blvd., Ste.400 | **Safekeeping:** Yes |
| L: 16.00 | Arlington. VA 22209 | **Accepts foreign:** Yes |
| **Rec:** 25.24 | First Chicago Trust    800-446-2617 | **Auto. inv.:** Yes |
| **Div.:** 2.13 | $25 - $250,000/year | **Disc.:** No |
| **Paid on:** | Every 5 days beginning varies | |
| 1.4.7.10-16 | FEES: Div: 5% to $3 + 3¢/sh.; Cash: $5 + 3¢/sh.; Auto. Inv.: $2 + 3¢/sh.; Cert: $0!; | |
| **Since:** 1994 | Term: $15 + 12¢/sh.; Sells daily, by phone, mail, fax, or Internet, at market, for $15 + | |
| | 12¢/sh. | |

## ✳ **Minnesota Mining & Manufacturing ♥**

| | | |
|---|---|---|
| **MMM/NYSE** | **Diversified mfr.** | **Shares to qualify:** 1 |
| H: 127.00 | 3M Center 225-1S-15 | **Safekeeping:** Yes |
| L: 80.50 | St. Paul. MN 55144-1000 | **Accepts foreign:** Yes |
| **Rec:** 109.85 | Wells Fargo Bank    800-401-1952 | **Auto. inv.:** Yes |
| **Div.:** 2.40 | $10 - $10,000/quarter | **Disc.:** No |
| **Paid on:** | Every 30 days beginning 1/12 | |
| 3.6.9.12-12 | FEES: Div: $0!; Cash: $0!; Auto. Inv.: $0; Cert: $0!; Term: $0; Sells daily, by mail or fax, at | |
| **Since:** 1917 | market, for $8 + 10¢/sh. | |

## ✳ **Modine Manufacturing Co. ♥**

| | | |
|---|---|---|
| **MODI/NASD** | **Auto & truck parts** | **Shares to qualify:** 1 /de ($500) |
| H: 32.00 | 1500 DeKoven Ave. | **Safekeeping:** Yes |
| L: 19.00 | Racine. WI 53403-2552 | **Accepts foreign:** Yes |
| **Rec:** 28.00 | Wells Fargo Bank    800-468-9716 | **Auto. inv.:** Yes |
| **Div.:** 1.00 | $10 - $5,000/month | **Disc.:** No |
| **Paid on:** | Every 5 days beginning varies | |
| 3.6.9.12-2 | FEES: Div: $0!; Cash: $0!; Auto. Inv.: $0; Cert: $10; Term: $0; Sells within 5 bus. days, by | |
| **Since:** 1959 | mail or phone, at avg. price, for $10 + 15¢/sh. | |

## * Molex, Inc.-A ⊗

**MOLXA/NA** — **Mfr. electronic instruments & controls**

H: 43.93
L: 24.62
Rec: 27.73
Div.: 0.10
Paid on:
1.4.7.10-25
Since:1990

2222 Wellington Ct.
Lisle. IL 60532

Computershare Investor Svcs.    312-360-5315
$100 - $100,000/year
Every 5 days beginning varies

FEES: Div: $0; Cash: $5 + 10¢/sh.; Auto. Inv.: $1.50 + 10¢/sh.; Cert: $0; Term: $10 + 10¢/sh.; Sells within 5 bus. days, by mail, at market, for $10 + 10¢/sh.

**Shares to qualify:** 1 /de ($500)
**Safekeeping:** Yes
**Accepts foreign:** Yes
**Auto. inv.:** Yes
**Disc.:** No

---

## * Monmouth Capital Corp. ♥

**MONM/NAS** — **Real estate**

H: 3.50
L: 2.37
Rec: 3.10
Div.: 0.20
Paid on:
12-15
Since:1963

125 Wyckoff Rd.
Eatontown. NJ 07724

Mellon Inv. Svcs.    800-526-0801
$500 - $40,000/month
Every 30 days beginning 1/15

FEES: Div: $0!; Cash: $0!; Cert: $0!; Term: $0,Does not sell through the plan

**Shares to qualify:** 1
**Safekeeping:** No
**Accepts foreign:** Yes
**Auto. inv.:** No
**Disc.:** Div 5% Cash: 5%

---

## * Monmouth REIT ♥

**MNRTA/NA** — **REIT**

H: 6.51
L: 4.75
Rec: 6.24
Div.: 0.58
Paid on:
3.6.9.12-15
Since:1969

3499 Rt. 9 North- Ste. 3-C
Freehold. NJ 07728

Mellon Inv. Svcs.    800-526-0801
$500 - $1,000/month
Every 30 days beginning 1/15

FEES: Div: $0!; Cash: $0!; Cert: $0!; Term: $0,Does not sell through the plan

**Shares to qualify:** 1
**Safekeeping:** No
**Accepts foreign:** Yes
**Auto. inv.:** No
**Disc.:** Div 5% Cash: 5%

---

## * Montana Power Co. (The)

**MTP/NYSE** — **Telecomm., electric & gas, mining**

H: 39.93
L: 6.40
Rec: 6.80
Div.: 0.00
Paid on:
DIV. SUSP.
Since:--

40 East Broadway
Butte. MT 59701-9394

Montana Power Co.    800-245-6767
$25 - $60,000/year
Every 15 days beginning 1/13-1/28

FEES: Div: n/o; Cash: 3¢/sh.; Auto. Inv.: $0; Cert: $0; Term: $0; Sells biweekly, by mail or fax, at market, for 5¢/sh.

**Shares to qualify:** 1 /de ($100)
**Safekeeping:** Yes
**Accepts foreign:** Yes
**Auto. inv.:** Yes
**Disc.:** No

---

## * MONY Group Inc. (The) ⊗

**MNY/NYSE** — **Insurance holding co.**

H: 51.37
L: 31.60
Rec: 36.56
Div.: 0.45
Paid on:
DECEMBER-22
Since:1999

1740 Broadway
New York. NY 10019

First Chicago Trust    800-926-6669
$100 - $250,000/year
Every 5 days beginning varies

FEES: Div: 5% to $3 + 5¢/sh.; Cash: $5 + 5¢/sh.; Auto. Inv.: $2 + 5¢/sh.; Cert: $0; Term: $15 + 5¢/sh.; Sells daily, by phone, mail, fax, or Internet, at avg. price, for $15 + 5¢/sh.

**Shares to qualify:** 1 /de ($3000)
**Safekeeping:** Yes
**Accepts foreign:** Yes
**Auto. inv.:** Yes
**Disc.:** No

---

## * Moore Corp. Ltd. ♥

**MCL/NYSE** — **Business forms & info. handling prods.**

H: 7.50
L: 2.31
Rec: 7.28
Div.: 0.20
Paid on:
1.4.7.10-1
Since:1933

1200 Lakeside Dr.
Bannockburn. IL 60015-6000

Montreal Trust    800-663-9097
$50 - $5,000/quarter (Cdn.)
Every 90 days beginning 1/12

FEES: Div: $0; Cash: $0; Cert: $0; Term: $0,Does not sell through the plan

**Shares to qualify:** 1
**Safekeeping:** No
**Accepts foreign:** Yes
**Auto. inv.:** No
**Disc.:** No

---

## * Morgan Stanley Asia-Pacific Fund, Inc.

**APF/NYSE** — **Closed-end fund**

H: 10.50
L: 7.35
Rec: 7.90
Div.: 0.05
Paid on:
7-15
Since:N/A

c/o Morgan Stanley ,1221 Ave. of the Americas
New York. NY 10020

American Stock Transfer    800-278-4353
$100 - $3,000/year
Every 180 days beginning 1/9

FEES: Div: $0!; Cash: comm.; Cert: $0; Term: $0; Sells weekly, by mail, at market, for 4¢/sh.

**Shares to qualify:** 1
**Safekeeping:** No
**Accepts foreign:** Yes
**Auto. inv.:** No
**Disc.:** No

---

## Morgan Stanley Dean Witter & Co. ♥

**MWD/NYSE** | Financial services

H: 110.00
L: 44.10
**Rec:** 55.89

**Div.:** 0.92
**Paid on:**
1.4.7.10-2
**Since:** 1993

1585 Broadway
New York. NY 10036

M.S. Dean Witter Trust FSB     800-622-2393
$100 - $40,000/year
Every 15 days beginning 1/2

FEES: Div: $0; Cash: $0; Auto. Inv.: $0; Cert: $0; Term: $0; Sells irregularly, by mail, at avg. price, for $5 + comm.

**Shares to qualify:** 1 /de ($1000)
**Safekeeping:** Yes
**Accepts foreign:** No
**Auto. inv.:** Yes
**Disc.:** No

---

## Motorola, Inc. ⊗

**MOT/NYSE** | Electronics

H: 37.25
L: 10.50
**Rec:** 18.00

**Div.:** 0.16
**Paid on:**
1.4.7.10-13
**Since:** 1942

1303 East Algonquin Rd.
Schaumburg. IL 60196

Computershare Investor Svcs.     800-704-4098
$100 - $120,000/year
Every 5 days beginning varies

FEES: Div: $0!; Cash: $5 + 10¢/sh.; Auto. Inv.: $1.50 + 10¢/sh.; Cert: $0!; Term: $12.50 + 10¢/sh.; Sells within 5 bus. days, by mail, at market, for $12.50 + 10¢/sh.

**Shares to qualify:** 1 /de ($500)
**Safekeeping:** Yes
**Accepts foreign:** Yes
**Auto. inv.:** Yes
**Disc.:** No

---

## Municipal Mortgage & Equity, L.L.C. ♥

**MMA/NYSE** | Mortgage and financing

H: 24.50
L: 20.25
**Rec:** 24.50

**Div.:** 1.71
**Paid on:**
2.5.8.11-1
**Since:** 1997

218 N. Charles St., Ste. 500
Baltimore. MD 21201-4019

Registrar & Transfer     800-368-5948
$100 - $5,000/quarter
Every 90 days beginning 2/1

FEES: Div: $0!; Cash: $0!; Cert: $0!; Term: $0,Does not sell through the plan

**Shares to qualify:** 1
**Safekeeping:** Yes
**Accepts foreign:** Yes
**Auto. inv.:** No
**Disc.:** No

---

## Myers Industries, Inc. ♥

**MYE/NYSE** | Equipment dist. plastic mfg.

H: 14.54
L: 8.75
**Rec:** 12.90

**Div.:** 0.24
**Paid on:**
1.4.7.10-1
**Since:** 1971

1293 South Main St.
Akron. OH 44301

First Chicago Trust     201-324-0498
$50 - $2,500/quarter
Every 90 days beginning 1/2

FEES: Div: $0!; Cash: $0!; Cert: $0!; Term: $0; Sells daily, by mail, at avg. price, for $10 + 12¢/sh.

**Shares to qualify:** 1
**Safekeeping:** Yes
**Accepts foreign:** No
**Auto. inv.:** No
**Disc.:** No

---

## Mylan Laboratories ♥

**MYL/NYSE** | Pharmaceutical products

H: 34.40
L: 20.15
**Rec:** 32.93

**Div.:** 0.16
**Paid on:**
1.4.7.10-15
**Since:** 1983

1030 Century Bldg., 130 Seventh St.
Pittsburgh. PA 15222

American Stock Transfer     212-936-5100
$50 - $5,000/quarter
Every 90 days beginning 1/15

FEES: Div: $0!; Cash: $0!; Cert: $0; Term: $0; Sells weekly, by mail, at market, for $7.50 + comm.

**Shares to qualify:** 25
**Safekeeping:** Yes
**Accepts foreign:** No
**Auto. inv.:** No
**Disc.:** No

---

## Mystic Financial, Inc. ♥

**MYST/NASD** | Bank holding company

H: 16.10
L: 12.50
**Rec:** 15.00

**Div.:** 0.32
**Paid on:**
2.5.8.11-15
**Since:** N/A

60 High St.
Medford. MA 02155-3820

Registrar & Transfer     800-368-5948
$100 - $2,500/quarter
Every 90 days beginning 2/15

FEES: Div: $0!; Cash: $0!; Cert: $0!; Term: $0; Sells within 10 bus. days, by mail, at avg. price, for $10 + comm.

**Shares to qualify:** 25
**Safekeeping:** Yes
**Accepts foreign:** Yes
**Auto. inv.:** No
**Disc.:** No

---

## Nash Finch Co. ♥

**NAFC/NASD** | Wholesale & retail food distribution

H: 35.90
L: 8.75
**Rec:** 35.10

**Div.:** 0.36
**Paid on:**
3.6.9.12
**Since:** 1926

Box 355
Minneapolis. MN 55440-0355

Wells Fargo Bank     800-468-9716
$10 - $1,000/month
Every 30 days beginning varies

FEES: Div: $0!; Cash: $0!; Cert: $0!; Term: $0!; Sells daily, by mail, at market, for $10 + 10¢/sh.

**Shares to qualify:** 1
**Safekeeping:** No
**Accepts foreign:** Yes
**Auto. inv.:** No
**Disc.:** No

---

## ✻ Nashua Corp. ♥

**Office equipment**

NSH/NYSE
H: 10.25
L: 3.02
**Rec:** 7.10

**Div.:** 0.00
**Paid on:**
DIV. SUSP.
**Since:** --

44 Franklin St.
Nashua. NH 03064-2665

BankBoston     781-575-3100
$100 - $5,000/quarter
Every 45 days beginning 2/15

FEES: Div: n/o; Cash: $0; Cert: $0; Term: $0; Sells within 10 bus. days, by mail, at market, for $0

**Shares to qualify:** 1
**Safekeeping:** Yes
**Accepts foreign:** Yes
**Auto. inv.:** No
**Disc.:** No

---

## ✻ National City Corp. ♥

**Banking**

NCC/NYSE
H: 32.70
L: 18.50
**Rec:** 31.85

**Div.:** 1.18
**Paid on:**
2.5.8.11-1
**Since:** 1936

Box 5756, Dept. 2101
Cleveland. OH 44101-0756

National City Bank     800-622-6757
$20 - $25,000/month
Every 30 days beginning 1/2

FEES: Div: $0!; Cash: $0!; Auto. Inv.: $0; Cert: $0; Term: $0; Sells weekly, by mail, at market, for comm.

**Shares to qualify:** 1
**Safekeeping:** Yes
**Accepts foreign:** Yes
**Auto. inv.:** Yes
**Disc.:** No

---

## ✻ National Commerce Financial ♥

**Banking**

NCF/NYSE
H: 27.87
L: 17.75
**Rec:** 25.75

**Div.:** 0.15
**Paid on:**
1.4.7.10-2
**Since:** 1970

One Commerce Sq.
Memphis. TN 38150

Bank of New York     800-524-4458
$100 - $3,500/month
Every 45 days beginning 1/2

FEES: Div: $0!; Cash: $0!; Cert: $0!; Term: $0; Sells weekly, by mail, at avg. price, for 7¢/sh.

**Shares to qualify:** 1
**Safekeeping:** Yes
**Accepts foreign:** Yes
**Auto. inv.:** No
**Disc.:** No

---

## ✻ National Data Corp. ♥

**Information processing**

NDC/NYSE
H: 38.93
L: 21.20
**Rec:** 34.05

**Div.:** 0.16
**Paid on:**
2.5.8.11
**Since:** 1977

National Data Plaza
Atlanta. GA 30329-2010

SunTrust Bank, Atlanta     800-568-3476
$25 - $1,000/quarter
Every 30 days beginning 1/30

FEES: Div: $0!; Cash: $0!; Cert: $0!; Term: $0; Sells weekly, by mail, at market, for 5¢/sh.

**Shares to qualify:** 1
**Safekeeping:** Yes
**Accepts foreign:** No
**Auto. inv.:** No
**Disc.:** No

---

## ✻ National Fuel Gas ♥

**Utility-gas**

NFG/NYSE
H: 64.50
L: 44.85
**Rec:** 48.28

**Div.:** 2.02
**Paid on:**
1.4.7.10-15
**Since:** 1903

10 Lafayette Sq.
Buffalo. NY 14203-1899

Computershare Investor Svcs.     800-648-8166
$100 - $120,000/year
Every 7 days beginning varies

FEES: Div: $0!; Cash: $0!; Auto. Inv.: $0; Cert: $0!; Term: $15 + 12¢/sh.; Sells weekly, by mail or phone, at avg. price, for $15 + 12¢/sh.

**Shares to qualify:** 1 /de ($1000)
**Safekeeping:** Yes
**Accepts foreign:** Yes
**Auto. inv.:** Yes
**Disc.:** No

---

## ✻ National Health Investors ♥

**REIT**

NHI/NYSE
H: 13.00
L: 4.87
**Rec:** 12.59

**Div.:** 2.56
**Paid on:**
2.5.8.11-10
**Since:** N/A

Box 1102
Murfreesboro. TN 37133-1102

SunTrust Bank, Atlanta     800-568-3476
$100 - $5,000/quarter
Every 30 days beginning 1/10

FEES: Div: $0; Cash: $0; Cert: $0; Term: $0; Sells biweekly, by mail, at market, for 8¢/sh.

**Shares to qualify:** 1
**Safekeeping:** Yes
**Accepts foreign:** Yes
**Auto. inv.:** No
**Disc.:** No

---

## ✻ National Service Industries, Inc.

**Lighting equip., specialty chemicals**

NSI/NYSE
H: 26.50
L: 17.81
**Rec:** 23.61

**Div.:** 1.32
**Paid on:**
2.5.8.11-1
**Since:** 1937

1420 Peachtree St., N.E.
Atlanta. GA 30309-3002

First Chicago Trust     877-342-5674
$25 - $350,000/year
Every 7 days beginning varies

FEES: Div: $0!; Cash: 3¢/sh.; Auto. Inv.: $0; Cert: $0!; Term: $0; Sells daily, by mail or phone, at market, for $15 + 12¢/sh.

**Shares to qualify:** 1 /de ($600)
**Safekeeping:** Yes
**Accepts foreign:** Yes
**Auto. inv.:** Yes
**Disc.:** No

---

✻ DRIP enrollment through Temper Enrollment Service (see page 180).     **121**

## ✱ Nationwide Financial Services-A ⊗

| | | |
|---|---|---|
| **NFS/NYSE** | **Annuity & life insurance products** | **Shares to qualify:** 1 /de ($500) |
| H: 51.43 | One Nationwide Plaza | **Safekeeping:** Yes |
| L: 33.10 | Columbus. OH 43215 | **Accepts foreign:** Yes |
| **Rec:** 46.49 | First Chicago Trust     800-317-4445 | **Auto. inv.:** Yes |
| **Div.:** 0.48 | $100 - $120,000/year | **Disc.:** No |
| **Paid on:** | Every 7 days beginning varies | |
| 1.4.7.10-15 | FEES: Div 5% to $3 + 3¢/sh.; Cash: $5 + 3¢/sh.; Auto. Inv.: $2 + 3¢/sh.; Cert: $0;  Term: | |
| **Since:** 1997 | $0; Sells daily, by mail or phone, at market, for $15 + 12¢/sh. | |

## ✱ Nature's Sunshine Products, Inc. ♥

| | | |
|---|---|---|
| **NATR/NASD** | **Herbal products manufacturer** | **Shares to qualify:** 1 |
| H: 13.31 | Box 19005 | **Safekeeping:** Yes |
| L: 5.68 | Provo. UT 84605-9005 | **Accepts foreign:** Yes |
| **Rec:** 12.49 | American Stock Transfer     800-278-4353 | **Auto. inv.:** No |
| **Div.:** 0.13 | $20 - $20,000/year | **Disc.:** No |
| **Paid on:** | Every 30 days beginning 1/10 | |
| 2.5.8.11-8 | FEES: Div $0!; Cash: $0!; Cert: $0!; Term: $0!; Sells weekly, by mail, at avg. price, for 4¢/sh. | |
| **Since:** N/A | | |

## NCR Corp.

| | | |
|---|---|---|
| **NCR/NYSE** | **Computer services** | **Shares to qualify:** 1 /de ($500) |
| H: 53.68 | 1700 South Patterson Blvd. | **Safekeeping:** Yes |
| L: 32.37 | Dayton. OH 45479 | **Accepts foreign:** Yes |
| **Rec:** 38.65 | American Stock Transfer     800-627-2303 | **Auto. inv.:** Yes |
| **Div.:** 0.00 | $25 - $10,000/investment | **Disc.:** No |
| **Paid on:** | Every day days beginning vary | |
| DIV. SUSP. | FEES: Div: n/o; Cash: $2.50 + 10¢/sh.;  Auto. Inv.: $2.50 + 10¢/sh.; Cert: $0;  Term: $15 | |
| **Since:** -- | + 10¢/sh.; Sells daily, by phone, mail, fax, or Internet, at market, for $15 + 10¢/sh. | |

## ✱ Neiman Marcus Group-A ♥

| | | |
|---|---|---|
| **NMGA/NYSE** | **Retail stores** | **Shares to qualify:** 1 |
| H: 40.01 | 27 Boylston St., Box 9187 | **Safekeeping:** Yes |
| L: 27.06 | Chestnut Hill. MA 02467-9187 | **Accepts foreign:** No |
| **Rec:** 31.28 | Boston Eq.     800-730-4001 | **Auto. inv.:** No |
| **Div.:** 0.00 | $25 - $2,500/45 days | **Disc.:** No |
| **Paid on:** | Every 45 days beginning 1/10 | |
| DIV. SUSP. | FEES: Div: n/o; Cash: $0!; Cert: $0!; Term: $0; Sells within 10 bus. days, by mail, at market, | |
| **Since:** -- | for $0! | |

## ✱ Neiman Marcus Group-B ♥

| | | |
|---|---|---|
| **NMGB/NYSE** | **Retail stores** | **Shares to qualify:** 1 |
| H: 38.00 | 27 Boylston St., Box 9187 | **Safekeeping:** Yes |
| L: 25.00 | Chestnut Hill. MA 02467-9187 | **Accepts foreign:** No |
| **Rec:** 30.00 | BankBoston     800-730-4001 | **Auto. inv.:** No |
| **Div.:** 0.00 | $25 - $2,500/45 days | **Disc.:** No |
| **Paid on:** | Every 45 days beginning 1/10 | |
| DIV. SUSP. | FEES: Div: n/o; Cash: $0!; Cert: $0!; Term: $0; Sells within 10 bus. days, by mail, at market, | |
| **Since:** -- | for $0! | |

## ✱ Nestle SA

| | | |
|---|---|---|
| **NSRGY/NAS** | **Food & beverage** | **Shares to qualify:** 1 |
| H: 53.95 | c/o Morgan Guaranty Trust, Box 9073 | **Safekeeping:** Yes |
| L: 53.00 | Boston. MA 02205-9948 | **Accepts foreign:** Yes |
| **Rec:** 53.35 | Morgan Guaranty Trust Co.     800-428-4237 | **Auto. inv.:** No |
| **Div.:** 1.05 | $20 - $60,000/year | **Disc.:** No |
| **Paid on:** | Every 30 days beginning 1/7 | |
| 6-26 | FEES: Div: 5¢/sh.; Cash: 5¢/sh.; Cert: $0; Term: $0; Sells daily, by mail, at market, for | |
| **Since:** N/A | 15¢/sh. | |

## ✱ New America High Income Fund, Inc.

| | | |
|---|---|---|
| **HYB/NYSE** | **Closed-end fund** | **Shares to qualify:** 1 |
| H: 3.68 | c/o State St. Bk. & Trust, Box 8200 | **Safekeeping:** No |
| L: 2.50 | Boston. MA 02266-8200 | **Accepts foreign:** Yes |
| **Rec:** 3.02 | State St. Bank     800-426-5523 | **Auto. inv.:** No |
| **Div.:** 0.36 | $100 - $500/quarter | **Disc.:** No |
| **Paid on:** | Every 90 days beginning 3/31 | |
| MONTHLY-30 | FEES: Div: comm.; Cash: 75¢ + comm.; Cert: $0; Term: $0; Sells irregularly, by mail or | |
| **Since:** N/A | phone, at market, for $2.50 + 15¢/sh. | |

---

## New England Business Service, Inc. ⊗
**\***

| | |
|---|---|
| **NEB/NYSE** | **Office supplies** |
| H: 21.87 | 500 Main St. |
| L: 14.68 | Groton. MA 01471 |
| **Rec:** 18.98 | |
| **Div.:** 2.40 | BankBoston 800-736-3001 |
| **Paid on:** | $50 - $100,000/year |
| 2.5.8.11-20 | Every 7 days beginning Wed. |
| **Since:** N/A | |

**Shares to qualify:** 1 /de ($250)
**Safekeeping:** Yes
**Accepts foreign:** Yes
**Auto. inv.:** Yes
**Disc.:** No

FEES: Div: $1.25; Cash: $5 + 8¢/sh.; Auto. Inv.: $2.50; Cert: $0; Term: $0; Sells weekly, by mail, at market, for $10 + 15¢/sh.

---

## New Germany Fund (The)
**\***

| | |
|---|---|
| **GF/NYSE** | **Closed-end fund** |
| H: 14.25 | c/o Deutsche Bk.Securities, 280 Park Ave., 7-East |
| L: 6.17 | New York. NY 10017 |
| **Rec:** 6.38 | |
| **Div.:** 0.08 | Investors Bank & Trust Co. 800-356-2754 |
| **Paid on:** | $100 - $36,000/year |
| 9.11-13 | Every 30 days beginning 1/15 |
| **Since:** N/A | |

**Shares to qualify:** 1
**Safekeeping:** Yes
**Accepts foreign:** Yes
**Auto. inv.:** No
**Disc.:** No

FEES: Div: $0!; Cash: comm.; Cert: $0!; Term: $0,Does not sell through the plan

---

## New Ireland Fund

| | |
|---|---|
| **IRL/NYSE** | **Closed-end fund** |
| H: 16.25 | c/o Amer.Stk., 40 Wall St., 46th Fl. |
| L: 11.50 | New York. NY 10005 |
| **Rec:** 12.31 | |
| **Div.:** 0.13 | American Stock Transfer 800-278-4353 |
| **Paid on:** | $100 - $3,000/year |
| 12-20 | Every 365 days beginning 1/15 |
| **Since:** N/A | |

**Shares to qualify:** 1
**Safekeeping:** No
**Accepts foreign:** No
**Auto. inv.:** No
**Disc.:** No

FEES: Div: comm.; Cash: comm.; Cert: $0; Term: $0; Sells weekly, by mail or fax, at market, for 4¢/sh.

---

## New Jersey Resources Corp. ♥
**\***

| | |
|---|---|
| **NJR/NYSE** | **Utility-gas** |
| H: 46.00 | 1415 Wyckoff Rd., Box 1468 |
| L: 37.26 | Wall. NJ 07719 |
| **Rec:** 43.80 | |
| **Div.:** 1.76 | Boston Eq. 800-817-3955 |
| **Paid on:** | $25 - $60,000/year |
| 1.4.7.10-3 | Every 15 days beginning 1/2 |
| **Since:** 1951 | |

**Shares to qualify:** 1 /de
**Safekeeping:** Yes
**Accepts foreign:** Yes
**Auto. inv.:** Yes
**Disc.:** No

FEES: Div: $0; Cash: $0; Auto. Inv.: $0; Cert: $0; Term: $0; Sells daily, by mail or phone, at market, for 10¢ to 15¢/sh.

---

## New Plan Excel Realty Trust ♥
**\***

| | |
|---|---|
| **NXL/NYSE** | **REIT** |
| H: 17.99 | 1120 Ave. of the Americas |
| L: 11.81 | New York. NY 10036 |
| **Rec:** 17.10 | |
| **Div.:** 1.65 | BankBoston 800-730-6001 |
| **Paid on:** | $100 - $20,000/quarter |
| 1. 4.7.10-19 | Every 90 days beginning 1/2 |
| **Since:** 1972 | |

**Shares to qualify:** 1
**Safekeeping:** Yes
**Accepts foreign:** Yes
**Auto. inv.:** No
**Disc.:** No

FEES: Div: $0!; Cash: $0!; Cert: $0; Term: $15 + 15¢/sh.; Sells within 7 bus. days, by mail or fax, at market, for $15 + 15¢/sh.

---

## New York Times Co.-A ♥
**\***

| | |
|---|---|
| **NYT/NYSE** | **Media** |
| H: 47.98 | 229 West 43rd St. |
| L: 32.62 | New York. NY 10036-3959 |
| **Rec:** 46.30 | |
| **Div.:** 0.50 | First Chicago Trust 800-414-6280 |
| **Paid on:** | $10 - $3,000/quarter |
| 3.6.9.12 | Every 90 days beginning 3/15 |
| **Since:** N/A | |

**Shares to qualify:** 1
**Safekeeping:** Yes
**Accepts foreign:** No
**Auto. inv.:** No
**Disc.:** No

FEES: Div: $0; Cash: $0; Cert: $0; Term: $10 + 12¢/sh.; Sells weekly, by mail or fax, at market, for $10 + 12¢/sh.

---

## Newell Rubbermaid Inc. ⊗
**\***

| | |
|---|---|
| **NWL/NYSE** | **Mfr. consumer & indust. prod.** |
| H: 29.50 | 6833 Stalter Dr., Ste. 100 |
| L: 18.25 | Rockford. IL 61108 |
| **Rec:** 23.67 | |
| **Div.:** 0.84 | First Chicago Trust 800-317-4445 |
| **Paid on:** | $25 - $250,000/year |
| 3.6.9.12-3 | Every 5 days beginning varies |
| **Since:** 1947 | |

**Shares to qualify:** 1 /de ($250)
**Safekeeping:** Yes
**Accepts foreign:** No
**Auto. inv.:** Yes
**Disc.:** No

FEES: Div: 5% to $3 + 3¢/sh.; Cash: $5 + 3¢/sh.; Auto. Inv.: $2 + 3/sh.; Cert: $0; Term: $15+ 12¢/sh.; Sells daily, by phone, mail, fax, or Internet, at market, for $15+ 12¢/sh.

---

**\*** DRIP enrollment through Temper Enrollment Service (see page 180).   **123**

## * Newmil Bancorp, Inc. ♥

| | |
|---|---|
| **NMIL/NASD** | **Bank holding company** |
| H: 15.80 | 19 Main St., Box 600 |
| L: 9.50 | New Milford, CT 06776 |
| **Rec:** 14.55 | American Stock Transfer    800-937-5449 |
| **Div.:** 0.44 | $100 - $1,000/quarter |
| **Paid on:** | Every 90 days beginning 2/16 |
| 2.5.8.11-16 | |
| **Since:** N/A | FEES: Div: $0!; Cash: $0!; Cert: $0!; Term: $0, Does not sell through the plan |

**Shares to qualify:** 1
**Safekeeping:** Yes
**Accepts foreign:** Yes
**Auto. inv.:** No
**Disc.:** No

---

## * Newport Corp.

| | |
|---|---|
| **NEWP/NASD** | **Scientific & technical instruments** |
| H: 192.06 | 1791 Deere Ave. |
| L: 19.99 | Irvine. CA 92606 |
| **Rec:** 21.53 | Wells Fargo Bank    800-468-9716 |
| **Div.:** 0.02 | $25 - $10,000/investment |
| **Paid on:** | Every 7 days beginning varies |
| 1-9 & 7-9 | |
| **Since:** 1978 | FEES: Div: 2% to $1.50 + 5¢/sh. ; Cash: $3 + 5¢/sh.; Auto. Inv.: $1; Cert: $0; Term: $10 + 10¢/sh.; Sells daily, by mail, fax or phone, at market, for $10 + 10¢/sh. |

**Shares to qualify:** 1 /de ($250)
**Safekeeping:** No
**Accepts foreign:** Yes
**Auto. inv.:** Yes
**Disc.:** No

---

## Newport News Shipbuilding ⊗

| | |
|---|---|
| **NNS/NYSE** | **Shipbuilding, defense** |
| H: 65.68 | 4101 Washington Ave. |
| L: 37.87 | Newport News. VA 23607-2770 |
| **Rec:** 63.62 | First Chicago Trust    800-519-3111 |
| **Div.:** 0.16 | $50 - $250,000/year |
| **Paid on:** | Every 5 days beginning varies |
| 2.5.8.11-VARIES | |
| **Since:** 1997 | FEES: Div: 5% to $3 + 10¢/sh.; Cash: $5 + 10¢/sh.; Auto. Inv.: $2 + 10¢/sh.; Cert: $0; Term: $0; Sells monthly, by mail or phone, at market, for $15 + 12¢/sh. |

**Shares to qualify:** 1 /de ($500)
**Safekeeping:** Yes
**Accepts foreign:** Yes
**Auto. inv.:** Yes
**Disc.:** No

---

## * Nicor Inc. ♥

| | |
|---|---|
| **GAS/NYSE** | **Utility-gas** |
| H: 43.87 | Box 3014 |
| L: 32.18 | Naperville. IL 60566-7014 |
| **Rec:** 37.97 | Nicor Inc.    630-305-9500 |
| **Div.:** 1.76 | $50 - $5,000/month |
| **Paid on:** | Every 30 days beginning 1/2 |
| 2.5.8.11-1 | |
| **Since:** 1954 | FEES: Div: $0!; Cash: $0!; Cert: $0!; Term: $0, Does not sell through the plan |

**Shares to qualify:** 1
**Safekeeping:** Yes
**Accepts foreign:** Yes
**Auto. inv.:** No
**Disc.:** No

---

## * Nike, Inc.-B ⊗

| | |
|---|---|
| **NKE/NYSE** | **Consumer footware** |
| H: 60.06 | One Bowerman Dr. |
| L: 34.93 | Beaverton. OR 97005 |
| **Rec:** 49.44 | First Chicago Trust    800-756-8200 |
| **Div.:** 0.48 | $50 - $250,000/year |
| **Paid on:** | Every 5 days beginning varies |
| 1.4.7.10-2 | |
| **Since:** 1984 | FEES: Div: 5% to $3 + 3¢/sh.; Cash: $5 + 3¢/sh.; Auto. Inv.: $2 + 3¢/sh.; Cert: $0; Term: $15 + 12¢/sh.; Sells daily, by phone, mail, fax, or Internet, at market, for $15 + 12¢/sh. |

**Shares to qualify:** 1 /de ($500)
**Safekeeping:** Yes
**Accepts foreign:** Yes
**Auto. inv.:** Yes
**Disc.:** No

---

## * NiSource Inc. ♥

| | |
|---|---|
| **NI/NYSE** | **Utility-gas & electric & water** |
| H: 32.55 | 801 E. 86th Ave. |
| L: 19.93 | Merrillville. IN 46410 |
| **Rec:** 25.18 | Mellon Inv. Svcs.    888-884-7790 |
| **Div.:** 1.16 | $25 - $5,000/quarter |
| **Paid on:** | Every 30 days beginning 1/20 |
| 2.5.8.11-20 | |
| **Since:** 1987 | FEES: Div: $0!; Cash: $0!; Cert: $0!; Term: $5 + 7¢/sh.; Sells biweekly, by mail or fax, at market, for $5 + 7¢/sh. |

**Shares to qualify:** 1
**Safekeeping:** Yes
**Accepts foreign:** Yes
**Auto. inv.:** No
**Disc.:** No

---

## * Nokia Corp.

| | |
|---|---|
| **NOK/NYSE** | **Telecommunication systems & equip.** |
| H: 53.75 | c/o CitibankShrhldr. Svcs., Box 2502 |
| L: 16.90 | Jersey City. NJ 07303-2502 |
| **Rec:** 19.00 | Citibank    877-665-4223 |
| **Div.:** 0.25 | $50 - $100,000/year |
| **Paid on:** | Every 15 days beginning 1st, 15th or both |
| 4-10 | |
| **Since:** 1995 | FEES: Div: 4¢/sh.; Cash: $2.50 + 4¢/sh.; Auto. Inv.: $2.50 + 4¢/sh.; Cert: $10; Term: $0; Sells daily, by mail or phone, at market, for $10 + 4¢/sh. |

**Shares to qualify:** 1 /de ($250)
**Safekeeping:** Yes
**Accepts foreign:** Yes
**Auto. inv.:** Yes
**Disc.:** No

---

## ✳ Nordson Corp. ♥

**NDSN/NASD**
**H:** 32.99
**L:** 22.00
**Rec:** 26.22
**Div.:** 0.56
**Paid on:**
1.3.6.9-28
**Since:** 1963

**Machinery**
28601 Clemens Rd.
Westlake. OH 44145-1148

National City Bank      800-622-6757
$10 - $4,000/quarter
Every 30 days beginning 1/31

FEES: Div: $0; Cash: $0; Cert: $0; Term: $5; Sells monthly, by mail, fax , or phone, at market, for 8¢ to 20¢/sh.

**Shares to qualify:** 1
**Safekeeping:** Yes
**Accepts foreign:** Yes
**Auto. inv.:** No
**Disc.:** No

---

## ✳ Norfolk Southern Corp.

**NSC/NYSE**
**H:** 24.00
**L:** 11.93
**Rec:** 20.43
**Div.:** 0.24
**Paid on:**
3.6.9.12-10
**Since:** 1982

**Railroads**
3 Commercial Pl.
Norfolk. VA 23510-9250

Bank of New York      800-432-0140
$10 - $3,000/quarter
Every 90 days beginning 3/10

FEES: Div: 5% to $2.50; Cash: 5% to $2.50; Cert: $0; Term: $5,Does not sell through the plan

**Shares to qualify:** 1
**Safekeeping:** No
**Accepts foreign:** Yes
**Auto. inv.:** No
**Disc.:** No

---

## ✳ North Fork Bancorp ♥

**NFB/NYSE**
**H:** 32.75
**L:** 16.87
**Rec:** 32.04
**Div.:** 0.84
**Paid on:**
2.5.8.11-15
**Since:** 1994

**Banking**
275 Broadhollow  Rd.
Melville. NY 11747

First Chicago Trust      800-317-4445
$200 - $15,000/month
Every 30 days beginning 1/15

FEES: Div: $0!; Cash: $0!; Cert: $0!; Term: $10 + 10¢/sh.; Sells daily, by phone, mail, fax, or Internet, at market, for $10 + 10¢/sh.

**Shares to qualify:** 1
**Safekeeping:** Yes
**Accepts foreign:** Yes
**Auto. inv.:** No
**Disc.:** No

---

## ✳ Northeast PA Financial Corp. ♥

**NEP/ASE**
**H:** 15.25
**L:** 10.12
**Rec:** 15.00
**Div.:** 0.40
**Paid on:**
2.5.8.11-25
**Since:** N/A

**Bank holding company**
12 E. Broad St.
Hazleton. PA  18201

Registrar & Transfer      800-368-5948
$100 - $1,000/quarter
Every 90 days beginning 2/25

FEES: Div: $0!; Cash: $0!; Cert: $0!; Term: $20; Sells weekly, by mail, at market, for $20

**Shares to qualify:** 50
**Safekeeping:** Yes
**Accepts foreign:** Yes
**Auto. inv.:** No
**Disc.:** No

---

## ✳ Northrop Grumman Corp. ♥

**NOC/NYSE**
**H:** 99.10
**L:** 72.87
**Rec:** 79.02
**Div.:** 1.60
**Paid on:**
3.6.9.12-VARIES
**Since:** 1951

**Aerospace, defense**
1840 Century Park East
Los Angeles. CA  90067-2199

First Chicago Trust      800-756-8200
$100 - $1,000/month
Every 30 days beginning 1/15

FEES: Div: $0!;  Cash: $0!; Cert: $0!; Term: $0,Does not sell through the plan

**Shares to qualify:** 1
**Safekeeping:** No
**Accepts foreign:** Yes
**Auto. inv.:** No
**Disc.:** No

---

## ✳ Northwest Bancorp, Inc. ♥

**NWSB/NAS**
**H:** 13.00
**L:** 6.93
**Rec:** 10.27
**Div.:** 0.24
**Paid on:**
2.5.8.11-14
**Since:** N/A

**Bank holding company**
Liberty St. at Second Ave.
Warren. PA  16365

American Stock Transfer      800-278-4353
$25 - $5,000/month
Every 30 days beginning 1/2

FEES: Div: $0; Cash: $0; Cert: $0; Term: $10 ; Sells within 5 bus. days, by mail, at market, for $10

**Shares to qualify:** 5
**Safekeeping:** Yes
**Accepts foreign:** Yes
**Auto. inv.:** No
**Disc.:** No

---

## ✳ Northwest Natural Gas Co. ♥

**NWN/NYSE**
**H:** 27.50
**L:** 21.65
**Rec:** 24.74
**Div.:** 1.24
**Paid on:**
2.5.8.11-15
**Since:** 1950

**Utility-gas**
220 N.W. Second Ave.
Portland. OR  97209

Northwest Natural      503-220-2590
$0 - $50,000/year
Every 30 days beginning 1/15

FEES: Div: $0!; Cash: $0!; Auto. Inv.: $0; Cert: $0!;  Term: $0; Sells weekly, by mail or fax, at market, for 4¢/sh.

**Shares to qualify:** 1
**Safekeeping:** Yes
**Accepts foreign:** Yes
**Auto. inv.:** Yes
**Disc.:** No

---

✳ DRIP enrollment through Temper Enrollment Service (see page 180).     **125**

## ✱ NorthWestern Corp. ♥

**NOR/NYSE**
**H:** 26.75
**L:** 19.12
**Rec:** 21.89
**Div.:** 1.19
**Paid on:**
3.6.9.12-1
**Since:** 1947

**Utility-electric & gas, service-misc.**
600 Market St. West
Huron. SD 57350
NorthWestern        800-677-6716
$10 - $10,000/month
Every 30 days beginning 1/2
FEES: Div $0!; Cash: $0!; Auto. Inv.: $0; Cert: $0!; Term: $0; Sells weekly, by mail, at market, for 6¢/sh.

**Shares to qualify:** 1 /de ($500)
**Safekeeping:** Yes
**Accepts foreign:** Yes
**Auto. inv.:** Yes
**Disc.:** No

---

## ✱ NSTAR ♥

**NST/NYSE**
**H:** 44.56
**L:** 33.93
**Rec:** 43.01
**Div.:** 2.06
**Paid on:**
2.5.8.11-1
**Since:** 1890

**Utility-electric**
800 Boylston St.
Boston. MA 02199-8003
BankBoston        800-338-8446
$50 - $60,000/year
Every 30 days beginning 1st bus. day
FEES: Div: $0!; Cash: $0!; Auto. Inv.: $0; Cert: $0!; Term: 5% to $15 + comm.; Sells within 5 bus. days, by mail or phone, at market, for 5% to $15 + comm.

**Shares to qualify:** 1 /de ($500)
**Safekeeping:** Yes
**Accepts foreign:** Yes
**Auto. inv.:** Yes
**Disc.:** No

---

## ✱ NTELOS Inc.

**NTLO/NASD**
**H:** 41.25
**L:** 14.37
**Rec:** 17.54
**Div.:** 0.00
**Paid on:**
DIV. SUSP.
**Since:** --

**Communications**
401 Spring Ln., Ste. 300, Box 1990
Wavnesboro. VA 22980
NTELOS Inc.        888-221-4239
$50 - $10,000/quarter
Every 30 days beginning 1/29
FEES: Div: n/o; Cash: $0!; Cert: $0; Term: comm.; Sells monthly, by mail, at market, for comm.

**Shares to qualify:** 1
**Safekeeping:** Yes
**Accepts foreign:** Yes
**Auto. inv.:** No
**Disc.:** No

---

## ✱ Nucor Corp. ♥

**NUE/NYSE**
**H:** 56.50
**L:** 29.50
**Rec:** 47.39
**Div.:** 0.68
**Paid on:**
2.5.8.11-12
**Since:** 1973

**Metals, parts**
2100 Rexford Rd.
Charlotte. NC 28211
American Stock Transfer        800-937-5449
$10 - $1,000/month
Every 30 days beginning 1/11
FEES: Div: $0!; Cash: $0!; Cert: $0!; Term: $10 + 4¢/sh.; Sells weekly, by mail, at market, for $10 + 4¢/sh.

**Shares to qualify:** 1
**Safekeeping:** No
**Accepts foreign:** Yes
**Auto. inv.:** No
**Disc.:** No

---

## ✱ NUI Corp. ♥

**NUI/NYSE**
**H:** 33.93
**L:** 20.10
**Rec:** 22.97
**Div.:** 0.98
**Paid on:**
3.6.9.12-15
**Since:** 1893

**Utility-gas**
550 Route 202-206, Box 760
Bedminster. NJ 07921-0760
American Stock Transfer        800-937-5449
$25 - $60,000/year
Every 7 days beginning Wed.
FEES: Div: $0!; Cash: $0!; Auto. Inv.: $0; Cert: $0!; Term: $10 + 12¢/sh.; Sells daily, by mail, at market, for $10 + 12¢/sh.

**Shares to qualify:** 1 /de ($125)
**Safekeeping:** Yes
**Accepts foreign:** No
**Auto. inv.:** Yes
**Disc.:** No

---

## ✱ Occidental Petroleum Corp. ♥

**OXY/NYSE**
**H:** 31.10
**L:** 19.06
**Rec:** 27.44
**Div.:** 1.00
**Paid on:**
1.4.7.10-15
**Since:** 1975

**Oil & gas**
10889 Wilshire Blvd.
Los Angeles. CA 90024-4201
Mellon Inv. Svcs.        800-622-9231
$50 - $1,000/month
Every 30 days beginning 1/15
FEES: Div: $0!; Cash: $0!; Cert: $5; Term: $15 + 3¢ to 12¢/sh.; Sells monthly, by mail or phone, at market, for $15 + 3¢ to 12¢/sh.

**Shares to qualify:** 25
**Safekeeping:** Yes
**Accepts foreign:** No
**Auto. inv.:** No
**Disc.:** No

---

## ✱ OceanFirst Financial Corp. ♥

**OCFC/NASD**
**H:** 27.08
**L:** 18.75
**Rec:** 25.92
**Div.:** 0.84
**Paid on:**
2.5.8.11-18
**Since:** N/A

**Bank holding co.**
975 Hooper Ave.
Toms River. NJ 08754-2009
American Stock Transfer        800-937-5449
$100 - $5,000/quarter
Every 90 days beginning 2/18
FEES: Div: $0!; Cash: $0!; Cert: $0!; Term: 4¢/sh.; Sells upon termination, by mail, at market, for 4¢/sh.

**Shares to qualify:** 1
**Safekeeping:** Yes
**Accepts foreign:** Yes
**Auto. inv.:** No
**Disc.:** Div 3% Cash: 3%

---

✱ DRIP enrollment through Temper Enrollment Service (see page 180).  **126**

## Office Depot, Inc. ⊗

**Office supplies**

ODP/NYSE
H: 13.24
L: 6.00
**Rec:** 12.00
**Div.:** 0.00
**Paid on:** N/0
**Since:** N/A

2200 Old Germantown Road
Delray Beach. FL 33445

Mellon Inv. Svcs.   800-681-8059
$25 - $100,000/year
Every 5 days beginning varies

**Shares to qualify:** 1 /de ($250)
**Safekeeping:** Yes
**Accepts foreign:** Yes
**Auto. inv.:** Yes
**Disc.:** No

FEES: Div: n/o; Cash: $5; Auto. Inv.: $3.50; Cert: $0; Term: $15 + 12¢/sh.; Sells within 3 bus. days, by mail or phone, at market, for $15 + 12¢/sh.

---

## OGE Energy Corp. ♥

**Utility-electric & gas**

OGE/NYSE
H: 24.75
L: 18.93
**Rec:** 21.25
**Div.:** 1.33
**Paid on:** 1.4.7.10-30
**Since:** 1946

Box 321
Oklahoma City. OK 73101-0321

Mellon Inv. Svcs.   888-216-8114
$25 - $100,000/year
Every 7 days beginning varies

**Shares to qualify:** 1 /de ($250)
**Safekeeping:** Yes
**Accepts foreign:** Yes
**Auto. inv.:** Yes
**Disc.:** No

FEES: Div: $0; Cash: $0; Auto. Inv.: $0; Cert: $0; Term: $0; Sells weekly, by phone, mail, fax, or Internet, at market, for $10 + 12¢/sh.

---

## Ohio Casualty Corp. ⊗

**Insurance**

OCAS/NASD
H: 14.34
L: 6.12
**Rec:** 13.60
**Div.:** 0.00
**Paid on:** DIV. SUSP.
**Since:** --

9450 Seward Rd.
Fairfield. OH 45014

First Chicago Trust   800-317-4445
$10 - $60,000/year
Every 30 days beginning 1/2

**Shares to qualify:** 1
**Safekeeping:** Yes
**Accepts foreign:** Yes
**Auto. inv.:** Yes
**Disc.:** No

FEES: Div: n/o; Cash: $5; Auto. Inv.: $2; Cert: $0; Term: $0; Sells daily, by phone or mail, at market, for $15 + 12¢/sh.

---

## Old National Bancorp ⊗

**Banking**

OLDB/NASD
H: 30.05
L: 20.36
**Rec:** 26.30
**Div.:** 0.68
**Paid on:** 3.6.9.12-15
**Since:** N/A

Box 718
Evansville. IN 47705-0718

Old National Bancorp   800-677-1749
$50 - $30,000/month
Every 30 days beginning 1/1

**Shares to qualify:** 1 /de ($500)
**Safekeeping:** Yes
**Accepts foreign:** Yes
**Auto. inv.:** Yes
**Disc.:** Div 3% Cash: 0%

FEES: Div: $0; Cash: $5; Auto. Inv.: $0; Cert: $0; Term: 15¢/sh. ; Sells monthly, by mail, at market, for 15¢/sh.

---

## Old Republic International Corp. ♥

**Insurance**

ORI/NYSE
H: 32.06
L: 21.25
**Rec:** 27.37
**Div.:** 0.60
**Paid on:** 3.6.9.12-15
**Since:** 1941

307 North Michigan Ave.
Chicago. IL 60601

First Chicago Trust   201-324-0313
$100 - $5,000/quarter
Every 90 days beginning 3/1

**Shares to qualify:** 1
**Safekeeping:** Yes
**Accepts foreign:** No
**Auto. inv.:** No
**Disc.:** No

FEES: Div: $0; Cash: $0; Cert: $0; Term: $0; Sells daily, by phone, mail, fax, at market, for 12¢/sh.

---

## Olin Corp. ⊗

**Chemicals**

OLN/NYSE
H: 23.18
L: 14.90
**Rec:** 15.90
**Div.:** 0.80
**Paid on:** 3.6.9.12-10
**Since:** 1926

501 Merritt 7, Box 4500
Norwalk. CT 06856-4500

Mellon Inv. Svcs.   800-306-8594
$50 - $5,000/month
Every 30 days beginning 1/10

**Shares to qualify:** 1
**Safekeeping:** Yes
**Accepts foreign:** Yes
**Auto. inv.:** No
**Disc.:** No

FEES: Div: 5% to $2.50; Cash: 5% to $2.50 + $5; Cert: $5; Term: $0; Sells monthly, by mail or phone, at market, for $15 + comm.

---

## OM Group ♥

**Specialty chemicals**

OMG/NYSE
H: 63.98
L: 40.12
**Rec:** 62.25
**Div.:** 0.52
**Paid on:** 2.5.8.11-31
**Since:** 1994

50 Public Sq., 3500 Terminal Twr.
Cleveland. OH 44113-2204

National City Bank   800-622-6757
$10 - $5,000/month
Every 30 days beginning 1/31

**Shares to qualify:** 1
**Safekeeping:** Yes
**Accepts foreign:** Yes
**Auto. inv.:** No
**Disc.:** No

FEES: Div: $0; Cash: $0; Cert: $0; Term: $0; Sells monthly, by phone or mail, at market, for comm.

---

## * Omega Healthcare Investor ♥

| | | |
|---|---|---|
| **OHI/NYSE** | REIT | **Shares to qualify:** 1 |
| H: 6.68 | 900 Victors Way, Ste.350 | **Safekeeping:** Yes |
| L: 1.35 | Ann Arbor. MI 48108 | **Accepts foreign:** Yes |
| **Rec:** 3.60 | First Chicago Trust     800-519-3111 | **Auto. inv.:** Yes |
| **Div.:** 1.00 | $1000 - $20,000/year | **Disc.:** Div: 5% Cash: 0% |
| **Paid on:** | Every 30 days beginning 1/15 | |
| 2.5.8.11-15 | FEES: Div: $0!; Cash: $0!;  Auto. Inv.: $0;  Does not sell through the plan | |
| **Since:** 1992 | | |

## * Omnicare, Inc. ♥

| | | |
|---|---|---|
| **OCR/NYSE** | Health care | **Shares to qualify:** 1 |
| H: 26.00 | 1600 RiverCenter II, 100 East River Ctr. Blvd. | **Safekeeping:** No |
| L: 10.25 | Covington. KY 41011 | **Accepts foreign:** Yes |
| **Rec:** 24.26 | First Chicago Trust     800-317-4445 | **Auto. inv.:** No |
| **Div.:** 0.09 | $10 - $1,000/month | **Disc.:** No |
| **Paid on:** | Every 30 days beginning 1/18 | |
| 3.6.9.12-10 | FEES: Div: $0!; Cash: $0!; Cert: $5; Term: $5; Sells daily, by mail or phone, at market, for | |
| **Since:** 1989 | $10 + 12¢/sh. | |

## * Omnova Solutions Inc. ♥

| | | |
|---|---|---|
| **OMN/NYSE** | Manufacturer of chemical products | **Shares to qualify:** 1 /de ($500) |
| H: 7.28 | 175 Ghent Rd. | **Safekeeping:** Yes |
| L: 4.37 | Fairlawn. OH 44333-3300 | **Accepts foreign:** Yes |
| **Rec:** 6.95 | Bank of New York     800-524-4458 | **Auto. inv.:** Yes |
| **Div.:** 0.20 | $50 - $10,000/investment | **Disc.:** No |
| **Paid on:** | Every 7 days beginning varies | |
| 2.5.8.11-30 | FEES: Div: $0!; Cash: $0!;  Auto. Inv.: $0; Cert: $0!;  Term: $10 + 10¢/sh.; Sells weekly, by | |
| **Since:** 1999 | mail or phone, at market, for $10 + 10¢/sh. | |

## * ONEOK, Inc. ♥

| | | |
|---|---|---|
| **OKE/NYSE** | Diversified energy company | **Shares to qualify:** 1 /de ($250) |
| H: 25.31 | 100 West Fifth St., Box 871 | **Safekeeping:** Yes |
| L: 14.37 | Tulsa. OK 74102-0871 | **Accepts foreign:** Yes |
| **Rec:** 17.32 | First Chicago Trust     888-764-5595 | **Auto. inv.:** Yes |
| **Div.:** 0.62 | $25 - $10,000/investment | **Disc.:** No |
| **Paid on:** | Every 5 days beginning varies | |
| 2.5.8.11-15 | FEES: Div: $0!; Cash: $0!;  Auto. Inv.: $0; Cert: $0!;  Term: $0; Sells daily, by phone, mail, | |
| **Since:** 1939 | fax, or Internet, at market, for $10 + 10¢/sh. | |

## * Otter Tail Corporation ♥

| | | |
|---|---|---|
| **OTTR/NASD** | Utility-electric | **Shares to qualify:** 1 /de ($100) |
| H: 31.00 | Box 496 | **Safekeeping:** Yes |
| L: 20.75 | Fergus Falls. MN 56538-0496 | **Accepts foreign:** Yes |
| **Rec:** 29.00 | Otter Tail Corporation     800-664-1259 | **Auto. inv.:** No |
| **Div.:** 1.04 | $10 - $5,000/month | **Disc.:** No |
| **Paid on:** | Every 30 days beginning 1/2 | |
| 3.6.9.12-10 | FEES: Div: $0!; Cash: $0!; Cert: $0!; Term: $0; Sells monthly, by mail or fax, at avg. price, | |
| **Since:** 1938 | for $0 | |

## * Owens & Minor, Inc. ♥

| | | |
|---|---|---|
| **OMI/NYSE** | Medical supplies | **Shares to qualify:** 1 |
| H: 21.00 | Box 27626 | **Safekeeping:** No |
| L: 11.87 | Richmond. VA 23261-7626 | **Accepts foreign:** No |
| **Rec:** 17.80 | Bank of New York     800-524-4458 | **Auto. inv.:** No |
| **Div.:** 0.28 | $25 - $25,000/year | **Disc.:** No |
| **Paid on:** | Every 30 days beginning 1/25 | |
| 3.6.9.12-31 | FEES: Div: $0!; Cash: $0!; Cert: $0!; Term: $5 + 10¢/sh.; Sells weekly, by mail, at market, | |
| **Since:** 1932 | for $5 + 10¢sh. | |

## * PAB Bankshares, Inc. ♥

| | | |
|---|---|---|
| **PAB/ASE** | Bank holding company | **Shares to qualify:** 1 |
| H: 13.00 | Box 3460 | **Safekeeping:** Yes |
| L: 8.68 | Valdosta. GA 31604-3460 | **Accepts foreign:** Yes |
| **Rec:** 11.21 | Registrar & Transfer     800-368-5948 | **Auto. inv.:** No |
| **Div.:** 0.44 | $50 - $5,000/year | **Disc.:** No |
| **Paid on:** | Every 90 days beginning 1/16 | |
| 1.4.7.10-15 | FEES: Div: $0!; Cash: $0!; Cert: $0!; Term: $0; Sells daily, by mail, at market, for 6¢/sh. | |
| **Since:** N/A | | |

## ✳ Pacific Century Financial Corp. ♥

**BOH/NYSE** — **Banking**

H: 27.44
L: 11.06
Rec: 27.18
Div.: 0.72
Paid on:
3.6.9.12-14
Since:1898

Box 2900
Honolulu. HI 96846

Continental Stock Transfer    800-509-5586
$25 - $5,000/quarter
Every 30 days beginning 1/10

FEES: Div $0!; Cash: $0!; Auto. Inv.: $0; Cert: $0!; Term: $0; Sells weekly, by mail, at market, for $2 + comm.

**Shares to qualify:** 1 / de ($250)
**Safekeeping:** Yes
**Accepts foreign:** Yes
**Auto. inv.:** Yes
**Disc.:** No

---

## ✳ Pall Corp. ♥

**PLL/NYSE** — **Filters**

H: 26.25
L: 17.93
Rec: 24.02
Div.: 0.68
Paid on:
2.5.8.11-19
Since:1974

25 Harbor Park Dr.
Port Washington. NY 11050-4630

Wachovia    800-633-4236
$100 - $5,000/month
Every 30 days beginning 1/10

FEES: Div: $0!; Cash: $0!; Cert: $0; Term: $0; Sells weekly, by mail or fax, at avg. price, for 8¢/sh.

**Shares to qualify:** 50
**Safekeeping:** Yes
**Accepts foreign:** Yes
**Auto. inv.:** No
**Disc.:** No

---

## ✳ Pan Pacific Retail Properties, Inc. ♥

**PNP/NYSE** — **REIT**

H: 26.27
L: 18.87
Rec: 26.24
Div.: 1.82
Paid on:
1.4.7.10-15
Since:N/A

1631-B South Melrose Dr.
Vista. CA 92083

Bank of New York    800-524-4458
$100 - $25,000/quarter
Every 90 days beginning 1/15

FEES: Div: $0!; Cash: $0!; Auto. Inv.: $0; Cert: $5; Term: $5 + comm.; Sells daily, by mail or phone, at avg. price, for $5 + comm.

**Shares to qualify:** 1 / de ($250)
**Safekeeping:** Yes
**Accepts foreign:** Yes
**Auto. inv.:** Yes
**Disc.:** Div 2% Cash: 2%

---

## ✳ Parker-Hannifin Corp. ♥

**PH/NYSE** — **Motion control components**

H: 50.10
L: 31.00
Rec: 45.35
Div.: 0.72
Paid on:
3.6.9.12-5
Since:1949

6035 Parkland Blvd.
Cleveland. OH 44124-4141

National City Bank    800-622-6757
$10 - $5,000/month
Every 30 days beginning 1/2

FEES: Div: $0!; Cash: $0!; Cert: $0!; Term: $0; Sells weekly, by mail, at market, for 5¢/sh.

**Shares to qualify:** 1
**Safekeeping:** Yes
**Accepts foreign:** Yes
**Auto. inv.:** No
**Disc.:** No

---

## ✳ Parkway Properties Inc. ♥

**PKY/NYSE** — **REIT**

H: 35.25
L: 27.37
Rec: 32.55
Div.: 2.52
Paid on:
3.6.9.12-28
Since:1986

1 Jackson Pl., Ste. 1000, 188 E. Capitol St.
Jackson. MS 39225

Computershare Investor Svcs.    877-588-4124
$100 - $10,000/month
Every 30 days beginning last bus. day/month

FEES: Div: $0!; Cash: $0!; Auto. Inv.: $0; Cert: $0!; Term: $10 + 10¢/sh.; Sells within 5 bus. days, by mail or fax, at market, for $10 + 10¢/sh.

**Shares to qualify:** 1 / de ($100)
**Safekeeping:** Yes
**Accepts foreign:** Yes
**Auto. inv.:** Yes
**Disc.:** Div 3% Cash: 3%

---

## ✳ Patriot Bank Corp. ♥

**PBIX/NASD** — **Bank holding co.**

H: 12.19
L: 5.62
Rec: 10.85
Div.: 0.37
Paid on:
2.5.8.11-31
Since:N/A

Box 1090
Pottstown. PA 19464-0289

Registrar & Transfer    800-368-5948
$100 - $5,000/quarter
Every 90 days beginning 2/28

FEES: Div: $0; Cash: $0; Auto. Inv.: $0; Cert: $0; Term: $10 + comm.; Sells weekly, by mail, at market, for $10 + comm.

**Shares to qualify:** 100
**Safekeeping:** Yes
**Accepts foreign:** Yes
**Auto. inv.:** Yes
**Disc.:** No

---

## ✳ Paychex, Inc. ♥

**PAYX/NASD** — **Accounting service**

H: 61.25
L: 30.61
Rec: 39.12
Div.: 0.36
Paid on:
2.5.8.11-15
Since:1988

911 Panorama Trail South
Rochester. NY 14625-0397

American Stock Transfer    800-937-5449
$100 - $10,000/investment
Every day days beginning daily

FEES: Div: $0!; Cash: $0; Auto. Inv.: $0; Cert: $0; Term: $15; Sells daily, by phone, mail, fax, or Internet, at market, for $15 + 10¢/sh.

**Shares to qualify:** 1 / de ($250)
**Safekeeping:** Yes
**Accepts foreign:** Yes
**Auto. inv.:** Yes
**Disc.:** No

---

✳ DRIP enrollment through Temper Enrollment Service (see page 180).    **129**

## ✳ Penney (J.C.)

**JCP/NYSE** | Retail department stores

H: 29.50
L: 8.62
Rec: 26.62

Box 10001
Dallas. TX 75301

Mellon Inv. Svcs.    800-842-9470

**Div.:** 0.50
**Paid on:**
2.5.8.11-1
**Since:** 1930

$25 - $10,000/month
Every 7 days beginning 1/7

**Shares to qualify:** 1 /de ($250)
**Safekeeping:** Yes
**Accepts foreign:** Yes
**Auto. inv.:** Yes
**Disc.:** No

FEES: Div: $0;  Cash: $1.50 + 6¢/sh.;  Auto. Inv.: $0;  Cert: $0;  Term: $0; Sells daily, by mail or phone, at market, for $15 + 6¢/sh.

---

## ✳ Pennichuck Corp. ♥

**PNNW/NAS** | Utility-water

H: 35.00
L: 22.50
Rec: 29.00

Four Water St., Box 448
Nashua. NH 03061

Boston Eq.    800-730-4001

**Div.:** 1.00
**Paid on:**
2.5.8.11-15
**Since:** 1917

$100 - $3,000/quarter
Every 90 days beginning 2/15

**Shares to qualify:** 1 /de ($500)
**Safekeeping:** Yes
**Accepts foreign:** Yes
**Auto. inv.:** No
**Disc.:** Div 5% Cash: 0%

FEES: Div: $0;  Cash: $0;  Cert: $0;  Term: $0,Does not sell through the plan

---

## ✳ Pennrock Financial Services Corp. ♥

**PRFS/NASD** | Financial holding co.

H: 23.00
L: 13.50
Rec: 22.00

1060 Main St., Box 580
Blue Ball. PA 17506

American Stock Transfer    800-937-5449

**Div.:** 0.76
**Paid on:**
1.4.7.10-10
**Since:** N/A

$25 - $10,000/quarter
Every 90 days beginning 1/10

**Shares to qualify:** 100
**Safekeeping:** Yes
**Accepts foreign:** Yes
**Auto. inv.:** No
**Disc.:** No

FEES: Div: $0!; Cash: $0!; Cert: $1; Term: $10 + 4¢/sh.; Sells within 15 bus. days, by mail, at market, for $10 + 4¢/sh.

---

## ✳ Penns Woods Bancorp, Inc. ♥

**PWOD/OTC** | Bank holding co.

H: 34.00
L: 26.50
Rec: 31.12

300 Market St.
Williamsport. PA 17701

Registrar & Transfer    800-368-5948

**Div.:** 1.00
**Paid on:**
3.6.9.12-28
**Since:** N/A

$50 - $2,000/quarter
Every 90 days beginning 3/28

**Shares to qualify:** 1
**Safekeeping:** Yes
**Accepts foreign:** Yes
**Auto. inv.:** No
**Disc.:** No

FEES: Div: $0;  Cash: $0;  Cert: $5;  Term: $5,Does not sell through the plan

---

## ✳ Pennsylvania Commerce Bancorp, Inc. ♥

**COBH/NASD** | Bank holding company

H: 38.00
L: 21.90
Rec: 35.00

100 Senate Ave., Box 8599
Camp Hill. PA 17011-8599

Commerce Bank/Harrisburg, NA    717-975-5630

**Div.:** STK.
**Paid on:**
N/A
**Since:** N/A

$100 - $5,000/quarter
Every 90 days beginning 3/31

**Shares to qualify:** 1
**Safekeeping:** Yes
**Accepts foreign:** Yes
**Auto. inv.:** No
**Disc.:** Div 3% Cash: 3%

FEES: Div: $0!; Cash: $0!; Cert: $0!; Term: $0; Sells quarterly, by mail, at market, for $25

---

## ✳ Pennsylvania REIT ♥

**PEI/NYSE** | REIT

H: 25.05
L: 16.81
Rec: 22.80

200 South Broad St., 3rd Fl.
Philadelphia. PA 19102

American Stock Transfer    800-278-4353

**Div.:** 2.04
**Paid on:**
3.6.9.12-15
**Since:** 1962

$250 - $5,000/month
Every 30 days beginning last bus. day/month

**Shares to qualify:** 1 /de ($250)
**Safekeeping:** Yes
**Accepts foreign:** Yes
**Auto. inv.:** No
**Disc.:** Cash: 1%

FEES: Div: $0!; Cash: $0!; Cert: $0!; Term: 4¢/sh.; Sells daily, by mail, at market, for 4¢/sh.

---

## ✳ Pennzoil-Quaker State Co. ♥

**PZL/NYSE** | Automotive consumer products

H: 16.00
L: 9.00
Rec: 11.20

Box 4531
Houston. TX 77210-4351

PZ Shareowner Services    888-795-7862

**Div.:** 0.10
**Paid on:**
3.6.9.12-15
**Since:** N/A

$50 - $60,000/year
Every 30 days beginning 1/15

**Shares to qualify:** 1
**Safekeeping:** Yes
**Accepts foreign:** Yes
**Auto. inv.:** Yes
**Disc.:** No

FEES: Div: $0!; Cash: $0!; Auto. Inv.: $0; Cert: $0!; Term: $0; Sells weekly, by mail, at avg. price, for $15 + 7¢/sh.

---

✳ DRIP enrollment through Temper Enrollment Service (see page 180).    **130**

## Pentair, Inc. ♥

**PNR/NYSE**
H: 37.30
L: 20.62
**Rec:** 35.94

**Div.:** 0.72
**Paid on:**
2.5.8.11-15
**Since:** 1976

**Manufacturing**
1500 County Rd. B2 West
St. Paul, MN 55113-3105
Wells Fargo Bank    877-536-3554
$10 - $3,000/quarter
Every 30 days beginning 1/12
FEES: Div $0!; Cash: $0!; Auto. Inv.: $0; Cert: $0!; Term: $0; Sells daily, by mail or fax, at market, for $10 + 10¢/sh.

**Shares to qualify:** 1
**Safekeeping:** Yes
**Accepts foreign:** Yes
**Auto. inv.:** Yes
**Disc.:** No

---

## People's Bank ♥

**PBCT/NASD**
H: 28.37
L: 18.68
**Rec:** 25.88

**Div.:** 1.36
**Paid on:**
2.5.8.11-15
**Since:** N/A

**Savings bank**
850 Main St.
Bridgeport, CT 06604
Mellon Inv. Svcs.    800-953-2592
$100 - $10,000/month
Every 7 days beginning varies
FEES: Div $0!; Cash: $0!; Cert: $0!; Term: $0; Sells daily, by mail or phone, at avg. price, for $15 + 8¢/sh.

**Shares to qualify:** 1 /de ($250)
**Safekeeping:** Yes
**Accepts foreign:** Yes
**Auto. inv.:** No
**Disc.:** No

---

## Peoples Bancorp of NC

**PEBK/NASD**
H: 19.30
L: 11.62
**Rec:** 19.00

**Div.:** 0.40
**Paid on:**
3.6.9.12-19
**Since:** N/A

**Bank holding co.**
Box 467
Newton, NC 28658-0467
Registrar & Transfer    800-368-5948
$25 - $2,500/quarter
Every 90 days beginning 3/19
FEES: Div $0!; Cash: $1.50; Auto. Inv.: 75¢; Cert: $5; Term: $5; Sells within 7 bus. days, by mail or fax, at avg. price, for $10 + comm.

**Shares to qualify:** 1
**Safekeeping:** Yes
**Accepts foreign:** Yes
**Auto. inv.:** Yes
**Disc.:** No

---

## Peoples BancTrust Co., Inc. ♥

**PBTC/NASD**
H: 13.75
L: 9.14
**Rec:** 12.00

**Div.:** 0.36
**Paid on:**
3.6.9.12-15
**Since:** N/A

**Bank holding company**
310 Broad St., Box 799
Selma, AL 36702-0799
Peoples BancTrust Co. Attn.    334-875-1000
$100 - $2,000/quarter
Every 90 days beginning 3/15
FEES: Div: $0; Cash: $0; Cert: $0; Term: $0,Does not sell through the plan

**Shares to qualify:** 25
**Safekeeping:** Yes
**Accepts foreign:** Yes
**Auto. inv.:** No
**Disc.:** No

---

## Peoples Energy Corp. ♥

**PGL/NYSE**
H: 46.93
L: 31.40
**Rec:** 37.70

**Div.:** 2.04
**Paid on:**
1.4.7.10-15
**Since:** 1939

**Utility-gas**
130 E. Randolph Dr., Box 2000
Chicago, IL 60690-0755
Peoples Energy Corp.    800-228-6888
$25 - $100,000/year
Every 15 days beginning 1/2
FEES: Div: $0!; Cash: $0!; Auto. Inv.: $0; Cert: $0!; Term: $0; Sells weekly, by mail or fax, at market, for 8¢/sh.

**Shares to qualify:** 1 /de ($250)
**Safekeeping:** Yes
**Accepts foreign:** Yes
**Auto. inv.:** Yes
**Disc.:** No

---

## Peoples First, Inc. ♥

**PPFR/OTC**
H: 21.50
L: 15.00
**Rec:** 20.25

**Div.:** 0.48
**Paid on:**
2.5.8.11-15
**Since:** N/A

**Bank holding co.**
24 South Third St.
Oxford, PA 19363
American Stock Transfer    800-278-4353
$50 - $2,500/quarter
Every 90 days beginning 2/15
FEES: Div: $0!; Cash: $0!; Cert: $0!; Term: $0!; Sells quarterly, by mail, at market, for $0!

**Shares to qualify:** 1
**Safekeeping:** Yes
**Accepts foreign:** Yes
**Auto. inv.:** No
**Disc.:** No

---

## Pep Boys ♥

**PBY/NYSE**
H: 13.98
L: 3.31
**Rec:** 11.94

**Div.:** 0.27
**Paid on:**
1.4.7.10-26
**Since:** N/A

**Auto parts retailer**
3111 West Allegheny Ave.
Philadelphia, PA 19132
American Stock Transfer    800-937-5449
$100 - $10,000/quarter
Every 90 days beginning 1/23
FEES: Div: $0; Cash: $0; Cert: $0; Term: $0; Sells weekly, by mail or fax, at market, for 4¢/sh.

**Shares to qualify:** 1
**Safekeeping:** Yes
**Accepts foreign:** Yes
**Auto. inv.:** No
**Disc.:** No

---

## PepsiAmericas, Inc. ⊗

**PAS/NYSE**

**Beverages**

H: 17.00
L: 10.93
Rec: 14.78
Div.: 0.04
Paid on: 4-3
Since: 1950

3880 Dain Rauscher Plaza, 60 S. 6th St.
Minneapolis. MN 55402

First Chicago Trust     800-446-2617
$50 - $120,000/year
Every 7 days beginning varies

Shares to qualify: 1 /de ($250)
Safekeeping: Yes
Accepts foreign: Yes
Auto. inv.: Yes
Disc.: No

FEES: Div: 5% to $3 + 3¢/sh.; Cash: 5% to $5 + 3¢/sh.; Auto. Inv.: $2 + 3¢/sh.; Cert: $0;
Term: $0; Sells daily, by mail, fax , or phone, at market, for $15 + 12¢/sh.

---

## PepsiCo Inc. ♥

**PEP/NYSE**

**Beverages and snack foods**

H: 49.93
L: 40.25
Rec: 45.66
Div.: 0.58
Paid on: 3.6.9-31 & 1-1
Since: 1965

Anderson Hill Rd.
Purchase, NY 10577

Bank of New York     800-226-0083
$25 - $5,000/month
Every 15 days beginning 15th & 30th

Shares to qualify: 5
Safekeeping: Yes
Accepts foreign: Yes
Auto. inv.: No
Disc.: No

FEES: Div: $0!; Cash: $0!; Cert: $0!; Term: $0; Sells weekly, by mail, at market, for $5 +
10¢/sh.

---

## PerkinElmer Inc. ♥

**PKI/NYSE**

**Mfr. scientific instruments & equipment**

H: 60.50
L: 21.27
Rec: 29.73
Div.: 0.28
Paid on: 2.5.8.11-10
Since: 1965

45 William St.
Wellesley. MA 02181-4078

Mellon Inv. Svcs.     877-711-4098
$25 - $5,000/month
Every 30 days beginning 1/2

Shares to qualify: 1
Safekeeping: Yes
Accepts foreign: Yes
Auto. inv.: No
Disc.: No

FEES: Div: $0!; Cash: $0!; Cert: $0; Term: $0; Sells weekly, by mail or phone, at market, for
$15 + 12¢/sh.

---

## Petroleum & Resources Corp.

**PEO/NYSE**

**Investment co.**

H: 32.65
L: 24.37
Rec: 26.10
Div.: 0.52
Paid on: 3.6.9-1 & 12-27
Since: N/A

Seven St. Paul St., #1140
Baltimore. MD 21202

Bank of New York     800-432-8224
$50 - $25,000/investment
Every day days beginning daily

Shares to qualify: 1 /de ($500)
Safekeeping: Yes
Accepts foreign: Yes
Auto. inv.: Yes
Disc.: No

FEES: Div: 10% to $2.50 + 5¢/sh.; Cash: $2.50 + 5¢/sh.; Auto. Inv.: $2.50 + 5¢/sh.;
Cert: $0; Term: $10 + 5¢/sh.; Sells weekly, by mail, fax or phone, at avg. price, for $10 +
5¢/sh.

---

## Pfizer Inc. ♥

**PFE/NYSE**

**Drugs, consumer products**

H: 48.06
L: 34.10
Rec: 41.10
Div.: 0.44
Paid on: 3.6.9.12-12
Since: 1901

235 East 42nd St.
New York. NY 10017-5755

First Chicago Trust     800-733-9393
$50 - $120,000/year
Every 7 days beginning Thurs.

Shares to qualify: 1 /de ($500)
Safekeeping: Yes
Accepts foreign: Yes
Auto. inv.: Yes
Disc.: No

FEES: Div: $0!; Cash: $0!; Auto. Inv.: $0; Cert: $0!; Term: $15 + comm.; Sells daily, by
mail, at avg. price, for $15 + comm.

---

## Pharmacia Corp. ⊗

**PHA/NYSE**

**Drugs**

H: 64.00
L: 40.00
Rec: 44.68
Div.: 0.54
Paid on: 2.5.8.11-2
Since: 1996

100 Route 206 North
Peapack. NJ 07977

Mellon Inv. Svcs.     888-312-8333
$100 - $250,000/year
Every 5 days beginning varies

Shares to qualify: 1 /de ($1000)
Safekeeping: Yes
Accepts foreign: Yes
Auto. inv.: Yes
Disc.: No

FEES: Div: 5% to $3 + 3¢/sh.; Cash: $5 + 3¢/sh. ; Auto. Inv.: $2 + 3¢/sh.; Cert: $0!;
Term: $15 + 12¢/sh.; Sells daily, by phone, mail, fax, or Internet, at market, for $15 +
12¢/sh.

---

## Phelps Dodge

**PD/NYSE**

**Metals**

H: 57.00
L: 36.00
Rec: 37.37
Div.: 0.50
Paid on: 3.6.9.12-10
Since: 1987

2600 North Central Ave.
Phoeniz. AZ 85004

Mellon Inv. Svcs.     800-279-1240
$100 - $10,000/month
Every 7 days beginning varies

Shares to qualify: 10 /de ($1000)
Safekeeping: Yes
Accepts foreign: Yes
Auto. inv.: Yes
Disc.: No

FEES: Div: $0!; Cash: 12¢/sh.; Auto. Inv.: $0; Cert: $0!; Term: $15 +12¢/sh.; Sells
monthly, by phone, mail, fax, or Internet, at avg. price, for $15 + 12¢/sh.

---

## ✱ Philadelphia Suburban Corp. ♥

**PSC/NYSE**
**Utility-water**

H: 26.30
L: 16.95
**Rec:** 26.27

762 W. Lancaster Ave.
Brvn Mawr. PA 19010-3489

**Div.:** 0.62
**Paid on:**
3.6.9.12-1
**Since:** 1939

BankBoston     800-205-8314
$50 - $250,000/year
Every Tues./Fri. days beginning Tuesday

**Shares to qualify:** 5 /de ($500)
**Safekeeping:** Yes
**Accepts foreign:** No
**Auto. inv.:** Yes
**Disc.:** Div 5% Cash: 0%

FEES: Div: $0!; Cash: $0!; Auto. Inv.: $0; Cert: $0!; Term: $15 + 12¢/sh.; Sells daily, by mail or phone, at market, for $15 + 12¢/sh.

---

## ✱ Philip Morris ♥

**MO/NYSE**
**Tobacco, food, & brewing**

H: 53.88
L: 26.06
**Rec:** 44.11

120 Park Ave.
New York. NY 10017-5592

**Div.:** 2.12
**Paid on:**
1.4.7.10-10
**Since:** 1928

First Chicago Trust     800-442-0077
$10 - $60,000/year
Every 30 days beginning 1/10

**Shares to qualify:** 1
**Safekeeping:** Yes
**Accepts foreign:** Yes
**Auto. inv.:** Yes
**Disc.:** No

FEES: Div: $0!; Cash: $0!; Auto. Inv.: $0; Cert: $0!; Term: $0; Sells daily, by mail, fax , or phone, at market, for $10 + 12¢/sh.

---

## ✱ Phillips Petroleum Co. ♥

**P/NYSE**
**Oil refining, chemicals**

H: 70.00
L: 51.50
**Rec:** 57.94

17 Phillips Bldg.
Bartlesville. OK 74004

**Div.:** 1.44
**Paid on:**
3.6.9.12-1
**Since:** 1934

Mellon Inv. Svcs.     800-356-0066
$50 - $10,000/month
Every 7 days beginning Fri.

**Shares to qualify:** 1 /de ($500)
**Safekeeping:** Yes
**Accepts foreign:** Yes
**Auto. inv.:** Yes
**Disc.:** No

FEES: Div: $0!; Cash: $0!; Auto. Inv.: $0; Cert: $0!; Term: $15 + 5¢/sh.; Sells weekly, by mail or phone, at market, for $15 + 5¢/sh.

---

## ✱ Piccadilly Cafeterias Inc. ♥

**PIC/NYSE**
**Restaurants**

H: 3.18
L: 1.01
**Rec:** 1.15

Box 2467
Baton Rouge. LA 70821

**Div.:** 0.00
**Paid on:**
DIV. SUSP.
**Since:** --

State St. Bank     800-633-4236
$100 - $5,000/quarter
Every 90 days beginning 1/2

**Shares to qualify:** 1
**Safekeeping:** Yes
**Accepts foreign:** No
**Auto. inv.:** No
**Disc.:** Div 5% Cash: 0%

FEES: Div: n/o; Cash: $0!; Cert: $0; Term: 5¢/sh.; Sells daily, by mail, at market, for 5¢/sh.

---

## ✱ Piedmont Natural Gas ♥

**PNY/NYSE**
**Utility-gas**

H: 39.43
L: 26.50
**Rec:** 33.00

Box 33068
Charlotte. NC 28233

**Div.:** 1.54
**Paid on:**
1.4.7.10-15
**Since:** 1977

American Stock Transfer     800-937-5449
$25 - $120,000/year
Every 7 days beginning Wednesday

**Shares to qualify:** 1 /de ($250)
**Safekeeping:** Yes
**Accepts foreign:** Yes
**Auto. inv.:** Yes
**Disc.:** Div 5% Cash: 0%

FEES: Div: $0!; Cash: $0!; Auto. Inv.: $0; Cert: $0!; Term: $0; Sells daily, by mail, at market, for comm.

---

## ✱ Pier 1 Imports Inc. ♥

**PIR/NYSE**
**Retailing**

H: 14.89
L: 9.00
**Rec:** 11.80

Box 961020
Fort Worth. TX 76161-0020

**Div.:** 0.16
**Paid on:**
2.5.8.11-24
**Since:** N/A

Mellon Inv. Svcs.     888-884-8086
$50 - $5,000/month
Every 7 days beginning varies

**Shares to qualify:** 1 /de ($500)
**Safekeeping:** Yes
**Accepts foreign:** Yes
**Auto. inv.:** Yes
**Disc.:** No

FEES: Div: $0; Cash: $0; Auto. Inv.: $0; Cert: $0; Term: $0; Sells weekly, by mail , at avg. price, for $15 + 12¢/sh.

---

## ✱ Pinnacle West Capital Corp.

**PNW/NYSE**
**Utility-electric**

H: 56.68
L: 39.06
**Rec:** 43.90

Box 52133
Phoenix. AZ 85072-2133

**Div.:** 1.50
**Paid on:**
3.6.9.12-1
**Since:** 1993

Pinnacle West Capital Corp.     800-457-2983
$0 - $150,000/year
Every 15 days beginning 1st bus. day

**Shares to qualify:** 1 /de ($50)
**Safekeeping:** Yes
**Accepts foreign:** Yes
**Auto. inv.:** Yes
**Disc.:** No

FEES: Div: 2¢/sh.; Cash: 2¢/sh. ; Auto. Inv.: $0; Cert: $0; Term: $0; Sells weekly, by phone, mail, fax, or Internet, at avg. price, for 2¢/sh.

---

## ✳ Pioneer Standard Electronics ♥

**PIOS/NASD** | Dist. of indus. & end user elec. prods.

H: 15.00
L: 9.00
**Rec:** 12.13

6065 Parkland Blvd.
Cleveland. OH 44124

National City Bank    800-622-6757

**Div.:** 0.12
**Paid on:**
7-14
**Since:** 1965

$25 - $5,000/month
Every 30 days beginning 1/2

FEES: Div: $0!; Cash: $0!; Cert: $0!; Term: $5; Sells weekly, by mail, at market, for $5 + 8¢ to 20¢/sh.

Shares to qualify: 1
Safekeeping: Yes
Accepts foreign: Yes
Auto. inv.: No
Disc.: No

---

## ✳ Pitney Bowes ♥

**PBI/NYSE** | Business equipment

H: 42.87
L: 24.00
**Rec:** 41.10

1 Elmcroft Rd., MSC 6140
Stamford. CT 06926-0700

First Chicago Trust    800-648-8170

**Div.:** 1.16
**Paid on:**
3.6.9.12-12
**Since:** 1934

$100 - $3,000/quarter
Every 30 days beginning 1/15

FEES: Div: $0!; Cash: $0!; Cert: $0!; Term: $0; Sells daily, by mail or phone, at market, for $15 + 12¢/sh.

Shares to qualify: 1
Safekeeping: Yes
Accepts foreign: Yes
Auto. inv.: No
Disc.: No

---

## ✳ Pizza Inn, Inc. ♥

**PZZI/NASDA** | Food supplier & distributor

H: 3.75
L: 1.43
**Rec:** 2.10

5050 Quorum Dr., Ste. 500
Dallas. TX 75240

American Stock Transfer    800-278-4353

**Div.:** 0.24
**Paid on:**
1.4.7.10-22
**Since:** N/A

$25 - $5,000/quarter
Every 90 days beginning 1/27

FEES: Div: $0!; Cash: $0!; Cert: $0!; Term: 4¢/sh.; Sells within 10 bus. days, by mail, at market, for 4¢/sh.

Shares to qualify: 1
Safekeeping: Yes
Accepts foreign: Yes
Auto. inv.: No
Disc.: No

---

## ✳ PMC Capital, Inc. ⊗

**PMC/ASE** | Financial

H: 10.00
L: 6.75
**Rec:** 8.04

18111 Preston Rd., Ste. 600
Dallas. TX 75252

American Stock Transfer    212-936-5100

**Div.:** 0.80
**Paid on:**
1.4.7.10-10
**Since:** 1981

$50 - $5,000/month
Every 30 days beginning 1/5

FEES: Div: $0!; Cash: $3; Cert: $0!; Term: $0; Sells weekly, by mail, at market, for 4¢/sh.

Shares to qualify: 15
Safekeeping: No
Accepts foreign: Yes
Auto. inv.: No
Disc.: No

---

## ✳ PNC Financial Services Group ♥

**PNC/NYSE** | Banking

H: 75.81
L: 54.87
**Rec:** 67.53

249 Fifth Ave., 29th Fl.
Pittsburgh. PA 15222

Mellon Inv. Svcs.    800-982-7652

**Div.:** 1.92
**Paid on:**
1.4.7.10-24
**Since:** 1865

$50 - $5,000/month
Every 30 days beginning 1/2

FEES: Div: $0!; Cash: $0!; Auto. Inv.: $0; Cert: $0!; Term: $0; Sells weekly, by mail or phone, at market, for $15 + 10¢/sh.

Shares to qualify: 1
Safekeeping: Yes
Accepts foreign: Yes
Auto. inv.: Yes
Disc.: No

---

## ✳ Pocahontas Bancorp, Inc. ♥

**PFSL/NASD** | Bank holding co.

H: 9.35
L: 6.31
**Rec:** 9.05

203 West Broadway
Pocahontas. AR 72455

Registrar & Transfer    800-368-5948

**Div.:** 0.26
**Paid on:**
1.4.7.10-3
**Since:** N/A

$25 - $5,000/quarter
Every 90 days beginning 1/2

FEES: Div: $0!; Cash: $0!; Cert: $5; Term: $5; Does not sell through the plan

Shares to qualify: 50
Safekeeping: Yes
Accepts foreign: Yes
Auto. inv.: No
Disc.: No

---

## ✳ Polaroid Corp.

**PRD/NYSE** | Photographic equip. & film

H: 18.50
L: 0.91
**Rec:** 1.46

784 Memorial Dr.
Cambridge. MA 02139

BankBoston    800-730-4001

**Div.:** 0.00
**Paid on:**
DIV. SUSP.
**Since:** --

$10 - $3,000/quarter
Every 90 days beginning 3/30

FEES: Div: 5% to $2.50; Cash: 5% to $2.50; Cert: $0; Term: $0; Sells within 10 bus. days, by mail, at market, for 5% to $5 + comm.

Shares to qualify: 1
Safekeeping: Yes
Accepts foreign: No
Auto. inv.: No
Disc.: No

---

## ∗ PolyOne Corp. ⊗

**POL/NYSE**

H: 10.70
L: 4.56
**Rec:** 10.17

**Div.:** 0.25
**Paid on:**
3.6.9.12-12
**Since:** 1958

**Specialty chemicals**

200 Public Sq., Ste.36-5000
Cleveland. OH 44114-2304

First Chicago Trust       800-446-2617
$25 - $250,000/year
Every 5 days beginning varies

FEES: Div: 5% to $3 + 3¢/sh.; Cash: $5 + 3¢/sh.; Auto. Inv.: $2 + 3¢/sh.; Cert: $0!;
Term: $15 + 12¢/sh.; Sells daily, by phone, mail, fax, or Internet, at market, for $15 +
12¢/sh.

**Shares to qualify:** 1 /de ($250)
**Safekeeping:** Yes
**Accepts foreign:** Yes
**Auto. inv.:** Yes
**Disc.:** No

---

## ∗ Popular, Inc. ♥

**BPOP/NASD**

H: 35.23
L: 19.37
**Rec:** 34.91

**Div.:** 0.80
**Paid on:**
1.4.7.10-1
**Since:** 1923

**Banking**

Box 362708
San Juan. PR 00936-2708

Popular,Inc..Attn:       787-764-1893
$25 - $10,000/month
Every 30 days beginning 1/15

FEES: Div: $0; Cash: $0; Cert: $0; Term: $0; Sells Friday, by mail, at market, for comm.

**Shares to qualify:** 1 /de ($100)
**Safekeeping:** Yes
**Accepts foreign:** Yes
**Auto. inv.:** No
**Disc.:** Div 5% Cash: 0%

---

## ∗ Potlatch Corp. ♥

**PCH/NYSE**

H: 36.87
L: 28.56
**Rec:** 34.09

**Div.:** 0.60
**Paid on:**
3.6.9.12-5
**Since:** 1955

**Paper & lumber products**

601 W. Riverside Ave., Ste. 1100
Spokane. WA 99201

Computershare Investor Svcs.       312-360-5100
$25 - $1,000/month
Every 30 days beginning 1/2

FEES: Div: $0!; Cash: $0!; Cert: $0!; Term: $0; Sells daily, by mail, at market, for 7¢ to
10¢/sh.

**Shares to qualify:** 1
**Safekeeping:** No
**Accepts foreign:** Yes
**Auto. inv.:** No
**Disc.:** No

---

## ∗ Potomac Electric Power ♥

**POM/NYSE**

H: 27.00
L: 20.08
**Rec:** 21.90

**Div.:** 1.00
**Paid on:**
3.6.9.12-31
**Since:** 1904

**Utility-electric**

Box 97256
Washinaton. DC 20090-7256

Potomac Elec. Pwr. Co.       800-527-3726
$25 - $5,000/month
Every 30 days beginning 1/30

FEES: Div: $0!; Cash: $0!; Cert: $0!; Term: $0; Sells weekly, by mail or fax, at market, for $5
+ 4¢/sh.

**Shares to qualify:** 1
**Safekeeping:** Yes
**Accepts foreign:** Yes
**Auto. inv.:** No
**Disc.:** No

---

## ∗ PPG Industries ⊗

**PPG/NYSE**

H: 59.75
L: 36.00
**Rec:** 54.53

**Div.:** 1.68
**Paid on:**
3.6.9.12-12
**Since:** 1899

**Coatings, glass & chemicals, fiberglass**

One PPG Pl., #40E
Pittsburgh. PA 15272

Mellon Inv. Svcs.       800-648-8160
$100 - $10,000/month
Every 7 days beginning varies

FEES: Div: $0; Cash: $6 + 12¢/sh.; Auto. Inv.: $3 + 12¢/sh.; Cert: $0; Term: $15
+12¢/sh.; Sells daily, by mail or phone, at market, for $15 +12¢/sh.

**Shares to qualify:** 1 /de ($500)
**Safekeeping:** Yes
**Accepts foreign:** Yes
**Auto. inv.:** Yes
**Disc.:** No

---

## ∗ PPL Corp. ♥

**PPL/NYSE**

H: 62.36
L: 28.00
**Rec:** 42.99

**Div.:** 1.06
**Paid on:**
1.4.7.10-1
**Since:** 1945

**Utility-electric**

2 North Ninth St.
Allentown. PA 18101-1179

PPL Corp.       800-345-3085
$0 - $80,000/year
Every 30 days beginning 1/2

FEES: Div: $0!; Cash: $0!; Cert: $0!; Term: $0; Sells weekly, by mail or fax, at market, for
10¢/sh.

**Shares to qualify:** 1
**Safekeeping:** Yes
**Accepts foreign:** Yes
**Auto. inv.:** No
**Disc.:** No

---

## ∗ Praxair, Inc. ♥

**PX/NYSE**

H: 54.00
L: 30.31
**Rec:** 47.10

**Div.:** 0.68
**Paid on:**
3.6.9.12-15
**Since:** 1992

**Industrial gas**

39 Old Ridgebury Rd.
Danburv. CT 06810-5113

Bank of New York       800-432-0140
$50 - $24,000/year
Every 30 days beginning 1/30

FEES: Div: $0!; Cash: $0!; Cert: $5; Term: $5; Sells within 10 bus. days, by mail, at market,
for $5

**Shares to qualify:** 1
**Safekeeping:** Yes
**Accepts foreign:** Yes
**Auto. inv.:** No
**Disc.:** No

---

∗ DRIP enrollment through Temper Enrollment Service (see page 180).     **135**

## ✳ Prentiss Properties Trust ⊗

**PP/NYSE**
H: 27.81
L: 23.70
**Rec:** 27.70
**Div.:** 2.14
**Paid on:**
1.4.7.10-16
**Since:** 1997

REIT
3890 W. Northwest Hwy., Ste. 400
Dallas. TX 75220

First Chicago Trust    800-446-2617
$100 - $5,000/month
Every 30 days beginning 1/2

FEES: Div: 5% to $3/quarter; Cash: $5; Auto. Inv.: $2; Cert: $0!; Term: $15 + 12¢/sh.;
Sells daily, by mail or phone, at market, for $15 + 12¢/sh.

**Shares to qualify:** 1 /de ($500)
**Safekeeping:** Yes
**Accepts foreign:** Yes
**Auto. inv.:** Yes
**Disc.:** Div: 0% Cash:
          0%-5%

---

## ✳ Presidential Realty -B ♥

**PDLB/ASE**
H: 7.10
L: 5.00
**Rec:** 6.75
**Div.:** 0.64
**Paid on:**
3.6.9.12-30
**Since:** 1980

REIT
180 South Broadway
White Plains. NY 10605

American Stock Transfer    800-937-5449
$100 - $10,000/quarter
Every 30 days beginning 1/10

FEES: Div: $0!; Cash: $0!; Cert: $0; Term: $0; Sells weekly, by mail, at market, for 4¢/sh.

**Shares to qualify:** 1
**Safekeeping:** No
**Accepts foreign:** Yes
**Auto. inv.:** No
**Disc.:** Div: 5% Cash: 0%

---

## ✳ Pride International, Inc. ♥

**PDE/NYSE**
H: 32.66
L: 13.36
**Rec:** 13.78
**Div.:** 0.00
**Paid on:**
N/0
**Since:** N/0

Oil well drilling
5847 San Felipe, Ste. 3300
Houston. TX 77057

American Stock Transfer    800-278-4353
$500 - $10,000/month
Every 30 days beginning 1/31

FEES: Div: n/o; Cash: $0!; Cert: $0!; Term: $0; Sells weekly, by mail or fax, at market, for
4¢/sh.

**Shares to qualify:** 1 /de ($1000)
**Safekeeping:** Yes
**Accepts foreign:** Yes
**Auto. inv.:** No
**Disc.:** No

---

## ✳ Procter & Gamble

**PG/NYSE**
H: 79.31
L: 55.96
**Rec:** 71.87
**Div.:** 1.52
**Paid on:**
2.5.8.11-15
**Since:** 1891

Consumer prod., food & beverages
Box 5572
Cincinnati. OH 45201-5572

Procter & Gamble Co.    800-764-7483
$100 - $120,000/year
Every 7 days beginning varies

FEES: Div: 5% to $1 + 3¢/sh.; Cash: $2.50 + 3¢/sh.; Auto. Inv.: $1 + 3¢/sh.; Cert: $0;
Term: 3¢/sh.; Sells daily, by mail, at avg. price, for $2.50 + 3¢/sh.

**Shares to qualify:** 1 /de ($250)
**Safekeeping:** Yes
**Accepts foreign:** Yes
**Auto. inv.:** Yes
**Disc.:** No

---

## ✳ Progress Energy

**PGN/NYSE**
H: 49.37
L: 35.25
**Rec:** 42.71
**Div.:** 2.12
**Paid on:**
2.5.8.11-1
**Since:** 1937

Utility-electric
Box 1551, Shareholder Relations
Raleigh. NC 27602-1551

State St. Bank    800-633-4236
$50 - $10,000/month
Every 15 days beginning 1/2

FEES: Div: $0!; Cash: .035¢/sh.; Auto. Inv.: $0; Cert: $0!; Term: $0; Sells daily, by mail,
fax , or phone, at avg. price, for .035¢/sh.

**Shares to qualify:** 1 /de ($250)
**Safekeeping:** Yes
**Accepts foreign:** Yes
**Auto. inv.:** Yes
**Disc.:** No

---

## ✳ Progressive Return Fund ⊗

**PGF/NYSE**
H: 12.18
L: 8.95
**Rec:** 9.38
**Div.:** 0.06
**Paid on:**
9-22
**Since:** N/A

Closed-end fund
c/o Bear Stearns, 575 Lexington Ave., 9th Fl.
New York. NY 10022

Boston Eq.    800-730-6001
$100 - $100,000/year
Every 7 days beginning varies

FEES: Div: $0; Cash: $5 + 8¢/sh.; Auto. Inv.: $0; Cert: $0; Term: $0; Sells weekly, by mail,
at avg. price, for $10 + 15¢/sh.

**Shares to qualify:** 1 /de ($250)
**Safekeeping:** Yes
**Accepts foreign:** Yes
**Auto. inv.:** Yes
**Disc.:** No

---

## ✳ ProLogis Trust ♥

**PLD/NYSE**
H: 24.68
L: 19.43
**Rec:** 22.63
**Div.:** 1.38
**Paid on:**
2.5.8.11-VARIES
**Since:** 1994

REIT
14100 East 35th Pl.
Aurora. CO 80011

Boston Eq.    800-956-3378
$200 - $5,000/month
Every 15 days beginning varies

FEES: Div: $0!; Cash: $0!; Auto. Inv.: $0; Cert: $0!; Term: $15 + 12¢/sh.; Sells within 3
bus. days, by phone, mail, fax, or Internet, at market, for $15 + 12¢/sh.

**Shares to qualify:** 1 /de ($200)
**Safekeeping:** Yes
**Accepts foreign:** Yes
**Auto. inv.:** Yes
**Disc.:** Div: 2% Cash: 2%

---

## Promistar Financial Corporation ♥

**PRFC/NASD**
H: 24.47
L: 15.62
**Rec:** 23.90
**Div.:** 0.84
**Paid on:**
3.6.9.12-1
**Since:** N/A

**Bank holding company**
551 Main St.
Johnstown. PA 15901

Laurel Trust Co.   814-536-2110
$20 - $2,500/quarter
Every 90 days beginning 3/1

**Shares to qualify:** 1
**Safekeeping:** Yes
**Accepts foreign:** Yes
**Auto. inv.:** No
**Disc.:** No

FEES: Div: $0; Cash: $0; Cert: $5; Term: $0; Sells daily, by mail, at market, for comm.

---

## Prospect Street Income Shares, Inc.

**CNN/NYSE**
H: 8.81
L: 6.75
**Rec:** 7.61
**Div.:** 0.84
**Paid on:**
1.4.7.10-14
**Since:** N/A

**Closed-end fund**
Highland Capital Mgmt.,13455 Noel Rd.,Ste.1300
Dallas. TX 75240

Bank of New York   800-432-8224
$25 - $unlimited
Every 30 days beginning 1/2

**Shares to qualify:** 1
**Safekeeping:** No
**Accepts foreign:** Yes
**Auto. inv.:** No
**Disc.:** No

FEES: Div: $0!; Cash: comm.; Cert: $0!; Term: $0,Does not sell through the plan

---

## Protective Life Corp. ♥

**PL/NYSE**
H: 35.00
L: 19.00
**Rec:** 31.04
**Div.:** 0.56
**Paid on:**
3.6.9.12-1
**Since:** 1926

**Insurance**
Box 2606
Birmingham. AL 35202

Bank of New York   800-524-4458
$25 - $6,000/quarter
Every 90 days beginning 3/1

**Shares to qualify:** 1
**Safekeeping:** Yes
**Accepts foreign:** Yes
**Auto. inv.:** No
**Disc.:** No

FEES: Div: $0!; Cash: $0!; Cert: $0!; Term: $0; Sells weekly, by mail, at market, for 20¢/sh.

---

## Provident Bankshares Corp. ♥

**PBKS/NASD**
H: 25.75
L: 12.85
**Rec:** 22.95
**Div.:** 0.78
**Paid on:**
2.5.8.11-11
**Since:** 1988

**Bank holding company**
114 East Lexington St.
Baltimore. MD 21202

BankBoston   866-820-0125
$100 - $10,000/quarter
Every 30 days beginning 1/30

**Shares to qualify:** 1
**Safekeeping:** No
**Accepts foreign:** Yes
**Auto. inv.:** No
**Disc.:** No

FEES: Div: $0!; Cash: $0!; Cert: $0!; Term: $0,Does not sell through the plan

---

## Providian Financial ⊗

**PVN/NYSE**
H: 67.00
L: 39.71
**Rec:** 45.40
**Div.:** 0.12
**Paid on:**
3.6.9.12-15
**Since:** 1969

**Financial services, consumer loans**
201 Mission St.
San Francisco. CA 94105

First Chicago Trust   800-317-4445
$50 - $250,000/year
Every 30 days beginning 1/15

**Shares to qualify:** 1 /de ($500)
**Safekeeping:** Yes
**Accepts foreign:** Yes
**Auto. inv.:** Yes
**Disc.:** No

FEES: Div: 5% to $3 + 3¢/sh.; Cash: $5 + 3¢/sh.; Auto. Inv.: $2 + 3¢/sh.; Cert: $0; Term: $15 + 12¢/sh.; Sells daily, by phone, mail, fax, or Internet, at market, for $15 + 12¢/sh.

---

## Public Service Co. of NM

**PNM/NYSE**
H: 37.80
L: 18.43
**Rec:** 29.19
**Div.:** 0.80
**Paid on:**
2.5.8.11-19
**Since:** 1996

**Utility-electric, gas**
Alvarado Sq., Box 1047
Albuquerque. NM 87103-9924

PNM Shareholder Records Dept.   800-545-4425
$50 - $5,000/month
Every 30 days beginning 1/2

**Shares to qualify:** 1 /de ($50)
**Safekeeping:** Yes
**Accepts foreign:** Yes
**Auto. inv.:** Yes
**Disc.:** No

FEES: Div: comm.; Cash: comm.; Auto. Inv.: $0; Cert: $0; Term: comm.; Sells weekly, by mail or fax, at market, for 2.5¢/sh.

---

## Public Service Enterprise Group ♥

**PEG /NYSE**
H: 51.55
L: 34.81
**Rec:** 46.19
**Div.:** 2.16
**Paid on:**
3.6.9.12-31
**Since:** 1907

**Utility-electric, gas**
Box 1171
Newark. NJ 07101-1171

Public Service Enterprise   800-242-0813
$50 - $125,000/year
Every 15 days beginning 1/15

**Shares to qualify:** 1 /de ($250)
**Safekeeping:** Yes
**Accepts foreign:** Yes
**Auto. inv.:** Yes
**Disc.:** No

FEES: Div: $0!; Cash: $0!; Auto. Inv.: $0; Cert: $0; Term: $0; Sells biweekly, by mail or fax, at market, for $10 + 2¢/sh.

---

## * Puget Energy, Inc.

**PSD/NYSE**
H: 28.00
L: 20.63
**Rec:** 24.13
**Div.:** 1.84
**Paid on:**
2.5.8.11-15
**Since:**1943

Utility-electric, gas
Box 97034
Bellevue. WA 98009-9734
Mellon Inv. Svcs.     800-997-8438
$50 - $100,000/year
Every 7 days beginning varies
FEES: Div: comm.; Cash: comm.; Cert: $0; Term: $0; Sells weekly, by mail or phone, at market, for $5 + 6¢/sh.

**Shares to qualify:** 1 /de
**Safekeeping:** Yes
**Accepts foreign:** Yes
**Auto. inv.:** No
**Disc.:** No

---

## * Quaker Chemical Corp. ♥

**KWR/NYSE**
H: 20.99
L: 15.87
**Rec:** 19.40
**Div.:** 0.82
**Paid on:**
1.4.7.10-30
**Since:**N/A

Specialty chemicals
Elm & Lee Sts.
Conshohocken. PA 19428
American Stock Transfer     800-278-4353
$300 - $24,000/year
Every 15 days beginning 15th & 30th /month
FEES: Div: $0; Cash: $0; Auto. Inv.: $0; Cert: $0; Term: $0; Sells within 5 bus. days, by mail, at market, for $7.50 + 4¢/sh.

**Shares to qualify:** 1
**Safekeeping:** Yes
**Accepts foreign:** Yes
**Auto. inv.:** Yes
**Disc.:** No

---

## * Quanex Corp. ♥

**NX/NYSE**
H: 27.55
L: 16.37
**Rec:** 27.01
**Div.:** 0.64
**Paid on:**
3.6.9.12-31
**Since:**1988

Mfr. steel bar, aluminum flat products,
1900 W. Loop South, Ste.1500
Houston. TX 77027
American Stock Transfer     800-937-5449
$50 - $10,000/quarter
Every 30 days beginning 1/2
FEES: Div: $0!; Cash: $0!; Auto. Inv.: $0; Cert: $0!; Term: $10 + 4¢/sh.; Sells weekly, by mail or fax, at market, for $10 + 4¢/sh.

**Shares to qualify:** 1 /de ($250)
**Safekeeping:** Yes
**Accepts foreign:** Yes
**Auto. inv.:** Yes
**Disc.:** No

---

## * Questar Corp.

**STR/NYSE**
H: 33.75
L: 19.93
**Rec:** 22.98
**Div.:** 0.70
**Paid on:**
3.6.9.12-VARIES
**Since:**1932

Integrated nat. gas holding co.
Box 45433
Salt Lake Citv. UT 84145-0433
Questar Corp.,Shareholders     801-324-5885
$50 - $100,000/year
Every 30 days beginning 1/31
FEES: Div: 5¢/sh.; Cash: 5¢/sh.; Cert: $0!; Term: $0,Does not sell through the plan

**Shares to qualify:** 1 /de ($250)
**Safekeeping:** Yes
**Accepts foreign:** Yes
**Auto. inv.:** Yes
**Disc.:** No

---

## * R.J. Reynolds Tobacco Holdings, Inc. ⊗

**RJR/NYSE**
H: 62.70
L: 30.37
**Rec:** 52.05
**Div.:** 3.50
**Paid on:**
1.4.7.10-1
**Since:**1999

Holding company
Box 2866
Winston-Salem. NC 27102-2866
Bank of New York     877-679-5701
$50 - $250,000/year
Every 7 days beginning varies
FEES: Div: 5% to $3 + 3¢/sh.; Cash: $5 + 3¢/sh.; Auto. Inv.: $2 + 3¢/sh.; Cert: $0; Term: $0; Sells weekly, by mail or phone, at market, for $15 + 10¢/sh.

**Shares to qualify:** 1 /de ($500)
**Safekeeping:** Yes
**Accepts foreign:** Yes
**Auto. inv.:** Yes
**Disc.:** No

---

## * RadioShack Corp. ⊗

**RSH/NYSE**
H: 72.93
L: 24.70
**Rec:** 24.98
**Div.:** 0.22
**Paid on:**
1.4.7.10-15
**Since:**1987

Retails consumer electr. & computers
Box 17180
Fort Worth. TX 76102
BankBoston     888-218-4374
$50 - $150,000/year
Every 15 days beginning 1/10
FEES: Div: $0; Cash: $5 + 4¢/sh.; Auto. Inv.: $2.50 + 4¢/sh.; Cert: $0; Term: $0; Sells daily, by mail, at market, for $15 + 10¢/sh.

**Shares to qualify:** 1 /de ($250)
**Safekeeping:** Yes
**Accepts foreign:** No
**Auto. inv.:** Yes
**Disc.:** No

---

## * Raven Industries, Inc. ♥

**RAVN/NASD**
H: 18.66
L: 9.83
**Rec:** 17.68
**Div.:** 0.52
**Paid on:**
1.4.7.10-15
**Since:**N/A

Mfr. plastic, electronics & sewn
205 E. 6th St., Box 5107
Sioux Falls. SD 57117-5107
Wells Fargo Bank     800-468-9716
$100 - $15,000/quarter
Every 90 days beginning 1/15
FEES: Div: $0!; Cash: $0!; Auto. Inv.: $0; Cert: $0; Term: $10 + 10¢/sh.; Sells daily, by mail, at market, for $10 + 10¢/sh.

**Shares to qualify:** 1
**Safekeeping:** Yes
**Accepts foreign:** Yes
**Auto. inv.:** Yes
**Disc.:** No

---

## ✶ Rayonier Inc.

**RYN/NYSE** | **Wood manufacturing**

H: 46.97
L: 31.25
**Rec:** 46.52
**Div.:** 1.44
**Paid on:**
3.6.9.12-30
**Since:** 1994

50 North Laura St.
Jacksonville. FL 32202

Bank of New York    800-432-0140
$50 - $5,000/quarter
Every 5 days beginning 1/6

FEES: Div: $0; Cash: $1.50; Cert: $7; Term: $5; Sells weekly, by mail, at avg. price, for $3 + 7¢/sh.

**Shares to qualify:** 1
**Safekeeping:** Yes
**Accepts foreign:** Yes
**Auto. inv.:** No
**Disc.:** No

---

## ✶ Raytheon Co. -A ♥

**RTN/NYSE** | **Aerospace, defense, elec. & appliances**

H: 36.68
L: 24.67
**Rec:** 27.80
**Div.:** 0.80
**Paid on:**
1.4.7.10-31
**Since:** 1964

141 Spring St.
Lexington. MA 02421

Boston Eq.    800-360-4519
$10 - $25,000/quarter
Every 30 days beginning 1/25

FEES: Div: $0; Cash: $0; Cert: $0; Term: $2.50 +15¢/sh.; Sells within 10 bus. days, by phone or mail, at market, for $10 + 15¢/sh.

**Shares to qualify:** 1
**Safekeeping:** Yes
**Accepts foreign:** Yes
**Auto. inv.:** No
**Disc.:** No

---

## ✶ Reader's Digest Assn., Inc. -A ⊗

**RDA/NYSE** | **Magazine, book publishing**

H: 41.87
L: 20.50
**Rec:** 21.37
**Div.:** 0.20
**Paid on:**
2.5.8.11-1
**Since:** 1990

Reader's Digest Rd.
Pleasantville. NY 10570-7000

Mellon Inv. Svcs.    800-242-4653
$100 - $10,000/month
Every 7 days beginning varies

FEES: Div: $0; Cash: $5 + 12¢/sh.; Auto. Inv.: $0; Cert: $0; Term: $0; Sells weekly, by mail or phone, at market, for $15 + 12¢/sh.

**Shares to qualify:** 1 /de ($1000)
**Safekeeping:** Yes
**Accepts foreign:** Yes
**Auto. inv.:** Yes
**Disc.:** No

---

## ✶ Reader's Digest Assn., Inc.-B ⊗

**RDB/NYSE** | **Magazine, book publishing**

H: 38.00
L: 19.60
**Rec:** 20.65
**Div.:** 0.20
**Paid on:**
2.5.8.11-1
**Since:** 1992

Reader's Digest Rd.
Pleasantville. NY 10570-7000

Mellon Inv. Svcs.    800-230-2771
$100 - $10,000/month
Every 7 days beginning varies

FEES: Div: $0; Cash: $5 + 12¢/sh.; Auto. Inv.: $0; Cert: $0; Term: $15; Sells weekly, by mail or phone, at market, for $15

**Shares to qualify:** 1 /de ($1000)
**Safekeeping:** Yes
**Accepts foreign:** Yes
**Auto. inv.:** Yes
**Disc.:** No

---

## ✶ Redwood Empire Bancorp ♥

**REBC/NASD** | **Bank holding company**

H: 34.25
L: 19.12
**Rec:** 34.00
**Div.:** 0.80
**Paid on:**
1.4.7.10-15
**Since:** N/A

111 Santa Rosa Ave., Box 402
Santa Rosa. CA 95402-0402

Mellon Inv. Svcs.    800-522-6645
$100 - $5,000/month
Every 30 days beginning 1/15

FEES: Div: $0!; Cash: $0!; Auto. Inv.: $0; Cert: $0!; Term: $2.50; Sells daily, by mail, at avg. price, for $2.50

**Shares to qualify:** 1
**Safekeeping:** Yes
**Accepts foreign:** Yes
**Auto. inv.:** Yes
**Disc.:** No

---

## ✶ Redwood Trust, Inc. ♥

**RWT/NASD** | **REIT**

H: 24.35
L: 14.12
**Rec:** 23.41
**Div.:** 2.28
**Paid on:**
1.4.7.10-21
**Since:** N/A

591 Redwood Hwy., #3100
Mill Valley. CA 94941

Mellon Inv. Svcs.    888-877-2882
$500 - $5,000/month
Every 30 days beginning 1/21

FEES: Div: $0; Cash: $0; Cert: $0; Term: $15 + 12¢/sh.; Sells monthly, by mail, at market, for $15 + 12¢/sh.

**Shares to qualify:** 1 /de ($500)
**Safekeeping:** Yes
**Accepts foreign:** No
**Auto. inv.:** No
**Disc.:** Cash: 0-2%

---

## ✶ Regions Financial Corp. ♥

**RGBK/NASD** | **Banking**

H: 32.99
L: 20.06
**Rec:** 32.00
**Div.:** 1.12
**Paid on:**
1.4.7.10-1
**Since:** 1971

417 North 20th St., Box 10247
Birmingham. AL 35202-0247

First Chicago Trust    800-524-2879
$25 - $120,000/year
Every 7 days beginning Wednesday

FEES: Div: $0!; Cash: $0!; Auto. Inv.: $0; Cert: $0!; Term: $0; Sells daily, by phone or mail, at market, for $15 + 12¢/sh.

**Shares to qualify:** 1 /de ($1000)
**Safekeeping:** Yes
**Accepts foreign:** Yes
**Auto. inv.:** Yes
**Disc.:** No

---

✶ DRIP enrollment through Temper Enrollment Service (see page 180).    **139**

## ✻ Reliant Energy

**REI/NYSE** | Utility-electric, gas

H: 50.45
L: 26.98
**Rec:** 31.55

Box 4505
Houston. TX 77210

Reliant Energy          800-231-6406
$50 - $120,000/year
Every 5 days beginning varies

**Div.:** 1.50
**Paid on:**
3.6.9.12-10
**Since:** 1921

**Shares to qualify:** 1 /de ($250)
**Safekeeping:** Yes
**Accepts foreign:** Yes
**Auto. inv.:** Yes
**Disc.:** No

FEES: Div: 3¢ to10¢/sh. ; Cash: 3¢ to10¢/sh.; Auto. Inv.: $0; Cert: $0; Term: $0; Sells weekly, by mail, fax , or phone, at avg. price, for 3¢/sh.

---

## Reliv International, Inc.

**RELV/NASD** | Food processing

H: 2.00
L: 1.00
**Rec:** 1.15

136 Chesterfield Industrial, Box 405
Chesterfield. MO 63006

American Stock Transfer     888-333-0203
$50 - $10,000/transaction
Every 7 days beginning varies

**Div.:** 0.00
**Paid on:**
DIV. SUSP.
**Since:** N/A

**Shares to qualify:** 1 /de ($100)
**Safekeeping:** Yes
**Accepts foreign:** Yes
**Auto. inv.:** Yes
**Disc.:** No

FEES: Div: 2% to $2.50; Cash: $2.50 + 10¢/sh.; Auto. Inv.: $2.50 + 10¢/sh.; Cert: $0; Term: $0; Sells weekly, by mail, at market, for $15 + 10¢/sh.

---

## ✻ Republic Bancorp Inc. ♥

**RBNC/NASD** | Banking

H: 16.10
L: 7.55
**Rec:** 15.40

1060 East Main St.
Owosso. MI 48867

State St. Bank     800-257-1770
$10 - $5,000/month
Every 30 days beginning 1/2

**Div.:** 0.34
**Paid on:**
1.4.7.10-3
**Since:** 1992

**Shares to qualify:** 1
**Safekeeping:** Yes
**Accepts foreign:** No
**Auto. inv.:** No
**Disc.:** No

FEES: Div: $0!; Cash: $0!; Cert: $0!; Term: $5 + comm.; Sells monthly, by mail, at market, for $5 + comm.

---

## ✻ Reynolds & Reynolds Co.-A ♥

**REY/NYSE** | Integrated info. mgt. sys. to auto, health

H: 23.44
L: 16.31
**Rec:** 23.40

Box 2608
Davton. OH 45401

Wells Fargo Bank     800-468-9716
$100 - $5,000/month
Every 30 days beginning 1/13

**Div.:** 0.44
**Paid on:**
1.4.6.9-13
**Since:** 1961

**Shares to qualify:** 1
**Safekeeping:** Yes
**Accepts foreign:** Yes
**Auto. inv.:** Yes
**Disc.:** No

FEES: Div: $0!; Cash: $0!; Auto. Inv.: $0; Cert: $0; Term: $0; Sells daily, by mail or fax, at market, for $10 + 10¢/sh.

---

## ✻ RGC Resources Inc. ♥

**RGCO/NASD** | Utility

H: 21.25
L: 17.75
**Rec:** 19.70

Box 13007
Roanoke. VA 24030

First Union Nat'l Bank     800-829-8432
$25 - $30,000/year
Every 30 days beginning 1/4

**Div.:** 1.12
**Paid on:**
2.5.8.11-1
**Since:** 1944

**Shares to qualify:** 1 /de ($100)
**Safekeeping:** Yes
**Accepts foreign:** Yes
**Auto. inv.:** Yes
**Disc.:** No

FEES: Div: $0!; Cash: $0!; Auto. Inv.: $0; Does not sell through the plan

---

## ✻ RLI Corp. ♥

**RLI/NYSE** | Insurance

H: 46.15
L: 36.75
**Rec:** 42.20

9025 North Lindbergh Dr.
Peoria. IL 61615-1431

Wells Fargo Bank     800-468-9716
$25 - $2,000/month
Every 30 days beginning 1/15

**Div.:** 0.64
**Paid on:**
1.4.7.10-15
**Since:** 1976

**Shares to qualify:** 1
**Safekeeping:** Yes
**Accepts foreign:** No
**Auto. inv.:** No
**Disc.:** No

FEES: Div: $0!; Cash: $0!; Cert: $0!; Term: $10 + 10¢/sh.; Sells daily, by mail or fax, at market, for $10 + 10¢/sh.

---

## ✻ Roadway Corporation ⊗

**ROAD/NASD** | Trucking

H: 30.30
L: 16.00
**Rec:** 24.21

1077 Gorge Blvd., Box 471
Akron. OH 44309-0471

Computershare Investor Svcs.     800-991-8947
$50 - $100,000/year
Every 7 days beginning varies

**Div.:** 0.20
**Paid on:**
VARIES
**Since:** N/A

**Shares to qualify:** 1 /de ($250)
**Safekeeping:** Yes
**Accepts foreign:** Yes
**Auto. inv.:** Yes
**Disc.:** No

FEES: Div: $0!; Cash: $5 + 10¢/sh.; Auto. Inv.: $1.50 + 10¢/sh.; Cert: $0!; Term: $10 +10¢/sh.; Sells within 5 bus. days, by mail, at market, for $10 + 10¢/sh.

---

## ✱ Robbins & Myers, Inc. ♥

**RBN/NYSE** | Pumps, valves, mixers & reactor sys.

H: 29.25
L: 21.12
**Rec:** 26.30

1400 Kettering Tower
Dayton, OH 45423

National City Bank  800-622-6757

**Div.:** 0.22
**Paid on:**
1.4.7.10-30
**Since:** 1989

$50 - $5,000/quarter
Every 30 days beginning 1/30

**Shares to qualify:** 1 /de ($500)
**Safekeeping:** Yes
**Accepts foreign:** Yes
**Auto. inv.:** No
**Disc.:** No

FEES: Div: $0!; Cash: $0!; Cert: $0!; Term: $0; Sells weekly, by mail, at market, for 5% to $5

---

## ✱ Rockwell Automation ⊗

**ROK/NYSE** | Global electronic controls & comm.

H: 49.45
L: 14.40
**Rec:** 16.70

777 East Wisconsin Ave., Ste. 1400
Milwaukee, WI 53202

Mellon Inv. Svcs.  800-204-7800

**Div.:** 0.66
**Paid on:**
3.6.9.12-4
**Since:** 1948

$100 - $100,000/year
Every 7 days beginning varies

**Shares to qualify:** 1 /de ($1000)
**Safekeeping:** Yes
**Accepts foreign:** Yes
**Auto. inv.:** Yes
**Disc.:** No

FEES: Div: $0; Cash: $5 + 10¢/sh.; Auto. Inv.: $0; Cert: $0; Term: $0; Sells weekly, by mail or phone, at market, for $15 + 12¢/sh.

---

## ✱ Roslyn Bancorp, Inc.

**RSLN/NASD** | Savings banks

H: 31.33
L: 18.62
**Rec:** 31.14

One Jericho Plaza
Jericho, NY 11753

Registrar & Transfer  800-368-5948

**Div.:** 0.68
**Paid on:**
3.6.9.12-15
**Since:** N/A

$100 - $5,000/quarter
Every 30 days beginning 1/15

**Shares to qualify:** 25
**Safekeeping:** Yes
**Accepts foreign:** No
**Auto. inv.:** No
**Disc.:** No

FEES: Div: $0!; Cash: $2.50; Cert: $0!; Term: $0; Sells within 10 bus. days, by mail, at avg. price, for $10 + comm.

---

## ✱ Rouse Co. ♥

**RSE/NYSE** | Real estate developers

H: 29.20
L: 23.25
**Rec:** 28.55

10275 Little Patuxent Pkwy.
Columbia, MD 21044-3456

Bank of New York  800-524-4458

**Div.:** 1.42
**Paid on:**
3.6.9-31 &
**Since:** 1978

$50 - $unlimited
Every 90 days beginning 3/30

**Shares to qualify:** 1
**Safekeeping:** Yes
**Accepts foreign:** No
**Auto. inv.:** No
**Disc.:** No

FEES: Div: $0!; Cash: $0!; Cert: $0!; Term: $0; Sells weekly, by mail, at market, for comm.

---

## ✱ Rowe Cos. (The) ♥

**ROW/NYSE** | Furniture

H: 4.87
L: 2.41
**Rec:** 2.43

2121 Gardner St.
Elliston, VA 24087

Wachovia  800-633-4236

**Div.:** 0.14
**Paid on:**
1.4.7.10-10
**Since:** N/A

$25 - $5,000/month
Every 30 days beginning 1/15

**Shares to qualify:** 1
**Safekeeping:** Yes
**Accepts foreign:** Yes
**Auto. inv.:** No
**Disc.:** No

FEES: Div: $0!; Cash: $0!; Cert: $0!; Term: 5¢/sh.; Sells daily, by mail, at avg. price, for 5¢/sh.

---

## ✱ Royce Focus Trust, Inc.

**FUND/NASD** | Closed-end fund

H: 7.15
L: 5.12
**Rec:** 6.20

1414 Ave. of the Americas
New York, NY 10019

BankBoston  800-426-5523

**Div.:** 0.00
**Paid on:**
DIV. SUSP.
**Since:** --

$100 - $unlimited
Every 30 days beginning 1/15

**Shares to qualify:** 1
**Safekeeping:** Yes
**Accepts foreign:** Yes
**Auto. inv.:** No
**Disc.:** No

FEES: Div: $0; Cash: 75¢ + comm.; Cert: $0; Term: $2.50 + 15¢/sh.; Sells within 3 bus. days, by mail, at avg. price, for $2.50 + 15¢/sh.

---

## ✱ Royce Micro-Cap Trust, Inc.

**OTCM/NAS** | Closed-end fund

H: 11.87
L: 8.12
**Rec:** 10.77

1414 Ave. of the Americas
New York, NY 10019

BankBoston  800-426-5523

**Div.:** 0.09
**Paid on:**
3.6.9.12-23
**Since:** N/A

$100 - $unlimited
Every 30 days beginning 1/15

**Shares to qualify:** 1
**Safekeeping:** Yes
**Accepts foreign:** Yes
**Auto. inv.:** No
**Disc.:** No

FEES: Div: $0; Cash: 75¢ + comm.; Cert: $0; Term: $2.50 + 15¢/sh.; Sells within 3 bus. days, by mail, at avg. price, for $2.50 + 15¢/sh.

---

## ✱ Royce Value Trust, Inc.

**RVT/NYSE**
H: 16.76
L: 13.25
**Rec:** 15.85
**Div.:** 1.48
**Paid on:**
3.6.9.12-23
**Since:** N/A

**Closed-end fund**

1414 Ave. of the Americas
New York. NY 10019

BankBoston       800-426-5523
$100 - $unlimited
Every 30 days beginning 1/15

FEES: Div: $0; Cash: 75¢ + comm.; Cert: $0; Term: $2.50 + 15¢/sh.; Sells within 3 bus. days, by mail, at avg. price, for $2.50 + 15¢/sh.

**Shares to qualify:** 1
**Safekeeping:** Yes
**Accepts foreign:** Yes
**Auto. inv.:** No
**Disc.:** No

---

## ✱ RPM, Inc. ♥

**RPM/NYSE**
H: 10.50
L: 7.75
**Rec:** 10.21
**Div.:** 0.50
**Paid on:**
1.4.7.10-30
**Since:** 1969

**Speciality chemicals & paints**

Box 777
Medina. OH 44258

National City Bank       800-988-5238
$25 - $5,000/month
Every 15 days beginning 1/10

FEES: Div: $0!; Cash: $0!; Auto. Inv.: $0; Cert: $0!; Term: $0; Sells weekly, by mail, at avg. price, for $0!

**Shares to qualify:** 1
**Safekeeping:** Yes
**Accepts foreign:** Yes
**Auto. inv.:** Yes
**Disc.:** No

---

## ✱ Ruddick Corp ♥

**RDK/NYSE**
H: 17.20
L: 9.81
**Rec:** 15.24
**Div.:** 0.36
**Paid on:**
1.4.7.10-1
**Since:** 1976

**Food supermarkets, thread**

2000 Two First Union Ctr.
Charlotte. NC 28282

First Union Nat'l Bank       800-829-8432
$20 - $3,000/month
Every 30 days beginning varies

FEES: Div: $0!; Cash: $0!; Cert: $0; Term: $0; Sells daily, by mail, at market, for $0

**Shares to qualify:** 1
**Safekeeping:** Yes
**Accepts foreign:** Yes
**Auto. inv.:** No
**Disc.:** No

---

## ✱ Rurban Financial Corp. ♥

**RBNF/OTC**
H: 15.25
L: 11.62
**Rec:** 15.25
**Div.:** 0.48
**Paid on:**
1.4.7.10-2
**Since:** N/A

**Bank holding co.**

401 Clinton St.
Defiance. OH 43512

Registrar & Transfer       800-368-5948
$50 - $5,000/month
Every 30 days beginning 1/2

FEES: Div: $0!; Cash: $0!; Auto. Inv.: $0; Cert: $0!; Term: $0; Sells within 15 bus. days, by mail, at market, for $0

**Shares to qualify:** 1
**Safekeeping:** Yes
**Accepts foreign:** Yes
**Auto. inv.:** Yes
**Disc.:** No

---

## ✱ Russell Corp. ♥

**RML/NYSE**
H: 20.84
L: 12.12
**Rec:** 17.45
**Div.:** 0.56
**Paid on:**
2.5.8.11-20
**Since:** 1963

**Textiles & apparel**

3350 Riverwood Pkwy., Ste. 1600
Atlanta. GA 30339

SunTrust Bank, Atlanta       800-568-3476
$50 - $2,000/month
Every 30 days beginning 1/20

FEES: Div: $0; Cash: $0; Cert: $0; Term: $0; Sells within 7 to 10 bus. days , by mail, at market, for 8¢/sh.

**Shares to qualify:** 50
**Safekeeping:** Yes
**Accepts foreign:** Yes
**Auto. inv.:** No
**Disc.:** No

---

## ✱ Ryder System, Inc. ♥

**R/NYSE**
H: 23.19
L: 14.81
**Rec:** 19.30
**Div.:** 0.60
**Paid on:**
3.6.9.12-20
**Since:** 1976

**Transportation**

3600 NW 82nd Ave.
Miami. FL 33166

BankBoston       781-575-3170
$25 - $60,000/year
Every 30 days beginning 1/20

FEES: Div: $0!; Cash: $0!; Cert: $0!; Term: $1 to $10 + comm.; Sells within 7 to10 bus. days, by phone or mail, at market, for $1 to $10 + comm.

**Shares to qualify:** 1
**Safekeeping:** Yes
**Accepts foreign:** No
**Auto. inv.:** No
**Disc.:** No

---

## ✱ Ryerson Tull Inc. ♥

**RT/NYSE**
H: 13.99
L: 6.93
**Rec:** 11.35
**Div.:** 0.20
**Paid on:**
2.5.8.11-1
**Since:** 1995

**Steel distribution**

2621 West 15th Pl.
Chicago. IL 60608

Computershare Investor Svcs.       312-360-5300
$25 - $10,000/month
Every 30 days beginning 1/24

FEES: Div: $0; Cash: $0; Cert: $0; Term: $0; Sells weekly, by mail, at market, for 7¢/sh.

**Shares to qualify:** 1
**Safekeeping:** No
**Accepts foreign:** Yes
**Auto. inv.:** No
**Disc.:** No

---

✱ DRIP enrollment through Temper Enrollment Service (see page 180).

## ✱ S.Y. Bancorp, Inc. ♥

**SYI/ASE** | **Banking**

H: 36.00
L: 18.87
**Rec:** 32.55

1040 East Main St., Box 32890
Louisville. KY 40232-2890

Stock Yards Bank & Trust    502-625-2456
$50 - $5,000/quarter
Every 90 days beginning 1/2

**Div.:** 0.44
**Paid on:**
1.4.7.10-1
**Since:** N/A

**Shares to qualify:** 1
**Safekeeping:** No
**Accepts foreign:** No
**Auto. inv.:** No
**Disc.:** No

FEES: Div: $0; Cash: $0; Cert: $0; Term: $10,Does not sell through the plan

---

## ✱ S&T Bancorp, Inc. ♥

**STBA/NASD** | **Bank holding company**

H: 27.00
L: 17.25
**Rec:** 24.54

800 Philadelphia St.
Indiana. PA  15701-0190

American Stock Transfer    800-937-5449
$25 - $2,500/month
Every 30 days beginning 1/15

**Div.:** 0.92
**Paid on:**
1.4.7.10-25
**Since:** N/A

**Shares to qualify:** 1
**Safekeeping:** Yes
**Accepts foreign:** Yes
**Auto. inv.:** No
**Disc.:** No

FEES: Div: $0; Cash: $0; Cert: $0; Term: $0; Sells weekly, by mail, at market, for comm.

---

## ✱ Salomon Bros. Fund

**SBF/NYSE** | **Capital appreciation fund**

H: 18.68
L: 12.50
**Rec:** 13.95

7 World Trade Ctr., 38th Fl.
New York. NY  10048

Bank of New York    800-432-8224
$25 - $unlimited
Every 7 days beginning Friday

**Div.:** 0.12
**Paid on:**
3.5.8.11.12-VARI
**Since:** N/A

**Shares to qualify:** 1
**Safekeeping:** Yes
**Accepts foreign:** No
**Auto. inv.:** Yes
**Disc.:** No

FEES: Div: comm.; Cash: comm.; Auto. Inv.: comm.; Cert: $0; Term: comm.; Sells weekly, by mail or fax, at market, for comm.

---

## ✱ Salomon Bros. High Income Fund Inc. ♥

**HIF/NYSE** | **Closed-end fund**

H: 14.00
L: 11.10
**Rec:** 12.12

7 World Trade Ctr., 38th Fl.
New York. NY 10048

American Stock Transfer    800-937-5449
$250 - $unlimited
Every 30 days beginning 1/2

**Div.:** 1.20
**Paid on:**
MONTHLY-24
**Since:** N/A

**Shares to qualify:** 1
**Safekeeping:** No
**Accepts foreign:** Yes
**Auto. inv.:** No
**Disc.:** No

FEES: Div: $0!; Cash: $0!; Cert: $0!; Term: $0,Does not sell through the plan

---

## ✱ Sanderson Farms, Inc. ⊗

**SAFM/NASD** | **Food processing**

H: 14.32
L: 5.93
**Rec:** 13.05

225 North 13th Ave., Box 988
Laurel. MS 39441-0988

Mellon Inv. Svcs.    888-810-7452
$50 - $10,000/month
Every 7 days beginning varies

**Div.:** 0.20
**Paid on:**
1.4.7.10-20
**Since:** N/A

**Shares to qualify:** 1 /de ($500)
**Safekeeping:** Yes
**Accepts foreign:** Yes
**Auto. inv.:** Yes
**Disc.:** No

FEES: Div: 5% to $10 + 12¢/sh.; Cash: $5 + 12¢/sh.; Auto. Inv.: $5 + 12¢/sh.; Cert: $0; Term: $15 + 12¢/s h.; Sells weekly, by mail, at market, for $15 + 12¢/sh.

---

## ✱ Sandy Spring Bancorp ♥

**SASR/NASD** | **Bank holding company**

H: 38.38
L: 20.68
**Rec:** 37.75

17801 Georgia Ave.
Olnev. MD 20832

American Stock Transfer    800-937-5449
$100 - $5,000/quarter
Every 90 days beginning 3/18

**Div.:** 0.88
**Paid on:**
3.6.9.12-18
**Since:** N/A

**Shares to qualify:** 1
**Safekeeping:** No
**Accepts foreign:** Yes
**Auto. inv.:** No
**Disc.:** No

FEES: Div: $0!;  Cash: $0!; Cert: $0!; Term: $0,Does not sell through the plan

---

## ✱ Sara Lee Corp. ♥

**SLE/NYSE** | **Food & consumer products**

H: 25.31
L: 18.25
**Rec:** 19.40

3 First National Plaza
Chicago. IL 60602-4260

Computershare Investor Svcs.    312-360-5157
$10 - $5,000/quarter
Every 45 days beginning 1/2

**Div.:** 0.58
**Paid on:**
1.4.7.10-1
**Since:** 1946

**Shares to qualify:** 1
**Safekeeping:** Yes
**Accepts foreign:** Yes
**Auto. inv.:** No
**Disc.:** No

FEES: Div: $0!; Cash: $0!; Cert: $0!; Term: 5% to $10 +10¢/sh.; Sells weekly, by mail, at market, for 5% to $10 + 10¢/sh.

---

## * SBC Communications

**SBC/NYSE**

**Telecommunications**

| | |
|---|---|
| H: 59.00 | 175 E. Houston, Box 2933 |
| L: 38.20 | San Antonio. TX 78299-2933 |
| Rec: 44.52 | First Chicago Trust 800-351-7221 |
| Div.: 1.02 | $50 - $120,000/year |
| Paid on: | Every 7 days beginning varies |
| 2.5.8.11-1 | |
| Since:1984 | |

**Shares to qualify:** 1 /de ($500)
**Safekeeping:** Yes
**Accepts foreign:** Yes
**Auto. inv.:** Yes
**Disc.:** No

FEES: Div: 5% to $2 + 3¢ to 5¢/sh.; Cash: $2.50 + 3¢ to 5¢/sh.; Auto. Inv.: $1 + 3¢ to 5¢/sh.; Cert: $0; Term: $0; Sells daily, by phone or mail, at avg. price, for $10 + 10¢/sh.

---

## * SCANA Corp.

**SCG/NYSE**

**Utility-electric, gas**

| | |
|---|---|
| H: 31.12 | 1426 Main St. |
| L: 24.92 | Columbia. SC 29201-2845 |
| Rec: 27.32 | SCANA Corp. 800-763-5891 |
| Div.: 1.20 | $25 - $100,000/year |
| Paid on: | Every 15 days beginning 1/2 |
| 1.4.7.10-1 | |
| Since:1946 | |

**Shares to qualify:** 1 /de ($250)
**Safekeeping:** Yes
**Accepts foreign:** No
**Auto. inv.:** Yes
**Disc.:** No

FEES: Div: 6¢/sh.; Cash: 6¢/sh.; Auto. Inv.: $0; Cert: $0; Term: $0; Sells Wednesday, by mail or fax, at market, for 18¢/sh.

---

## * Schawk, Inc. ♥

**SGK/NYSE**

**Prepress graphic arts design**

| | |
|---|---|
| H: 11.50 | 1695 River Rd. |
| L: 8.56 | Des Plaines. IL 60018 |
| Rec: 10.90 | First Chicago Trust 800-446-2617 |
| Div.: 0.13 | $50 - $100,000/year |
| Paid on: | Every 7 days beginning varies |
| 3.6.9.12-30 | |
| Since:1983 | |

**Shares to qualify:** 1
**Safekeeping:** Yes
**Accepts foreign:** Yes
**Auto. inv.:** Yes
**Disc.:** No

FEES: Div: $0!; Cash: $0!; Auto. Inv.: $0; Cert: $0!; Term: comm.; Sells daily, by mail, fax , or phone, at market, for $15 + 12¢/sh.

---

## * Schering-Plough Corp. ♥

**SGP/NYSE**

**Drugs, consumer products**

| | |
|---|---|
| H: 60.00 | 2000 Galloping Hill Rd. |
| L: 33.86 | Kenilworth. NJ 07033 |
| Rec: 38.40 | Bank of New York 800-432-0140 |
| Div.: 0.64 | $25 - $36,000/year |
| Paid on: | Every 15 days beginning 1/10 |
| 2.5.8.11-30 | |
| Since:1952 | |

**Shares to qualify:** 1
**Safekeeping:** Yes
**Accepts foreign:** No
**Auto. inv.:** No
**Disc.:** No

FEES: Div: $0!; Cash: $0!; Cert: $0!; Term: $2.50 + comm.; Sells weekly, by mail, at market, for $2.50 + comm.

---

## * Schnitzer Steel Industries, Inc. ♥

**SCHN/NASD**

**Steel & iron**

| | |
|---|---|
| H: 16.62 | 3200 Northwest Yeon Ave., Box 10047 |
| L: 12.00 | Portland. OR 97296-0047 |
| Rec: 13.00 | Bank of New York 800-524-4458 |
| Div.: 0.20 | $50 - $10,000/investment |
| Paid on: | Every 7 days beginning varies |
| 2.5.8.11-26 | |
| Since:1994 | |

**Shares to qualify:** 1 /de ($500)
**Safekeeping:** Yes
**Accepts foreign:** Yes
**Auto. inv.:** Yes
**Disc.:** No

FEES: Div: $0!; Cash: $0!; Auto. Inv.: $0; Cert: $0!; Term: $0; Sells weekly, by mail, at avg. price, for $5 + 10¢/sh.

---

## * Schwab (Charles) Corp. ♥

**SCH/NYSE**

**Financial**

| | |
|---|---|
| H: 40.43 | 101 Montgomery St. |
| L: 13.14 | San Francisco. CA 94104 |
| Rec: 13.83 | Wells Fargo Bank 800-468-9716 |
| Div.: 0.04 | $10 - $5,000/month |
| Paid on: | Every 30 days beginning last bus. day/month |
| 2.5.8.11-28 | |
| Since:1989 | |

**Shares to qualify:** 1
**Safekeeping:** Yes
**Accepts foreign:** Yes
**Auto. inv.:** Yes
**Disc.:** No

FEES: Div: $0!; Cash: $0!; Auto. Inv.: $0; Cert: $0!; Term: $0; Sells daily, by mail, at market, for $10 + 10¢/sh.

---

## * Scientific-Atlanta ♥

**SFA/NYSE**

**Communications equipment**

| | |
|---|---|
| H: 94.00 | Box 465447 |
| L: 21.00 | Lawrenceville. GA 30042 |
| Rec: 26.60 | Bank of New York 800-524-4458 |
| Div.: 0.04 | $25 - $40,000/year |
| Paid on: | Every 30 days beginning 1/15 |
| 3.6.9.12-22 | |
| Since:1976 | |

**Shares to qualify:** 1
**Safekeeping:** Yes
**Accepts foreign:** No
**Auto. inv.:** No
**Disc.:** No

FEES: Div: $0!; Cash: $0!; Cert: $3; Term: $3; Sells weekly, by mail, at market, for $5

---

## Scudder New Asia Fund

**✱**

| | |
|---|---|
| **SAF/NYSE** | **Closed-end fund** |
| H: 14.25 | c/o Zurich Scudder Inv., 345 Park Ave. |
| L: 8.15 | New York. NY 10154-0004 |
| **Rec:** 8.30 | Kemper Service Co.     800-621-1048 |
| **Div.:** 0.15 | $100 - $3,000/semiannually |
| **Paid on:** | Every 180 days beginning 2/15 |
| 1-14 & 3-31 | FEES: Div: $0!; Cash: 75¢ + comm.; Cert: $0; Term: $0; Sells daily, by mail, at market, for |
| **Since:** N/A | $2.50 + 15¢/sh. |

**Shares to qualify:** 1
**Safekeeping:** No
**Accepts foreign:** Yes
**Auto. inv.:** No
**Disc.:** Div 5% Cash: 0%

---

## Sea Containers Ltd. -A ♥

**✱**

| | |
|---|---|
| **SCRA/NYSE** | **Marine cargo containers, hotels, ferries,** |
| H: 29.68 | 1155 Ave. of the Americas |
| L: 13.66 | New York. NY 10036 |
| **Rec:** 17.05 | Boston Eq.     800-730-4001 |
| **Div.:** 0.30 | $100 - $15,000/quarter |
| **Paid on:** | Every 90 days beginning 2/21 |
| 2.5.8.11-21 | FEES: Div: $0; Cash: $0; Cert: $0; Term: $0; Sells daily, by mail, at market, for 5% to $15 + |
| **Since:** 1992 | comm. |

**Shares to qualify:** 50
**Safekeeping:** Yes
**Accepts foreign:** Yes
**Auto. inv.:** No
**Disc.:** Div 3% Cash: 0%

---

## Seacoast Financial Services Corp. ♥

**✱**

| | |
|---|---|
| **SCFS/NASD** | **Bank holding company** |
| H: 19.21 | 791 Purchase St. |
| L: 9.43 | New Bedford. MA 02740 |
| **Rec:** 15.77 | Registrar & Transfer     800-368-5948 |
| **Div.:** 0.36 | $100 - $5,000/quarter |
| **Paid on:** | Every 90 days beginning 2/19 |
| 2.5.8.11-19 | FEES: Div: $0!; Cash: $0!; Auto. Inv.: 75¢; Cert: $0!; Term: $0; Sells within 10 bus. days, |
| **Since:** N/A | by mail, at market, for $10 + comm. |

**Shares to qualify:** 100
**Safekeeping:** Yes
**Accepts foreign:** Yes
**Auto. inv.:** Yes
**Disc.:** No

---

## Sears, Roebuck & Co. ⊗

**✱**

| | |
|---|---|
| **S/NYSE** | **Retail** |
| H: 47.80 | 3333 Beverly Rd., B5-161A |
| L: 27.75 | Hoffman Estates. IL 60179 |
| **Rec:** 44.74 | First Chicago Trust     800-732-7780 |
| **Div.:** 0.92 | $50 - $150,000/year |
| **Paid on:** | Every 7 days beginning varies |
| 1.4.7.10-3 | FEES: Div: 5% to $3 + 3¢/sh.; Cash: 5% to $7.50 + 3¢/sh.; Auto. Inv.: $1 + 5% to $7.50 |
| **Since:** 1935 | + 3¢/sh.; Cert: $0; Term: $0; Sells daily, by phone or mail, at avg. price, for $15 + 12¢/sh. |

**Shares to qualify:** 5 /de ($500)
**Safekeeping:** Yes
**Accepts foreign:** Yes
**Auto. inv.:** Yes
**Disc.:** No

---

## Second Bancorp, Inc. ♥

**✱**

| | |
|---|---|
| **SECD/NASD** | **General banking** |
| H: 23.00 | 108 Main St. S.W. |
| L: 12.12 | Warren. OH 44481 |
| **Rec:** 22.00 | American Stock Transfer     800-278-4353 |
| **Div.:** 0.68 | $50 - $5,000/quarter |
| **Paid on:** | Every 30 days beginning 1/30 |
| 1.4.7.10-30 | FEES: Div: $0; Cash: $0; Cert: $0; Term: $0; Sells weekly, by mail, at market, for $5 + comm. |
| **Since:** 1940 | |

**Shares to qualify:** 1
**Safekeeping:** No
**Accepts foreign:** Yes
**Auto. inv.:** No
**Disc.:** Div 5% Cash: 5%

---

## Selective Insurance Group ♥

**✱**

| | |
|---|---|
| **SIGI/NASDA** | **Insurance** |
| H: 28.21 | 40 Wantage Ave. |
| L: 15.25 | Branchville. NJ 07890-1000 |
| **Rec:** 25.40 | First Chicago Trust     800-446-2617 |
| **Div.:** 0.60 | $100 - $1,000/quarter |
| **Paid on:** | Every 90 days beginning 3/1 |
| 3.6.9.12-1 | FEES: Div: $0!; Cash: $0!; Cert: $0!; Term: $0; Sells daily, by mail or phone, at market, for |
| **Since:** 1976 | $10 + 12¢/sh. |

**Shares to qualify:** 1
**Safekeeping:** No
**Accepts foreign:** Yes
**Auto. inv.:** No
**Disc.:** No

---

## SEMCO Energy Inc. ♥

**✱**

| | |
|---|---|
| **SEN/NYSE** | **Utility-gas** |
| H: 16.93 | 405 Water St., Box 5026 |
| L: 13.18 | Port Huron. MI 48061-5026 |
| **Rec:** 14.68 | Wells Fargo Bank     877-536-3549 |
| **Div.:** 0.84 | $25 - $100,000/year |
| **Paid on:** | Every 5 days beginning varies |
| 2.5.8.11-15 | FEES: Div: $0; Cash: $0; Auto. Inv.: $0; Cert: $0; Term: $0; Sells weekly, by mail or fax, at |
| **Since:** 1955 | market, for $10 + 6¢/sh. |

**Shares to qualify:** 1 /de ($250)
**Safekeeping:** Yes
**Accepts foreign:** Yes
**Auto. inv.:** Yes
**Disc.:** No

---

## Sempra Energy ♥

**SRE/NYSE**
H: 28.61
L: 17.31
**Rec:** 26.62
**Div.:** 1.00
**Paid on:**
1.4.7.10-15
**Since:** 1909

Utility-electric, gas
101 Ash St.
San Diego. CA 92101
First Chicago Trust     877-773-6772
$25 - $150,000/year
Every 7 days beginning Tuesday

| | |
|---|---|
| Shares to qualify: 1 /de ($500) | |
| Safekeeping: Yes | |
| Accepts foreign: Yes | |
| Auto. inv.: Yes | |
| Disc.: No | |

FEES: Div: $0!; Cash: $0!; Auto. Inv.: 50¢; Cert: $0; Term: $10 + 3¢/sh. ; Sells daily, by phone or mail, at market, for $10 + 3¢/sh.

---

## Senior Housing Properties Trust ♥

**SNH/NYSE**
H: 13.23
L: 8.50
**Rec:** 13.19
**Div.:** 1.20
**Paid on:**
2.5.8.11-22
**Since:** 1999

REIT
400 Centre St.
Newton. MA 02458
State St. Bank     800-426-5523
$0 - $10,000/quarter
Every 90 days beginning 2/22

| | |
|---|---|
| Shares to qualify: 1 | |
| Safekeeping: No | |
| Accepts foreign: Yes | |
| Auto. inv.: No | |
| Disc.: No | |

FEES: Div: $0!; Cash: $0!; Cert: $0!; Term: $2.50 + comm.; Sells weekly, by mail or phone, at market, for $2.50 + comm.

---

## Sensient Technologies Corp. ♥

**SXT/NYSE**
H: 23.99
L: 17.00
**Rec:** 19.85
**Div.:** 0.53
**Paid on:**
3.6.9.12-1
**Since:** 1934

Flavors, colors, food ingredients
777 East Wisconsin Ave.
Milwaukee. WI 53202-5304
Wells Fargo Bank     800-468-9716
$25 - $1,500/month
Every 30 days beginning 1/30

| | |
|---|---|
| Shares to qualify: 1 | |
| Safekeeping: Yes | |
| Accepts foreign: Yes | |
| Auto. inv.: No | |
| Disc.: No | |

FEES: Div: $0!; Cash: $0!; Cert: $0!; Term: $0; Sells biweekly, by mail or fax, at market, for comm. + 3¢ to 5¢/sh.

---

## ServiceMaster Co. ♥

**SVM/NYSE**
H: 12.84
L: 8.25
**Rec:** 11.99
**Div.:** 0.40
**Paid on:**
1.4.7.10-30
**Since:** 1970

Consumer and other services
One ServiceMaster Way
Downers Grove. IL 60515-1700
Computershare Investor Svcs.     888-834-0744
$25 - $5,000/month
Every 30 days beginning 1/25

| | |
|---|---|
| Shares to qualify: 1 | |
| Safekeeping: Yes | |
| Accepts foreign: Yes | |
| Auto. inv.: Yes | |
| Disc.: No | |

FEES: Div: $0!; Cash: $0!; Auto. Inv.: $1.50; Cert: $0!; Term: 7¢/sh.; Sells weekly, by mail, at market, for 7¢/sh.

---

## Shell Trans. & Trading Co. plc ADR

**SC/NYSE**
H: 54.25
L: 44.37
**Rec:** 47.25
**Div.:** 1.11
**Paid on:**
5-29
**Since:** 1898

Energy holding co. of Shell Oil in UK
c/o BNY,101 Barclay St., 22 West
New York. NY 10286
Bank of New York     888-269-2377
$25 - $unlimited
Every 30 days beginning 1/10

| | |
|---|---|
| Shares to qualify: 1 | |
| Safekeeping: Yes | |
| Accepts foreign: Yes | |
| Auto. inv.: No | |
| Disc.: No | |

FEES: Div: $2.50 + 7¢/sh.; Cash: $2.50 + 7¢/sh.; Cert: $5; Term: $0; Sells weekly, by mail, at market, for $5 + 7¢/sh.

---

## Sherwin Williams Co. ♥

**SHW/NYSE**
H: 27.25
L: 18.87
**Rec:** 22.32
**Div.:** 0.58
**Paid on:**
3.6.9.11-12
**Since:** 1979

Manufacturer & retailer of paint
101 Prospect Ave., NW
Cleveland. OH 44115
Bank of New York     800-524-4458
$10 - $2,000/month
Every 30 days beginning 1/22

| | |
|---|---|
| Shares to qualify: 1 | |
| Safekeeping: Yes | |
| Accepts foreign: Yes | |
| Auto. inv.: No | |
| Disc.: No | |

FEES: Div: $0!; Cash: $0!; Cert: $0!; Term: $0; Sells monthly, by mail, at market, for $0!

---

## Sierra Pacific Resources

**SRP/NYSE**
H: 19.43
L: 10.56
**Rec:** 15.94
**Div.:** 0.80
**Paid on:**
2.5.8.11-1
**Since:** N/A

Utility-gas, water, electricity
Box 30150
Reno. NV 89520-3150
Sierra Pacific Resources,     800-662-7575
$50 - $100,000/year
Every 30 days beginning 1/1

| | |
|---|---|
| Shares to qualify: 1 /de ($250) | |
| Safekeeping: Yes | |
| Accepts foreign: Yes | |
| Auto. inv.: No | |
| Disc.: No | |

FEES: Div: $0; Cash: 5¢/sh.; Cert: $0; Term: $0; Sells daily, by mail, at market, for 6¢/sh.

---

## ✱ SIFCO Industries, Inc. ♥

**SIF/ASE** | Precision forging, turbine eng.

H: 7.45
L: 4.40
**Rec:** 7.20

970 East 64th St.
Cleveland. OH 44103-1694

National City Bank    800-622-6757

**Div.:** 0.00
**Paid on:**
DIV. SUSP.
**Since:** --

$20 - $3,000/quarter
Every 30 days beginning 1/2

**Shares to qualify:** 1
**Safekeeping:** Yes
**Accepts foreign:** Yes
**Auto. inv.:** No
**Disc.:** No

FEES: Div: n/o; Cash: $0!; Cert: $0!; Term: $0; Sells weekly, by mail, at market, for 20¢/sh.

---

## ✱ Sizeler Property Investors Inc. ⊗

**SIZ/NYSE** | REIT

H: 10.09
L: 6.87
**Rec:** 10.05

2542 Williams Blvd.
Kenner. LA 70062

Bank of New York    800-524-4458

**Div.:** 0.92
**Paid on:**
3.6.9.12-8
**Since:** 1987

$50 - $20,000/month
Every 30 days beginning 1/31

**Shares to qualify:** 1 /de ($500)
**Safekeeping:** Yes
**Accepts foreign:** Yes
**Auto. inv.:** Yes
**Disc.:** Div 3% Cash: 3%

FEES: Div: $0; Cash: 5% to $3 + 10¢/sh.; Auto. Inv.: 5% to $3 + 10¢/sh.; Cert: $0; Term: $5; Sells weekly, by mail, at market, for 5% to $3 + 10¢/sh.

---

## ✱ Sky Financial Group

**SKYF/NASD** | Financial svcs.

H: 20.40
L: 12.61
**Rec:** 20.40

10 East Main St.
Salineville. OH 43945

Bank of New York    888-683-4901

**Div.:** 0.72
**Paid on:**
1.4.7.10-10
**Since:** N/A

$50 - $10,000/month
Every 7 days beginning varies

**Shares to qualify:** 1 /de ($500)
**Safekeeping:** Yes
**Accepts foreign:** Yes
**Auto. inv.:** Yes
**Disc.:** No

FEES: Div: $0!; Cash: $2 + 5¢/sh.; Auto. Inv.: $1 + 5¢/sh.; Cert: $0!; Term: $0; Sells daily, by phone or mail, at market, for $10 + 5¢/sh.

---

## ✱ Slade's Ferry Bancorp ♥

**SFBC/NASD** | Banking

H: 13.30
L: 8.31
**Rec:** 13.00

100 Slade's Ferry Ave., Box 390
Somerset. MA 02726

Slade's Ferry Bancorp    508-675-2121

**Div.:** 0.36
**Paid on:**
1.4.7.10-12
**Since:** 1961

$100 - $5,000/year
Every 30 days beginning 1/15

**Shares to qualify:** 1
**Safekeeping:** Yes
**Accepts foreign:** No
**Auto. inv.:** No
**Disc.:** No

FEES: Div: $0!; Cash: $0!; Cert: $0!; Term: $0,Does not sell through the plan

---

## ✱ Smith (A.O.) Corp.-B ♥

**AOS/NYSE** | Mfg. of electric motors, heating

H: 20.10
L: 11.18
**Rec:** 17.12

Box 245008
Milwaukee. WI 53224-9508

Wells Fargo Bank    800-468-9716

**Div.:** 0.52
**Paid on:**
2.5.8.11-15
**Since:** 1940

$0 - $5,000/quarter
Every 90 days beginning 2/15

**Shares to qualify:** 1
**Safekeeping:** No
**Accepts foreign:** Yes
**Auto. inv.:** No
**Disc.:** No

FEES: Div: $0; Cash: $0; Cert: $0; Term: 12¢/sh. + comm.; Sells biweekly, by mail or fax, at market, for comm.

---

## ✱ Smucker (J.M.) ♥

**SJM/NYSE** | Food products

H: 29.00
L: 18.12
**Rec:** 27.03

Strawberry Lane
Orrville. OH 44667

Computershare Investor Svcs.    800-942-5909

**Div.:** 0.64
**Paid on:**
3.6.9.12-1
**Since:** 1949

$20 - $1,500/month
Every 30 days beginning 1/2

**Shares to qualify:** 1
**Safekeeping:** Yes
**Accepts foreign:** Yes
**Auto. inv.:** No
**Disc.:** No

FEES: Div: $0!; Cash: $0!; Cert: $0!; Term: $0; Sells weekly, by mail, at market, for $0!

---

## ✱ Snap-on Inc. ♥

**SNA/NYSE** | Manufacturing of tools

H: 32.43
L: 21.00
**Rec:** 25.97

Box 1430
Kenosha. WI 53141-1430

First Chicago Trust    800-446-2617

**Div.:** 0.96
**Paid on:**
3.6.9.12-10
**Since:** 1939

$100 - $150,000/year
Every 7 days beginning Friday

**Shares to qualify:** 1 /de ($500)
**Safekeeping:** Yes
**Accepts foreign:** No
**Auto. inv.:** Yes
**Disc.:** No

FEES: Div: $0!; Cash: $0!; Auto. Inv.: $2; Cert: $0!; Term: 12¢/sh. + comm.; Sells daily, by mail, fax , or phone, at market, for $15 + 12¢/sh.

---

## ✳ SNB Bancshares, Inc. ♥

| | | |
|---|---|---|
| SNBJ/NASD | Bank holding co. | Shares to qualify: 50 |
| H: 17.00 | 2918 Riverside Dr., Box 4748 | Safekeeping: Yes |
| L: 12.25 | Macon. GA 31208 | Accepts foreign: Yes |
| Rec: 14.50 | Registrar & Transfer    800-368-5948 | Auto. inv.: No |
| Div.: 0.32 | $100 - $2,500/quarter | Disc.: No |
| Paid on: | Every 90 days beginning 3/25 | |
| 3.6.9.12-25 | FEES: Div: $0!;  Cash: $0!;  Cert: $0!;  Term: $20,Does not sell through the plan | |
| Since: N/A | | |

## ✳ Solutia Inc. ⊗

| | | |
|---|---|---|
| SOI/NYSE | Mfg. of chemical-based materials | Shares to qualify: 1 |
| H: 15.81 | Box 66760, Investor Relations 3N | Safekeeping: Yes |
| L: 10.18 | St. Louis. MO 63166-6760 | Accepts foreign: Yes |
| Rec: 13.74 | First Chicago Trust    888-446-2617 | Auto. inv.: Yes |
| Div.: 0.04 | $25 - $100,000/year | Disc.: No |
| Paid on: | Every 30 days beginning 1/12 | |
| 12-12 | FEES: Div: 2.5% to $4;  Cash: 2.5% to $4;  Auto. Inv.: $1; Cert: $0;  Term: $0; Sells daily, | |
| Since: 1997 | by mail, fax , or phone, at market, for $10 + 12¢/sh. | |

## ✳ Sonoco Products Co.

| | | |
|---|---|---|
| SON/NYSE | Industrial & consumer packaging | Shares to qualify: 1 /de ($250) |
| H: 26.00 | North Second St., A46 | Safekeeping: Yes |
| L: 16.56 | Hartsville. SC 29550 | Accepts foreign: Yes |
| Rec: 25.66 | State St. Bank    800-633-4236 | Auto. inv.: Yes |
| Div.: 0.80 | $10 - $100,000/year | Disc.: No |
| Paid on: | Every 5 days beginning 1/5 | |
| 3.6.9.12-10 | FEES: Div: $0!;  Cash: 10¢/sh.;  Auto. Inv.: 10¢/sh.;  Cert: $0!;  Term: $0; Sells weekly, by | |
| Since: 1900 | mail or phone, at market, for 10¢/sh. | |

## Sonoma Valley Bank

| | | |
|---|---|---|
| SBNK/OTC | Banking | Shares to qualify: 1 /de ($250) |
| H: 23.80 | 202 West Napa St., Box 1228 | Safekeeping: Yes |
| L: 15.47 | Sonoma. CA 95476 | Accepts foreign: Yes |
| Rec: 21.00 | American Stock Transfer    800-937-5449 | Auto. inv.: Yes |
| Div.: STK. | $25 - $10,000/investment | Disc.: No |
| Paid on: | Every daily days beginning varies | |
| N/A | FEES: Div: n/o;  Cash: $2.50 + 10¢/sh.;  Auto. Inv.: $2.50 + 10¢/sh.;  Cert: $0;  Term: | |
| Since: N/A | $7.50 + 10¢/sh. Sells weekly, by mail or fax, at market, for $7.50 + 10¢/sh. | |

## ✳ Sotheby's Holdings, Inc. ♥

| | | |
|---|---|---|
| BID/NYSE | Auctioneer | Shares to qualify: 1 |
| H: 28.25 | 1334 York Ave. | Safekeeping: No |
| L: 15.53 | New York. NY 10021 | Accepts foreign: Yes |
| Rec: 17.01 | Mellon Inv. Svcs.    800-851-9677 | Auto. inv.: No |
| Div.: 0.00 | $100 - $5,000/month | Disc.: No |
| Paid on: | Every 30 days beginning 1/15 | |
| DIV. SUSP. | FEES: Div: n/o;  Cash: $0;  Cert: $0;  Term: $10 + comm.;  Sells weekly, by mail or phone, at | |
| Since: -- | market, for $10 + comm. | |

## ✳ South Financial Group, Inc. (The) ♥

| | | |
|---|---|---|
| TSFG/NASD | Bank holding company | Shares to qualify: 1 |
| H: 22.00 | Box 1029 | Safekeeping: Yes |
| L: 8.37 | Greenville. SC 29602 | Accepts foreign: No |
| Rec: 18.44 | Registrar & Transfer    800-368-5948 | Auto. inv.: Yes |
| Div.: 0.44 | $25 - $10,000/month | Disc.: Div 5% Cash: 0% |
| Paid on: | Every 30 days beginning 1/2 | |
| 2.5.8.11-1 | FEES: Div: $0;  Cash: $0;  Auto. Inv.: $0; Cert: $0;  Term: $0; Sells irregularly, by mail, at | |
| Since: 1994 | market, for comm. | |

## ✳ South Jersey Industries, Inc. ♥

| | | |
|---|---|---|
| SJI/NYSE | Utility-gas | Shares to qualify: 1 /de ($100) |
| H: 32.25 | 1 South Jersey Plaza | Safekeeping: No |
| L: 26.37 | Folsom. NJ 08037-9917 | Accepts foreign: Yes |
| Rec: 31.31 | SJI Dividend Reinvestment Plan    888-SJI-3100 | Auto. inv.: No |
| Div.: 1.48 | $25 - $100,000/year | Disc.: Div 2% Cash: 2% |
| Paid on: | Every 90 days beginning 1/2 | |
| 1.4.7.10-3 | FEES: Div: $0!;  Cash: $0!;  Cert: $0!;  Term: $0; Sells weekly, at market, for $2.50 + | |
| Since: N/A | 5¢/sh. | |

---

## Southern Co. ♥

| | | |
|---|---|---|
| **SO/NYSE** | **Utility-electric** | **Shares to qualify:** 1 /de ($250) |
| H: 35.72 | Box 54250 | **Safekeeping:** Yes |
| L: 20.89 | Atlanta. GA 30308-0250 | **Accepts foreign:** Yes |
| **Rec:** 23.15 | SCS Stockholder Services    800-554-7626 | **Auto. inv.:** Yes |
| **Div.:** 1.34 | $25 - $150,000/year | **Disc.:** No |
| **Paid on:** | Every 15 days beginning 10th & 25th/month | |
| 3.6.9.12-6 | | |
| **Since:** 1946 | FEES: Div: $0!; Cash: $0!; Auto. Inv.: $0; Cert: $0!; Term: $0; Sells within 5 bus. days, by mail, at avg. price, for 6¢/sh. | |

## Southern Financial Bancorp, Inc. ♥

| | | |
|---|---|---|
| **SFFB/NASD** | **Banking** | **Shares to qualify:** 1 |
| H: 26.51 | 37 East Main St. | **Safekeeping:** Yes |
| L: 11.37 | Warrenton. VA 20186 | **Accepts foreign:** Yes |
| **Rec:** 24.95 | Mellon Inv. Svcs.    800-851-9677 | **Auto. inv.:** No |
| **Div.:** 0.48 | $100 - $1,000/quarter | **Disc.:** No |
| **Paid on:** | Every 90 days beginning 2/20 | |
| 2.5.8.11-20 | | |
| **Since:** 1992 | FEES: Div: $0!; Cash: $0!; Cert: $0!; Term: $0; Sells within 10 bus. days, by mail, at market, for fee + comm. | |

## Southern Michigan Bancorp ♥

| | | |
|---|---|---|
| **SOMC/OTC** | **Bank holding company** | **Shares to qualify:** 1 |
| H: 18.50 | 51 West Pearl St. | **Safekeeping:** Yes |
| L: 13.00 | Coldwater. MI 49036 | **Accepts foreign:** Yes |
| **Rec:** 15.05 | Registrar & Transfer    800-368-5948 | **Auto. inv.:** No |
| **Div.:** 0.60 | $25 - $5,000/quarter | **Disc.:** No |
| **Paid on:** | Every 90 days beginning 1/20 | |
| 1.4.7.10-20 | | |
| **Since:** NA | FEES: Div: $0!; Cash: $0!; Cert: $0!; Term: $0; Sells weekly, by mail, at market, for $0 | |

## Southern Peru Copper Corp. ♥

| | | |
|---|---|---|
| **PCU/NYSE** | **Copper mining** | **Shares to qualify:** 1 |
| H: 15.87 | 180 Maiden Lane | **Safekeeping:** Yes |
| L: 11.31 | New York. NY 10038 | **Accepts foreign:** Yes |
| **Rec:** 11.42 | Bank of New York    800-524-4458 | **Auto. inv.:** No |
| **Div.:** 0.19 | $25 - $1,000/month | **Disc.:** No |
| **Paid on:** | Every 30 days beginning 1/2 | |
| 3.6.9.12-1 | | |
| **Since:** 1996 | FEES: Div: $0!; Cash: $0!; Cert: $0!; Term: $0!; Sells weekly, by mail, at avg. price, for $0! | |

## Southern Union Co.

| | | |
|---|---|---|
| **SUG/NYSE** | **Natural gas distributor** | **Shares to qualify:** 1 /de ($250) |
| H: 27.93 | 504 Lavaca , Ste. 800 | **Safekeeping:** Yes |
| L: 16.56 | Austin. TX 78701 | **Accepts foreign:** Yes |
| **Rec:** 22.35 | BankBoston    800-736-3001 | **Auto. inv.:** Yes |
| **Div.:** STK. | $50 - $100,000/year | **Disc.:** No |
| **Paid on:** | Every 15 days beginning 1/5 | |
| N/0 | | |
| **Since:** 1994 | FEES: Div: $0; Cash: $2.50 + 15¢/sh.; Auto. Inv.: $0; Cert: $0; Term: $10 + 15¢/sh.; Sells weekly, by mail, at market, for $10 + 15¢/sh. | |

## Southtrust Corp. ♥

| | | |
|---|---|---|
| **SOTR/NASD** | **Banking** | **Shares to qualify:** 1 |
| H: 26.61 | Box 2554 | **Safekeeping:** Yes |
| L: 13.12 | Birmingham. AL 35290 | **Accepts foreign:** No |
| **Rec:** 25.87 | American Stock Transfer    800-937-5449 | **Auto. inv.:** Yes |
| **Div.:** 0.56 | $25 - $10,000/month | **Disc.:** No |
| **Paid on:** | Every 30 days beginning 1/2 | |
| 1.4.7.10-1 | | |
| **Since:** 1944 | FEES: Div: $0; Cash: $0; Auto. Inv.: $0; Cert: $0; Term: $0; Sells weekly, by mail or phone, at market, for 4¢/sh. | |

## Southwest Gas Corp. ♥

| | | |
|---|---|---|
| **SWX/NYSE** | **Utility-gas, & gas distrib.** | **Shares to qualify:** 1 /de ($100) |
| H: 24.67 | Box 98511 | **Safekeeping:** Yes |
| L: 17.12 | Las Vegas. NV 89193-8511 | **Accepts foreign:** Yes |
| **Rec:** 22.95 | Southwest Gas Corp.    702-876-7280 | **Auto. inv.:** Yes |
| **Div.:** 0.82 | $25 - $100,000/year | **Disc.:** No |
| **Paid on:** | Every 15 days beginning 10th & 25th /month | |
| 3.6.9.12-1 | | |
| **Since:** 1956 | FEES: Div: $0!; Cash: $0!; Auto. Inv.: $0!; Cert: $0!; Term: 3¢ to 5¢/sh.; Sells weekly, by mail, at market, for 3¢ to 5¢/sh. | |

## Southwest Georgia Financial Corp. ♥

**SGB/ASE** | **Banking services**
H: 16.35
L: 14.12
**Rec:** 15.80

**Div.:** 0.52
**Paid on:**
1.4.7.10-30
**Since:** N/A

201 First St. S.E.
Moultrie. GA 31768

American Stock Transfer    800-278-4353
$5 - $5,000/month
Every 30 days beginning varies
FEES: Div: $0; Cash: $0; Auto. Inv.: $0; Cert: $0; Term: $0; Sells weekly, by mail, at market, for 4¢/sh.

**Shares to qualify:** 1
**Safekeeping:** Yes
**Accepts foreign:** Yes
**Auto. inv.:** Yes
**Disc.:** No

---

## Southwest Water Co. ♥

**SWWC/NAS** | **Utility-water**
H: 15.62
L: 9.60
**Rec:** 13.50

**Div.:** 0.22
**Paid on:**
1.4.7.10-20
**Since:** 1960

225 N. Barranca Ave., Ste. 200
West Covina. CA 91791-1605

Mellon Inv. Svcs.    800-356-2017
$25 - $3,000/quarter
Every 90 days beginning 1/20
FEES: Div: $0; Cash: $0; Cert: $0; Term: $0,Does not sell through the plan

**Shares to qualify:** 1
**Safekeeping:** Yes
**Accepts foreign:** Yes
**Auto. inv.:** No
**Disc.:** Div 5% Cash: 0%

---

## Southwestern Energy Co. ⊗

**SWN/NYSE** | **Diversified-gas**
H: 16.35
L: 7.12
**Rec:** 11.84

**Div.:** 0.00
**Paid on:**
DIV. SUSP.
**Since:** --

Box 1408
Favetteville. AR 72602-1408

First Chicago Trust    800-446-2617
$25 - $120,000/year
Every 5 days beginning varies
FEES: Div: n/o; Cash: $5 + 3¢/sh.; Auto. Inv.: $2 + 3¢/sh.; Cert: $0!; Term: $0; Sells daily, by phone, mail, fax, or Internet, at market, for $10 + 12¢/sh.

**Shares to qualify:** 1 /de ($250)
**Safekeeping:** Yes
**Accepts foreign:** Yes
**Auto. inv.:** Yes
**Disc.:** No

---

## Sovereign Bancorp Inc. ♥

**SOV/NYSE** | **Banking**
H: 13.50
L: 6.56
**Rec:** 11.02

**Div.:** 0.10
**Paid on:**
2.5.8.11-15
**Since:** 1987

Box 12646
Reading. PA 19612

Mellon Inv. Svcs.    800-685-4524
$50 - $5,000/quarter
Every 90 days beginning 2/15
FEES: Div: $0!; Cash: $0!; Cert: $0!; Term: $0; Sells daily, by mail, at market, for $15 + 6¢/sh.

**Shares to qualify:** 1
**Safekeeping:** Yes
**Accepts foreign:** No
**Auto. inv.:** No
**Disc.:** Div 5% Cash: 0%

---

## Sovran Self Storage, Inc. ♥

**SSS/NYSE** | **REIT**
H: 27.80
L: 17.87
**Rec:** 26.15

**Div.:** 2.32
**Paid on:**
1.4.7.10-22
**Since:** 1995

5166 Main St.
Williamsville. NY 14221

American Stock Transfer    800-278-4353
$100 - $10,000/month
Every 30 days beginning 1/22
FEES: Div: $0!; Cash: $0!; Cert: $0!; Term: $10 + 4¢/sh.; Sells within 10 bus. days, by mail, at market, for $10 + 4¢/sh.

**Shares to qualify:** 1 /de ($100)
**Safekeeping:** Yes
**Accepts foreign:** Yes
**Auto. inv.:** No
**Disc.:** Div 2% Cash: 2%

---

## Spain Fund (The)

**SNF/NYSE** | **Closed-end fund**
H: 13.25
L: 8.30
**Rec:** 8.97

**Div.:** 0.94
**Paid on:**
1.4.7.10-7
**Since:** N/A

c/o All. Capital,1345 Ave. of the Amer.
New York. NY 10105-0302

State St. Bank    800-219-4218
$100 - $unlimited
Every 180 days beginning 1/15
FEES: Div: $0; Cash: 75¢; Cert: $0; Term: $0; Sells within 10 bus. days, by mail or phone, at market, for $2.50 + comm.

**Shares to qualify:** 1
**Safekeeping:** No
**Accepts foreign:** Yes
**Auto. inv.:** No
**Disc.:** Div 5% Cash: 0%

---

## Sprint Corp. (FON Group) ♥

**FON/NYSE** | **Telecommunications**
H: 36.81
L: 19.06
**Rec:** 22.26

**Div.:** 0.50
**Paid on:**
3.6.9.12-30
**Since:** 1939

Box 11315
Kansas Citv. MO 64112

UMB Bank, N.A.    816-860-7786
$25 - $5,000/quarter
Every 30 days beginning 1/30
FEES: Div: $0; Cash: $0; Cert: $0; Term: $2; Sells weekly, by mail or fax, at market, for $2 + comm.

**Shares to qualify:** 1
**Safekeeping:** Yes
**Accepts foreign:** Yes
**Auto. inv.:** No
**Disc.:** No

---

## St. Paul Cos. (The) ♥

**SPC/NYSE** | Insurance | **Shares to qualify:** 1
H: 57.00 | 385 Washington St. | **Safekeeping:** Yes
L: 39.57 | Saint Paul. MN 55102 | **Accepts foreign:** Yes
**Rec:** 43.01 | | **Auto. inv.:** No
| Wells Fargo Bank    888-326-5102 | **Disc.:** No
**Div.:** 1.12 | $10 - $60,000/year |
**Paid on:** | Every 30 days beginning 1/17 |
1.4.7.10-17 | FEES: Div: $0!; Cash: $0!; Cert: $0!; Term: $5; Sells daily, by phone or fax, at market, for $5
**Since:** 1872 | + 15¢/sh.

## Standard Commercial Corp. ♥

**STW/NYSE** | Tobacco | **Shares to qualify:** 1
H: 19.30 | Box 450 | **Safekeeping:** Yes
L: 3.75 | Wilson. NC 27894-0450 | **Accepts foreign:** Yes
**Rec:** 19.05 | | **Auto. inv.:** No
| First Union Nat'l Bank    800-829-8432 | **Disc.:** No
**Div.:** 0.20 | $25 - $3,000/quarter |
**Paid on:** | Every 30 days beginning 1/15 |
N/A | FEES: Div: $0!; Cash: $0!; Cert: $0!; Term: $0; Sells bimonthly, by mail or fax, at market, for
**Since:** N/A | 5¢/sh.

## Standard Register ♥

**SR/NYSE** | Business forms & handling | **Shares to qualify:** 1
H: 19.51 | Box 1167 | **Safekeeping:** Yes
L: 11.75 | Davton. OH 45401 | **Accepts foreign:** Yes
**Rec:** 18.60 | | **Auto. inv.:** Yes
| State St. Bank    800-633-4236 | **Disc.:** No
**Div.:** 0.92 | $25 - $60,000/year |
**Paid on:** | Every 30 days beginning 1/5 |
3.6.9.12-1 | FEES: Div: $0!; Cash: $0!; Auto. Inv.: $0; Cert: $0!; Term: $0; Sells daily, by mail or fax, at
**Since:** 1927 | avg. price, for 5¢/sh.

## Stanley Works ⊗

**SWK/NYSE** | Machinery, tools, hardware, consumer | **Shares to qualify:** 1 /de ($250)
H: 45.80 | 1000 Stanley Dr. | **Safekeeping:** Yes
L: 18.43 | New Britain. CT 06053 | **Accepts foreign:** Yes
**Rec:** 45.43 | | **Auto. inv.:** Yes
| State St. Bank    800-543-6757 | **Disc.:** No
**Div.:** 0.96 | $100 - $150,000/year |
**Paid on:** | Every 7 days beginning varies |
3.6.9.12-31 | FEES: Div: $2; Cash: $5; Auto. Inv.: $2 + 5¢/sh.; Cert: $0; Term: $15 + 12¢/sh.; Sells
**Since:** 1876 | within 4 bus. days, by mail or phone, at market, for $15 + 12¢/sh.

## State Auto Financial Corp. ♥

**STFC/NASD** | Insurance | **Shares to qualify:** 1
H: 18.00 | 518 East Broad St. | **Safekeeping:** Yes
L: 11.25 | Columbus. OH 43215 | **Accepts foreign:** Yes
**Rec:** 15.75 | | **Auto. inv.:** No
| National City Bank    800-622-6757 | **Disc.:** No
**Div.:** 0.12 | $10 - $3,000/quarter |
**Paid on:** | Every 90 days beginning 1/2 |
3.6.9.12-31 | FEES: Div: $0!; Cash: $0!; Cert: $0!; Term: $0; Sells weekly, by mail, at market, for $2.50
**Since:** 1991 |

## State Bancorp, Inc. ♥

**STB/ASE** | Bank holding co. | **Shares to qualify:** 1
H: 18.25 | 699 Hillside Ave. | **Safekeeping:** Yes
L: 11.90 | New Hvde Park. NY 11040 | **Accepts foreign:** No
**Rec:** 17.48 | | **Auto. inv.:** No
| Wells Fargo Bank    800-468-9716 | **Disc.:** Div 5% Cash: 5%
**Div.:** 0.53 | $100 - $10,000/quarter |
**Paid on:** | Every 90 days beginning 1/6 |
1.4.7.10-6 | FEES: Div: $0!; Cash: $0!; Cert: $0!; Term: $5 + 10¢/sh.; Sells daily, by mail, at market, for
**Since:** 1987 | $5 + 10¢/sh.

## State Street Corp. ⊗

**STT/NYSE** | Financial services | **Shares to qualify:** 10
H: 68.40 | 225 Franklin St. | **Safekeeping:** Yes
L: 38.76 | Boston. MA 02110 | **Accepts foreign:** No
**Rec:** 52.32 | | **Auto. inv.:** Yes
| State St. Bank    800-426-5523 | **Disc.:** No
**Div.:** 0.40 | $100 - $25,000/month |
**Paid on:** | Every 30 days beginning 1/15 |
1.4.7.10-15 | FEES: Div: 5% to $3; Cash: $3.50; Auto. Inv.: $2.50; Cert: $0; Term: $0; Sells daily, by
**Since:** 1910 | mail or phone, at market, for $10 + comm.

---

✴ DRIP enrollment through Temper Enrollment Service (see page 180).    **151**

## ✳ Sterling Bancorp ♥

**STL/NYSE**
**Regional banks**

| | |
|---|---|
| H: 30.60 | |
| L: 14.77 | |
| **Rec:** 30.45 | |

430 Park Ave., 4th Fl.
New York. NY 10022-3505

Mellon Inv. Svcs.      800-851-9677

**Div.:** 0.64
**Paid on:**
3.6.9.12-30
**Since:** N/A

$150 - $4,500/month
Every 30 days beginning varies

FEES: Div: $0!; Cash: $0!; Cert: comm.; Term: comm.; Sells weekly, by mail, at market, for comm.

**Shares to qualify:** 5
**Safekeeping:** Yes
**Accepts foreign:** Yes
**Auto. inv.:** No
**Disc.:** No

---

## ✳ Sterling Financial Corp. ♥

**SLFI/NASDA** | **Bank holding company**

| | |
|---|---|
| H: 26.00 | |
| L: 15.00 | |
| **Rec:** 24.30 | |

101 N. Pointe Blvd.
Lancaster. PA 17601-4133

Bank of Lancaster County     717-735-5602

**Div.:** 0.76
**Paid on:**
1.4.7.10-1
**Since:** N/A

$50 - $2,500/quarter
Every 90 days beginning 1/2

FEES: Div: $0!; Cash: $0!; Cert: $15; Term: $5; Sells within 10 bus. days, by mail, at market, for $15 + comm.

**Shares to qualify:** 25
**Safekeeping:** Yes
**Accepts foreign:** No
**Auto. inv.:** No
**Disc.:** No

---

## ✳ Stifel Financial Corp. ♥

**SF/NYSE** | **Financial**

| | |
|---|---|
| H: 14.93 | |
| L: 10.68 | |
| **Rec:** 12.13 | |

501 North Broadway
St. Louis. MO 63102

UMB Bank, N.A.     816-860-7787

**Div.:** 0.12
**Paid on:**
2.5.8.11-24
**Since:** 1993

$25 - $5,000/month
Every 90 days beginning 2/24

FEES: Div: $0!; Cash: $0!; Cert: $0; Term: $0; Sells weekly, by mail, at market, for 10¢ to 12¢/sh.

**Shares to qualify:** 1
**Safekeeping:** Yes
**Accepts foreign:** Yes
**Auto. inv.:** No
**Disc.:** No

---

## ✳ Stilwell Financial, Inc.

**SV/NYSE** | **Financial services**

| | |
|---|---|
| H: 54.50 | |
| L: 23.27 | |
| **Rec:** 29.20 | |

920 Main St., 21st Fl.
Kansas Citv. MO 64105

UMB Bank, N.A.     800-884-4225

**Div.:** N/A
**Paid on:**
1.4.7.10-31
**Since:** 2000

$50 - $5,000/quarter
Every 90 days beginning 1/18

FEES: Div: 5¢/sh.; Cash: 5¢/sh.; Cert: $0; Term: $5; Sells weekly, by mail, at market, for $5 + comm.

**Shares to qualify:** 1
**Safekeeping:** Yes
**Accepts foreign:** Yes
**Auto. inv.:** No
**Disc.:** No

---

## ✳ Storage USA, Inc. ♥

**SUS/NYSE** | **REIT**

| | |
|---|---|
| H: 37.75 | |
| L: 27.12 | |
| **Rec:** 37.68 | |

165 Madison Ave., Ste.1300
Memphis. TN 38103

First Union Nat'l Bank     800-829-8432

**Div.:** 2.84
**Paid on:**
4.7.10-11 &
**Since:** 1994

$50 - $25,000/quarter
Every 90 days beginning 3/31

FEES: Div: $0; Cash: $0; Cert: $0; Term: $5; Sells bimonthly, by mail or fax, at market, for $5 + comm.

**Shares to qualify:** 1
**Safekeeping:** Yes
**Accepts foreign:** Yes
**Auto. inv.:** No
**Disc.:** No

---

## ✳ Strayer Education Inc. ♥

**STRA/NASD** | **Schools**

| | |
|---|---|
| H: 54.70 | |
| L: 17.50 | |
| **Rec:** 47.06 | |

8550 CinderBed Rd.
Newinaton. VA 22122

American Stock Transfer     800-278-4353

**Div.:** 0.26
**Paid on:**
1.4.7.10-26
**Since:** N/A

$200 - $25,000/year
Every 30 days beginning 1/15

FEES: Div: $0!; Cash: $0!; Cert: $0!; Term: $10 + comm.; Sells within 5 bus. days, by mail, at market, for $10 + comm.

**Shares to qualify:** 1
**Safekeeping:** Yes
**Accepts foreign:** Yes
**Auto. inv.:** No
**Disc.:** No

---

## ✳ Stride Rite Corp. (The)

**SRR/NYSE** | **Apparel, retail & mfr. of shoes**

| | |
|---|---|
| H: 9.99 | |
| L: 4.81 | |
| **Rec:** 8.96 | |

Box 9191
Lexinaton. MA 02420-9191

Boston Eq.     781-575-3170

**Div.:** 0.20
**Paid on:**
3.6.9.12-15
**Since:** 1955

$10 - $1,000/month
Every 45 days beginning 2/1

FEES: Div: 5% to $2.50; Cash: 5% to $2.50 ; Cert: $0; Term: $0,Does not sell through the plan

**Shares to qualify:** 1
**Safekeeping:** Yes
**Accepts foreign:** Yes
**Auto. inv.:** No
**Disc.:** No

---

## ✱ Suffolk Bancorp ♥

| SUBK/NASD | Banking | Shares to qualify: 1 |
|---|---|---|
| H: 50.25 | 6 West 2nd St., Box 9000 | Safekeeping: Yes |
| L: 27.00 | Riverhead. NY 11901 | Accepts foreign: Yes |
| Rec: 48.00 | | Auto. inv.: No |
| | American Stock Transfer    800-937-5449 | Disc.: Div 3% Cash: 3% |
| Div.: 1.12 | $300 - $5,000/quarter | |
| Paid on: | Every 90 days beginning 1/2 | |
| 1.4.7.10-1 | | |
| Since: 1890 | FEES: Div: $0; Cash: $0; Cert: $0; Term: $15 + comm.; Sells weekly, by mail or fax, at market, for $15 + comm. | |

## ✱ Summit Properties ♥

| SMT/NYSE | Property management | Shares to qualify: 1 /de ($100) |
|---|---|---|
| H: 27.20 | 309 E. Morehead St., Ste. 200 | Safekeeping: Yes |
| L: 21.93 | Charlotte. NC 28202 | Accepts foreign: Yes |
| Rec: 26.09 | | Auto. inv.: No |
| | First Union Nat'l Bank    800-829-8432 | Disc.: Div 3% Cash: 3% |
| Div.: 1.85 | $100 - $10,000/month | |
| Paid on: | Every 30 days beginning 1/2 | |
| 2.5.8.11-15 | | |
| Since: 1994 | FEES: Div: $0; Cash: $0; Cert: $0; Term: $0; Sells monthly, by mail, fax , or phone, at market, for 2¢/sh. | |

## ✱ Sun Bancorp, Inc. ♥

| SUBI/NASD | Banking | Shares to qualify: 1 |
|---|---|---|
| H: 16.50 | 2 South Market St., Box 57 | Safekeeping: Yes |
| L: 12.62 | Selinsgrove. PA 17870 | Accepts foreign: Yes |
| Rec: 15.88 | | Auto. inv.: Yes |
| | SunTrust Bank, Atlanta    888-374-1545 | Disc.: No |
| Div.: 0.60 | $50 - $10,000/month | |
| Paid on: | Every 30 days beginning last Friday of each month | |
| 3.6.9.12-15 | | |
| Since: N/A | FEES: Div: $0; Cash: $0; Auto. Inv.: $0; Cert: $0; Term: $3; Sells daily, by mail or in person, at market, for $0 | |

## ✱ Suncor Energy Inc. ♥

| SU/NYSE | Integrated oil & gas company | Shares to qualify: 1 |
|---|---|---|
| H: 30.00 | 112 4th Ave. 5 W., Box 38 | Safekeeping: Yes |
| L: 19.37 | Calgary. Alta. T2P 2VS Canada | Accepts foreign: Yes |
| Rec: 27.35 | | Auto. inv.: No |
| | Computershare Trust Co. of    800-558-0046 | Disc.: No |
| Div.: 0.22 | $100 - $5,000/quarter Cdn. | |
| Paid on: | Every 90 days beginning 3/30 | |
| 3.6.9.12-25 | | |
| Since: 1990 | FEES: Div: $0!; Cash: $0!; Cert: $0!; Term: comm.,Does not sell through the plan | |

## Sunoco Inc. ⊗

| SUN/NYSE | Oil & energy | Shares to qualify: 1 /de ($250) |
|---|---|---|
| H: 42.73 | Ten Penn Ctr., 1801 Market St. | Safekeeping: Yes |
| L: 24.56 | Philadelphia. PA 19103-1699 | Accepts foreign: Yes |
| Rec: 34.95 | | Auto. inv.: Yes |
| | First Chicago Trust    800-888-8494 | Disc.: No |
| Div.: 1.00 | $50 - $250,000/year | |
| Paid on: | Every 5 days beginning varies | |
| 3.6.9.12-10 | | |
| Since: 1925 | FEES: Div: $0; Cash: $5 + 3¢/sh.; Auto. Inv.: $2 + 3¢/sh.; Cert: $0; Term: $15 + 12¢/sh.; Sells daily, by phone, mail, fax, or Internet, at market, for $15 + 12¢/sh. | |

## SunSource, Inc. ♥

| SDP/ASE | Industrial products & services | Shares to qualify: 25 |
|---|---|---|
| H: 10.15 | 3000 One Logan Sq. | Safekeeping: Yes |
| L: 2.87 | Philadelphia. PA 19103 | Accepts foreign: Yes |
| Rec: 10.07 | | Auto. inv.: No |
| | Registrar & Transfer    800-368-5948 | Disc.: No |
| Div.: 0.00 | $100 - $2,500/quarter | |
| Paid on: | Every 90 days beginning 1/10 | |
| N/O | | |
| Since: N/O | FEES: Div: n/o; Cash: $0!; Cert: $0!; Term: $10 + comm.; Sells within 10 bus. days, by mail, at avg. price, for $10 + comm. | |

## ✱ SunTrust Banks Inc. ♥

| STI/NYSE | Banking | Shares to qualify: 1 |
|---|---|---|
| H: 70.90 | Box 4418, Center 645 | Safekeeping: Yes |
| L: 41.62 | Atlanta. GA 30302-4418 | Accepts foreign: Yes |
| Rec: 70.12 | | Auto. inv.: Yes |
| | SunTrust Bank, Atlanta    800-568-3476 | Disc.: No |
| Div.: 1.60 | $10 - $60,000/year | |
| Paid on: | Every 30 days beginning 1/15 | |
| 3.6.9.12-15 | | |
| Since: 1985 | FEES: Div: $0!; Cash: $0!; Auto. Inv.: $0!; Cert: $0!; Term: $0; Sells biweekly, by mail, at market, for 9¢/sh. | |

## ∗ Superior Industries Int'l, Inc. ♥

| | | |
|---|---|---|
| **SUP/NYSE** | **Auto & truck parts** | **Shares to qualify:** 1 |
| H: 44.85 | 7800 Woodley Ave. | **Safekeeping:** Yes |
| L: 27.68 | Van Nuvs. CA 91406 | **Accepts foreign:** Yes |
| **Rec:** 43.03 | Mellon Inv. Svcs.    800-851-9677 | **Auto. inv.:** No |
| **Div.:** 0.44 | $50 - $5,000/quarter | **Disc.:** No |
| **Paid on:** | Every 90 days beginning 1/23 | |
| 1.4.7.10-16 | FEES: Div: $0!; Cash: $0!; Cert: $5; Term: $5; Sells weekly, by mail, at market, for $15 + | |
| **Since:**1985 | comm. | |

## ∗ Supervalu, Inc. ♥

| | | |
|---|---|---|
| **SVU/NYSE** | **Food wholesaler and retailer** | **Shares to qualify:** 1 |
| H: 21.05 | Box 990 | **Safekeeping:** Yes |
| L: 11.75 | Minneapolis. MN 55440 | **Accepts foreign:** No |
| **Rec:** 20.25 | Wells Fargo Bank    800-468-9716 | **Auto. inv.:** No |
| **Div.:** 0.56 | $10 - $3,000/quarter | **Disc.:** No |
| **Paid on:** | Every 30 days beginning 1/15 | |
| 3.6.9.12-15 | FEES: Div: $0!; Cash: $0!; Cert: $0!; Term: $10 + 10¢/sh.; Sells daily, by mail, at market, for | |
| **Since:**1936 | $10 + 10¢/sh. | |

## ∗ Susquehanna Bancshares ⊗

| | | |
|---|---|---|
| **SUSO/NASD** | **Banking** | **Shares to qualify:** 1 /de ($250) |
| H: 37.99 | 26 North Cedar St., Box 1000 | **Safekeeping:** Yes |
| L: 12.87 | Lititz. PA 17543-7000 | **Accepts foreign:** Yes |
| **Rec:** 21.54 | Bank of New York    800-524-4458 | **Auto. inv.:** Yes |
| **Div.:** 0.76 | $50 - $25,000/year | **Disc.:** No |
| **Paid on:** | Every 7 days beginning varies | |
| 2.5.8.11-21 | FEES: Div: $0!;  Cash: $5 + 10¢/sh.;  Auto. Inv.: $5 + 10¢/sh.; Cert: $0!; Term: $0; Sells | |
| **Since:**1982 | weekly, by mail, at market, for $10 + 10¢/sh. | |

## ∗ Sussex Bancorp ♥

| | | |
|---|---|---|
| **SBB/ASE** | **Bank holding company** | **Shares to qualify:** 1 |
| H: 10.80 | 399 Route 23 | **Safekeeping:** Yes |
| L: 7.43 | Franklin. NJ 07416 | **Accepts foreign:** Yes |
| **Rec:** 10.60 | American Stock Transfer    800-278-4353 | **Auto. inv.:** No |
| **Div.:** 0.28 | $100 - $3,000/quarter | **Disc.:** Div 3% Cash 0% |
| **Paid on:** | Every 90 days beginning 1/25 | |
| 1.4.7.10-25 | FEES: Div: $0!;  Cash: $0!; Cert: $0!; Term: $0,Does not sell through the plan | |
| **Since:**1998 | | |

## ∗ Synovus Financial Corp.

| | | |
|---|---|---|
| **SNV/NYSE** | **Banking** | **Shares to qualify:** 10 /de ($250) |
| H: 37.43 | Box 120 | **Safekeeping:** Yes |
| L: 18.75 | Columbus. GA 31902-0120 | **Accepts foreign:** Yes |
| **Rec:** 34.32 | State St. Bank    800-503-8903 | **Auto. inv.:** Yes |
| **Div.:** 0.51 | $50 - $250,000/year | **Disc.:** No |
| **Paid on:** | Every 7 days beginning varies | |
| 1.4.7.10-1 | FEES: Div: $0!; Cash: $2.50 + 8¢/sh.;  Auto. Inv.: $0; Cert: $0!;  Term: $0; Sells weekly, by | |
| **Since:**1930 | mail, at market, for $10 + 15¢/sh. | |

## ∗ Sysco Corp. ⊗

| | | |
|---|---|---|
| **SYY/NYSE** | **Food distribution** | **Shares to qualify:** 1 |
| H: 30.43 | 1390 Enclave Pkwy. | **Safekeeping:** Yes |
| L: 20.25 | Houston. TX 77077-2099 | **Accepts foreign:** Yes |
| **Rec:** 27.80 | BankBoston    800-730-4001 | **Auto. inv.:** Yes |
| **Div.:** 0.28 | $100 - $10,000/month | **Disc.:** No |
| **Paid on:** | Every 30 days beginning 4th Fri. of each month | |
| 1.4.7.10-VARIES | FEES: Div: $0!; Cash: $5 + 5¢/sh.;  Auto. Inv.: $5 + 5¢/sh.; Cert: $0!;  Term: $0; Sells | |
| **Since:**1970 | weekly, by mail, at avg. price, for $10 + 15¢/sh. | |

## ∗ Taiwan Fund (The)

| | | |
|---|---|---|
| **TWN/NYSE** | **Closed-end fund** | **Shares to qualify:** 1 |
| H: 19.06 | Taiwan Fund, 225 Franklin St. | **Safekeeping:** No |
| L: 9.25 | Boston. MA 02266-8200 | **Accepts foreign:** Yes |
| **Rec:** 10.01 | State St. Bank    800-426-5523 | **Auto. inv.:** No |
| **Div.:** 0.00 | $100 - $3,000/semiannually | **Disc.:** Div 5% Cash 0% |
| **Paid on:** | Every 180 days beginning 2/15 | |
| 1-15 | FEES: Div: $0!; Cash: 75¢ + comm.; Cert: $0!; Term: $2.50 +15¢/sh.; Sells daily, by mail, | |
| **Since:**N/A | at market, for $2.50 + 15¢/sh. | |

## ✱ Tanger Factory Outlet Centers, Inc. ♥

**SKT/NYSE** | Outlet centers | **Shares to qualify:** 1
H: 23.62 | 1400 W. Northwood St., Box 29168 | **Safekeeping:** No
L: 19.50 | Greensboro. NC 27429 | **Accepts foreign:** No
**Rec:** 21.70 | | **Auto. inv.:** No
| Boston Eq.    781-575-3170 | **Disc.:** No
**Div.:** 2.44 | $100 - $25,000/quarter |
**Paid on:** | Every 30 days beginning 1/15 |
2.5.8.11-15 | FEES: Div: $0!; Cash: $0!; Cert: $0!; Term: $5 + comm.; Sells within 6 bus. days, by mail, at
**Since:** N/A | market, for $5 + comm.

## ✱ Target Corp. ⊗

**TGT/NYSE** | Retail stores | **Shares to qualify:** 1 /de ($500)
H: 40.43 | 777 Nicollet Mall | **Safekeeping:** Yes
L: 21.62 | Minneapolis. MN 55402 | **Accepts foreign:** Yes
**Rec:** 37.85 | | **Auto. inv.:** Yes
| First Chicago Trust    800-317-4445 | **Disc.:** No
**Div.:** 0.22 | $50 - $100,000/year |
**Paid on:** | Every 7 days beginning varies |
3.6.9.12-10 | FEES: Div: 5% to $3 + 10¢/sh.; Cash: $5 + 10¢/sh.; Auto. Inv.: $2 + 10¢/sh.; Cert: $0!;
**Since:** 1965 | Term: $10 +12¢/sh.; Sells daily, by mail or phone, at market, for $10 + 12¢/sh.

## ✱ Taubman Centers, Inc. ⊗

**TCO/NYSE** | Operates & develops shopping centers | **Shares to qualify:** 1 /de ($250)
H: 14.23 | 200 East Long Lake Rd., Ste. 300 | **Safekeeping:** Yes
L: 10.25 | Bloomfield Hills. MI 48303 | **Accepts foreign:** Yes
**Rec:** 14.01 | | **Auto. inv.:** Yes
| Mellon Inv. Svcs.    888-877-2889 | **Disc.:** No
**Div.:** 1.00 | $25 - $25,000/month |
**Paid on:** | Every 7 days beginning varies |
1.4.7.10-20 | FEES: Div: $0!; Cash: $5 + 12¢/sh.; Auto. Inv.: $5 + 12¢/sh.; Cert: $0!; Term: $15 +
**Since:** 1993 | 12¢/sh.; Sells daily, by mail, at market, for $15 + 12¢/sh.

## ✱ TCF Financial Corp.

**TCB/NYSE** | Bank holding company | **Shares to qualify:** 1
H: 49.80 | 200 Lake St. East, MC EX0-02-C | **Safekeeping:** Yes
L: 30.50 | Wavzata. MN 55391-1693 | **Accepts foreign:** Yes
**Rec:** 49.52 | | **Auto. inv.:** No
| Boston Eq.    800-730-4001 | **Disc.:** No
**Div.:** 1.00 | $25 - $25,000/quarter |
**Paid on:** | Every 30 days beginning 1/31 |
2.5.8.11-31 | FEES: Div: $0!; Cash: $1; Cert: $0; Term: $0; Sells within 10 days, by mail, at market, for
**Since:** 1988 | $15

## ✱ Teche Holding Company ♥

**TSH/ASE** | Bank holding co. | **Shares to qualify:** 100
H: 19.50 | 211 Willow St. | **Safekeeping:** Yes
L: 12.50 | Franklin. LA 70538 | **Accepts foreign:** Yes
**Rec:** 19.35 | | **Auto. inv.:** No
| Registrar & Transfer    800-368-5948 | **Disc.:** No
**Div.:** 0.50 | $25 - $2,000/quarter |
**Paid on:** | Every 90 days beginning 3/30 |
3.6.9.12-29 | FEES: Div: $0!; Cash: $0!; Cert: $0; Term: $10,Does not sell through the plan
**Since:** 1995

## ✱ Technitrol Inc. ♥

**TNL/NYSE** | Electronic, mechanical products | **Shares to qualify:** 10
H: 76.12 | 1210 Northbrook Dr., Ste. 385 | **Safekeeping:** Yes
L: 19.60 | Trevose. PA 19053 | **Accepts foreign:** Yes
**Rec:** 26.05 | | **Auto. inv.:** No
| Registrar & Transfer    800-368-5948 | **Disc.:** No
**Div.:** 0.13 | $50 - $5,000/quarter |
**Paid on:** | Every 90 days beginning 2/2 |
1.4.7.10-30 | FEES: Div: $0; Cash: $0; Cert: $15; Term: $25,Does not sell through the plan
**Since:** 1975

## ✱ TECO Energy ♥

**TE/NYSE** | Utility-electric, metals & mining | **Shares to qualify:** 1
H: 33.18 | Box 111 | **Safekeeping:** Yes
L: 23.81 | Tampa. FL 33601 | **Accepts foreign:** Yes
**Rec:** 29.21 | | **Auto. inv.:** No
| BankBoston    800-650-9222 | **Disc.:** No
**Div.:** 1.38 | $25 - $100,000/year |
**Paid on:** | Every 30 days beginning 1/15 |
2.5.8.11-15 | FEES: Div: $0!; Cash: $0!; Cert: $0!; Term: $0; Sells within 10 bus. days, by mail, at market,
**Since:** 1900 | for $10 + 15¢/sh.

## Tektronix ⊗

| | |
|---|---|
| **TEK/NYSE** | **Electronic instruments & controls** |
| H: 40.50 | 26600 S.W. Pkwy., Box 1000 |
| L: 20.60 | Wilsonville. OR 97070-1000 |
| **Rec:** 21.05 | Mellon Inv. Svcs.      800-411-7025 |
| **Div.:** 0.24 | $100 - $10,000/month |
| **Paid on:** | Every 7 days beginning varies |
| 1.4.7.10-25 | FEES: Div: 5% to $10 + 12¢/sh.;  Cash: $5 + 10¢/sh.;  Auto. Inv.: $5 + 12/sh.; Cert: $0; |
| **Since:** N/A | Term: $0; Sells daily, by mail, at market, for $15 + 12¢/sh. |

Shares to qualify: 20 /de ($500)
Safekeeping: Yes
Accepts foreign: Yes
Auto. inv.: Yes
Disc.: No

---

## Teleflex Inc. ♥

| | |
|---|---|
| **TFX/NYSE** | **Multi-industry manufacturer** |
| H: 50.99 | 155 S. Limerick Rd. |
| L: 31.81 | Limerick. PA 19468 |
| **Rec:** 46.88 | American Stock Transfer      800-278-4353 |
| **Div.:** 0.68 | $50 - $2,500/month |
| **Paid on:** | Every 30 days beginning 1/15 |
| 3.6.9.12-15 | FEES: Div: $0!; Cash: $0!; Cert: $0!; Term: $0; Sells within 7 bus. days, by mail, at market, |
| **Since:** N/A | for $15 + 4¢/sh. |

Shares to qualify: 10
Safekeeping: Yes
Accepts foreign: Yes
Auto. inv.: No
Disc.: No

---

## Telephone & Data Systems ♥

| | |
|---|---|
| **TDS/ASE** | **Telecommunications** |
| H: 122.87 | 30 North LaSalle St., Ste. 4000 |
| L: 80.60 | Chicago. IL 60602-2507 |
| **Rec:** 104.50 | Computershare Investor Svcs.      877-337-1575 |
| **Div.:** 0.54 | $10 - $5,000/quarter |
| **Paid on:** | Every 30 days beginning 1/2 |
| 3.6.9.12-31 | FEES: Div: $0!;  Cash: $0!;  Cert: $0!; Term: $0,Does not sell through the plan |
| **Since:** 1974 | |

Shares to qualify: 10
Safekeeping: Yes
Accepts foreign: Yes
Auto. inv.: No
Disc.: Div: 5% Cash: 0%

---

## TELUS Corporation ♥

| | |
|---|---|
| **TU/NYSE** | **Telecommunications** |
| H: 26.81 | Floor 30, 10020 100th St. |
| L: 15.66 | Edmonton. AB. Canada T5J 0N5 |
| **Rec:** 15.67 | Computershare Trust Co. of      800-558-0046 |
| **Div.:** 0.91 | $100 - $20,000/year (Cdn.) |
| **Paid on:** | Every 30 days beginning 1/2 |
| 1.4.7.10-1 | FEES: Div: $0; Cash: $0; Cert: $0; Term: $0; Sells within 14 bus. days, by mail, at market, |
| **Since:** N/A | for $8.50 + 4¢/sh. |

Shares to qualify: 1
Safekeeping: No
Accepts foreign: Yes
Auto. inv.: No
Disc.: Div: 5% Cash: 0%

---

## Temple-Inland ♥

| | |
|---|---|
| **TIN/NYSE** | **Containers, paper, fin'l svcs.** |
| H: 62.15 | Box 40 |
| L: 34.62 | Austin. TX 78767 |
| **Rec:** 60.46 | First Chicago Trust      201-324-1225 |
| **Div.:** 1.28 | $25 - $1,000/quarter |
| **Paid on:** | Every 90 days beginning 3/15 |
| 3.6.9.12-15 | FEES: Div: $0!; Cash: $0!; Cert: $0!; Term: $0; Sells daily, by mail, fax or phone, at market, |
| **Since:** 1984 | for $10 + 10¢/sh. |

Shares to qualify: 1
Safekeeping: Yes
Accepts foreign: No
Auto. inv.: No
Disc.: No

---

## Tenet Healthcare Corp. ♥

| | |
|---|---|
| **THC/NYSE** | **Health care** |
| H: 57.00 | Box 31907 |
| L: 28.06 | Santa Barbara. CA 93130 |
| **Rec:** 55.40 | Bank of New York      800-524-4458 |
| **Div.:** 0.00 | $10 - $1,000/month |
| **Paid on:** | Every 30 days beginning 1/15 |
| DIV. SUSP. | FEES: Div: $0!; Cash: $0!; Cert: $0!; Term: $3 + 5¢/sh.; Sells within 5 bus. days, by mail, at |
| **Since:** -- | market, for $3 + 5¢/sh. |

Shares to qualify: 1
Safekeeping: Yes
Accepts foreign: Yes
Auto. inv.: No
Disc.: No

---

## Tennant Co. ♥

| | |
|---|---|
| **TNC/NYSE** | **Floor maintenance equipment** |
| H: 53.37 | 701 N. Lilac Dr. |
| L: 36.20 | Minneapolis. MN 55440 |
| **Rec:** 36.60 | Wells Fargo Bank      800-468-9716 |
| **Div.:** 0.80 | $50 - $5,000/quarter |
| **Paid on:** | Every 90 days beginning 3/15 |
| 9-15 12-31 | FEES: Div: $0; Cash: $0; Cert: $0; Term: $10 + 10¢/sh.; Sells daily, by phone or mail, at |
| **Since:** 1933 | market, for $10 + 10¢/sh. |

Shares to qualify: 1
Safekeeping: Yes
Accepts foreign: Yes
Auto. inv.: No
Disc.: No

---

## Texaco Inc.

**TX/NYSE**
H: 73.90
L: 48.68
**Rec:** 69.64
**Div.:** 1.80
**Paid on:**
3.6.9.12-10
**Since:** 1903

**Fully integrated oil company**

2000 Westchester Ave.
White Plains. NY 10650-0001

Texaco Inc.    800-283-9785
$50 - $120,000/year
Every 3x/month days beginning 10,20,30th

FEES: Div: 4¢/sh.; Cash: 4¢/sh.; Auto. Inv.: $0; Cert: $0; Term: $0; Sells biweekly, by mail or fax, at market, for 4¢/sh.

**Shares to qualify:** 1 /de ($250)
**Safekeeping:** Yes
**Accepts foreign:** Yes
**Auto. inv.:** Yes
**Disc.:** No

---

## ✻ Textron, Inc. ♥

**TXT/NYSE**
H: 60.50
L: 40.68
**Rec:** 55.95
**Div.:** 1.30
**Paid on:**
1.4.7.10-1
**Since:** 1942

**Aerospace, diversified manufacturer**

40 Westminster St.
Providence. RI 02903

First Chicago Trust    800-519-3111
$25 - $120,000/year
Every 30 days beginning 1/1

FEES: Div: $0!; Cash: $0!; Auto. Inv.: $1; Cert: $0; Term: $10 + 12¢/sh.; Sells daily, by phone or mail, at market, for $10 + 12¢/sh.

**Shares to qualify:** 1
**Safekeeping:** Yes
**Accepts foreign:** Yes
**Auto. inv.:** Yes
**Disc.:** No

---

## ✻ Thai Fund

**TTF/NYSE**
H: 5.00
L: 2.63
**Rec:** 3.52
**Div.:** 0.00
**Paid on:**
N/A
**Since:** N/A

**Closed-end fund**

c/o Boston EquiServe, Box 8040
Boston. MA 02266

Boston Eq.    800-730-6001
$100 - $3,000/semiannually
Every 180 days beginning 2/15

FEES: Div: comm.; Cash: comm.; Cert: $0; Term: $0; Sells bimonthly, by mail, at market, for $0

**Shares to qualify:** 1
**Safekeeping:** No
**Accepts foreign:** No
**Auto. inv.:** No
**Disc.:** Div 0-5% Cash: 0%

---

## ✻ Thistle Group Holding Co. ♥

**THTL/NASD**
H: 10.40
L: 7.56
**Rec:** 9.96
**Div.:** 0.28
**Paid on:**
1.4.7.10-15
**Since:** N/A

**Unitary thrift holding company**

6060 Ridge Ave.
Philadelphia. PA 19128

Registrar & Transfer    800-368-5948
$100 - $1,000/quarter
Every 90 days beginning 1/13

FEES: Div: $0; Cash: $0; Cert: $0; Term: $10 + comm.,Does not sell through the plan

**Shares to qualify:** 100
**Safekeeping:** Yes
**Accepts foreign:** Yes
**Auto. inv.:** No
**Disc.:** No

---

## ✻ Thomas & Betts Corp. ♥

**TNB/NYSE**
H: 23.90
L: 13.06
**Rec:** 20.82
**Div.:** 1.12
**Paid on:**
1.4.7.10-1
**Since:** 1934

**Manufacturer**

8155 T&B Blvd., 4A-31
Memphis. TN 38125-8888

First Chicago Trust    800-446-2617
$10 - $24,000/year
Every 30 days beginning 1/2

FEES: Div: $0!; Cash: $0!; Cert: $0; Term: $0; Sells daily, by mail, fax , or phone, at market, for $15 + 12¢/sh.

**Shares to qualify:** 1
**Safekeeping:** Yes
**Accepts foreign:** Yes
**Auto. inv.:** No
**Disc.:** No

---

## ✻ Thomas Industries ♥

**TII/NYSE**
H: 29.50
L: 18.25
**Rec:** 26.45
**Div.:** 0.34
**Paid on:**
1.4.7.10-1
**Since:** 1955

**Mfr. compressors & vacuum pumps**

Box 35120
Louisville. KY 40232-5120

National City Bank    800-622-6757
$25 - $3,000/month
Every 30 days beginning 1st bus. day /month

FEES: Div: $0!; Cash: $0!; Cert: $0; Term: $0; Sells daily, by mail, at market, for comm.

**Shares to qualify:** 1
**Safekeeping:** Yes
**Accepts foreign:** Yes
**Auto. inv.:** No
**Disc.:** No

---

## ✻ Thornburg Mortgage, Inc. ♥

**TMA/NYSE**
H: 18.45
L: 8.00
**Rec:** 16.10
**Div.:** 1.60
**Paid on:**
2.5.8.11-18
**Since:** 1993

**REIT**

119 East Marcy St., Ste. 201
Santa Fe. NM 87501

Continental Stock Transfer    800-509-5586
$100 - $5,000/month
Every 30 days beginning 1/15

FEES: Div: $0!; Cash: $0!; Cert: $0!; Term: comm.,Does not sell through the plan

**Shares to qualify:** 1 /de ($500)
**Safekeeping:** Yes
**Accepts foreign:** Yes
**Auto. inv.:** No
**Disc.:** Div 0-5% Cash: 0-5%

---

## * Tidewater Inc.

**TDW/NYSE** | **Offshore oil & gas services** | **Shares to qualify:** 1
H: 52.95 | 601 Poydras St., Ste. 1900 | **Safekeeping:** Yes
L: 31.60 | New Orleans. LA 70130 | **Accepts foreign:** Yes
**Rec:** 32.85 | | **Auto. inv.:** No
| BankBoston 781-575-3170 | **Disc.:** No
**Div:** 0.60 | $25 - $5,000/quarter |
**Paid on:** | Every 45 days beginning 2/3 |
2.5.8.11-3 | FEES: Div: 5% to $2.50 + comm.; Cash: 5% to $2.50 + comm.; Cert: $0; Term: $0; Sells
**Since:** N/A | daily, by mail, at market, for 5% to $5 + 15¢/sh.

---

## * Timken Co. ⊗

**TKR/NYSE** | **Industrial products, bearings, alloy** | **Shares to qualify:** 1 /de ($1000)
H: 18.65 | Box 6928, GNE-04 | **Safekeeping:** Yes
L: 12.56 | Canton. OH 44706-0928 | **Accepts foreign:** Yes
**Rec:** 15.70 | | **Auto. inv.:** Yes
| First Chicago Trust 800-555-9898 | **Disc.:** No
**Div:** 0.72 | $100 - $250,000/year |
**Paid on:** | Every 7 days beginning varies |
3.6.9.12-VARIES | FEES: Div: $0!; Cash: $3 + 10¢/sh.; Auto. Inv.: $1; Cert: $0; Term: $0; Sells weekly, by
**Since:** 1922 | mail or phone, at market, for $15 + 12¢/sh.

---

## * Tompkins Trustco, Inc. ♥

**TMP/ASE** | **Bank holding company** | **Shares to qualify:** 1
H: 41.00 | Box 460 | **Safekeeping:** No
L: 23.50 | Ithaca. NY 14851 | **Accepts foreign:** Yes
**Rec:** 38.30 | | **Auto. inv.:** No
| Bank of New York 800-524-4458 | **Disc.:** No
**Div.:** 1.12 | $25 - $3,000/quarter |
**Paid on:** | Every 30 days beginning 1st bus. day |
3.6.9.12-15 | FEES: Div: $0; Cash: $2; Cert: $0; Term: $2.50 + comm.; Sells witihin 5 bus. days, by mail,
**Since:** 1935 | at market, for $2.50 + comm.

---

## * Torchmark Corp.

**TMK/NYSE** | **Insurance & financial** | **Shares to qualify:** 1
H: 41.95 | 3700 S. Stonebridge Dr. | **Safekeeping:** Yes
L: 25.68 | McKinnev. TX 75070 | **Accepts foreign:** Yes
**Rec:** 41.72 | | **Auto. inv.:** No
| First Chicago Trust 800-446-2617 | **Disc.:** No
**Div:** 0.36 | $100 - $3,000/45 days |
**Paid on:** | Every 45 days beginning varies |
2.5.8.11-1 | FEES: Div: 5% to $2.50 + 10¢/sh.; Cash: $2.50 + 10¢/sh.; Cert: $0; Term: 5% to $2.50 +
**Since:** 1933 | 10¢/sh.; Sells within 10 bus. days, by mail, at market, for $10 + 12¢/sh.

---

## * Toro Co. (The) ♥

**TTC/NYSE** | **Machinery** | **Shares to qualify:** 1
H: 48.99 | 8111 Lyndale Ave. South | **Safekeeping:** Yes
L: 27.25 | Bloominaton. MN 55420-1196 | **Accepts foreign:** Yes
**Rec:** 48.90 | | **Auto. inv.:** No
| Wells Fargo Bank 800-468-9716 | **Disc.:** No
**Div.:** 0.48 | $10 - $1,000/month |
**Paid on:** | Every 30 days beginning 1/12 |
1.4.7.10-12 | FEES: Div: $0; Cash: $0; Cert: $0; Term: $10 + 10¢/sh.; Sells daily, by mail or fax, at
**Since:** 1984 | market, for $10 + 10¢/sh.

---

## * Total System Services, Inc.

**TSS/NYSE** | **Credit card data processing serv.** | **Shares to qualify:** 10 /de ($250)
H: 35.84 | Box 120 | **Safekeeping:** Yes
L: 14.87 | Columbus. GA 31902-0120 | **Accepts foreign:** Yes
**Rec:** 31.74 | | **Auto. inv.:** Yes
| State St. Bank 800-503-8903 | **Disc.:** No
**Div.:** 0.06 | $50 - $250,000/year |
**Paid on:** | Every 30 days beginning 1/31 |
1.4.7.10-1 | FEES: Div: $0; Cash: $2.50 + 8¢/sh.; Auto. Inv.: 8¢/sh.; Cert: $0; Term: $10 + 15¢/sh.;
**Since:** 1990 | Sells weekly, by mail, at market, for $10 + 15¢/sh.

---

## * TransCanada Pipelines Ltd. ♥

**TRP/NYSE** | **Natural gas pipeline** | **Shares to qualify:** 1
H: 12.80 | Box 1000, Station M | **Safekeeping:** No
L: 8.68 | Calqarv. Alta. T2P 4K5 Canada | **Accepts foreign:** Yes
**Rec:** 12.62 | | **Auto. inv.:** No
| Computershare Trust Co. of 800-558-0046 | **Disc.:** No
**Div.:** 0.59 | $35 - $7,000/quarter |
**Paid on:** | Every 90 days beginning 1/31 |
1.4.7.10-30 | FEES: Div: $0!; Cash: $0!; Cert: $0!; Term: $0,Does not sell through the plan
**Since:** 1964 |

---

* DRIP enrollment through Temper Enrollment Service (see page 180).  **158**

## ✳ Transocean Sedco Forex ⊗

**RIG/NYSE** | **Oil well svcs. & equipment** | **Shares to qualify:** 1 /de ($500)
H: 65.50 | 4 Greenway Plaza, 11th Fl. | **Safekeeping:** Yes
L: 28.90 | Houston. TX 77046 | **Accepts foreign:** Yes
**Rec:** 29.53 | | **Auto. inv.:** Yes
| Bank of New York    877-397-7229 | **Disc.:** No
**Div.:** 0.12 | $25 - $5,000/investment |
**Paid on:** | Every 7 days beginning varies |
3.6.9.12-15 | FEES: Div: $1 to $5 + 10¢/sh.; Cash: $5 + 10¢/sh.; Auto. Inv.: $5 + 10¢/sh.; Cert: $0;
**Since:** N/A | Term: $10 + 10¢/sh.; Sells daily, by mail or phone, at market, for $10 + 10¢/sh.

## ✳ Tredegar Corp. ♥

**TG/NYSE** | **Diversified mfr. plastic & metal prods.** | **Shares to qualify:** 1
H: 23.68 | 1100 Boulders Pkwy. | **Safekeeping:** Yes
L: 14.68 | Richmond. VA 23225 | **Accepts foreign:** Yes
**Rec:** 20.76 | | **Auto. inv.:** No
| American Stock Transfer    800-937-5449 | **Disc.:** No
**Div.:** 0.16 | $25 - $4,000/month |
**Paid on:** | Every 30 days beginning 1/2 |
1.4.7.10-1 | FEES: Div: $0!; Cash: $0!; Cert: $0!; Term: $0; Sells weekly, by mail, at market, for 4¢/sh.
**Since:** 1989 |

## ✳ Tribune Co. ⊗

**TRB/NYSE** | **Publishing, broadcasting, education** | **Shares to qualify:** 1 /de ($500)
H: 46.50 | 435 North Michigan Ave. | **Safekeeping:** Yes
L: 33.12 | Chicago. IL 60611-4041 | **Accepts foreign:** No
**Rec:** 41.07 | | **Auto. inv.:** Yes
| First Chicago Trust    800-446-2617 | **Disc.:** No
**Div.:** 0.44 | $50 - $120,000/year |
**Paid on:** | Every 5 days beginning Thurs. |
3.6.9.12-8 | FEES: Div: 5% to $3 + 10¢/sh.; Cash: $5 + 10¢/sh.; Auto. Inv.: $2 + 10¢/sh.; Cert: $0;
**Since:** 1903 | Term: $0; Sells within 5 bus. days, by phone or mail, at market, for $10 + 12¢/sh.

## ✳ TriCo Bancshares ♥

**TCBK/NASD** | **Bank holding co.** | **Shares to qualify:** 1
H: 20.27 | 63 Constitution Dr. | **Safekeeping:** Yes
L: 14.50 | Chico. CA 95973 | **Accepts foreign:** Yes
**Rec:** 19.01 | | **Auto. inv.:** No
| Mellon Inv. Svcs.    800-356-2017 | **Disc.:** Div 4% Cash: 0%
**Div.:** 0.80 | $100 - $1,000/quarter |
**Paid on:** | Every 90 days beginning 3/30 |
3.6.9.12-30 | FEES: Div: $0!; Cash: $0!; Cert: $5; Term: $5; Sells within 10 bus. days, by mail or phone,
**Since:** N/A | at market, for $15

## ✳ Tricon Global Restaurants, Inc. ⊗

**YUM/NYSE** | **Operates quick service restaurants** | **Shares to qualify:** 1 /de ($250)
H: 48.75 | 1441 Gardiner Lane | **Safekeeping:** Yes
L: 25.87 | Louisville. KY 40213 | **Accepts foreign:** Yes
**Rec:** 43.60 | | **Auto. inv.:** Yes
| Boston Eq.    888-439-4986 | **Disc.:** No
**Div.:** 0.00 | $25 - $250,000/year |
**Paid on:** | Every 7 days beginning Friday |
DIV. SUSP. | FEES: Div: n/o; Cash: $5 + 3¢/sh.; Auto. Inv.: $2 + 3¢/sh.; Cert: $0!; Term: $15 +
**Since:** -- | 12¢/sh.; Sells weekly, by mail or phone, at market, for $15 + 12¢/sh.

## ✳ Troy Financial Corp.

**TRYF/NASD** | **Bank holding company** | **Shares to qualify:** 1
H: 21.00 | 433 River St. | **Safekeeping:** Yes
L: 10.43 | Troy. NY 12180 | **Accepts foreign:** Yes
**Rec:** 20.80 | | **Auto. inv.:** No
| Registrar & Transfer    800-368-5948 | **Disc.:** No
**Div.:** 0.40 | $100 - $2,500/quarter |
**Paid on:** | Every 90 days beginning 2/28 |
2.5.8.11-28 | FEES: Div: $0!; Cash: $1.50; Cert: $0!; Term: $0; Sells within 10 bus. days, by mail, at avg.
**Since:** N/A | price, for $10 + comm.

## ✳ TrustCo Bank Corp NY ♥

**TRST/NASD** | **Banking** | **Shares to qualify:** 1 /de ($25)
H: 14.25 | Box 1082 | **Safekeeping:** Yes
L: 9.75 | Schenectadv. NY 12301-1082 | **Accepts foreign:** Yes
**Rec:** 13.54 | | **Auto. inv.:** Yes
| TrustCo Bank    518-381-3601 | **Disc.:** No
**Div.:** 0.60 | $25 - $unlimited |
**Paid on:** | Every 7 days beginning varies |
1.4.7.10-1 | FEES: Div: $0!; Cash: $0!; Auto. Inv.: $0; Cert: $0!; Term: $0; Sells within 10 bus. days, by
**Since:** N/A | mail, at market, for $0

## * TRW Inc. ♥

**TRW/NYSE**
H: 52.75
L: 29.37
**Rec:** 43.07
**Div.:** 1.40
**Paid on:**
3.6.9.12-15
**Since:** 1950

**Air bags, defense, automotive**
1900 Richmond Rd.
Cleveland. OH 44124-3760
TRW Inc. Shareholder Services        216-291-7654
$10 - $1,000/45 days
Every 45 days beginning 1/30
FEES: Div: $0!; Cash: $0!; Cert: $0!; Term: $0; Sells every 45 days, by mail or fax, at market, for 8¢/sh.

**Shares to qualify:** 1
**Safekeeping:** Yes
**Accepts foreign:** Yes
**Auto. inv.:** No
**Disc.:** No

---

## * Twin Disc, Inc. ♥

**TDI/NYSE**
H: 17.81
L: 13.06
**Rec:** 15.05
**Div.:** 0.70
**Paid on:**
3.6.9.12-1
**Since:** 1934

**Mfr. ind. equip.**
1328 Racine St.
Racine. WI 53403
Firstar Bank        800-637-7549
$10 - $2,000/month
Every 90 days beginning 3/1
FEES: Div: $0; Cash: $0; Cert: $0; Term: $0; Sells biweekly, by mail or fax, at market, for $0

**Shares to qualify:** 1
**Safekeeping:** No
**Accepts foreign:** Yes
**Auto. inv.:** No
**Disc.:** No

---

## * TXU Corp. ♥

**TXU/NYSE**
H: 50.00
L: 33.25
**Rec:** 47.00
**Div.:** 2.40
**Paid on:**
1.4.7.10-1
**Since:** 1945

**Utility-electric**
Box 130059
Dallas. TX 75313-0059
TXU Business Services        800-828-0812
$25 - $250,000/year
Every 5 days beginning varies
FEES: Div: $0!; Cash: $0!; Auto. Inv.: $0; Cert: $0!; Term: 7¢/sh.; Sells weekly, by mail or fax, at market, for $10 + 7¢/sh.

**Shares to qualify:** 1 /de ($500)
**Safekeeping:** Yes
**Accepts foreign:** No
**Auto. inv.:** Yes
**Disc.:** No

---

## * Tyco International Ltd. ♥

**TYC/NYSE**
H: 63.21
L: 40.15
**Rec:** 53.77
**Div.:** 0.05
**Paid on:**
2.5.8.11-1
**Since:** 1975

**Fire prot., elec. comp., health care prod.**
One Tyco Park
Exeter. NH 03833
Mellon Inv. Svcs.        800-685-4509
$50 - $10,000/month
Every 7 days beginning varies
FEES: Div: $0; Cash: $0; Auto. Inv.: $0; Cert: $0; Term: $2.50 + 12¢/sh.; Sells weekly, by phone, mail, fax, or Internet, at market, for $2.50 + 12¢/sh.

**Shares to qualify:** 1
**Safekeeping:** Yes
**Accepts foreign:** Yes
**Auto. inv.:** Yes
**Disc.:** No

---

## * Tyson Foods-A ♥

**TSN/NYSE**
H: 15.50
L: 8.55
**Rec:** 10.70
**Div.:** 0.16
**Paid on:**
3.6.9.12-15
**Since:** 1976

**Integrated poultry business**
Box 2020
Springdale. AR 72765-2020
First Chicago Trust        800-317-4445
$50 - $unlimited
Every 7 days beginning Thurs.
FEES: Div: $0!; Cash: $0!; Auto. Inv.: $1; Cert: $0!; Term: $0; Sells daily, by phone or mail, at market, for $15 + 10¢/sh.

**Shares to qualify:** 1 /de ($250)
**Safekeeping:** Yes
**Accepts foreign:** Yes
**Auto. inv.:** Yes
**Disc.:** No

---

## * U.S. Bancorp ♥

**USB/NYSE**
H: 26.06
L: 15.37
**Rec:** 24.64
**Div.:** 0.75
**Paid on:**
1.4.7.10-15
**Since:** 1863

**Banking**
601 Second Ave. South
Minneapolis. MN 55402-4302
Firstar Bank        800-637-7549
$50 - $25,000/quarter
Every 30 days beginning 1/15
FEES: Div: $0!; Cash: $0!; Auto. Inv.: $0; Cert: $0!; Term: $0; Sells weekly, by mail or fax, at avg. price, for 3¢/sh.

**Shares to qualify:** 1
**Safekeeping:** Yes
**Accepts foreign:** Yes
**Auto. inv.:** Yes
**Disc.:** No

---

## * UAL Corp. ⊗

**UAL/NYSE**
H: 54.68
L: 30.50
**Rec:** 34.54
**Div.:** 0.20
**Paid on:**
2.5.8.11-1
**Since:** 2000

**Holding co.**
Box 66100
Chicago. IL 60666
Computershare Investor Svcs.        800-647-4488
$25 - $50,000/year
Every 5 days beginning varies
FEES: Div: 75¢; Cash: $5 + 10¢/sh.; Auto. Inv.: $1.50 + 10¢/sh.; Cert: $0; Term: $10 + 10¢/sh.; Sells weekly, by mail, at market, for $10 + 10¢/sh.

**Shares to qualify:** 1 /de ($250)
**Safekeeping:** Yes
**Accepts foreign:** Yes
**Auto. inv.:** Yes
**Disc.:** No

---

## UGI Corp. ♥

**UGI/NYSE**
H: 28.11
L: 21.37
**Rec:** 28.09
**Div.:** 1.60
**Paid on:**
1.4.7.10-1
**Since:** 1885

**Utility-gas & electric, propane**
Box 858
Valley Forge, PA 19482
Mellon Inv. Svcs.    800-756-3353
$25 - $3,000/quarter
Every 30 days beginning 1/4
FEES: Div: $0!; Cash: $0!; Cert: $0!; Term: $2.50 + 10¢ to12¢/sh.; Sells within 10 bus. days, by mail or phone, at market, for $2.50 + 10¢ to12¢/sh.

**Shares to qualify:** 1
**Safekeeping:** Yes
**Accepts foreign:** Yes
**Auto. inv.:** No
**Disc.:** No

---

## UIL Holdings Corp.

**UIL/NYSE**
H: 56.00
L: 42.87
**Rec:** 47.75
**Div.:** 2.88
**Paid on:**
1.4.7.10-1
**Since:** 1900

**Utility-electric**
157 Church St., Box 1564
New Haven, CT 06506-0901
American Stock Transfer    800-937-5449
$25 - $10,000/investment
Every 5 days beginning varies
FEES: Div: 2% to $1.50 + 10¢/sh.; Cash: $2.50 + 10¢/sh.; Auto. Inv.: $2.50 + 10¢/sh.; Cert: $0; Term: $7.50 + 10¢/sh.; Sells weekly, by phone, mail, or Internet, at market, for $7.50 + 10¢/sh.

**Shares to qualify:** 1 /de ($250)
**Safekeeping:** Yes
**Accepts foreign:** Yes
**Auto. inv.:** Yes
**Disc.:** No

---

## Ultramar Diamond Shamrock ♥

**UDS/NYSE**
H: 56.25
L: 23.18
**Rec:** 47.20
**Div.:** 0.50
**Paid on:**
3.6.9.12-5
**Since:** 1992

**Refining oil, retail marketing**
Box 696000
San Antonio, TX 78269-6000
Registrar & Transfer    800-368-5948
$100 - $25,000/year
Every 90 days beginning 3/5
FEES: Div: $0!; Cash: $0!; Cert: $0!; Term: $0; Sells weekly, by mail, at market, for $0!

**Shares to qualify:** 1
**Safekeeping:** Yes
**Accepts foreign:** Yes
**Auto. inv.:** No
**Disc.:** No

---

## UMB Financial Corp. ♥

**UMBF/NAS**
H: 44.41
L: 32.87
**Rec:** 42.74
**Div.:** 0.80
**Paid on:**
1.4.7.10-2
**Since:** N/A

**Financial**
1010 Grand Blvd., Box 419226
Kansas City, MO 64141-6226
UMB Bank, N.A.    816-860-7891
$50 - $3,000/quarter
Every 30 days beginning 1/2
FEES: Div: $0!; Cash: $0!; Cert: $0!; Term: $3; Sells weekly, by mail, at market, for $3

**Shares to qualify:** 1
**Safekeeping:** Yes
**Accepts foreign:** Yes
**Auto. inv.:** No
**Disc.:** No

---

## UNB Corp. ♥

**UNBO/NASD**
H: 20.12
L: 11.50
**Rec:** 19.01
**Div.:** 0.50
**Paid on:**
3.6.9.12-15
**Since:** N/A

**Bank holding company**
Box 24190
Canton, OH 44701
United National Bank    800-773-4862
$500 - $5,000/month
Every 30 days beginning varies
FEES: Div: $0; Cash: $0; Cert: $0; Term: $0; Sells daily, by mail, at avg. price, for $0

**Shares to qualify:** 1
**Safekeeping:** Yes
**Accepts foreign:** Yes
**Auto. inv.:** No
**Disc.:** No

---

## Union National Financial Corp. ♥

**UNNF/OTC**
H: 14.50
L: 11.75
**Rec:** 12.25
**Div.:** 0.42
**Paid on:**
2.5.8.11-5
**Since:** N/A

**Bank holding company**
P.O. Box 567
Mount Joy, PA 17552
Union Nat'l Community    717-653-1441
$100 - $1,000/quarter
Every 90 days beginning 2/15
FEES: Div: $0!; Cash: $0!; Cert: $10; Term: $10; Sells monthly, by mail, at market, for $10 + comm.

**Shares to qualify:** 1
**Safekeeping:** No
**Accepts foreign:** No
**Auto. inv.:** No
**Disc.:** No

---

## Union Pacific Corp. ♥

**UNP/NYSE**
H: 60.70
L: 37.50
**Rec:** 54.98
**Div.:** 0.80
**Paid on:**
1.4.7.10-1
**Since:** 1898

**Transportation, railroad**
1416 Dodge St.
Omaha, NE 68179
Computershare Investor Svcs.    800-317-2512
$10 - $60,000/year
Every 30 days beginning 1/2
FEES: Div: $0!; Cash: $0!; Cert: $0!; Term: $0; Sells weekly, by mail, at market, for $0!

**Shares to qualify:** 1
**Safekeeping:** Yes
**Accepts foreign:** Yes
**Auto. inv.:** No
**Disc.:** No

---

## ✱ Union Planters National Bank ♥

| | | |
|---|---|---|
| **UPC/NYSE** | **Banking** | **Shares to qualify:** 1 |
| H: 46.20 | 7650 Magna Dr. | **Safekeeping:** Yes |
| L: 29.06 | Belleville. IL 62223 | **Accepts foreign:** Yes |
| **Rec:** 46.04 | Union Planters Bank  800-900-4548 | **Auto. inv.:** No |
| **Div.:** 2.00 | $100 - $2,000/quarter | **Disc.:** No |
| **Paid on:** | Every 90 days beginning 3/1 | |
| 2.5.8.9-15 | | |
| **Since:** 1987 | FEES: Div: $0!; Cash: $0!; Cert: $0!; Term: $0,Does not sell through the plan | |

## ✱ UnionBanCal Corp. ♥

| | | |
|---|---|---|
| **UB/NYSE** | **Banking** | **Shares to qualify:** 1 |
| H: 38.40 | Box 45000 | **Safekeeping:** Yes |
| L: 18.31 | San Francisco. CA 94145 | **Accepts foreign:** Yes |
| **Rec:** 38.07 | Computershare Investor Svcs.  213-360-5100 | **Auto. inv.:** No |
| **Div.:** 1.00 | $25 - $3,000/quarter | **Disc.:** Div: 5% Cash: |
| **Paid on:** | Every 90 days beginning 1/10 | 0% |
| 1.4.7.10-7 | | |
| **Since:** N/A | FEES: Div: $0; Cash: $0; Cert: $2.50; Term: $0,Does not sell through the plan | |

## ✱ UniSource Energy Corp. ♥

| | | |
|---|---|---|
| **UNS/NYSE** | **Utility-electric** | **Shares to qualify:** 1 /de ($250) |
| H: 25.99 | Box 711, Dept. DA406 | **Safekeeping:** Yes |
| L: 14.12 | Tucson. AZ 85702 | **Accepts foreign:** Yes |
| **Rec:** 17.17 | Bank of New York  888-269-8845 | **Auto. inv.:** Yes |
| **Div.:** 0.40 | $50 - $unlimited | **Disc.:** No |
| **Paid on:** | Every 15 days beginning 10th & 25th | |
| 3.6.9.12-10 | FEES: Div: $0!; Cash: $0!; Auto. Inv.: $0; Cert: $0!;  Term: $5; Sells weekly, by mail or | |
| **Since:** 2000 | phone, at market, for $5 + 10¢/sh. | |

## ✱ United Bancorp, Inc. ♥

| | | |
|---|---|---|
| **UBCP/NASD** | **Banking** | **Shares to qualify:** 1 |
| H: 13.97 | 201 South Fourth St. | **Safekeeping:** Yes |
| L: 8.80 | Martins Ferrv. OH 43935-0010 | **Accepts foreign:** Yes |
| **Rec:** 13.45 | American Stock Transfer  800-278-4353 | **Auto. inv.:** No |
| **Div.:** 0.52 | $100 - $5,000/quarter | **Disc.:** No |
| **Paid on:** | Every 90 days beginning 3/20 | |
| 3.6.9.12-18 | FEES: Div: $0; Cash: $0; Cert: $0; Term: $0; Sells weekly, by mail, at market, for $0 | |
| **Since:** N/A | | |

## ✱ United Bankshares, Inc. ♥

| | | |
|---|---|---|
| **UBSI/NASD** | **Banking** | **Shares to qualify:** 1 |
| H: 28.25 | 514 Market St., Box 1508 | **Safekeeping:** No |
| L: 17.25 | Parkersburq. WV 26101 | **Accepts foreign:** Yes |
| **Rec:** 26.99 | Mellon Inv. Svcs.  800-756-3353 | **Auto. inv.:** No |
| **Div.:** 0.92 | $25 - $10,000/quarter | **Disc.:** No |
| **Paid on:** | Every 90 days beginning varies | |
| 1.4.7.10-1 | FEES: Div: $0!; Cash: $0!; Cert: $0!; Term: $0,Does not sell through the plan | |
| **Since:** N/A | | |

## ✱ United Community Financial Corp. ♥

| | | |
|---|---|---|
| **UCFC/NASD** | **Bank holding company** | **Shares to qualify:** 100 |
| H: 8.87 | 275 Federal Plaza West, Box 1111 | **Safekeeping:** Yes |
| L: 5.93 | Younastown. OH 44501-1111 | **Accepts foreign:** No |
| **Rec:** 7.30 | Registrar & Transfer  800-368-5948 | **Auto. inv.:** No |
| **Div.:** 0.30 | $100 - $3,000/quarter | **Disc.:** No |
| **Paid on:** | Every 90 days beginning 3/15 | |
| 3.6.9.12-15 | FEES: Div: $1.50!; Cash: $0; Cert: $0; Term: $5,Does not sell through the plan | |
| **Since:** N/A | | |

## ✱ United Dominion Realty Trust ♥

| | | |
|---|---|---|
| **UDR/NYSE** | **REIT** | **Shares to qualify:** 1 |
| H: 14.37 | 400 East Cary St. | **Safekeeping:** Yes |
| L: 9.37 | Richmond. VA 23219-3816 | **Accepts foreign:** Yes |
| **Rec:** 14.08 | Mellon Inv. Svcs.  888-237-5723 | **Auto. inv.:** No |
| **Div.:** 1.08 | $50 - $25,000/quarter | **Disc.:** No |
| **Paid on:** | Every 90 days beginning 1/31 | |
| 1.4.7.10-31 | FEES: Div: $0!; Cash: $0!; Cert: $0!; Term: $5; Sells within 13 bus. days, by mail , at | |
| **Since:** 1973 | market, for $5 + comm. | |

## ✱ United Industrial Corp. ♥

**UIC/NYSE** | Equipment

H: 17.78
L: 9.37
**Rec:** 15.63

**Div.:** 0.40
**Paid on:**
2.5.8.11-30
**Since:** N/A

570 Lexington Ave.
New York. NY 10022

American Stock Transfer      800-278-4353
$100 - $5,000/month
Every 30 days beginning 1/10

**Shares to qualify:** 1
**Safekeeping:** Yes
**Accepts foreign:** No
**Auto. inv.:** No
**Disc.:** No

FEES: Div: $0!; Cash: $0!; Cert: $0!; Term: $10 + comm.; Sells within 5 bus. days, by mail, at avg. price, for $10 + comm.

---

## ✱ United National Bancorp ♥

**UNBJ/NASD** | Banking

H: 25.25
L: 15.00
**Rec:** 23.21

**Div.:** 0.80
**Paid on:**
2.5.8.11-1
**Since:** N/A

1130 Route 22 East, Box 6000
Bridgewater. NJ 08807-0010

Registrar & Transfer      800-368-5948
$50 - $100,000/year
Every 7 days beginning varies

**Shares to qualify:** 1 /de ($100)
**Safekeeping:** Yes
**Accepts foreign:** Yes
**Auto. inv.:** Yes
**Disc.:** No

FEES: Div: $0!; Cash: $0!; Auto. Inv.: $0; Cert: $0!; Term: $0; Sells weekly, by mail or fax, at market, for 10¢/sh.

---

## ✱ United Technologies ♥

**UTX/NYSE** | Aerospace, elevator systems

H: 87.50
L: 58.62
**Rec:** 73.98

**Div.:** 0.90
**Paid on:**
3.6.9.12-10
**Since:** 1936

One Financial Plaza
Hartford. CT 06101

First Chicago Trust      800-519-3111
$100 - $120,000/year
Every 30 days beginning 1/10

**Shares to qualify:** 10
**Safekeeping:** Yes
**Accepts foreign:** Yes
**Auto. inv.:** No
**Disc.:** No

FEES: Div: $0!; Cash: $0!; Cert: $0!; Term: $10 + 12¢/sh.; Sells weekly, by mail or phone, at market, for $10 + 12¢/sh.

---

## ✱ Unitil Corp. ♥

**UTL/ASE** | Public utility holding company

H: 30.75
L: 22.75
**Rec:** 23.45

**Div.:** 1.38
**Paid on:**
2.5.8.11-15
**Since:** 1985

6 Libery Lane West
Hampton. NH 03842-1720

Boston Eq.      800-736-3001
$25 - $5,000/quarter
Every 90 days beginning 2/15

**Shares to qualify:** 1
**Safekeeping:** Yes
**Accepts foreign:** No
**Auto. inv.:** No
**Disc.:** No

FEES: Div: $0!; Cash: $0!; Cert: $0!; Term: $0; Sells within 10 days, by mail, at market, for $15 + 12¢/sh.

---

## ✱ Unitrin, Inc. ⊗

**UTR/NYSE** | Insurance

H: 41.93
L: 28.56
**Rec:** 37.40

**Div.:** 1.95
**Paid on:**
3.5.9.12-25
**Since:** N/A

One East Wacker Dr.
Chicago. IL 60601

First Union Nat'l Bank      800-829-8432
$50 - $100,000/year
Every 5 days beginning varies

**Shares to qualify:** 1 /de ($500)
**Safekeeping:** Yes
**Accepts foreign:** Yes
**Auto. inv.:** Yes
**Disc.:** No

FEES: Div: 5% to $5 + 5¢/sh.; Cash: $5 + 5¢/sh.; Auto. Inv.: $5 + 5¢/sh.; Cert: $0; Term: $15 + 5¢/sh.; Sells daily, by mail or phone, at market, for $15 + 5¢/sh.

---

## ✱ Unity Bancorp, Inc. ♥

**UNTY/NASD** | Bank holding company

H: 5.37
L: 1.93
**Rec:** 4.90

**Div.:** 0.00
**Paid on:**
2.5.8.11-25
**Since:** N/A

64 Old Highway 22
Clinton. NJ 08809

First City Transfer Co.      732-906-9227x
$100 - $2,500/quarter
Every 90 days beginning 2/25

**Shares to qualify:** 1
**Safekeeping:** No
**Accepts foreign:** No
**Auto. inv.:** No
**Disc.:** No

FEES: Div: $0!; Cash: $0!; Cert: $0!; Term: $3, Does not sell through the plan

---

## ✱ Universal Corp. ♥

**UVV/NYSE** | Leaf tobacco, bldg. prod., agri-prod.

H: 41.47
L: 22.56
**Rec:** 39.45

**Div.:** 1.28
**Paid on:**
2.5.8.11-2
**Since:** 1984

Box 25099
Richmond. VA 23260

Wells Fargo Bank      800-468-9716
$10 - $1,000/month
Every 30 days beginning 1/2

**Shares to qualify:** 1
**Safekeeping:** No
**Accepts foreign:** No
**Auto. inv.:** Yes
**Disc.:** No

FEES: Div: $0!; Cash: $0!; Auto. Inv.: $0; Cert: $0!; Term: $0; Sells weekly, by mail, at market, for 5¢/sh.

---

✱ DRIP enrollment through Temper Enrollment Service (see page 180).      **163**

## ✳ Universal Health Realty Income Trust ♥

**UHT/NYSE**

**REIT**

367 South Gulph Rd., Box 61558
King of Prussia. PA 19406-0958

H: 23.99
L: 16.75
**Rec:** 21.77

Boston Eq.    800-730-6001
$25 - $50,000/month
Every 30 days beginning 1/30

**Div.:** 1.86
**Paid on:**
3.6.9.12-31
**Since:** 1987

**Shares to qualify:** 1
**Safekeeping:** Yes
**Accepts foreign:** Yes
**Auto. inv.:** No
**Disc.:** No

FEES: Div: $0!; Cash: $0!; Cert: $0!; Term: $0!; Sells daily, by mail, at market, for 5% to $10

---

## ✳ Univest Corp. of Pennsylvania ♥

**UVSP/OTC**

**Bank holding company**

14 N. Main St., Box 197
Souderton. PA 18964-0197

H: 33.75
L: 19.50
**Rec:** 33.10

United National Bank    215-721-2400
$100 - $5,000/quarter
Every 90 days beginning 1/2

**Div.:** 0.84
**Paid on:**
1.4.7.10-1
**Since:** N/A

**Shares to qualify:** 1
**Safekeeping:** Yes
**Accepts foreign:** Yes
**Auto. inv.:** Yes
**Disc.:** No

FEES: Div: $0; Cash: $0; Auto. Inv.: $0; Cert: $0; Term: $5 + comm.; Sells within 30 days, by mail, at market, for $5 + comm.

---

## ✳ Unocal Corp. ⊗

**UCL/NYSE**

**Oil exploration and production**

2141 Rosecrans Ave., Ste. 4000
El Segundo. CA 90245

H: 40.12
L: 30.25
**Rec:** 35.20

Mellon Inv. Svcs.    800-279-1249
$50 - $10,000/month
Every 30 days beginning 1/10

**Div.:** 0.80
**Paid on:**
2.5.8.11-10
**Since:** 1916

**Shares to qualify:** 25
**Safekeeping:** Yes
**Accepts foreign:** No
**Auto. inv.:** No
**Disc.:** No

FEES: Div: 5¢/sh.; Cash: 5% to $3 + 5¢/sh.; Cert: $5; Term: $15 + 5¢/sh.; Sells daily, by mail or phone, at market, for $15 + 5¢/sh.

---

## ✳ UNUMProvident Corp. ⊗

**UNM/NYSE**

**Life & health insurance**

2211 Congress St. (B118)
Portland. ME 04122

H: 33.75
L: 19.25
**Rec:** 27.50

First Chicago Trust    800-446-2617
$100 - $60,000/year
Every 30 days beginning 1/15

**Div.:** 0.59
**Paid on:**
2.5.8.11-15
**Since:** 1987

**Shares to qualify:** 1
**Safekeeping:** Yes
**Accepts foreign:** Yes
**Auto. inv.:** Yes
**Disc.:** No

FEES: Div: 5% to $3 + 3¢/sh.; Cash: $5 + 3¢/sh.; Auto. Inv.: $2 + 3¢/sh.; Cert: $0!; Term: $15 + 12¢/sh.; Sells daily, by phone, mail, fax, or Internet, at market, for $15 + 12¢/sh.

---

## ✳ USEC Inc. ⊗

**USU/NYSE**

**Chemical manufacturing**

6903 Rockledge Dr.
Bethesda. MD 20817

H: 10.95
L: 3.87
**Rec:** 7.75

BankBoston    888-485-2938
$50 - $250,000/year
Every 7 days beginning varies

**Div.:** 0.55
**Paid on:**
3.6.9.12-15
**Since:** 1998

**Shares to qualify:** 1 /de ($250)
**Safekeeping:** Yes
**Accepts foreign:** Yes
**Auto. inv.:** Yes
**Disc.:** No

FEES: Div: 5% to $3; Cash: $5 + 5¢/sh.; Auto. Inv.: $2 + 5¢/sh.; Cert: $0; Term: $15 + 12¢/sh.; Sells daily, by phone, mail, fax, or Internet, at market, for $15 + 12¢/sh.

---

## ✳ UST Inc. ♥

**UST/NYSE**

**Tobacco, wine**

100 West Putnam Ave.
Greenwich. CT 06830

H: 32.70
L: 14.87
**Rec:** 31.24

State St. Bank    800-730-4001
$10 - $10,000/month
Every 15 days beginning varies

**Div.:** 1.84
**Paid on:**
3.6.9.12-30
**Since:** 1912

**Shares to qualify:** 1
**Safekeeping:** Yes
**Accepts foreign:** Yes
**Auto. inv.:** No
**Disc.:** No

FEES: Div: $0!; Cash: $0!; Cert: $0!; Term: $0; Sells within 5 days , by mail, at market, for 5% to $5 + comm.

---

## USX-Marathon Group ♥

**MRO/NYSE**

**Oil & gas**

600 Grant St., Rm. 611
Pittsburgh. PA 15219-4776

H: 33.73
L: 25.25
**Rec:** 30.00

USX Corp.    412-433-4801
$50 - $10,000/month
Every 7 days beginning Friday

**Div.:** 0.92
**Paid on:**
3.6.9.12-10
**Since:** 1901

**Shares to qualify:** 1 /de ($500)
**Safekeeping:** Yes
**Accepts foreign:** Yes
**Auto. inv.:** Yes
**Disc.:** Div: 0-3% Cash:
0-3%

FEES: Div: $0!; Cash: $0!; Auto. Inv.: $0; Cert: $0; Term: $0; Sells weekly, by mail, fax , or phone, at market, for 5¢/sh.

---

✳ DRIP enrollment through Temper Enrollment Service (see page 180).    **164**

## USX-U.S. Steel Group ♥

**X/NYSE**
H: 22.00
L: 12.68
**Rec:** 19.57
**Div.:** 0.40
**Paid on:**
3.6.9.12-10
**Since:** 1901

Steel products manufacturer
600 Grant St., Rm. 611
Pittsburgh, PA 15219-4776
USX Corp.    866-433-4801
$50 - $10,000/month
Every 7 days beginning Friday
FEES: Div: $0!; Cash: $0!; Auto. Inv.: $0; Cert: $0; Term: $0; Sells weekly, by mail, fax , or phone, at market, for 5¢/sh.

**Shares to qualify:** 1 /de ($500)
**Safekeeping:** Yes
**Accepts foreign:** Yes
**Auto. inv.:** Yes
**Disc.:** Div 0-3% Cash: 0-3%

---

## ✳ UtiliCorp United Inc. ♥

**UCU/NYSE**
H: 37.85
L: 22.62
**Rec:** 31.13
**Div.:** 1.20
**Paid on:**
3.6.9.12-12
**Since:** 1939

Utility-electric, gas
Box 13287
Kansas City, MO 64199-3287
First Chicago Trust    800-884-5426
$50 - $10,000/month
Every 30 days beginning 1/12
FEES: Div: $0!; Cash: $0!; Auto. Inv.: $0; Cert: $0!; Term: $0; Sells daily, by mail, fax , or phone, at market, for $15 + 12¢/sh.

**Shares to qualify:** 1 /de ($250)
**Safekeeping:** Yes
**Accepts foreign:** Yes
**Auto. inv.:** Yes
**Disc.:** Div 5% Cash: 0%

---

## ✳ Valley National Bancorp ♥

**VLY/NYSE**
H: 32.02
L: 23.85
**Rec:** 28.78
**Div.:** 1.06
**Paid on:**
1.4.7.10-1
**Since:** 1936

Banking
1455 Valley Rd.
Wayne, NJ 07470
American Stock Transfer    800-278-4353
$50 - $5,000/month
Every 30 days beginning 1/2
FEES: Div: $0!; Cash: $0!; Auto. Inv.: $0; Cert: $0!; Term: $0; Sells weekly, by mail, at market, for 4¢/sh.

**Shares to qualify:** 1
**Safekeeping:** Yes
**Accepts foreign:** No
**Auto. inv.:** Yes
**Disc.:** No

---

## ✳ Valspar Corp ⊗

**VAL/NYSE**
H: 36.91
L: 19.75
**Rec:** 33.72
**Div.:** 0.54
**Paid on:**
1.4.7.10-15
**Since:** 1964

Mfr. chemicals, paints & coatings
1101 Third St. South
Minneapolis, MN 55415
Mellon Inv. Svcs.    800-842-7629
$100 - $10,000/month
Every 7 days beginning varies
FEES: Div: $0; Cash: $5 + 12¢/sh.; Auto. Inv.: $3 + 12¢/sh.; Cert: $0; Term: $15 + 12¢/sh.; Sells weekly, by mail or phone, at market, for $15 + 12¢/sh.

**Shares to qualify:** 1 /de ($1000)
**Safekeeping:** Yes
**Accepts foreign:** Yes
**Auto. inv.:** Yes
**Disc.:** No

---

## ✳ Vectren Corp. ♥

**VVC/NYSE**
H: 26.50
L: 18.56
**Rec:** 20.05
**Div.:** 1.02
**Paid on:**
3.6.9.12-1
**Since:** 2000

Utility-gas, electric
Box 209
Evansville, IN 47702-0209
First Chicago Trust    800-446-2617
$25 - $50,000/year
Every 30 days beginning 1/1
FEES: Div: $0!; Cash: $0!; Auto. Inv.: $2; Cert: $0!; Term: $15 + 12¢/sh.; Sells weekly, by mail or phone, at market, for $15 + 12¢/sh.

**Shares to qualify:** 1
**Safekeeping:** Yes
**Accepts foreign:** Yes
**Auto. inv.:** Yes
**Disc.:** No

---

## ✳ Venator Group ♥

**Z/NYSE**
H: 18.00
L: 9.75
**Rec:** 17.19
**Div.:** 0.00
**Paid on:**
DIV. SUSP.
**Since:** --

Retail stores
112 West 34th St.
New York, NY 10120
First Chicago Trust    800-519-3111
$20 - $60,000/year
Every 30 days beginning 1/2
FEES: Div: n/o; Cash: $0!; Cert: $0!; Term: $0; Sells daily, by mail, fax , or phone, at market, for $10 + 12¢/sh.

**Shares to qualify:** 1
**Safekeeping:** Yes
**Accepts foreign:** No
**Auto. inv.:** No
**Disc.:** No

---

## ✳ Verizon Communications, Inc.

**VZ/NYSE**
H: 59.37
L: 39.06
**Rec:** 53.93
**Div.:** 1.54
**Paid on:**
2.5.8.11-1
**Since:** 1984

Telecommunications
1095 Ave. of the Americas, Rm. 3619
New York, NY 10036
Boston Eq.    800-631-2355
$50 - $200,000/year
Every 7 days beginning Monday
FEES: Div: $1 to $2 + 3¢/sh.; Cash: $2.50 + 3¢/sh.; Auto. Inv.: $1 + 3¢/sh.; Cert: $0; Term: $10 + 7¢/sh.; Sells weekly, by mail or phone, at avg. price, for $10 + 7¢/sh.

**Shares to qualify:** 1 /de ($1000)
**Safekeeping:** Yes
**Accepts foreign:** Yes
**Auto. inv.:** Yes
**Disc.:** No

---

✳ DRIP enrollment through Temper Enrollment Service (see page 180).    **165**

## * VF Corp.

**VFC/NYSE**
H: 42.70
L: 22.06
**Rec:** 36.59
**Div.:** 0.92
**Paid on:**
3.6.9.12-20
**Since:** 1952

**Apparel, casual**
628 Green Valley Rd., Ste. 500
Greensboro. NC 27408

First Chicago Trust    201-324-1225
$10 - $3,000/quarter
Every 90 days beginning 3/20

**Shares to qualify:** 1
**Safekeeping:** No
**Accepts foreign:** Yes
**Auto. inv.:** No
**Disc.:** No

FEES: Div: 5% to $2.50; Cash: 5% to $2.50; Cert: $0; Term: $0; Sells daily, by mail, at market, for $10 + 12¢/sh.

---

## * Visteon Corp. ⊗

**VC/NYSE**
H: 21.72
L: 9.75
**Rec:** 20.50
**Div.:** 0.24
**Paid on:**
3.6.9.12-1
**Since:** N/A

**Automotive supplier**
5500 Auto Club Dr., Ste. 2W229
Dearborn. MI 48126

First Chicago Trust    877-881-5962
$50 - $250,000/year
Every 7 days beginning varies

**Shares to qualify:** 1 /de ($1000)
**Safekeeping:** Yes
**Accepts foreign:** Yes
**Auto. inv.:** Yes
**Disc.:** No

FEES: Div: 5% to $5 + 3¢/sh.; Cash: $5 + 3¢/sh.; Auto. Inv.: $1 + 3¢/sh.; Cert: $0; Term: $15 + 12¢/sh.; Sells daily, by phone, mail, fax, or Internet, at market, for $15 + 12¢/sh.

---

## * Volvo AB-B ⊗

**VOLVY/NAS**
H: 44.31
L: 19.18
**Rec:** 19.54
**Div.:** 0.78
**Paid on:**
5-2
**Since:** 1935

**Swedish auto mfr.**
570 Lexington Ave., 20th Fl.
New York. NY 10022

Citibank    877-248-4237
$50 - $100,000/year
Every 7 days beginning varies

**Shares to qualify:** 1 /de
**Safekeeping:** Yes
**Accepts foreign:** Yes
**Auto. inv.:** Yes
**Disc.:** No

FEES: Div: 10¢/sh.; Cash: $5 + 10¢/sh.; Auto. Inv.: $5 + 10¢/sh.; Cert: $0; Term: $10 + 12¢/sh.; Sells daily, by mail or phone, at market, for $10 + 12¢/sh.

---

## * Vulcan Materials Co. ⊗

**VMC/NYSE**
H: 55.30
L: 36.50
**Rec:** 49.09
**Div.:** 0.90
**Paid on:**
3.6.9.12-10
**Since:** 1957

**Construction, industrial chemicals**
Box 385014
Birmingham. AL 35238-5014

First Chicago Trust    800-519-3111
$10 - $60,000/year
Every 30 days beginning 1/10

**Shares to qualify:** 1
**Safekeeping:** Yes
**Accepts foreign:** Yes
**Auto. inv.:** Yes
**Disc.:** No

FEES: Div: 5% to $3 + 3¢/sh.; Cash: $5 + 3¢/sh.; Auto. Inv.: $2 + 3¢/sh.; Cert: $0; Term: $15 + 12¢/sh.; Sells daily, by phone, mail, fax, or Internet, at market, for $15 + 12¢/sh.

---

## * W Holding Co.

**WBPR/NAS**
H: 17.00
L: 8.56
**Rec:** 16.04
**Div.:** 0.25
**Paid on:**
MONTHLY-15
**Since:** N/A

**Bank holding company**
19 West McKinley St., Box 1180
Mavaquez. PR 00681

Bank of New York    888-269-2377
$50 - $5,000/investment
Every 7 days beginning varies

**Shares to qualify:** 1 /de ($100)
**Safekeeping:** Yes
**Accepts foreign:** Yes
**Auto. inv.:** Yes
**Disc.:** No

FEES: Div: $1.50 + 7¢/sh.; Cash: $2 + 7¢/sh.; Auto. Inv.: $2 + 7¢/sh.; Cert: $5; Term: $0; Sells daily, by mail or phone, at market, for $5 + 7¢/sh.

---

## * W.P. Carey & Co. ♥

**WPC/NYSE**
H: 21.80
L: 16.25
**Rec:** 21.70
**Div.:** 1.70
**Paid on:**
1.4.7.10-15
**Since:** N/A

**Real estate**
50 Rockefeller Plaza
New York. NY 10020

Mellon Inv. Svcs.    800-200-8690
$500 - $25,000/month
Every 30 days beginning 1/21

**Shares to qualify:** 1 /de ($500)
**Safekeeping:** Yes
**Accepts foreign:** Yes
**Auto. inv.:** Yes
**Disc.:** No

FEES: Div: $0!; Cash: $0!; Auto. Inv.: $0; Cert: $0!; Term: $0; Sells daily, by mail or phone, at market, for $15 + 12¢/sh.

---

## * Wal-Mart Stores ⊗

**WMT/NYSE**
H: 58.75
L: 41.43
**Rec:** 53.60
**Div.:** 0.28
**Paid on:**
1.4.7.10-VARIES
**Since:** 1973

**Operates discount stores**
702 S.W. 8th St.
Bentonville. AR 72716-8001

First Chicago Trust    800-438-6278
$50 - $150,000/year
Every day days beginning daily

**Shares to qualify:** 1 /de ($250)
**Safekeeping:** Yes
**Accepts foreign:** Yes
**Auto. inv.:** Yes
**Disc.:** No

FEES: Div: $0!; Cash: $5 + 10¢/sh.; Auto. Inv.: $1 + 10¢/sh.; Cert: $0; Term: $0; Sells daily, by phone or mail, at market, for $20 + 10¢/sh.

---

## Walgreen Co. ⊗ *

**WAG/NYSE** | **Retail stores** | **Shares to qualify:** 1 /de ($50)

H: 45.75
L: 31.00
**Rec:** 37.32

**Div.:** 0.14
**Paid on:**
3.6.9.12-12
**Since:**1933

200 Wilmont Rd., MS 2261
Deerfield. IL 60015

Computershare Investor Svcs.      888-368-7346
$50 - $60,000/year
Every 7 days beginning varies
FEES: Div: $0!; Cash: $5 + 10¢/sh.; Auto. Inv.: $1.50 + 10¢/sh.; Cert: $0!; Term: $0;
Sells weekly, by mail or fax, at market, for $10 + 10¢/sh.

**Safekeeping:** Yes
**Accepts foreign:** Yes
**Auto. inv.:** Yes
**Disc.:** No

---

## Walt Disney Co. ⊗

**DIS/NYSE** | **Recreation, film** | **Shares to qualify:** 10 /de ($1000)

H: 41.93
L: 26.00
**Rec:** 27.42

**Div.:** 0.21
**Paid on:**
12-17
**Since:**1957

500 South Buena Vista St.
Burbank. CA 91521-9722

Walt Disney Co.                818-553-7200
$100 - $250,000/year
Every 5 days beginning varies
FEES: Div: $0; Cash: $5 + 3¢/sh.; Auto. Inv.: $1; Cert: $0; Term: $10 + 3¢/sh. ; Sells
within 5 bus. days, by mail or fax, at market, for $10 + 3¢/sh.

**Safekeeping:** Yes
**Accepts foreign:** Yes
**Auto. inv.:** Yes
**Disc.:** No

---

## Warwick Community Bancorp, Inc. ♥ *

**WSBI/NASD** | **Bank holding co.** | **Shares to qualify:** 100

H: 18.75
L: 11.06
**Rec:** 18.63

**Div.:** 0.38
**Paid on:**
3.6.9.12-30
**Since:**N/A

18 Oakland Ave.
Warwick. NY 10990

Registrar & Transfer      800-368-5948
$100 - $2,000/quarter
Every 90 days beginning 3/30
FEES: Div: $0!; Cash: $0!; Cert: $0!; Term: $10,Does not sell through the plan

**Safekeeping:** Yes
**Accepts foreign:** Yes
**Auto. inv.:** No
**Disc.:** No

---

## Washington Mutual, Inc. ♥

**WM/NYSE** | **Banking** | **Shares to qualify:** 1

H: 42.99
L: 21.08
**Rec:** 41.37

**Div.:** 0.92
**Paid on:**
2.5.8.11-15
**Since:**1986

1201 3rd Ave., WMT0735
Seattle. WA 98101

Mellon Inv. Svcs.      800-234-5835
$50 - $3,500/month
Every 15 days beginning 1/2
FEES: Div: $0!; Cash: $0!; Auto. Inv.: $0; Cert: $0!; Term: $15 + 12¢/sh.; Sells weekly, by
mail or phone, at market, for $15 + 12¢/sh.

**Safekeeping:** No
**Accepts foreign:** Yes
**Auto. inv.:** Yes
**Disc.:** No

---

## Washington REIT *

**WRE/NYSE** | **REIT** | **Shares to qualify:** 1 /de ($250)

H: 25.00
L: 18.25
**Rec:** 24.45

**Div.:** 1.33
**Paid on:**
3.6.9.12-31
**Since:**1961

6110 Executive Blvd., Ste. 800
Rockville. MD 20852

First Chicago Trust      877-386-8123
$100 - $25,000/month
Every 7 days beginning varies
FEES: Div: $0!; Cash: 3¢/sh.; Auto. Inv.: $0; Cert: $0!; Term: $0; Sells daily, by phone,
mail, or Internet, at market, for $15 + 12¢/sh.

**Safekeeping:** Yes
**Accepts foreign:** Yes
**Auto. inv.:** Yes
**Disc.:** No

---

## Washington Trust Bancorp, Inc. ♥ *

**WASH/NAS** | **Banking** | **Shares to qualify:** 1

H: 22.62
L: 13.37
**Rec:** 20.50

**Div.:** 0.52
**Paid on:**
1.4.7.10-15
**Since:**N/A

23 Broad St.
Westerlv. RI 02891

Washington Trust Bancorp      401-348-1200
$25 - $10,000/quarter
Every 90 days beginning 1/15
FEES: Div: $0!; Cash: $0!; Auto. Inv.: $0; Does not sell through the plan

**Safekeeping:** Yes
**Accepts foreign:** No
**Auto. inv.:** Yes
**Disc.:** No

---

## Waste Management, Inc. ⊗ *

**WMI/NYSE** | **Waste management, energy** | **Shares to qualify:** 1 /de ($500)

H: 31.85
L: 21.00
**Rec:** 30.00

**Div.:** 0.01
**Paid on:**
10-19
**Since:**1976

1001 Fannin, Ste. 4000
Houston. TX 77002

Computershare Investor Svcs.      800-969-1190
$50 - $100,000/year
Every 7 days beginning 1/7
FEES: Div: $0!; Cash: $5 + 10¢/sh.; Auto. Inv.: $1.50 + 10¢/sh.; Cert: $0; Term: $0; Sells
weekly, by mail, at market, for $10 + 10¢/sh.

**Safekeeping:** Yes
**Accepts foreign:** Yes
**Auto. inv.:** Yes
**Disc.:** No

---

## ✳ Wausau-Mosinee Paper Corp. ♥

**WMO/NYSE** | Paper & lumber

H: 14.00
L: 7.56
**Rec:** 12.20

**Div.:** 0.34
**Paid on:**
2.5.8.11-15
**Since:** 1960

1244 Kronenwetter Dr.
Mosinee. WI 54455-9099

Continental Stock Transfer     800-509-5586
$25 - $5,000/quarter
Every 90 days beginning 2/15

**Shares to qualify:** 1
**Safekeeping:** Yes
**Accepts foreign:** No
**Auto. inv.:** No
**Disc.:** No

FEES: Div: $0!; Cash: $0!; Cert: $0!; Term: 7¢ to 10¢/sh.; Sells weekly, by mail, at market, for 7¢ to 10¢/sh.

---

## ✳ Waypoint Financial Corp.

**WYPT/NASD** | Bank holding co.

H: 14.25
L: 9.00
**Rec:** 14.00

**Div.:** 0.34
**Paid on:**
2.5.8.11-15
**Since:** N/A

235 N. Second St.
Harrisburg. PA 17101

Registrar & Transfer     800-368-5948
$250 - $2,500/quarter
Every 90 days beginning 2/15

**Shares to qualify:** 1
**Safekeeping:** Yes
**Accepts foreign:** Yes
**Auto. inv.:** No
**Disc.:** Div 10% Cash: 0%

FEES: Div: $0!; Cash: $1.50; Cert: $0; Term: 4¢/sh.; Sells weekly, by mail, at market, for 4¢/sh.

---

## ✳ WebsterFinancial Corp. ♥

**WBST/NASD** | Banking

H: 36.38
L: 21.56
**Rec:** 36.10

**Div.:** 0.68
**Paid on:**
2.5.8.11-1
**Since:** N/A

Webster Plaza
Waterbury. CT 06702

American Stock Transfer     800-278-4353
$100 - $10,000/month
Every 90 days beginning 2/12

**Shares to qualify:** 1
**Safekeeping:** Yes
**Accepts foreign:** Yes
**Auto. inv.:** No
**Disc.:** No

FEES: Div: $0; Cash: $0; Cert: $0; Term: fee; Sells weekly, by mail, at market, for comm.

---

## ✳ Weingarten Realty Investors-A ♥

**WRI/NYSE** | REIT

H: 47.55
L: 38.78
**Rec:** 47.55

**Div.:** 3.16
**Paid on:**
3.6.9.12-15
**Since:** 1958

Box 924133
Houston. TX 77292-4133

Mellon Inv. Svcs.     800-550-4689
$100 - $25,000/month
Every 30 days beginning 1/15

**Shares to qualify:** 1 /de ($500)
**Safekeeping:** Yes
**Accepts foreign:** Yes
**Auto. inv.:** Yes
**Disc.:** No

FEES: Div: $0; Cash: $0; Auto. Inv.: $0; Cert: $0; Term: $0; Sells weekly, by mail or phone, at market, for $15 + 12¢/sh.

---

## ✳ Weis Markets, Inc. ♥

**WMK/NYSE** | Retail stores

H: 42.75
L: 31.45
**Rec:** 32.30

**Div.:** 1.08
**Paid on:**
2.5.8.11-26
**Since:** N/A

1000 S. Second St.
Sunbury. PA 17801-0471

American Stock Transfer     800-937-5449
$10 - $3,000/quarter
Every 90 days beginning 2/26

**Shares to qualify:** 50
**Safekeeping:** Yes
**Accepts foreign:** No
**Auto. inv.:** No
**Disc.:** No

FEES: Div: $0; Cash: $0; Cert: $0; Term: $0; Sells weekly, by mail, at market, for comm.

---

## ✳ Wells Fargo & Co. ⊗

**WFC/NYSE** | Banking

H: 56.37
L: 39.62
**Rec:** 46.00

**Div.:** 1.04
**Paid on:**
3.6.9.12-1
**Since:** 1939

Sixth & Marquette Ave.
Minneapolis. MN 55479-1016

Wells Fargo Bank     877-840-0492
$25 - $10,000/month
Every 7 days beginning Thursday

**Shares to qualify:** 1 /de ($250)
**Safekeeping:** Yes
**Accepts foreign:** Yes
**Auto. inv.:** Yes
**Disc.:** No

FEES: Div: 4% to $4 + 3¢/sh.; Cash: $3 + 3¢/sh.; Auto. Inv.: $1; Cert: $0; Term: $10 + 3¢/sh. ; Sells daily, by phone or mail, at avg. price, for $10 + 3¢/sh.

---

## ✳ Wendy's International, Inc. ♥

**WEN/NYSE** | Restaurant

H: 27.93
L: 17.93
**Rec:** 26.77

**Div.:** 0.24
**Paid on:**
3.5.8.11-VARIES
**Since:** 1976

Box 256
Dublin. OH 43017-0256

American Stock Transfer     800-278-4353
$20 - $20,000/year
Every 30 days beginning 1/10

**Shares to qualify:** 1
**Safekeeping:** Yes
**Accepts foreign:** Yes
**Auto. inv.:** Yes
**Disc.:** No

FEES: Div: $0!; Cash: $0!; Auto. Inv.: $0; Cert: $0!; Term: $0; Sells weekly, by mail or fax, at market, for $2 + 4¢/sh.

---

✳ DRIP enrollment through Temper Enrollment Service (see page 180).     **168**

## WesBanco, Inc. ♥

**WSBC/NAS** | Banking
H: 27.75
L: 17.00
**Rec:** 24.75

**Div.:** 0.92
**Paid on:**
1.4.7.10-1
**Since:** N/A

1 Bank Plaza
Wheeling, WV 26003

Fifth Third Bank    800-837-2755
$10 - $5,000/quarter
Every 90 days beginning 1/2

FEES: Div: $0; Cash: $0; Auto. Inv.: $0; Cert: $0; Term: $0; Sells weekly, by mail, at market, for comm.

**Shares to qualify:** 1
**Safekeeping:** Yes
**Accepts foreign:** No
**Auto. inv.:** Yes
**Disc.:** No

---

## West Pharmaceutical Services Inc. ♥

**WST/NYSE** | Packaging, pharmaceutical svcs.
H: 28.35
L: 18.62
**Rec:** 26.96

**Div.:** 0.76
**Paid on:**
2.5.8.11-3
**Since:** 1970

101 Gordon Dr.
Lionville, PA 19341

American Stock Transfer    800-937-5449
$50 - $5,000/month
Every 30 days beginning 1/2

FEES: Div: $0!; Cash: $0!; Cert: $0!; Term: 4¢/sh.; Sells weekly, by mail, at market, for 4¢/sh.

**Shares to qualify:** 1
**Safekeeping:** Yes
**Accepts foreign:** No
**Auto. inv.:** No
**Disc.:** No

---

## Westamerica Bancorporation ♥

**WABC/NAS** | Banking
H: 43.93
L: 28.37
**Rec:** 39.85

**Div.:** 0.84
**Paid on:**
2.5.8.11-15
**Since:** 1983

Box 1250, Inv. Relations, A-2B
Suisun City, CA 94585-1250

Computershare Investor Svcs.    877-588-4258
$100 - $3,000/month
Every 30 days beginning 1/15

FEES: Div: $0!; Cash: $0!; Cert: $5; Term: $15 + 10¢/sh.; Sells monthly, by mail or phone, at avg. price, for $15 + 10¢/sh.

**Shares to qualify:** 1
**Safekeeping:** No
**Accepts foreign:** Yes
**Auto. inv.:** No
**Disc.:** No

---

## Westbank Corp. ♥

**WBKC/NAS** | Bank holding company
H: 9.90
L: 6.62
**Rec:** 9.60

**Div.:** 0.40
**Paid on:**
1.4.7.10-20
**Since:** N/A

225 Park Ave.
West Springfield, MA 01089-3310

Park West Bank & Trust    413-747-1470
$0 - $10,000/quarter
Every 90 days beginning 1/20

FEES: Div: $0!;  Cash: $0!; Cert: $0!; Term: $0, Does not sell through the plan

**Shares to qualify:** 10
**Safekeeping:** Yes
**Accepts foreign:** No
**Auto. inv.:** No
**Disc.:** No

---

## Westcoast Energy Inc. ♥

**WE/NYSE** | Gas pipeline operations
H: 24.56
L: 17.68
**Rec:** 23.73

**Div.:** 0.89
**Paid on:**
3.6.9.12-30
**Since:** 1967

1333 West Georgia St.
Vancouver, BC V6E 3K9 Canada

Computershare Trust Co. of    800-558-0046
$50 - $5,000/quarter Cdn.
Every 90 days beginning varies

FEES: Div: $0!; Cash: $0!; Cert: $0!; Term: $0, Does not sell through the plan

**Shares to qualify:** 1
**Safekeeping:** Yes
**Accepts foreign:** Yes
**Auto. inv.:** No
**Disc.:** Div: 5% Cash: 0%

---

## Western Digital Corp.

**WDC/NYSE** | Mfr. computer hard drives
H: 6.81
L: 2.18
**Rec:** 3.69

**Div.:** 0.00
**Paid on:**
DIV. SUSP.
**Since:** --

8105 Irvine Center Dr., Box 19665
Irvine, CA 92713-9665

American Stock Transfer    888-200-3165
$25 - $10,000/investment
Every day days beginning daily

FEES: Div: n/o; Cash: $2.50 + 10¢/sh.; Auto. Inv.: $2.50 + 10¢/sh.; Cert: $0; Term: $7.50 + 10¢/sh.; Sells daily, by phone, mail, fax, or Internet, at market, for $7.50 + 10¢/sh.

**Shares to qualify:** 1 /de ($250)
**Safekeeping:** Yes
**Accepts foreign:** Yes
**Auto. inv.:** Yes
**Disc.:** No

---

## Western Resources, Inc. ♥

**WR/NYSE** | Utility-electric
H: 25.87
L: 16.62
**Rec:** 18.10

**Div.:** 1.20
**Paid on:**
1.4.7.10-1
**Since:** 1926

Box 889
Topeka, KS 66601-0889

Western Resources    800-527-2495
$50 - $10,000/month
Every 15 days beginning 1/2

FEES: Div: $0!; Cash: $0!; Auto. Inv.: $0; Cert: $0; Term: 7.5¢/sh.; Sells weekly, by mail or fax, at avg. price, for 7.5¢/sh.

**Shares to qualify:** 1 /de ($250)
**Safekeeping:** Yes
**Accepts foreign:** Yes
**Auto. inv.:** Yes
**Disc.:** Div: 3% Cash: 0%

---

## ✱ Westvaco Corp. ♥

**W/NYSE** | Paper, chemicals
H: 30.62
L: 22.70
**Rec:** 26.31 | 299 Park Ave.
New York. NY 10171

**Div.:** 0.88 | Bank of New York    800-432-0140
**Paid on:** | $25 - $5,000/quarter
1.4.7.10-1 | Every 7 days beginning varies
**Since:** 1896 | FEES: Div: $0!; Cash: $0!; Auto. Inv.: $0; Cert: $0!; Term: $0; Sells weekly, by mail, at market, for 5¢/sh.

Shares to qualify: 1 /de ($250)
Safekeeping: Yes
Accepts foreign: Yes
Auto. inv.: Yes
Disc.: No

## ✱ Weyerhaeuser Co. ⊗

**WY/NYSE** | Forestry & wood products
H: 63.50
L: 36.06
**Rec:** 57.95 | Box 2999
Tacoma. WA 98477-2999

**Div.:** 1.60 | Mellon Inv. Svcs.    800-561-4405
**Paid on:** | $100 - $25,000/quarter
3.6.9.12-4 | Every 30 days beginning 1/2
**Since:** 1933 | FEES: Div: 4% to $1.50; Cash: $5 + comm.; Cert: $5; Term: $5 + comm.; Sells weekly, by mail or phone, at market, for $15 + comm.

Shares to qualify: 1
Safekeeping: Yes
Accepts foreign: Yes
Auto. inv.: No
Disc.: No

## ✱ WGL Holdings, Inc.

**WGL/NYSE** | Utility-gas
H: 31.50
L: 24.81
**Rec:** 27.63 | 1100 H St. NW
Washington. DC 20080

**Div.:** 1.26 | Bank of New York    800-330-5682
**Paid on:** | $25 - $20,000/quarter
2.5.8.11-1 | Every 30 days beginning 1/2
**Since:** 1852 | FEES: Div: 10¢/sh.; Cash: 10¢/sh.; Cert: $0; Term: $0; Sells weekly, by mail or fax, at market, for 10¢/sh.

Shares to qualify: 1
Safekeeping: Yes
Accepts foreign: Yes
Auto. inv.: No
Disc.: No

## ✱ Whirlpool Corp. ⊗

**WHR/NYSE** | Household appliances
H: 71.93
L: 31.50
**Rec:** 67.69 | 2000 N. M-63, MD 2800
Benton Harbor. MI 49022-2692

**Div.:** 1.36 | First Chicago Trust    800-446-2617
**Paid on:** | $100 - $250,000/year
3.6.9-15 & | Every 7 days beginning varies
**Since:** 1929 | FEES: Div: 5% to $3 + 3¢/sh.; Cash: $5 + 3¢/sh.; Auto. Inv.: $2 + 3¢/sh.; Cert: $0!; Term: $0; Sells daily, by phone or mail, at market, for $15 + 12¢/sh.

Shares to qualify: 1 /de ($1000)
Safekeeping: Yes
Accepts foreign: Yes
Auto. inv.: Yes
Disc.: No

## ✱ Whitney Holding Co. ♥

**WTNY/NASD** | Bank holding company
H: 47.03
L: 33.12
**Rec:** 46.93 | Box 61260
New Orleans. LA 70161-1260

**Div.:** 1.52 | Bank of New York    800-432-0140
**Paid on:** | $50 - $5,000/quarter
1.4.7.10-1 | Every 90 days beginning 1/2
**Since:** 1962 | FEES: Div: $0; Cash: $0; Cert: $0; Term: $0, Does not sell through the plan

Shares to qualify: 1
Safekeeping: Yes
Accepts foreign: Yes
Auto. inv.: No
Disc.: No

## ✱ Wilmington Trust Co. ♥

**WL/NYSE** | Banking
H: 67.00
L: 46.00
**Rec:** 66.09 | 1100 N. Market St., Rodney Sq. North
Wilmington. DE 19890-0001

**Div.:** 1.92 | Wells Fargo Bank    800-999-9867
**Paid on:** | $10 - $5,000/quarter
2.5.8.11-15 | Every 30 days beginning 1/15
**Since:** 1914 | FEES: Div: $0!; Cash: $0!; Auto. Inv.: $0; Cert: $0!; Term: $10 + 10¢/sh.; Sells daily, by mail or fax, at market, for $10 + 10¢/sh.

Shares to qualify: 1
Safekeeping: Yes
Accepts foreign: No
Auto. inv.: Yes
Disc.: No

## ✱ Winn-Dixie Stores, Inc. ♥

**WIN/NYSE** | Retail stores
H: 33.12
L: 13.43
**Rec:** 23.39 | Box B
Jacksonville. FL 32203-0297

**Div.:** 1.02 | First Chicago Trust    888-822-5593
**Paid on:** | $10 - $10,000/month
MONTHLY-1 | Every 30 days beginning 1/2
**Since:** 1934 | FEES: Div: $0!; Cash: $0!; Auto. Inv.: $1; Cert: $0!; Term: $10; Sells daily, by mail, fax, or phone, at market, for $10 + 12¢/sh.

Shares to qualify: 10
Safekeeping: Yes
Accepts foreign: No
Auto. inv.: Yes
Disc.: No

---

## * Winston Hotels, Inc. ♥

**WXH/NYSE** | REIT

H: 10.77
L: 6.87
**Rec:** 9.70

**Div.:** 1.12
**Paid on:**
1.4.7.10-18
**Since:**1994

2626 Glenwood Ave., Ste. 200
Raleigh. NC 27608

Branch Banking & Trust     800-213-4314
$100 - $10,000/month
Every 7 days beginning Wednesday

FEES: Div: $0!; Cash: $0!; Auto. Inv.: $0; Cert: $0!; Term: $0; Sells within 3 bus. days, by mail, at avg. price, for 5¢/sh.

**Shares to qualify:** 1 /de ($250)
**Safekeeping:** Yes
**Accepts foreign:** Yes
**Auto. inv.:** Yes
**Disc.:** Div: 0% Cash:
0-5%

---

## * Wisconsin Energy Corp. ♥

**WEC/NYSE** | Utility-electric, gas

H: 24.62
L: 17.87
**Rec:** 23.04

**Div.:** 0.80
**Paid on:**
3.6.9.12-1
**Since:**1942

231 West Michigan St., Box 2949
Milwaukee. WI 53201

Boston Eq.     800-558-9663
$25 - $100,000/quarter
Every 15 days beginning 1/2

FEES: Div: $0!; Cash: $0!; Auto. Inv.: $0; Cert: $0!; Term: $0!; Sells daily, by phone or mail, at market, for $15 + 5¢/sh.

**Shares to qualify:** 1 /de ($250)
**Safekeeping:** Yes
**Accepts foreign:** Yes
**Auto. inv.:** Yes
**Disc.:** No

---

## * Woodward Governor Co. ♥

**WGOV/NAS** | Electronic inst. & controls

H: 91.00
L: 29.75
**Rec:** 75.32

**Div.:** 0.93
**Paid on:**
3.6.9.12-1
**Since:**N/A

5001 North Second St.
Rockford. IL 61125

American Stock Transfer     800-278-4353
$25 - $1,000/quarter
Every 90 days beginning 3/1

FEES: Div: $0!; Cash: $0!; Cert: $0!; Term: $0; Sells within 10 bus. days, by mail, at market, for comm.

**Shares to qualify:** 1
**Safekeeping:** No
**Accepts foreign:** Yes
**Auto. inv.:** No
**Disc.:** No

---

## * Worthington Industries ♥

**WOR/NYSE** | Metals

H: 14.80
L: 6.37
**Rec:** 14.00

**Div.:** 0.64
**Paid on:**
3.6.9.12-27
**Since:**1968

1205 Dearborn Dr.
Columbus. OH 43085

Boston Eq.     800-730-4001
$50 - $5,000/month
Every 30 days beginning 1/31

FEES: Div: $0!; Cash: $0!; Auto. Inv.: $0; Cert: $0!; Term: $0; Sells within 10 bus. days, by mail, at market, for $0

**Shares to qualify:** 1
**Safekeeping:** Yes
**Accepts foreign:** Yes
**Auto. inv.:** Yes
**Disc.:** No

---

## * WPS Resources Corp. ♥

**WPS/NYSE** | Utility-electric, gas

H: 39.00
L: 29.81
**Rec:** 33.75

**Div.:** 2.10
**Paid on:**
3.6.9.12-20
**Since:**1953

Box 19001
Green Bay. WI 54307-9001

WPS Resources Corp.     800-236-1551
$25 - $100,000/year
Every 15 days beginning 5th & 20th

FEES: Div: $0!; Cash: $0!; Auto. Inv.: $0; Cert: $0!; Term: $0; Sells within 5 bus. days, by mail or fax, at market, for 25¢/sh.

**Shares to qualify:** 1 /de ($100)
**Safekeeping:** Yes
**Accepts foreign:** Yes
**Auto. inv.:** Yes
**Disc.:** No

---

## * Wrigley (Wm. Jr.) Co. ♥

**WWY/NYSE** | Chewing gum prod.

H: 50.96
L: 35.09
**Rec:** 50.08

**Div.:** 0.76
**Paid on:**
2.5.8.11-1
**Since:**1923

410 North Michigan Ave.
Chicago. IL 60611-4287

First Chicago Trust     800-446-2617
$50 - $5,000/month
Every 30 days beginning 1st bus. day /month

FEES: Div: $0!; Cash: $0!; Cert: $0!; Term: $0; Sells monthly, by mail, at avg. price, for $0!

**Shares to qualify:** 1
**Safekeeping:** Yes
**Accepts foreign:** Yes
**Auto. inv.:** No
**Disc.:** No

---

## * Xcel Energy Inc. ♥

**XEL/NYSE** | Utility-electric & gas

H: 31.85
L: 24.06
**Rec:** 26.90

**Div.:** 1.50
**Paid on:**
1.4.7.10-20
**Since:**1949

800 Nicollet Mall, Ste. 3000
Minneapolis. MN 55402-2023

Wells Fargo Bank     877-778-6786
$50 - $100,000/year
Every 7 days beginning Friday

FEES: Div: $0; Cash: $0; Auto. Inv.: 5¢/sh.; Cert: $0; Term: $0; Sells within 15 bus. days, by mail, fax or phone, at avg. price, for $10 + 10¢/sh.

**Shares to qualify:** 1 /de ($1000)
**Safekeeping:** Yes
**Accepts foreign:** Yes
**Auto. inv.:** Yes
**Disc.:** No

---

## ✱ Xerox Corp. ♥

**XRX/NYSE**
H: 18.50
L: 3.75
**Rec:** 8.32
**Div.:** 0.00
**Paid on:**
DIV. SUSP.
**Since:** --

**Business equipment**
800 Long Ridge Rd., Box 1600
Stamford. CT 06904

Boston Eq.      800-828-6396
$10 - $5,000/month
Every 30 days beginning 1/2

FEES: Div: n/o; Cash: $0; Cert: $0; Term: $10 + 15¢/sh.; Sells weekly, by mail, at market, for $10 + 15¢/sh.

**Shares to qualify:** 1
**Safekeeping:** Yes
**Accepts foreign:** Yes
**Auto. inv.:** No
**Disc.:** No

---

## ✱ XTO Energy Inc. ♥

**XTO/NYSE**
H: 21.73
L: 8.33
**Rec:** 13.74
**Div.:** 0.04
**Paid on:**
1.4.7.10-15
**Since:** 1993

**Oil & gas development, production**
810 Houston St., Ste. 2000
Fort Worth. TX 76102-6298

Mellon Inv. Svcs.      888-877-2892
$50 - $10,000/month
Every 7 days beginning varies

FEES: Div: $0; Cash: $0; Auto. Inv.: $0; Cert: $0; Term: $15 + 12¢/sh.; Sells weekly, by mail or phone, at market, for $15 + 12¢/sh.

**Shares to qualify:** 1 /de ($500)
**Safekeeping:** Yes
**Accepts foreign:** Yes
**Auto. inv.:** Yes
**Disc.:** No

---

## ✱ Yahoo! Inc. ⊗

**YHOO/NASD**
H: 140.00
L: 11.37
**Rec:** 15.42
**Div.:** 0.00
**Paid on:**
N/0
**Since:** N/0

**Internet media co.**
3420 Central Exp.
Santa Clara. CA 95051

Boston Eq.      877-946-6487
$50 - $150,000/year
Every Tues. & Thurs. days beginning Tues.

FEES: Div: n/o; Cash: $5 + 5¢/sh.; Auto. Inv.: $2 + 5¢/sh.; Cert: $0; Term: $10 + 12¢/sh.; Sells daily, by phone, mail, fax, or Internet, at market, for $10 + 12¢/sh.

**Shares to qualify:** 1 /de ($250)
**Safekeeping:** Yes
**Accepts foreign:** Yes
**Auto. inv.:** Yes
**Disc.:** No

---

## ✱ York International Corp. ⊗

**YRK/NYSE**
H: 36.79
L: 19.00
**Rec:** 35.00
**Div.:** 0.60
**Paid on:**
3.6.9.12-29
**Since:** 1991

**Mfr. climate control systems, HVAC**
631 South Richland Ave.
York. PA 17403

Mellon Inv. Svcs.      800-437-6726
$100 - $10,000/month
Every 7 days beginning varies

FEES: Div: $0; Cash: $5; Auto. Inv.: $0; Cert: $0; Term: $0; Sells weekly, by mail or phone, at market, for $15 + 12¢/sh.

**Shares to qualify:** 1 /de ($1000)
**Safekeeping:** Yes
**Accepts foreign:** Yes
**Auto. inv.:** Yes
**Disc.:** No

---

## ✱ Zions Bancorp ♥

**ZION/NASD**
H: 64.00
L: 40.62
**Rec:** 58.51
**Div.:** 0.80
**Paid on:**
1.4.7.10-25
**Since:** N/A

**Banking**
One South Main
Salt Lake City. UT 84111

Zions First Nat'l Bank      801-524-4624
$10 - $5,000/quarter
Every 90 days beginning 1/20

FEES: Div: $0!; Cash: $0!; Cert: $0!; Term: $0,Does not sell through the plan

**Shares to qualify:** 1
**Safekeeping:** No
**Accepts foreign:** No
**Auto. inv.:** No
**Disc.:** No

---

## ✱ Zweig Fund (The)

**ZF/NYSE**
H: 10.75
L: 9.15
**Rec:** 9.49
**Div.:** 0.88
**Paid on:**
1.4.7.10-VARIES
**Since:** 1987

**Capital appreciation fund**
900 3rd Ave., c/o Zweig Advisors
New York. NY 10022

State St. Bank      800-272-2700
$100 - $3,000/month
Every 30 days beginning 1/15

FEES: Div: 5¢/sh.; Cash: 5¢/sh.; Auto. Inv.: $0; Cert: $0; Term: $0; Sells daily, by mail or phone, at market, for 5¢/sh.

**Shares to qualify:** 1
**Safekeeping:** Yes
**Accepts foreign:** No
**Auto. inv.:** Yes
**Disc.:** No

---

# Closed-End Funds

The following listing includes closed-end funds that offer direct investment plans. Dividends may be irregular, and cash may be accepted as seldom as once or twice a year. Although fund names may describe their general category, they are no guarantee of the exact securities held. In addition, potential investors should be wary of fees, fund turnover, and capital gains distributions.

* Adams Express Co.
* Allmerica Securities Trust
* Argentina Fund Inc. (The)
* ASA Ltd.
* Austria Fund (The)
* Bancroft Convertible Fund, Inc.
* Blue Chip Value Fund, Inc.
* Brazil Fund, Inc. (The)
* Brazilian Equity Fund (The), Inc.
* Canadian General Investments, Inc.
* Central European Equity Fund
* Chile Fund (The), Inc.
* CNA Income Shares, Inc.
* Cornerstone Strategie Return Fund, Inc.
* Dresdner RCM Global Strategic Income Fund
* Duff & Phelps Utilities Income Inc.
* Ellsworth Convertible Growth & Income Fund
* Emerging Markets Floating Rate Fund Inc.
* Emerging Markets Income Fund Inc. (The)
* Emerging Markets Income II Fund Inc. (The)
* Emerging Markets Telecomm. Fund, Inc.
* First Australia Prime Income Fund, Inc.
* Gabelli Convertible Securities Fund, Inc.
* Gabelli Equity Trust, Inc.
* Gabelli Global Multimedia Trust
* Germany Fund (The)

* Independent Bank Corp. (MA)
* India Fund
* Indonesia Fund, Inc. (The)
  Irish Investment Fund
* Italy Fund Inc. (The)
* Korea Fund, Inc. (The)
* Liberty ALL-STAR Equity Fund
* Liberty ALL-STAR Growth Fund, Inc.
* Lincoln Nat'l Convert. Securities Fund
* Lincoln Nat'l Income Fund
* Morgan Stanley Dean Witter Asia-Pacific Fund, Inc.
* New America High Income Fund, Inc.
* New Germany Fund (The)
* Petroleum & Resources Corp.
* Progressive Return Fund
* Royce Focus Trust, Inc.
* Royce Micro-Cap Trust, Inc.
* Royce Value Trust, Inc.
* Salomon Bros. Fund
* Salomon Bros. High Income Fund Inc.
* Scudder New Asia Fund
* Spain Fund (The)
* Taiwan Fund (The)
* Thai Fund
* Zweig Fund (The)

**\* Available through the Temper Enrollment Service**

# American Depository Receipts (ADRs)

The following listing includes foreign companies that trade as American Depository Receipts (ADRs) and are offered under standard high-fee plans sponsored by plan administrators. The standard terms are as follows:

Bank of New York: Minimum initial investment $200; enrollment fee $10; cash investment fee $5 plus 10¢ per share; reinvestment fee 5% up to $5 plus 10¢ per share; invests weekly; sales fee $5 plus 10¢ per share.

Citibank: Minimum initial investment $250; enrollment fee $10 plus 10¢ per share; cash investment $5 plus 10¢ per share; reinvestment fee 10¢ per share; invests weekly; sales fee $10 plus 12¢ per share.

Morgan Guaranty Trust: Minimum initial investment $250; enrollment fee $15; cash investment fee $5 plus 12¢ per share; reinvestment fee 5% up to $2.50; invests weekly; sales fee $5 plus 12¢ per share.

Both Bank of New York's "Global BuyDirect" and Morgan Guaranty's "Shareholder Services Plan" allow investments from $50 to $100,000 per year, with automatic investing, subject to fees. The third agent, Citibank, has launched an "International Direct Investment" plan with the same cash limits, and currently offers 15 ADR companies, which include Akzo Nobel N.V., AEGON N.V., CRH plc, Deutsche Telekon AG, Elsevier N.V., Pioneer Electronic Corp., Reed Int'l plc, Sulzer Medica, Ltd., and Nokia. Its fees for Nokia and Hanson are lower, as shown in the general listing.

## ADRs with DRIPs

ABN AMRO Holdings N.V.
Adecco SA
AEGON N.V.
AFP Provida
Akzo Nobel NV
Alcatel Alsthom SA
Allied Irish Banks, plc
AMCOR Ltd.
AMVESCAP plc
Anangel-American Shipholdings Ltd.
Anglogold Ltd.
Anntenna TV
APT Satellite
Aracruz Celulose SA
ARCADIS NV
ARM Holdings plc
Ashanti Goldfields Co.
Asia Pulp & Paper Co. Ltd.
Asia Satellite Tele. Holdings Ltd.
ASM Lithography Holding NV
AstraZeneca Group plc
* Aventis
* AXA SA
Baltimore Technologies plc
Banco BHIF, SA
Banco Bilbao Vizcaya
Banco Comercial Portugues SA ADS
Banco Ganadero (common)
Banco Ind. Colombiano, SA
Banco Rio de la Plata, SA
Banco Santiago
Banco Wiese Limitado
Bank of Ireland
Bank of Tokyo-Mitsubishi
Barclays Bank plc
BE Semiconductor Industries
Beijing Yanhua Pet. Co. Ltd.
Benetton Grp. SpA
Biora AB
Blue Square-Israel Ltd.
BOC Group plc (The)
Boral Ltd.
* BP Amoco plc
British Airways plc
British American Tobacco plc
British Energy plc
British Telecommunications plc
Cadbury Schweppes plc
Canon Inc.
Cantab Pharmaceuticals plc
Carlton Communications plc

Chicago Bridge & Iron Co. N.V.
China Eastern Airlines Corp.
China Southern Airlines Co. Ltd.
China Telecom Ltd.
CNH Global N.V.
Coca-Cola FEMSA
Companhia Brasileira de Distribuicao
Companhia Paranaense de Energia
Compania Cervecerias Unida SA
Compania de Minas Buenaventura
Cresud S.A.C.I.F. y A.
CRH plc
CSR Ltd.
DaimlerChrysler AG
Dassault Systemes SA
De Rigo S.p.A.
Delta Galil Industries
Deutsche Telekom AG
Diageo plc ADS
Digitale Telekabel AG
Ducati Motor Holding
Durbam Roodeport Deep Ltd.
ECsoft Group plc.
Eidos plc
ELAN Corp., plc
Electrolux, AB
Elsevier N.V.
Embratel Participacoes SA
Empresas ICA, SA de C.V.
Empresas Telex-Chile
Endesa SA
Energis plc
ENI SpA
EON AG
Epcos AG
Equant NV
Espirito Santo Financial Grp., SA
Fiat SpA
Fila Holding S.p.A.
Flamel Technologies
Formula Systems Ltd.
France Telecom
Fresenius Medical Care AG
Gallaher Group plc
General Cable
GlaxoSmithKline plc
Groupe AB ADS
Groupe Danone
Grupo Casa Saba SA de C.V.
Grupo Elektra, SA de C.V.
Grupo Imsa, SA de C.V.

**\* Available through the Temper Enrollment Service**

Grupo Industrial Durango, SA
Grupo Tribasa
Guangshen Railway Co. Ltd.
* Hanson plc
Harmony Gold Mining Co. Ltd.
Havas Advertising
* HSBC Holding plc ADR
Huaneng Power Int'l, Inc.
Ilog SA
Imperial Chemical Ind. plc
Imperial Tobacco Group plc
Industrias Bachoco
Industrie Natuzzi SPA ADS
ING Groep N.V.
Insignia Solutions plc
IRSA Inversiones y Representaciones SA
Ispat International N.V.
Jazztel plc
Jefferson Smurfit plc
Koor Industries Ltd.
Korea Electric Power Corp.
Kyocera Corp.
Lihir Gold Ltd. ADS
LM Ericsson Telephone Co.
Logitech International SA
Luxottica Grp. ADS
LVMH Moet Hennessy L.V.
Macronix Int'l. Co. Ltd.
Maderas y Sinteticos Sociedad Anonima
Magyar Tavkozlesi Rt. (MATAV)
Makita
Matav-Cable Systems Media
Matsushita Electric Ind. Co.,Ltd.
Mavesa, SA
Merant plc
Metso Corp.
Modern Times Group
Movil@ccess SA de CV
National Australia Bank Ltd.
NEC Corp.
Nera A.S. ADS
* Nestle SA
New York Broker Deutschland
Nice Systems Ltd.
Nippon Telephone & Telegraph Corp.
* Nokia Corp.
Norsk Hydro A.S.
Novo Nordisk A/S
Novogen Ltd.
Nuevo Grupo Iusacell
OAO Rostelecom
OAO Tatneft
Oce-van der Grinten N.V.
Orbital Engine Corp. Ltd.
P.T. IndoSat
P.T. Pasifik Satelit Nusantara
P.T. Telkom
P&O Princess Cruises plc
Pacific Dunlop Ltd.
Pepsi-Gemex, SA de C.V.
Pfeiffer Vacuum Technology AG
Pioneer Electronic Corp.
Pohang Iron & Steel Co. Ltd.
Portugal Telecom
PowerGen plc
Rangold & Exploration Co.
Rank Group plc (The)
Reed International plc
Repsol S.A. ADS
Reuters Group plc
Rio Tinto plc

Royal Ahold
Royal Dutch Petroleum Co.
Ryanair
Sanpaolo di Torino-IMI
Santander Central Hispano Bank & Trust Ltd.
Santos Ltd.
Sappi Ltd.
Savia SA de C.V.
Sawako Corp.
Scoot.com plc
SCOR
Scottish Power plc
Senetek plc ADS
* Shell Trans. & Trading Co. plc ADR
Shire Pharmaceuticals plc
Signet Group plc
Siemens AG
Sinopec Shanghai Petrochemical
SmartForce plc
Sociedad Quimica y Minera
Sony Corp.
STET Hellas Telecomm. SA
STMicroelectronics NV
Sulzer Medica
Super-Sol Ltd.
Supermercados Unimarc SA
Swedish Match AB
TDK Corp.
Tele2 AB
Tele Celular Sul Participacoes SA
Tele Centro Oeste Celular Participacoes SA
Tele Leste Celular Participacoes SA
Tele Nordesto Celular Participacoes SA
Tele Norte Celular Participacoes SA
Tele Norte Leste Participacoes SA
Tele Sudeste Celular Participacoes SA
Telecom Argentina Stet-France Telecom SA
Telecom Corp. of New Zealand Ltd.
Telecom Italia SpA
Telecomunicacoes Brasileiras SA
Telefonica del Peru SA
Telefonos de Mexico, SA de C.V.
Telemig Celular Participacoes SA
Telesp Celular Participacoes SA
Telesp Participacoes SA
Telewest Communications plc
Telstra Corp. Ltd.
Thomson Multimedia
Tomkins plc
Total Fina Elf SA
Toyota Motor Corp.
Tricom, SA
Tubos de Acero de Mexico SA
TV Azteca
Unilever N.V.
Unilever plc
VersaTel Telecom Int'l N.V.
VimpelCom
Vina Concha y Toro, SA
Vodafone Group plc
* Volvo AB
* W Holding Co.
Wacoal Corp.
Waterford Wedgewood plc
Wavecom SA
Westpac Banking Corp.
Xeikon, N.V.
Xenova Grp. plc
Yanzhou Coal Mining Co. Ltd.
Zindart Ltd.

**\* Available through the Temper Enrollment Service**

# General Instructions About Registration

## Overview (more specific information can be found on the following pages)

### Individual Name:

Enter your full name, address, and Social Security number. If your first name is an initial, you must send proof (a copy of your birth certificate, passport, SS card).

### Other Than Single Registration:

Indicate the proper form of registration. For example, JT TEN for joint tenancy accounts, where the surviving tenant receives the property automatically.

### Minor Registrations–USA:

Uniform Gift to Minors Act or Uniform Transfer to Minors Act: In the United States, name the adult first as custodian for the child and indicate the state, for example, "John Doe, custodian for Jane Doe, UGTMA(UTMA) of NY." Use the child's SS number.

### Minor Registrations–Canada:

Uniform Gift to Minors Act or Uniform Transfer to Minors Act: For Canadians, name the adult first as trustee for the child, then the minor's name followed by "a minor," e.g., "John Doe in trust for Jane Doe, a minor." Note: For other countries, consult a lawyer.

### Trusts:

For registrations involving trust agreements, be sure to indicate the date: "Robert Doe, trustee, UTA-DTD 1/1/90 for the benefit of (FBO) Jane Doe, beneficiary." (If the Temper Enrollment Service is handling the transaction, you must send copies of the first page and the signature page showing trustee, trust name, and date. Temper will not open an account without this information.)

For IRA accounts, enter the name of the custodian first, then the name of the IRA and the date the account was established: "XYZ Bank, custodian for John Doe under IRA plan dated ____."

### Corporations, Partnerships, and Investment Clubs:

For registrations involving corporations, partnerships, or investment clubs, be sure to include the full name of the entity. (If Temper is handling the transaction, it requires proof of the entity's existence, such as the certificate of incorporation, partnership agreement, or investment club agreement.)

## W-9 Forms:

Certain companies require a signed W-9 form in order to open an account. If you are using the Temper Enrollment Service to establish your account with the following companies, sign and return a W-9 form with your order: AFL, BC, CB, CTWS, CV, D, GAS, ITT, MKC, OK, PZL, SLE, SNV, and SO.

## Enrollment Cards:

In addition to a W-9 form, if you are using the Temper Enrollment Service, you should send a signed enrollment card along with your order form when ordering the following companies: AFL, ALE, BN, CTL, CV, GAS, ITT, JCI, MSEX, NCC, NWN, PZL, SNV, STR, and UPC.

To obtain forms, call 800-295-2550, or contact Temper by mail at 555 Theodroe Fremd Ave., Suite B-103, Rye, New York 10580.

# Whose Name Should It Be In?

How should you own your stocks? Of course, you can own them outright, by yourself (in law, called fee simple), and dispose of them as you wish. But suppose you buy property with one or more persons, or just want to designate someone as co-owner. In general, you have the following options.

## Joint Tenants with Right of Survivorship

If there is someone whom you would like to have the property after your death, a convenient form of ownership is "joint tenancy with the right of survivorship" (JT TEN).

On the death of one of the joint tenants, acquiring sole title does not require probate of a will, or any intestacy proceedings absent a will. The surviving tenant receives the property automatically. (Registering in the individual name after the death of the joint tenant may require presentation of a death certificate, and in some states, an estate-tax waiver.)

Creating a joint tenancy does not remove the property from the taxable estate of the first to die. Therefore, if there is a taxable estate (there may not be because the marital or charitable deduction may eliminate estate taxes), responsibility for the tax will fall on the estate unless it can be proved that the assets were the property of the surviving tenant. (Regardless of whether or not there is a federal tax due, there is the responsibility to file a federal tax return if the gross estate is $675,000 for the year 2000, $700,000 for the year 2001, and gradually increasing to $1 million in the year 2006.)

For married joint tenants, the IRS presumes that half of the property is part of the estate of the first to die—unless there are canceled checks or other proof that all the property, or a different portion of it, was purchased by the surviving tenant.

Parents (or grandparents) may wish to establish joint tenancies with adult children, if they wish to transfer property without probate or the public disclosure of a will. Friends or roommates may elect the joint tenancy registration in order to establish that the property will go directly to the surviving tenant and not to the heirs of the decedent.

Be aware that creation of a joint tenancy establishes immediate rights in the other joint tenant, and those rights cannot be severed by the creator of the joint tenancy. So you won't be able to change your mind and remove a joint tenant at a later date, unless the joint tenant agrees.

Although joint tenancy is convenient for married couples, in some cases, it may impede sophisticated estate planning for owners of large estates. (In some states, joint tenancy between husbands and wives has the special designation of "tenancy by the entirety" but its characteristics are the same as those of the traditional joint tenancy with rights of survivorship. See below.)

Joint tenancy can be a problem in the case of a second marriage, especially if each spouse has children from a previous marriage. When the first spouse dies, it is the survivor who will inherit the jointly held property, not the children of the spouse who died. Tenancy in common would be a better choice in that situation if you wanted to protect the children.

When deciding whether to hold property jointly, consider the ramifications for estate planning, which will vary according to state law, so you may want to consult an attorney. That's especially true in the 10 "community property" areas (Arizona, California, Idaho, Louisiana, Nevada, New Mexico, Puerto Rico, Texas, Washington, and Wisconsin), where each spouse owns 50% of all property acquired during a marriage.

You can leave cash without a will, in some states, by creating bank accounts in trust for another. No formal trust instrument is required and the beneficiary does not acquire any interest in the property until the death of the owner. There is no tax benefit to these accounts.

### Tenants by the Entirety

This is a special type of joint tenancy between a husband and wife. Upon the death of one spouse, the property automatically passes to the surviving spouse. The advantage of tenancy by the entirety (TBE) is that, in some states, a creditor of one spouse may not collect against property held in a TBE, whereas in a JT TEN, a creditor of only one joint tenant may move against that tenant's share in the property.

### Tenants in Common

For persons who wish to maintain their own legal interest in property, but desire to share with another the acquisition and cost of maintenance, "tenancy in common" is an appropriate form of ownership. With this registration, the tenants are equal owners (unless they otherwise agree) and have the right to transfer their respective ownership interest, either while living or at death. In the latter case, the property would pass according to the provisions of a will, or, if there is no will, to the heirs according to state law. Any income earned by the property would be taxed equally to the tenants in common, unless, by agreement, the tenancy is not to be equal. Any such agreement should be in writing to avoid the possibility of disputes.

## Minors

In all states, 18 is the age of majority (except for Alabama and Nebraska, where the minimum age is 19, and for Mississippi, where the minimum age is 21; it is also 21 in Puerto Rico).

Registration of stock in the name of minors is not advisable since the sale or transfer of the stock can be difficult. Transfer agents may not process a sale or assignment by a minor and they may require a court-appointed guardian, not a natural guardian. For this reason, it is preferable to register stock for minors under the Uniform Gift to Minor's Act.

## Uniform Gift to Minors Act

The Uniform Gift to Minors Act or the Uniform Transfer to Minors Act is a popular form of ownership for property to be given to minors. All states have adopted one or the other of these acts, as has the District of Columbia, but not Puerto Rico.

Under these acts, the named custodian manages the property for the minor until he or she reaches majority (or, in some states, until age 21). One can remove the property from one's own estate by naming someone other than oneself as custodian. In this case, the tax responsibility for the income would fall to the child and be taxed at his or her rate. (Be sure to name an alternative custodian, because under many state laws, a court proceeding may be necessary to name a successor custodian if the beneficiary is under age 14.)

## Trusts

A trust is a legal device by which property is held by a named trustee for the benefit of another. Trusts are useful in the following situations: (1) where the trust creator seeks to protect the beneficiary from his or her own fiscal irresponsibility, creditors of the beneficiary, or marital claims on the beneficiary; (2) where the beneficiary is unable to manage his or her own financial affairs; (3) where the creator desires to provide income to a beneficiary, but does not wish such person to receive the principal of the trust; (4) where the creator desires to remove the property from his or her estate, in accordance with the rules of the IRS. The income generated by the trust can be distributed to the beneficiary and would be taxable to the beneficiary.

### Corporations, Partnerships, and Investment Clubs

You may wish to register your stock in the name of an entity with which you are involved, such as your business or investment club. Remember to use the tax identification number of the entity when registering.

A corporation is an association of one or more shareholders having a legal identity separate and distinct from the purpose of running a business. An investment club is usually a partnership made up of people interested in investing within a group.

### TODs to Avoid Probate

A "transfer on death" (TOD) registration provides automatic transfer of ownership at the owner's death. You might name an adult child, for instance. At your death, the ownership changes immediately after presentation of a death certificate and a medallion signature guarantee. The Temper Enrollment Service will not process TOD registrations.

TOD registration is now available in 38 states: Alabama, Alaska, Arizona, Arkansas, Colorado, Connecticut, Delaware, Florida, Idaho, Illinois, Indiana, Iowa, Kansas, Maryland, Michigan, Minnesota, Mississippi, Missouri, Montana, Nebraska, Nevada, New Hampshire, New Jersey, New Mexico, North Dakota, Ohio, Oklahoma, Oregon, Pennsylvania, South Carolina, South Dakota, Tennessee, Utah, Virginia, Washington, West Virginia, Wisconsin, and Wyoming.

# How Does the Temper Enrollment Service Work?

You can use the enrollment service offered by Temper of the Times Communications, Inc., a member of the NASD and an affiliate of *The Moneypaper*, to become enrolled in the direct investment plan of any company indicated with an asterisk in this Guide. The Temper service will do all the paperwork to get the account opened and get you enrolled in a DRIP.*

Temper will purchase and transfer the number of shares you order (which must be at least the minimum necessary to qualify for the plan you choose, but may be as many as 100 shares) and request that you be enrolled in the plan as a shareholder.

Once your account is established, you will be able to send investments directly to the transfer agent for the company; in some instances, the company acts as its own transfer agent. No further fees are paid to the Temper Enrollment Service. The charge to become enrolled is $30; however, subscribers to any Moneypaper Inc. publication are charged a discounted service fee of $15 if the stock is featured in the current issue of the publication; otherwise, subscribers pay $20. Temper acknowledges your order as soon as it is received. You will receive a "Confirmation/Account Statement" after the stock(s) you ordered have been purchased. This statement will state the purchase price, service fee, and commission paid for each stock. The confirmation will be accompanied by either a refund check or a request for additional money, as applicable.

Temper is in contact with the transfer agents until the account is opened. Status reports/notifications are sent if there is an excessive delay in opening an account. You are expected to remit enough money to cover the cost of the share(s), the service fee(s), and a 10% refundable cushion against any upward movement in the market price of the stock. Any excess funds will be returned to you with the final accounting, at which time you will be billed for any underpayment.

Here is how it works: Your order is entered and acknowledged. With your acknowledgment, you are informed of your order number and given the opportunity to review and make any corrections to the registration. If the registration is correct, you do not need to return the notification. If a correction is required, it is important that you respond immediately. It's crucial that your name and Social Security number are correct for tax purposes, as well as to avoid bothersome and expensive corrections after the account is open.

### Enrollment Fee (per company)

|  | Featured Stocks | Other Stocks |
|---|---|---|
| Subscribers | $15 | $20 |
| Nonsubscribers | $30 | $30 |

## How Long Does It Take?

Each company plan is different and each transfer agent has its own method of operating. Some companies automatically enroll you in the plan without your first signing an authorization form. Some will open an account on a book-entry basis. In some cases, a stock certificate will be sent to you by the company's transfer agent or by the **Temper Enrollment Service**. The enrollment service will make every effort to get the account open in the quickest and most efficient manner. However, it depends on the participation of the transfer agents, and some agents are more competent than others. Certain agents require that the shareholder himself or herself request the enrollment form.

## Special Gift Offers

Subscribers to *The Moneypaper* have requested a means to help their friends and relatives enroll in DRIPs. From time to time, *The Moneypaper* editors will select a group of stocks based on certain criteria as appropriate for gift giving. Those companies are packaged by the Temper Enrollment Service at a fixed price (which includes the service fee and a nonrefundable cushion). The fixed price is established to facilitate the transaction in that no request for additional funds or refunds will be necessary.

About 100 companies are always available to give as gifts at www.giftsofstock.com. The stocks offered at that Site change from time to time and you are invited to visit the site as often as you wish to review the LIST OF STOCKS.

**Come visit Giftsofstock.com**

---

### Visit Our Web Sites!

If you have access to the Internet and would like to search for any changes that may have taken place after this Guide was printed, log in at **www.directinvesting.com**. You'll find a constantly updated listing of companies that offer plans. The company names and number of shares required are listed for the general public, but to view the plan details, you need a password, which you can acquire by registering at that site.

As a *Moneypaper* subscriber, you can review the plans by entering your subscription number as user name and your last name as your password. (Must be entered as capital letters.)

Also, at **www.moneypaper.com**, you can find recent news, INVEST%, the MP 63 Index (updated daily), opportunities to give gifts of stock with enrollment in DRIPs, and other valuable information.

**Enter your subscription or membership # here** (for your handy reference)

---

For subscription or membership information, call 1-800-388-9993. (As a subscriber you get discounts on enrollment fees.)

---

**ISBN #: 0966154509**

## That's All There Is to It

Below are some reminders on how to avoid the more common errors made by individuals using the Temper Enrollment Service to join DRIPs.

1. Do not forget to include your name, address, and Social Security number on the order form. Also, don't use an initial for your first name, unless that is your legal name and you can prove it.

2. If the stock is to be registered in any way other than the individual name of the subscriber, the proper form of registration must be given. An explanation of the various forms of registration, "Whose Name Should It Be In?," can be found on page 177 of this Guide.

3. The service fee to become enrolled is $30. However, subscribers to any Moneypaper Inc. publication pay only $15 for companies featured in the current issue. Otherwise, the service fee is $20.

4. The brokerage commission or "markup" for one qualifying share is 50 cents. The charge is up to $1 for two to 20 shares; for more than 20 shares, the markup is 5 cents per share up to 100 shares ($5).

5. Do not combine payments to Temper with payments to *The Moneypaper*. For instance, don't combine your DRIP payment with a check to *The Moneypaper* for a subscription renewal. These are two different companies.

6. The subscriber $15 and $20 service fees are available to you, a member of your immediate family who lives at the same address, or another paid subscriber. The nonsubscriber service fee is $30.

7. Pay for your stock order(s) by check or money order (payable to Temper of the Times) and send it to 555 Theodore Fremd Ave., Suite B-103, Rye, New York 10580. An order form is available online at www.directinvesting.com, or fax your request to 914-921-9318.

- - - - - - - - - - - - - - - - - - - - - - - - - - - - - - -

# Investment Alert

To take advantage of the immediate and easy access afforded by the Internet, when we have thoughts to share between issues, we will do so by email. In addition, so that DRIP investing can be even more affordable, we are offering a sale price on enrollment service fees for one company as part of this *Investment Alert*.

Visit: **www.directinvesting.com/moneypaper/stockoftheday.cfm** or provide us with your name and email address below.

---

Name

---

Email address

P.S.: Your privacy is guaranteed. The Moneypaper does not sell or rent its email lists.

Mail to: 555 Theodore Fremd Ave., Suite B-103, Rye, New York 10580

# Subscribe to
# THE **MONEY**PAPER

*The Moneypaper* guides you to the best investments for your money with specific, unhedged recommendations, and details exactly what steps to take. Every month, you get:

- The Editor's  perspective on current topics of interest

- A suggested portfolio of DRIP stocks with a common theme, including capsule descriptions of the companies

- Contrarian Michael Burke's thoughts for the month

- Timely suggestions and information culled from other publications, ranging from professional journals to the New York Times

- And beyond stocks, tips on personal finance: taxes, retirement, insurance, real estate—and more

*The Moneypaper* provides a clear, coherent plan that really works. It guides you to the best places for your money with specific, unbiased recommendations. It tells you exactly what steps to take and how to take them.

*The Moneypaper's* goal is to help you achieve wealth and security by becoming a self-reliant, self-directed investor.

Note: Only full-term paid subscribers are entitled to a lower fee when they use the enrollment service of  fered by Temper of the Times Communications, Inc. Subscribers

**Turn for additional benefits**

are char ged $15 in most cases, instead of the $30 fee char ged to nonsubscribers.

Your subscription entitles you to receive 12 monthly issues of *The Moneypaper*, delivered to your home.

In addition:

- You may read the current issue of *The Moneypaper* online and have access to back issues.

- You can access INVEST% online. INVEST% is our contrarian formula-driven investment guide that can help you avoid chasing rising prices and/or selling into a panic.

- Free access online to "Slash the Cost of Investing."

- You get a substantial discount when you use the enrollment service of fered by Temper of the Times Communications, Inc. The fee is $15 for stocks featured in the current issue (an issue is current until the 15th of the month following publication). Otherwise, the fee for subscribers is $20. Nonsubscribers always pay $30.

------------------------------------------------

# Subscribe to
# Direct Investing

If you have an interest in owning the very best stocks for your personal objectives, you need *Direct Investing*. We created this publication for people like you who invest through DRIPs — bringing up-to-the-minute performance information to help you take advantage of the very best opportunities!

Published twice each month, *Direct Investing* focuses exclusively on companies with direct investment plans, analyzing company performance and making recommendations, including how much to invest in which companies, and when.

And there are special features that make every issue of *Direct Investing* an even more useful resource. In the Bargain Corner, for example, you will find good stocks that are currently languishing and so can be picked up at bargain prices in anticipation of their eventual recovery.

Your subscription entitles you to receive 24 issues of *Direct Investing*, delivered to your home.

### *In Each Issue:*

Portfolio Picks: include something that's been lacking in your portfolio with these choices.

Bargain Corner: buy a stock that has a bright future when it recovers from its discounted sale price.

Model portfolio: select a portfolio with themes ranging from speculative to the bluest of the blue chips.

**Turn for additional benefits**

Commentary: find out what's going on in a particular industry.

Company Updates: decide how much to invest in the MP 63 companies for which investment dates are approaching.

News Briefs: latest news and changes in DRIP plans.

Keep ahead of the pack and on top of your DRIP companies with the timely information in *Direct Investing*!

In addition:

- You may read the current issue of *Direct Investing* online and have access to back issues.

- You can access INVEST% online. INVEST% is our contrarian formula-driven investment guide that can help you avoid chasing rising prices and/or selling into a panic.

- Free access online to "Slash the Cost of Investing."

- You get a substantial discount when you use the enrollment service offered by Temper of the Times Communications, Inc.The fee is $15 for stocks featured in the current issue (an issue is current until the 15th of the month following publication). Otherwise, the fee for subscribers is $20. Nonsubscribers always pay $30.

---

# Notes

# Notes

# Notes

# Notes